'A lovely book, hugely funny at times' Rod Liddle, *Spectator*

'A joy and a treasure trove ... Do not leave your county without it.' *Oldie*

'*Engel's England* is a fascinating example of his exceptional talents: erudite, emotive, enthusiastic in a witty, perceptive, irreverent style that's utterly enjoyable, whether you agree with him or not.' *Camden Review*

'A lovely, engaging ... has the perfect light, humorous touch' *New*

'My old friend Matthew Engel has w... unexpectedly, the book reveals a deeply hidden ...tiful book ... Rather ... de.' Simon Barnes, *Eastern Daily Press*

'Matthew Engel, the most stylish and entertaining of authors, has written an enchanting book.' *Northern Echo*

'Wonderful' Richard Coles, *Saturday Live, Radio 4*

'Engel is mostly positive about the places he visits, warm about the people he meets and often very funny ... He's a class act.' *British Journalism Review*

'Timely and engaging ... genially celebrates the best that the country has to offer, while offering a salutary warning of how much there is to lose.' *Field*

MATTHEW ENGEL was born in Northamptonshire (Chapter 38) and lives in Herefordshire (Chapter 40) with his wife, daughter and various animals. He wrote for the *Guardian* for nearly twenty-five years and is now th... for ...ll ...nes. For twelve years, ... His previous books ... *Extracts from the Rea...*

ENGEL'S ENGLAND

Thirty-nine counties, one capital and one man

MATTHEW ENGEL

P

PROFILE BOOKS

ıperback edition published in 2015

ırst published in Great Britain in 2014 by
Profile Books Ltd
3 Holford Yard
Bevin Way
London WC1X 9HD
www.profilebooks.com

Copyright © Matthew Engel, 2014, 2015
Map illustrations by Susannah English

1 3 5 7 9 10 8 6 4 2

Typeset in Garamond by MacGuru Ltd
info@macguru.org.uk

Printed and bound in Great Britain by
CPI Group (UK) Ltd, Croydon CR0 4YY

A CIP catalogue record for this book is available from the British Library.

ISBN 978 1 84668 572 9
eISBN 978 1 84765 928 6

Mixed Sources
Product group from well-managed
forests and other controlled sources
www.fsc.org Cert no. TT-COC-002227
© 1996 Forest Stewardship Council
FSC

CONTENTS

To Laurie and the past; to Vika and the future

ENGLAND

The thirty-nine counties and one capital

INTRODUCTION

When my son, Laurie, was about eight, I tried to explain to him which country we lived in. Since our home was barely five miles from the Welsh border and we crossed it without thinking all the time, it was not just a theoretical question: when we went into Wales, we entered a different country, but then again we didn't.

So I told him as succinctly as I could about England, Scotland, Wales and, heaven help us, the two Irelands; about Britain, Great Britain, the United Kingdom and the British Isles (a term now increasingly considered politically incorrect, some pedants preferring 'North-west European Archipelago' or 'Islands of the North Atlantic'). He got the hang of the outlines remarkably quickly. But the more I said, the less I understood the subject myself, and the more I realised how bizarre these distinctions were; grasping the three-fold nature of the Christian God was a doddle in comparison.

I also realised that explaining the subject through sport, our normal topic of conversation, would make matters worse. Each sport organises itself along different national lines. Feeling bolshie, I once pointed out to a British Olympic official that the term 'Team GB' was wrong because that excludes Northern Ireland. He replied in a gotcha tone of voice that the alternative, Team UK, would exclude the Isle of Man and the Channel Islands. At any given moment, other countries may have more violently expressed divisions, but they generally know who, where and what they are.

In this century, as nationalism grew in Scotland and, to a lesser extent, Wales, the English began to chafe against their own bonds. One of the great successes of the new Celtic consciousness was the way it finessed any taint of racism: for these purposes, a Scot was someone who lived in Scotland. Attempts to find a matching English nationalism always seemed cranky.

England and Britain were once considered almost synonymous. If you met a compatriot abroad he was English unless he told you forcefully he wasn't. Until the late twentieth century 'United Kingdom' was reserved for the most formal occasions, like best china; and there were certainly no such people as 'Brits'. Within the new more inclusive vocabulary the English have found themselves a little lost.

The Scots could safely rail against English overlordship; the English became stuck in a general alienation that was difficult to express. Their lives were changing, at the mercy of forces beyond their control – a fragile economy, technological change, Brussels, bloody foreigners – and it was hard to know what to do about it. Meanwhile, all the wealth and power that England did possess was pouring inexorably into one corner of the country, the South-East, a process that was bad news even for those who lived there, at least if they were not homeowners. All this in a country whose name cannot be reliably found in drop-down internet menus. Are we U for United Kingdom, B for Britain, G for Great Britain or E for England?

It was against this background, in the financially difficult spring of 2011, with the country half-heartedly governed by David Cameron's coalition, that I set off.

This is a travel book about England, in the spirit and the footsteps of other travellers round this strange land: Defoe, Cobbett, Priestley, if it is not too pretentious to mention them. The difference is that this book is divided into the historic, ancient and traditional counties, the divisions of England that collectively withstood a thousand years of epic history but not the idiocy of the 1970s. It is not a gazetteer, nor a guidebook, nor a compendium of England's best anything.

This is emphatically not a book about local government, nor is it a prolonged whinge about the iniquities of the 1972 Local Government Act, though that will crop up as appropriate, to explain why the counties in this book are those of Defoe, Cobbett and Priestley and not those used by modern Whitehall. And a little background is essential in advance.

For a start, as people kept asking me, why cover just England, and not GB, UK or the whole archipelago? Firstly, there was the euphonious coincidence of my un-English surname, which lent itself to an obvious title. Secondly, the historic counties of Scotland and Wales – now almost all formally abolished – were primarily just administrative units and never had the wider resonance of those in England. This is not true of Ireland, where the frontier between the twenty-six counties now in the Republic and the six still attached to the UK is at the forefront of the island's tortured history. There is a happier side to that: everyone in Ireland can instantly recognise the perceived characteristics of a Corkman, Kerryman or Dub; and the former Taoiseach Brian Cowen was widely known as BIFFO – 'Big Ignorant Fucker From Offaly'. But all that is another book entirely.

Thirdly, *ars longa, vita brevis*. It would have been lovely to spend time exploring the mountains of Sutherland or the 35,000 acres of Clackmannanshire, 'the Wee County', which is one-third the size of England's pygmy, Rutland. But for any author, the prime object of writing a book is to get the damn thing finished and published, and three years' travel is long enough. Above all, it is unexamined England, so little understood even by its own inhabitants, that fascinates me, and where I felt that exploring the microscopic pieces of the puzzle might produce some insights into the big picture.

The idea of the county goes so far back in English history that exact dates are impossible. The best I can discover is as follows: Kent was probably recognisable as Cantium when Christ was a lad. Like Essex, it was an independent kingdom in the fifth century AD. The idea of a shire (*scir* = a division) originated in Wessex not much later. There are references to Hampshire and Devonshire from the eighth century. In the early tenth century, when Wessex conquered Mercia under Edward the Elder, son of Alfred the Great, the term spread into the Midlands.

When they arrived, the Normans did not attempt to interfere with these arrangements, but changed the nomenclature: the *ealdorman*, the Anglo-Saxon officer in charge of a shire, mutated into a *comes* or count, and thus the shire became known as *comitatus*, or county. As England was more or less pacified, united and systematised, the concept spread into the Danelaw and the barbarous North (and even more barbarous Wales). Not all shires made it into full-blown counties. In the early days Yorkshire was divided into subordinate shires, including Hallamshire and Richmond-shire, whose names persisted though their roles disappeared. The walled town of Winchcombe in Gloucestershire was regarded as Winchcombe-shire between about 1007 and 1016, its presumed millennium being marked by a bell-ringing commemoration in 2007. But by the Middle Ages England was a country of counties in a manner that would remain fundamentally unchanged for the best part of a millennium.

Oh, there were all kinds of anomalies and bits of weirdness which were gradually tidied up. There were counties palatine (Lancashire, Cheshire and Durham) that were directly under the control of a local princeling. There were counties corporate, boroughs that were regarded as self-governing although nearly all still fell under the jurisdiction of the Lord Lieutenant for military purposes; to this day, on feeble evidence, Bristol fancies itself as a separate county. There were enclaves and exclaves. There were ancient liberties like the Soke of Peterborough and the Isle of Ely. Yorkshire was divided into three ridings (a thirding) and Lincolnshire into three parts. Most of the counties were divided into hundreds, areas big enough to offer a hundred men at arms. But some counties had wapentakes instead, while Kent had lathes and Sussex rapes.

The very distinctions show just how important the county was in the lives of the people. The monarch was in the far distance; authority was channelled through the Lord Lieutenant and the sheriff, though the sheriff's power later devolved on the justices of the peace. Counties developed their own laws, dialects, customs, farming methods, building styles. They formed the tapestry of the nation. In 1911 P. H. Ditchfield asked in the preface to his book *Counties of England*: 'Why should Devonshire farmers shoot their apple-trees on New Year's Day to make them fruitful, singing curious verses, and those of Surrey or Sussex be ignorant of the custom? Why should a dark man bring luck as a first-foot on the same day in Lancashire, and a fair man in Shropshire?' The answer is that these were real places that had real differences and inspired real loyalties.

The Local Government Act of 1888 brought the new-fangled notion of democracy to the hierarchical shires by establishing county councils, while giving the larger municipalities independence within the counties by designating them county boroughs. The biggest change came in London, where the disorganised administration of the capital, outside the City itself, was given some sense by carving chunks from surrounding counties and creating the London County Council. Until this point, the monarch, Parliament and Eros were all living in Middlesex, which was somewhat absurd.

Elsewhere, the integrity of the counties was respected. There was very minor tinkering with borders and some of the counties were subdivided: the ridings of Yorkshire and parts of Lincolnshire acquired separate councils, but the people remained unarguably Tykes and Yellowbellies. Indeed, county identity was perhaps stronger than ever around the turn of the twentieth century. In peacetime, county cricket was at the heart of the sporting calendar; and, come 1914, the young men marched proudly off to war in their county regiments. This was a mistake, since it meant they died in clusters and, when the bugles sounded from sad shires, they often did so en masse from the same shire, which was bad for morale.

The map of England was almost entirely left alone until the early 1960s, when the London County Council was expanded to take in the outer ring of suburbs as the new Greater London Council. This fitted with the orthodoxy of the time that large metropolitan areas should be planned holistically; more importantly, it served the ruling Conservatives' purposes since the old inner-urban LCC was almost always a Labour-led nuisance. The Labour Party huffed and puffed and then, characteristically, allowed the act to come into force as planned after it had returned to power. The main effect was the total abolition of Middlesex, but the outcry was limited: Middlesex had long since become amorphous suburbia and it survived both as a cricket team and (crucially) as a postal address.

The lack of uproar encouraged the Labour government, under Harold Wilson, to start on the rest of the country. It set up a royal commission under a classic Whitehall committee man, Sir John Maud (later Lord Redcliffe-Maud). His report, issued in 1969, was not to be confused with the MAUD report of 1941 (Military Application of Uranium Detonation), which started the British atom bomb project, and actually led to remarkably little devastation in comparison. The new Maud report proposed dividing England into eight provinces and sixty-one numbered units, nearly all of them 'unitary', so that virtually all local government would be in the hands of city-based regions, governing half a million people or more, checked from below only by local parish councils, which, after much thought, were graciously to be allowed to continue. Existing boundaries were considered irrelevant: the map was redrawn from scratch.

The aim was to 'revitalise' local government, then in the hands of 1,210 different authorities. A civil servant who worked on the report told me, with some passion, of the idealism that lay behind it. Though full of staid old farts, the committee had reported in the spirit of the 1960s: bigger trumped smaller; new trumped old. Down with the slums! Up with the tower blocks! Their report almost totally ignored local loyalties, and so did the initial newspaper commentaries.

The report was never implemented. The Conservatives regained power under Ted Heath in 1970 and constructed their own version of reform, based on the dear old counties which they usually controlled. The 1970s proved to be a more sentimental, rustically minded decade: hereabouts began the renewed enthusiasm for country cottages, real ale and (too late) steam trains. However, the minister involved was Peter Walker, a dashing, dodgy, self-conscious moderniser, and the counties he proposed were only loosely based on the ancient ones. The Heath government as a whole, whose one great achievement was Britain's entry into Europe, was deeply in love with biggism.

This time there would be 380 councils. Since these proposals bore some resemblance to existing reality, people understood more easily what they meant and began to fight for their own history. The proposals were not immutable: the women of Barlborough, Derbyshire, marched on Westminster and averted absorption into Sheffield. But the government soon tired of the arguments: Herefordshire was festooned with posters opposing merger with Worcestershire but got dragged to the altar regardless, kicking and screaming. Most surprising of all was the near-silence of Yorkshire. The bold-as-brass, shout-the-odds, proud Tykes and terriers allowed their county to be sliced, diced and divvied up. No bite, nary even a bark.

Some protesters were mollified by assurances that the proposals were entirely about local government and would have nothing to do with history, geography or loyalty. Cricket, for instance, simply ignored the 1972 act. But these intentions were thwarted for two main reasons. After the changes took effect in 1974 the Post Office this time insisted that the new county names should be used. And the media, led by the BBC, slavishly followed.

Local government remained the most consistently worthless of all British institutions. Indeed it got worse. This was largely due to central government's insistence on untrammelled power: the new metropolitan county councils, including and especially the GLC, terminally irritated Margaret Thatcher and in 1986 were liquidated. Another decade later, with the sole exception of Cumbria, all the other made-up county names – Avon, Cleveland, Hereford and Worcester, Humberside – had also gone.

Except that they hadn't really. Because no one knew where anywhere was any more. Is Sunderland now in County Durham, where it spent a good eight centuries? In the county of Tyne and Wear (which lasted only slightly longer than Winchcombeshire), as Wikipedia still insists? Is it Sunderland, Sundld, which is what my AA atlas calls it? Or, as most search engines imply, does it exist only as a football team? The AA ('Britain's Clearest Mapping'), trying desperately to follow the endless shifts in council boundaries, also awards county status to such confections as Halton, Kirklees, Knowsley, Sandwell and Trafford, remote centres of power even to locals, meaningless to outsiders. Other atlases and websites use different formulae. My special favourite is 'Wigan, Wigan', which makes it on to the BBC Weather website. So good they named it twice!

Contrast this with America. Everyone knows it's Boston, Massachusetts, Chicago, Illinois, and Memphis, Tennessee: ('Long-distance information, give me Memphis, Tennessee!'). An American president can nuke Moscow in an instant, but cannot possibly interfere with the domestic arrangements of Memphis City Council. The current British government is far more subtle than Mrs Thatcher. It preaches 'localism' while at the same time whittling away at the two major areas of authority left with councils: education and planning.

The communities secretary, Eric Pickles, has expressed support for traditional counties and abandoned a rule barring the erection of signs denoting their historic boundaries. But councils don't have enough money to mend the roads, never mind anything else. And a sign is meaningless when Royal Mail is agitating to get county names off envelopes entirely. No traditions attach themselves to a postcode.

Even modern birthing practices conspire against local loyalties. Maternity hospitals are increasingly centralised, so whole swathes of the country will be filled with children born in another county, or even across national borders. And the populace are themselves guilty. If, by some strange fluke, a decision is taken locally and does not come down from Brussels, Westminster, Whitehall or the distant HQ of an avaricious multinational, the cry goes up, 'Unfair! Postcode lottery!'

This absence of local pride and engagement was noted by Raymond Seitz, the US Ambassador to Britain in the early 1990s. Seitz was a notable Anglophile, but he regretted, for instance, the dreary car number plates that resulted from Britain's inability to permit diversity. 'Its licence plates are unimaginative and uninformative. There is no "Kent: The Garden County" or "Cumbria: Land o' Lakes". I wonder what games British children play on long trips.'

To me, the destruction of local pride in general, and the counties in particular, is a tragedy. Not a thousand-dead tragedy, but a slow-burn, almost unnoticed disaster leading to an irrevocable loss of self-respect. Not a deliberate act, but a case of criminal negligence. A crime against history, a crime against geography. Of course, mobility and mass media and globalisation make some degree of homogenisation inevitable. But that means it is even more urgent to cherish the things that make our own small patch of the planet special.

It is not just the US where they do things differently. In France and Germany and Belgium, no one needs a government to preach localism: the strength of the *commune* or the pull of *Heimat* is very strong. In Scotland and Wales the nations themselves have awoken from slumber. In England people know less and less what they are and where they are. You can see the consequences in sad, once self-governing northern county boroughs like Dewsbury, their town halls echoing and empty. And you can see it on the Berkshire Downs, where the White Horse of Uffington has probably been a symbol of local pride for a couple of thousand years, and specifically Berkshire pride for eleven hundred. It was then moved to Oxfordshire. Decisions like this instantly rendered inoperative such adornments of the nation's cultural heritage as the *Victoria County History* series and Pevsner's *Buildings of England*. The benefit was negligible, the loss incalculable.

Though much is taken, much abides. And although this book is something of an elegy, it is also a celebration of the remarkable and continuing distinctiveness of every part of England. It is the product of a three-year journey – to be more exact, a series of journeys, since real life did not cease – through thirty-nine counties and one capital: an average of just over one a month.

To others, my wanderings appeared unexotic. Once I sent a friend an email saying 'Am in Grimsby.' 'Bloody hell,' he replied. 'You're like some third-rate Henry Kissinger – couldn't you have said you were in Rio?' Another time I really was going abroad, to Crete with the family. But obviously part of my brain refused to believe it. So somehow I managed to start a message to a colleague with the words 'Just off for a week in Crewe'.

As the project continued, people would ask me if I had a favourite county. But I soon ceased to answer. Since no one else seemed to cherish the counties, I found myself acquiring a mother's fierce protectiveness. These were my forty children. Some had become gratifyingly more famous of late, like pushy Essex and tarty Cheshire, even though certain aspects of their celebrity might cause a little maternal concern; some found it ever harder to assert themselves and make their way in the world, so they needed my care even more; some were frankly exasperating. But I never had a dull day. And I never met a county I didn't love.

Despite all the pressures towards uniformity, each one is still individual, unique. My tone of voice may occasionally be sharp, as a mother's should be, and some readers may say I have been unkind to their county or home town. But I do hope my underlying affection shines through.

The notion that there are forty counties is an old one. Thomas Moule stated it as a fact in *The English Counties Delineated* (1839). Charlotte M. Mason used the title *The Forty Shires* for a book in 1881, implying it was a well-known phrase. She begins: 'The writer ventures to hope the following pages may help to acquaint English children with their native land in the only way in which England can be practically known – county by county.' And I applaud the sentiment.

My forty chapters are not quite hers, though. Mason, like Moule, included Monmouthshire as part of England, which was technically correct from 1542 to 1974. And though the 1974 changes were almost all terrible, this one tidied up an obvious piece of nonsense. It is not entirely clear why the 1542 Laws in Wales Act should have omitted Monmouthshire: I thought at first it was either some Machiavellian Tudor manoeuvre or a straightforward cock-up. Monmouthshire was then far more Welsh than it is now, and for many purposes in those intervening 432 years the standard formulation was 'Wales and Monmouthshire'. It was never truly an English county. Rhodri Morgan, the erudite former First Minister of Wales, thinks this anomaly arose from an earlier act which rejigged the judicial circuits – then vital cogs in the governmental machine. This took Monmouth out of the Welsh circuit and on to the Oxford circuit, apparently to even up the populations. In other words, it was an example of precisely the kind of insensitive tinkering that was repeated over and over again at the very time this ancient mistake was finally being corrected.

On the other hand, Mason did not count London. Her book was published seven years before the formation of the London County

Council, when the city was simply the City and the rest was in one of the Home Counties. It seems to me ludicrous to suggest that Westminster Bridge still links Middlesex and Surrey, and I don't.

London had to be included as a separate chapter for what might be called technical reasons: the publisher, Andrew Franklin, said a lot of books can be sold in London and I'd better include it or else. It was only much later that I realised that he was also right on a higher plane. All the counties exist in apposition to London, their nature determined by the extent to which Londonishness pervades them. In a sense, the entire book is about London.

And there is no longer any clear definition of a county. The recent history is so shambolic I've just had to decide that I know a county when I see one. As a rough guide, I have used the 1955 *AA Handbook* because (a) it pre-dates the twists and turns of the past half-century and makes sense; (b) I possess a copy; and (c) it is a glorious evocation of bygone England. Opening the book at random, I was able to discover, on a single spread, hotels called the King's Arms in Berkhamsted, Herts (**), Berwick-upon-Tweed, Nthmb (***) and Bicester, Oxon (**, telephone Bicester 15), all offering B&B for twenty shillings or less, with dinner for as little as five and sixpence; dogs in Berkhamsted at manager's discretion only. And when I wrote each chapter, I added another piece to my 'Victory Plywood Jig Saw Puzzle', showing all the counties (but ducking the London conundrum), which must be of similar vintage.

The order of my chapters may not look immediately logical. I considered proceeding in alphabetical order, which sounded boring, or grouping them by regions, which sounded very boring. So I went as the spirit moved me. There were things I wanted to do at a particular time of year, and I wanted variety: big and small; coastal and inland; urban and rural. I also wanted to finish with the three places where I have lived almost all my life: Northamptonshire, where I grew up; London, where I grew a little wiser; and Herefordshire, where I settled. Sometimes I went back to a county to tie up a loose end, but they appear in chronological order of my main visit, and are written as I found them, without hindsight.

I went to the northernmost, southernmost, westernmost and easternmost bits of England (two of these are the same place; one of the others is a dump); the wettest, the driest, the lowest, the highest (though only one of these is unarguable). The seasons changed around me, and I have tried not to condemn a place just because the weather was shitty. But there were places within counties that I liked and those I didn't. The opinions I formed were often far removed from those I expected to form. Not everyone will agree, but they are honest opinions and my own. If you find a factual mistake (and there are bound to be quite a few in such a book), please let me know (matthew@matthewengel.co.uk) to allow for possible corrections, but do so gently and politely, because it will have been an honest mistake.

When required, updates appear in italics after each chapter.

My website, matthewengel.co.uk, will have further updates and talking points and quirky footnote-y material that failed to make the book for fear of denuding all the forests of Scandinavia.

By way of subtext, I visited all forty-one (Anglican) cathedrals and lit a candle to my late son in each. This meant going to a lot of Choral Evensong, partly for pleasure and partly to avoid paying the admission charges; principle not meanness, you understand.

And everywhere I met wonderful people, many of whom are thanked by name at the back of the book. They helped me not only out of the goodness of their hearts, though that was plentiful, but also because in most cases, I believe, they got pleasure from talking about their village, their town and, sometimes above all, their county. The question I kept asking was, 'How do I find the essence of this county?' The answers often led me to fascinating discoveries.

It is easy to get depressed about England, so confused, so ill-used, so wet and so grey. But there was something I believed when I set out that I believe even more strongly now I have finished: that this is the most beautiful and fascinating country on earth.

Matthew Engel
Herefordshire, September 2014

1. *I'll be with you in plum blossom time*

Hearts at peace, under an english heaven
rupert brooke

WORCESTERSHIRE

The 'Springtime in the Vale' coach trip left the country park outside Evesham just after 10 a.m. This was the outing formerly known as the Blossom Trail tour. But blossom and bus timetables are uneasy bedfellows. 'It's a bit of a revamped blossom tour,' explained our guide, Angela from Wychavon District Council. 'Either the blossom was too early, or we were too late, or vice versa, so we've rebranded it.'

There was another uneasy party to this arrangement. I'm a train man: I don't like buses. And simply being here spoke to one of my deepest fears. Everyone has their own particular alarm about old age: pain, infirmity, mental decay. My own holy terror is of being so bored and lonely that I succumb to booking seven-day coach tours to 'Glorious Devon' or 'Loch Lomond and the Trossachs'. As it was, I found myself – as happens less and less often – some way below the average age of the thirty-strong company, although Fred the driver had trouble believing my protest that I was not entitled to the £1 pensioner discount.

But it had seemed churlish to spurn the bus trip. Angela and Fred knew where Worcestershire's best blossom might be; I didn't. And for once everything was in sync. An infamously savage December had been succeeded by a bland January and February, and a kindly March. The upshot was that on this Wednesday, 6 April, the plum trees were in full cry. These are the traditional harbingers of the brief and glorious Midland spring; they are followed by riots of pear, cherry and apple blossom before the orchards calm down, stop showing off and get on with the serious business of producing fruit.

Furthermore, this was no ordinary 6 April. It was a fabulous 6 April: the sky deep blue, the sun blazing down, the air midsummer-warm.

The tour had definitely been given more of a revamp than a rebrand. Once we got going, we saw heaps of plum blossom, but only in the distance. Angela had other priorities. Within minutes, we stopped at a farm shop for plum-jam nibbles washed down with thimbles of local apple juice. That lasted half an hour. We went on to Croome Park, designed by Capability Brown, mucked up by the RAF and then by the M5, now being restored by the National Trust, which has had difficulty replanting some of the trees in their old places, since they are ill-suited to the southbound fast lane.

At Croome Park we were encouraged to visit the toilets, the coffee shop and the redundant Georgian church of Croome D'Abitot, once the quasi-private chapel of the Earls of Coventry. This was an hour-long stop, which was a bit leisurely for the toilet but not quite long enough to visit Croome Court, the Coventrys' ancestral home which fell on confused times after the tenth earl was killed during the Dunkirk retreat, and the estate was sold off. The house then had spells as a Catholic boys' school, a country house hotel, a base for the Hare Krishna movement, the home of a property developer or two, the offices of an insurance company and a police training centre. The motorway came through in the 1960s, perhaps the only decade in the past 250 years when such a thing would have been possible without either the Coventrys or public opinion screaming blue murder.

Which is, I think, all very interesting, but nothing to do with plum blossom. And then, when we reboarded Fred's coach, we were taken straight to the centre of Evesham and decanted for a *two-hour* stop, this time to have lunch. By now, I was hearing mutinous murmurs from the rows behind me. 'I came to see the countryside, not the town,' moaned a woman from Worcester.

Some of the party probably lived in Evesham and might have walked home for lunch. Evesham is a pretty town, especially on a day like this, though it is of an unfortunate size (pop.: 22,000) which means it has a good many chain stores of a not especially useful kind (Edinburgh Woollen Mill, Body Shop, Burton) but no Marks & Spencer. It does have a particularly hideous 24-hour Tesco on the edge of town. My friend Jane Mason, who was to give me board and lodging that evening, once complained to the manager: 'Can't you turn the sign off at night? This is a rural area and you can see it from everywhere, even the riverbank.' 'That's the point,' he replied.

Before the supermarket came, the last major event in Evesham was a kerfuffle in 1265 when rebel soldiers led by Simon de Montfort were trapped by the bend in the River Avon. With no Tesco sign to suggest a line of retreat, they had the river on three sides and forces loyal to Henry III on the fourth; they were duly massacred. De Montfort was slain and cut in pieces, with body parts being awarded, in the manner of the *corrida*, to various loyalist generals. Roger, the first Baron Mortimer, was given the head and sent it home to his wife, as one of the most original and thoughtful of all love tokens. Perhaps it was stamped A SOUVENIR OF EVESHAM, or MY HUSBAND WENT TO EVESHAM AND ALL I GOT WAS THIS LOUSY HEAD.

I would have retrieved my car and gone off on my own but for an assurance from Angela that we really were going to see blossom in the hour that would remain between us regrouping at 3 p.m. and saying goodbye at 4. The destination was The Lenches, a group of five villages and hamlets, Rous Lench, Church Lench, Ab Lench, Atch Lench and Sheriff's Lench, famous for their mistletoe-covered old orchards. I just wanted to lie on the warming ground and stare through the flowers at the perfect sky.

So, after 3, Angela pointed out the homes of a few minor celebrities and I sat back contentedly, savouring the prospect ahead and that lovely phrase: *plum blossom*. Perhaps only cherry blossom can match it for euphony, I was thinking, though that has become tainted by association with boot polish. The coach jogged gently along the lanes. The sun streamed through the window. I must have closed my eyes. And the next thing I knew we were back in the car park, being ushered off.

Very cross, I drove straight back to Atch Lench, where there is a large community orchard, saved from the bulldozers in 1999 by a consortium of concerned villagers. The gate was open and it was at last possible to bond with the springtime. England stretched down the hill and far beyond; a soft spring breeze ruffled the grass; the trees were stark white against the sky. Plum blossom is not just a pretty phrase. It is more beautiful in reality than its rivals, purer in its whiteness, more delicate, more vulnerable. It symbolises all the hope of the year. But the breeze was driving the first blooms to the ground: April not a week old – day one of the financial year – and already the first hint of melancholy. It felt like a scene that had been enacted in the Lenches for thousands of springtimes.

Actually not. The Vale of Evesham was originally famous for vegetables (including asparagus), cereals and sheep. Then came the great agrarian depression of the late nineteenth century. According to John Edgeley – the acknowledged local expert – the first big orchards near here were then planted just over the Gloucestershire border by Lord Sudeley.

Soon they spread into Worcestershire, and Evesham's neighbour Pershore became famous for two plums, the Pershore Yellow Egg and the Pershore Purple. Fresh plums, previously an upper-class delicacy, became widely available, and plum jam and tinned plums ubiquitous. However, this heyday lasted barely half a century. By the 1950s cold storage was enabling the nascent supermarkets to bring in fresh plums from more trustworthy climes.

The vulnerability of plum blossom is very real. Because it comes so early, it is at risk from equinoctial gales and late frosts. Many gardeners believe plum trees fruit in alternate years, which is sort of, but not precisely, true. With plums, it is always famine or feast. My neighbour on the bus remembered her mother, in pre-war Birmingham, getting word that they were being sold off at a farthing a pound, one-tenth of a modern penny: 'She made a hundred pounds of plum jam that year.' In such seasons, the slender boughs often get snapped by the sheer weight of fruit.

My theory is that English soft fruit, unreliable though it is, always tastes best because it is on the edge of its range and so ripens more slowly. That's another argument that wouldn't go down well with a Tesco manager.

I realised only with hindsight what an appropriate place Worcestershire was for the start of this journey. Nowhere better represents the England of the imagination: the idealised, disembodied England of folk memory and fantasy.

Small towns, all of them close to each other, nestle in the lowlands, the hills never far from view. Each of them became famous for producing something now more likely to come from thousands of miles away: plums from Pershore; nails and buttons from Bromsgrove; carpets from Kidderminster; needles from Redditch; salt from Droitwich. They are separated by villages that are absurdly rich in thatch and half-timbering and ecclesiastical overstatement, rather less rich in natural vibrancy. Broadway is a theme park of bogus Englishness, maintained for tourists. But there are others just as nice and far less famous, like Elmley Castle, which appear to have been hijacked by commuters to Worcester and Brum.

Perhaps no county has been mucked around so much by boundary-fiddlers. Small-scale land swaps with neighbours have gone on for centuries. Until 1911 the south-western suburbs of Birmingham were part of Worcestershire. Long after that, the county included parts of the Black Country, including Dudley, retained as an island enclave in hostile territory.

(Dudley was built up by the seventeenth-century ironmaster Dud Dudley, who one might have assumed was an American blues musician.)

Most of the guidebook writers were so appalled by this aspect of Worcestershire they recoiled in horror: 'Hideous,' said Hutchinson's *Britain Beautiful*. In the late twentieth century, Worcestershire had a brief, discreditable reign as an occupying power when the absurd county of Hereford and Worcester was created, and little Herefordshire was crushed under the Worcester jackboot. (I may be overdramatising just a fraction.) Even now, Worcestershire has a pleasingly irrational shape, full of peninsulas and inlets, ensuring that Broadway and Tenbury Wells are in and Tewkesbury is out.

The imperial overlordship of Herefordshire was an uncharacteristic phase. The typical Worcestershire town has generally been dozy, inward-looking, entire of itself. Perhaps that's why, in the 1640s, Worcester was the Faithful City, the one that failed to get the message about the swing from the king: the first to declare for Charles I; the last to surrender – more Royalist even than Oxford. There was a sense at the time that Worcestershire could remain loyal and be self-sufficient if necessary, though the passage of armed convoys down the Severn to reach the sea might have got a little wearing after a while.

And now there cannot be a town in the kingdom that feels as removed from surrounding reality as Malvern. As I left Evesham for the forty-minute drive, Jane Mason's husband, Nick, said he couldn't understand why anyone retired to Malvern because everything was uphill. When I arrived, I went to see George Chesterton, a former Worcestershire cricketer and later deputy head of Malvern College, who explained that was the secret of its success: it keeps 'em fit. 'People come to Malvern to die,' he said, 'and then they don't.' At eighty-eight, thoroughly perky, having spent almost his entire life in the town, he was the evidence for his own case.

What a distinctive town this is. 'In my childhood,' wrote Jonathan Keates in the late 1970s, 'it always seemed full of old ladies and schoolgirls – the former have, alas, broken ranks, but the latter remain in force – four girls' boarding schools, the famous Malvern College for boys, and six prep schools.'

Since then, the balance of power has switched back again. The second-division schools have all closed (Chesterton recited them to me: 'Lawnside, The Abbey, Douglas House, Ellerslie ...') and the old ladies and gentlemen dominate the place. It is a town where men go out in jackets and ties for no obvious purpose; and the menswear department of Brays may be the last in Britain to display pyjamas prominently in the window.

On the one hand, Malvern is the most English of towns. On the other, it feels curiously foreign, like an Indian hill station in the last years of the Raj – Simla or 'Snooty Ooty'. In some ways, it seems dull as ditchwater: 'Hey, let's go and buy some pyjamas.' Yet the setting is freaky, dreamlike. The hills, as Keates put it, are 'triumphant in their suddenness', and the town girdles them, the atmosphere changing street by street. Sometimes one seems to be in an Italian painting. Next moment the Rhondda.

And ditchwater you never get in Malvern. The place grew rich because of the purity of the water that permeates the rock and escapes through dozens of springs. It is not that Malvern Water contains any healthy minerals: its secret is an absence of anything *un*healthy. There was a local verse about the town's eighteenth-century pioneer:

> *Malvern Water*
> *Says Dr John Wall*
> *Is famed for containing*
> *Nothing at all.*

Which, in that pre-sanitary era, was in itself a benefit. Wall's ideas mutated into the nineteenth-century pseudo-science of hydropathy, which was held to cure anything. *Everyone* came to Malvern: Florence Nightingale was a regular; Henry James was anxious to improve his bowel movements. Hydropathy can hardly have done anyone much harm, unlike the billions of plastic bottles which cater to the modern version of the obsession and then infest the oceans. On that basis, it sounded like good news that the works producing bottled Malvern Water were closed down in 2010 by its owners, Coca-Cola, even though the Queen, a great enthusiast, was said to be unamused.

Initiates use God's benison more wisely. The most popular spring is Hay Slad, the great gusher that pours out of the hillside in West Malvern. Always a line of cars, I was told ... people from as far afield as America and Australia ... you'll see it. It took some finding; and when I finally discovered Hay Slad – not signposted, just an open secret – there was no one around at all. So I wandered up the road to have lunch at the Brewers Arms, in a garden overlooking Herefordshire ('Best Pub View in Britain 2005'). When I got back to the spring, one of the locals, Philippa Lee, was filling two dozen bottles, all glass. 'Plastic leeches into the water,' she said.

Does everyone come here? 'People don't talk about it, they just do it. Tea tastes rubbish made with anything else.'

'So where does the water come from?'

'No one knows. It's not run-off from the hills, it's from somewhere deep in the earth. If it's ever been through anyone, it was hundreds or thousands of years ago. Since we've got this facility, we might as well use it, though I always feel guilty when I leave it running. I keep thinking I should turn the tap off.'

Finally, bottle no. 24 went into one of her bags-for-life. 'Right,' she said. 'I'll get home. If the neighbours hear the clink, they'll think I'm on the booze.'

The author James Lees-Milne, born in Wickhamford, wrote that Worcestershire was 'pre-eminently an autumnal county ... smells of the muddy river after rain, of hops and cider apples, of walnuts, blackberries, Michaelmas daisies and rotting sycamore leaves'. Nonsense: it's a springtime county.

Since 1899, Worcestershire has had first-class cricket, which has given the county a celebrity it would never have had otherwise. First and foremost, Worcester is renowned as the most beautiful of county grounds, with its encircling trees that do not quite obscure the view of the cathedral. It is in fact an ugly ground in a beautiful setting. The old pavilion was quite charming, but got demolished because it was regularly inundated, along with the playing area, whenever the Rivers Severn and Teme felt a bit full. The new pavilion, though believed to have Noah's Ark qualities, is in keeping with the Worcester tradition of repulsive modern architecture. 'Words fail me,' wrote Lees-Milne of the city centre.

What is wholly spring-like is the tradition (now more often breached than observed) that touring teams – especially Australian ones – begin their visits to England in Worcester. In the 1930s Donald Bradman came here three times and on every visit made a double-century. In 1948 he returned, and failed – out for 107, watched (judging by the number of people who have said they were there) by a crowd of at least half a million.

These famous matches all took place at the end of April, beginning of May, the customary start of the cricket season. However, the game's rulers have great faith in global warming and in 2011 the opening match,

Worcestershire v Yorkshire, was scheduled for 8 April. Their trust was rewarded. It was another peach of a day. Or a plum. And a surprisingly large crowd survived the horrendous one-way system and made their way into the ground to begin their pre-match rituals. They chatted with old acquaintances, poured tea from their Thermoses and read their *Daily Telegraph*s.

The first day of the season always has a special buzz of anticipation. The players, who usually look as though a day's cricket is a less enticing option than a shift in a call centre, certainly felt it. As the cathedral clock struck 11, Ryan Sidebottom of Yorkshire bowled the opening delivery; the Worcestershire captain, Daryl Mitchell, defended routinely to mid-off, and all the fielders fizzed with enthusiasm as though the bowler had taken a wicket at the first attempt. The spectators, however, chatted with old acquaintances, poured tea from their Thermoses, and read their *Daily Telegraph*s.

They weren't wrong, because the cricket soon settled into a gentle, pleasant rhythm. It seemed safe to nip out to visit the cathedral, something I had never done in decades of watching cricket here. The great architectural historian Alec Clifton-Taylor implied I was no bad judge, and that Worcester Cathedral was best observed from across the river – i.e. from the cricket ground. The local building stone was 'friable New Red sandstone' and the masonry had 'suffered cruelly at the hands of time'. He was also appalled by the Victorian restoration ('platitudinous ... very nasty ... horrible ... lamentable'). Luckily, he never saw the new cricket pavilion. Anyway, embarking on this book, I had set myself a subsidiary task: to light a candle for my late son, Laurie, in every Anglican cathedral in England, and I duly went across to start the list by ticking off Worcester.

The building is particularly long and thin and if – of the two struggling institutions – the Church should precede county cricket into oblivion, the cricketers could take it over and use the nave for net practice. They would comfortably fit in two wickets, one behind the other.

Not being wholly certain which bits Clifton-Taylor most wanted me to hate, I concentrated on finding Worcester's three most significant memorials. King John lies buried here, in accordance with his wishes – under a Purbeck marble effigy close to the altar. However, the accompanying notice to visitors refers to his reign as a 'tyranny', which is presumably not what he requested. Close by is the chantry dedicated to Arthur, Prince of Wales, elder brother of Henry VIII and first husband of Catherine of

Aragon. He died suddenly, aged fifteen, in 1502, with all kinds of consequences. His funeral lasted four days. 'I should like the same,' commented
Barbara, one of the guides.

However, Arthur's remains are no longer in the chantry. 'He's somewhere in the cathedral,' said Barbara, 'but we're not quite sure exactly
where.' There is a third memorial hereabouts, to a man who – from less
promising beginnings than Arthur's – did rule England: Stanley Baldwin,
son of a Worcestershire ironmaster, prime minister for seven years in three
separate spells between 1923 and 1937 and regarded with awe for his saga-
city and skill. 'No man has ever left in such a blaze of affection,' wrote
Harold Nicolson on his retirement. When war came, Baldwin was blamed
for Britain's failure to rearm and reviled almost unanimously. His death,
in 1947, was little noticed. He was cremated, his ashes being brought here
and tucked away under a discreet memorial just inside the west wall. 'Can
I see it?' I asked Barbara. No. It turned out the stone was hidden under
the deck of seats used for concerts – notionally temporary but now virtually permanent. 'You might be able to see it in August when they clear the
nave,' she said. 'Oh no, not this year. It's our turn to hold the Three Choirs.'

Baldwin's reputation has recovered somewhat. He is now mainly
thought of, if at all, as an unpretentious rustic, emblematic of his own
county. This is not a unanimous view, though. A few years back, before
the seats went up, a man asked to be pointed towards Baldwin's ashes. 'He
jumped up and down on the spot,' reported Barbara, 'and said, "I've been
wanting to do that for years."'

I walked back to the cricket in the sunshine, past the largest convoca-
tion of swans I have ever seen. On the way, I heard a distant cry of 'Owzat?',
and by the time I was back, the Worcestershire batting had started to collapse. The crowd was now approaching 3,000, quite extraordinary for a
Friday in early April. I wandered round, engaged in a few conversations,
eavesdropped on others. Topics included: rugby union, the December
snowstorms, the winter climate in Rome, French holidays, the plight of
freelance cricket journalists (that was in the press box), Aston Villa goal-
keepers, the virtues of Thatchers cider, the difference between a Honda
and a Toyota, train times from Wolverhampton, and the breeding of lab-
radoodles. I even heard two people discussing the cricket.

The fifth wicket fell with the score on 129. 'Someone's going in,' a
man said urgently. Of course, you might think, it's cricket: one batsman is
out, another goes in. But I am an old hand here and knew otherwise. The

someone in question was wearing a navy-blue sweater, not cricket whites, and he was heading not for the middle but through a glass door into a small wooden building. It was 2.50 p.m., nearly an hour before official tea-time, but the most glorious ritual on the cricket circuit was under way: tea in the Ladies' Pavilion at Worcester.

By the time I arrived – and I moved fast – the queue was already snaking out of the glass door on to the steps. By the time I reached the counter the first of the lemon sponge cakes was already disappearing. But there were plenty more in reserve, and twenty-three types of cake in all, provided by the ladies of the county, as if this were a village fete rather than a professional sporting event. I added a slice of cherry and sultana to the lemon sponge, ordered two cups of tea (not for my imaginary friend, but to avoid queuing for seconds), paid £3 and returned to the secondary delight of watching the cricket.

The pleasures of Worcester are not always so decorous. This is a beery town and the long bar in the old pavilion used to be a heck of a place after play. I have never once gone to bed in Worcester other than rat-arsed. Fortunately for my increasingly delicate constitution, I was heading home before nightfall. But there was something healthy I wanted to do first.

I drove back south towards Pershore and, after a few wrong turnings and enquiries, parked near the romantically neglected churchyard at Great Comberton. This is the start of the route (or one route) up Bredon Hill, northerly outcrop of the Cotswolds and great sentinel of southern Worcestershire. In the churchyard I saw the stone commemorating Robert and Lily Lee, 'a dearly loved father and mother'. It gave their dates (1891–1966 for Robert, 1899–1981 for Lily) and added simply: 'In Summertime on Bredon'. What a gorgeous summation of two lives, a marriage, a family, their love, a village, of Worcestershire and of England.

In summertime on Bredon ... began Housman,

My love and I would lie
And see the coloured counties,
And hear the larks so high
About us in the sky.

My love being otherwise engaged (which was a long-term issue for Housman), I was alone save for a bag of sherbet lemons, somewhat stuck together. The route was poorly marked, which was pleasing since it made me feel more of a traveller than a tourist, and not a problem, since the summit was quite obvious. I scrambled the last bit among some stunted hawthorns and emerged into an improbably lush, flat meadow.

I heard no larks, though a couple of buzzards hovered. I saw a few ramblers and runners. But even the evidence of humanity was muted. The landmark on the top is Parsons Folly, built as a summerhouse for John Parsons, MP and country squire, in the eighteenth century and now requisitioned and rendered fit for purpose, with uncharacteristic good taste, by a mobile phone company. Naturally, some visitors have left their markers, but not in ink: they had shifted the rocks lying around the folly to form their names – KEV AND PAT WOZ ERE ... TOBY ... EVIE ... ADAM ... RYAN ... CALUM – in a way that could be recycled by others.

They say you can see eight of the coloured counties from here on a clear day. Some say fourteen. I couldn't tell. Nature doesn't give them different colours, as the old mapmakers did. And anyway, as the sun grew lower and the heaven-sent day drew to a close, the air was growing hazy. But one could see enough colours. Every shade of green from pea to bottle; the white of the houses; the yellow of the early rape fields; the grey-brown of the church towers; the bluish tinge of the Avon and of what looked like rippling lakes but were actually fields covered by polytunnels.

It was stunning. And to think I was setting out to visit *all* the coloured counties. Maybe the other thirty-eight (plus London) would be as lovely as this one. What joy! What an adventure!

April 2011

~~~~~~~

In 2012 a local company with six employees deflected Coca-Cola's opposition and began calling its product Holywell Malvern Spring Water – sold only in glass bottles. George Chesterton died, aged ninety, in November 2012.

Three years on, my eyes still well with tears whenever I think of the inscription on Robert and Lily Lee's gravestone.

2. *Do you know how the shower works, Jesus?*

BEDFORDSHIRE

Then, next thing, I was at the gates of Mordor, otherwise known as the Ibis Hotel, Luton Airport: a couple of hours' flying time from almost anywhere in Europe; an unimaginable distance from Bredon.

Luton Airport stands as a representation of England as it changed, for better and worse, in the second half of the twentieth century. It developed as a base for charter airlines in the early days of package holidays and acquired a particular place in the cultural history of flight: typifying its transition from being exotic, risky, thrilling and luxurious to commonplace, safe, dull and disgusting. In the late 1970s the young actress Lorraine Chase, looking exquisite, appeared with a white-suited roué in an unforgettable advert set on an elegant terrace outside a Palladian mansion, somewhere near the Mediterranean. 'Were you truly wafted here from paradise?' purred the vile smoothie. The goddess replied in pure Eliza Doolittle, pre-Higgins: 'Naaa, Lu'on Airpor'.' (The ad was for Campari, though it may not have been very effective. Until I checked, my memory said Wall's Cornetto.)

I have myself been wafted to distant places from Luton, though not often. I remember the security hall, filled with offensively bossy notices written in capital letters: it was much how one imagines the induction centre at Guantanamo Bay. I also remember a winter flight back from Zurich. In Switzerland there was a foot and a half of fresh snow; my train across the country was ninety seconds late. In Luton there had been a light dusting; chaos reigned. The plane was delayed five hours because the land-ing runway was blocked, and we returned to an emergency bus timetable, carefully organised so as to deposit us on the frozen wastes of Luton Air-port Parkway Station at 2.10 a.m., thus missing the hourly all-night service to King's Cross by precisely one minute.

I took intense satisfaction in the fact that, this time, unlike every other guest at the Ibis Hotel, I did not have to fly anywhere. I was here because Luton Airport was in Bedfordshire, a fact probably unknown to everyone else in the hotel.

Modern counties, with their public relations officers and marketing departments and tourist boards, like self-promotion. They try to infil-trate themselves into the minds of those passing through with signs and catchy slogans. You would have thought this was particularly relevant for a county with a lot of through traffic (M1, A1, A5, A6 and all three main railway lines to the North). Not in the least. Bedfordshire survived the 1974 reorganisation intact and, up till 2009, its borders had remained unchanged – bar minor tinkering – since Saxon times. Technically, that remains the case. But it is now divided into three 'unitary areas' and thus has no county council with any duty of care for the name and its heri-tage. The Bedfordshire signs were removed and sold on eBay for £6 each (having reportedly cost £2,000 to erect). As they leave, motorists are told where they are going, without knowing where they have just been. The only indication I had – and this was temporary, though not very tempo-rary – was that the M1 went down to 50 mph for the entire length of the county because of roadworks between Junctions 10 and 13.

It is not as if the county doesn't lend itself to slogans. During the 1990s craze for 'Do It' puns ('Rugby players do it with oval balls'; 'Cardiologists do it till your heart stops' etc.), a competition run by the *Daily Mail* was won by the suggestion 'Luton Town Do It in Beds'. Vera Lynn sang

> *Up the wooden hill to Bedfordshire*
> *Heading for the land of dreams ...*

Turvey

River Ouse

BEDFORD

Cardington

Sandy

Biggleswade

Old Warden

Stewartby

Eversholt

WATLING

Toddington

Leighton Buzzard

Luton

Dunstable

STREET

Whipsnade

And Lorraine Chase had come-to-Beds eyes.

Perhaps, too, no county has more need of marketing. Bedfordshire has no mountains, no coastline, no cathedral. No racecourse, no first-class cricket team and, in 2011, no League football team. It is the most nondescript of counties: Britain's New Jersey. The state of Idaho, struggling for a catchphrase, used to say on its number plates 'Famous Potatoes'. What might Bedfordshire say? Its main distinction is its lack of self-respect.

Even the *Victoria County History* struggles to get excited: 'a county of comparatively little interest to the vertebrate palaeontologist ... the name of Bedfordshire is not connected to any of the more striking memories of early Church history ... few distinctive characteristics ... a thoroughfare from one part of the kingdom to another ...' (If not necessarily a quick thoroughfare.) In the early 1980s, when the now-defunct *Illustrated London News* was doing a series on all the counties, my friend Frank Keating suggested to the editor that I might do the piece on Northamptonshire, my home county. No chance, said the editor. 'Already arranged.' Then he perked up. 'Can he do Bedfordshire? No one else wants it.'

'Is there *anything* distinctive about the county?' I asked the local naturalist Conor Jameson. 'Um, um,' he replied. 'It's probably distinguished by its averageness.'

That average is brought down not only by Luton Airport but by Luton itself: a middlingly dreary town in terms of looks that has somehow made itself wholly unloved. The English characteristic of good-natured tolerance never took root here. In 1919 the official celebration of the end of the First World War was marked in Luton by rioters burning down the town hall. In the 1970s and 1980s the town was known as a hotbed of pro-IRA sentiment. Since then, the pace of unpleasantness has quickened. There was said to be an Islamist militant cell here even before 2005, when the four London suicide bombers made it their last stop on the way to blowing up themselves and fifty-two strangers on the London transport system. Their visit had not inspired them to choose life and light rather than death and infamy. In 2009 local Muslims infuriated their neighbours by protesting against soldiers returning from Afghanistan ('Luton twinned with Yemen,' said the *Mail* columnist Richard Littlejohn). This in turn gave rise to the white backlash group, the English Defence League, which is thought to have emerged from Luton's football-hooligan class. It was also here that an entire family of chavs kept a slave, tortured him and then finally, in 2009, hacked him to pieces.

The only major institution now named after the county is the University of Bedfordshire, which is a mutation and rebranding of the University of Luton, which passed into folk myth (no doubt unfairly) as the ultimate pretend university where they would readily dish out to all-comers first-class honours in basket weaving or strip pontoon. Maybe Luton itself could be rebranded: it really does not help a place to have a name so redolent of the toilet.

It is possible to avoid Luton and the M1 by taking Watling Street, the A5, through the once-grand staging-post town of Dunstable. In pre-railway days the Old Sugar Loaf Hotel was one of the most famous coaching inns of England. Moll Flanders stopped there, as did Queen Victoria (though not at the same time). It is now a loud, chirpy, bog-standard pub with TV screens all round the bar flashing up messages like TRY OUR TASTY BASKET MEALS! and BUY 5 COFFEES AND RECEIVE YOUR 6TH FREE. That would keep you awake in the traffic jams. It is almost impossible to park nearby even if you wanted and such a struggle to run a business in Dunstable that even the charity shops steer clear. Building after building was empty when I went through.

And yet you only have to head a couple of miles west and you can see how Bedfordshire maintains its averageness. Suddenly you are on Dunstable Downs, 700 feet up; the air is fresh and, westward, look, the land is bright. At the official viewing spot the scene is somewhat spoiled when you turn round and see the nasty new visitors' centre. But my weatherman-friend Philip Eden, who lives at Whipsnade, showed me his secret view from a barley field: clear across to Ivinghoe Beacon and way beyond – to the Cotswolds on a clear day. You can also just glimpse the penguin enclosure.

Whipsnade has something far more surprising than the view and the zoo. For Bedfordshire does, after all, have a cathedral: an imitation more touching than anything made of stone – a tree cathedral, created by a local grandee, Edmund Kell Blyth, to commemorate his First World War comrades. Not a memorial, he said, but a symbol of 'faith, hope and reconciliation'. It was not immediately successful: as soon as he finished planting it, the next war began. But it has survived all the horrors. It has the shape and scale of the real thing: a porch of oaks; a nave of limes; a chancel of silver birches; transepts of tulip trees and chestnuts. It is a quiet, numinous place. The South-East being gripped by drought that spring, I thought it politic not to light a candle.

Someone summed up Bedfordshire to me as 'a county of ugly towns and pretty villages'. And the second half of that is undoubtedly true. There is stunning stone-built Turvey; prosperous Eversholt with its splendid cricket field, its own communal swimming pool and a street called Witts End (which I'm often at); and, above all, there is Old Warden, full of thatch and leaded lights without a rough edge in sight, so pristine one would be frightened to fart in bed for fear of a harsh letter from the parish council. Old Warden was advertising a black-tie summer ball, starting with Pimm's and canapés, with tickets at £50 a head. Oh, the simple joys of merrie England! Even Toddington, famous for its motorway service station and racked by traffic, has a charming church and village green. It also still had, in 2011, *seven* pubs, believed to be a record for any English village. Indeed, I don't know any county with such handsome pubs – top beer, too, now that the south London staple Youngs is brewed in Bedford alongside much-loved Charlie Wells. The Royal Society for the Protection of Birds is based in a country house set in parkland just outside Sandy. Conor Jameson works there and talked to me eloquently of the joys of the Greensand Ridge, a landmark for migratory birds that crosses the county.

And Bedford is an unexpectedly pretty town. It went upmarket in the late nineteenth century thanks to the appeal of the good local schools run by the Harpur Trust. It seems settled, content, unexpectedly refined. St Paul's Church, in the centre of town, was the wartime setting for the BBC's Daily Service, which would be described as coming from 'Somewhere in England'.

Somewhere in England: it's a good description of Bedfordshire.

In contrast to Luton, Bedford has a sense of community. This is exemplified by its newspaper, *Bedfordshire on Sunday*, a freesheet started in 1977 by a rip-roaring local journalist called Frank Branston who got thrown out of the bland and fearful *Bedfordshire Times* because he kept trying to write stories exposing corruption. 'It was like a thirty-year revenge mission for Frank,' said his successor as editor, Steve Lowe.

An exquisitely successful mission: eventually his baby eclipsed the *Times* and took over its old office. Branston's paper was something else: part redtop tabloid, part *Private Eye*, it avoided village news and cheque presentations and delighted in enraging the bourgeoisie. Branston eventually became Bedford's first elected mayor and won a second term before he died suddenly, in 2009. His creation – now corporately owned by the Iliffe group – lives on, a little more placidly than before. 'We miss Frank,' said

Lowe. 'It was his newspaper, his personality. But Iliffe said they wouldn't interfere and they haven't. It's just that the law makes it harder for us to do what we used to do. We were forever monstering people and we did get sued an awful lot.' When I went to the office, an old bloke in front of me was complaining: 'No one's delivered to Roxton for three weeks.' Normal freesheets do not draw this kind of response. Its success suggests a place with hidden depths.

I wandered down to the River Ouse, bordered by gardens full of lilacs and early roses, with school eights gliding by. Pevsner was enchanted by the riverbank: 'Few English towns can be compared'. He missed the turning to Albany Road, an ordinary-looking street of Edwardian terraces, architecturally undistinguished but potentially the most famous street in the world.

For this is the home of the Panacea Society, a religious sect founded at the end of the first war under the leadership of Mabel Barltrop (a name that might have been invented by either Agatha Christie or Alan Bennett), who lived at no. 12. The Society gathered enough adherents – who knew Mabel under the more heavenly-sounding name of Octavia – to acquire a large property portfolio and a war chest now thought to exceed £30 million.

Though almost forgotten beyond Bedford, the Panacea Society is fashionably feminist: its fundamental tenet is that God is fourfold – father and son; mother and daughter. It is also very British, venerating a string of obscure British prophets, the most significant being Joanna Southcott, daughter of an eighteenth-century Devonian farmer, who left some of her writings in a sealed box, now held at an undisclosed location, thought to be 18 Albany Road, three doors down from Mabel's. This can only be opened, Southcott decreed, 'in a time of a grave national danger' on the instructions of twenty-four bishops of the Church of England.

In the 1920s, when Britain was full of bereaved young women, the society struck a chord and ran a poster campaign that made it famous: CRIME BANDITRY DISTRESS AND PERPLEXITY WILL INCREASE UNTIL THE BISHOPS OPEN JOANNA SOUTHCOTT'S BOX. Anyone who has observed the Church of England will be aware how difficult it is to get twenty-four bishops to agree on anything. And so crime, banditry, distress and perplexity have duly increased.

Much of this information I found on the society's website. This did not mention what members once told a TV documentary team: that the society believes Bedford to be the centre of the Garden of Eden. They added that a room (also thought to be in no. 18) had been prepared for Jesus' return, complete with en suite facilities.

All religions, including the most successful, require a suspension of everyday rational thought. In the cold light of a Channel 4 documentary, they would all sound ridiculous, especially if they originated not in Jerusalem, but in a terraced house in Bedford. It is socially acceptable to believe in the virgin birth, but not in Joanna Southcott's Box. So the Panacea Society grew sheepish and suspicious. When I rang the office bell and asked if they had any information, a gruff man told me: 'We don't just give out information. You'd need to write in and say why you want to know.' How was he so sure I wasn't a bishop?

There was one group who found worldly salvation in Bedford. I discovered their remnants, most of them by now over eighty, at their Thursday afternoon group in a Methodist church near the centre of town. The main difference between this club and the average British pensioners' group was the refreshment. No tea urn. At the Club Prima Generazione Italiani, they served tiny cups of strong coffee.

The Italians came to Bedford in the early 1950s because – with post-war employment booming – the locals no longer wanted or needed to work in the brickworks that then dominated the Bedfordshire landscape. The big firms began to recruit in southern Italy, where the grinding poverty meant there were many takers: strong young men keen to earn money unimaginable in the *Mezzogiorno*.

Some of those men were at Park Road church, still powerfully built, no longer young. They thought the streets of Bedford would be paved with gold. They were shocked by what they found. 'I thought when they said "hostel", that was the same as a hotel,' said Piras from Sardinia. They slept six to eight in a room; they hated the food (in 1950s England, pasta meant Heinz spaghetti); and, after they had paid for their accommodation and bus fares, there was little enough to send back.

To make more money, they had to take the toughest jobs: on piece-work and inside the 'chamber', the kiln itself, which could get unspeakably hot, especially towards the end of the week. 'On Monday, after it had been cooled for the weekend, it was not so bad,' said Domenico from Campobasso. 'But by Friday if I touched the floor it burned my hand. Every hour I had to change my shirt, it was so wet.' 'My husband had gloves made from

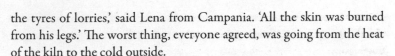

the tyres of lorries,' said Lena from Campania. 'All the skin was burned from his legs.' The worst thing, everyone agreed, was going from the heat of the kiln to the cold outside.

Because they worked hard, the men were accepted soon enough. At home, it was harder, with the neighbours complaining about the noise and the cooking smells. The womenfolk could be isolated, although many got work in the Meltis factory, making that delight of a 1950s childhood, New Berry Fruits. I suspect things started to get easier in the 1960s, which was when the British discovered Italy (often flying from Luton Airport) and ceased to think of their neighbours as Martians. Most of the migrants went home eventually, but some stayed, although it was noticeable that, even sixty years on, almost everyone at Park Road was far more comfortable speaking Italian. Their children grew up British, with the girls in particular chafing against their mothers' notions of teenage decorum. And now, as the *prima generazione* moves on, Bedford's Italian culture is fading too. 'Once there was an Italian shop on every street, and sometimes two,' said Carmela Semeraro, the community historian and organiser of the Thursday group. 'Now there are only two left in Bedford.'

The brickworks have gone too. The largest in the world, run by the London Brick Company at Stewartby, was said to produce 650 million bricks a year. And that was just one site: there were 130 chimneys on the road between Bedford and Bletchley alone. Stewartby closed in 2008 and production moved to Peterborough, on the same brick-friendly layer of clay, but with more modern plant. On the otherwise deserted site I discovered a lone watchman supervising the exit of the day's last lorry carrying away the old spoil. The four Stewartby chimneys – more than 200 feet high – are not being demolished: the heritage people stepped in. Outside a battered sign read: GRADE II LISTED CHIMNEYS AND KILNS FOR SALE OR TO LET. The kilns might make bijou garden flats, I suppose, but it is not obvious what use there might be for the chimneys, which would have drawbacks as family homes, despite the sensational view from the roof terrace.

So they will remain, along with the two great airship sheds at Cardington, which have had little use since the R101 left there in 1930 on its doomed journey to France. There it crashed in flames, killing forty-eight passengers and crew and, with them, the dream that airships would be the transport of the future. The sheds stand like beached whales, towering above the poplars – symbols, like the Stewartby chimneys, of a county that desperately needs some kind of symbolism. Otherwise, it will eventually lose what little identity it has and really will be just Somewhere in England.

Perhaps the RSPB could set up an offshoot, the Royal Society for the Protection of Bedfordshire. Perhaps the Panacea Society could be a little less secretive with the notion of Bedford as the Garden of Eden. But what if Mabel's heirs were half right, and Jesus actually turned up in a room with en suite at the Ibis Hotel, Luton Airport, instead? That might be a very interesting and profound statement.

May 2011

~~~~~~

The last resident member of the Panacea Society died in 2012 and it ceased to exist as a religious community. It is now under control of a trust which, grown weary of furtiveness, has a museum, open for a short period every Thursday. It intends to continue to abide by the conditions for opening the box, which is 'in a safe and secure location'. The profusion of pubs in little Toddington was too good to be true: by the end of 2012 the seven had dwindled to four. Luton Town returned to the Football League in 2014 after five years in exile.

3. *Adventures in the state-your-business belt*

SURREY

We were standing, Matthew Banner and I, on the western edge of Box Hill. On a ridge to the north-east, looking very out of place, was the show-offy eighteenth-century pile of Norbury Park. But since this was later owned by Leopold Salomons, who gave Box Hill to the nation, it would have been mean to complain.

That one house aside, nothing. Mile after mile of what looked like virgin forest. We could have been Lewis and Clark on the Rockies, stout Cortez on a peak in Darien. It was a moment for wild surmise. Where on earth were we? 'That's Heathrow Airport over there,' said Matthew. 'You'd see it very clearly in the winter when there's no leaf cover.'

We went back to the most famous part of the hill, the southern slope by the Salomons memorial. On the warm summer's morning there were women in bikinis, sunbathing. Ahead of them lay this vision: Leith Hill, the highest point in south-east England; a few Italianate lollipop trees atop the foothills; and a seemingly empty plain stretching to

Chanctonbury Ring, the South Downs, the horizon and the sea.

'Over there, hidden by the ridge,' said Matthew, pointing south-east, 'that's Gatwick. And there, those are the suburbs of Dorking. You can see the main railway line there, and there's another below us. That's the A24 just there ...'

'And what are those white things, the ones that look like the sails of a yacht?'

'That's the sewage works.'

Surrey truly is a miraculous county, the world's biggest trompe l'oeil. Somewhere round here, there are millions of people. But they are hidden among the trees: shy woodland creatures, probably nocturnal – trolls or goblins or hobbits. Maybe that's why the river that flows past Box Hill is called the Mole. Again and again, this place takes one's breath away: from the top of the stand at Epsom racecourse, all you see, if you gaze beyond the horses, are treetops stretching towards infinity, like the New Guinea rainforest. Surrey is called the most wooded county in England and I believe it. There is an iron law in journalism that it must always be referred to as 'leafy Surrey'; subeditors probably think that's the official title, like Royal Berkshire. Technically, it's only leafy between April and the end of October, when you can't see Heathrow from Box Hill. So why not twiggy, boughy or trunky? Shouldn't be there a close season on using the word 'leafy', as with grouse shooting?

In my mind's eye, Surrey has always been associated with green: Green Line buses, the green station signs of the old Southern Region. And the leafiness means it stays green even after a drought-spring like this one. But there are contrasts too. Looking north from the Hog's Back, I fancied myself on the Blue Mountains in New South Wales: 'I see the vision splendid of the sunlit plains extended'. Well, as I say, there was a drought. And it had been a pretty brief glimpse. The Hog's Back is the A31 dual carriageway, not a place to get distracted by visions.

For it's all an illusion. You may not be able to see the airports from Box Hill but you can hear the planes right enough: we were only a few miles from Ockham, one of the four stacks which pilots must meander around when awaiting a landing slot at Heathrow. George Meredith, who lived nearby, referred to the valley below Box Hill as 'a soundless gulf'. He died in 1909, two months before Blériot crossed the Channel and some years before the motorcycling community discovered Ryka's burger bar at Burford Bridge, began flocking there on summer weekends like starlings,

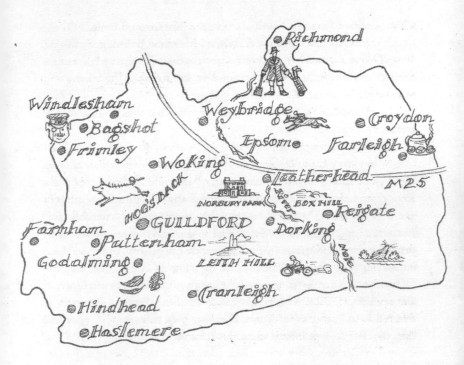

staging ton-up races down the A24 and, sometimes, writing themselves off on the Mickleham bends.

That's entirely typical. Surrey is visually exhilarating but aurally vexatious. The racket is constant but no one else appears to notice. In Farnham, pretty and Georgian, the bleepers on the pedestrian crossings were set to ear-splitting levels; maybe it's the only way they could be heard above the planes. Every road in the county seemed constantly busy, even in the middle of the day. And here was me thinking the entire adult population was whisked to Waterloo sometime around sunrise, leaving Surrey to the young, the old, the feckless and about half a dozen surviving farm workers.

It's a bad-tempered county too. On the roads, someone is always in your face or up your arse. There is a myth that drivers in London are mean and aggressive; it's not true (the cyclists excepted) – the only way to survive on the roads there is by give-and-take. Then these gentle souls get out of town and, whump, all their pent-up motoring misanthropy comes out. No one gives an inch. There is still something of the 1930s about Surrey, when a chap might take his popsy out in the jalopy for a spin round Brooklands, have a few jars at the roadhouse and a canoodle in the dicky seat down Lovers' Lane. But there are no quiet lanes any more. My constant companion, Kathy, the Irish satnav voice, was spooked by this county and regularly disorientated. Once this forced me to execute a nine-point turn on a sandy track. In the midst of this operation, I was assailed by a herd of cyclists, taking no prisoners.

The epitome of Surrey is Seven Hills Road in Weybridge: huge houses set among the tall trees and the rhododendrons, nearly all of them with sylvan names: Squirrels Wood, The Beeches, Hill Pines, Fox Oak, The Spinney. The only exception I spotted was Millstones, presumably named by an owner who needed multiple mortgages or hated his children. But I may have missed some: if I had slowed down a fraction to check the names, someone would have nuzzled my rear bumper. These houses must constitute second prize in life's lottery (we will come to the first prize later). Yet just turning right when they exit their security gates in the morning constitutes a further gamble for these winners. The traffic is always fast and the drivers furious. What are they furious about? Because they *don't* live on Seven Hills Road? Or because they *do*?

Money and property are the Surrey obsessions. One of the county magazines, *So Surrey* – witless even by the low standards of this genre – had 'The New £150,000 Aston Martin' on its cover. Its rival, *Surrey Life*, channelled the *Sunday Times* rich list and revealed that nos. 1, 2 and 3 were all local residents (or homeowners anyway): Lakshmi Mittal of Cranleigh, Alisher Usmanov of Guildford and Roman Abramovich of Stoke D'Abernon. The front few pages of the *Surrey Advertiser* homes supplement were taken up by places all valued deep into seven-figure territory; eight is not uncommon; nine not unthinkable. On the web there was a mansion in Windlesham for sale at £70 million. Exact size unknown, since different agents counted different numbers of bedrooms, twenty-two, twenty-three, twenty-four, somewhere in that region. Not forgetting heated marble driveways, three swimming pools, squash court, bowling alley and a galleried landing that is 'a replica of Versace's home in Miami'.

Staring at the colour pictures of sumptuous interiors and neatly mown weedless lawns, one sensed something dismal about these places: they seemed vapid, sterile, loveless. I know people normally tidy up before the estate agent takes photographs, but there is another property-selling theory – that you should casually strew the lawn with children's bikes and a football, and suffuse the house with the smell of freshly baked apple pie. Hard to imagine these houses had ever heard children's laughter or smelt an apple pie. This is the heart of what the writer Gordon Burn once called 'the state-your-business belt'.

One felt most of the sales marked the end of more than one era and that the marriage was being disposed of too. Further back came the adverts for flats, and every Surrey town I saw was echoing to the construction of new blocks of what are usually now called apartments, boltholes for refugees from relationships that have fractured under the pressure of living in Surrey.

But the wealth is in part another illusion. Surrey is not homogeneous, even its post-1965 incarnation after its urban north-east was ceded to Greater London in exchange for a chunk of meat carved from the carcass of murdered Middlesex. You can take a tram these days from Croydon to Wimbledon that goes through much of ex-Surrey, most of it a bit grim. Surrey County Hall, weirdly, is still in Kingston, which is no longer part of the territory it administers.

Some people think of Surrey in quadrants: more urban north of the M25; a bit snootier west of the A3. But overall it is quite obviously wealthy. That, says Wendy Varcoe of the Community Foundation for Surrey, is the trouble: 'Our challenge is to make people aware that there's a problem. If you're wealthy, it's a lovely place to live. If you're not, the services aren't geared to you.'

I met Wendy at Ockford Ridge, a 1930s ex-council estate above Godalming, regarded with a slight shudder by most of the residents of that most Surreyish of towns as 'up there'. It does not look deprived, and indeed has been gentrified by young couples fleeing the million-pound houses below. The main complaint I heard was about a woman who always left her overflowing dustbin on the pavement.

But there's stuff beneath the surface and always has been. I met a woman who came from Birmingham to work in the nursery school: 'I was teaching in Handsworth and I thought I'd seen it all. When I first got here the kids said, "We're not going to do what you tell us." I was spat on, I was kicked.'

'How old were these kids?'

'Three and four.'

Terry Broomfield, who grew up on the estate, got into the grammar school in 1947. His parents, humiliatingly, sent him with football boots rather than rugby boots. 'Oh, you wouldn't know about such things,' he was told dismissively on Day 1. 'You're from Ockford Ridge.' In retirement, he still hadn't budged and was working hard for the community.

'The doctor's surgery used to be in the High Street. Now it's out of town and 250 yards from a bus stop. And a lot of people have to take two buses to get there at all. Well, if you're ill, you might not be able to walk 250 yards. We get forgotten.' Terry drove me round and pointed out, with some pride, a house where a murder took place. 'That's the private estate, Miltons Crescent,' he explained.

'So that's not Ockford Ridge?'

'Oh, no,' he said, talking mock-posh. 'That's Miltons Crescent. Phwah!'

Naturally, the news reports all said it was Ockford Ridge.

I fall in love with place names and then regret it. Once, I took a bus hundreds of miles because I couldn't resist the sound of Sweetwater, Texas. It was a dump, of course. I kept rolling the names of Surrey towns round my tongue, but one look in my copy of the Surrey Pevsner stopped me bothering. This was the only volume in the series almost wholly written by that much-missed critic and wanderer Ian Nairn. He was more reliably trenchant than the series' eponymous master: ABINGER (beloved of E. M. Forster): 'a little suburbanized'; ASH: 'sad'; BRAMLEY: 'nondescript'; BYFLEET: 'shattered ... beneath contempt'; CAPEL: 'nondescript' ... all the way down to WRECCLESHAM: 'a few very battered cottages and a bad church'.

I couldn't resist Bagshot, purely because of the name, redolent of the days when every lounge bar in England, possibly under a similar regulation to the one governing the use of 'leafy Surrey', always had a mustachioed military figure at the bar with a name like that. 'Mornin', Major Bagshot. A pint of the usual?' Long before Pevsner, Daniel Defoe had called Bagshot the town 'good for nothing' and he wasn't wrong. I couldn't see a pub that would have suited the major. Or me.

I had to go on to Camberley, not utterly dismissed by Pevsner, but really because of Betjeman:

By roads 'not adopted', by woodlanded ways,
She drove to the club in the late summer haze,

Into nine-o'clock Camberley, heavy with bells
And mushroomy, pine-woody, evergreen smells.

I parked by Pine Avenue (unadopted) and scrunched my way down the gravel road past houses called Stony Ridge, Stumpers and Squirrels Lea. Some of the houses did have a vaguely Betjemanesque quality but most had been extended, remodelled, infilled. There was an occasional whiff of pine. But I heard no bells: just the jets from Gatwick; the roar of the traffic on the M3; the hammering of builders; the whine of hedge trimmers and the whirr of mowers, controlled by jobbing gardeners who arrive in American-style pickup trucks and are not encouraged to let mushrooms show their faces. In the autumn, they probably use leaf blowers. At moments when everything stopped except the M3, it was possible to detect an understorey of birdsong. That kind of silence does occur in Surrey but, I think, less frequently than in any other county.

I went to Puttenham under the Hog's Back, home of the last hop garden in Surrey, and singled out in 2007 by the connoisseur of villages, Clive Aslet, for its peacefulness and for the sign in the charmingly named pub, the Good Intent, welcoming 'muddy boots, dogs and children'. I sat in the pub garden: a siren was wailing from the main road; next door someone was using a power drill, which might have been annoying had it not been outcompeted by a mega-decibel cooling unit or something at the back of the pub. The beer was OK. Then I spotted the sign. It now read: 'Please remove or clean properly your shoes or boots to protect the carpet. Thank you.' The road to the Good Intent is paved with hell.

I tried heaven instead and went to Guildford Cathedral to light my candle. The building is modern, almost contemporaneous with Coventry, but laid out in the Gothic manner without the curly, twirly bits. It is not much loved. Pevsner-Nairn, however, was kindly, calling it 'noble and subtle, with a queer power of compelling not reverence but contemplation'. I tried to sit and contemplate but, when I stared skywards, I noticed the ceiling had developed dark blotches, as though it had a fungal disease. Then a thirty-strong conga line passed by, suddenly and bafflingly. They were apparently Dutch choristers, rehearsing for the evening concert. I also needed a pee. None of this was conducive to contemplation. The cathedral is, however, available for 'drinks receptions and gala dinners' and I am sure it is conducive to those.

In any case, I had an invitation – to go back to Seven Hills Road and climb, from the runners-up zone to the podium reserved for life's real champions: the St George's Hill estate. This place is famous for two reasons, which happen to be totally contradictory. Surrey may be a county of paradoxes but there is nothing to match this.

In the 1640s a London cloth merchant called Gerrard Winstanley responded to the collapse of his business by retreating to Surrey to farm. He began hearing voices and seeing visions, as people did in that overwrought decade. In April 1649, three months after Charles I was executed, Winstanley and a small group of settlers put together a few rickety huts and began planting crops on the St George's Hill common, preaching some kind of combination of love, peace and the abolition of private property. The earth, said Winstanley, should be 'a common treasury'. They called themselves the Diggers or the True Levellers.

Respectable local opinion was outraged and a group of vigilantes wrecked one field by ploughing in the crop; soldiers destroyed another. One officer sent to investigate said 'the business is not worth the writing'. Another observer called the Diggers 'a company of crackbrains'. They did not last long, had little impact and were largely forgotten for more than three centuries, until the 1960s, another overwrought decade, when the mood of the times – and the researches of the historian Christopher Hill – helped push them into public consciousness. We have had a play, a film, a song by Leon Rosselson and, in 2009, *The Complete Works of Gerrard Winstanley*, published by the Oxford University Press, which has no truck with any of that common treasury nonsense, at £189. Plus the fact that in 1999 a new group of Diggers arrived and decided that the time had come again.

However, by now St George's Hill had changed a bit. It certainly was not common land. The reverse. Just before the First World War, a builder called George Tarrant had bought the property and built 105 family homes, mostly in the 'Surrey style', influenced by Lutyens and the Arts and Crafts movement, each with at least an acre of land, suitable for the plutocrats of the day, with a golf course and tennis club on hand.

The years passed. St George's Hill became a byword for luxurious and exclusive living: more private and less nouveau than its rivals like Wentworth and Woldingham. The golf course, set amid the pines with a clubhouse in tartan baronial style, became much admired and enjoyed. It was a gorgeous place for a drink on a hot afternoon. The estate acquired an international reputation, appealing in particular to the new breed of Russian oligarch. Meanwhile, the cult of Winstanley was starting to take shape. And finally, on a springtime Saturday in 1999, the 350th anniversary of the Diggers' arrival, the worlds collided.

A sculptor and lettercutter called Andrew Whittle had been commissioned to produce a stone to commemorate Winstanley for an exhibition. He was taken with the idea: 'There was no known grave and he seemed like a worthy character,' Whittle explained. One thing led to another, and thus he found himself marching through the gates of St George's Hill with a group of activists to do a bit of ranting (in the very specific, seventeenth-century sense) and erect the stone in a permanent site on the hill. So they duly trundled the stone up the hill and across the golf course – startling a couple of ladies waiting to tee off – to a bit of spare ground in the woods. All this had been agreed by the Residents' Association.

That's what Whittle thought he was doing, anyway. But two things he didn't know. Firstly, these Diggers (300 of them, they claimed; probably more like thirty) were not planning just to commemorate their predecessors, but to emulate them – only this time they were not going to be pushed out. They had a marquee and a supply of perfectly good food thrown out as unsaleable by the supermarkets. Secondly, as Whittle explained, the residents had changed their minds: 'First of all, they thought it was fine. A free bit of art, thank you. Then they found out who Winstanley was. Suddenly, they got very cold feet.'

Millenarian socialism did not go down well with the Cromwellian establishment in 1649. It was never likely to be popular, with the real millennium approaching, on Britain's richest estate, especially not among the Russians who had reached here by getting rid of the communists. History now began to repeat itself to an uncanny degree. The Diggers made big statements; the locals harassed them – one activist got punched and, said Whittle: 'I remember a Mercedes with blacked-out windows that stopped so they could lob golf balls at us'; the water company which owned the patch of land being used for the camp, got heavy and went to court; and the whole thing fizzled out in a fortnight.

There was one loose end: the stone which had been temporarily dug in was now homeless and, although it was rather beautiful, had become very unpopular on the hill, where it was thought to be a potential magnet for tourists, ramblers, idealists and other riff-raff. Elmbridge Council did agree to find a home for it. And so now it stands in the woods, half-hidden in the summer by bracken, close to Weybridge Station, by the junction with Cobbetts Hill, which gives it some historical resonance (William Cobbett, a far more effective radical than Winstanley, was also a Surrey lad: born and buried at Farnham). There is an information board, covered with dust and bird shit, but quite helpful, offering a not very convincing Diggers' trail round the area. It does not include St George's Hill.

By 2011 the proportion of ex-Soviets on the estate was estimated at between a quarter and a third. Many of the houses were empty, or nearly always empty, because they were owned by people who had boltholes everywhere. When I was there, one had just been taken over by squatters. The original houses are very attractive but hardly any are protected by listing, so the gig now – I was told – goes like this: resident sells to developer for £3 million; developer spends £500,000 on demolishing the house and £3 million on putting up a more sumptuous replacement, then sells for £10 million to a Russian or a footballer.

St George's Hill is a very pretty place, offering what is usually called an enviable lifestyle. The houses are shielded by a riot of Surrey shrubbery, as well as high walls and security gates to offer protection from anyone not filtered out by the guards at the entrances to the estate. But the grass alongside the rampant rhododendrons is cut uniformly, like a fairway, which looks ridiculous: a foreign billionaire's conception of England. 'A nice place to live,' said one advert. A nice place to endure house arrest while cowering from your enemies, perhaps. But to *live*? It's miles to the shops and Lord knows how you borrow a cup of sugar from a neighbour.

What would Winstanley have thought? Well, here's the funniest thing of all. After the Diggers' thing collapsed, he came into money and land, farmed near Cobham and became a churchwarden, constable and overseer of the poor. He would probably have fancied one of George Tarrant's houses.

Surely there must be somewhere in Surrey with which I could fall in love? So many of these places looked so beautiful, but further investigation made them seem intolerable (and usually intolerant as well). Flicking through Pevsner, I found something unexpected: FARLEIGH: 'A tiny hamlet on the North Downs, quite unspoiled – almost the most rural in Surrey. Flint and brick farms and barns. This extraordinary place is four miles from the centre of Croydon.' The edition was dated 1971. Doubtless it must have been wrecked by now. I could see this for myself, write a few more angry paragraphs, damn Surrey to hell and move on.

It was Friday evening; the traffic was just starting to ease off, the weather was cooling down and Kathy the satnav was becoming calmer. She directed me along the M25 and up the steep hill towards Warlingham. Even this bit was a revelation: more like a Shropshire lane than the lanes they have in – ghastly word – 'countrified' Surrey. I passed somewhere called Halliloo House, nothing special as a property, but I could see what had inspired the name.

Then out of Warlingham, pleasantly unpretentious, to Farleigh. I passed the Harrow, an unappealing pub with a packed car park that was obviously very Surrey. Then things changed. This was not like any normal boundary: it was like walking through the wardrobe into a parallel world.

The grass on Great Farleigh Green grew high, set about with ox-eye daisies; there were twisted hawthorns instead of rhododendrons; horses grazed in thistly fields. I found my way to the church. It was small, Norman and stuccoed – in continuous use for worship since 1086, the rector, Rev. Alan Middleton, told me later. There was a breeze now and everything felt fresh. Nearby there was a tatty riding centre; across the road bits of machinery and a collection of old tyres. Normally, this might be annoying. But after days in Surrey, it was a revelation: like an English English village, not an oligarch's notion of it, a place where people might even tend their own garden and let their children play in it. Here was a place where a man might breathe and a dog might crap.

A bloke on a bicycle rode out of the woods. His name was Peter and he stopped for a chat. Stopped for a chat! In Surrey!

'I didn't know this place,' I said.

'Weird, isn't it? You wouldn't believe we're a couple of miles from Croydon. I tell people at work I pass horses, cows and sheep and they don't believe me. Mind you, we're 600 feet up. Gets a bit naughty in the wintertime.'

Not only is this not like Surrey, for a few years in the 1960s it was officially moved – into Greater London. That notion was so mad and the locals so determined that they fought and won. The history is that the land was owned by Merton College, Oxford, which refused to allow any development when the south London suburbs began their march towards the sea. The college was too rich to care, too dozy or too high-minded (too rich, probably). Then came the Green Belt legislation and suddenly the land could not be developed. Thus it has remained, in this glorious time warp.

There has been some change: one farm has become a golf course; a few new houses have been allowed, and some residents insist on behaving as though they were elsewhere in Surrey and lock their front gates. But otherwise it remains astonishingly untouched. There is also a hall at the back of the church, useful for parish meetings – where people can get het up if developers find Farleigh on the map and start getting ideas – and also deanery synods. Alan Middleton said he was attending a particularly dull one of these when a horse suddenly appeared at the window and stared in. 'I'm sure he was laughing.'

The church itself is well attended. It uses an old-fashioned prayer book and on summer Sundays the congregation serve cream teas all afternoon, followed at 8 by candlelit compline with a guest speaker. 'Everyone wants to come,' says the rector. 'It's very popular among those who like a certain kind of religion.' You bet! I'm a cream-tea-and-candlelit-compline Christian, and I'm Jewish.

I resolved to return, not to Surrey, but here – to unSurrey. I had found it. Halliloo, indeed, Halliloo-loo-jah!

June 2011

~~~~~~

I was not imagining the blotches at Guildford Cathedral. In 2014 the cathedral's website said there was a 'serious risk of closure' because of the state of the ceiling.

4. *Oh, my name it means nothing*

DURHAM

The day of the 127th Durham Miners' Gala dawned bright, with a hint of threat. As the crowds gathered good-naturedly on the streets leading into Durham city, clouds gathered more menacingly on the horizon. There was what felt like a conscious decision to ignore them. This may be a metaphor for the fate of the coal industry.

The first thing outsiders learn about the Gala is that it's pronounced 'Gayla'. The second thing is that it isn't necessarily. Most of the locals say 'Garla'. I think this is a lesson in advanced Englishism, not just an unexpected pronunciation like Leominster/Lemster but something more complex. Maybe in Durham there are multiple layers of initiation and in some inner sanctum it really is called 'the Gayla'. It's also called The Big Meeting.

There's actually not much call for outsiders to call it anything at all. They are not unwelcome, just not expected. The signposting is useless. This may be because the event comes under the aegis of the National Union of Mineworkers, no longer the country's most vibrant organisation (in July

2011 its homepage was still wishing members a Happy New Year) but also because Durham is a bit introspective. The people are not unwelcoming, the complete reverse. Nor, in the city, are they unused to tourists. But they still seem surprised to see any. They greet visitors from distant Herefordshire with the same kindly bemusement ('You're not from here, are you?') with which they might greet ET.

It's not a big meeting either. It's a middle-sized meeting. The Communist paper, the *Morning Star*, still clinging on for dear life, reported that 'trade union leaders addressed 130,000 people'. They did nothing of the kind. They addressed about a thousand or two. Maybe 130,000 were in town, but the Gala has multiple purposes. It is a political meeting; it is a funfair; it is an informal brass band festival; it is an obeisance to history; it is a church service; it is a piss-up.

Bourgeois Durham recoils. 'It was all right when it was families coming for picnics,' one woman working at the cathedral told me as she prepared to leave town. 'Now it's just an excuse to get drunk.' Families do come, though they may not be the sort normally seen round the ancient cathedral. In the shadow of the walls, I saw a man pointing out his four-year-old to his mate. 'He's a little shit, that one,' he said. 'Gunna be a copper.'

The Gala-goers march through the streets behind their smartly uniformed bandsmen and their lovingly crafted banners – some representing historic miners' lodges, some representing still-thriving unions – to the Old Racecourse by the river. A small minority stood listening to repetitive speeches from an endless cavalcade of union leaders and old lefties. The speakers were behind a banner provided by the *Morning Star* and in front of a funfair sideshow called Jungle Madness. The speeches contained the same mixture of ever-changing topical references and unchanging slogans that have formed the basis of left-wing politics throughout my adult life: 'We must all work for a new Labour government but it must be a *true* Labour government ... Brothers and sisters, we are under attack from the government ... They've got an ideological hatred of working people ... WE OPPOSE THE CUTS!'

The vast majority of the 130,000, or whatever, were either out of earshot – the sound system was mercifully useless – or just not listening. They were having fun. But then the clouds, which had been quietly moving towards critical mass all morning, suddenly exploded. There was a single but ferocious thunderclap and an overwhelming downpour. The speakers

Chopwell

Jarrow

Sunderland

Consett

PENNINES

DURHAM

Wheatley Hill

Peterlee

Trimdon Grange

Hartlepool

Escomb

Bishop Auckland

River Tees

paused and huddled under umbrellas. I was given sanctuary behind the desk of a stall manned by the North-East Shop Stewards' Network, which I will always remember with gratitude. The locals, famously insouciant about the weather, took little notice. The big fairground rides like the Waltzer and the Hard Rock continued as before, just as busy. Maybe the rain was an added thrill.

When it eased and Dennis Skinner MP began banging on, I followed the banner of the Dean and Chapter Lodge which I assumed, with a name like that, must be heading for the cathedral. Actually, they were heading home to Ferryhill, whence they came. Dean and Chapter was the name of Ferryhill's old pit because the Church was the landowner.

The cathedral was packed anyway. Probably more people heard the current dean, the Very Reverend Michael Sadgrove, welcome them than listened to Dennis Skinner. In accordance with tradition, new banners were brought in to be blessed. Those from Easington and Eppleton collieries were given a place of honour, draped in black, to mark the six-tieth anniversary of major pit disasters: eighty-one killed at Easington in May 1951; nine at Eppleton five weeks later. 'This is the day,' said Sadgrove, 'when I am reminded who this cathedral really belongs to.'

Durham used to be dominated by a unique coalition: the coal indus-try and the Church, both once impregnable: the one now effectively van-ished, except from folklore; the other facing the future with alarm. As the dean well knew, their relationship in this county was never straightfor-ward, and the question of what belonged to whom was at the heart of the problem.

On the eve of the Gala, I overheard an American tourist describe Dur-ham Cathedral as 'quite impressive'. *Quite?* OK, but not as classy as Min-neapolis or Little Rock, then?

Apart from anything else, Durham is the most unignorable cathedral in England. It stands on both a promontory and a peninsula, where the River Wear does a sharp U-turn. It looks like a defensive position, I said to Michael Sadgrove. Exactly, he replied. The Saxon followers of St Cuth-bert discovered the site a century after the Vikings had chased them out of Lindisfarne. Then the Normans arrived and, having harried, devastated and subdued the North, they built their own cathedral, dedicating it to Cuthbert as a sop to local opinion, and placed it under the control of a bishop who turned into a prince. Durham did not become a county like any other; it was never a *shire*. It was a quasi-independent nation, run by a bishop who had his own army, parliament, courts and coinage. Though its independence waned after the Reformation, it remained a palatinate, a statelet, until 1836: arguably more of a country than Wales.

And much of the land was owned directly by the Church. This became worthwhile when lead and silver mining took off in the early days of the Industrial Revolution. These industries were based in the west of the county: rugged, remote, now almost wholly depopulated. The silver was worked out, and the price of lead plummeted – just as the coal indus-try, in the eastern half of Durham, took off, creating another bonanza for the diocese. The mine owners, the Church among them, grew rich. The colliers did not grow rich but they had steady work: low-paid, dangerous and often horrendous, but reliable, less cyclical than Durham's other great industries of shipbuilding and steel.

For a century Durham was defined by Church and coal. But it was a stormy marriage. In 1892 Bishop Westcott brokered a peace deal that ended a particularly bitter strike. In the 1930s the miners were so livid with Bishop Henson (who had denounced the Jarrow march as 'organised mob pressure') that they tried to throw him in the river on Gala Day. Actually, they had the wrong man: it was his dean, dressed in bishop's robes because he had once been Bishop of Calcutta. In 1984 Bishop Jenkins, the scholar-iconoclast who dared to admit to doubts about the Gospels, vociferously backed the miners' strike. And to this day the cathedral authorities are acutely sensitive about the contrast between the opulence of their build-ing and the poverty of the diocese. Despite its magnificence, Durham Cathedral does not charge admission.

The night before the Gala it had been almost empty. The afternoon was rainy, and at Choral Evensong the congregation was slightly outnum-bered by the choir. They sang Harold Darke's arrangement of the Mag-nificat in A Minor, beautifully. The audience huddled alongside them in the seventeenth-century choir stalls, awestruck. It was as if a troupe of West End stars were putting on the performance of their lives at a sparsely attended matinee.

In return we recited the Apostles' Creed as though we were certain of its truth:

I believe in the Holy Spirit,
the holy catholic Church,
the communion of saints,
the forgiveness of sins,
the resurrection of the body,
and the life everlasting.

But as I mouthed the words, I was finalising my plan, for a rare, I think unique, Friday-night double. I had asked a local expert, Mike Amos of the *Northern Echo*, where I should go to capture the spirit of County Dur-ham. He didn't even stop to think. 'Wheatley Hill dog track,' he replied.

It was below the village, the other side from the closed-down pit, just below the closed-down pub. It comprised some of the ugliest buildings in the palatinate: a mixture of breezeblocks and Meccano. The kennels looked as though they had burned down (they had). Nearby were several tethered ponies, munching in reasonable contentment. Sometimes they get raced on a Sunday evening. The official County Durham signs still call it Land of the Prince Bishops. I think of it as the Land of the Tethered Pony.

This is part of a secret world, hiding in plain sight, as mystical in its way as Choral Evensong. Wheatley Hill is a 'flapping track', beyond the reach of the authorities that control greyhound racing, just about subject to the laws of England, but basically operating to codes that might have been understood, in some circles, at the time of the Apostles. They have been racing here on Friday nights since no one knows when. 'It hasn't changed much,' said Tommy White from Hartlepool, who had been smoking his roll-ups here for sixty years. And it was going long before he arrived.

'It used to be Tuesday night and Saturday morning too. That was good. I could come here in the morning, do Houghton on a Saturday afternoon and Easington or Stockton on Saturday night.' He had just had half a lung out. 'Nothing will stop me coming to the dogs,' he said. Or smoking his roll-ups. Tommy was an old seacoaler, the most characteristic of marginal Durham jobs: wading into the sea, netting the coal waste that was either dumped into the water or emerged from seams deep under the seabed and drifted in on the tide and the easterlies, staining the beach black. There was enough coal in the waste to make some kind of living.

Wheatley Hill was even more marginal. The greyhounds were unloaded from white vans by men who looked as though they drove white vans. Their charges had simpler and more robust names than is normal at fancier tracks: Seek & Destroy; Mad Dog; Black Mick; Black Lass; Walk of Shame; RU Trying; Could Be Hassle; Whacko; Slip; Cash Only; Snotty Nose; Twin. Nothing here was fancy, except for the mechanical hare, which was covered in pink, green and blue and looked like a dead parrot. The prize money was very unfancy: £15 for the winner in most races with a fiver for second.

The logic that drove events at Wheatley Hill was somewhat confusing. The official race timetable was merely a basis for negotiation. The only two bookmakers present stood around chatting under signs saying 'No Bets Taken Before Race'. I would have almost been willing to believe that at Wheatley Hill bets were only taken after the result, but I was assured this was a ban on bets being struck in the bar earlier in the evening.

You had to be quick to get on at all. Neither bookmaker began to think about chalking the odds until the announcer said 'Seconds to Go', whereupon they would, very often, chalk up each of the six runners at 2 to 1, which would give them a theoretical profit margin of 100 per cent. But theory does not get anyone far at Wheatley Hill.

Everyone knew everyone (except me). Everyone seemed to know what was going on in any particular race (except me). And there was always something going on. Money changed hands but there were no receipts: everyone was known by their name or nickname. Including me, by the end of the evening: I was 'the Welsh author', which was at least half-right.

'It's a very fair track, Wheatley Hill,' said Tommy. 'An excellent galloping track, I don't care what anyone else says. But Askern's the place …'

'Ascot?'

No, As-*kern*, near Doncaster. The Ascot of flapping. 'You can get a proper bet on there. You can't get fifteen hundred quid here if you go down on your knees. You get all the good dogs there. Mind you, lads like us, we want to race our dogs against Jack Russells really.'

Tommy had a dog running in the fourth race. He pointed to it on the racecard: Bailey's Bullet. It was running in the name of a Mr McCloud. I looked puzzled.

'You don't ever race under your own name,' explained Tommy. 'Not if you've got a reputation.'

'But everyone knows it's your dog.'

'Course they do. If I had a man in an iron mask lead the dog round, they'd know it was mine.'

I got the impression I should steer clear of Bailey's Bullet. But it ran well, came close, finished third. He made a 'that was a near thing' face.

'What would you have done if it had won?'

'Been very upset,' said Tommy. 'I backed the winner.'

I started talking to one of the bookmakers, Alan Dobbin. 'You make money?' I asked.

'Oh, yeah.'

'Everyone I've met makes money.'

'Aye.'

'Track makes money?'

'Some.'

'Miraculous, isn't it?'

'Definitely.'

I believe in the Holy Spirit,
the holy catholic Church,
the communion of saints,
the forgiveness of sins,
the resurrection of the body,
and the life everlasting.

I had not made money. I had started by obeying my betting rules, one of which is never to bet when I know absolutely nothing. But a man can only have so much self-control. Before the last race Tommy said that, on form, Cosy Toes couldn't lose but that his dog Twin should definitely come second. There was nothing else to touch him.

Cosy Toes was heavy odds-on, so the bookmakers chalked up prices without the favourite. Twin 5 to 4, so I could make money if he won or came second to Cosy Toes.

Cosy Toes got beaten, Twin was nowhere at all. I was feeling mildly aggrieved but sportingly went to the kennels to give Twin a pat.

'You said on form that was impossible,' I whined.

Tommy gave me a pitying look. 'You don't take any notice of form in flapping,' he said.

The pit in Wheatley Hill closed in 1968, a decade in which the number of mines in County Durham was halved. More went before and after the great confrontation of 1984: the wicked witch Margaret Thatcher pitted against the arrogant dolt Arthur Scargill. In 1993 Durham's last, at Wearmouth, closed down and the new Sunderland football stadium was built on the site. A colony of shrimps, living in an underground lagoon, was rescued. The mine itself was not.

Five years earlier, the last shipyard had closed in Sunderland, once the largest shipbuilding town in the world. The great steelworks in Consett had already gone; so had the Shildon Wagon Works, which built most of British Railways' goods wagons. That's now a museum.

Since then the bigger cities and towns in the North-East have reinvented themselves, but in an evanescent kind of way. They assemble cars in Sunderland, but only as long as it suits the Japanese owners. Hartlepool has a marina and can now laugh at itself. When I first went there I was told, with deadly earnest, 'Don't mention the monkey.' During the Napoleonic Wars, a monkey was found on the beach, presumably having escaped from a passing ship. However, it refused to explain its presence to the locals. So they hanged it as a French spy. Having been derided for years by opposing supporters as monkey-hangers, the football club employed a monkey mascot, under the name of H'Angus Monkey. The mascot then stood for election as mayor, got in, took off his monkey suit, reverted to his real name and was later re-elected.

It is still hard to work out what most people do in these places. The heritage is fading into history, shaped by Gala-style nostalgia. But pit villages had a very strange attitude to their mines. Fathers with a smidgin of ambition wanted their sons to escape. Yet the mining life – its harshness, its traditions, its camaraderie – was at the core of their being. Now the relationship with the past is just as ambivalent. The county is cleaner and their lives are gentler. And yet. What's Durham *for*? What are the people *for*?

Tom Thubron's father didn't want his sons to go down the pit, and they didn't. Tom, having gone into the shipyards and then the Merchant Navy, became ordained and ended up as Wheatley Hill's vicar, not a normal career trajectory. Many of his contemporaries left school on the Friday and worked their first shift at the pit on the Monday. Not all the jobs were terrible – there was surface and ancillary work – but many were tough in a way that has become unimaginable. The adversity bred comradeship inside the pit and beyond, in the rituals of the coalfield: football, bowls, the clubs, leek growing, pigeon fancying. 'There was a tradition of never missing a shift,' says Tom Thubron. 'You were honest and you never let your mates down. And miners were polite, civilised, respectful. That kind of tradition was in the genes.' The pit boys married the prettiest girl they could find and in the fullness of time the girls grew into matriarchs, dominating the homes, belting the kids and providing their own kind of strength for the village.

Since the pit closed, the population of Wheatley Hill has halved. The working men's club and the 'Conshie' (the Constitutional Club, a lightly disguised Conservative Club, though it might never have seen a real Conservative) have both faded, especially since the smoking ban. The bowling green was terminally vandalised long ago. And the brass band packed up. Before electronic payouts, there was always quite a gathering at the post office first thing for the benefit payments. Many men are known to have been on the sick for years.

'There are a lot of black people nowadays,' someone whispered.

'*Really?*' This was an immigration pattern I had failed to pick up.

'The black economy. Drawing benefits and doing painting and decor-
ating. That sort of thing.'

Tom Thubron says Wheatley Hill's decline began long before the
pit closure. The Attlee government wanted to shift people into the new
towns of Peterlee and Newton Aycliffe, and banned expansion in villages
like Wheatley Hill, which were classed as Category D, a term still used
casually in Durham. By 1964, 121 of the county's villages were placed on
the planning equivalent of Death Row – new development was banned;
property that became available was subject to compulsory purchase and
demolition.

In the end, hardly any of the condemned villages were actually executed; they were just left maimed. When the pit did close, there was nothing else. If the men found other work, it would be elsewhere: they would
have to move completely or commute so far they would become tangential
to the community. Or they would stay at home and rot: on the black, on
the sick, on the dole.

The women went out to work, in low-paid flexi-jobs, like supermarkets or care homes. So the old family life collapsed too: a more extreme
version of what happened in households across Britain. There is not much
left on Wheatley Hill's Front Street but there are plenty of takeaways. As
I drove past on the way to the dogs, the only people about were a group
of women or maybe girls – their faces were so raddled it was hard to tell –
drinking lager out of cans and swearing at each other.

Wheatley Hill does not look dead. The Category D threat having
been lifted, most of the houses are new, complete with plastic windows,
faux-leaded lights, satellite dishes and conservatories. Tom Thubron says
the place is far better than a few years back, when everything seemed to be
dying. The old miners' welfare hall has been converted into a community
centre, Greenhills, where they offer lunches, belly dancing, 'boxercise' and
over-50s fitness classes with tai chi and aerobics. But the centre is locked
up in the evenings. 'Hardly anyone goes out at night now,' said Tom.

There is still power produced in the village. There are half a dozen
wind turbines scattered about, providing at least enough electricity to
keep most of Wheatley Hill's TV sets going. Their movement made me
think irresistibly of the over-50s doing something aerobic.

Durham is full of places with peculiar resonance. There is Chopwell –
'Little Moscow', complete with Marx Terrace and Lenin Terrace. There is

Blackhall, where a ski lift contraption, the 'aerial flight', used to take the coal waste out to sea, which was handy in *Get Carter* when Michael Caine wanted to dispose of Ian Hendry. There is Bishop Auckland, where, until 2010, the successor to the prince-bishops lived in Auckland Castle ('a flat within the castle', the church's PR people would insist defensively).

It had never occurred to me that Bishop Auckland actually had anything to do with bishops because to me it meant football. In the days when I knew a lot about football teams and little about British hypocrisy, Bishop Auckland used to dominate the FA Amateur Cup, now long defunct but then a very big deal. That was why so many other of these Durham towns sounded familiar – Tow Law, Shildon, Consett, Ferryhill, Crook: they all had top-flight amateur clubs. And Crook was the operative word. 'Of course it wasn't amateur,' said Mike Amos. 'The notion was ludicrous. A lot of the players came up from Manchester twice a week and they didn't do that because they liked the air. Everybody knew it was shamateur. There was a maximum wage in the professional game and you could do very well as an amateur.'

Close by is Escomb, where an essentially unchanged Saxon church – tiny at ground level but nearly as high as a cathedral – has been in almost continuous use for worship since AD 670. That's, what, forty-five, fifty generations? Trying to consider that concept is like contemplating the immanence of God. And then there is Jarrow, a town with a double place in English history. Here it was, in the eighth century, around the time the third generation was praying for salvation in Escomb Church, that the Venerable Bede produced dozens of remarkable works of scholarship, all without a laptop.

For most of the twentieth century, Jarrow had a more powerful association. It was the symbol of the depression of the 1930s thanks to the Jarrow marchers, 207 of them, who tramped to London in October 1936 to protest against poverty and unemployment.

Jarrow is on the south bank of the Tyne, and boomed with the shipbuilding industry. When that bust, it bust. Palmers yard, which employed the overwhelming majority of Jarrow men, collapsed in 1932. It was then sold to a consortium of shipyard owners whose aim was to reduce overcapacity and protect their own firms; they made very sure the yard did not reopen. The government was not sympathetic. 'Jarrow must work out its salvation,' said Walter Runciman, president of the Board of Trade. By 1935, unemployment in the town had reached 72.9 per cent. This number was rapidly reduced, but only by amalgamating the labour exchange with the one next door in Hebburn, whose yard was flourishing. Thus the next official figure, magically, was below 40 per cent.

The march did not achieve anything concrete. Unemployment in Jarrow eased only with the outbreak of war. But it imprinted the image of hunger, poverty and suffering on the rest of the nation (most of which was doing quite nicely), where it remains to this day, forever associated with Jarrow. Bede has been elbowed aside, confined to a museum called Bede's World.

There is a bronze of the marchers in the centre of Jarrow, outside Morrisons. It is a handy spot to sit and have a smoke. Jarrow is not now obviously poverty-stricken: it is an easy commute across the Tyne to Newcastle, with three metro stations and a new road tunnel. But one did sense a certain poverty of expectation and aspiration.

Bede probably had more books than the Jarrow public library. And the Morrisons car park reminded me, more than anywhere else in Britain, of Chunky, Mississippi, a small town I discovered one sultry morning when I was searching for the obesity capital of the United States, and which lived up to its name because everyone I saw weighed at least twenty stone. This is the modern manifestation of the 1930s: the poverty that leads not to malnutrition but to obesity. And depravity. On the gents' toilets inside Morrisons there was a sign warning unaccompanied boys not to enter, for fear of funny men.

I met the Mawsons, Bob and Joan, in the cemetery at Trimdon Grange. It was a name I knew because of a song, 'The Trimdon Grange Explosion', written by Tommy Armstrong, the Pitman Poet (1848–1920), and revived in 1969 by Alan Price:

> *Let us not think of tomorrow,*
> *Lest we disappointed be;*
> *All our joys may turn to sorrow,*
> *As we all may daily see …*

It was not the first, last or worst pit disaster, but, in a small village, seventy-odd miners died on a February afternoon in 1882. The inquest failed to discover the precise cause. There is a sort of memorial in the village: a pit wheel dedicated on one side to the miners' leader, Peter Lee, who gave his name to Peterlee, and the other to the victims.

Joan Mawson told me that one of her relatives was among the dead:

John Edmund or Edmunds. She thought he might have been her grand-mother's brother, but she was vague, the way people are about great-uncles, especially if they died long before they were born. Yet Joan had always lived in Trimdon Grange: she grew up across from the old slagheap that used to blow its contents on to the windowsills whenever the wind got up.

Bob took me to see their neighbour, Les Rowell, who had been down the pits, some of the time on his hands and knees working a two-foot seam. Les had a more than normally thick Durham accent and was addicted to 'pitmatic', the miners' equivalent of naval jackspeak. He talked enthusiasti-cally for some minutes about hedgehogs, cows, bulls, gripes, goves, bath-gates, straps and pigheads, all of them apparently items of mine equipment.

'It's all gobbledegook to me,' said Bob, twenty-five years at ICI.

'Les, can you just tell me what it was like down there?' I wailed.

'Bloody dusty and bloody noisy.'

I became intrigued by Joan's Great-Uncle John. He was buried not in Trimdon Grange but, along with most of the others, in neighbour-ing Trimdon under what looks like a war memorial. The number of dead is astonishingly variable for such a disaster, where surely everyone must have been known: sixty-nine according to the inquest report; seventy-four according to the memorial. The Mawsons had some documents: one referred to 'John Edmund, boy'; another said he was aged seventeen. The side of the memorial listing the youngest miners is crumbling: it's impos-sible to tell whether his name had an S at the end or whether he was thir-teen or eighteen. Definitely not seventeen or sixteen – you could tell from the shape of the numbers – but sixteen is clearly what it says on the nearby stone, which was moss-covered but readable.

Tommy Armstrong concluded:

> Death will pay us all a visit;
> They have only gone before.
> We may meet the Trimdon victims
> Where explosions are no more.

I thought of Bob Dylan: 'Oh, my name it means nothing, my age it means less.' In Durham Cathedral, I lit a candle for John Edmunds as well as for my own son.

I had been to Trimdon before. In 1983 the Sedgefield Constituency

Labour Party unexpectedly chose a quick-tongued and presentable young lawyer from London as their candidate for Parliament. As he made his reputation, the locals grew increasingly proud: of their boy, who was rising so quickly up the political ladder, and of themselves, for spotting him.

When Tony Blair became party leader and then prime minister, the Trimdon Labour Club became his touchstone and his Durham HQ. At election time, the press would gather and drink the bar dry. Sometimes I was among them, including the last such occasion: the day of Blair's resignation, as both PM and MP, in 2007.

Shortly afterwards the club closed. Rumour was that it was only a back-door subsidy from London that had kept it going and, once Blair went, so did the subsidy. But it soon reopened: as the Green Bar, Lounge and Function Room. Trimdon had three other pubs, but none had a function room, so the Green could corner the wedding market. The manager, Lyn Walsh, took me down there and it all came back to me: I even remembered the banquette I had stood on to watch his resignation speech.

'Have you thought of renaming it the Tony Blair Room?' I asked. She gave me a very dirty look.

It seems unlikely that Tony Blair ever wandered down the road to look at the Trimdon Grange memorial. This was a man who did not even know the number of British soldiers killed in Iraq, the war he started. Tom Thubron had been an admirer, a friend even: 'I liked him.'

'What do you think of him now?'

'Power corrupts,' he replied.

July 2011

～～～～～～

The very next week after my visit to Wheatley Hill, a man from Stockton-on-Tees appeared before Hartlepool magistrates and admitted causing unnecessary suffering to greyhounds running on flapping tracks by feeding them boiled cannabis when he wanted them to lose and Viagra tablets when he wanted them to win. The Viagra, he said, made them 'run their heads off'. He was banned for life from keeping greyhounds but allowed to retain up to twenty ferrets. I am not making this up.

5. *Watch the wall, my darling*

DEVON

August Bank Holiday: Britain is covered with a blanket of low cloud and gloom, literal and metaphorical. Beset by an economic squeeze and a paltry exchange rate, a large portion of the British population has forgone its customary continental holiday and stayed home, wallowing in the misery of it all.

Much of the North is sodden, the South-East heading towards drought. The South-West is different. Devon, in August 2011, looked exactly the way England ought to look in late summer: a riot of rich green laid out as if to please the fertility gods.

And much of the country – at least those with any dosh left – seemed to know it. They converged on Devon, as of old, especially on the roads along the banks of the Dart leading to the riverside village of Dittisham (*Dit'sham*). Roads? That's not the word, really. There are country lanes and then there are Devon lanes. Most of the rural South is characterised by grass verges and hedgerows. Here they have Devon banks, solid obstacles without an inch of give designed to shelter the cattle from the west wind. Overtaking becomes near-unthinkable once you leave the A38. Close to Dittisham, it is difficult to pass a pedestrian without the risk of burying them in the brambles and the far more worrying danger of scratching the wing mirror.

All over the South Hams, locals and visitors were taking part in the traditional holiday-time motorised folk dance to get by without bashing into banks, buttresses and garden walls. It is like a sideways limbo mixed with a Maori haka. The inhabitants are able to execute the steps with practised elegance, if not much grace: the trick is to use a show of aggression, then make the visitors do the reversing – especially if the opposition comprises a nerve-wracked woman from north London with a Range Rover full of infants. In places, especially on the overgrown tracks leading to the beaches or where the spring tide in the creeks laps across the tarmac, it is hard enough even for one car to get by. In Dartmouth, I watched a 30,000-ton cruise liner trying to escape the harbour on what looked to me like an iffily low tide. But that was nothing compared to the terrifying sight of the double-decker 93 bus to Kingsbridge trying to barrel its way through Stoke Fleming.

There was a time when none of this mattered. Dittisham was a fishing village with a sideline in plum growing. Now the old cottages have turned into holiday homes, each with a Range Rover or BMW outside, if the owners can manoeuvre it anywhere close. The locals are not grumbling about this: they took their profits, sold out and moved out. Or they are revelling in it. It was impossible to get served in the Ferry Boat Inn. And outside the poshed-up Anchorstone Café someone – maybe the owner – was yelling into a mobile (Lord knows how he got a signal) that he had never been busier. Someone told me a house in the village recently went for £8 million. No one thinks that implausible.

But the dance season does not last long, at least not at its bank holiday intensity. Less than two weeks later I was back in Devon, walking along the stony beach at Budleigh Salterton, a place straight out of inter-war comedy. 'No one but a monumental bore would have thought of having a honeymoon in Budleigh Salterton,' a character says in Noël Coward's *Blithe Spirit*. And it still got a laugh in London when Alison Steadman played the crazed old medium Madame Arcati in 2011.

The town, it's true, does seem a little elderly. But on the beach, when I arrived, the scene was very romantic: a Turneresque September day of

sun, cloud, wind, spume and spits of rain; pines to the east, sheer cliffs to the west. A lone fisherman was the only other figure on the shingle. Hoping for bass on the flood tide, he was finding only dogfish, which may be a metaphor for life. The Longboat Café was not just closed, but closed with eighteen separate padlocks. It was a signal that summer was over and that Devon was once again guarding its secrets.

Secrets! And lies! Was there ever a place so full of them? Along the coast at Slapton Sands the seas hide one of the greatest mysteries of the war. In 1943 the area was evacuated because the shore was a remarkable facsimile of the Utah and Omaha beaches chosen for the Normandy landings. After the population was dispersed, the Allies undertook months of exercises to prepare for the invasion, complete with live firing for added realism, which had some unfortunate consequences in itself.

Six weeks before D-Day came a full-scale dress rehearsal for the Utah landing, known as Operation Tiger. What happened next was detailed in a locally published account, *Preparing for D-Day*, by Arthur L. Clamp. The exercise, he said, was very successful: 'one incident, however, marred this event'. His tone suggested a sharp downpour had afflicted the village fete. Instead: 'two German E-boat flotillas ... stumbled on the exercise taking place during the hours of darkness. Two landing craft full of troops were sunk and one was damaged causing the death of about 700 men – more than were killed on Utah Beach during the actual invasion.'

The disaster was hushed up and relatives fobbed off, which was understandable given the overriding imperative of the moment. But official embarrassment ensured the cover-up continued long after the war. There is what looks like a memorial in the car park at Slapton, close by the ice cream van. But this was a gift from the US Army to thank the locals for uncomplainingly getting out of their way. No word of the dead, nearly all of whom were American. It took a local obsessive, Ken Small, to give them any honour. He spent years fighting bureaucratic obstructionism to raise a tank, lost in the disaster, from the depths. It is now preserved further along the beach, as an inadequate and rather inappropriate monument.

Just south of Slapton, on this east-facing stretch of coast, is Hallsands, once a thriving crab-fishing village. In 1896 an industrialist called Sir John Jackson was given a licence to dredge the shingle there to expand the Devonport dockyard: nearly three-quarters of a million tons were removed. The locals were alarmed right from the start and foresaw that it would destroy first their livelihoods and then their homes. Sir John's representative assured them there was no danger because sand would come in to fill the gaps. Guess who was right? The village was savagely damaged over the years ahead and piffling compensation was offered, until in 1917 the combination of a high tide and a roaring sou'easter destroyed Hallsands once and for all.

There are still dark rumours that the Lynmouth floods of 1952, which killed twenty-four people, were caused by the RAF playing with cloud-seeding in an exercise known as Project Cumulus. Certainly, the whole scheme was scrapped very quickly thereafter, and crucial files have gone missing. No wonder Agatha Christie was inspired by Devon. It reeks of cover-up and deception. Even visitors play the game. Personally, I've found an absolutely scrumptious beach but I'm buggered if I will reveal where it is. And I noticed, as I talked to people for this chapter, that while everyone was friendly and charming and talkative, they were more than normally reluctant to reveal their names.

I think this stems from two separate traditions. One is the wariness of country folk the world over when confronted by a stranger making notes. But in Devon this collides with the even more mysterious and frequently nefarious habits of those who live by the coast and their wits. The salty tang of the sea is mixed with a whiff derived from centuries of dodgy dealing: illicit red diesel, smuggled brandy and maybe the hint of something from the marijuana farms that lurk in the remote combes.

> *If you wake at midnight, and hear a horse's feet,*
> *Don't go drawing back the blind, or looking in the street,*
> *Them that ask no questions isn't told a lie.*
> *Watch the wall, my darling, while the Gentlemen go by.*

And it hasn't all gone away. In January 2007 the cargo ship *Napoli* ran into trouble in a Channel storm and was beached in Lyme Bay, a mile off Branscombe. Soon afterwards, the containers began floating ashore, awakening atavistic memories from deep within Devon's soul. By the time the police had got their boots on, everything from empty oak barrels and packs of nappies to 200 BMW motorcycles had been scooped up. The romanticism of this re-enactment of Devonian heritage was somewhat spoiled by the devastation of a Swedish family, emigrating to South Africa to open a winery, who saw on TV their most sentimental possessions (and their barrels) being carted off by scavengers. And the locals found themselves elbowed aside by some pretty nasty gangs from Liverpool and Birmingham.

Still, the incident has become suffused with a nostalgic glow and, more thoughtfully, immortalised by Steve Knightley from the folk duo Show of Hands, a brilliant chronicler of the underside of West Country life. He incorporated Kipling's poem into a song called 'The Napoli', which had the chorus:

> *Flotsam, jetsam, call it what you like*
> *I got a big oak barrel and a German motorbike.*

Lyme Bay to eBay, tell me where's the sin
Everyone's a wrecker 'neath the skin.

Sorry, but Devon does make one burst into song a lot.

When Adam and Eve were dispossessed
Of the garden, hard by Heaven,
They planted another one down in the west –
'Twas Devon, glorious Devon.

And that's the reason why people pay £8 million for houses in inaccessible fishing villages with an uncertain climate. The notion of Devon is embedded in the image of home the British took with them when they built their empire. 'Devon-shyer' cream teas (not very nice ones) are served on Australian trains. There are Hotels Devon or Devonshire in Kenya, New Zealand, Sri Lanka, South Africa, Canada, wherever. Other counties have rivers, the sea, moors, hills, all of those. But Devon has hardly any flat at all, except on the high plateaux. It's all crinkles or, as one local male put it, one long line of breasts.

Just about every town is on the slant, sometimes precipitously so: Modbury, South Molton, North Tawton, Torrington, Totnes, Kingsbridge, Hatherleigh ... plus Ottery St Mary, which is not just on a hillside but has streets with a camber that would suit an Olympic velodrome. And that's just the inland places, never mind the vertiginous coastal resorts. On the Malvern principle, they must be healthy. A friend of mine went to the doctor, who thought he might have angina. 'I live in Dartmouth,' the patient replied. 'I think I'd know if I had angina.'

There are beautiful places all over England, but Devon doesn't do anything else. I went round and round this large county (surpassed in size by only Yorkshire and Lincolnshire), reversing in the face of oncoming traffic more often than a coalition government, but I discovered only four ugly places: parts of Plymouth (OK, most of Plymouth); Paignton, where a hideous cinema separates the town from the sea; Westward Ho!; and Bigbury. And in each of these cases God was on absolutely ace form but the planners were not. Devonians shudder at the very mention of Princetown, the grim-visaged prison town on top of Dartmoor. True, the housing stock, weary and discoloured, has the unmistakable look of being built to government spec and maintained to government standards. But

Princetown is not ugly. Even the prison itself, far from dominating the town, nestles discreetly underneath it. In the Pennines it would pass as a redundant cotton mill, be transformed into an arts centre and be leeched off by the entire community selling cream teas, second-hand books and knick-knacks.

But there is just too much competition here. From Abbots Bickington to Zeal Monachorum, from Exmoor to the Tamar, this is a lovely county. It is still possible to use John Betjeman's 1936 Shell Guide and revel in his judgement and enjoyments without feeling a sense of utter depression at what has been lost. Mind you, his views are somewhat subjective. DODDISCOMBSLEIGH: 'The people in these parts are very friendly, and blackberries are juicy and ripe.'

Do you know? I think the old rascal might have scored.

Absent a Doddiscombsleigh wench with ripe lips and an undertaste of blackberry, my Devon epiphany came the day I went to Dartmoor and turned west from Bovey Tracey, past Haytor towards Widecombe in the Moor (pronounced Widdy-combe, as in the name of the politician, dancer and professional virgin, Ann Widdecombe). By the happiest of coincidences, it was the second Tuesday in September, the day of Widecombe Fair, a fact that will either reduce you to blank incomprehension or an immediate rendition of Devon's most famous folk song.

> Tom Pearce, Tom Pearce, lend me your grey mare,
> All along, down along, out along lee,
> For I want for to go to Widecombe Fair,
> Wi' Bill Brewer, Jan Stewer, Peter Gurney,
> Peter Davy, Dan'l Whiddon, Harry Hawk,
> Old Uncle Tom Cobley and all,
> Old Uncle Tom Cobley and all.

Traffic was banned from the village for the day and we had to park in the teeth of a gale, high on the moor near Rippon Tor, and take a double-decker bus, an even scarier proposition in those lanes than in Stoke Fleming. I sat, with childlike wonder, at the front of the top deck, which was clouted so hard by one overhanging branch that I got a headache.

But the view, oh my, the view. In one of the fields above the village, there was a row of silage bales wrapped in a plastic whose green was just a touch jarring. Otherwise, there was nothing that was not totally adorable. And in the midst of the picture, bathed in sunlight, in the lee of the hill – Widecombe, only a little tich of a place, laid out as if for a medieval tournament. There were just a few houses, a couple of pubs sustained by tourists, and a church, St Pancras, 'the cathedral in the moor', so improbably grand that it might easily live up to its name with the nave serving as a platform and trains waiting in each of the aisles.

There was no wind here. And for the fair, the village was packed, even on a working Tuesday, with a nice throng of trippers and locals watching the shearing competitions and the bale-tossing and the tug o' war. In some respects it might not have changed much since the late nineteenth century, soon after there really was a Thomas Cobley Esq. in the vicinity, when the Rev. Sabine Baring-Gould (author of 'Onward, Christian Soldiers') heard the song and brought it into the national consciousness.

There is probably less public drunkenness at Widecombe Fair now. It has certainly become more self-referential: there is the Uncle Tom Cobley mechanical model; the Uncle Tom Cobley downhill race; the Uncle Tom Cobley junior race; the grand parade of prize-winning horses led by Uncle Tom Cobley, played by a suitably genial and bearded villager. I can find nothing bad to say about Widecombe whatever, except this: just listen to the bloody song – it's brutal.

Tom Pearce kindly lent them his mare; these seven wretches clambered on, knackered her and left her to rot. It broke his heart.

> So Tom Pearce's old mare, her took sick and died,
> All along, down along, out along lee,
> And Tom he sat down on a stone and he cried,
> Wi' Bill Brewer, Jan Stewer, Peter Gurney,
> Peter Davy, Dan'l Whiddon, Harry Hawk,
> Old Uncle Tom Cobley and all,
> Old Uncle Tom Cobley and all.

Cobley has passed into the language. And the victim? Forgotten.

Devon is England's only county with two completely separate coastlines, and the two have very little to say to each other. Separated by the hulking great obstacle of Dartmoor, linked only feebly by road or rail, there is a vast gulf in status.

The north coast is by far the fiercer, bleaker, more rugged of the two. South and east of the moor is the rich, red, fertile soil supposed to be characteristic of Devon. North-west of it lie the culm grasslands: heavy clay soils, difficult to work, with about five feet of rain a year belting in from the west – 'mud and rushes country', according to Anthony Gibson, for many years the National Farmers' Union's south-west regional director. 'There's a Bermuda triangle between Hatherleigh, Holsworthy and Torrington into which hundreds of farm businesses have disappeared,' he says.

'In the old days you could milk cows on it. But there's been a big decline in the number. There's a bit of a switch to beef: the Devon cattle – the ruby reds – do well on rough grassland. But there's always been a big turnover of farmers here. It's not like east Devon, round Honiton, say, where most of the farmers can trace themselves back on their farms for centuries.'

There is not much call for B&B and holiday cottages in the triangle. And in the towns, far from the bright lights, one senses teenagers in particular leading lives of quiet desperation. Lord knows, the places are still pretty enough. I took a particular shine to wind-tossed Torrington, with its tight terraced houses marching up the hill. It captivated me when I passed three greengrocers in the first two minutes. There are also two independent butchers, two bakers producing their own bread and the Mole & Haggis Bookshop. One assumed this all comes about because the big supermarkets are only a rumour. Oh, no, insisted the woman in John Patt's Country Store: 'It's the customer care.'

Hatherleigh, according to Betjeman, is 'unexpected but squalid'. (So he didn't score there, then.) It seems most unkind. But it was devastated by the 2001 foot and mouth epidemic. And the market, the beating heart of the town since the thirteenth century, lies under threat of development. Already the livestock and the Tuesday pannier market have been separated: the animal sales are dwindling away, while the other has become a West Country phenomenon. 'There's a world here the supermarkets don't understand,' said Dan Garnett ('Dan the Fishman'). 'You've got toilets that should be condemned, a café out of *Brief Encounter*. But the Tuesdays have just got bigger and bigger.'

Dan the Fishman operates out of Clovelly, the most famous of all Devon fishing villages and the only one that has to be entered through the gift shop, accompanied by a demand for £5.95 admission. The place itself is a wonder of conservation, thanks to the determination of the Hamlyns and Rouses, who have owned Clovelly Court since 1738. The cobbled steps tumble down to the sea past wattle-and-daub houses of infinite cuteness that have transfixed, delighted and horrified visitors for generations.

In 1925 Hilaire Belloc wrote the classic account, observing from the cliff top as

> up that cleft swirled, surged, pushed, strenuously and unfailingly, one mass of packed, dark-clothed mortality, closely hemmed in by the cottages (I wondered that their walls stood the strain), and looking from where we stood very much like black pressed German caviare, the acrid stuff which is sold for the destruction of the race. This wedge had its base upon the seashore and was filled with a communal desire, with a mass mind, impelling it to attempt the height – a hopeless task! For the char-a-banc crowd above could not have been pierced by cavalry ...

Nearly nine decades of mass tourism after that, on an early autumn afternoon, Clovelly was nowhere near so vile. A little unpleasant, perhaps – there was something peculiarly cynical about the gift shop – and my first instinct was to feel a deep sense of pity for the residents, who have only to step outside to be gawped at.

But Clovelly is also a source of wonder. Here, truly, is somewhere without cars – hence, in 1925, the parked chars-a-banc. The donkeys, who were the villagers' beasts of burden, have been retired, so goods can only be delivered, and rubbish collected, by hand-pulled sledges. Heaven knows how you would get a fire engine or ambulance in an emergency, but maybe no one gets ill because the fitness regime of Dartmouth is, through daily necessity, even more strenuous in Clovelly. The street is slightly straiter and steeper than the equivalent leading down to the quayside in billionaires' Dittisham. However – and it took me a little time to realise this – there is one huge difference. The houses are not for sale. A view and ambience that would be priceless anywhere else in Devon may be available to anyone at a very reasonable rent on application to the estate.

There are distinct downsides to this. For better or worse, residents sign away some of their rights as free-born modern Britons: they have to live in the houses, not just spend weekends there; they have to maintain the gardens; satellite dishes, problematic anyway because of the lie of the land, are allowed only if they are totally out of sight. Great, you may say. But the inhabitants also seemed not just sensibly reluctant to offer their names but scared witless, since their presence depends wholly on the squire's goodwill. The idea that families have lived there for generations seems to be a myth; several sources told me that a lot of the residents were on housing benefit – that way the estate can be certain of receiving its rent. 'I know they look nice,' one unusually communicative woman told me, 'but most of the houses are cold – no double glazing – damp and higgledy-piggledy.'

Still, she was not remotely unhappy. 'Because the people all really live here, it's a proper community. We do look out for each other. It's very safe. No one ever locks their door.'

'What, even with all these strangers around?'

'Well, no one's ever going to nick my telly. They'd have to carry it up to the top. Someone left the pub without paying last year. The police were waiting for him by the time he reached the car park.'

A few hours later – though it was a hell of a trek – I was back on the south coast, staying, thanks to the kindness of friends, in a different kind of idealised home: a rented holiday house officially described as 'smart'. This meant that if you set foot outside your bedroom after midnight every light in the building came on. Naturally, none of us were smart enough to work out how to adjust the damn things.

But the view was, if anything, even more sensational than at Clovelly. This was Salcombe, where the entrance to the Kingsbridge River offers the nearest thing Britain has to Sydney Harbour. Or at least what Sydney Harbour might look like had we sent out the aristocrats and mill own-ers rather than the convicts. Across the bay is East Portlemouth, a village slightly less accessible than the South Pole, which was convulsed a couple of years back by a dispute about the construction of six low-cost houses for locals. The homeowners, few of them full-time residents, reacted as though the council had proposed siting the world's entire population of refugees, Romanies and riff-raff by their beloved beaches. They lost the argument and the houses were built. There have, as yet, been no reports of riots in East Portlemouth.

Later I went to visit the publisher Tom Jaine at his base at Allaleigh, near Dartmouth, where he handed me a well-researched potted history. Allaleigh has not been more than a hamlet since the Middle Ages. In 1891 there were only eight inhabited houses and fifty-two people, all the occupations being agricultural save for one market gardener and one carter. Circa 2007 there were thirty-one people in ten houses, the residents including – besides a publisher – an agronomist, a gift manufacturer, a carpenter, a care worker, a retired art teacher, an estate agent, a film-maker, a silversmith, a doctor and a management consultant.

These conflicts and changes are played out, though usually more subtly than in Devon, throughout desirable Britain, and summed up by Steve Knightley in Show of Hands' song 'Country Life':

> *... And the red brick cottage where I was born*
> *Is the empty shell of a holiday home*
> *Most of the year there's no one there*
> *The village is dead and they don't care*
> *Now we live on the edge of town*
> *Haven't been back since the pub closed down*
> *One man's family pays the price*
> *For another man's vision of country life.*

But there is a paradox. The holiday homes are often there because the long-standing owners have taken their profits and gone where there is work. The film-makers and publishers are often sensitive and conscientious stewards of the land, and supporters of local shops and schools and pubs and sometimes even churches that would close down without them. Incomers are people too.

Back at Budleigh Salterton, the annual literary festival was just beginning. Carol Ann Duffy, the Poet Laureate, was reading from her work in the Public Hall. She would make a plausible Madame Arcati, I reckon, but she was in the wrong place: she was just reciting poetry. The real Budleighan event was taking place up the hill at the Venture Hall, organised by the local spiritualist churches, with the role of Arcati played by Nick, a carpenter from Cullompton.

The venue was no more than a glorified Scouts' hut, but it was packed: nearly a hundred crowded in and they had to hunt for extra chairs. Nick, a burly bloke with a crew-cut and the air of an affable copper, was nothing like the batty woman dabbling with darkened rooms and ectoplasm one might have hoped for. But then carpenters have a good reputation in spiritual matters, so there was no reason not to have faith. Until he started.

He did warn us: 'Mediumship is not an exact science. It depends on the atmosphere, the energy in the room.'

Now, Budleigh is not a place obvious for its energy but the audience – overwhelmingly female, mostly *d'un certain age* – had not come to scoff. They had all, in the nature of things, lost loved ones. And they wanted news.

Nick, however, did not inspire a great deal of confidence. 'We are separated by a thin veil, the veil of senses,' he said. He rocked back, put on a pensive face, then implied that he had made contact with someone beyond. He singled out a woman in a striped jersey: 'I feel there was a problem with his throat.'

'No,' came the confident reply. But a woman just in front nodded and caught his eye. Perhaps it was her father? Nick switched targets.

'Thin white hair?'

'White hair, not thin.'

'He worked with his hands?'

'No.'

'A love of being outside? He loved chrysanthemums?'

'No.'

'The reason I said yes,' the woman explained, 'was that he'd had a tracheotomy and couldn't speak. Perhaps you can't hear him.'

And so it went on. Nick's technique was to opt for short-odds favourites. 'I feel a farming connection?' 'He wore braces?' 'Was there a military background?' 'An association with a crucifix?' We were talking fathers and grandfathers who lived through the first half of the twentieth century: agriculture, military service, religion and braces were all pretty good bets. Even so, he struggled to pick winners.

He switched to a woman at the back, out of my line of vision.

'Would you understand a father in the spirit world?'

'No, he's still alive.'

'Would you understand a grandfather?'

'No, they both died before I was born.'

'I feel he lived near lakes.'

'No, we were in Belgium.'

It was like watching a cartoon character – Tom chasing Jerry, maybe – climbing a sheer precipice, clinging on to stunted trees that kept snapping while he reached for the next and that snapped too. Occasionally, Nick got something close enough to a hit and then imparted a message from the spirit world, that they should love their family and make more space in their lives. Then he restored the veil and drew the evening to a hasty close.

Budleigh Salterton was not impressed. But they didn't think he was a phoney. 'He was a bit slow,' one woman said to me on the way out. 'This lady from Exmouth who's coming next month, I think she's very good.'

Me, I don't feel the need for instructions from beyond. I would like some reassurance that heaven looks much like Devon (perhaps with a more trustworthy summer and less traffic). But, unlike Nick, I believe heaven also likes to guard its secrets.

August/September 2011

~~~~~~~

In March 2014 outline planning permission was granted for 106 houses on Hather-leigh market – livestock sales will cease, although there will be space for the pannier market to continue.

6. *Here be bores, and boars*

GLOUCESTERSHIRE

It was coming up to 9 a.m. on a late October morning; a cold autumn rain was falling and there were just a dozen of us on the riverbank outside the pub: ten adults and two children, plus a brown mongrel bitch who seemed to be relishing the occasion more than anyone.

We were there to witness Britain's most extraordinary natural phenomenon, something so astonishing that if it happened anywhere more exotic we would fly off to see it, come home with our pictures and everyone would say: 'Oooh, I'd love to see that.'

But it has a downbeat name and it isn't even the Mississippi Bore or the Nile Bore or the Dordogne Bore. It's the Severn Bore, and the nearer people are to it, the more blasé they get. The dozen on the bank had come variously from Cornwall, Sussex, Leicester, Leeds, Nottingham and Herefordshire. There was one young couple, from just up the road in West Dean. They admitted they were a bit unusual. 'My dad's lived on the river at Westbury for sixty-four years,' said the bloke. 'Never seen it.' There are some exceptions to this rule, though: 'Dave with the hot dog van at Newnham, he knows a lot about it.'

Twice a day the tide comes in from the Atlantic and funnels its way up the Bristol Channel, which has a huge tidal range, second only to the Bay of Fundy in Canada. When it heads through the estuary and towards the river, the space available gets both narrower and shallower. So the water forms itself into a wave. It then enters the Severn, which is placidly meandering towards the sea until it meets the wave, travelling north. On the road, that would produce a right pile-up. On the river, it produces the bore, which races up here – to the Severn Bore Inn outside Minsterworth – and all the way to Gloucester, where, ever since a series of weirs were built in the nineteenth century, it has faded away. In the old days, it could reach upstream to Worcester. Theoretically, the bore happens twice a day. In practice, it is only noticeable a hundred-odd times a year, and spectacular maybe a couple of dozen.

Similar phenomena occur on other rivers, about a dozen of them in Britain. But all are titchy in comparison with the Severn Bore except the one on the Qiantang River in China, which regularly causes mayhem among the small boats in Hangzhou Harbour. (Yes, it's just the silver medal for England yet again.) But here we are in sleepy old Gloucestershire in an era when we have messed up almost everything on the planet. Yet the Severn Barrage – which would destroy the bore – is still just a fantasy. And so we have a continuing demonstration of nature's raw, untamed power. Where the hell are the school geography classes?

Part of the problem, I suppose, is that it is not quite as spectacular as all that. It's not a tsunami: it's three to six feet high. It's also unpredictable: the complex nine-year cycle that governs the bore is calculable from the tide tables, but the reality is affected by wind and water levels and what seems like sheer caprice. The Environment Agency and a few enthusiasts give bores a star rating in advance. But, as one expert put it, 'it's an art not a science'. This one was graded as two- or three-star, depending which website you used. For a four- or five-starrer in fine weather at a weekend, maybe a hundred would be here. But they could easily go away, shrugging: 'Is that IT?' And the timing is guesswork: it might be early, though in my experience of about half a dozen bores, it has always been late. It's like waiting for a train on a dismal country platform. And this morning was particularly dismal.

But, as the rain beat down, there were a couple of bonuses. One was

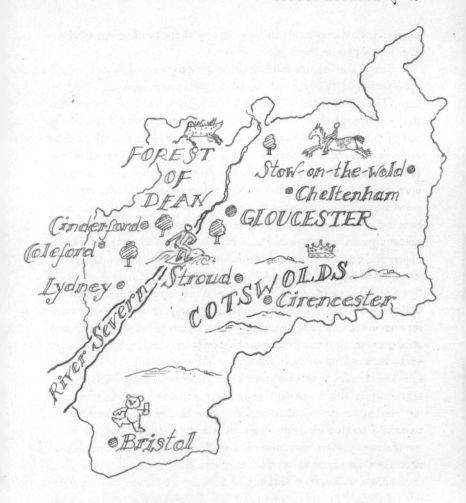

that expectations were low, as they are about most things in an English October. The other was that the powerboat owners who wreck the experience for everyone else with their racket (and allegedly dissipate the wave as well) had not bothered to appear. There were just half a dozen surfers in the water, waiting to ride the wave. And when it finally appeared, a mere twelve minutes late, it arrived with a very satisfying whoosh, and all the neophytes were contented. 'That was really good,' said one of the Nottingham party, heading into the pub for a well-earned full English.

The surfers were less happy. 'Missed it, didn't I?' said one, as he trudged back through the car park. But he added, with a connoisseur's eye: 'Lovely peel on that one, though.'

'That was NOT fun!' said one of his mates.

'Why not?'

'Hit a bloody tree.'

The bore reaches 13 mph, and thus cannot normally outrun a car on the A48 to Gloucester, even with its 50 limit, so it is possible to drive north and catch the wave two or three times more. The surfers, their routine well honed, were heading up towards Thomas Telford's old bridge at Over to have another go. After a quick sausage sarnie, I stayed, and stood alone to watch the aftermath.

What happens is that the tide rises for about an hour behind the wave, submerging much of the bank. In extreme cases, parked cars get drowned. The debris that had once wandered downstream was now rushing back up. Then very slowly, the river level fell again, and the tide grew increasingly languid. The branches and plastic bottles in the rearguard of this invasion slowed to a crawl and then to a halt. At that moment, the normal current reasserted itself and, reluctantly, they began to head back downstream – until the evening tide and the next bore arrives to hurtle them back again. Very disorientating for the bottles.

The corollary is that low tide on this river is very low. By mid-afternoon, all the sandbanks of the Lower Severn were exposed. I stood at Lydney Harbour, just above the original Severn Bridge and before the river starts to narrow, with John Thurston, a real Gloucestershire man, and stared across Saniger Sand towards Berkeley and the nuclear power station. There was far more sandbank visible than river.

'I could walk across that, couldn't I?'

'You *could*,' he said thoughtfully. 'You'd probably die, but you *could*.'

Later, an old riverman called Chris Witts warned me: 'It's Britain's most dangerous river. Don't ever be tempted. It just sucks you down, Severn mud.' I heard a story about four salmon-fishing brothers, all of whom had drowned, separately. No one could confirm it; no one disbelieved it. Maybe it's not such a bad thing for the predators that the salmon and the elver and the lamprey are all slowly disappearing from the river.

Gloucestershire has a human equivalent of the Severn Bore too. In Stow-on-the-Wold, perhaps the most self-conscious of all Cotswold towns (which is saying something), it happens every May and October. For fifty weeks a year the life of Stow, full of antiquery and teashoppery, meanders placidly on its own sweet way, just like the river. Then suddenly, whoomph, it is swamped by an onrushing tide. That's how Stow sees it.

Stow Fair began in 1476, always held to mark the feasts of St Philip and St James in May and of St Edward the Confessor in October. It mutated from a hiring fair into a horse sale, with attendant funfair centred on the market square. But then the official horse sale moved elsewhere and a stabbing put paid to the funfair. What's left, in a traveller-owned field just out of town, is, next to Appleby-in-Westmorland, the biggest Gypsy gathering in the country.

Most fairs of this size and antiquity send the local tourist information office into spasms of delight. Here the office ('Go-Stow') closes down. The pubs don't just shut their doors, they slam them. The Bell, nearest the field, appears to have emptied all its furniture. Up the road, the Royalist Hotel, 'the Oldest Inn in England, circa 947 AD', must have withstood the Conqueror, King John, the Wars of the Roses, Cromwell and the Abdication and remained staunch. Stow Fair is too much, though. About half the shops have stayed open, but cautiously, with the owners or their security men looking vigilant. Some of the shops have found other reasons to close. One café says it will reopen on Saturday 'because of work required in our bathrooms'. A clothes shop happened to decide it was stocktaking day. Greedy's Fish and Chips, a business fairly resistant to shoplifting, always stays open and rakes in the cash.

Groups of Gypsy teenagers stood around the square, oblivious to their effect on the locals. I have been here before, in May time, and seen the girls come dressed for clubbing, wearing heels half the height of the smaller cottages and somewhat shorter shorts, in lime greens and flamingo pinks. On a coolish October day, they were a touch more demure: the same heels but stretching up towards tight jeans or jodhpurs, even tighter tops and long, flowing hair. They are not oblivious to their effect on the Gypsy boys, all with gelled hair, big forearms and popping eyes, and all rendered seemingly speechless. About a hundred police stood around, staring intently even at my notebook, but they could find no infringement to engage them other than a breach of the back-seat seat-belt laws.

Why does Stow hate the fair so much? No, no, we don't hate it, they say. 'It's a bit of an anachronism,' one antiques dealer, Antony Preston, had told me. 'No one wants to stop them holding the fair. But it may not be right for a small town.' The complaints come down to two: one is petty theft, not just on the day but all week – 'Small stuff: chicken-stealing, wood taken from sheds, that sort of thing.'

But it's not so much what they take from Stow's lovingly-tended gardens, rather what they do there.

'They pee?' I enquired.

'Worse. The other thing.'

The fair field itself is marked by an official sign saying 'This is not an organised event', which is a formal disclaimer from the police, council and every other gorgio body imaginable. And indeed this is probably the largest untoileted event in the country, which explains the problem with 'the other thing'. But apart from that the fair organises itself. Though there are very few gorgios – representatives of the Muggle-world of non-Travellers – and hardly any Stowites at all, the atmosphere is welcoming and the police inside are relaxed. The most intent representatives of officialdom come from the RSPCA, anxiously scanning the tethered Welsh cobs and caged chickens.

There was a good turnout, because it was a fine week and dry underfoot. But this was not a happy week for the Travellers. The day before the fair, police, in force and in riot gear, had marched in to take possession of the Dale Farm site in Essex. The story dominated both the morning papers and the quiet conversations of the Gypsy menfolk at Stow. It's all very well for the authorities to turf them off one site, they said, but they have to offer *somewhere* to go.

The Gypsy Council tent had a big sign:

MYTH: Gypsies are foreign.
TRUTH: Romani Gypsies and Travellers have been part of British
    society for over 500 years.
MYTH: Gypsies are dirty.
TRUTH: Gypsy culture is built upon strict codes of cleanliness
    learned over centuries.
MYTH: Gypsies are criminals.
TRUTH: Gypsies and Travellers are overrepresented in prison
    because courts are more likely to give a custodial sentence.

And so on. Judged by what's on sale, though, Gypsy culture seems to fit a lot of clichés: bejewelled bra tops that would be a bit extreme on a belly-dancing night; furs 'as worn by Katie Price'; the girliest little-girl dresses left anywhere outside a Catholic confirmation ceremony; purple thigh boots of the sort normally favoured only by drag artists; armchairs that might have been liberated from Colonel Gaddafi's compound; and extra-chunky catapults that looked as though they could down a NATO bomber.

'How much are they?'

'Sixty-five,' replied the man.

'Sixty-five pence?' I said, suddenly interested.

'Quid,' he replied, more affably than the question deserved. 'Look at them. Beautifully crafted. Camel bone, buffalo horn.'

'What would I use it for?'

'Pheasants. On the way home.'

But no one was buying. It was that kind of year, and Gypsies were part of British society in that respect too. 'Lots of people,' said the Irishwoman selling handbags, 'nobody spending. Nobody's got any money. We won't sell enough to pay for the stall.'

Like many of the stallholders, she had plastic mesh at the front protecting the stock.

'What's that for?'

'There are a lot of teeves here,' she said.

'Are you a Gypsy?'

'Oh, yes,' she replied.

What *is* Gloucestershire? It is an exceptionally difficult county to encompass. A helpful character from the county council spread out a map and gave me a quick tour, using the council boundaries, which is how local government people always think, even if no one else does. The official pointed to Tewkesbury at the top. 'They're all very apathetic up there.' (This may have been a generalisation.) Then Stroud at the bottom. 'They're all very green down there.' (Ditto.)

In the middle are what Americans would call the twin cities – Gloucester and Cheltenham – except that one is a city and the other isn't. Gloucester has the cathedral but was sabotaged by dreadful post-war redevelopment from which it has never recovered. This is not a controversial judgement. Cheltenham, however, has maintained most of its spa-town charm, enhanced its reputation and become known for its festivals: literature, music, science, cricket and – most famously – drinking, which takes place for four days every March, accompanied by an ancillary horse-racing festival for those who misunderstand the main point of the gathering.

The county as a whole is marked by very high property prices except in the eastern part, the Cotswolds, where prices are exceptionally high. In those much-admired, to my eyes rather pallid-looking, cottages lurk locals who tend to be asset-rich and cash-poor, living in valuable houses they can't sell because they have to live somewhere. There was a story of a beautifully turned-out and much-liked Cotswold woman who would go into town every week to have her hair done. Suddenly, she was not seen around any more. When her body was found, sometime later, it emerged that she had been living in a freezing-cold rat heap.

There is a thin coating of celebrities, headed by Prince Charles and Princess Anne (performers in a well-loved British soap opera), above a thicker layer of upmarket society. Allied to them are the weekenders, east Gloucestershire being the outer limits of comfortable weekly commuting from London. Nowhere else in the country are the weekenders so signifi-cant a part of the economy and culture.

Their homes are not quite empty all winter, the way a Cornish holi-day home might be, but they are not quite full. Mostly, these part-timers do *try* to contribute. As a council official put it: 'When they buy their homes they tend to start out wanting to do everything local – going to the farmers' market, buying from the village shop. But after a while it just gets a bit exhausting. They've worked hard all week and they want to spend the time relaxing – reading, walking, that sort of thing – not trudging round buying things.'

There is one other area, conveniently coloured green on the map. That's the Forest.

The Forest! Throughout Gloucestershire, and some way beyond, the word only has to be mentioned to produce a frisson. No one ever has to ask which forest. The Forest of Dean has been a place with a mind and character and traditions of its own since medieval times. 'He's from the Forest' is one of those phrases that explains everything.

It forms something close to an island between the largely unbridged downstream sections of the Severn and the Wye. And it is a real forest: a place of darkness and mystery and danger that repelled outsiders for thousands of years. Especially as the locals were known to take potshots at passing riverboats. Even Lord Nelson, hunting for oak for England's wooden walls, only peeked from the outside. The nation's most gallant sailor declined to wander into the woods.

The Forest also had minerals – ironstone and coal in particular

– which offered a more regular source of income than forestry, and were enough to save the locals from the uttermost depths of poverty. This was a royal forest but also an industrial area. Thus the population remained stable and largely unnoticed by the outside world.

Inbreeding was one obvious consequence. But so was a remarkable sense of pride and tradition. Perhaps nowhere in the southern half of England is there such persistence of dialect. I met a young labourer in Lydney who still greets his mates with the pure-Forest phrase: 'How bist, o'but?' The dialect may be more self-conscious now but it's still there, along with the Forest's more industrial tastes: chapel, rugby, brass bands. Occasionally, a figure would emerge blinking into the light of the wider world, like the playwright Dennis Potter. And you can see where Potter's *noir*ishness came from, not to mention – a Forest word he was inclined to use himself – his 'stubbornyudedness'.

The Foresters have their rights, and they know them. When Edward I besieged Berwick-upon-Tweed in 1296, he called in miners from the Forest of Dean to undermine (literally) the town's fortifications. As a reward, he gave them free mining rights within the Forest in perpetuity. And there are still freeminers producing coal from shallow pits. It tends to come out in unmanageably large lumps but burns well enough, apparently. To exercise this right it is necessary to be born within the Forest – 'the Hundred of St Briavels' – and to have worked underground. These qualifications are getting harder to fulfil since the Coal Board pulled out, in 1964, and the maternity hospital in Cinderford shut down. But the right is there and is still exercised.

There are still, in ever-decreasing numbers, 'badgers', locals who can run their sheep in the Forest. Some have the right to 'estivers' – i.e. firewood. And there is pannage, permission to release your pigs in autumn to gorge themselves on acorns. Strictly speaking, these are not rights but privileges which can only be exercised with a permit. Rob Guest, former Deputy Surveyor of the Forest, was insistent on that point. And there is a particular problem with pannage. Any little piggies wandering out to snaffle some acorns are likely to come face to face with one of their long-lost and rather more voracious cousins. After an absence of several centuries, a sounder (that's the collective noun) of wild boar celebrated the millennium by escaping from a farm near Ross-on-Wye and returning to their ancestral home. There are now three separate populations, thought to be increasing rapidly. So far, the only reported human injury came about when a man tried to feed one while a small boy simultaneously hit it with a stick.

The boar have their supporters, who include sentimentalists, traditionalists, wildlife enthusiasts and shotgun-carrying boyos from the Welsh valleys who are happy to take on the ancient role as the boars' only predator, now that the monarch and court can no longer be bothered. The pro-boar contingent is not thought to include bluebells, dormice, ground-nesting birds like wood warblers, or anyone who likes neat verges. Much of the grass now looks as though it has been attacked by an alliance of giant moles and JCBs.

Nor does the pro-boar party include Rob Guest. 'Sooner or later, someone is going to be badly injured by one of these animals. It's probably going to involve a dog. Even the smaller animals are powerful and the bigger ones are fearful: about 250 kilos.'

'But they are part of the primeval forest, surely?'

'The difference is that (a) they would always have been hunted in the past and (b) you didn't have 35,000 people living close by and a million people coming in every year. With dogs.'

This is a problem that vexes Guest's successors at the Forestry Commission, and the Court of Verderers, a body dating back at least to 1218 – a blink of an eye in the Forest's history – which still meets in its courtroom in what is now the Speech House Hotel outside Coleford. The court retains some responsibility for the 'vert and venison', which is verderer-speak for the flora and fauna, including the wild boar. The four members are elected for life.

It happened that a vacancy on the court had arisen through death, with an election date set for Gloucester Cathedral on 29 November. 'It's the last old-fashioned election anywhere,' Guest told me. The vote is called by the high sheriff, confined to freeholders of the county (the City of Gloucester excluded) and conducted by a show of hands – none of your new-fangled secret-ballot nonsense. Rob Guest had resolved to stand; I resolved to attend.

As I headed out of the Forest, I picked up the freesheet, the *Review*.

IT'S THE SUPERSTORE DASH

FIRST SAINSBURY IN THE FOREST – 270 JOBS ON THE CARDS

Sainsbury's, the *Review* explained, had beaten Tesco and Asda to get a site in Cinderford, the Forest's largest town, and it would be a 32,000-square-foot store, equivalent to Morrisons in Ross-on-Wye – which is a local benchmark, in the way that newspapers always compare a large tract of land to 'the size of Wales'. The Foresters may also still be unworldly enough to imagine that a new supermarket really creates jobs instead of adding a few – mostly low-grade ones – at the expense of all the others that will vanish. Not just jobs in the small shops that will close but in the ancillary industries that serve them, from accountancy to plumbing. 'A breath of fresh air for Cinderford,' said the happy head of a haulage firm, who had managed to sell his prime site for this enterprise.

Some people in Gloucestershire take a different view. Stokes Croft is an old inner-city area of Bristol, mildly fashionable before it was cut off from the centre by the inner ring road and the notorious horror of the St James Barton roundabout, aka the Bear Pit. Later it had a different type of resident, some of them by 2011 living in a squat known as Telepathic Heights. This was remarkably handy for the shops, in particular a new branch of Tesco Express – the thirty-first branch of Tesco in Bristol – that was opening directly opposite them. Police raided the squat, where they found petrol bombs and made four arrests; a riot ensued and the new shop was duly trashed. Tesco prevailed of course, and was trading calmly but just a little fearfully when I passed by six months later, closing at 6 p.m. instead of the 11 p.m. at other branches, scared as they were of things going bump or boom in the night.

But Tesco does not sit easily in Stokes Croft. The police might stamp on Telepathic Heights but something was emerging from below which would be less easily eradicated. The guiding spirit was the graffito-genius Banksy, one of whose seminal works, *The Mild Mild West*, had been on a wall by the Jamaica Street junction for over a decade. It depicts a teddy bear about to throw a Molotov cocktail at a line of riot police. A letter writer to the *Western Daily Press* blamed Banksy for the riots and attacked the council for encouraging 'this anarchic graffiti and attitudes'. (Subediting on Bristol's morning paper has declined since the days when the editor threw typewriters at his staff.) The writer was presumably unaware that the Jamaica Street painting had been defaced with red paint in 2009 by a group who thought Banksy was a capitalist stooge.

The walls of Stokes Croft are full of contributions by wannabe Banksies. And the whole place was work in progress. It had elements of growing awareness ('The People's Republic of Stokes Croft'), self-awareness ('People's Republic of Stokes Croft T-shirts £10'), gentrification ('risotto of pumpkin, sage and Stilton'), degradation ('Massage Club. Staff Always Required') and homogenisation (Tesco Express). My sense was that categories two and three were likely to come out on top.

It was raining again on the day of the verderers' election. By the main door of the cathedral, officials sat handing out pieces of paper marked GUEST STANDING. I assumed I was supposed to take one, as an acknowledgement that, not being a freeholder in Gloucestershire (the City of Gloucester excluded), I was not entitled to vote or to sit down.

It took a while to realise that was in fact the ballot paper: Rob GUEST v Ian STANDING. Guest was the establishment candidate: not quite the country gentleman who would be calmly slotted in to fill these positions in the old days, but someone the gentlemen knew and trusted. Several people had told me he knew more about the Forest than anyone else alive. And he had told me he would not stoop to electioneering: busing in his supporters, that kind of stuff.

Standing, though, was not just standing – he was running. Hard. He had been the secretary of HOOF – Hands Off Our Forest – which had sprung up in response to the coalition government's plans, hastily dropped, to start selling off woodland. He was, someone said to me with a shudder, *political*. Despite the weather, several hundred people had turned up, many of them, the whispers suggested, bused in by this, shudder, *politician*. In theory, the electors could have popped in from the Cotswolds or anywhere else. There was no check and, anyway, heaven knows how you confirm whether anyone is actually a freeholder. But everyone seemed to know everyone else and had an inkling of what would happen.

The formalities can have changed little over the centuries. We were Oyez, Oyez, Oyez-ed and all persons were told to keep silent, which was difficult for the crying baby at the back. Then we all stood for the high sheriff who was in full fig – ruff, tights, buckled shoes and all – but somehow managed to sit cross-legged while the senior verderer, Robert Jenkins, droned on, milking his moment of glory.

The two candidates sat at the front, on opposing sides of the aisle, like the fathers at a particularly ill-starred wedding. Both were grey-bearded, but differently. Rob Guest had a full countryman's beard, a trustworthy kind of beard; Ian Standing had a suspiciously academic goatee. They were allowed to speak briefly. Both were courteous, even chivalrous, to their opponent, but the speeches were full of subtext that, in a very English, understated, coded way, summed up all the divisions of the modern countryside.

At the difficult art of cathedral oratory, Guest was superior: he spoke clearly and audibly. The Court of Verderers, he said, 'is not a political party, it is not a campaigning group. It is a *court*. It is the equivalent of a magistrates' court.' (There is a local myth that the court is still entitled to hang miscreants.) He did say that people were important as well as 'vert and venison', but the main issues, he said, were essentially technical: 'Here I feel I have something to offer.'

Standing was a bit of a mumbler. But he explained his own expertise: he was steeped in the history of this forest – his MA research focused on its seventeenth-century landscape. But now, he said, 'it is a complicated multi-purpose forest'. The three current verderers, sitting on the platform behind him, looked rather doubtful, as though uncertain what was meant by this word 'multi-purpose' but not liking the sound of it.

None of this mattered. Everything was preordained. When the vote was taken, a respectable but not overwhelming number of hands went up for Rob Guest. 'I don't think we're going to get this,' said a well-spoken woman near me. 'It's all going to turn into a political nightmare.' Then the Standing supporters were asked to indicate. It was what you might call a forest of hands. 'Oh, God,' said the woman.

The victor spoke graciously and said he was sorry there were not two seats: 'I think Rob would have served you equally well.' Behind him, his new colleagues said nothing, though they looked as though the waiter had just brought them a plate of particularly nasty turbot.

And so the battles for England's soul rage: violently in Stokes Croft between capitalist conformity and its enemies; understatedly in Gloucester Cathedral between different views of the English countryside; eternally on the Severn, between the sluggish current and the inrushing tide.

October/November 2011

~~~~~~~~~

Ian Standing, who seemed a very decent bloke, later told me that, at his first meeting, his fellow verderers 'were very warm and welcoming, and presented me with two ties.' But he was not yet ready to succumb: 'This forest needs a vision that will value it and protect it.' There was no internal argument about culling the wild boar, which had reached an estimated 800 by 2014, and a major anti-boar programme was planned. By then the Tesco Express in Stokes Croft had extended its opening hours, but only until 7 p.m.

7. *Bye-bye to the bile beans*

YORKSHIRE

Yorkshire day, 1 August, dawned warm and humid, but no rain seemed imminent. The group gathered at Walmgate, the easternmost gate to the city of York, at 10.45 a.m. The Yorkshire Declaration of Integrity was read for the first time:

> I declare ...
> That Yorkshire is three Ridings and the City of York with these boundaries of 1,136 years standing;
> That the address of all places in these Ridings is YORKSHIRE;
> That all persons born therein or resident therein and loyal to the Ridings are Yorkshire men and women;
> That any person or corporate body which deliberately ignores or denies the aforementioned shall forfeit all claims to Yorkshire status.
> These declarations made this Yorkshire Day 2011. YORKSHIRE

FOR EVER! GOD SAVE THE QUEEN!

This was greeted with a cheer from everyone present, a crowd totalling fifteen. There was a brace of Japanese tourists on the city wall and two ladies in the coffee shop; otherwise just the heedless traffic. Roger Sewell, chairman of the Yorkshire Ridings Society, said the turnout was always a bit thin at Walmgate. The eastern wall is the furthest from the city centre; the area is full of council flats and hardly a visitor hub. Things will warm up later, he said.

Every Yorkshire schoolboy used to know that they lived in the largest county (and the best). The three ridings were North, East and West, the word 'riding' deriving from 'thirding'; there never was a South Riding except in a novel. And, as the declaration said, York was not in a riding but an 'ainsty' of its own. Then in the great shake-up of 1974 the ridings were abolished and six separate bits of the county, some small, some substantial, were chopped off and merged with neighbouring, lesser counties. The West Riding was actually shared between seven different new authorities. These decisions caused controversy at the time but were not halted. Most of those who even remember the old county are now in bus-pass land; certainly most of this little group were.

We made the declaration by setting foot, just, in each of the ridings: outside Walmgate for the East Riding, Micklegate for the west, Bootham Bar for the north and inside Monkgate for the ainsty itself. It was read in English, in Latin, in Old English – full of references to Eoforwic-scire – and Old Norse, a prolix language which always took twice as long as the others. However, it was declaimed with great elan by a scholarly chap called Peter Hindle. 'It's an easier language if you've got a Yorkshire accent than if you're southern,' he said. 'Very flat vowels.' Sometimes the proclaimers preceded their declaration with a traditional Yorkshire opening: 'Eh-upp' or 'Nah then'.

And the crowd did build. By Micklegate there were a good two dozen of us. The group regards that one as the main event and insisted on it starting at 11.36 to mark the fact that it was 1,136 years since Eoforwic-scire first got a mention in the *Anglo-Saxon Chronicle*. There was also one declaration for luck, at the market in Parliament Street, where we were joined by the Deputy Lord Mayor, not a grand figure in robes and chain but a jolly bloke in a panama hat, and a girl called Amanda who had a Yorkist rose tattooed on her left shoulder.

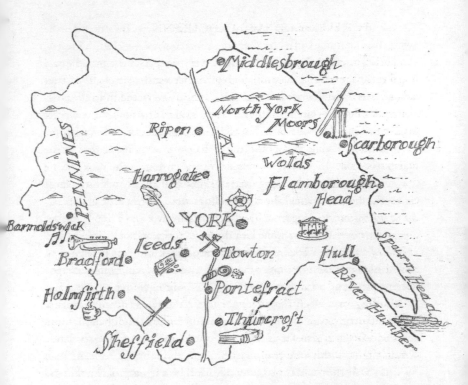

There was a large crowd at the market, shopping and eating their sandwiches. Most took no notice whatever. Roger had warned me it would be a bit like this: 'The trouble with York is that 70 per cent of the people on the streets are tourists.' But you could tell he was a bit disappointed. At Bootham Bar, where we gathered outside the Gents, and even Peter's theatrical Old Norse could not be heard above the traffic, we did seem particularly pathetic.

We tramped the walls from Bar to Bar, waving our flags. And the general response was simple indifference. A local resident, Carolyn Dougherty, who fetched up here from San Jose, California, explained to me that the great delight of Yorkshire was the number of eccentrics. So a dozen or so of them gathered together impressed no one.

Much of the conversation among the group concerned the iniquity of the 1972 Local Government Act, which not only dismembered Yorkshire but created the much-loathed, and now abolished, artificialities of

Cleveland and Humberside. 'I heard on the BBC News the other day the words Bridlington, North Humberside,' snorted someone. Judith Preston Anderson, a retired headmistress (there were several in the group), told me that she moved to Lincolnshire to take over a primary school and her first act was to get the words 'South Humberside' removed from the notepaper. 'All the old grannies gathered at the gate and said: "But you'll get sent to prison, Mrs Anderson." They wouldn't have dared, believe me.'

And I had some very complicated conversations about the precise status of Goole. There were even hints of dissension in the ranks of the society, between those who wanted to emphasise the county as a whole and those more concerned about the ridings. These are not the major topics of concern on the streets of Leeds and Bradford.

And yet beneath it all one can detect a barely audible rustle of success. Yorkshire Day was conceived by the society's founders in the 1970s, when the resentment of those who felt it still burned hot. They chose 1 August primarily because it is Minden Day, which celebrates the Battle of Minden, 1759, when the 51st Foot (later the King's Own Yorkshire Light Infantry) fought their way to victory over the French wearing roses in their coats. It is also the anniversary of the abolition of slavery across almost all the British Empire in 1834, brought about by the Yorkshireman William Wilberforce. It is also Lammastide in the Church calendar. 'And my husband's birthday,' added Judith.

In 2011, for the first time, the concept looked like gaining real traction. In the Test match at Nottingham, England beat India thanks to the bowling feats of the Yorkshireman Tim Bresnan. Both the radio commentators and the *Sun* made much of it being Yorkshire Day. In Whitehall the communities secretary, Eric Pickles, the bumptious ex-leader of Bradford Council, reportedly ordered his staff to fly the Yorkshire flag. This was also created by the society, and very handsome it is: a double white rose on a delicious ice-blue background. A blue of more southerly skies. There were various stunts across the county as well: an ice cream firm near Huddersfield made a special batch – Yorkshire pudding and gravy flavour; there was a Yorkshire Day cooking competition at Leconfield; and an evening of stories and music at Meltham Church Hall. One of the activists, Mark Graham of Stamford Bridge, was delighted to be told by his daughter that at the Leeds rock festival, which takes place later in August, there are regular chants of 'Yorkshire, Yorkshire'. Nothing like that happens anywhere else.

It was only when the Welsh Nationalist Gwynfor Evans threatened to starve himself to death unless the government provided a TV channel in Cymraeg that Welsh language and culture ceased to be a joke and started to revive. And it seems to me that the Yorkshire Ridings Society has become marginalised by its own moderation. As I left them, I felt that what the cause needed was a few Gandhian fanatics. And good Lord, there ought not to be a shortage round here.

In the drab open country between Tadcaster and Pontefract there occurred, on the bitter-cold Palm Sunday of 1461, what is now thought to be the grisliest day ever on English soil. This was the Battle of Towton, where the white-rose forces of Edward, Duke of York, routed the red-rose forces of the Lancastrian king, Henry VI, leaving thousands dead: 38,000 is the top-of-the-range figure. Many were slain on a field still known as Bloody Meadow. Others either froze or drowned in Cock Beck.

Most of the dead were Lancastrians. They had the numerical advantage but the Yorkist archers had the wind at their backs. The victory secured the kingship for Edward IV, whose heirs might have stayed on top for ever had Edward not died suddenly in 1483. This led to the murder of his sons (in most versions) by their uncle, who became Richard III until his own death at Bosworth handed the throne to Henry Tudor, who was more or less Lancastrian. The rest, as they say, is history.

Despite its gruesomeness, Towton is not a very well-known battle. However, a clearly marked trail had just opened to coincide with the 550th anniversary. On a clear day at Towton you can see the Drax power station; but I arrived in the midst of a filthy downpour. A cross of St George flew in the adjoining field, but that was simply to advertise a forthcoming ploughing match. There were, however, two wreaths at the foot of the tiny memorial, Dacre's Cross: one of them, improbably but charmingly, from the Military History Society of the West Midlands Police.

Towton actually takes up most of the second act of a Shakespeare play, but the play is *Henry VI Part III*, which is not high on the list of audience favourites. And indeed the Wars of the Roses have generally struggled to maintain their place in the nation's historical imagination, especially since school history became largely Hitler-centric. Their most obvious commemoration comes in the cricketing rivalry between Yorkshire and Lancashire, which is still real, though with little of its old intensity. Most half-interested people probably assume, as I did, that the counties were relevant to the conflicts of the fifteenth century, when they had already been in existence for half a millennium.

Evidently not. Then and now, dukedoms were titles unrelated to local connections: the Dukes of Devonshire are based in Derbyshire; the current Duke of York, Prince Andrew, does not go round saying 'Nah then' or 'Eh-upp'. According to Professor Michael Hicks, author of the recent work *The Wars of the Roses*, the Lancastrian heartland was actually Leicester. And although the Dukes of York had a castle at Sandal, near Wakefield, the centre of their power was Wales. The families that mattered in Yorkshire were the Percys and the Nevilles. Indeed, York itself was a hotbed of Lancastrian sympathy, as was the East Riding. The realities of Yorkshire rarely accord with the perception.

Still, the notion of Eoforwic-scire does date back more than 1,100 years, and the characteristics associated with Yorkshiremen also have a long history. 'A more stiff-necked, wilful and obstinate people did I ever know or hear of,' complained Archbishop Edwin Sandys, translated from London to York in 1577. The word 'tyke', otherwise a mongrel or boor, was applied to Yorkshiremen from at least 1700. In 1736 the ballad-opera *A Wonder, or An Honest Yorkshireman* was a West End hit, the title being a bit of a giveaway as to what London thought.

The line 'Eat all, sup all, pay nowt' seems to have a long provenance, as does the verse

> *Tha' can say what tha' likes to a Yorkshireman*
> *Tha' can do as tha' likes an' all;*
> *But tha'll gerrit all back an' more besides*
> *So mind what tha' sez, that's all.*

There would be no perception these days that Yorkshire people are any more dishonest than anyone else. But wilful, canny heading towards tight, and combative? All of these, and more, are part not just of their image but of their self-image. Boastful, too.

'What's the biggest county in England?' one of my favourite Yorkshiremen asked over dinner.

'Yorkshire,' I replied.

'What's the second biggest?'

I began to get suspicious. 'We are talking traditional counties?'

'Of course.'

'Well, Lincolnshire, then.'

'Wrong! The West Riding!' he announced triumphantly. (True, I now think, but only just.)

The ur-text on Yorkshireness these days is the Monty Python sketch:

'We lived for three months in a paper bag in a septic tank. We used to have to get up at six in the morning, clean the paper bag, eat a crust of stale bread, go to work down t' mill, fourteen hours a day, week-in week-out, for sixpence a week, and when we got home our dad would thrash us to sleep wi' his belt.'

'Looxury.'

It is a stereotype, of course: the hard-as-nails, mook-an'-brass, oop-by-his-bootstraps, University-of-Hard-Knocks northern businessman, so busy telling you how successful he is that he can't possibly have time to make money. He exists, though, and not just in Yorkshire. But Yorkshire is his spiritual home. And if anything, the notion of Yorkshireness has grown stronger since the county suffered its multiple amputations.

Accents that were a rarity in the media in the early days of the BBC became far more prevalent from the 1960s onwards. The cosy tones of J. B. Priestley once embodied the county. Later came harsher figures like Arthur Scargill, Geoffrey Boycott and Jimmy Savile. The last two bewildered the radio psychiatrist Dr Anthony Clare, supposedly unflappable as both a broadcaster and a shrink: Boycott told him cricket was not a team game; Savile, a lifelong bachelor, derided the notion of the word 'love', implying the whole thing was some kind of global hoax.*

The anthropologist Kate Fox saw the classic Yorkshire type as a self-conscious inversion of the English character. The English in general are even more squeamish about money than they are about sex. She regards the blunt Pythonesque Yorkshire businessman as a deliberate, very self-conscious reversal of this, even a parody. It is not a diagnostic condition that afflicts every male born in the Broad Acres; Yorkshiremen come in all flavours. And not every example is in business. My own favourite representation came from Peter Simple, the late, great *Daily Telegraph* columnist,

---

* I wrote that sentence before Savile was exposed as a mass sexual predator in 2012; I have retained it as written, on grounds of perceptiveness.

who invented Alderman Foodbotham, 'the 25-stone, crag-visaged, iron-watch-chained, grim-booted perpetual chairman of the Bradford City Tramways and Fine Arts Committee'. At least I thought Simple, aka Michael Wharton, had invented him until the day I first clapped eyes on Eric Pickles as a real-life Bradford councillor.

Not everyone looks like Alderman Footbotham or blusters like Arthur Scargill. For each county in this book, I have tried to distil the essence of the place. On Yorkshire Day I kept asking the enthusiasts where I might find that essence. They all replied that the whole point of the county was its diversity, which is fair enough. More acres in Yorkshire (3,882,851), they like to say, than letters in the King James Bible (3,228,076). (There are different versions of these figures, but the principle stands, for what it's worth.) Paul Jackson, editor of the *Dalesman*, told me that Yorkshire's size was the key to the strength of its identity. 'After the Industrial Revolution, when people came out of the Dales to find work, they tended to move to industrial areas within the county. Elsewhere, they would have been far more likely to move counties. I've traced my ancestry back to Nidderdale and round Settle in the 1800s. They went down to Leeds, Bradford and the Heavy Woollen District, but they didn't leave Yorkshire.'

Britain's Texas, it is sometimes called – a phrase I mentioned to Carolyn Dougherty, the Californian Tyke-ophile. 'No! Texans are mean,' she said. 'Yorkshire people aren't mean. Canny. But not mean-spirited. Very generous.' With the zeal of the convert, Carolyn listed for me her favourite safely dead Yorkshiremen: Sir George Cayley of Scarborough, who was tinkering with primitive flying machines before the close of the eighteenth century; William Scoresby, Arctic explorer and curate of Bessingby; and Squire Charles Waterton of Walton Hall, collector of South American animals and creator of the world's first bird sanctuary, a man who shot a donkey with a curare dart and then spent four hours resuscitating it with a bellows, so it lived on as a family pet for years. 'His personality was so charismatic I can still respond to it more than two centuries later,' she said.

Had they lived in London, such men might have been hailed as geniuses. But inventiveness in draughty northern manors and vicarages always tends to be taken for madness. Despite all its pretensions, moaned Foggy Dewhurst in *Last of the Summer Wine*, 'Yorkshire is not even one of the superpowers competing for the ideological leadership of the world.' His mate Cleggy moaned in reply: 'It all went wrong when they sacked Boycott.'

If Yorkshire were a country it would have a respectable population size, comparable with Ireland, Norway, Singapore and, come to think of it, Scotland. But it's not a country. It's not even a proper county any more. Imagine how Texas would respond if some Washington dumb-ass proposed shifting the panhandle to Oklahoma on the grounds that it would be more administratively convenient. Faced with the destruction of the county, allegedly proud Yorkshire folk behaved in a manner that did not invert Englishness, but epitomised it: they grumbled and did what they were told.

Still, much of the county, however we define it, has thrived over the past forty years. Leeds, in particular, has acquired a new pre-eminence. It may well be the most pleasant place to shop in the country, though I don't find much else pleasant about it. After the fall of Soviet Russia, Leeds became the global centre of excellence for fat-headed jobsworths. But I know smart London girls who have spurned Oxbridge because they think they will have more fun in Leeds. Enthusiasts rave, not only about Leeds and Harvey Nichols, but about the whole of Yorkshire's restaurants and galleries and concerts and all-round sophistication. All of which is true. But what they mean is that the place has been southernised. It has become a cheap (literally) version of the South-East, all part of homogenised England. Same shops, same architecture, same tastes.

Rugby league might stand as a symbol. Baffled by all oval-ball games, I once called it 'formation mugging' in print and a Yorkie colleague stopped speaking to me for years. Enthusiasts say it is a much better, faster game these days. But it is now nourished by marketing men and TV executives, not by its northern working-class roots. It is played in summer, and teams have names like Leeds Rhinos and Wakefield Wildcats. It values incomers like Catalans Dragons (*sic*) and London Broncos – who play in a Super League which is impervious to normal promotion and relegation – more than it values stalwart old teams like Featherstone Rovers. And even *their* ground has been renamed: goodbye, Post Office Road; hello, Bigfellas Stadium.

Because of the size of the place, there was little enough that ever actually united Yorkshire. Cricket was foremost. Yorkshire were county champions as often as not; they set the standard for all their rivals and they maintained the rule that the team comprised players all born inside the borders of historic Yorkshire. This led to the stories of women being rushed up the A1 as their contractions grew more frequent, with their husbands desperate to get across the frontier just in case the event brought forth a man-child.

The Yorkshire-born rule remained until 1992, long after the county's official existence had ceased and the team, partly because of the birthplace rule, had descended into vile-tempered mediocrity. This came to a head in 1983 when the club, as Cleggy said, got rid of Geoff Boycott, a cricketer of great ability, even greater determination, complete indifference to anyone else's feelings and a matchless ability to divide public opinion. A revolution ensued, with Boycott supporters – as obsessive as their hero – using the democratic procedures of a members' club to kick out the committee and get him reinstated. It mirrored the simultaneous goings-on nationally in the Labour Party in which the far left was trying to wrest control from the centrists. But the convulsions in Yorkshire County Cricket Club generated more passion.

Both insurgencies achieved short-term victories: the Yorkshire committee fell and Boycott was reinstated; Michael Foot became leader of the Labour Party. Both had similar long-term results. The cricket club's members lost their rights to do anything except pay up, turn up and shut up, and control passed to a classic Yorkshire businessman who ran it as he pleased. The team continued to be mediocre and membership withered, especially from the further edges of the county. The fixtures in Hull, Sheffield, Middlesbrough, Bradford and Harrogate were all abolished and nearly all the matches concentrated at Headingley in Leeds, a ground that would remain unpleasant if it were rebuilt by Frank Lloyd Wright. Yorkshire's tenure became funded, under a bizarre arrangement, by a local university (not the good one). Its fixture list has to be married up with that of the Rhinos next door. And at big matches the crowd got increasingly nasty-drunk and the stewards increasingly nasty-officious.

If not cricket, what now unites the county? Traditional Yorkshire had its own logic, even if it was not obvious. Professor Clive Upton, the expert on dialect at the University of Leeds, explained to me that the Humber–Ribble line has a vital linguistic significance, dividing northern English speech from Midland speech. The North and East Ridings were north of the line and the West Riding south of it: 'There was never any such thing as a typical Yorkshire speaker,' he explained. Paul Jackson broke it down even further, explaining that the word 'right' would be 'rait' in the West Riding, 'reet' in the East Riding and 'raat' in the North Riding. Dr Barrie Rhodes of the Yorkshire Dialect Society offered 'about': 'abaht' in the West, 'abut' in the East and 'aboot' in the North.

There are many relevant quirky habits and usages: the issue of whether 'dinner' happens at midday or in the evening has both a regional and a class dimension and extends far beyond Yorkshire. So does the endearment 'luv'. The lingering taste for tripe and offal extends across the Pennines to Lancashire. There are other usages that seem to be peculiarly Yorkshire, but whether they encompass the whole of Yorkshire or not is mysterious. Martin Wainwright, for many years northern editor of the *Guardian*, says Yorkshire people will say: 'Would you like it wrapping?' rather than 'wrapped'. And 'What do they call her?' instead of 'What's her name?'

Then there is 'I'll wait while three' instead of 'until'. And inversion: 'She's a lovely woman is Penny.' Or, as Jimmy Savile once said: 'It's wonderful, is death'.* Barrie Rhodes thought the most typical Yorkshire characteristic was 'ascribing an inanimate object with the capacity for desire': 'That window wants cleaning.'

Yorkshiremen traditionally send a pint of ale back unless it has a foaming head. And chips are still cooked in beef fat, not vegetable oil. But a lot of southerners like a foaming pint and beef fat was used in the Black Country. There was a time when Yorkshire people took the otherwise defunct English version of the 'tu' form – thou to denote affection or superiority, thee for formality – as seriously as any French academician, leading to the once-famous injunction: 'Don't thee thar me, thee thars them that thars thee.' This is now either defunct or confined to a few remaining old-timers in Barnsley working men's clubs, if anywhere.

I thought I might have made a breakthrough when I discovered Henderson's Spicy Relish, which, unlike Worcestershire Sauce (and indeed Yorkshire chips), is suitable for vegetarians and vegans. But it turned out to be a taste largely confined to Sheffield. There was Mather's Black Beer from Huddersfield (made without hops), but that hardly runs through the veins of the ridings. Is there anything left that is peculiarly and all-embracingly Yorkshire? Was there ever anything at all? Barrie Rhodes pointed out that the division into ridings meant that Yorkshire had not been united in an administrative sense since the kingdom of Jorvik collapsed in the tenth century. 'Yorkshire is really more an idea than an entity,' he said.

And yet what an idea! The champions of Yorkshire are not wrong. It is a

---

*Not for his reputation, it wasn't.

place of constant surprises and magical memories. And when I sat down to try to list a few – some garnered while researching this book, some from many years before – I found I couldn't stop.

1. Sitting in St George's Hall, Bradford, listening to that most Yorkshire of brass bands, Hammond's Saltaire (formerly Hammond's Sauce Works), playing that most Yorkshire of pieces, Holst's 'Moorside Suite'.

2. Going to Spurn Head, the strangest spit of land in the kingdom, where Yorkshire reaches out into the Humber and narrows to a few feet across; and the lifeboatmen, the only full-timers in the service, reverse traditional roles. Their station is so remote that they cannot leave while on call, and so their wives and kids scatter and the menfolk stay home all day, doing chores and cooking – unless and until their bells ring, and then they're gone.

3. Hull Fair, the largest in the kingdom by far, and the traditional end-of-season gathering for the showmen of England.

4. Huddersfield Station, the St Pancras of the North, fit for a grander train service, with its statue of Harold Wilson, fit for a grander prime minister.

5. Driving along Berry Brow near Huddersfield on a sunny autumn afternoon with the leaves hurtling towards the river.

6. The maples turning yellow in Meersbrook Park, Sheffield.

7. Watching county cricket at Bradford Park Avenue, the lost temple of Yorkshire sporting pride.

8. More cricket at Scarborough, the one place where Yorkshire allowed the game to be treated as fun, mainly because everyone was playing in an alcoholic haze.

9. Being met off the train by my friend Geoffrey Moorhouse, wearing, as I recall, an Aztec hat, at remote Dent Station on the Settle–Carlisle line, as the sun set on a frosty evening.

10. Watching Keighley, again with Geoffrey, play hopeless rugby league at run-down Lawkholme Lane in the days before, lordy, lordy, it was renamed Cougar Park – which one would like to believe is a reference to predatory middle-aged women rather than exotic beasts.

11. Geoffrey's funeral, years later, on a December day in Hawes: the light declining, the mist on the fells, the smoke rising from the

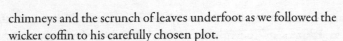

chimneys and the scrunch of leaves underfoot as we followed the wicker coffin to his carefully chosen plot.

12. White wine in the Dean of York's garden on a summer's afternoon after Eucharist in the Minster.

13. Striding out to the Cow and Calf on Ilkley Moor on a summer's morning, possibly baht 'at.

14. High tide at Flamborough Head with the waves dancing through the arches in the chalky cliffs.

15. The faded glory of the Cutlers' Hall in Sheffield.

16. The secretive crypt at Ripon Cathedral, constructed a trifling 1,450 years ago, on the instructions of the great scholar and traveller St Wilfrid, complete with niche for the saintly relics he brought back from his journeys.

17. Thirsk Races, under the Hambleton Hills.

18. The wonderful war memorial at Sledmere in the East Riding, built in the style of an Eleanor Cross, so that the men who died as cattle – like Harry Addison, carpenter, Walter Barker, footman, David Scott, agriculturalist, and William Webster, saddler – are memorialised in the manner of medieval saints.

19. Seeing a narrow boat on the Rochdale Canal outside Mytholmroyd, preceded by a phalanx of Canada geese, apparently guiding it forward like tugboats.

20. A sudden scene just outside the unremarkable (except for its name) West Riding village of Ulleskelf: autumnal lime trees; the sun on a field of ripe maize; a storm approaching and the sky turning violet; and where the hell's my camera?

In that moment I understood why Turner was so enraptured by Yorkshire, and why David Hockney went back to paint in Bridlington instead of Los Angeles.

Oh, and then there are those place names, few as strange or as obviously Danelaw as Ulleskelf, but rich with comedic possibilities: Wetwang, Fangfoss, Kirby Grindalythe, Sewerby, Penistone, Grimethorpe, Blubberhouses. And the ones that embody the rule expounded in *The Sunshine Boys* that places with a hard K are inherently funnier than those without: Heckmondwike, Giggleswick, Cleckheaton. And of course the Swaledale hamlet of Crackpot.

I was tempted to add the faded advert on a brick wall in Lord Mayor's

Walk, York: 'Nightly BILE BEANS Keep You HEALTHY BRIGHT EYED & SLIM'. I wanted to believe that people in York were still devoted to the laxative appeal of bile beans and perhaps were still dosing their children with Argotone Nose Drops and Radio Malt. It turns out this ad is regarded by local sophisticates as a much-cherished landmark, and it has already been repainted once.

The day that Yorkshire was sliced and diced was 1 April 1974, a day that for the zealots of the Yorkshire Ridings Society will live in infamy. Hardly noticed, amid it all, was the loss of the small Pennine town of Barnoldswick (usually known as Barlick), which was translated to the Pendle district of Lancashire. It's the sort of town I instinctively like: isolated but stable. Not unprosperous too – Rolls-Royce have built aero-engine parts here for decades, and Silent-night beds are just moving in. It also has a surprising number of shops, most of which will doubtless keel over as soon as Tesco comes to town.

Gordon Prentice, who became MP for Pendle in 1992, told me that in the early years he got a regular stream of letters from Barlick complaining about being moved. They tapered off but Lancashire has still not dared put up a sign announcing its imperium. Its subordinate body, Pendle, had one hidden behind greenery just after the turn-off from the main road to Blackburn. In town, where council property is safer from attack, Pendle was far more brazen. It took over the post office, opposite the bus shelters, thus occupying not just the most prominent but also what may be the ugliest and worst-maintained building not merely in Barlick, but possibly in England. The council should issue an enforcement notice on itself.

I resolved to stand near this monster and ask ten locals which county they (a) lived in and (b) wanted to be in. I was hoping, I suppose, for an outburst of fearsome Yorkshire irredentism. It didn't happen. I got one rebuff (male). Otherwise, all ten dutifully told me they were in Lancashire, some in a where's-this-leading kind of tone, as though, like the North Humberside grannies, they feared they might go to jail for the wrong answer. To the second question, four said Lancashire, three said Yorkshire and three didn't care.

One incomer told me he preferred Lancashire on political grounds: it was usually Labour-controlled, while the alternative, North Yorkshire, was invariably Tory. A teenage girl kindly switched off her iPod to talk to me, then looked disgusted: '*Yorkshire?* It's just the elderly people who think that.'

Barlick was always a bit divided: it was a cotton town, not a wool town; residents always found it a fraction quicker to go and do a big-shop in Lancashire not Yorkshire; and, even before 1974, the letters came through Colne, so the Post Office encouraged the use of Lancashire on envelopes. But the significant change came when the midwife stopped coming round town to deliver babies, and mothers were sent to mater-nity hospital. They could opt for Keighley, on the Yorkshire side, but the default position, if they were not bothered, was Burnley, the other way. So most locals under fifty were born in what is unarguably Lancashire.

David Stead, former chairman of the town council, is a Yorkie and proud of it. But he told me: 'When we were shifted, most of Barlick just accepted it. Barlickers knew who Barlickers were. We were very insular, still are. Nobody passes through, we're not on anyone's route. We're in Barlickshire, basically.' There is still some fun to be had. The town's water comes from Yorkshire but the sewage goes into Lancashire. So when the subject crops up, the Yorkies have a ready answer: 'You get all our crap.'

Some of Yorkshire has come back home: for instance, since Hum-berside was strangled, the flag of a revived East Riding Council flies over Bridlington's shingle. But it's all a complete dog's breakfast. And Middles-brough seems to have left Yorkshire behind completely: Clive Upton says there is even evidence that the accent has changed since the boundaries were moved, becoming more Geordie and less Yorkie.

In 1960 Clancy Sigal, a young American writer based in London, wrote a book that created a mild stir at the time. It was called *Weekend in Dinlock*, about a visit – less fleeting than the title suggests – to a Yorkshire mining village. Sigal arrived, at the invitation of a pitman-cum-artist called Davie, and found himself among creatures so alien that the early pages seem less like sociology or even anthropology, and more like zoology.

Sigal was an exotic in a white duffel coat, in a place he called 'dingy, narrow, primitive', wandering among people who might have been pyg-mies or gorillas or Martians, three hours from King's Cross: fighting-drunk men, put-upon wives. Mutual sympathy developed and, finally, Sigal was allowed to go down the pit himself:

> metallic fracturing explosions of picks sunk into coal ... shovels
> ramming into piles of loose coal ... five teams of men moving word-
> lessly in damp semi-darkness ... picks and shovels clanking and

plunging ... ten men in pit boots and leather belt and pit helmet and
naked to the gods of the interior earth ... the collier derives from
the very nakedness of his coal-smeared flesh a unique self-respect,
an unfleshly fraternity which is both elemental and deep-driven.

The account is somewhat fictionalised. Dinlock was really Thurcroft,
just outside Rotherham; Davie was really an aspirant writer called Len
Doherty. But Sigal's account had the resonance of truth. Thurcroft was an
extraordinary, self-contained world. Now it is easy to rattle through and
mistake it for a Rotherham suburb enjoying a little brittle prosperity: the
houses have generous gardens and look solid enough. But it's a Potemkin
village: lean on the place a little and there is nothing there.

Doherty achieved some reputation as a novelist, joined the Sheffield
Star and was named provincial journalist of the year. But he died young,
and it took a full morning of cornering old people round the shops before
I stopped getting blank looks and found Bill Williams, who could just
remember both Len and Clancy. The pit closed in 1991. The nearby brickworks also closed, and the waters of forgetfulness closed over them both.
There is a pitwheel at the entrance to the village, but it is not even Thurcroft's pitwheel, it comes from nearby Dinnington. There is nothing else
to mark the village's past except in the Gordon Bennett Memorial Hall
(named after a county councillor), where there is a handsome painting of
a pit in winter which turns out to be the pub sign of the Thurcroft Hotel.
That's now demolished, awaiting, with an air of helplessness, a developer
who wants to build houses in such a drab spot.

'What do the men do now?' I asked an old boy outside the hall.

'Not a lot. Quite a lot are unemployed. Some of them do roofing.
There's nothing here.'

And yet one essential truth of Sigal's excursion survives: in England
you can travel in no time to what might be distant galaxies. Less than an
hour from Thurcroft is Holmfirth, a classic Pennine millstone grit town
that has acquired celebrity as the setting of a TV sitcom. Holmfirth's fame
has proved remarkably persistent because the series, *Last of the Summer
Wine*, ran on BBC TV from 1973 to 2010, surviving the death of nearly all
the original cast – and the author's inspiration.

Formulaic though it became, it was a wonderful formula. The programme was always set in a perpetual late summer that never quite turned
to autumn, which was precisely its theme: three old buffers – Just William's

Outlaws as pensioners – making light mischief against the background of a haunting harmonica solo. It was a glorification of age, blithe spirits and community, with a light peppering of Yorkshireness. It will exist on cable and satellite for ever.

Holmfirth turned out to be both more upmarket and more distressed than I had expected: Pennine Wealth Management and Harrow's Wine Bar rubbing shoulders with a large cluster of charity shops. There was some minor but not very intrusive cashing-in. The Wrinkled Stocking Tea Room and the Summer Wine Shop and Exhibition were closed. Sid's Café, where Foggy, Clegg and Compo sat for years contemplating life, the universe and Nora Batty, was open. As is surprisingly normal in Yorkshire, the tea came in a mug, not a pot. It occurred to me that the decline of the teapot does not represent – as it does in the South – laziness and indifference, but a small manifestation of Yorkshire arrogance: we-know-how-to-make-tea-here-and-you-can-bluddy-lahk-it. There is something very Texan about this attitude. The half-dozen tea rooms in the county run by Bettys are an exception. But Bettys was founded by a Swiss immigrant called Frederick Belmont.

Fifty minutes and several valleys away is Hebden Bridge, which has been named (meaningless statistic alert) as the fourth funkiest town in the world and the most individual in Britain. It is also said, more convincingly, to be Britain's most lesbian-friendly town. I saw only one shop – William Holt greengrocer – that looked as though it had been there more than five minutes. Its neighbours included the Old Treehouse Children's Hairdresser (First Haircut: £10 including certificate and lock of hair) and Home Oh! It was hard to get a decent cuppa here too, because the cafés were obsessed with fruit-flavoured quasi-teas. If Kate Fox is right and Yorkshireness is an inversion of Englishness, Hebden Bridgeness has become an inversion of Yorkshireness. In its way it seemed to me as sad as Thurcroft.

In the licorice fields at Pontefract
My love and I did meet
And many a burdened licorice bush
Was blooming round our feet ...

I had thought this verse was a Betjemanesque joke and that the liquorice fields of Pontefract were as real as the spaghetti trees of southern Switzerland. Then I found myself on the outskirts of Pontefract, in the office of Chris Marshall, managing director of Tangerine Confectionery, 'the leading UK independent manufacturer of sugar confectionery and branded popcorn'.

'Do you know what those are round the flagpole?' he asked, waving his arm towards the window.

'Well, they look like roses,' I said.

In my defence, I had my reading glasses on. And I had never before seen a liquorice bush. The dozen or so round the flagpole, he thought, were probably the largest collection of them left in Pontefract, Britain, or indeed western Europe – although Marshall, a third-generation liquorice man, was planning a small plantation in his own garden.

Liquorice came from the Middle East, where it was prized for its multifarious medicinal qualities. The Cluniac monks apparently brought it to Pontefract in the Middle Ages, discovering by chance, said Marshall, that the area's sandy soils helpfully mimicked the plant's natural home. The taste for liquorice as a sweet came later, and eventually the town had seventeen local manufacturers and a hundred acres of liquorice fields.

A hundred acres did not sound a lot to me but essence of liquorice, distilled from the root, is said to be the sweetest natural substance on earth, and a little goes a very long way. Which means it is easy to transport. By the late Victorian era, when there were seventeen different makers of Pontefract Cakes, and demand was growing, it made sense to have new plantations in Turkey, where land and labour were cheaper and the weather more trustworthy.

The history of all the British confectionery brands that seem a changeless part of our lives is like a game of pass-the-parcel. And mostly the parcel has now been passed right out of Yorkshire. Rowntree's (owned by Nestlé) have gone from York. So have Terry's (owned by Kraft). Mackintosh's (Nestlé again) have gone from Halifax. But there are still two liquorice factories: Tangerine and the old firm of Dunhill, now owned by Haribo. But there are no liquorice allsorts made in Pontefract. Bassett's (owned by Kraft) make theirs – over-sweet to my taste – in Sheffield. Tangerine, who do supermarket own-brands, make theirs in Blackpool, where the late tycoon Garfield Weston built a new factory simply because he happened to love liquorice allsorts.

I love them too, and their health-giving qualities are undeniable:

Red hair she had and golden skin,
Her sulky lips were shaped for sin,
Her sturdy legs were flannel-slack'd
The strongest legs in Pontefract.

And then there is rhubarb. The rhubarb triangle, north of Wakefield and south of Morley and Rothwell, was once as mysterious as the drowning grounds of the Bermuda Triangle or the opium fields of the Golden Triangle. And its borders wavered depending who you asked. Now the EU has given Yorkshire Forced Rhubarb protected status, like Shetland Wool or Cornish Clotted Cream, with its boundaries clearly defined and the full might of Brussels waiting to descend on any producer from outside the area who falsely claims to be in it. The EU couldn't care less where all the opium comes from.

Rhubarb originated in Siberia, and the climate north of Wakefield proved equally favourable, for reasons that might seem obvious to anyone who has been there in winter with an east wind blowing, but more specifically arose from the area being both a frost pocket and in a rain shadow from the Pennines. There were once 200 producers, and special rhubarb expresses to Covent Garden. Now there are only eleven. 'It's extremely hard work and some would say only stupid Yorkshire people would do it,' said Janet Oldroyd-Hulme. 'We go on to the land at a time of year when most other farmers are off it.'

Mrs O-H is the fourth-generation boss of the splendidly Yorkshire-sounding firm of E. Oldroyd & Sons. She has her sons in the business, and a sixth generation being groomed. The principle handed down through the years is that exposure to light thickens and toughens the stalks, and that getting the plant out of the ground and into a darkened shed makes it sweeter and more tender. Thus, the growers insist, they can produce better rhubarb than anything that might come out of my garden. And they can get it into the shops in midwinter, when there is precious little else available that is both English and fresh.

There is a magnificent rhythm to the rhubarb grower's winter as each type succeeds another: from Timperley to Hammonds Early to Reed's Early Superb to the champagne varieties to Stockbridge Harbinger to Stockbridge Arrow to Queen Victoria and Prince Albert. In the war, when sweets were rationed, kids used to chew on sticks of rhubarb to get a sugar hit. But when the good times returned, rhubarb evoked bad memories and was bracketed with cabbage and sprouts. It is indeed a vegetable, even though it's eaten as a fruit, making rhubarb the exact reverse of a tomato. However, it is back in fashion, and champagne rhubarb is on every bistro menu though it has nothing to do with champagne.

But there is a problem, resulting from climate change: before it is taken into the sheds, the rhubarb needs frost to get the glucose going in the roots; only then can the growers raise the temperature to trick the plant into thinking it's spring.

'Climate change is shrinking the growing season,' said Mrs O-H.

'You mean, it's the exact reverse of everything else?'

'Yes. My dad used to take the Timperley into the forcing sheds in early November. You couldn't do that now.'

I was in her office on a mild November day, without even a hint of frost. The previous winter the ground had been so frozen that they couldn't dig the roots out, so that was no good either. There are other unhelpful changes. In the old days, the sulphates from all the sooty chimneys could be used as fertiliser. And the leftovers from the woollen mills were useful too, the 'shoddy': there was nothing like Pennine shoddy, she said, especially if it had the daggings – the pooey bits – still on it. Now the wool comes from all over, and weird Antipodean plants have been known to sprout in the fields as a result.

Just behind Oldroyd's field of early Timperley was a heap of what looked like sand and ash. But to the touch it felt woolly, if a bit coarse. It was shoddy. Or to put it the Yorkshire way: that's shoddy, is that.

The most prominent building in Dewsbury is an old mill, five storeys high and recently restored. 'ESTD 1856,' says the sign. 'MACHELL BROS LIMITED. SHODDY & MUNGO MANUFRS.'

Shoddy and mungo were both essentially recycled wool, the bottom end of the market. Hence, obviously, the adjective 'shoddy'. The noun has gone the way of Machells (pronounced May-chells), whose mill has predictably been turned into flats. Very desirable, one might think: centre of town, short walk to the station, easy commute into Leeds but far cheaper. The flats have not even been sold. They are owned by a housing association. 'Nothing wrong with a housing association,' said the Dewsbury journalist Margaret Watson.

Absolutely not. But if, as one would have expected, the Machells flats had been sold to yuppies from Leeds, the pub next door, the old Railway Tavern, would not be shut, it would be a wine bar. The next building would not be a snooker hall-cum-loan shop. The next two buildings would not have been pawnbrokers ('WANTED. GOLD AND SILVER!!'). And the rest of town might not be so full of pound shops broken up by the occasional amusement arcade. The only thriving business in the immediate vicinity was the Iqbal Hijab Centre. Nothing wrong with that either. But in the complex history of race relations in Britain, Dewsbury stands out as an unusually disastrous example.

This is a handsome stone town, a county borough – and thus answerable to no one between here and Whitehall – from 1913 to 1974, full of pride and good-natured rivalry, based on proximity and rugby league, with its neighbour Batley. We are in the Heavy Woollen District, where prosperity depended on the rougher end of the wool trade.

The mill owners began to run out of willing labour before they began to run out of customers and thus began to advertise in Pakistan. And the newcomers began arriving, to initial good-natured curiosity. And arriving and arriving and arriving. And then the original inhabitants began to disappear either to the distant edges of the borough or right out of it, leaving behind the newcomers and a white underclass.

When I drove into Dewsbury, there was a low afternoon sun; hunting a parking space, I accidentally turned down a one-way street. I was put right by four young Asians driving the correct way, who angrily waved me backwards. I acknowledged and started to reverse. But they kept coming towards me and, with solid traffic on the main road behind, I was stuck. I wound the window down and said, with uncharacteristic mildness: 'You might at least let me get out of this.' 'You shouldn't have fooking got into it, should you?' snarled the driver. Well, welcome to fooking Dewsbury.

When I mentioned this to one white Dewsburyite, he rolled his eyes in a what-do-you-expect-of-the-Asians kind of way. Yet the incident did not strike me as particularly Asian; it did strike me as rather Yorkshire, and very Dewsbury. It's a bad-tempered place. It didn't feel in any way dangerous, though. By 8 p.m. the centre was like one of those American small towns where almost everyone has fled to the suburbs, leaving behind a tiny residue of drunks, dogs and the occasional passing freight train. Here even the drunks were missing: most of the pubs in Dewsbury have shut down. One of them, the White Hart – formerly the haunt of the Masons and Rotarians – has become a Sharia Centre. There is no cinema, not so much as a bingo hall. Even McDonald's looked deserted.

It's not that much livelier in daylight: Marks & Spencer pulled out years ago; and the confident Victorian town hall has been a shell since Dewsbury county borough and the town were subsumed into an amorphous Huddersfield-centred splodge known as Kirklees. The market itself was thriving, although there were few young shoppers, and no one under eighty at the tripe stall.

Dewsbury did still have two weekly papers. I met two of the journalists. Margaret Watson, who joined the *Dewsbury Reporter* in 1958 and rose to be deputy editor, was still writing her column, 'The Way We Were' (sample headline: AUSTIN FRIARS HAS A RICH AND INTERESTING HISTORY), and is a local legend. She is kindly and friendly but fearful that I might be about to criticise her beloved Dewsbury. When I met her, she had a book coming out: *Dewsbury in Food and Photos*.

Danny Lockwood used to edit the *Reporter* and now edits an independent rival the *Press* (sample headline: GUN TERROR). He played amateur rugby league for Great Britain; on his website he calls himself 'Yorkshire's no. 1 columnist'; he is shaven-headed, voluble and a very Yorkshireish Yorkshireman. He was about to publish a book too, called *The Islamic Republic of Dewsbury*. Margaret and Danny are very fond of each other, a sort of mother and wayward son. Their Dewsburys are rather different. Danny took me round his version of it. It is not a cheerful one.

He showed me the estate where in 2008 a woman called Karen Matthews got herself involved in the abduction of her nine-year-old daughter, Shannon, one of her seven children by five different fathers. It was a case that transfixed the nation and, more than anything, created the image of Dewsbury as a dump. These are the new slums, identifiable not by the state of the buildings but by the state of the gardens, the worn-down faces of the women and the hopelessness of the teenagers.

We passed Dewsbury Minster, on a site used for worship for about 1,500 years. 'If the chips had fallen right, that would have been the cathedral, not Wakefield,' I said. 'The chips never fall right for Dewsbury,' he said bitterly.

Then he showed me Savile Town, an old area now almost wholly Asian and home to Markazi Masjid, a site used for worship for just over thirty years. Unlike the minster, it can hold 4,000 worshippers and furthermore is likely to get them. It is run by the Tablighi Jamaat, an organisation that appears to be fundamentalist in the sense of urging that followers adhere to the lifestyle of Muhammad, even – according to some accounts – to the point of brushing their teeth with a twig and sleeping on the ground. There have been moments when it has clearly brushed with terrorism, but most experts see its main characteristic as a flinty austerity.

It is very keen on recruiting young Muslims but does not proselytise among unbelievers. And Dewbury Muslims are more than normally wary of unbelievers. Hence the sign outside: 'UNAUTHORISED PERSONS NOT ALLOWED. TRESPASSERS WILL BE PROSECUTED'. Very un-minster-like. But we were greeted by a friendly young man called Imran with a long beard, shalwar kameez, Timberland boots and a Glasgow accent. He asked if we would like to look around. Perhaps he was unaware of local race relations. Yes, please, I said. And, after an interval, we were admitted. Danny was gobsmacked and, not being universally popular in this part of town, rather uneasy. This was not his Dewsbury at all. I am not normally more gung-ho than a rugby league international.

We were given a brief tour of the downstairs area, the main prayer hall being blocked off by a security fence. It was a place governed by clocks, like a City of London trading room, though these clocks showed the prayer times. Inside one large room, a group of acolytes sat cross-legged on the floor listening to a lesson that was in turn being relayed by loudspeaker to the sleeping quarters.

This was another large room, with maybe a hundred rugs and blankets on the floor. People stay here for a month or more, Imran told us. There was no furniture except a couple of washing machines in the far corner. It reminded me of an airport lounge during a strike by French air traffic controllers or a particularly ferocious blizzard. By now there was a certain amount of whispering and pointing going on, and Danny was growing very uneasy indeed. One sensed that if there were a secret crypt here to match St Wilfrid's at Ripon, we might not be invited to view it. So we said polite goodbyes.

But I couldn't get away from the thought of the Ripon crypt and the monks who would have been awestruck by Wilfrid's holy relics. They were probably much like these young men: intense, ascetic, God-fearing, credulous, biddable, naïve, half-crazed by unutterable longings. And it seemed to me that Yorkshire might have gone full circle.

August/November 2011

~~~~~~~~

Mather's Black Beer ceased production in 2013: it had previously benefited from a complicated quirk in the way duty was calculated. The Treasury closed the loophole in 2012, forcing a huge price rise, with predictable results (especially in Yorkshire). Barnoldswick has so far successfully resisted Tesco; opposition included town centre shopkeepers boarding up their windows as a sign of what would happen. In 2014 Margaret Watson, happily, was still writing her column ('Mill apprentice's tale brings back memories') and the Press *was still purveying its less rosy view of Dewsbury.*

In May 2014 voters in Yarm, near Middlesbrough, having spent half a lifetime in areas variously described as Teesside, Cleveland and Stockton on Tees, voted 1,288 to 177 to return to Yorkshire once and for all. The referendum was unofficial and the turnout was 24 per cent. The figures seem to convey accurately the sentiments of those who do care and the wretched indifference of the majority.

In July 2014 the first two stages of the Tour de France were held in Yorkshire. An estimated 2.5 million people hung around for hours to glimpse a few moments worth of Lycra, which was weird. Gary Verity of 'Welcome to Yorkshire' enthused beforehand: 'There are millions of people round the world who can't point to where Yorkshire is today on a map ... after this weekend everybody will know where Yorkshire is.' Unfortunately, people still could not point to Yorkshire on a map, the bloody fools having gone and moved it.

8. *Life on the edge*

SUSSEX

On 5 November I arrived in town at lunchtime, as advised, before the roads closed for the duration. Already, occasional explosions rent the air. Workmen were boarding up the windows of shops, nearly all of which were planning to close early. Waitrose was packed, pending its 4 p.m. shutdown. Friends acknowledged each other hurriedly, usually with a single-word greeting: 'Mad!' The atmosphere was that of a town in the southern United States given warning that a Category Five hurricane would score a direct hit just after nightfall.

But people were not leaving, they were pouring in.

Just after dark, I was standing next to Cliffe Bridge. The crowd was several deep now. I had spent the afternoon studying my programme and the twelve-page pullout supplement in the *Sussex Express*, but still hadn't got a clue what was about to happen. My understanding was that it might be an hour before the first parade. I asked a policeman if he knew. He shrugged. 'It's a massive mess,' he said. 'They do whatever they want and they get away with murder, basically.'

Moments later, the explosions became more intense, and from the top of School Hill there appeared several hundred marchers with firm tread, carrying burning crosses. It still seemed like Dixie, but now we were back in the 1930s and the Klansmen were marching across town to lynch themselves a few uppity suspects.

The sight was astonishing. And so was the sound. And that was only the start. The marching would go on for another *four hours*, and even then the night would be young. This was Bonfire Night in Lewes, perhaps the most gloriously individualistic town in England on what is emphatically its most gloriously individualistic night of the year. As the evening went on, I caught overtones of Remembrance Sunday, Mardi Gras, Saturnalia, Purim, the Gordon Riots of 1780, the Durham Miners' Gala, the Mexican *día de los muertos*, the First Intifada, the Battle of Little Big Horn, the Wicker Man, Sherman's March to the Sea, Up Helly Aa and the Northampton League of Pity fancy-dress party circa 1957. There is also a soupçon of April Fool's Day since, in the weeks beforehand, the *Sussex Express* goes on to red alert about news tip-offs in the expectation of being hoaxed.

The one event to which it bears no resemblance is the sanitised, organised, municipalised, be-careful-dear-sparklers-can-be-dangerous Guy Fawkes celebrations that now take place almost everywhere else in the country as an afterthought to Americanised Halloween. In Lewes the actual fireworks displays are the least of the evening's entertainment. It is nothing like an American Fourth of July, though there is a smidgen of Protestant Ulster marching on the Twelfth.

The burning crosses were just the start. They went on burning all night, along with the torches. Then came the bands. And the smugglers, all dressed in hooped jerseys (always called guernseys, but not alderneys or sarks) in the distinctive colours of the town's six different Bonfire Societies. On top of everything else, it also looked a bit like *The Pirates of Penzance*, as directed by Cecil B. DeMille. The smugglers were followed by an assortment of Red Indians, Aztecs, Mounties, Confederates, Cavaliers, Roundheads, Zulus, Battle of Britain pilots, harlequins, serving wenches and Romans. At one point, the Chanctonbury Ring Morris Men appeared, thrilled to be at an event where no one thought them remotely eccentric.

By now nearly every marcher, at least those over the age of ten, was carrying not a cross but a flaming torch which, when it got too hot to handle, was dumped on the ground to be picked up by a team of men with barrows.

The bands competed against constant explosions, some of them inches from my ears. I was a bit puzzled where they all came from, until I saw one of the smugglers – probably a chartered accountant in real life – casually take a banger out of his pocket, set the fuse and toss it on the ground, as though he were discarding a sweet wrapper. Each society stopped at the war memorial to stage a sort of pastiche Poppy Day ceremony, which was a gesture towards respectability and solemnity. But only a gesture.

In theory, Lewes Bonfire is based on the fact that seventeen Protestant martyrs were burned here under Bloody Mary. Sensitive Catholics still get upset and believe that the 'No Popery' banner that hangs over Cliffe High Street for the night is a manifestation of lingering, atavistic anti-Catholicism. Likewise the burning of Paul V, who became Pope in 1605 and allegedly encouraged the Gunpowder Plot. This is complete tosh. Someone told me 'No Popery' is in fact a corruption of 'No Pot-Pourri' and constitutes a rejection of the profusion of twee gift shops. That is at least more convincing than the idea that Lewes cares one way or another about a pope dead for four centuries.

The night is partly a celebration of pyromania and mayhem. It is partly a celebration of ritual, far more fun than religion, more fashionable than Freemasonry: the officials of the Cliffe Bonfire Society include a Captain of Tableau, a Captain of Effigies, of Aerials, of Tar Barrels, of Torches, of Firesite, of Banners, of Bands, of Programmes, of Fiery Pieces, of Street Fireworks. There is also a safety officer, though he may not be the greatest power in the organisation.

But above all it is a celebration of Lewes. Even on the other 364 days, it is, as a town, decidedly up itself. Lewes is still primarily a place of small shops, not all of them selling pot-pourri. It loves a fight, usually about far more relevant matters than Protestant martyrs. In 2006, when the mighty corporation that now owns the Lewes Arms stopped selling locally brewed Harvey's Bitter, there was a mass boycott until it caved in. When East Sussex County Council brought in a new parking regime, some of the more ardent pyrotechnicians began stuffing fireworks into the parking meter slots to sabotage them. The great eighteenth-century troublemaker Tom Paine was a regular in the White Hart on the High Street, spouting sedition. And his spirit lives on.

Bonfire is sustained by a unique alliance between local traditionalists, zealous youngsters and subversive academics. 'There's no corporate sponsorship, no council involvement,' enthused one resident. 'I think that's the heart of it – the people of Lewes doing it for themselves.' And the town does engage with it. The windows were being boarded up to guard against stray explosions, not looting. The women in Waitrose were saying 'Mad!' not 'Nightmare!' And, though the shops shut, the pubs stayed open with relish. It is hardly the ideal bonfire for small children. And my Brighton friend Paul Weaver stopped going the year some bloke came up to him in the street and started cuffing him about the temples. Paul understandably tried to thump him back. 'Don't be a cunt,' replied his tormentor. 'Your head's on fire.'

Bonfire Night in Lewes must be the only time and place in Britain where one can get attacked in the street *for one's own good.* Some dog owners regard it with genuine loathing; but even the police recognise they are up against superior forces. In the 1990s they tried to gain control by setting up loudspeakers. One year they threatened to arrest anyone who dropped a banger. They have given up and stand back, waiting – I suspect – for something to happen that would prove their instincts right so they can ban it all.

Just as the Harvey's might really be taking hold, the crowds disperse to the different bonfire sites on the edge of town where they burn their effigies: Guy, Paul V and their chosen enemy of the moment. Those on display this time included a very popular model of Rupert Murdoch and his henchwoman Rebekah Brooks, plus a banker with a four-foot prick, all the better to screw everyone. I went to the Cliffe fire-site, where they had opted for the recently deceased Colonel Gaddafi, who was packed with fireworks and supposed to self-destruct, though, as in real life, he proved very stubborn.

The guns finally fell silent around 2 a.m.; by dawn about a million broken bottles and spent fireworks had already been cleared away. Of an estimated crowd of 60,000, two people were seriously hurt with head injuries, not including anyone whose head hurt because of a hangover. There were fifteen arrests, mainly for possession of drugs, and drunken behaviour, in both cases a very small fraction of the total eligible. And Bonfire marches on, until the pope resumes his dominion over this realm, hell freezes over or the town incinerates itself.

This is not wholly a one-off, a demonstration of Lewes' indomitable and anarchic spirit. The bonfire season in East Sussex starts in September, so that a dozen different towns can stage their own smaller-scale versions before converging on Lewes as if it were staging some sporting grand final. Many parts of England maintain resistance to outside authority as part of their self-image. It is 99 per cent bluster, of course. And even Lewes lost its battle over parking charges: the council just redesigned the machines. But in Sussex the spirit of passive resistance lies deep. 'We won't be druv,' goes the local saying.

'There is no peasant in the world,' wrote Hilaire Belloc, 'so rooted in his customs and so determined to maintain them as is the Sussex peasant.' Belloc's book *The County of Sussex*, published in 1936, is largely an elegy for a dialect and a way of life that was already dying. But the bolshiness had not gone completely: 'Those who know Sussex and its people take a secret delight in observing that power of resistance still painfully at work,' he said. And it has not disappeared yet. Belloc thought it was strongest in West Sussex, the bit furthest from London. That's outdated now. The centre of defiance has clearly moved east to Brighton and Lewes. Some people who muddle fact and fiction and have little else to do argue whether Walmington-on-Sea, home of *Dad's Army*, is in Kent or Sussex. Stupid boys. It is obviously in Sussex. Walmington is the epitome of not being druv. I like to think Sussex was every bit as humorously obstreperous when the Conqueror arrived.

The original South Saxons were largely cut off, by marshes to the east and west, by the Downs to the north and the Channel to the south.

Nowadays, much of the county appears to have been Surreyised, at least to those without an especially keen eye for dew ponds, fingerposts and Wealden hall houses. But Sussex has a much gladder heart. Most of Surrey, wrote Ian Nairn in his introduction to the Sussex Pevsner, 'is fatally turned towards London'. Sussex, however, can look south, to the Downs and the sea, so its relationship with the capital 'becomes a kind of contract between equals rather than Surrey's meek subjugation'. The tile-hung cottages, the red-brick pubs and the flinty churches all seem that little bit more welcoming than in the county next door. It is possible, if not always easy, to find contemplative silence. However, the spirit that creates Lewes Bonfire has another, more sombre side.

Beachy Head is a short drive or bus ride out of Eastbourne. Few place names are as instantly evocative. It conjures up heroic images of wartime dogfights and of healthy walks over the springy turf: on a very clear day it is said you can see east to Dungeness and west to the Isle of Wight.

I was there on Guy Fawkes morning: it was a touch misty, though with a stiff breeze coming off the Downs. But there were shafts of sunlight out to sea: the water was calm, turquoise in patches, beautiful. Sussex looked lovely too; the breeze was fresh and it seemed impossible to feel anything but *joie de vivre*. Beachy Head, however, also conjures up suicide.

The chalk face, up to 530 feet high, is said to be the third most popular suicide destination in the world, after the Golden Gate Bridge in San Francisco and the Aokigahara Woods at the base of Mount Fuji (though these figures are inherently unreliable). Jumping off the Golden Gate sounds like a typically showy Californian thing to do, and a predilection for suicide lies deep in Japanese culture. But why here?

Some people – policemen, even – have talked about a mystical force that draws you towards the edge. Yet the vast majority of visitors are taking the air, walking their dogs, heading for the gift shop or pub – the Beachy Head, known locally as the Last Stop. At intervals along the edge there are crosses, placed by relatives left behind: the most bereft of all the bereft. One had a lone carnation lashed to it, buffeted by the wind. Nearby is a memorial to PC Harry Ward, until 1966 the Downs Ranger, who patrolled the cliffs on horseback. 'On numerous occasions he risked his life to save others,' says the inscription. Another stone offers Psalm 93, verse 4, in the inelegant 2001 translation: 'Mightier than the thunders of many waters, mightier than the waves of the sea, the Lord is high and mighty', adding that 'God is always greater than all of our troubles'. I am not sure either bit helps. By the bus stop, next to the Mr Whippy van, is a sign with the Samaritans' number. Mobile signals up here are uncertain.

Outside the Coastguard Centre is the 4×4 belonging to the Beachy Head Chaplaincy Team, perhaps the only vehicle in the country with flashing lights that constitute a cry of 'Let me through, I'm a Christian.' Patrols prowl the downland and six miles of cliff edge, looking for suicides. Their strike rate is very high. The chaplains issue terse reports detailing the number of searches each week, month and year, the number of 'despondent persons' found, plus – though they make this bit less obvious – the number of bodies recovered. The publicly available records go back to April 2010, and I could not find a month without a body. It would have been a record year for activity in 2010 but for the harsh winter weather that rendered the Downs almost inaccessible. The chaplaincy does not like talking to the media, for fear of increasing the numbers still further. On the other hand, it needs more volunteers. One can see the dilemma.

The volunteers do, however, like speaking to people on the cliffs, especially those who look like potential clients. And I suppose I fitted the profile: alone, wandering with no obvious purpose, a bit furtive. The young woman on duty in a red chaplaincy anorak seemed very pleasant and I felt my main duty was to reassure *her*. To begin with, I was on my way to my first Lewes Bonfire and wouldn't miss it for anything. What's more, I couldn't bring myself to go anywhere near the cliff edge: my legs turned to mush at the thought. They still do, as I write this paragraph, more than a hundred miles away. Mystical force, indeed.

But I felt later there was an unexpected connection between Beachy Head and Bonfire. Beachy Head has the odd sign warning of the dangers of falling. Parts of the cliff are roped off, with a single strand, because they are considered unstable, but the rope would not deter a potential suicide for a second. At other points there is nothing at all. One moment you are on springy open turf, then there is the drop.

In a funny way, I approve of this. In a country that has submitted itself to successive governments that have behaved more like governesses, Lewes Bonfire represents one gesture of defiance. And the invitation offered at Beachy Head also constitutes a rare recognition that, in the end, adults in a free society must exercise their own free will. Happily, most despondent persons – even those who get as far as the edge – are looking primarily for a way back into life, not a way out. But there will always be those who have come to Beachy Head, rationally, determinedly, having made a choice which cannot be argued away by a pleasant woman in a red anorak. It's a horrific choice, but a legitimate one.

Sussex is so varied and so enticing that it is full of fascinating places, not all of them as obvious as Beachy Head. Chanctonbury Ring, the ancient hill fort on top of the Downs near Washington, can be seen from Box Hill, though it's easy to miss the sign off the road to Steyning. All my road atlases ignore it, preferring nearby Cissbury Ring, probably because the name's shorter.

Belloc complained that even at Chanctonbury 'you may hear the machine-gun fire of a motor bicycle'. But a bikie would get set upon here these days (provided he did not have a hundred of his mates with him) and it is a quiet, contemplative place, reached through primeval woodlands. Most of the beech trees were savaged by the 1987 hurricane; their replacements are progressing slowly, to be threatened only by the next twice-a-millennium storm, now expected about twice a year. But on a Sunday afternoon, the only hint of a threat came from the gliders, circling like buzzards but neither as noisy nor as predatory. The gliders would have terrified the Iron Age defenders; up here, not much else could have perturbed them.

More secretive still is Pooh Bridge in the Ashdown Forest, close to A. A. Milne's home at Hartfield, whence he would set out on walks with Christopher Robin. The bridge is the Wembley Stadium of Poohsticks, a game with an important place in the national tapestry, because Milne's stories represented the perfect idealisation of English childhood, at least until Disney acquired the rights and turned them into something entirely different.

I tramped nearly a couple of miles from the main road, past signs that were tiny, unconvincing and – at crucial moments – completely absent. There were plenty of other signs, hinting that we were now dangerously close to the Surrey border: 'NO PARKING', 'NO TURNING', 'NO PICNICS', 'NO DOGS'. Even the Pooh Corner gift shop in the village had signs warning visitors off this journey. The residents, too old for Poohsticks, many of them living in 'cottages' about half the size of Versailles, evidently get pleasure at the sight of baffled Japanese tourists going round in circles.

Reassured by passing dog walkers, I finally found myself at a brook spanned by what was evocatively described as East Sussex County Council Bridge no. 8022. There was no other marker. It was a pretty spot, with hazels growing aslant the brook and a nearby oak turning autumn-fiery. I threw two twigs in the water and they set off, skilfully evading what looked like a container of motor oil, in the direction, one assumes, of East Sussex County Council Bridge no. 8023.

From a lower branch of the oak a rope dangled. It was over the fence in obviously private land but easily reachable by an adventurous child keen to swing across the brook. A nice gesture, perhaps. But I am inclined to think it was placed there by a refugee from Surrey and it was meant to persuade them to hang or drown themselves.

The jewels of Sussex are undoubtedly on the coast, in the pendant of shingly resorts that runs from Hastings to Bognor, each of them strange in its own particular way. Belloc loathed them: 'There is little of Sussex about them; they have not the Sussex method of building nor any of the lingering Sussex habits.' As a nautical man, he was inclined to make an exception for Hastings, 'a necessary sea-town'. But he was behind the times even then. Hastings, having been the chief of the Cinque Ports, was declining by the thirteenth century, according to Pevsner, got sacked twice by the French by the fourteenth and 'never recovered'.

It gets worse. I was greeted by the following sign on the A21: 'Hastings – Birthplace of television. Town Centre cameras in 24-hour operation'. The claim may have a sliver of truth in that John Logie Baird lived in Hastings in the early 1920s and clearly worked on his invention there. But the town otherwise made nothing of it. There was no museum or anything, just a plaque. So what on earth was the council trying to suggest? That visitors will arrive and say: 'Yippee! Let's get up at 4 a.m. tomorrow and see the TV cameras!'?

For some time, Hastings has had little else to attract visitors, and its boarding houses ended up being filled by social security claimants. It is a handsomely built town, though the Priory Meadow shopping centre, which replaced the grand old cricket ground, is very ugly and the seafront is a disaster. Part of the problem is that the main coast road runs next to the beach, and much of the promenade has been turned into a cycle raceway, leaving no safe haven for pedestrians.

The pier was closed long before most of it burned down in 2010. It was standing completely forlorn, with a sign announcing 'HASTINGS PIER IS STILL NOT BEING DEMOLISHED', which did not sound like sure and certain hope of resurrection. The town has been pinning its hope on the Jerwood Art Gallery, but my hunch is that the Louvre would struggle to find an audience in this town. If Hastings has a future, then surely it must be as a cheap and cheerful kind of resort. The crazy golf looked quite good, I thought.

Neighbouring Bexhill is very different. Its centrepiece, the modernist De La Warr Pavilion, has been refurbished and turned into a very funky arts centre. It was showing an Andy Warhol exhibition. People stood around looking at the six skulls, fifty Marilyns, ten Maos, the boxes of Brillo Pads and the nudes, one of them male and contemplating masturbation. I stared at the green pea and tomato soups, wondering if Bexhill's tastes might be better served by Brown Windsor or mock turtle.

Architecturally, the pavilion has been much praised over the years. Personally, I was more taken with the neighbouring homes in Marina Court Avenue, an Edwardian terrace built in Moghul style and rumoured to have been created for a maharaja and his entourage. They would be pretty even if they did not have long gardens leading directly down to the prom and the beach. It was dark, the moon was above the sea and everything was bathed in its light. There was no sound but the waves. One of the houses had an agent's board outside and I started fantasising about the possibility of life in Bexhill. It occurred to me that gardening might be tricky here given the need for salt-resistant plants. Also, there might be a problem with privacy so close to the beach. Nude sunbathing on the balcony would be especially problematic, though I don't suppose that would bother anyone who had been to the Warhol.

I confined my impulsiveness to booking into the Grand Hotel, Eastbourne, 'the only five-star hotel on the British coastline', which came slightly cheaper – if not *that* much cheaper – than the £695,000 requested by the vendors of Marina Court Avenue. Before dinner, I slumped into an armchair by the fire in the Great Hall, whence the BBC Light Programme used to broadcast concerts by the Palm Court orchestra. It was a very comfy armchair and a very beautiful room.

Although never, even in the darkest moments, tempted by Beachy Head, I have sometimes wondered about the perfect way to go. I think it was P. D. James who suggested 'in a hammock, on a summer's afternoon, with a distant hubbub of great-grandchildren'. That would do. But one could also settle for an armchair by the fire in the Grand Hotel, Eastbourne, having just finished a large gin and tonic, but not paid for it.

I skipped Worthing, having known it all too well. Eastbourne is sometimes called 'life's departure lounge' – a reference to the aged population, not to Beachy Head. But Worthing is the holding area at the gate. In later years, my parents had a holiday flat there. I would sometimes visit them and find they had aged twenty years since they left home the previous week. Then they would go back and return to normal. Senescence obviously being infectious, it seemed safest to steer clear. I did want to see the beach at Littlehampton, a town unsuited to any of Warhol's male nudes. (A basic knowledge of rhyming slang may be essential to comprehension of the preceding sentence.) But having driven round the one-way system three times, I gave up and stormed off to Bognor.

On the edge of Eastbourne, there are brick-built beach huts that look like houses. Bognor has a shantytown with houses that look like beach huts, which is taking eccentricity a bit far. Prime position on the seafront was commandeered by Butlins more than half a century ago. The holiday camp is surrounded by a high-security fence, cutting its territory off from the beach and lending the entire seafront the air of a prison. There is some argument about when, why or whether George V said: 'Bugger Bognor.' But Bognor has been duly buggered.

Which leaves Brighton. The much-missed columnist Keith Waterhouse is supposed to have described it as a town 'constantly helping police with their enquiries'. He also said it was possible to buy one's love a new pair of knickers at Victoria Station and have them off (and, indeed, it off) in the Grand Hotel inside two hours.

On one level, this seems unduly pessimistic. A fast train, not stopping after East Croydon ... a bit of luck with the taxi queue at the other end ... an hour and a half would seem perfectly possible. On the other hand, by 2011 it was no longer possible to buy knickers at Victoria Station. You could place a bet, in two separate venues; have a haircut or a vaccination; buy 'handmade sexy peel-rich citrus marmalade soap', and even a sandwich or a newspaper. But knickers, no. Perhaps regular users of the Brighton line have stopped wearing them.

Three months passed after saying an unfond farewell to Bognor before I could make this trip. I knew the place well enough to write about it from memory. But, hell, having gone to Dewsbury, there was no way I would miss out on Brighton. Even London that day was bitterly cold; snow was piled up throughout the Sussex countryside; the railway, which in 1970 gave way to Laurence Olivier and briefly restored kippers to the breakfast menu on the Brighton Belle, now treats passengers like kippers instead of serving them. But simply arriving there restores the spirits. The sun was out, looking a little wan but beckoning invitingly towards the seafront. And there, barrelling up West Street to greet me, was the Prince Regent.

This was not the original, you understand, but a bus, one of a couple of hundred Brighton & Hove buses named after local personalities. This is a delicious tradition. It was not invented in Brighton: it was done much earlier in, doubtless among other places, both Hereford and Northampton, where I remember nearly being run over by Alan Parkhouse, a nice man who had once been town clerk. Short of a more glittering cast list, both places gave up. In Brighton, however, the stars (prime qualification: being dead) queue up for inclusion. The oldest name on the list, and the most tangential, is Charles II, who spent just one night in town – fleeing the victorious Roundheads after the Battle of Worcester in 1651. He found a man, Nicholas Tettersell, captain of the coal brig *Surprise*, willing to transport him and his party to France, though Tettersell more than trebled the price after finding out who his chief passenger was. This strikes me as very Brighton indeed, mixing disdain for the ruling authorities with an eye to the main chance.

Before the day was out, I had also spotted Phyllis Pearsall (inventor of the A to Z street map), the 1950s crooner Donald Peers, Sir Terence Rattigan and Douglas Byng, the last two both leading members of Brighton's gay community in the old days when, to the uninitiated, the town was more associated with Graham Greene's Pinky than pink. The artist Eric Gill also has a bus named after him despite complaints that he should be banished because of his unconventional sex life. Adam Trimingham, the Brighton *Argus* columnist who advises the bus company on possible candidates, said that if that was to be a criterion, almost the entire fleet would have to be scrapped.

Outré sexuality has been part of the Brighton mix since at least the Prince Regent's time; it has a terrible drug problem, though it also has a great many drug users who don't perceive that as a problem; and the undertow of violence, captured by Greene, has not gone away, especially round the West Street clubs on a Friday and Saturday night. Brighton was and is poorer and rougher than its image suggests. Yet while so much of England has been squashed by conformity, Brighton's spirit remains unbroken. I saw a young lad dribbling a football amid the traffic on Queen's Drive, which was a pretty daft thing to do, and fairly unimaginable anywhere else.

How did Brighton retain its vibrancy? The turning point may well have been the defeat, in the early 1970s, of a plan for a motorway that would have destroyed the North Laine area. Some credit is given to the reforming Labour council that came to power in 1986, which pushed forward the marina and, among other things, made the North Laine a conservation area, which was a bold thing to do at that time for a district that had down-at-heel charm rather than grandeur. The decision was also taken to put the chain stores in Churchill Square, which is central but invisible.

The journalist Peter Nichols pinpoints the importance of the Tour de France, which hosted a stage of the race on a perfect day in 1994, with the TV pictures showing Brighton at its most seductive. Simon Fanshawe, the comedian and local activist, cites the significance of the Stomp dance troupe and Body Shop, started by the late Anita Roddick (now bus no. 912) in the North Laine in 1976. 'If you had come out with the idea for that in Hull, you would have got laughed out of court,' says Fanshawe. 'When Anita started here and said: "I'm going to do foot lotion made out of peppermints," they said: "Where's the shop?"'

Now Brighton has elected Britain's first Green MP and the Greens have taken over the council, which is more a fashion statement than a political one. But the nature of a place like Brighton is not determined by politics. I think the most significant thing is the shingle. If Brighton's beach were more child-friendly, it would have developed differently. But instead of being the place to take the family, it became the place to do the thing that starts a family, or to get away from the family, or break up a family, or not have a family. It turned into Britain's San Francisco.

And even on this bleak February morning, the sun was on the waters, and the beach – stony and scrunchy though it is – was still the place to go. And, at what seemed to be regular intervals, there were people at the water's edge. At first I thought they were fishermen. Then I wondered if this was some new Antony Gormley installation. Then I realised they were all just sitting there, contemplating infinity. If you believe that giving us the capability of *joie de vivre* is whatever passes for a divine plan – a route to not ending up at Beachy Head – then Brighton is a great place to contemplate infinity. There is a very Sussex sense of enjoyment that links a walk up Chanctonbury Ring, a game of Poohsticks, Bonfire in Lewes and all the delights of Brighton.

An old verse about San Francisco sprang to mind. It was written after the 1906 earthquake when the churches were destroyed but not the huge Hotaling liquor repository.

> *If, as they say, God spanked this town*
> *For being over-frisky,*
> *Why did he burn His churches down*
> *And save Hotaling's whiskey?*

I like to think God looks down on Brighton, shrugs his shoulders and says: 'Whatever.'

November 2011/February 2012

～～～～～

There were no reports of any deaths on Beachy Head in January 2012 (a comparatively mild month), but this record was sadly not maintained: 2012 turned into the chaplaincy's busiest year ever.

In July 2014 Eastbourne Pier followed the sad fashion set by Brighton West Pier and Hastings, and partially burned down. Eastbourne being a marginal constituency, the prime minister immediately promised funds for restoration.

9. *Ignorant Hobbledehoyshire (not)*

RUTLAND

On a mild February evening, with the snow still just about lying, members were summoned to the council chamber for the 201st meeting of the restored Rutland County Council. Also present were one representative of the local press, one member of the public and someone writing a book.

There were nineteen items on the agenda and all except one were rattled through in no time. The general tone was cordial, consensual and seemingly apolitical. One councillor arrived late. She happened to be Mrs Lucy Stephenson, daughter of the chairman, Edward Baines. Her apology was greeted with some mirth by her colleagues. 'Lack of parental control, there, chairman,' said one. 'Good thrashing,' muttered another. He was about three-quarters joking.

The council accepted without demur such matters as item 2.2: the Conservative-controlled Rutland Cabinet's recommendation to approve 'the Prudential Indicators and limits for 2012–13 to 2014–15 contained within Appendix A of Report no. 24/2012 including the Authorised Limit Prudential Indicator'.

It did, however, spend three-quarters of an hour discussing a report from the chief executive on 'members' support'. This, on the face of it, was merely a Rutlandish manifestation of the most boring conversation in the world: The Problems I'm Having With My Laptop (Nightmare!). There was a lot of talk about connectivity and the state of the local broadband alongside the question of whether members should conduct council business on their own laptops. It almost grew animated at one stage – 'Mr Roper, we are coming into the realms of debate,' warned the chairman – but not quite. Here we were in England's tiniest county: a place that is a byword for parochialism. There would be something wrong if the council meetings were not boring.

Then the one member of the public, a blogger called Martin, leaned across to me. 'They think the council's hacking their emails,' he hissed.

They, in this case, were the county's newest political party, holding four of the twenty-six seats: the Rutland Anti-Corruption Group, which is a big name for a political party in a very small county. Martin also whispered something to me about 'The Mystery' of Barleythorpe Hall.

But three of the four anti-corruption members had failed to turn up and the fourth, Brian Montgomery, said nothing. I rang him two days later, by which time I had already discovered that Barleythorpe Hall, a former old people's home, was long-derelict and there was a question about what had happened to some of the stainless-steel kitchen equipment.

'Are you saying the council is corrupt?' I asked Councillor Montgomery.

'It depends on how you define the word.'

'Are you saying the council is financially corrupt?'

'I don't think anyone is saying that anyone is financially corrupt.'

'So what are you saying?'

'We're saying the system is corrupt.'

But he could not explain how or why it was corrupt. It is a reasonable assumption that financial corruption exists in different forms in every council in England. But there are three reasons why it seems less plausible in Rutland than anywhere else. One look at the cabinet provided the first reason: they were better-heeled than any council cabinet I've ever seen, including several dressed in the clashing tweed checks worn only by the wealthiest country gentlemen. Which led on to reason two: they could

probably fund Rutland Council, with its minuscule budget, out of their Coutts' current accounts. The leader, Roger Begy, gave me reason three in the pub afterwards: 'You'd never get away with it,' he said. 'Everybody here knows everybody else's business.'

None of this means Rutland is innocent. I was baffled by the way the council press officer veered – after my visit – from extreme helpfulness to a blanket failure to reply to messages. One could only conclude he was acting under orders. This council is not used to any meaningful scrutiny. Maybe it is Chicago and not Camberwick Green. But the most reliable-seeming informant I could find offered no evidence. And if it were true, it would be heart-breaking because ...

... Rutland! The very name is the embodiment of the romance that lies behind this book. Whenever I mentioned that I was writing about

England's historic counties, people would reply: 'Oh, you mean Rutland?'

I used to read the Fern Hollow books to my son, full of animal characters – Lord Trundle of Trundleberry Manor, PC Hoppit, Parson Dimly, Farmer Bramble and Boris Blinks of the bookshop – all living in idyllic English countryside by a railway line, probably offering a service like Oakham's two direct trains to London a day: 'The animals of Fern Hollow are all good friends and neighbours and, if you are a stranger, they will make you feel at home in next to no time.' It had to be Rutland.

It was always the tiniest of English counties: in terms of acreage, from the moment it emerged in the twelfth century; in terms of population, certainly by the mid-eighteenth century. If you count the Isle of Wight as a county, which I don't, Rutland would have a rival. The island is said to be smaller than Rutland when the tide is in, but bigger when it's out. But it has nearly four times Rutland's population. There are only two towns, both attractive: Oakham and Uppingham. In the Domesday Book Rutland was considered part of Nottinghamshire, which it doesn't even border, a fact that offers an explanation for it splitting off in the first place, though not how Rutland survived untouched for 800 years.

Then came the mid-twentieth century and the growth of governmental tinkering. The county's independence was threatened just after the war, but it successfully resisted everything except the forced merger of Rutland Constabulary (twenty-nine men, one woman, one police car). The police's very success in crime prevention – there was barely any crime except speeding and poaching – made them expendable. In the early 1960s Whitehall called again: the county was recommended for merger with Leicestershire. More than 27,000 people signed a petition against the change, which was clever since there were only 13,000 on the electoral roll. A public inquiry was held in Oakham Castle (itself very small) and was graced by a forceful defence from the protesters' QC, Geoffrey Lane, who held up the report from the Local Government Commission and declaimed: 'The impression they obviously want to create is that you cross the frontier into Rutland, your car jolts into cart tracks, unshod illiterate children stand by the roadside brought into the world by their rude peasant mothers without the help of medical science.'

This appeared in *The Times* under the headline: 'RUTLAND PEOPLE NOT A LOT OF IGNORANT HOBBLEDEHOYS'. Perhaps more tellingly, the Lord Lieutenant, Mr Codrington, CMG, MC, of Preston Hall, happened to have dinner with the prime minister, Harold Macmillan – probably at Buck's or the Cavalry Club – and told him Rutland was taking things badly. The matter was fixed and Rutland survived for another decade. The system was ever corrupt. But sometimes benignly so.

It was an era, however, when it was not possible to stand in the way of what was deemed to be progress. The creation of Britain's largest man-made lake – what became known as Rutland Water – took 3 per cent of the county's not many acres, despite all the protests. And the next inundation of local government reform was unstoppable. Rutland was merged with Leicestershire, though merger was hardly the word. There were ninety-three seats on the new county council and Rutland had two of them.

Yet *the idea* of Rutland never went away. Indeed, it grew stronger. The year after Rutland was formally abolished, Eric Idle's *Rutland Weekend Television*, a spoof series about Britain's smallest TV station, began on BBC2. In the early days of CAMRA, Ruddles' Brewery in Oakham became seen as the epitome of a rural family-owned brewery that cared about its beer. Naturally, hardly anyone in the county cared who emptied their bins. They did care about being made to write 'Oakham, Leicestershire' on envelopes or being told they lived in Leicestershire on news bulletins. Signs did not always stay where they had been erected.

There were obvious political undercurrents – Leicestershire often being Labour; Rutland very un-Labour. In neighbouring counties, even among the gentry, Rutland is thought of as rich. There may have been a racial tinge too, Leicestershire's ethnic make-up being very different; perhaps also a sense that Rutland sounded better for property-price purposes. But one can be over-cynical. There was also an enormous affection for the place – because outsiders liked to know it was there, because residents liked being there.

Local opinion suggests that, had it been a bit bigger, Rutland might never have come back. It was being so ridiculously bijou – one-third the size of Westmorland – that made it so loveable. It was Ruritania, Fredonia, *Erewhon, Passport to Pimlico*. It had no business existing; it therefore seemed all the more important that it should.

In the 1990s the mood in government became more sympathetic, and Rutland saw its chance. And it found an improbable ally: the city of Leicester, which was also anxious to escape from Leicestershire County Council. And together they succeeded. Brian Montgomery was chairman of the district council, which was permitted to attend to minor matters during the occupation. 'I remember the night the decision went through.

We left Westminster when Big Ben struck one. We got back at 3 and had champagne. A bit like winning the Cup at Wembley.'

Soon the Post Office, which by then had postcodes so didn't care, agreed that letters could be addressed to Rutland again but declined to create a Rutland postcode. A pity: one could have fun with that –

RU1? IM2.

RU2? 00H!

However, buyers' remorse set in quickly. Maybe Rutland was a bit hobbledehoyish in its negotiations. 'We gave Rutland to Leicestershire with no debts and all its assets,' said Roger Begy. 'We got it back with £13 million in debts and very few assets.' Very soon the county had the highest council tax in the country. This has not changed significantly. Even the good news can seem bad. The council had just reduced short-stay car parking charges in the towns from 40p to 20p. Underneath the notice in Uppingham marketplace was a bad-tempered scrawl: 'Subsidised by all council tax payers'. The public toilets in Uppingham close at 5.30 p.m., which is either an extreme way of saving money or based on the assumption that only weirdos would be out any later.

Yet the notion of Rutland as idyll remains. 'A picture of a human, peaceful, slow-moving, pre-industrial England, with seemly villages [what a lovely word: *seemly*], handsome churches, great arable fields and barns,' wrote Professor W. G. Hoskins in his introduction to the 1963 Shell Guide. 'One would like to think that one day soon at each entrance to this little county, beside a glancing willow-fringed stream, there will stand a notice saying *Human Conservancy: Abandon the Rat-Race at This Point*.'

It is true that when I saw three local papers alongside each other in the Oakham newsagents, the *Rutland Mercury* headline was

DOCTORS IN PLAN FOR NEW SURGERY

the *Rutland Times* led with

KATIE CLOSES IN ON TALENT SHOW DREAM

and the *Leicester Mercury* had

POSTMASTER ABDUCTED IN ARMED RAID.

But I reckon you could find a Rutland-sized patch in every county in England as quiet and handsome and dreamy and seemly as this one. It just wouldn't constitute a separate county. And it is certainly possible to over-romanticise this place. I was keen to find Whitwell (population: 41), which in 1980 asked to twin with Paris (population: several million). When the mayor of Paris declined to accede to this reasonable request, Whitwell went ahead unilaterally, dragooning a passing Frenchman to represent his government and wave to the crowds from a 2CV while a celebration was held, complete with can-can dancers.

The restored council later played along and agreed to put up official signs saying 'Whitwell Twinned with Paris', which still stand. The joke is somehow infinitely funnier because it happened in Rutland rather than anywhere else. I am not sure the French got that.

I really wanted to adore Whitwell. It turned out to be a strung-out, litter-strewn, main-road village; and the Noel Arms, headquarters of the great jape, has no remembrance of it in its barn-like bar. It does have a sign in the Gents reading: 'JOINING THE NOEL AT WHITWELL REWARD PROGRAMME WILL ENABLE YOU TO START SAVING MONEY, RECEIVE EXCLUSIVE OFFERS AND EARN REWARDS.' I left before my sandwich arrived, which still meant I was there a long time.

Close by, though not as close as it was – unless you are flying crow-class – is Hambleton, where the clock on the old post office has no hands, and thus time stands still, which is sadly inappropriate. Upper Hambleton is now a wealthy village on a peninsula overlooking Rutland Water. I would have liked to visit Nether Hambleton. It suffered a different fate. It drowned, so that others might drink.

Nowadays Rutland Water is perceived as a great success: a major destination for fishermen and sailors. Hambleton Hall has become a much-lauded Michelin-starred hotel. On another smaller, artificial, peninsula, on the eastern shore, there is another lost village, Normanton, which was destroyed in 1764 because the local plutocrat Sir Gilbert Heathcote wished to enlarge his park. He pulled down the old church, too, and built a new one as a private chapel, with a baroque tower, which probably looked ridiculous even then. The church was spared when the valley was flooded, but it was shored up with rubble and concrete so the floor comes up to the windows. It has been deconsecrated but occasionally stages weddings.

Pevsner called this remnant church 'absurd and disproportionate', which is spot on. It looked to me as though it is slowly sinking into the deep. I was just thinking this might be a more humiliating fate for an old building than demolition – the equivalent of keeping a brain-dead patient on life support – when I found a small plaque: 'This church has been preserved entirely by voluntary effort ... as a memorial to the county of Rutland.'

But Rutland turned out not to need a memorial after all. And heaven be praised for that.

February 2012

~~~~~~~~

In June 2012 Rutland Council's strategic director for places, Aman Mehra, was found dead after being sent home from his job. The coroner's verdict was that he hanged himself. No connection with wider council matters has emerged. At the start of 2013 the council decided to sue the three remaining Anti-Corruption Group councillors. At the end of the year Private Eye *awarded Rutland Council the title Legal Bullies of the Year in its Rotten Boroughs Awards. The magazine reported that, before turning on the rebel councillors, Rutland had prosecuted Martin Brookes the blogger for 'harassing and stalking' the chief executive, Helen Briggs. The case was thrown out; Judge John Temperley said: 'Freedom of expression is an essential function of a democratic society.'*

10. *Buckethead and Puddingface*

HUNTINGDONSHIRE

It is just coming up to the top of the hour and on HCR 104FM, Hunting-don Community Radio, the host of *Drivetime*, Bill Hensley, is about to hand over – after the news, weather and jingles – to tonight's host of *Over to You*, Bill Hensley. If anything goes wrong, no doubt it will come to the ear of the station manager, Bill Hensley, who might wish to discuss the subject with the founder and managing director, Bill Hensley.

Huntingdon Community Radio does have other presenters. It must do: it runs twenty-four hours a day, broadcasting live from 7 a.m. to midnight. The schedule is similar to that of a typical BBC local station: undemanding music and chat by day, specialist music in the evening, a bit of variety at weekends ... the presentation somewhat rougher, but the staff-ing decidedly more generous. HCR has more than a hundred on its books and even has *Huntsford*, a thrice-weekly soap opera (omnibus on Sunday afternoons), set in a hairdressing salon.

True, no one gets paid: in BBC local radio, abolition of salaries is thus far merely an aspiration. But under the terms of the licence, there are adverts (£2.50 + VAT for a thirty-second spot) and sponsorship, *Hunts-ford* being proudly sponsored by the Right Cut, *Drivetime* by Fire and Safety Solutions, *Saturday Sport* by Huntingdon Town Football Club, the weather by Coversure Insurance Services.

It seemed extraordinary to me. And so did Bill Hensley. Crikey, what a fireball. Just short of sixty, with crew-cut grey hair, he presented his show in a loose-fitting blue short-sleeved shirt. It was surprising he did not have a row of biros in his breast pocket. One meets characters like this in Minnesota and Kansas, rarely in England. Aside from running this radio station, he was a Huntingdon town councillor, parish councillor in the village of Warboys, director of the Red Tile Wind Farm Trust, chair-man of Hospital Radio Hinchingbrooke, chairman of the Huntingdon & District Sea Cadets and a trustee of the Huntingdon Commemoration Hall. He also had a full-time job as sales manager of an electronics com-pany. In his spare time, when we met, he was getting divorced. He was also, very much by the way, chairman of the Huntingdonshire Society, the organisation devoted to the restitution of the county as a living entity. This has been a rather less successful operation than Huntingdon Com-munity Radio.

Huntingdonshire traditionally was England's second-smallest county. It became briefly bloated in the 1960s when it merged with the Soke of Peterborough, previously part of Northamptonshire. But come the big change of 1974, the whole kit and caboodle became part of Cam-bridgeshire. In 1995 the Local Government Commission which brought back Rutland specifically rejected Huntingdonshire's claims because there were objections in local government terms and 'there was no exceptional county allegiance'.

No one I spoke to disagreed with that assessment. This is Rootless England, the epitome of the Greater South-East, forty-five minutes from King's Cross, the crossroads of the A1 and the frantic A14. A place where people settle because it's easy to escape. When Rutland's identity was snatched away, people cared enough to conduct a little low-level sabotage. Here there were just a few sad letters to the *Hunts Post*. Membership of the Huntingdonshire Society, according to its chairman, had dwindled from fifty or sixty to 'about ten'. So how come community radio has been so suc-cessful in a place that struggles to find any sense of community?

Two reasons, said Bill Hensley, the first of them being Bill Hensley:

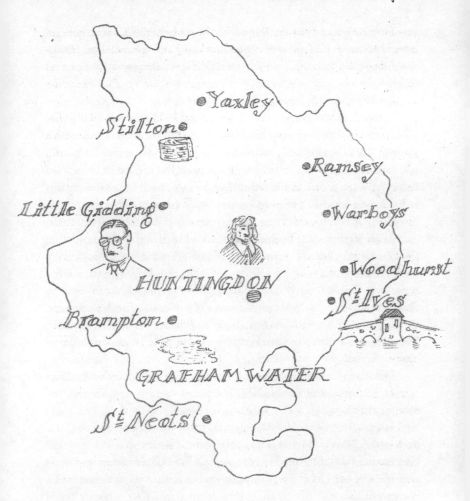

'It's successful because I have made it successful and I've pushed it and pushed it and pushed it.' How have you got all these sponsors? 'I'm a sales-man, remember.' All true, I'm sure: I loved his un-English lack of false modesty. The second derives precisely from the fragile sense of neighbour-liness. 'We get little old ladies ringing us up late at night: "What time is it?" "Ten o'clock." "Is that morning or evening?"'

Ours was a disjointed conversation, which must be the norm with Bill. We had to break off for his links, for on-air interviews with represen-tatives of the swimming club and a fair trade campaigner. He also had to nip down periodically to open the front door; I wouldn't have been surprised had he simultaneously chaired a meeting of the Sea Cadets. Small-town England needs Bill Hensleys to galvanise it. But mostly they move on.

Huntingdonshire has sent three people to rule over the nation. Oliver Cromwell (Lord Protector 1653–8) has a museum devoted to him in the old grammar school room in Huntingdon where he studied. It is dark and gloomy, which might have pleased him, but open on Sunday afternoons, which would not. There was Richard Cromwell, 'Tumbledown Dick', who lasted less than a year as his father's successor, but did marry a woman called Major, which might make him a distant kinsman of the third, John Major, MP for the area for twenty-two years and prime minister for seven.

There is a statue of Oliver on the Market Hill in St Ives. He is wearing a wide-brimmed hat and a ferocious expression and is pointing with his left hand, as though to an imaginary piece of litter. John Major rates only a bust on the first floor of Huntingdon Public Library, tucked away next to the map cabinets. The locals say it makes him look like Eric Morecambe, which is a bit to do with the big glasses and his air of mild amusement, and a bit to do with the general view of his term of office. Major completely cocked up the privatisation of the railways, but was otherwise not a nuisance, an admirable trait in a national leader and one he might have inherited from Tumbledown Dick. He is not otherwise commemorated except in the signs for 'Major Roadworks Ahead'.

He did, however, enjoy the greatest night of vindication known to perhaps any British leader, at least since Charles II came back to replace the Cromwell dynasty. On election day in 1992, after eighteen fraught months as prime minister, Major was assumed to be on his way to defeat and a place in history on a par with Tumbledown Dick. That night he stood on the podium in Huntingdon with one of the largest personal majorities ever recorded, 36,230, knowing he would be back in Downing Street. Unfortunately, on the podium alongside him was Lord Buckethead.

This was not a real Lord Buckethead of Buckethead Hall, owner of as many acres as a small county could reasonably offer. This was Lord Buckethead of the Gremloids Party, who had infiltrated himself into the election and received 107 votes, which, in a notably bizarre campaign, did not even put him bottom of the poll – he was eighth out of ten. Screaming Lord Sutch of the Monster Raving Loony Party came fifth, almost beating the Green candidate. Sutch had, however, been comprehensively out-loonied.

And thus it was, as the pictures of a triumphant Major went round the planet, there – far more arrestingly – was a man with a bucket on his head. It never happened to Oliver Cromwell.

Very flat, Huntingdonshire: itsy-bitsy hills, big arable fields, hardly any hedgerows. It was probably the most invisible county – Rutland at least having a reputation – even in the days when it was officially a county. In the north it shades into Fenland and there is a village called Ramsey Heights, which must be some kind of joke, like the little Don Estelle character in *It Ain't Half Hot Mum* being known as Lofty. Maybe Lord Buckethead is the local grandee.

The county probably has Britain's lowest point, amid the birches at Holme Fen, about nine feet below sea level. Holme Fen Posts, which measure how the peat has shrunk since the Fens were drained, is usually cited as the spot. But there is no marker, no flags, no one taking selfies to celebrate the achievement of their descent. Huntingdonshire doesn't make a fuss. Also, one deep winter pothole and there would probably be a new lowest point.

Rupert Barnes from the Huntingdonshire Society recommended a couple of villages: Ellington and Woodhurst. I could sort of see what he meant. Ellington has some very fine porches – but it was right next to the horrendous A14 and threatened by wind farms and seemed to me wholly unliveable. Woodhurst (Best Kept Village in Huntingdonshire, 1999) is more obviously good-looking and a splendid example of an Anglo-Saxon ring village, something that would be difficult to notice except from a hot-air balloon. More obviously still, it was, on a Friday morning, utterly deserted. No school, no pub, and the building with a fading General Stores sign had a couple of plant troughs blocking the front door. The fields of winter wheat were presumably being tended by one man and an extremely large tractor. Rural Huntingdonshire does feel unusually depressing.

It was, however, market day in St Ives and the joint was jumping. This has been a market town since shortly after Huntingdonshire, under Danish occupation in the late ninth century, began to acquire the foetal characteristics of a county. 'Morning, Sheila,' I heard the man on the flower stall shout. 'Did you wear your bikini yesterday?' (It had been unseasonably warm.) I never heard the response but I like to believe that pre-medieval market traders had equally cheeky banter in their repertoire. They bridged the Ouse here to bump up the market trade in 1107, and the stone bridge, which came three centuries later, still has a tiny mid-river chapel, available for (very small) weddings.

The chapel is dedicated not to St Ivo, who gave his name to the town, but to St Leger, who died after horrible tortures in the seventh century and is somewhat better known as a horse race. That's held in Yorkshire. The name St Ives more often conjures up Cornwall. This whole county seems condemned to obscurity. Take the largish village of Stilton, once a major coaching stop on the Great North Road. Stilton cheese got its name because the owners of the Bell Inn there sold it to travellers. The current landlords are now trying to make Stilton themselves, but have been banned from calling it Stilton because EU law insists that it can only be made in the East Midlands.

The A1 bypassed the village in 1958 and Stilton High Street must now be the widest cul-de-sac in England. Pevsner said the village was 'in a sad state of dereliction', though lately it has started to cash in on its name. But it did seem to be the epitome of Huntingdonshire, the county that cared too little about life to fight for it.

Huntingdonshire *was* once famous for something: cabmen. In the days when the *Daily Express* was the most powerful newspaper in the land and not a relic, the Beachcomber column, written by J. B. Morton, was a daily fixture. For more than half a century, amidst such characters as Mr Justice Cocklecarrot, the M'Babwa of M'Gonkawiwi, Big White Carstairs and Captain Foulenough, there would be references to the 'List of Huntingdonshire Cabmen', as for instance in the book review that appeared in the *Express* of 16 April 1953:

The new edition of the 'List of Huntingdonshire Cabmen' (long acknowledged as a standard work on the subject) is a book for the bedside. It can be opened anywhere. One or two mistakes should be corrected in the next edition. Palmer, F. L., is obviously a misprint for Palmer, F. G. On page 284, the name Ropesock is puzzling, and on page 136 there is no indication that Hitchwell, C. T. R., and Hitchwell, B. S., are, in fact, twins. The footnote on page 61 which tells us that Empson, N., is known as 'Tubby' is irrelevant and introduces a vulgar note. Still more regrettable is the information that Archer, W. W., is called 'Puddingface'. But these are minor blemishes, and easily remedied. They have no place in a serious factual work.

Not everyone found Beachcomber funny: it is said Lord Beaverbrook, the *Express*'s proprietor, was entirely baffled. But the relevant point here is Huntingdonshire. Without it, the joke does not work, or nothing like as well. It needs the four sonorous syllables, shared by only four other counties. But it also needs Huntingdonshire's essential obscurity and piddlingness. Rutland would never do: too brief a word, too obvious a choice. Do you understand what I'm saying? If not then, as Louis Armstrong supposedly said when asked what jazz is: 'Lady, if you gotta ask, you'll never know.'

Perhaps the most famous place of all in Huntingdonshire is barely even a place at all. You turn off down one quiet road and on to a lane that leads to a seventeenth-century religious retreat, founded by the MP and divine Nicholas Ferrar; a long-demolished stately home; a farm; a tiny church. It looks out placidly across what passes in Huntingdonshire as a valley. On the wood-panelled walls of the church is a scroll embroidered with a verse so unremittingly grim that one might think it came from the sternest of preachers:

> *You are not here to verify,*
> *Instruct yourself or inform curiosity*
> *Or carry report. You are here to kneel*
> *Where prayer has been valid.*

No author is given, though a crib sheet is close to hand. A battered and pencil-annotated copy of T. S. Eliot's poems was open on the nearby pew. In context, it sounds somewhat different.

The place and the poem is 'Little Gidding', the last of the Four Quartets, the one that begins:

> *Midwinter spring is its own season*
> *Sempiternal though sodden towards sundown,*
> *Suspended in time, between pole and tropic.*

The topographic references in the poem are accurate: Eliot talks of rounding a pigsty, which I was shown reverently, though it is now used as a bike store. Ferrar House is being used as a retreat again and the garden was a hub of early springtime activity. I got talking to one of the volunteer gardeners, a ruminative Ulsterman called Stephen Dalzell.

'When I work here in winter I can feel what Eliot meant,' he said. 'It's as though heaven and earth are very close together. There's a phrase that crops up in Celtic legend to describe somewhere like this. It's called a thin place.

'Seems very peaceful, doesn't it?' he added.

I nodded.

'Well, you can't see it now, but on the horizon is RAF Molesworth, which is just about the most secret place in the country. You see the lights at night.'

Funny thing is, as neither Stephen nor I knew at the time, that Eliot almost certainly never came here in winter. His only visit is believed to have been in May 1936. He carried report in the midst of wartime: the poem was published in 1942.

Another funny thing: the whole time I was in Huntingdonshire I never saw a cab, or a cabman.

March 2012

～～～～～～

Bill Hensley became mayor of Huntingdon in 2013 and was given a second term the following year. He was still broadcasting, but a little less. The soap opera Huntsford *was off the air in early 2014 due to 'internal politics'.*

11. *Between the old way and the Ooh-arr A*

CORNWALL

Cornish hagiography is a specialist subject. Across the rest of England the names of churches – St John's, St Mark's, St Mary's, St Anne's, St Peter's – read like the roll call in a 1950s primary school, where anyone with an unusual name was at risk of getting beaten up in the playground.

Yet Cornwall is a riot of saintly place names, the vast majority Celticly poetic and utterly distinctive, whose very mention conjures up summer afternoons, craggy cliffs, the smell of fish, the cry of seagulls and crowded car parks: St Austell, St Blazey, St Endellion, St Enodoc, St Erth, St Mawes, St Mellion, St Tudy ...

And then there are the church names to be relished and discovered only by the most assiduous Pevsnerite: Sts Ciricus and Julitta, St Maunanas, St Meriodocus, St Carantocus, St Crida, St Cruenna ... The list is beautiful and almost endless. These are not saints likely to achieve much recognition east of the Tamar, partly because they spent their time converting only the Cornish and also because the stories about them do require a certain suspension of disbelief: St Ia arrived floating on an ivy leaf, St Budoc was born in a floating barrel, and so on. Most of them make it on to the list of saints on the website Catholic Online, but that does list 892 of them beginning with the letter A alone.

All of which is by way of a feeble excuse for not knowing that 5 March, the feast day dedicated to (among others) St Adrian, St Oliva, St John Joseph of the Cross, St Carthach the Elder, St Colman of Armagh, St Theophilus, St Kieran of Saigir and St Gerasimus of the Jordan, is also the feast of St Piran, patron saint of tin miners and of Cornwall itself.

Thus it was that I managed to arrive at St Austell Station at lunchtime on 6 March, the day *after* St Piran's Day. Thus it was that I missed what is increasingly described as Cornwall's national day, missed the carnival parade through Bodmin, missed the tableau on the sand dunes at Perranporth, missed the bloody lot. And I kicked myself and cursed my ignorance from Saltash to Scilly.

All that was left, according to the *Western Morning News*, was a *yeth an werin* session that night at the Royal Standard, Gwinear. Not sure what a *yeth an werin* might be, I drove the hire car twenty-five miles through driving rain, avoiding three separate Road Closed signs. (This phenomenon seems peculiarly prevalent in Cornwall, an indication of either the state of the roads or a clampdown on separatist sentiment by English government forces.) It was a kind of mortification of the flesh.

The street outside the pub was rammed with cars. Inside the noise was deafening and I had to fight my way to the bar.

'Busy,' I said to the barman, gratefully accepting my pint. 'Must be quite an occasion.'

'Oh, yeah,' he replied. 'There's a leaving party, *and* there's a pool match against the Engine.'

'Isn't there some kind of Cornish event?'

'Oh,' he said dismissively. 'They're over there, that table in the corner.'

There were eight of them, mostly elderly. Among them was a figure with a long grey-white beard who, though no one was taking any notice, could only have been a former Grand Bard of *Gorseth Kernow* – the Cornish version of Eisteddfod – unless God himself had nipped into the Royal Standard for a quick one. This was Jori Ansell, Grand Bard of the *Gorseth* from 1991 to 1994, Bardic name Caradok, known to his friends as George, and, in his role as publications officer of the Cornish Language

Board, at least partly responsible for the current project of translating the Bible into Cornish. Not a million miles away from God, then.

Jori proved to be a courtly, well-spoken man who dealt with the arrival of this absurd interloper with infinite politeness. It was hardly the right moment for a chat with the likes of me because (a) the purpose of the *yeth an werin* is for like-minded linguists to converse in Cornish and (b), what with the pool match and the party, it was almost impossible to hear anything anyway. But he took time to explain that a few years ago there were only a few such groups in Cornwall but now there was a meeting somewhere almost every night of the week.

This did not seem like an obvious breeding ground for a revolution, especially given the ultra-loyalist name of the pub. But revolutions always emerge from unpromising circumstances: Marx pub-crawling his way up Oxford Street; Lenin meandering round London on the top deck of a bus; the perpetrators of the Easter Rising being regarded as complete eejits until the British did the Irish republican cause a historic good turn by martyring them.

From Huntingdonshire, which did not care about being a county, I had come to a county that increasingly felt the same way for the reverse reason – because it believed itself to be something more. Professor Philip Payton, Cornwall's leading historian, pointed out to me that the Celtic components of the United Kingdom have rediscovered and revived their own heritage in the reverse order in which they were incorporated into the English state: Ireland, annexed in 1801, fought its way out (bar the six northern counties) little more than a century later; Scotland (1707) has now been flirting with the exit; Wales, formally taken over in Tudor times, was asserting itself more sluggishly. So what about Cornwall, whose degree of separation was always vaguer? Is it incredible that it should go in the same direction? Into the 1960s both the Scottish and Welsh national-ists were considered a laughing stock, and not just by the English. So it might be wise not to be too dismissive of the Cornish.

I said *Dwr genes* (goodbye) to Jori Ansell: he corrected my pronun-ciation – hard g, not soft – and I shuffled off. But Cornish consciousness is not necessarily just the preserve of elderly eccentrics being drowned out in a noisy pub. A couple of years earlier, I had visited a class of eleven-year-olds at Hayle Community College and heard them singing:

> *Yith esa tiek a'n jevo ki*
> *Ha Tangi o y hanow*
> *T-A-N-G-I*
> *T-A-N-G-I*
> *T-A-N-G-I*
> *Ha Tangi o y hanow.*

It drove me nuts until I realised it was the song my children knew as

> *There was a farmer who had a dog*
> *And Bingo was his name-o ...*

This was part of a taster lesson in Cornish being offered along with German and Mandarin, both of which in theory might be more useful in the twenty-first century. But the kids were loving it. Here was something that was *theirs*, a secret code unknown to the rest of England. Yet there was also no hint of exclusivity. A girl whose family had just moved from Bolton was joining in every bit as enthusiastically as those who had surnames starting Tre-, Pol- or Pen- with great-grandparents buried in the churchyards at St Elwyn's and St Winierus.

Dick Cole is an archaeologist by training, but he has celebrated both his thirtieth and fortieth birthdays as leader of Mebyon Kernow, the Cornish Nationalists. He has a natural politician's easy manner, as yet unspoiled by the compromises and defensiveness of power. In late 2011, after nearly fifteen years of his leadership, his party managed to achieve its fifth seat on Cornwall Council. Loveday Jenkin from Praze-an-Beeble won the Wendron by-election – which, I would modestly claim, are the most euphonious eight words ever written about local government.

It has been a long old haul since the party's wild-eyed beginnings in 1951. The cause has become modest in its aims, respectable and increasingly mainstream. It is no longer just Mebyon Kernow that wants St Piran's Day to be made a Cornish bank holiday. It was not Mebyon Kernow's decision to call the new and Conservative-led unitary county council 'Cornwall Council', carefully omitting the contentious word 'county'.

MK has now marginalised two other separatist organisations: the Stannary Parliament, which claims a line of legitimacy dating back to Edward I but has not actually been elected by anyone in at least 250 years; and the Cornish Republican Army (christened by some clever London tabloid subeditor the Ooh-arr A). A while ago this shadowy and probably barely existent organisation made oblique threats against a couple of celebrity chefs, set fire to a derelict brewery, plastered a wall with graffiti and issued a defiant statement: 'We are NOT responsible for the damage in Redruth when an ornamental dog had its head removed.'

Cole was clear on the fundamentals: 'I take the view that Cornwall is the Cornish nation and not an English county. Here we have a distinct culture, a distinct Celtic language. We have a border along the Tamar which has hardly changed since AD 936. If you look at the names of the farms and the fields, they start to become Cornish a very few miles from the border. We have our own traditional music. We have our own sports. We have the DNA of nationhood.'

'In your wildest fantasies –' I began.

'You don't want to know about my wildest fantasies.'

'In your wildest *political* fantasies ... do you imagine going to Downing Street on equal terms, as leader of an independent nation, for bilateral negotiations with the prime minister of England?'

'We are not fantasising. We are not campaigning for outright independence. But long term, things change. The twenty-first century is not about independent countries. There is a whole new interrelationship between nations.'

Cornishness, however, is a particularly slippery concept, because there have never been frontier posts at the Tamar or entry restrictions; and, in the twentieth century, the idea of moving there began to seem attractive.

The problem was exemplified by the late, much-loved and very Cornish Liberal MP for Truro, David Penhaligon, who was asked at a meeting: 'What are you going to do about all this immigration, then?'

'Oo you talking about, boy?' replied Penhaligon. 'The blacks? Or the English?'

A few English people move to Scotland, Wales or Ireland to work or retire or buy a holiday home, but not that many. And they would always – unless they were exceptionally crass – take the place on its own terms. Moving to Cornwall does not involve the same mental leap. 'There has to be an accommodation,' says Cole. 'But there are a large number of people who expect the Cornish to do all the accommodating.'

Yet Cornwall is indeed accommodating in a way that the other Celtic countries are not. The writer Tim Heald, who lived in Fowey for fifteen years, was once doing a turn at the town's Daphne du Maurier festival. 'There was a man in a Viking headdress and a Cornish rugby shirt, the worst sort of local idiot. I said: "I bet you're from Essex", and of course he was.' It all fits with the Bolton lass loving her Cornish lesson. And the Yorkshireman I met with a black and white St Piran's flag in his lapel. For those who want to embrace it, Cornwall offers a sense of belonging that no other county can. Newcomers to Leeds don't suddenly proclaim themselves Yorkshiremen.

Cornwall is of course perceived as an exceptionally desirable place: the most beautiful girl in the class, eyed longingly by the boys and jealously by the rivals. Outsiders fall in love instantly with the coastline, the climate, the soft accent, the perception of gentleness.

But there is some perversity involved here. The climatic advantage is strongest in winter: Falmouth is four degrees centigrade warmer – that's almost a layer of clothing less – than Birmingham then, but one degree cooler in summer. Yet everything is closed in winter and hardly anyone goes there. Instead they pile in for August. And Cornwall's reputation for beauty is a modern construct, largely built up by the marketing skills of the old Great Western Railway. *Bradshaw's Monthly Descriptive Guide* of 1857 called it 'one of the least inviting of English counties ... a dreary waste'. The slow road and rail journeys down the Cornish spine are still very dreary: it was only by building its branch lines to the sea that the Great Western fixed the glories of Cornwall into the English consciousness.

Cornwall we can conjure up instantly; Cornishness, however, is more elusive. Cornish nationalism may be making headway; the language may be reviving two centuries after it died; but Cornish dialect and accent are actually fading faster than most in the face of the onslaught of immigration. The word 'emmet', dialect for ant, has achieved a life of its own as an alternative to 'grockle', the lowest form of tourist. Otherwise the sound of Cornwall is blurring into a kind of generalised Mummerset. And in east Cornwall most of the younger locals are actually Devonians, because the maternity hospitals are in Plymouth and Barnstaple.

Sir Tim Smit, founder of the Eden Project, finds Cornishness deep in the past, in its lost industrial power. Cornwall was the world's greatest producer of copper in the early nineteenth century; then copper gave way to tin; and tin gave way to nothing, and so the Cornish miners – known everywhere as 'Cousin Jacks' – set out to dig up distant parts of the planet. 'There are parts of the country where the industrial culture has died which have developed a loser culture,' says Smit. 'I don't find that here. Instead there is a sense of bereavement. And the tombstones are all the preserved mines and the sheds and the beam engines. Popular culture and the best Cornish writing are based on that heritage.'

He also thinks there is an underlying seriousness to Cornwall: 'The Methodist tradition is still strong. A lot of teetotalism still. There's an austerity, by desire not lack of wealth. If you want to fit in, you don't flaunt what you have. Historically, there were stately homes here but, because of the distances and the state of the roads, the upper echelon tended to find company which wasn't their class and status.

'So it was a more egalitarian place than most. There was more active headship from the big families and they defined themselves as being Cornish. They didn't see this as their country estate, they saw it as their home.' This is echoed by the businessman John Brown, who owns a restaurant in

St Mawes: 'You really do get a better class of landed gentry here. They're not just rich dickheads. They work.'

However, no one seems to have told the latest incomers about shabby chic. 'When I first moved to Cornwall,' said the ex-Fowey resident Tim Heald, 'a smart car was a rustbucket and a smart suit was your grandfather's. Now a smart car is a four-wheel drive and it's all bling.'

Fowey felt rather Italianate to me, with its narrow streets, its precipitous slopes, its umbrella-shaped pines and the sense that everything was just a little bit mad. If God did intend people to live here, He never imagined they would bring their Range Rovers. For those who don't wish to move the Chelsea tractor (who knows when another parking space might appear?), there is a twenty-six-mile walk north from the Fowey estuary to the Camel estuary, the Saints' Way, believed to be the route taken by many of Cornwall's sainted pilgrims as they shook off the sea from their ivy leaves and barrels and set about converting the benighted populace. It now leads to Padstow, the holy shrine erected by and for the soon-to-be canonised Rick Stein.

I have never come across a place as obsessed with television as Cornwall, not so much with watching it as appearing on it. It has more media tarts than Islington. 'We were on *Time Team*,' someone remarked casually. 'See Us on *Countryfile*' said a sign in Newlyn. 'Jamie's Top Ten Fish Available Here!' said another. Everywhere it was Rick Stein this, Caroline Quentin that, Jamie Oliver the other. 'Didn't you see us?' they will ask, bewildered that anyone could be so remiss.

And Padstow is the ultimate monument to the peculiar obsession with celebrity chefs, men with a flair for cooking and an even greater flair for self-promotion. They all have their shtick: there's a Cockney one and a winsome one and a rude one and a sweary one, and nobody remembers anything about the food. As a fashionable venue, north Cornwall generally has over the past two decades caught up and perhaps surpassed the climatically advantaged south, partly because of surfing, partly because of golf, but most obviously because of televised eating.

In comparison to Stein's presence in Padstow, St Bernadette in Lourdes is a shadowy and modest figure. 'We call this place Padstein now,' whispered the first local I met. His tone seemed to convey a mix of fear, bravado, affection (Stein was well known locally before he got famous), gratitude and generalised alienation, of the sort expressed by the Athenian who hated Aristides the Just because he was sick of hearing him called 'the Just'.

By early 2012 Stein had four restaurants in Padstow plus a deli, a patis-serie, a cookery school and forty guest bedrooms spread over six differ-ent locations. Of course he has brought heaps of money into the town, and most of the population, especially the long-standing property owners, have hitched a ride on the bandwagon. In the early post-war years some of the fishermen's cottages would have been worth less than a current serving of Rick's *fruits de mer* and Bollinger special cuvée.

But in Padstow, with Tesco commanding the high ground and Stein the waterside, there is not much room for anyone else except for Boots, the banks, a few non-Stein restaurants mopping up the overflow, and the usual shops selling overpriced instant clutter. As Cassius said of Caesar, and the Padstein-whisperer might have done: 'we petty men walk under his huge legs'.

Travelling between the two resorts by car, you would probably go through the main-road village of Bugle. I had been there once before, on a whimsical journalistic mission in 1997: this intriguing-sounding place had been named and shamed, along with various dingy inner-city spots, as possessing one of the ten worst-kept railway stations in Britain. The sta-tion was and is on the branch line to Newquay, and the train approaches it through the delicious woods of the Luxulyan Valley. But in 1997 it was indeed disgusting. Despite a quick clean-up before I could get there, new graffiti had immediately sprouted: 'Gavin is a babe' and 'Rob and Roger are shit'. The main topic of local conversation was a recent street murder.

Now, with Gavin presumably no longer a babe, the station was look-ing much sprucer. The village still looked grim, grey and rather sad, the epitome of inland Cornwall's drive-by country. It is one of those rare places named after its pub, though it does also have a well-regarded silver band (which does not include a bugle).

Bugle's existence always depended on the long-declining china clay industry, but it has had some fair years since the opening of the Eden Project – though by now even that was starting to make staff redundant. The village was looking less distressed too, partly because the china clay slagheaps had been cunningly grassed over. And there were new houses, many of them retro-style starter homes with stone facings, aimed at com-muting young couples priced out of the coastal fringes. There was also a new block of flats by the station which looked very inner-city indeed. A woman by the post office, who was telling me about the shortage of jobs, mentioned the flats unprompted: she thought they were horrid.

'So who lives in them?'

'People from up-country.' England beyond the Tamar, she meant. And she obviously did not mean the kind of up-country people who move to the coasts.

'But why would they come here if there aren't any jobs?'

'They think they'll find a better life here. *Then* they find out there aren't any jobs.'

Cornwall may be more nation than county, but if so it is certainly two nations rather than one. And only occasionally do the two meet. Drinkers enjoying a smoke and the sunshine outside the Ship in Mousehole might momentarily pause when they see the plaque to Charles Greenhaugh, the landlord who died in the Penlee lifeboat disaster in 1981. Which, apart from anything else, is a reminder of how, in the traditions of both Cornwall and the volunteer lifeboat service, the land and sea are all of a piece.

Sometimes one gets a reminder that not every visitor comes in a Mercedes or a Range Rover, as at almost-perfect Trevose Head, where a caravan site pops up from nowhere. Sometimes one gets a reminder, far starker than at Bugle, that in a county with no substantial towns, the migrants have to live somewhere. Outside both Wadebridge and St Austell the new houses march over the hillsides as if this were California or the occupied West Bank.

And perhaps nowhere on the island of Great Britain is there such a jarring disjunction between beauty and beastliness as on the very tip of it. For about two centuries the 105 acres of cliff top constituting the property of Land's End were owned by the Neave-Hill family. In 1982 Charles Neave-Hill, known as 'the 14th Master of Land's End', sold the estate to a Welsh property tycoon who easily outbid the National Trust. It was then bought and sold three more times in thirteen years before ending up with its present owners, a company now called Heritage Great Britain plc.

What an awful shame: I thought the National Trust was richer than *anyone*. This is a place one would call iconic were one the sort of person who used the word iconic. It is part of Great Britain's heritage, not part of Heritage Great Britain's heritage. But I had to approach Land's End through a faux-Doric portico that looked like a scale model of a Las Vegas casino. There was a cinema advertising a '4D' film, *The Curse of Skull Rock*, a couple of tat shops and a bar-restaurant with a fantastic view but a depressing menu.

The whole set-up was not even interestingly, Las Vegas-ishly, vulgar:

it was just mildly repulsive. I retreated to the First and Last pub in the nearest village, Sennen. However, the pub has always been bought and sold by the estate, so is also owned by Heritage Great Britain – and had stopped serving food at 1.30. One might like to run as far away from Land's End as possible. Alas, John O'Groats, notoriously dismal, is also owned by Heritage Great Britain. (I commend instead the beer and the crab soup in the Old Success, Sennen Cove, owned by St Austell Brewery.)

However, Land's End is not the last of England. Nor does the First and Last entirely live up to its name. The most westerly, and the most southerly, pub in England is the Turk's Head on the island of St Agnes, most distant of the Isles of Scilly, population 75-ish. A few hours after driving away from Land's End, seething, I was in the Turk's Head, having made the short flight to St Mary's, Scilly's bustling hub (in comparison), and then taken John Peacock's boat.

At lunchtime, the shipping forecast had been using the phrase Violent Storm Eleven, a step above Severe Gale Nine and Storm Ten, just below Hurricane Twelve. It is a formulation that sounds rather thrilling when the rain is beating against the curtained double glazing and the Rayburn is turned up, rather less so when about to set out into the Atlantic in a small boat.

As it turned out, the filthiest weather was to the north and the journey was merely what the islanders cheerfully called 'a bit bouncy'. Still, I was relieved and pleased to be safe in the Turk's Head, a pub that normally hunkers down for the winter, the resident population being so tiny and potential visitors wary of the bounce. But it had opened specially for a quiz night: Nicki and Rob had fresh barrels on the real ale pumps, and a dozen people, about one-sixth of the adult population, took the chance of a get-together. Along with a single stranger.

It is not *that* difficult to get here. But Land's End itself is a good six hours by car or train from London (nearly half that time has to be spent negotiating Cornwall), and not much quicker, when you've done all the messing about, even if you fly to Newquay. Then there are the two separate island hops. St Agnes is an outpost of an outpost of an outpost.

Beyond here there are just a few malevolently jagged bits poking out of the sea, lying in wait for mariners who stray too close. To help them steer clear is the Bishop Rock lighthouse, which, in the days of the transatlantic liners, was the first hint of home, a landmark as resonant as the

White Cliffs. The next parish, heading due west, is, by my reckoning, Pouch Cove, Newfoundland. I can't vouch for its ale.

The stranger took some weighing up. Then I was invited to join one of the quiz teams. And, since I knew that George IV came before William IV, that Nixon was elected US president in 1968 and that it was Lesley Gore who had a hit in 1963 with 'It's My Party', all of which helped our team to victory ... why, by closing time, I was practically an islander.

It was a tempting thought. Just before dusk, an all-but-full moon, looking tropically huge, had risen next to the lighthouse. Later it shimmered on the sandbar, as it does in the Caribbean. The wind was still stiff but the treetops it tousled were palm trees, and when it whistled through the protective hedges, it made a noise like birdsong. Otherwise, there was no light, and no sound.

By morning the gale had blown itself out and the sun was beating down. I walked around St Agnes, which is easy enough, and across the sandbar to the deserted neighbouring islet of Gugh (rhymes with Hugh). The bumblebees were in business; asters were out in the gardens and violets by the roadside: more like May than early March. Winter is always a rumour here. When even the tiny Land's End airfield was snowbound in December 2010, St Agnes had a few flakes and the gentlest touch of frost. This time the weather had actually been too mild for Fran Hicks, the flower grower: the early blooms had raced away far too fast for their own good, or his. The dairy farmer Tim Hicks, so his wife Sue confided, has sensitive skin: 'Sometimes, if he forgets his suncream in February, he gets burned.'

The name Hicks has been here for four centuries, as has Legg. I walked away from the pub with Harry Legg, Kit the fisherman's boy, just back from university. All over rural Britain bright young kids leave home because they sense no choice: there is nothing there for them. On St Agnes, to an extraordinary extent, they return. Harry has joined his dad on the boat; he also fixes people's computers. He was about to move into the house built by his great-great-great-great-grandfather. This is not unusual. 'There are about a dozen graduates on the island, most of them islanders,' said Fran Hicks, who is one of them. 'They want to be here. I can only think it comes from a very deep sense of belonging.'

The notion of moving to Cornwall is one aspect of the English dream, one that comes true too often for Cornwall's liking. And the idea of moving to St Agnes would be the ultimate expression of that: a remote, unpolluted island with only a sniff of winter, but also a post office-shop, real ale in the pub, a cricket pitch and the *Daily Telegraph* arriving (Violent Storm Elevens permitting) on the morning boat.

The islanders, however, do not consider this to be Cornwall. They are, they insist, not Cornish but Scillonian. No one could satisfactorily explain the difference. But it is true that, under current local government arrangements, the 2,000 people of Scilly have their own toytown unitary council, so tiny it makes Rutland seem like Shanghai and mocks all the theories of size that Whitehall normally uses to decide who should run what. It is also true that St Agnes doesn't feel very Celtic: there are no Tregunnas, Penberthys or Polzeaths in the churchyard along with all the Hickses and Leggs. The Scilly historian R. L. Bowley said that the Celtic heritage faded quickly because the islands had to be garrisoned and so fresh settlers kept arriving.

However, according to Philip Payton, the field names across the Scillies tend to be Cornish, which would pre-date the gravestones. And the island's customs are deeply Cornish. The characteristic sport, as it is all along the Cornish coast, is gig racing. This involves replicas (or, on St Agnes, an original) of the small boats that used to race out to passing vessels to drop on a pilot who could guide them to London or Bristol. This is historic business turned into tradition and fun. As with third-world taxi drivers hustling for passing tourists, winning that race could make the difference between prosperity and starvation.

And there is a hidden power: the Duke of Cornwall, aka the Prince of Wales. Across rural Cornwall, the Duchy, as the dominant landowner, has fingers in all sorts of pies, so much so that in late 2011 an information tribunal ruled that it was a public authority not a private estate, and thus subject to public scrutiny and potential judicial review. The Scilly Isles are all owned, lock, stock and almost everything but the Turk's Head barrels, by the Duke of Cornwall.

Prince Charles came to St Agnes a while back to inspect this distant colony. 'Camilla was a bit nervous about the helicopter ride,' recalled Sue Hicks. 'But she liked the egg sandwiches.' Fran Hicks believes the Duchy has been the island's salvation, preventing the establishment of a normal property market and a takeover by outsiders and holiday-home owners.

Chris Simmonds, the schoolteacher's husband, an incomer, a food scientist and one of my team-mates in the quiz, explained to me that this was an island of multitaskers long before the word was invented. 'You are welcomed here for what you can contribute. The island's not big enough to have an electrician or a plumber or a doctor. There wouldn't be enough work. So everybody does several things. You don't want to be the person who's receiving the whole time.' He is a co-responder, ready to be bleeped for a medical emergency. I sense that knowing about George IV, Nixon and Lesley Gore might not, day in, day out, quite cut it.

But I have this in common with the Hicks and Legg boys: I ache to go back. Only one thing worries me about St Agnes. On my walk, I picked up a plastic bottle by the shore, thinking of putting it in the recycling; I'm obsessive that way. Then I saw another. And another, and another, and ... there were thousands of them: more Coca-Cola than the islanders could have ever drunk; jetsam blown here by wind and tide. And if this is what has happened to one clump of rocks on one lovely, little island, what the hell is going on out on the ocean?

The spring spreads slowly north-eastwards from St Agnes. In Scilly, dairy cattle can normally be left outside all winter, which might only be advisable on the mainland on a few south-facing slopes near Land's End. In Britain the definitive sign of spring is always the daffodil. And west Cornwall and Scilly grow a fifth of the world's supply.

The daff was the making of Scilly. When the first Isles of Scilly daffodil show was held in 1886, the *Gardeners' Chronicle* predicted: 'It speaks of new prosperity for the Islanders, of the banishment of famine, of the establishment of industry and of the promotion of happiness.'

For a time St Agnes depended on daffodils. But the small fields, extra freight costs and uncertain sea conditions cancelled out its climatic advantages. Fran Hicks now concentrates on growing ultra-tender specialist varieties, the tazettas; others have just given up, the final straw being the sense that mainland winters were getting more Scillonian. So the business has shifted. Daffodil growers are not global-warming sceptics. 'When we were children we used to go for a Christmas Day walk to try and find the first daffodil,' said James Hosking of Fentongollan Farm near Truro. 'Now it would be much earlier. Admittedly we've got some early varieties. But mostly it's climate.' For the same reason, Cornish growers have been threatened by rivals from Lincolnshire, although a couple of retro-style freezes have put a check on that.

Hosking is a fourth-generation daffodil grower, by no means the biggest: but he has seventy different varieties in his catalogue, from Abba and Actaea to White Lion and Winifred van Graven; and about fifteen million blooms a year, spread over 170 acres, mostly rented, because this crop needs constant rotation. It has another problem: mechanised picking is impossible – the job still requires endless bend-and-stretch. Osteopathy may be considered a dependent industry.

In the old days, the pickers were fishermen kept shore-bound by the weather, china clay workers between shifts, and housewives looking for holiday money. But fishing and china clay dwindled, and the womenfolk preferred warmer, more reliable jobs in supermarkets. Hosking tried the local unemployed, but daffodil growers are very sceptical about the work ethic of young Cornish males. So the East Europeans took over.

He was happy to let me talk to his pickers and I tracked them to a field at Polwhele. They were reticent, partly because their English is fragile, partly out of an understandable wariness, and partly because they are on piecework and interruptions are not welcome. The theory of daffodil picking has changed in that the market insists now that they must be picked completely unopened for long life, even though that weakens the intensity of the colour. So if you see a lovely blooming field of Cornish daffodils, it probably means something has gone wrong. Modern tomatoes and apples are picked primarily for looks; daffodils are not. Funny old world.

The method has not changed a bit, though. 1–2–3–4–5–6–7–8–9–10 ... that's a bunch ... even them up ... cut off the bottoms ... rubber band out of pocket ... tie them together ... throw down for collection. That's 7p ...

1–2–3–4–5–6–7–8–9–10, bunch, even, cut, band, tie, throw. Another 7p ...

1–2–3–4 ...

Eighty bunches a box, and the best pickers can do twenty boxes a day, which means £112. Two dozen is not unheard of. Less Stakhanovite workers might only manage twelve or thirteen boxes. Fall much below that and the piecework rate dips below the minimum wage; Fentongollan has to make up the difference, which is not a tenable situation for the employer, so non-improvers have to be fired. My back hurt just watching, and I thought that Cornwall could add to its list of saints Andreas Pavel of São Paulo, inventor of the personal stereo.

However, the workers I met were not unhappy.

'Do you like the work?' I asked Vesi from Bulgaria.

'I like the country,' she said carefully. 'I like the farm. I like the people on the farm. And I like to earn the money.'

'It's hard but it's usual, I think,' said Lena from Lithuania. 'For

Lithuania, it's much money. As a teacher you earn less. This way I can buy a house.'

Back home Vesi was a kitchen designer and Lena worked for a phone company. Like most of the workers, they are Fentongollan regulars. The economics are harsh, but evidently realistic. One day East European property prices will rise and daffodil picking will not be a route to home ownership.

I think then Hosking will have to make daff picking a sport. It could compete with gig racing and the Cornish form of wrestling as a local attraction. Instead of paying everyone, there could be winner-take-all prizes for the men who can bust the twenty-five-box barrier. That would get the lads up in the morning.

March 2012

~~~~~~~

St Piran's Day 2014 was more Cornish than ever: the county was without a rail link to most of England after the sea had washed away the main line in Devon. St Agnes was also battered by the stormy winter: much of the footpath on the south-west side was washed away; one lump of stone dumped over the quay weighed about five tons. Otherwise, Chris Simmonds told me, the island was flourishing: enrolment in the primary school, which had fallen as low as two, was into double figures (just). Despite the gales, it had not been such a bad winter for plastic detritus: Simmonds explained that the debris on the rocks arrived not on the prevailing winds but when it blew northerly or easterly. 'We get an awful lot of suntan lotion, not something used by mariners on the big tankers. It comes from the beaches of northern Europe.'

In April 2014 the Cornish were given minority status under Council of Europe rules. This offers the same rights as the Welsh, Scottish and Irish to be protected against discrimination and have their views taken into account by government. It does not involve any extra money, though.

In March 2015 researchers announced in the journal Nature *that the Devon-Cornwall border was not just historic, but genetic. After the largest-ever study of Britain's DNA, Professor Peter Donnelly said: 'The geographical boundary of the Tamar River in the south and Bodmin Moor in the north seemed to have kept the counties from intermarrying for millennia.'*

12. *Covered in blotches*

WARWICKSHIRE

I stood on the bank with my daughter, and after a while the waterbus came along. It was small and pink and empty and it felt a bit daft when Rory the helmsman recited the safety information, as he must do a hundred times a day, every time anyone comes aboard. 'If anyone should fall in, we advise all passengers not to panic,' he said. 'Please don't swallow or consume the water, it's actually quite dirty.' Rory didn't have much of a Brummie accent, but he said it in the downbeat, matter-of-fact tone that meant we could hardly be anywhere else.

And so we set off from the picturesquely named Gas Street Basin past Old Turn Junction, round the Oozells Street Loop, then via Telford's new route and the narrows into the Worcester and Birmingham Canal and back again to Gas Street.

I have taken a waterbus across Sydney Harbour, the Star Ferry in Hong Kong, the ferries across the Bosphorus, the Circle Line in New York. The astonishing thing about this one was the quiet. Apart from the chugging of the engine, a recorded, half-audible commentary and Rory's dire warnings when anyone boarded, there was hardly a sound. Momentarily, I heard a dust cart clearing some bottles; the air conditioning at the Blue Mango Indian Brasserie may have been a bit noisy. Otherwise, barely a squawk. By the water's edge a goose was sitting on a clutch of eggs. She looked totally secure.

Birmingham has been the crossroads of England since modern travel began. Now there is Spaghetti Junction, a couple of miles up the road; before that it was New Street Station, even closer; before that it was arguably Oozells. We could see the Convention Centre, the Hyatt and the Crowne Plaza. And Birmingham's much-admired latest regeneration has turned the derelict warehouses into apartment blocks and the rusting old narrow boats into party vessels. Yet all was peaceful.

We walked along the towpath in the sunshine, had tea in the pretty Canalside Café and a chat with a couple from Shropshire who had pottered down from Norbury Junction in a sixty-six-footer called *Python*. There is no mode of transport more conducive to conversation than the narrowboat: you can walk your dog along the towpath faster than it can chug. It was lovely here, we agreed. 'Bit dodgy further down. You wouldn't want to moor there,' they said. 'We came under Spaghetti Junction. That was weird. Lager cans everywhere. Covered in graffiti.'

Oh, Birmingham! Birmingham! What is it about Birmingham?

> Brummagem: 'Counterfeit, sham, cheap and showy (1637)'
>   – *OED*
> 'Flash, pinchbeck, brummagem, tinsel, shoddy' – *Roget*
> 'One has not great hopes of Birmingham. I always say there is
>   something direful in the sound' – *Jane Austen*
> 'I feel as if my throat wanted sweeping like an English chimney' –
>   *Robert Southey*
> 'The frontier station of the Land of Mordor' – *E. R. Dodds*
> 'A disgusting town' – *Evelyn Waugh*

My own favourite quote is from Lady Trevor-Roper, the very grand country-house-going wife of the historian Hugh. Told that some friends had gone to Birmingham for the weekend, she enquired: 'Oh, whose place is that?'

The point is that it was nobody's place. Birmingham grew primarily because it didn't mind who turned up from the seventeenth century onwards: 'It awarded almost perfect freedom to all who chose to come,' according to one Victorian account. 'Dissenters and Quakers and heretics of all sorts were welcomed and undisturbed ... no trade unions, no trade guilds, no companies existed, and every man was free to come and go.'

The most instructive thing to do in Birmingham after the canal trip is to head across town to Hurst Street, where the National Trust has, almost miraculously, preserved what are said to be the last back-to-backs in Britain. These are real back-to-backs, not the normal Victorian terraces joined on two sides with a yard, a privy and alleyway separating them from the row behind. These houses are joined on three sides, so that those at the rear are accessible only through an alleyway leading into a yard with wash-houses and thunderboxes shared by a dozen or more families, creating the rough-and-ready communalism (and no doubt the stench) of a Chinese *hutong*.

Three of the homes have been recreated in the way they might have looked for three generations who lived and plied their trades there: a Jewish clock-hands maker of the eighteenth century; a man who made glass eyes for stuffed animals (and maybe live humans) in the nineteenth century; and a twentieth-century locksmith. Just three of Birmingham's thousand trades.

The English ought to marvel at this city. If the North was the engine room of the Industrial Revolution, Birmingham was its workshop. But they don't marvel, they recoil, as Waugh did. All that freedom, all that coming and going, meant it was a city that was constantly reinventing and rebuilding itself. Unfortunately, the post-war reconstruction of the centre – car-oriented, insensitive, tasteless – entrenched its image for a new generation. What's it they say? More canals than Venice, more trees than Paris, more hills than Rome, more parks than anywhere. But other cities somehow arrange it all better.

It's partly because the football teams, the modern indicator of civic pride, have been underachievers for decades. It's partly the accent, always bottom of the charts in popularity polls, which is why call centres are sited elsewhere. It's partly what they say in that accent. Miserablism is the shared Brummie religion, and expressed in such deadpan tones that one never quite knows to what extent the grumbling is self-conscious and self-deprecating.

I know nowhere else in the world so morbidly obsessed with its health. This may date back to the *hutongs*. And it seems to infest the rest of Warwickshire too. I once overheard a woman outside Marks & Spencer, Nuneaton, say to her companion: 'Our Elsie's legs are covered in blotches.' She sounded so *proud*.

However, there is not much else to connect Birmingham to the rest of Warwickshire. Carl Chinn, university professor and professional-Brummie personality (born 1956), insisted to me: 'Growing up, we were very proud of being in Warwickshire. Very proud of the cricket team. Very proud of being Shakespeare's county.' But Wasim Khan (born 1971), who went on to play cricket for Warwickshire, had never heard of it as a teenager: 'Birmingham City we understood – after all, we lived in Birmingham, didn't we? Supported the Blues ... Copied songs we'd heard taking the piss out of Villa. Yeah, we knew about Birmingham OK. But where was this Warwickshire? Well, who cared?'

Warwickshire is said to date back to the early eleventh century, but in 1974 Birmingham, Coventry and everything in between – comprising three-quarters of the population – was taken out to be called West Midlands. Has anyone, ever, cared about 'West Midlands'? 'Come on, West Midlands!' Do me a favour. It is, I think, one factor in Birmingham's rootlessness and miserablism. Far from the only one. But one. Official modern Warwickshire is just a rural rump, very Tory, which overnight was reduced from being the fourth most populous county to the twenty-ninth.

Birmingham's exponential growth meant that an unusual degree of minor tinkering with the county boundaries took place in the century before 1974. And it seems fair to say that expulsion from Warwickshire caused less distress in Birmingham than in traditionalist enclaves like Sutton Coldfield or Solihull, or indeed its rival, Coventry. But Birmingham and Coventry do have one big thing in common: both were wrecked more wholeheartedly by their planners than the Germans ever managed. And in Coventry that is saying something.

On the night of 14 November 1940, Coventry's old city centre was destroyed by the Luftwaffe in the most infamous of all Nazi raids. Hundreds died, more than a thousand were hurt. Most visibly, the cathedral – the medieval church of St Michael, promoted in 1918 after Coventry became a city – was ravaged by incendiary bombs. The decisive blow was that iron girders, put in to *strengthen* the roof, buckled in the heat and thus destroyed the masonry which otherwise might have survived.

The fourteenth-century tower and much of the walls did come through unscathed. And the first and best decision was to retain them as a symbol of both remembrance and reconciliation. The ruin feels almost like a walled garden: very strange, very moving. The new cathedral was much admired at the time, though that time was 1961, an era when architects were full of crap. Sir Basil Spence was constrained from over-exuberance by the proximity of the old building. His creation's great virtue is its humility. But it does feel a bit like an air terminal. And Sutherland's Christ does look as though he is dressed as grandma. Against that, the flock-of-birds motif above the choir stalls is compelling, and the morning light through John Piper's stained glass unforgettable.

You can also climb the steep steps to the top of the old tower and get rewarded by what might be a fine view. Except that modern Coventry is in the way. To the north: the city centre and ring road (ghastly); to the east: Coventry University (repulsive); to the west IKEA, a rectangle in deep blue (revolting); to the south: a general mishmash. The only things that might be worth seeing are too close.

The pedestrian precinct that replaced Coventry's old centre was also much praised at the time, even by such a robust judge as Ian Nairn, who called it 'probably the best thing of its kind in Europe'. But it is cold and sterile. One local explained that Leamington grew in importance after Coventry was bombed because the locals had to go there to shop, and got into the habit of it. Many never went back.

I stopped by the rugged cross at Meriden which is supposed to mark the centre of England. In any other country this might be a major tourist trap. But this is England. The cross is pretty enough, surrounded by tulips and gillyflowers, with a few initials carved almost apologetically in the soft, mossy stone.

The marker showing the presumed geographic centre of the forty-eight contiguous US states is certainly the biggest thing in Lebanon, Kansas. Meriden's cross is not even the biggest thing on Meriden village green: it is dwarfed by a memorial to the cyclists who died in both world wars, though quite why cyclists warrant a special war memorial is a little mysterious.

One problem is that measuring the centre of a country is not an exact application of science. Lebanon's claim is not undisputed, and Meriden's position has certainly had pretenders: Lillington, Copston Magna, Minworth. I suppose the name Meriden just sounds like middle England. It certainly looks like a place where everyone reads the *Daily Mail.* Not a world-class tourist attraction, though. There is only one of those in Warwickshire.

If you come into Stratford-upon-Avon by the leisure centre, you are greeted by the offices of Shakespeares Solicitors. In town you can stay in Cymbeline House, As You Like It Cottage, Twelfth Night, Hamlet House, First Night guest house or Curtain Call. Fancy staying on? You can run the Shakespeare Marathon and, when that gets too hard, see out your days at the Hathaway Court retirement home until you're ready for the Shakespeare Hospice. Even the pubs are protected from yobboes by Bard-Watch (you're barred, geddit?) Unexpectedly, the town centre is not full of obvious possibles like the Othello coffee shop, Midsummer Night's Dream bedding and the Romeo and Juliet dating agency. But that's only because rents are so high that the centre is dominated by chain stores.

Stratford is a one-trick town, but by golly it's a good trick. It is baffling why people from all over the world with only a passing interest, if that, in Shakespeare's work should be so obsessed with the small, overcrowded and frankly larcenous town he came from. The Shakespeare Birthplace Trust, which runs the five main sites in the town, has reported booming business, especially from China.

But what's so interesting about any writer's life? Now, taken as a whole, Shakespeare's body of work may well be superior to my own in every particular, except perhaps consistency of spelling. But I don't imagine that his life, taken up by the process of writing, can have been any less dull. Duller even, Microsoft Pinball and Free Cell not being available to add spice to the writer's day on the versions of Windows issued prior to 1616. Life? What life?

I decided to take the open-top hop-on, hop-off bus tour, although, sadly, intermittent downpours rendered the top deck unusable. I suppose I hoped to tuck myself behind some Americans who would say some quotably amusing things the way people do whenever Alan Bennett gets on a bus: 'Say, is this where Shakespeare wrote *David Copperfield*?' 'Are we going to Julius Caesar's birthplace?' 'Hey, Elsie, your legs are covered in blotches.'

In fact, when I got on, there was no one else on the bus at all. I opted to hop off at Anne Hathaway's Cottage. The sun was out now and there was a queue to get in, with, in front of me, a group of teenage American girls who took my line on the absurdity of this exercise. 'We'll do what we did at Winston Churchill,' one whispered conspiratorially. 'Remember? We went in, we went out, we had ice cream and we went shopping.' Good plan. I whipped through quickly, but by the time I was out they were long gone.

They couldn't even have taken time to indulge in the opportunity for self-expression afforded by the message board near the gift shop which had Post-it notes for comment: the tiny ones with barely room for a haiku, never mind a sonnet. A sample:

This is so fantastic. I'm so glad I came – Susannah, Calif, USA
Paul and Louise In Love forever xxx
Greetings from Boise, ID
Harry Styles I ♥ You
Claire and Hayley on our secret holiday
I know what you did last summer – Emilio
WOW Rating: ***** By Rosie 7 years old
To Shakespeare: Thank you for the genius in your writing.
[Shakespeare? Shakespeare? Oh, him!]
and
We loved the Easter Egg Hunt!

The gift shop, alongside Diamond Jubilee tea pots and an Olympic Games apron, had a T-shirt with a quote from *The Merry Wives of Windsor*: 'There is money. Spend it; spend it; spend more.' An assistant was able to confirm my supposition that a book entitled *Sex in Elizabethan England* was outselling *The Complete Works*.

My Brummie sister-in-law, Susan, suggested I should take a bus round Birmingham: the no. 11 outer circular, which has a firm place in the city's folklore. It was a fine trip for a tourist, she said, something she had always wanted to do but had never quite got round to.

The bus took some finding: no. 11 on the West Midlands travel website is a Coventry route. This was because there is no No.11 in Birmingham as such but two different routes – the 11A going anticlockwise and the 11C clockwise. Fatefully, it was the 11A that arrived at Acocks Green first.

I was greeted at the top of the stairs by half a kebab, lying flat with the onion beginning to suppurate. At the back was a young couple, drinking cans of lager; the man spoke largely in an incoherent jumble but from the tone of his voice he was teaching a baby, which I couldn't actually see, simple vocabulary: 'ma', 'da', 'fucking hell'. Alongside me was a group of young girls, all somewhat obese. 'Shall we go Froydee?' 'No, we can't go Froydee. Mum's in court Froydee.'

Acocks Green became Yardley became Stechford became Erdington. The houses were not at all unpleasant and often quite handsome – mid-Victorian railwaymen's cottages, late Victorian terraces, Edwardian villas, interwar semis, seasidey bungalows. But as townscape they formed an incoherent jumble, like the bloke at the back's conversation. There was, as they say of towns in the American west, no there there.

I embarked on a train of thought that this was a product of Birmingham's history: all that growth, all that openness, all that coming and going. The place was not rooted anywhere. Not in Warwickshire, not in England, barely even on Earth. 'All right, mate,' the man said sweetly to his infant. 'Shut the fuck up.'

He got off with his girl and his can of lager shortly afterwards, but there was no baby. Or if there was, they had left it behind. The fat girls went too, to be succeeded by two pre-pubescent boys in tracksuits and hoodies who lit a roll-up. Or maybe a joint; it was hard to tell above the smell of onion. I decided that, despite the forthcoming excitement of passing Winson Green prison, perhaps I would go back the way I came. The kebab was still above the stairs, turning septic. The 11C was much quieter, presumably attracting a far higher class of clientele, people who are clockwise rather than anti.

Next morning I did go to Winson Green, taking a ride on Birmingham's single lonely tram line and then walking past the terraces of evocatively named Nineveh Road. Every house in the street bar one had the floral-patterned net curtains that in Britain have become a reliable indicator of Asianness: families as discreet and house-proud as the British of two generations ago. One home had a little sign in the window, '2 ROOM TO LET INDIAN FAMILY', perhaps just ambiguous enough to avoid prosecution, but still a throwback to the days when white families had these houses and placed adverts with NC in the corner: No Coloureds. The little front gardens, however, were all neglected.

Nineveh Road reaches Soho Road, where every business appears to be Asian-run, except the betting shops. The dominant feature is the Sikh temple, proudly advertising its new free schools, primary and secondary. And at the corner of Hamstead Road, where Handsworth turns into Lozells, the Asian Resource Centre offered 'FREE COFFEE MORNINGS, ALL NATIONS WELCOME'. It listed some examples: Pakistani, Indian, Afro-Caribbean, Bengali, Chinese, Vietnamese. Some might think there is an ethnic group missing. But actually it is not really an ethnic group represented in Lozells.

The vicar of Lozells, the Rev. Jemima Prasadam, 'Auntie Jemima', built a considerable reputation for her dedication and fortitude on the streets when the area was convulsed by rioting in 2005. Finding her was not easy. There was a crowd of men outside the impressive New Testament Church of God, but when I asked where the Church of England was, they were as bewildered as if I had asked about the Kirk of the Wee Frees or the Masorti Synagogue. I found it eventually: an obscure modern single-storey building, St Paul & St Silas, successor to two large Victorian churches, St Paul, now a nursery, and St Silas, so grand it has its own square, but now given over to the Pentecostalists.

The church was locked, and it was some weeks before I could track her down and months before I could come back to meet her. Famously, she is *everywhere* in Lozells all week; the only way was to return on a Sunday morning. Before doing that, I popped into the New Testament Church of God – just one of a stack of revivalist churches on and around Lozells Road. It offered five big screens, theatrical lights, five singers on stage, a band and a warm welcome to a crowd of about 150. Elderly black ladies in black hats swayed and clapped to a succession of rather samey gospel songs. We prayed for Mrs Olive Thomas, who had suffered the loss of an aunt, and for the rich, who didn't understand. And we praised God and said Hallelujah a great deal.

Attendance at the harvest festival service down the road at St Paul & St Silas was bumped up above a couple of dozen by the presence of a fraternal delegation from suburban Sutton Coldfield. Auntie Jemima turned out to be even tinier than her congregation and looked like a little Indian bird. But she did her utmost to offer a touch of hot-gospel vibrancy, which is not easy in a near-empty room. Over tea afterwards, I raised the question of numbers.

'Well,' she said, 'a hundred years ago we would have had 120. Now we have twenty. But this is God's territory and we take the challenge. You know, other churches have more and they take care of their people. But the good old Anglicans. We go Out There.'

She may be on to something. The Sikh free school up the road will be well funded and probably a huge success. But it will be full of Sikhs, strengthening the mutual incomprehension between Birmingham's communities for generations to come. Lozells needs Jemima to be Out There.

It is only a short walk, if not a pleasant one, to the last resting place of the man who was once Birmingham's most famous son: Joseph Chamberlain (1836–1914), father of the now more famous Neville.

He remains the best-known resident of Key Hill Cemetery, challenged only by Alfred Bird, inventor of Bird's Custard. But it took me a full hour and a half to find the Chamberlain family tomb, which can only be reached by trampling over assorted Caddicks, Rylands and Harrolds. It is marked by a stake, which is not much use if you don't know what the stake signifies.

As mayor, Joe Chamberlain transformed this city in a manner more associated with an American mayor than a British one, clearing slums, cleaning the water supply, creating public amenities. Then he went to Westminster and – without ever becoming prime minister – became the most gifted, potent, admired and reviled politician in the country.

In *Portrait of Birmingham* Vivian Bird (no known connection with custard) wrote how the city 'went en fête for Joseph's seventieth birthday, with a civic banquet, mass rallies in six parks, and bunting across every street'. The obscurity of his grave is a symbol of the fate of British local democracy.

Bird – writing in 1970 – tried to say the right thing about the mass immigration that was under way but could not help mentioning that his middle-class suburb was just over the River Cole from increasingly Asian Sparkhill: 'I am not the only Hall Green resident who watches for signs of encroachment on "our side of the river".'

Back in Lozells, I went into a Sudanese internet café and got talking to a young man. 'You look at Soho Road,' he said. 'It doesn't look like the UK. It makes me angry. It is a bit extreme.'

His name was Beruke. From Ethiopia.

April/October 2012

～～～～～

In 2014 Warwickshire County Cricket Club rebranded their team, for the purpose of Twenty20 matches only, as the Birmingham Bears, causing great irritation to their supporters in Coventry, Nuneaton and Leamington etc., and also to the writer of this book. Even more irritatingly, this mutant won the tournament.

13. *The sound of the froghorn*

SUFFOLK

We were walking – my friend Simon Barnes and I – by the reed beds that lead down to the sea at Minsmere, perhaps the holiest shrine of the British conservation movement. He was engaged in giving me a full-scale lecture on the purpose of the reserve. But a practised birdwatcher is like a secret agent. He never once took his eyes off everything around him. The difference is that Simon, without missing a beat, kept telling me what he saw.

'The whole point,' he was saying, 'is that a reed bed wants to become an oak forest. *Shoveller.* Left to themselves, the reeds would slowly deposit humus and dry up and eventually the scrubby stuff would *reed warbler, no, sedge warbler* take over. Brambles and so on. Then would come the pioneer trees, largely *pair of lapwings* birch or alders, continuing the process until, eventually, the climax vegetation arrives, and over the course of a millennium the canopy would close.

'The whole point of management is to prevent that happening. An allotment is trying to become an oakwood. So is a flower bed. Or a farmer's field. The reed bed is being farmed for bitterns by being cut *gadwall* on a rotational basis so the reeds come back new and young and fresh, which is just the habitat that bitterns like. *Swift! First of the season!*

But we did not see a bittern, even though the whole place was being designed for their benefit. Hardly anyone ever sees a bittern. It is a sort of heron but an extremely shy one: its reedy world meets all its needs. In any case, only a few dozen breed in Britain each year, all in East Anglia and one small reserve in Lancashire. Under the circumstances, it needs to advertise its presence to avoid complete extinction. Loudly. The boom of the bittern is a characteristic sound of the Suffolk countryside. But by now the grey morning had turned to drizzle and, despite their penchant for damp surroundings, bitterns find rain very unerotic and keep quiet.

We did see the avocets, the monarchs of Minsmere, who made this whole place possible. In the early days of the Second World War, with invasion a serious threat, it was decided that this lonely, low-lying stretch of coastline was indefensible. The army built a line of concrete posts to deter the tanks and then allowed the sea to come through the gaps, so that the carefully drained coastal farmland became a mere again. Suddenly, up popped the avocets, who had not bred in Britain for a hundred years. At the time the Royal Society for the Protection of Birds had fewer than 10,000 members. Now it has over a million, with the avocet as its symbol.

What a perfect symbol it is too: a lovely, sinuous creature, from its slender legs to its curly beak, far too exotic-looking for these drab climes. Ruthless, though: it goes head-down every few seconds, like a metronome or a nodding donkey, to slash the nearest aquatic insect with that luscious beak. No birder I, but this was riveting.

We wandered off eventually and walked along the beach. But by now the drizzle had turned to rain and the rain had turned to downpour. I had on some gear I had worn on a trip to the South Pole, but it was no protection against Suffolk in April. We found another hide, full of birders in dripping-wet anoraks, all groaning about the weather. Simon, being a successful author of wildlife books and local with it, counts as a personality in these parts. And suddenly he was spotted, as though he were a shoveller or a gadwall.

'You tell people when to come to Minsmere,' a woman was saying to her friend, 'and you say late April or early May. But now look at it. *Simon Barnes.*'

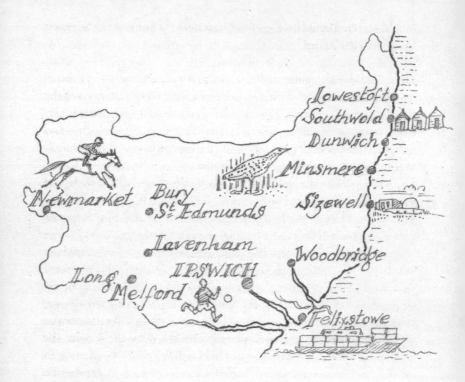

She came over to say hello, and Simon introduced his friend Matthew. And she held out her hand and said: 'Whetton Coles.' We talked about the weather for a bit while I considered the etiquette of asking why Mr and Mrs Coles might have called their baby girl Whetton. The moment passed, which was lucky, as it was some hours later when I realised that, far from performing the un-English act of introducing herself, she had in fact uttered the most English phrase of them all: 'Wet and cold.'

Simon and I had a nice lunch in the Eels Foot Inn (a local joke) in East-bridge. The rain had stopped now, and we went for a post-prandial wander and found ourselves by the Minsmere River, which runs along the southern edge of the reserve. Suddenly, Simon held up his hand and shushed.

It was not a boom: there was no B. And it was not that loud, though audible enough across the coastal marshes. 'Oom ... oom ... oom.' A couple making love in the next hotel room? A frog with mild constipation? That other characteristic sound of the east coast, a foghorn? Some combination of the above – an amorous froghorn, perhaps?

Whatever, I could hold my head high from the Stour to the Waveney. I had heard the bittern.

As a child, I had regular nightmares about inundation. Still do sometimes. Long before the terrible Indian and Pacific Ocean tsunamis of the early twenty-first century, I spent holidays on Bournemouth beach nervously conning the horizon just in case one turned up. My horror was and is mixed with fascination. I love to watch stormy seas pounding the walls or raging rivers bursting into water meadows.

Suffolk taunts me. Normally, the land is *there* and the sea is *there*, and that's that. Here you never quite know. How many outsiders think of Ipswich as a port? On a map Woodbridge looks miles inland. But if you pass through by train, there is a boatyard that stretches alongside the line for what seems like a mile or more. There are no north–south roads anywhere near the coast ('too crumbly, squishy and volatile,' says Simon). In some places there is no route seaward of the A12, about eight miles from the notional edge of England. Beyond that, there is terra-not-all-that-firma, estuaries, rivers, meres and marsh and the very Suffolk habitat known as sandling heath, merging and unmerging with the tides, the seasons, the years and the eons while the opportunist North Sea lies in wait like a wolf at the door. It is the mud from all the estuaries, I was told, that makes the Suffolk sea so peculiarly brown, even on bright days.

This is a very mysterious place to an inlander. The coastline is dominated by the dome of the Sizewell B power station. Even at Minsmere, it pokes up behind the reed beds, looking like a rising full moon. Not ugly, just unearthly. Alongside that seems to go the unworldly. Edward FitzGerald translated the *Rubáiyát* here; W. G. Sebald walked this coast for his idiosyncratic meditation on world history, *The Rings of Saturn*, which included, in a very Sebaldian way, the story of Major Le Strange of Henstead, who died in 1992, leaving his entire estate to his housekeeper, who had dined with him every day for more than thirty years, having adhered to his original condition that she should do so in total silence. Was this real? The cutting looked authentic. But the combination of Sebald and Suffolk is most unsettling.

In 2009 I found, tucked away and unsignposted in the little town of Leiston, Summerhill School, whose very existence had beguiled us as children. The school where lessons are optional! The school where kids make the rules! It was founded by A. S. Neill in 1921 and was still run by his daughter, Zoë Readhead, and still wholly true to itself, if somewhat out of fashion. I was welcomed warmly and allowed in to The Meeting, the thrice-weekly gathering that makes the rules: one person, one vote, be they principal or infant. The upshot is that Summerhill has what must be the thickest rule book of any school in England, possibly thicker than the book governing VAT regulations, a testament to children's innate love of order and fairness, as long as the rules are theirs. When Zoë Readhead talked about children being 'successful', she made quotation-mark signs with her fingers.

The Suffolk accent is also mysterious. Anyone with half an ear and a reasonable knowledge of Britain can make a reasonable stab at identifying and perhaps amateurishly imitating maybe a dozen of the best-known accents. But even good actors usually turn Norfolk and Suffolk into a bastardised Mummerset.

Rivalry between Norfolk and Suffolk has for years manifested itself mainly at football, where Norwich City and Ipswich Town have long performed better than is expected from teams beyond the big conurbations. The differences between the counties are subtle: Suffolk these days is a bit richer, partly from being closer to London; the Norfolkologist Keith Skipper thinks it's less deferential. He is also kind about its accent: 'Suffolk is Norfolk dialect set to music.' Simon Barnes thinks rivalry with Norfolk is not the urgent one: 'It's more important now to make it clear that Suffolk is not Essex than to say it's not Norfolk.'

Suffolk's image is indisputably rural. Ipswich Town are known as 'Tractor Boys' in the papers and 'sheepshaggers' on the terraces. Yet the town now sprawls for miles until it almost merges with Woodbridge. And this is nowhere near the outer limits of London commuterdom.

Forced to break off this chapter to spend a day in London, I arrived at Saxmundham Station at 6 a.m., just nicking the last parking place, to the disgust of one regular on the 6.14 to Ipswich, whom I heard chuntering about the iniquity of such a thing all the way to Wickham Market. It was another cold, bleak morning and, outside major disaster zones, I have never seen a crowd quite as grim-faced as that gathered on Platform 2 to get on the connecting 7.09 to Liverpool Street.

In Suffolk, though, this seems out of character. Most people have no wish to travel anywhere else, which is lucky, because the A12 going north quickly turns into a cart track. In the unlikely event of the road ahead not being occupied by a juggernaut or a tractor or an unjustified 30 mph limit, there will appear in front of you an elderly couple in a red Nissan

Micra, travelling at a speed low enough to be incredibly irritating but high enough to be impassable. I suspect they are paid by the council to deter any purposeful movement whatever.

The most striking thing about the county, though, is the extent to which it is so palpably show-offy. All those pink-cheeked houses! You wouldn't get away with them in Yorkshire, not even in Hebden Bridge. They would be an aberration in Cornwall. 'Am I not incredibly beautiful?' the very stones are saying. 'Is not my pargeting extremely fine?' 'Is my thatch not immaculate?'

This is most obvious in west Suffolk, where the old wool-based opulence has been fortified by the wagonloads of Waitrosey weekenders. Take Long Melford, with a parish church that can only be described as arrogant. Long? The village/town/megalopolis stretches downhill (and then a little way up again) for two miles, slowly becoming less prosperous the further you get from God's Very Large House. Or Lavenham, where the much-loved half-timbered houses have been twisted into bizarre shapes, one is tempted to imagine, not by the ravages of time but in a self-conscious effort to look quainter than their neighbours.

And then there is Newmarket, so close to Suffolk's western border that the Cesarewitch, one of the most famous of all its races, actually starts in Cambridgeshire. On a fresh, dewy, spring morning, there are few more beautiful spots to be than the foot of Warren Hill, or on the edge of the Heath with the first lot of horses glistening from their morning workout and Ely Cathedral shimmering in the distance. It's pointless to consider Newmarket in terms of the county as a whole: it is perhaps the least diversified town left in the kingdom, and the most introverted, and the most distinctive – 'a one-horse-town with 3,000 horses'. Like horse racing in general, Newmarket is based on a strange alliance of toffs and oiks, with the bourgeoisie almost wholly absent. 'Which is why,' explained one resident, 'the best restaurant in town is Pizza Express.'

However, the essence of Suffolk, which is on the whole relentlessly bourgeois, is to be found near the water. Take four coastal towns with totally different stories, two of them disastrous, two of them successful – or, as Zoë Readhead of Summerhill would say – 'successful'. All of them illustrating Suffolk's contradictions.

The first is Dunwich, which 850 years ago was one of the largest and most prosperous ports in England. But it was built on shifting sands and collapsing cliffs. Our lives are all like that, I suppose, but Dunwich's case was a bit extreme. In 1286 that deadly North Sea combination – a stormy nor'easter and a spring tide – destroyed much of the town, but, even more disastrously in economic terms, the spit washed across the harbour mouth and blocked the entrance. The trade moved elsewhere and, with the cliffs eroding at the rate of a yard a year, Dunwich slowly tumbled into the sea, though it infamously maintained two MPs until the 1832 Reform Act.

There are at least a dozen churches under the sea, their bells (so it is said) giving out ghostly peals on blowy nights, the last of them, All Saints, finally going under in 1919. Dunwich now has a beach with a café (looking sensibly impermanent), a few cottages, a pub and a fascinating museum. The whole place panders to my obsessive fears, though it took me until 2009 before I finally got there and indulged them. The man in the museum told me that day that he expected the sea would claim the building in seventy years' time.

I mentioned this to Jane Hamilton, the museum's education officer, who was in charge the day I returned: 'On that reckoning, you've got sixty-seven years left.' Not necessarily, she said, because Dunwich disappears in fits and starts. 'That figure was based on a council seventy-five-year line that put the sea just on the far side of the museum. In fact there hasn't been much erosion the last few years.'

But how do you get the building insured? Not a problem, she said. 'The insurance companies are only bothered about what's going to happen in any given year. They don't care about seventy years' time. It's the same when you take out dog insurance. They're very happy to take your money until the dog's nine or ten.' In actuarial terms, indeed, Dunwich's life expectancy is considerably better than my own, never mind my dog's.

An hour south and the coast had a very different feel. I was standing by the Spa Pavilion in Felixstowe. The tulips were blooming and the place seemed as sleepy and Edwardian and unchanging as Budleigh Salterton. But past the pier, there was an extraordinary sight: a line of giant cranes, looking like the invaders in *War of the Worlds*.

Felixstowe is Britain's biggest port. Ask that as a quiz question and hardly anyone outside Suffolk or the shipping business would have a clue. Yet it handles twice as many containers as its nearest rival, Southampton, and is the only UK port in the global top fifty – 6,000 containers coming in or out every day. Shanghai would have 60,000, but still. 'Felixstowe,' says the port's corporate affairs officer, Paul Davey, 'is better known in China than it is in the UK.'

This story is Dunwich in reverse. Felixstowe only acquired a port in 1875 and for decades it was insignificant, pottering around with a bit of agricultural trade. It was so small that when the Attlee government introduced the National Dock Labour Scheme in 1947 Felixstowe was too trivial to qualify. Which turned out to be crucial.

Until then, dockers had been employed on a brutally casual basis, standing outside desperately trying to catch the foreman's eye. No work, no pay, like a struggling actor. The reform completely reversed the balance of power and ultimately the unions negotiated lifetime job security. When containerisation came in around 1966, cutting freight costs considerably, they saw it as a threat, as indeed it was: one container ship could replace nine conventional cargo ships. But the dockers had the muscle to keep the containers out. Felixstowe's owners, exempt from the scheme, saw their opportunity. And to their own tiny workforce, it meant more jobs, not fewer. 'I think the Port of London had 50,000 dockers at one time,' said Davey. 'Now it's about 500. We had fifty, now it's 2,500.'

Felixstowe had other advantages. As Britain's trade moved first towards Europe and then to Asia, it had geography on its side: ships flitting between the big European ports – Rotterdam, Antwerp, Hamburg – could easily fit in Felixstowe. And, unlike the old big-city ports, it had room to expand: specifically on to a stretch of marshland reluctantly bought by Trinity College, Cambridge, in the 1930s as a makeweight when it was buying some nearby farms. Since then, this port has paid for a great deal of the port Trinity dons enjoy at high table.

The docks are a mile and a world away from the Spa Pavilion and the tulips: it is a vast and private place, with lorries piling out day and night on to the A14, and fifty-eight train movements a day, with a new rail terminal being built. It has its own fire, ambulance and statutory police service. Along the shoreline the containers are stacked up to nine-high in the different-coloured liveries of the major freight companies: from the air, they must look like a child's building blocks. Recently, the port of Ningbao in China asked Felixstowe for a twinning arrangement. 'We didn't know too much about Ningbao,' said Davey. 'Turns out it's got a population of six and a half million. Felixstowe's 30,000.'

I was intrigued by the notion of the handful of third-world sailors who crew those behemoths coming ashore for their brief visit to Felixstowe and hastily ravishing the womenfolk before heading off to Hamburg or wherever to repeat the exercise the next night.

'Where do they go?' I asked Davey. 'The fleshpots of Felixstowe?'

'They're too tired. Anyway, there are no fleshpots in Felixstowe.'

The past and present sometimes blend just as successfully but more attractively. Just north of Dunwich is Southwold: 'one of the happiest and most picturesque seaside-towns in England'.

Pevsner wrote that more than half a century ago and it is, if anything, even more true now. One theory is that Southwold and Aldeburgh owe their modern success to the *closure* of their railways, thus making them more exclusive for the car-owning middle class. Sebald, who arrived on foot, was especially taken with the Sailors' Reading Room, a building too much like a Victorian schoolroom to attract the other German migrant Pevsner. It was open, according to *The Rings of Saturn*, from seven in the morning to midnight but 'almost always deserted but for one or two of the surviving fishermen and seafarers sitting in silence in the armchairs'.

The opening hours had certainly shortened when I arrived, and there was not much to read, just that rusting old hulk of a newspaper, the *Daily Express*, and the Ipswich morning paper, the *East Anglian Daily Times*, which – like the reading room itself – is a remarkable survivor. A new sign on the table read: 'The Sunday newspapers have been discontinued as they do not seem to get read.'

Mostly the reading room is a quaint museum, the wood-panelled wall filled with figureheads and photos and scale models of old ships like the beach yawl *Bittern* (which I hope had a froghorn) and the steamer *Southwold Belle*. There is a members-only back room with a snooker table. Three old boys – all genuine longshore fishermen, I think – were reading the papers companionably and far from silently. 'Place next door to Buffy Baggott's,' said one (I'm sure that's what he said). 'Fifteen hundred a calendar month. Bit steep!'

Southwold has fine pubs and Adnams Beer, whose brewery has moved only from the town centre to the outskirts. But there is something even more special: Southwold Pier, rebuilt at the turn of this century.

Bypass the bog-standard amusement arcade at the pier entrance, ignore even the improbably alluring pier restaurant (cod with chorizo, butterbean, herb cassoulet and curly kale) and walk down to the Under the Pier Show, an amusement arcade appealing even to people who hate amusement arcades (my wife). It was created by an inventor called Tim Hunkin and comprises a collection of homemade slot machines and what I suppose you might call rides, mixing Heath Robinson engineering, post-modern irony and a large dollop of genius. My special favourite – beating even Whack a Banker ('You lost ... So it's business as usual') – is Micro-Break ('the fast, efficient holiday'), a wonderful pastiche of the travel industry as it caters to people stupid enough to go further than Southwold.

It is then necessary to leave just before the hour or half-hour to go outside and see Hunkin's towering achievement, the water clock, which culminates in ... but no, you have to see it.

When I told Suffolk friends I was going to Lowestoft, they responded rather like my mum when I told her I was heading to a war zone. Its reputation is Southwold in reverse: having failed to make much impact on the sun-and-sea market, the family market, the youth market, the elderly market, the dirty weekend market, the clean weekend market, the stag party market, the hen party market and the day trip market, the town is reckoned to have done well with the cider-and-meths drinkers' market.

But my destination was not the town itself. The aim was to touch England and the UK's most easterly point: 52°28' N , 1°45' E. Lowestoft Ness.

There was no visible sign on Whaploade Road, the main coastal route out of town. Instead I parked near quite a pretty cricket ground-cum-park and a caravan site that might have been attractively positioned had the concrete sea wall not rendered the sea invisible. Thinking I needed to head back south, I walked along the wall for the thick end of a mile into a wind coming straight from the South Pole that, in defiance of geography, appeared to have skipped the tropics altogether. Later I realised that, precisely because this was such an easterly outpost, the wind was carrying all the cold of the North Sea straight into my face. A kindly dog walker said I was on the right track, pointing to a tower that looked like some sort of landmark.

To landward now was the Bird's Eye factory; to seaward was a sign saying 'Beach closed due to sharp spikes and concrete blocks'. The wall opened out into a longer platform, like the deck of an aircraft carrier. Were the place a fraction more attractive, everything would have been covered in graffiti, but no vandal would be desperate enough to come here. T¹ landmark turned out to be some kind of chimney belonging to ⸰

sewage works, with a rusting metal seat attached for the benefit of tourists on which it seemed unlikely that any human buttocks had ever rested. I was alone except for a single birdwatcher.

On the ground at the easternmost point itself was something called the Euroscope – i.e. it was paid for by European funds – showing the compass points of more welcoming tourist resorts like Dogger Bank and the Indefatigable Gas Field. To the south-west was a wind turbine, said to be the UK's tallest (certainly the most easterly) and an ancient gasometer.

The correct route, I later discovered, was to have turned right at Atlas Autos and then left into Gasworks Road, past the barbed wire with the plastic bags hanging from it. Much later, I discovered the Ness Point website, written by someone aware that the 'tourist offer' is not necessarily all it might be. 'Currently all there is for a tourist to see apart from the wonderful sea views is the Euroscope which some people have called "a thing on the floor".' The site also says: 'These are very exiting times for both Lowestoft and Ness Point.' Honest, it said exiting. Tim Hunkin is not the only ironist in these parts.

The birdwatcher said there had been some changes: 'The sewage outflow used to be just over there,' he said, pointing at the waves. 'But they moved it now.'

'So that's an improvement, anyway,' I said.

'Not really. You used to get all the gulls coming to feed on the sewage, especially the rare ones. It's not nearly so good now.'

And not an avocet or bittern in sight.

April 2012

〜〜〜〜〜〜

In 2014 the Ness Point website was still reporting 'exiting times': no mention of anything happening.

14. *Mayday! Mayday!*

OXFORDSHIRE

In my niece's house in North Hinksey, I put the alarm on for 4.30. Scared of sleeping through it, I thus hardly slept at all. I tiptoed out at 5 and could have walked into town had the rain not been absolutely bombarding. So I drove, a triumph of hope over experience even at that time of the morning. Oxford sets complex intellectual challenges so that entrance is barred to all but the most intelligent aspirants. This applies to motorists as well as students.

I came up with wrong answers on the Botley Road, then on the complex one-way system, the dead ends and the D.Phil.-level parking regulations, and still ended up dumping the car illegally and having to hail a cab to get as far as was feasible down the High.

As 6 a.m. approached, the streets were already full, and noisy. Some people were coming out of nightclubs (on a Tuesday!), some were in evening dress, or remnants of it. Virtually all of them were young; many of them were drunk; most of them, one imagines, were students residing in the ancient colleges, both because it was hard to get there otherwise at such an hour and because of the elevated nature of their discourse: 'Come on, you guys' ... 'Pretty *fucking* awesome' ... 'And she was, like, paralytic in KFC, y'know' ...

By now, the rain had eased to a light drizzle. I fought my way on to Magdalen Bridge, where it was just possible to see ghostly figures moving below the pinnacles of Magdalen College's great tower. On the stroke of 6, in keeping with ancient tradition, they began the May morning carol:

> *Te Deum Patrem colimus,*
> *Te laudibus prosequimur ...*

Something like that, anyway. The chief recipient of the *Hymnus Euchar-isticus*, the rising sun, was having a very long lie-in. It was also difficult for the audience on the bridge to hear because the pre-6 a.m. hubbub had stilled only a fraction. As the hymn turned to madrigals, conversation grew louder and the choir, 144 feet above us, was having trouble compet-ing, even with amplifiers.

Finally, the bells rang out and everyone drifted away. A few years ago, it was customary – young gentlemen, high spirits, drink taken – to mark May Day in Oxford by jumping into the Cherwell. In 2005, with river lev-els unusually low, forty of them got hurt ('Barmpots today, rulers tomor-row,' said the *Sun*) and for several years police closed the bridge for the duration.

By 2012 the authorities had relented a little. But it was impossible even to see the river, never mind jump in it. It was protected by three lines of security fences and one line of unsmiling guards. There was also, puz-zlingly, a line of green flags, the universal indicator of safe bathing. Hardly anyone was confused: only three people tried to beat the system, accord-ing to the *Oxford Mail*, and none of them made it. The whole occasion was a bit joyless somehow, and I trudged off to buy a coffee and pastry to wake and cheer myself up.

In the coffee shop, a young man – merry even for May – came over and pleaded: 'May Day hug, May Day hug'. So that's why it's the inter-national distress call, I thought. 'A bit early in the morning,' I grumped. Within moments I repented, thinking my reply was just a bit over-English and stuffy. It made no difference. By then he had given me my hug anyway.

Seventeen days later, on a more clement morning, at a less trying hour, a smaller, more decorous gathering collected outside what is regarded as the city church, St Michael's at the North Gate, on Cornmarket Street at the far end of the High. It was Ascension Day, the fortieth day after Easter, and the city rector, Bob Wilkes, was to lead all-comers on a tour of the city, to beat the bounds of his parish.

This is an English rite of spring at least as deeply rooted as May Day. A few villages across the country still organise a nice country walk, touching markers in the field margins and hedgerows. In Oxford, there being a shortage of hedgerows, it works a little differently: the marker stones are in all kinds of weird places. About seventy of us gathered and were handed canes more normally used these days for tying sweet peas or runner beans. Bob Wilkes' departing cry was: 'To Boots!'

And so he led us on the merriest dance: two hours, twenty-nine stones, each of which he would chalk and we would whack with the cry: 'Mark! Mark! Mark!' This exercise pre-dates mapping: the parish was the fount of authority in most people's lives, and it was important for everyone to know where its writ began and ended. It was especially important for the elders to impress this on the young, and sometimes they would impress it extra hard by whacking their heads against the stones.

'Nobody's supposed to tell you this,' one of the priests on the walk murmured to me, 'but the real reason was that illegitimate children were a charge on the parish. The young men had to be told where the boundaries were to make sure that, when they played, they played away so that someone else would pay for the consequences.'

Actually, *everyone* told me that: the churchmen love the story. And it is always a thrill to feel a connection with the reality of ancient lives. In this parish the ceremony dates back at least to 1428, but the rector thinks it is probably far older. It certainly felt more authentic than May Day.

After Boots, Bob led us into the Clarendon Centre and to Zara's basement, where the stone was at the back of the shoe racks. Then a sudden change of scene, and it was into the garden of St Peter's College, where the stone was half-entangled in vine (pause here for orange juice and bikkies and three cheers for the college for their kindness).

Then under St Peter's wisteria-covered pergola, back out into the streets. Stone 8 was lost in the cellar of O'Neill's Irish bar, which was decreed too dingy to enter, so we decided any old stone would do and whacked that. Past the Bodleian and the Radcliffe Camera, into Brasenose College (coffee and pastries, three more cheers). The only other church still observing the custom, the university church of St Mary the Virgin, had got to Brasenose first – the boundaries meet there. Had we coincided, we might have had to stage a rapper dance with our canes.

Then to the Vincent's Club bike shed, and Marks & Spencer, where four of the city parishes meet, a point marked by a cross on the floor just by the tights, leggings and bikinis. 'Marks! Marks! Marks!' suggested Bob, who was a most genial host. There is of course no more appropriate place for a delegation from this church to visit than an even greater temple which is also dedicated to St Michael.

We also hit (literally) a shop in the covered market ('Mark! Mark! Market!'), and marched through Monsoon and the kitchens of Wagamama before finishing at Lincoln College. There the stone is by a back door to Brasenose, known as the needle's eye, so narrow that Bob had to proceed on his own to mark Stone 29, while the rest of us were led into the refectory for light luncheon and ivy beer, to be followed by three more cheers and undergraduates throwing hot pennies to schoolboys by Jeremy Taylor's staircase. By now we were so drenched in Oxonian arcana that at any moment one felt Great Tom would chime 101 times and the fellows of All Souls might start doing unspeakable things to a mallard.

Having avoided being struck with a stick throughout, two things did strike me. The first was that only in Oxford could seventy-odd people carrying a cross, staffs and canes process through the middle of Marks & Spencer without anyone batting an eyelid. The second was how the ceremony showed off the glorious medieval hugger-mugger of the place. In Oxford, far more than in Cambridge, everything nestles tightly against everything else: town and gown; high and low; vaulted halls and grubby basements; churches, colleges and commerce; Carfax and cars; God, quad and Bod.

I was so enchanted by the whole occasion that when later I strolled down to Magdalen Bridge, now free of drunks and security men, I almost jumped off it, for sheer joy.

When we were in Wagamama's kitchens I caught a sign that read: 'PPE. Don't risk it.' Those initials could be the shibboleth that distinguishes the two Oxfords. What do they stand for? Politics, philosophy and economics? Not much use when rushing out an order for chicken and prawn teppanyaki. Personal protection equipment.

Another question. Name the biggest university in Oxford? The 2012–13 figures, the latest available, suggest the right answer is the obvious one, but in terms of full-time undergraduates it's almost a dead heat between the University of Oxford and the Other One: based way out east, in unremarkable buildings, long past Magdalen Bridge and the roundabout where the tour buses give up and turn round, and not requiring a galaxy of A* A-levels to gain admission. This is Oxford Brookes University, the old polytechnic, elevated in status in 1992, along with the other downbeat polys, in a fit of governmental egalitarianism. Actually, it had the reverse effect: making the old class-ridden stratification of tertiary education something even more prescriptive and almost Hindu in its fine gradations and complexity.

Brookes turned into a success story. From its inception, it was rather good, and innovative, allowing students to put together unusual modules: accounting and history of art, for example, which is a sound basis on which to run an art gallery. Some say it has become less innovative, since almost every university does that kind of stuff now. But it still has pockets of excellence: architecture and nutrition among them.

It had three permanent advantages, though: location, location, location. Local rumour is that the obscure name was chosen (Brookes was a former principal) so it would be high in the alphabetical list of universities. But what mattered was the O not the B. Immediately, students poured in from overseas, confident that no one back home would grasp the difference between studying *at* Oxford and *in* Oxford. But it worked for home-based kids too, especially posher ones who had the balls to go to job interviews and say they went to 'Oxford slight cough University'. And, in the meantime, it's a much nicer place to be a student than Wolverhampton.

There is, however, a third class of young person in Oxford: the locals. In the old days the college menials – the cooks and the porters and the scouts – lived in rented homes nearby. Now the city has turned into Paris: the centre is full of smart *arondissements*, while the workers have been shoved off towards and beyond the *périphérique*. If your first thought on hearing PPE is the Wagamama meaning, out you go to Barton or Blackbird Leys. 'It's a circular gentrification project that operates like a blast radius,' says the Oxford-based film-maker Jon Spira.

Spira's debut film, *Anyone Can Play Guitar*, highly regarded if little shown, was a celebration of the Oxford music scene, which, he says, is unique: 'You look at any of the cities with music scenes that everyone talks about, Liverpool, Manchester, Bristol, Sheffield ... they were based on a single sound and a handful of bands all doing the same thing, which was always short-lived. Oxford has been a boot camp for bands and movements – Radiohead, Supergrass, Riot Grrrl, twee music, shoegaze, math rock.' He could be making this stuff up, but most of it is on Wikipedia. If you can make it there, you can make it anywhere, goes the thesis.

Does this have *anything* to do with university? Nothing to do with the students. 'But my theory is this,' says Jon. 'It's a very inspirational place to grow up. The most amazing people in the world come through Oxford.

I think there's something in the air here.' Not all of it is agreeable. 'You feel an outcast. The university has all these beautiful buildings which you never get to go in. The students come here for three years and they get all that. You're an exile in your own city.'

I got an inkling of what he meant when I went to Oxford Cathedral to light my candle. It's actually part of Christ Church, Oxford's snootiest college, and getting there requires walking across the vast acreage of Tom Quad; it is not at all obvious that one is welcome. I paused momentarily before following my normal rule in moments of uncertainty – keep walking briskly until someone points a gun – and marched past the bowler-hatted flunkeys. It was worth the small risk that they had shoot-to-kill instructions. The cathedral is beautiful, intimate in a chapel-y kind of way, and someone kindly scurried off to find a candle for me because there were none in the shrine. But an Oxford ragamuffin might not feel exactly welcome.

Still, Jon Spira is right about the inspiration. In 1991 the Blackbird Leys estate, the epitome of the Oxford *banlieues*, became briefly notorious when riots started following a crackdown on joyriding. The joyriding involved not just nicking the cars but using them for show-off stunt drives. It was a kind of performance art.

Oxford is a first-class city at the heart of a two-two sort of county. Yet it no longer stands unchallenged as Oxfordshire's chief tourist attraction. Forget Blenheim Palace, forget Churchill's grave. This new phenomenon is Bicester Village, an outlet centre on the outskirts of the once-obscure town of Bicester, which is now better known in China, Brazil and Russia than any of the dreaming spires: 130 shops, nearly all of them belonging to chains even I had heard of; three million visitors a year, many of them arriving by air from Beijing and Shanghai via bus from London.

When I arrived, on a dank Friday afternoon, it was busy – if not quite weekend-frantic – and at a guess nearly half the shoppers were Asian. The shops are all wood-clad: impermanent-looking but gaily painted. My first thoughts were that I had been transported to the village in *The Prisoner* or to some New England movie-set town where something *terrible* was about to happen to the inhabitants.

Nothing in the windows looked cheap to me. And I was beginning to feel the whole thing was ludicrous when I was suddenly spotted by my photographer mate Rick and his girlfriend, Leanne, who is in the fashion trade and understands these places. She explained that although not necessarily cheap, Bicester was cheap*er*. 'If you crave a £1,000 bag and it's worth £250 and you see it for £350, it's a bargain.' So we sat down, had tea and a laugh, and I felt better and went and had another stroll round.

Look, I only bought two shirts, a tie and two pairs of shoes, which I really needed, and honest they were bargains so just shut up, will you? I came to scoff and I stayed to pay.

The original point of Oxfordshire was its positioning: the crossroads of the Wessex–Mercia trade routes. Hence too the positioning of Bicester: an hour from London, just far enough to make visitors feel they have been out in the country. And geography still governs the whole nature of the county. It attracts both weekenders and commuters, a deadly combination.

Take Kingham: 'England's Favourite Village', according to a panel put together by *Country Life* in 2004. Of all the surveys of this kind, this one has had a unique resonance, so much so that Kingham-England's-favourite-village has almost become its official title, like Henley-on-Thames or Stow-on-the-Wold. Absurd, of course – no human can have visited every village. Kingham ticks plenty of boxes (looks, pubs, school, cricket team ...) but the crucial part is that it has a railway station: eighty-six minutes from London. Not fast but doable.

Which of course bumps up the property prices and attracts a particular sort of wannabe villager. The station, like many of those built by the Great Western Railway, is a long way from the village itself, past the *cordon sanitaire* that divides the old now-posh bit from the new unposh bit and then a fair distance again: hardly walkable on a wet or frosty morning. The station car park looked like an Audi showroom.

Oxfordshire's weekenders became notorious after the 2010 election because of what is now known as the Chipping Norton set, various dubious media-trash figures who socialised with each other and with the new prime minister, David Cameron, whose presence could be explained away by his being the local MP. For the others, the attraction was simply proximity to London, which tends to produce undesirable neighbours with the least commitment. Chipping Norton itself is a solid, workaday kind of town, even though its chief landmark, the tweed mill, has long since been turned into 'apartments'. Its inhabitants responded to the publicity by voting for a Labour councillor in 2012.

Most Oxfordshire towns are far more preening: Woodstock; Burford;

red-brick, riverside Goring; Henley, for heaven's sake ... all of them places just a little bit too good to be true to themselves. I was far more taken with Bampton, which used to be known (and, self-deprecatingly, sometimes still is known) as Bampton-in-the-Bush, because the communications were so terrible. It is still out of the way, unless you arrive by RAF jet to Brize Norton, yet it is as handsome as any town in the Cotswolds.

Then I drove east, through Berkshire and the Goring Gap, on a whim and a mission. I had a sudden notion to return to the White House at Ipsden, the pub we used to visit illicitly near my old school. Ipsden is very different from Cotswold Oxfordshire. This is high country: hedgeless fields of maize and rape with views clear across to the Didcot power station. The White House closed in 1995, I discovered, and had become a soft furnishings shop. Soft furnishings or gastro? Which outcome would the old landlord 'Father' (I don't think he had any other name) have hated most? He had very few furnishings, none of them soft. And the only food I remember was pickled eggs.

The village shop in dinky little North Stoke had gone too. And so, as I well knew, had the school. Carmel College – known in its day as 'the Jewish Eton' – went under in murky circumstances in 1997, and the handsome site by the Thames had still found no proper use fifteen years later. The gates were festooned with 'Keep Out' signs, which I decided to ignore. Bloody funny, I thought: after all those years when they were so determined to keep me in and stop me going to the White House.

The place was derelict. It looked somewhere between a Detroit slum and the room laid for Miss Havisham's wedding breakfast. I stood on the pretty little bridge over the cut into the river. This one, I am sure, I did jump off once. No. I'm a scaredy-cat; I was probably pushed.

May 2012

15. *And no knickers*

CHESHIRE

On the first day of the May meeting at Chester, where racing dates back at least to the early sixteenth century, the horse that attracted most attention was an unraced two-year-old colt in the opening race, the Lily Agnes Stakes.

This was mainly because of the identity of his owners. This was the first-ever runner in the pink-and-white colours of Mr and Mrs W. Rooney, Mr Rooney being Wayne Rooney, a Manchester United and England footballer who had become rather famous.

The second point of discussion was the horse's name, Pippy, for reasons expressed rather elegantly in the following day's *Racing Post*: 'Racecourse rumour was rife ... not so much with reports of sparkling workouts as with the information that the origins of the horse's name were rooted in, shall we say, the gynaecological.'

Whatever, Pippy came stone last. But the name of the winner was also intriguing: All Fur Coat. Now, I had always understood that the horse-racing authorities maintained a team of young men with filthy minds whose job was to sniff out hidden meanings in horse names submitted for registration by owners whose wealth may have arrived faster than their discretion (as in the case of Rooney, whose *weekly* wage had just been reported at £250,000).

They are meant to maintain the sport's dignity by catching such suggestions as Wear the Fox Hat or Superbum (its rudeness depends on the stress) or, indeed, Pippy (a vagina – urbandictionary.com). And they must have had a collective off day, because All Fur Coat might be considered at least a marginal case. It is the first half of an old northern saying whose second half forms the title of this chapter.

I have always understood it to mean a state of dress where outward show disguised hidden poverty, like the well-turned-out woman in Gloucestershire whose body was found amid squalor. But there is a collateral meaning, implying a certain over-readiness in the pippy area.

Ach, what the hell? My own selection, Tharawal Lady (Tharawal – an Aboriginal tribe of New South Wales, no offence seemingly intended), came fourth, which set the tone for a disastrous meeting betting-wise. But I adore racing at Chester, anyway. It is a unique racecourse, on the Roodee, a small patch of green below the city walls with a tight track full of turns, more suited to greyhounds than thoroughbreds, and full of singular problems to solve for horses, jockeys and punters.

There is a singular problem for the racecourse management too, since the best view is obtained not from the expensive stands, which are invariably jammed solid, but free of charge from the ramparts above. I suspect many regular racegoers, as the great baseball player and Malapropist Yogi Berra said of a popular restaurant, might say of Chester: 'Nobody goes there. It's too crowded.'

On the other hand, the atmosphere is unique. The course is so close to the centre of a city that is traffic-clogged even in a normal week that arrival by car is insane bordering on impossible. So the crowd progresses from the station through the city and, by the time they have reached the Eastgate clock and the surprisingly named Watergate begins, the racegoers far outnumber the shoppers and the whole place feels as it might have done a century or two ago. It would be no surprise if the ticket touts and hustlers waiting for custom in the Rows were joined by circus freaks or pea-and-thimble men.

The free view is not a significant problem because, frankly, hardly

anyone comes to watch the racing. This year I went on the Thursday, Ladies Day, a northern *hommage* to, and pastiche of, the equivalent day at Royal Ascot. And the horses were the least of the attractions. Wearing saddles and number cloths, they were more demurely clad than half the humans.

On the train, I found myself sitting opposite a woman whose dangly earrings were involved in a photo-finish with her hemline. And the pageant to the station was full of dress-alikes. The style was quasi-regal, that is to say a mix of Gypsy queen and drag queen. Coral was supposed to be flavour of the season, but it just looked pink to me. The prevailing colour scheme was the Rooney racing silks, but without the white: pink mini-dresses and pink shoes, mainly on heels so high that no Chinese peasant with her feet bound could have suffered such discomfort. The substantial portion of skin on display was pink with a tendency towards mottling, and there was the odd outbreak of pink hair too. Some of the women were pretty. But only some. The overall effect as they tittuped and clattered past the Rows was rather alarming: Chester may not have experienced an invasion quite so overwhelming since Augustus's 20th Legion marched in.

The young men were in suits and ties, which is the dress code for the County Enclosure. They mostly wore the ties disrespectfully, loosening them even before arrival at the course. Something similar happens at Australia's great race day, the Melbourne Cup, where the women also dress as they might for clubbing, and the men wear suits, but they don't loosen their ties until much later, conscious as they are that the day is an obeisance to the nearest thing Australia has to a national religion.

In Melbourne the women's fashions are usually more appropriate to the weather. In Chester it had been raining on more than off for weeks, with further downpours forecast. That clearly was going to make no difference whatever to the wearers ('I don't care if it does bloody rain. I've chosen my bloody outfit and that's bloody final'), certain – and correctly so – that they were the centre of attention, and not necessarily clear that there was any alternative entertainment. ("Orses? What piggin' 'orses? Nobody said anything about piggin' 'orses!')

There were no religious undertones, though one did sense that Ladies Day at Chester could stand as the national day of an independent Cheshire, to be presided over by the local spiritual leaders, Mr and Mrs W. Rooney.

The boundaries of Cheshire were much fiddled with in the 1974 reorganisation. Nonetheless Cheshire's image has sharpened in the four subsequent decades. Just like Essex, and for much the same reason. In the North-West, Cheshire fulfils the function of both Essex and Surrey, or, as someone once said of white-ruled Rhodesia, Surrey with the lunatic fringe on top.

Only one major aspect of modern English post-industrial life is centred on the North-West and that's football, so inevitably its young megamillionaires set the tone of the area where most of them live. However, I believe there was always a touch of loucheness about Cheshire. Between the wars its great houses were far enough from London, yet easy enough to reach, and so became convenient venues for goings-on.

Cheshire was then, and to some extent still is, a major centre of industry: chemicals, soap, shipbuilding, oil refineries and cars – Vauxhall in Ellesmere Port and Bentley in Crewe. Tucked away just below Winsford, there are still huge heaps of surprisingly sandy-looking stuff: actually the rock salt which there is never enough of to pour on the roads in cold winters. I like the idea of all those imported East European football stars ending up so close to the salt mines.

In the romantic imagination, though, Cheshire was always a place of dairy cows luxuriating in deep-green fields amid half-timbered houses. In modern times its most memorable monument has become the Jodrell Bank radio telescope, peering above the hedgerows and into the heavens by the railway line to Manchester just north of Goostrey. More and more the county exists now only in apposition to the cities to its north, Liverpool and especially Manchester. Cheshire (like Bedfordshire and Berkshire) no longer has a county council whose job is to nurture it. The footballers are left to set the tone and the fashion.

And the county town is suffering. Chester is a beautiful fake, showily tarted up like the racegoers: most of the black-and-white buildings are not medieval, as they pretend, but Victorian imitations. (And much of the twentieth-century infilling is disgusting – that's the real Watergate Scandal.) The city has not been Cheshire's centre of gravity since at least the Industrial Revolution. However the boundaries are drawn, it is nowhere near the middle of the county but on the western edge, guarding against marauding Welshmen. Stuff seems to wither here somehow: the old League football club went spectacularly bust; there is no professional theatre. If Cheshire wants to be entertained, be it sport or culture, it mostly heads to Manchester.

Chester is best known now for *Hollyoaks*, the most quietly enduring of British soap operas. It has been going since 1995, little noticed even by the tabloids, though it is a staple for the teen magazines. It was devised for Channel 4 by Phil Redmond, inventor of *Grange Hill* and *Brookside*, and a legend in this business, in an attempt to get a series that was both younger and more middle class than the TV norm. The setting is Hollyoaks Community College, which is a notional further education college. According to Mark Lawson, who is an expert on these matters, the point of using a college is that it offers a natural means of bringing the characters together and is also a magnificent way of getting rid of them organically: they can graduate or get another job. In something like *EastEnders* they have to die some horrible death that the producers haven't already used. 'Very canny, Phil, about the grammar of it,' says Lawson, who somehow manages to fit watching this stuff into a busy life as broadcaster and writer.

From my experience as a viewer (one episode), most of the characters are in their late teens or early twenties with busy sex lives. The target audience appears to be a slightly younger age group, mostly female, who would like busier sex lives. The script is cliché-ridden and thus the authentic voice of the young middle class. No one seems to be doing any studying. And the female characters appear to be dressed for Chester Races, just on the off chance it's the right week.

According to Wikipedia, so this must be true, storylines since 1995 have included: 'drug addiction, murder, arson, hit-and-run, abortion, suicide, homelessness, financial problems, interracial relationships, racism, religion, bisexuality, homosexuality, homophobia, sexual confusion, alcoholism, rape, cancer, child abuse, domestic violence, anorexia/bulimia, incest, sexual harassment, general bullying, carbon monoxide poisoning, living with epilepsy, HIV, pupil-teacher relationships, self-harm, schizophrenia, OCD, gambling addiction, shoplifting, fostering, teenage pregnancy, SIDS, miscarriage, kidnapping, brain aneurysm, Gender Identity Disorder and surrogacy.'

All very Cheshire, I dare say.

Liverpool and Manchester have very different relationships with their southern hinterland. Liverpool looks across from its gleaming waterfront to the Wirral peninsula as New York does to the Jersey shore. From the Mersey ferry, Cheshire looks like the municipal dump, and the dominant landmark is a ventilation shaft.

The Wirral has always returned the contempt and was exceedingly cross about being bundled out of Cheshire and into 'Merseyside' after 1974, especially as the home insurers upped their premiums as a result. The Wirral is a mishmash, and little known too, somewhere outsiders almost never penetrate except when the Open Golf is staged amid the bungalows of Hoylake. Years ago I did a series for the *Guardian* called Fourth Division England, about the mostly downbeat towns whose struggling clubs made up the lower reaches of the Football League.

I decided to include Tranmere Rovers. 'Where's Tranmere?' someone in the office enquired, reasonably enough.

'Birkenhead,' I replied.

'Where's Birkenhead?'

When I rang Directory Enquiries, I was asked if I meant Berkhamsted.

Birkenhead was the biggest town in historic Cheshire, though Chester has overtaken it since the days when Cammell Laird turned out a ship every twenty days. The ferry itself is a quaint survival, used mainly by cyclists: other commuters from the Wirral into the city go by car or train. In the autumn of 2011, I took the 7.50 ferry from the Pier Head to Seacombe, against the flow, with two other passengers. Most of the day the boat does tourist trips. On a fine morning, though, with the sun rising behind Liverpool's Old Church, there may not be a lovelier journey to work anywhere in Britain.

I had no idea what to do in Seacombe. But the three-mile promenade between there and New Brighton is pedestrianised and has encouraging markers every 100 metres. The sun was out and the view across the glinting Mersey to the Liverpool skyline was splendid. The walk felt carefree as well as car-free. At Egremont I spotted a small boy heading to school on his own, kicking a football as his grandfather might have done. He may even have been whistling.

The problem here is Cheshire. The beach, if that is the correct word, is disgusting. It's full of folklore: at Guinea Gap in 1849 the locals found a hoard of old coins washed ashore; I spotted two lorry tyres, a football, a good many bricks, an industrial trolley, lumps of concrete and what looked like a giant's condom. And if that lot doesn't put off potential sunbathers, the signs will. At Magazine Prom there were *thirteen* separate warning logos and messages along the shoreline.

DO NOT ...

DIVE

USE INFLATABLES

JUMP

SAND YACHT

BEWARE ...

LARGE SURF OR HIGH BREAKING WAVES

QUICKSAND

SAILING

SLIPWAY

STRONG WINDS

SUBMERGED OBJECTS

TIDES

PERSONAL WATERCRAFT

SLIPPERY SURFACES

Plus five other notices warning of soft sand, silt and mud near the breakwaters; rising tides; tidal flooding on the road; authorised vehicles on the roadway; and 'Beware of slippery surfaces due to algae and marine growth'. Apart from that, there was nothing to worry about.

By the time I got to New Brighton, where the river meets the open sea, the submerged objects were no longer an official threat; kitesurfing had been added, though. The *Daily Mail*, around the same time, found a dozen warnings at a paddling pool in Canvey Island, Essex, that had never had an accident. Pending further claims, the Wirral's thirteen must stand as the record.

There is one further risk in New Brighton: abject depression. It was a resort designed in the 1830s to rival its south coast namesake: 'As New Brighton is likely to become a favourite and fashionable Watering Place, several gentlemen have proposed to erect there a handsome Hotel,' said a contemporary report. With the railways just getting started, it should have been perfect timing. But it never happened for New Brighton. In 1900 came a tower that was bigger than Blackpool's (621 feet v 500) but it was taken down just twenty years later. Though the fresh breezes made it a fair enough place from which to take the train into Liverpool, it did not become a favourite and fashionable Watering Place. And it never will. The seafront was redeveloped in the 1960s with predictably unfortunate results. And the map by the seafront makes the town sound more like an archaeological site than a resort: 'Former site of the Tower' ... 'Former site of the Pier' ... 'Former site of the Pool' ...

Manchester's Cheshire is altogether different. Its heart is the footballing triangle bounded by Alderley Edge, Wilmslow and the stinkingly prosperous village of Prestbury, where flows the pleasant River Bollin, though nowhere near as fast as the lively Bollinger.

The centre of it all is a nothingy sprawl of a village called Mottram St Andrew. And the centre of that, in so far as it has one, is a little cul-de-sac called Collar House Drive, home – according to reports – of the aforesaid Mr and Mrs W. Rooney. I assume theirs was the house with the bird-box security cameras and the 'PRIVATE LAND. NO PARKING' signs.

This area has been affluent since the railway reached Alderley Edge in 1842. It has long attracted wealthy footballers. And its reputation for hedonism is not new either. In 1999 the Rev. David Leaver left his parish in Wilmslow with this tribute to the locals: 'I have never met people who are quite so obsessed with money. Who are so far removed from any sense of spiritual values, let alone organised Christian worship ... In this part of north Cheshire the questions seem essentially materialistic: How much money do you earn? What car do you drive? How big is your car?'

One resident shocked by this was the then TV presenter Stuart Hall: 'He's got it all wrong. When my friends come round we sit in our kitchen and enjoy a steak and kidney pie and a glass of very ordinary claret.' Even these days it is said that Wayne Rooney's tastes are so homely that he always orders pizza margarita. One advantage of being as successful as Rooney is that it is possible to stop trying to impress anyone, eat what you want to eat, be what you want to be.

It is easy to caricature this area. There is still a layer of the comfy old *Manchester Guardian*-reading bourgeoisie, who age gracefully attending the birdwatching and rambling groups organised by the Wilmslow Guild. But old people give way to young; old money gives way to new; old taste gives way to no taste at all. There is even a clash between old and new football money: the generation who got rich and moved here in the early days of the Premier League boom became appalled at the McMansions that were constructed for the new mega-million men of Manchester City.

On a wet Friday morning Mottram St Andrew was far from a peaceful idyll. The place was alive with the sound of construction. The trees were festooned with planning notices seeking to demolish discreet old houses and replace them with indiscreet new ones. Outside one site I heard a builder talking into his mobile discussing some proposed design feature: 'It was supposed to be ducks,' he said, with some exasperation. 'Now it's reindeer.' Very possibly real ones. Top of the range on offer was a three-storey eight-bedroom listed Georgian hall on Macclesfield Road, carefully restored to look modern, with pool, gym, cinema and tennis court: £8.75 million. Every *Hollyoaks* watcher's wildest fantasy.

There are fads and fashions in this market that have a life of their own. There is, or was, a craze for American black walnut flooring: no better than oak, say the experts, but vastly more expensive. It's what their mates have. Footballers slightly less famous than Rooney still have to impress.

And yet only a few miles away is Knutsford, where old money is likely to hold on until the day comes when Knutsford FC of the Cheshire League are taken over by Arab sheikhs to compete with United and City. This was the original of Mrs Gaskell's *Cranford*. When the novel was – rather freely – adapted by the BBC in 2007, they opted to film it in Lacock in Wiltshire, which is everyone's idea of what mid-nineteenth-century England ought to have looked like. The main drag in Knutsford, King Street, is genuinely Georgian, but poses problems: it is narrow, traffic-clogged and full of chain stores. And its most prominent building, the Gaskell Memorial Tower, would seem a bit odd in the midst of Mrs Gaskell's most famous work.

The tower was built in 1908 by a local glove merchant and architectural patron called Richard Harding Watt, whose contribution to Knutsford reduced Pevsner to spluttering rage. As well as the tower, he was responsible, in Legh Road, for what Pevsner called 'the maddest sequence of villas in all England' and 'a witches' sabbath'. I think they are a splendid jumble of architectural styles – here a bit baronial, here Italianate, here a curly bit – which Watt built using whatever he could collect from demolition contractors. They have far more going for them than that bland almost £9 million buggered-up Georgian hall on offer to the footballers. The Legh Road Watt house that came on the market in 2010 looked a snip to me at £2.35 million. Fastidious Pevsnerites should know it would not look remotely out of place in southern California.

And, after all, what was *Cranford* if not a pioneering form of soap opera? And what is southern California if not a very distant outpost of Cheshire?

May 2012

~~~~~~~

In 2014 Wayne Rooney's salary was reportedly increased to £300,000 a week. After two seasons in training Pippy had raced seventeen times and won just once: on the fourth-division all-weather track at Wolverhampton. His total earnings, £6,501, equalled – by my rough calculation – Rooney's earnings in about three minutes playing football. And, poor Pippy, for all the innuendo in his name, had been gelded. Unlike Stuart Hall, who in 2013 and 2014 was sentenced to a total of five years' imprisonment for historic sexual offences. Steak and kidney pie, indeed!

16. *Location, location*

KENT

When Rose and James Rouse retired from commuterdom, they bought a house overlooking St Margaret's Bay, tucked inside a couple of headlands high above the Straits of Dover. Their garden is sheltered from every wind except a straight-up sou'easter, and palm, fig and olive trees thrive there as if they were in a more southerly country. Which they almost are.

In front of them, the busiest shipping route in the world: 350 ships a day passing through the straits east-west, with another 150 going between England and France. And behind that, the not-so-distant shore. One of the neighbouring houses is called Calais View. On a summer's evening, when the sun moves into the right position, it is possible, with a good pair of binoculars, to tell the (French) time by the clock on the Calais *mairie*, and see the back of Napoleon's statue on *la colonne de la grande armée* outside Boulogne. That's what they told me. Rose's welcoming email had, however, contained a very English warning: the view, she said, 'does have a tendency to disappear in the mist as soon as visitors arrive'.

The day had been near-perfect. In Broadstairs, I had padded across the sands in T-shirt and shorts, licking a gelato. It changed the moment I reached the outskirts of Dover. But this was not mist. It was old-fashioned English fog. By the time I got to the Rouses' house, it was barely possible to glimpse the Channel, never mind Bonaparte's bum.

So they offered me a gin and tonic and a roast chicken dinner; James got out his Imray nautical chart and explained the geography; and, before the midsummer dusk, the weather had abated a little. The coastguard cutter *Valiant* hove into view; the Dover lifeboat passed by, towing a boat. 'Probably got stuck on the Goodwin Sands,' said James.

After dark, the Varne lightship made its presence known, and the buoy on the south-western edge of the Goodwins. 'It'll be beautiful again by morning,' I said cheerfully as James showed me to my room. 'Perhaps,' he replied. You can guess the next bit. By the time he took me up on the White Cliffs next morning, it was foggier than ever. Oh well, as the old *Daily Mail* headline had it: 'FOG IN CHANNEL. CONTINENT ISOLATED.'

Assuming that 'abroad' is not all an elaborate hoax, the South Foreland lighthouse, just along from here, is the nearest point in the British Isles to the rest of the world: less than twenty-one miles to the Channel swimmers' destination of Cap Gris Nez; about the same distance as it is to Ashford, as long as you travel by crow rather than the M20. It is this stretch of water, both its narrowness and its very existence, that has defined England since the land link was broken (without a referendum) about 8,000 years ago.

Kent has been the obvious target of external threat, from Caesar's landing – probably near Walmer – to the German bombardments of the Second World War, when the area round St Margaret's was known as Hellfire Corner. The iconography of war continues to dominate Kent. Even the local bitter is called Spitfire.

It has also been the route in and out of Britain for less aggressive purposes, from St Augustine's landing in AD 597 to the Channel Tunnel. Because Augustine settled here, Canterbury became the centre of English Christianity, a position that still matters more than 1,400 years later: the sixteen-strong selection panel that chose Justin Welby as the 105th Archbishop of Canterbury, a line started by Augustine, comprised six members from East Kent and one representing all the foreigners in Christendom.

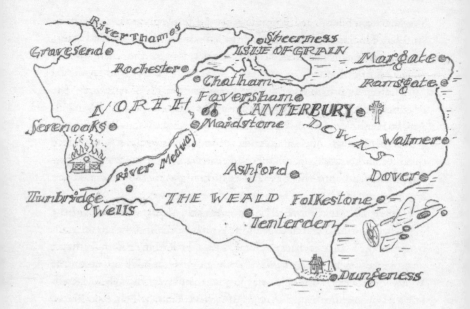

Yet Canterbury's real potency derived not from its 105 archbishops but from one: the forty-first, Thomas Becket, whose martyred bones were enshrined within the cathedral for more than three centuries, until Henry VIII – who understood the power of symbolism – got rid of them.

One way and another, no one has ever been able to rule England without securing not just the coastline but Kent itself: London's rear. And this task has always been a little problematic. Caesar himself referred to *Cantium*, so this county is almost certainly the most ancient of all. It was an independent kingdom until the end of the eighth century, when it was conquered first by Mercia and then by Wessex, which devised the system of shires to maintain the governance of most of England. However, Wessex did not attempt to split up this place, as they did others. 'I suspect they found Kent rather indigestible,' said John Barnes, scholar and former chairman of the Kent Education Committee. And thus the boundaries of this kingdom would have remained pretty much unchanged from the Dark Ages to the 1960s.

Kent is now renowned as the HQ of opposition to progressive thought of all kinds. In their 1985 play *Pravda*, David Hare and Howard Brenton created a thinly disguised version of Rupert Murdoch: the

South African newspaper tycoon Lambert Le Roux, played in London by Anthony Hopkins. In one scene he spelled out his recipe for the perfect newspaper. 'A page of letters,' he said evenly, before pausing with glorious relish. 'All from Kent.'

Yet Kent's prickliness was not always on the side of authority. The Peasants' Revolt (1381), led by Wat Tyler of Maidstone; Jack Cade's march against Henry VI (1450); Wyatt's Rebellion against Bloody Mary (1554) – they all came out of Kent. Even now one might say that it is necessary to hold Kent to rule England: whenever the marginals round the Medway start falling to Labour on a general election night, the Tories know they are done for.

These days Kentish rebelliousness generally takes the form of writing to the papers or, at worst not voting Tory, rather than heading for the capital, capturing the courtiers, beheading them and displaying their heads on pikes, kissing each other – which is how Cade's men added insult to fatal injury. The last great Kentish outrage was probably in 1913, when the suffragettes burned down the Tunbridge Wells cricket pavilion. I do like to imagine the meeting where that idea was cooked up: 'Sisters! I have a plan that will shake the male establishment to its very foundations!'

Despite the suffragettes' best efforts, cricket lives on at Tunbridge Wells, and the annual festival is one of the few of these events left on the county circuit. In Kent – perhaps even more than Yorkshire – cricket remains the one great expression of the county's identity. In the old days the fixture list would move in a steady eastward direction from Blackheath and Gravesend in May towards Dover and Folkestone in August. Now even Kent play almost all their home matches in one place, where the signs at the city boundary proclaim 'Canterbury – World heritage site and home of Kent County Cricket', as though the two were directly connected.

There are Kentishmen, born west of the River Medway, and men of Kent, born to the east. The division hardly ranks alongside Sunnis and Shias and is not a staple of conversation, even on the cricket grounds, though I heard a story of two missionaries bickering about the subject in the Solomon Islands, to the bemusement of the locals. It is somewhat confusing, since the Medway wanders around more than most rivers and in the upper reaches flows south-north, north-south and all sorts. In Tonbridge it flows in several channels at once. The Medway is a practical modern division too, since to the east commuting to London becomes a decidedly optimistic enterprise: the railways of Kent have always been notorious, a situation only marginally alleviated by the new fast trains into St Pancras. And man of Kent is more emphatic, implying someone truly belonging to the county. Kent*ish* sounds altogether more half-hearted. There is an Association of Kentish Men and Men of Kent, with eighteen branches that do good works and are open also to Fair Maids of Kent and Kentish Maids, and no doubt Unfair Maids, Fair Unmaids and indeed anyone else with the slightest Kent connection.

Tunbridge Wells is famously the capital of the Kentish letter-writing habit that Lambert Le Roux so admired: 'Disgusted, Tunbridge Wells' was reputedly invented by the local paper, the *Kent and Sussex Courier*, in the 1930s as a means of publishing phoney letters when the real ones ran short.

As a spa, the town was never much cop: the waters, despite tasting nasty, were quickly shown to be useless. But it discovered its niche as a retirement village for old colonials and their widows. I find Tunbridge Wells handsome and soothing. I love the acid-soil gardens too: this is a place that rests on its rhododendrons as well as its laurels.

On the face of it, Tunbridge Wells is everything you would expect it to be: one of the most imposing buildings in town is a neo-Georgian pile on London Road. A particularly fine post office, perhaps? It turns out to be the bridge club. And the main church is named not after a saint but 'King Charles the Martyr', built in the 1670s, shortly after the Stuart restoration. Which seems to fit with Lambert Le Roux's view of Kent, and our own. But, even in Tunbridge Wells, not everything is as obvious as it seems.

The two slopes that lead to the Pantiles, the now unpantiled shopping centre, are called Mount Sion and Mount Ephraim, names that reek of Puritan influence. And in the 1930s King Charles the Martyr was an improbable stronghold of Low Church thinking. Lord Clonmore, in his wonderfully eccentric 1935 Shell Guide to Kent, says that 'Tunbridge Wells may be considered a fair rival to Tennessee'. Well, lordy, lordy.

What Tunbridge Wells now represents is an idealised version of one aspect of England. And the same can be said of Kent as a whole. Travellers were always entranced: 'plantations and husbandrie in such admirable order, as infinitely delighted me' – John Evelyn; 'very little land which cannot, with propriety, be called good' – William Cobbett.

Especially if they had just returned from exile, glimpsed the white cliffs and then ...

On, on! Through meadows managed like a garden,
A paradise of hops and high production;
... after years of travel by a bard in
Countries of greater heat but lesser suction. –

Byron, not quite on top form

There is a historic reason for Kent's well-cultivated look. Before the Conquest, the default method of inheritance in Kent was not primogeniture but *gavelkind*, whereby the land was divided between all the male heirs. Thus Kent had relatively small farms, all nourished and loved, with very few wild places. (There was a third form of inheritance: borough English, whereby the youngest son copped the lot. Possessing two elder brothers, I regret the rarity of this system.) *Gavelkind* went together with comparative prosperity, self-reliance and the touchiness that produced all the rebellions. Along with good soil and a relatively benign summer climate, it also produced the place that to this day fancies itself as the Garden of England. 'Kent, Sir,' said Mr Jingle in *Pickwick Papers*. 'Apples, cherries, hops and women.'

Hops were Kent's most distinctive product, and the source of the most distinctive visitors: the hoppers – the families who came down en masse on special trains from London for the end-of-August harvest to pick all day, earn a little money, drink till chucking-out time, snore through the night in huts and generally scare the bourgeoisie witless. In 1934, so Dr S. Nicol Galbraith, medical officer for south-west Kent, told the *Observer*, two officials *actually slept* in one of the huts to experience the conditions. There had been no fatalities on any of the 314 hop gardens in his area, he reported, and no complaints from the pickers. 'Nevertheless,' he added, 'everyone concerned, especially the officials, will heave a sigh of relief when the lively Londoners pack up and return to town.' What a wealth of Kentish euphemism is in that word 'lively'. Disgusted would have phrased it differently.

The hoppers' holidays disappeared after the war, partly through their own increased prosperity, partly through mechanisation, and then through the decline of English ale, which meant that continental high-yielding hops replaced the old Kent varieties like Goldings and Fuggles (first propagated by one Richard Fuggle). So the hop gardens dwindled and the oast houses were converted into bijou cottages. Of late the rise of the microbreweries has led to a small-scale recovery. But the lively Londoners have long since been replaced by a few passing Ukrainians.

The apple industry's story is not dissimilar. The National Fruit Collection at Brogdale, near Faversham, has 2,300 different types of apple: all the supermarkets in Britain would sell about ten types. Things reached rock bottom in the 1970s and 80s, when the French Golden Delicious took over, there were grants to grub up old orchards, and the industry and the apples both rotted. But here again there has been a stabilisation: a small-scale trend towards farmers' markets and diversity and localism. Yet the supermarkets' control of the distribution chain has grown only tighter and they want apples that look pretty and stay that way. James Smith, a fifth-generation farmer at Linton, near Maidstone, told me he was experimenting with a yellowy new apple called Opal that he hopes the supermarkets might bite on, because it actually tastes nice.

And then there are cherries, another variation on the same theme. The Kent countryside used to be dominated by great cherry trees, supposedly fifty, sixty feet high. But the size of the trees made picking uneconomic and, in wet summers, the fruit would split before anyone could get to it. Turkey and Spain – cheaper labour, better weather – cleaned up. Nearly all the old orchards vanished. And then there was a little pushback. A new rootstock from Germany allowed for dwarf trees, and polytunnels made the crop more reliable.

As a young man Mike Austen, a retired farmer now working as a guide at Brogdale, used to climb up a ladder with sixty 'stales', or rungs – eight inches between each of them – to pick the cherries in his father's orchard with a basket tied to either his waist or the ladder.

'Was it terrifying?'

'Only when the wind blew.'

In a good year (which 2012 was not) Kent cherries are unquestionably the best in the world. And, as a cherry-holic, I became obsessed, as -holics of all kinds do. The mission was to find a surviving orchard with sixty-foot trees. Sources suggested there might be one by the A2 east of Sittingbourne. And just outside Teynham I did find an ancient orchard, full of cherries ripening towards crimson, on ancient gnarled trees with ancient ladders, broad at the bottom, propped up against them. But they had been well pruned and I doubt if any tree can have been above thirty-five feet.

Over the road was an oast house converted into a white clapboarded cottage that looked as scrumptious as the cherries. Outside was a pinky-gold rose in full cry; its very feminine fragrance wafted through the summer morning, mingling with the hint of diesel fumes from the A2. A Kentish scent. Or scent of Kent. Whichever.

Which brings us, to complete the Jingle-list, to women. I had glimpsed a wonderful specimen on the train to Tunbridge Wells: raven hair, Renoir complexion, lips like, well, cherry – perhaps with an undertaste of hops and apple. Her male companion was talking to her in low, anxious tones.

Then finally she spoke, loudly: 'I'm not fuckin' puttin' up with this any more. I've fuckin' had enough. Fuck it.' She alighted at High Brooms Station. Maybe Kentish women now have to comply with supermarket standards and are grown for looks rather than taste.

Canterbury was rammed solid with tourists, mostly French schoolchildren. The French famously never used to leave the country; now their children are ubiquitous, to no obvious purpose. The cathedral is tucked away behind a pay-wall, literally: reluctant to enforce payment for entry to a place of worship, Canterbury's solution is to place the moneychangers outside the temple and make people pay just to enter the precincts. Since this is not a very visible cathedral, the effect is to render it so irrelevant that the city is more about Fenwicks, Debenhams and M&S than Augustine, Becket and Chaucer.

Kent is the only county with two ancient-foundation cathedrals. Rochester is a midget in comparison, in terms of both size and grandeur, but it is a lot more beckoning. It stands above the high street, which is now given over to the local author in a manner that makes Stratford look restrained by comparison. There was the Dickens House Wine Emporium, the Dickens Café, Peggotty's Parlour, Pips of Rochester, Expectations (a pub), Sweet Expectations, Mrs Bumbles, Little Dorrit Revival (ethnic clothing and gifts), Copperfields Antiques and A Taste of Two Cities (Indian and Bangladeshi cuisine).

The traffic has been diverted since Dickens's day, and the little bits of modern infilling are discreet, so it's all very pleasant, though after a while Dickens's ubiquity becomes overwhelming. I fancied that Nat West might be a Thames-side cut-throat (rather appropriate, on reflection) in *Our Mutual Friend* and Pizza Express some Italian showman in *Nicholas Nickleby*.

Inland Kent is full of likeable towns, many of them filled with croco-
diles of blazered, well-mannered children (I was very taken by Faversham),
and often outrageously beautiful villages like Chiddingstone, which boasts
the oldest shop in the country, which has certainly existed since 1593 and
still has some Tudor counters to prove it.

The owner, Sallie Stevens, had been trying to sell it for some time. But
though one deal had fallen through, she was unperturbed – 'They messed
about. I'm in no hurry' – and clearly addicted to the place. Sallie was a
perky, welcoming chatelaine, who served tea and was happy to let visitors nose round. 'In its way Chiddingstone is perfect,' said Pevsner, and it's
hard to argue, with the castle, seat of the Streatfeilds, shop, pub and school
in a line of beauty across from the church. But Sallie's shop is not quite a
village store in the traditional sense. The window is full of local jewellery
and paintings of cats, with just a small stock of emergency provisions at
the back: cans of beans and nappies and toilet paper and teabags, plus two
freezers offering ready meals for one or two. A ready meal for two, in my
experience, means barely enough for one. Perhaps life in Chiddingstone is
sadder than it appears.

Eventually I realised there were indeed two Kents, though not those
separated by the Medway. The real difference is between the inland and
the long, three-sided coastline. By the sea, beautiful is not the word that
springs to mind. Dickensian, maybe – but not in the sense of Peggotty's
Parlour. The coast is a necklace of poverty, as one local put it, round an
exquisite neck.

North-east Kent is dominated by three islands: Grain, Sheppey and
Thanet, all now physically connected to the mainland yet somehow disconnected, unworldly, spoken of, if at all, by people elsewhere in Kent –
men of, fair maids of and ish-men – with a slight shudder. In the middle is
Sheppey, full of prisons, old people's homes and caravan sites, and it is not
clear which of those might be regarded as the worst in which to end up.

Thanet is dominated by Margate, a shattered seaside resort with
shops called Tatters, Scrag Bag and Bling Bling Bling!, though God
knows this is not a place which ought to be attempting irony. The seafront is dominated by an ugly new art gallery, the Turner Contemporary,
which won great plaudits for an eponymous exhibition when it opened in
2011. I saw no sign of the regeneration it promised. I did see an exhibition
by Tracey Emin, who was brought up in Margate. It mainly comprised

daubs of naked women in vaguely masturbatory poses. The other visitors were nearly all over eighty or under ten, and looked confused. One elderly gent was at the reception desk, asking plaintively: 'What happened to that exhibition about the Queen? I wanted to see that.'

North of the Medway towns lies the Isle of Grain. On the opening page of *Great Expectations* Pip talks about 'five little stone lozenges, each about a foot and a half long, which were arranged in a neat row beside their grave, and were sacred to the memory of five little brothers of mine – who gave up trying to get a living, exceedingly early in that universal struggle'. In so far as any work of fiction can be rooted in a real place, there can be little doubt that this one starts in the graveyard at Cooling, next to the marshes, themselves bordered by the 'low leaden line' of the Thames estuary, and that it was here that Pip was confronted by Magwitch and the cheery, well-remembered greeting: 'Keep still, you little devil, or I'll cut your throat.'

Dickens himself came out here for larky picnics from his home at Gad's Hill and, as one American guest recalled, once set a tablecloth on a flat gravestone and emptied the hamper on to it. And here, surrounding the tombs of Micheal (*sic*) and Jane Comport, are thirteen heartbreakingly small lozenges – to my eyes more like torpedoes or curiously shaped fish – of tiny Comports and closely related Bakers, who died aged between one month and seventeen months between 1771 and 1854, six years before the opening chapter of the novel was serialised. Given that there are thirteen graves here and only five in the book, this must be a rare case of a novelist, especially one who was a journalist by training and instinct, taking reality and understating it for dramatic purposes.

But this entire corner of Kent feels stranger than fiction. It was no day for picnics when I went to Cooling: I arrived in one of the cloudbursts that characterised the summer of 2012, so intense that the narrow lane to Allhallows and Allhallows-on-Sea started to flood and I hastily turned round for fear I would be stranded for ever in the marshes and forced to threaten children for food, like Magwitch. I returned later, on a morning of wan sunshine, and made it to Allhallows-on-Sea, walking along the deserted shingle, piled high with cockle shells.

This, according to Ian Jack of the *Guardian*, is 'the Ozymandias of seaside resorts', destined in the 1930s to have '5,000 houses, several hotels, a zoo and Britain's largest swimming pool, with a wave-making machine'. Then the war came. Instead it acquired a few houses, mainly occupied by exiled Cockneys, a caravan park and a fine view of the Grain oil-fired power station. And soon, in the dreams of Boris Johnson, the mayor of London, it is due to have an even more spectacular view of London's next airport, to be built out in the estuary, to blight the lives of much of Kent and Essex while relieving the pressure on the eardrums of Johnson's own voters.

The coastline perks up after it reaches the eastern edge of Kent. Broadstairs is the star turn. Though it was a Tuesday in term time, the sands were packed when I was there (in contrast to deserted Margate), mainly with school parties. One was from an Islington primary, one of whose teachers complained that it was a poor choice for the annual outing: 'There's nothing to do here.' Nearby was a smaller group, from a local private school, in smart blue polo shirts and shorts. These children knew exactly what to do, and were using their spades to bury each other. Behind us was yet another Dickens shrine, Betsey Trotwood's House. Having overdosed on Dickens, I asked the lady at the tourist information booth if she could direct me to the boyhood home of Edward Heath. 'That's a first,' she said.

The prosperous bit of coast stretches as far as St Margaret's. Then comes Dover, which shares with London and Edinburgh the honour of having its own name in French. It is only by going to Dover that one can understand the appeal of Canterbury. Cruise liners dock here, for heaven's sake. Sensible operators get the passengers out fast, preferably with the coach curtains drawn, up to Dover Castle, the White Cliffs and beyond. In Dover, Poundland has a bigger branch than Marks & Spencer.

There is a seafront, which can be accessed from town by a dingy subway marked 'Seafront and Factory Outlet'. It is dominated by a large block of neo-Stalinist council flats and what might be a defunct hotel, a multistorey car park or an office block belonging to an extremely secret branch of British intelligence. One can only conclude that MI7, or whoever is in the blacked-out block, had determined that to protect the nation's security it is necessary to make England's front line so repulsive that any enemy would take one look and conclude the country was not worth fighting for.

It would be easy to imagine Dover was the most depressed and depressing town in the kingdom, were it not so close to Folkestone. And Margate. And, across the Sussex border, Hastings. In the midst of this lot, there is a far more fascinating place. And that, truly, is the end of the line.

The Romney, Hythe and Dymchurch Light Railway runs thirteen and a half miles from Hythe to Dungeness, the southernmost point of Kent.

It is a fifteen-inch-gauge railway, opened in 1927, when improbable lines elsewhere in the country were just starting to close, and the tiny carriages were somewhat more accessible for the average holidaymaker than they are in the supersize era.

It was the fantasy of a pair of racing drivers from the whizz-bang-prang era, Captain J. E. P. Howey and Count Louis Zborowski, who was killed before the line could open when he wrapped himself round a tree at Monza, as one did. Howey was rich enough and determined enough to carry his dream through to fruition.

And what a wonder it is. It does not connect with any mainline railway; it hardly seems to connect with the real world at all. It takes sixty-eight minutes to do the length of the line, at an average speed of just under 12 mph. Yet it survives and thrives, and even has a life beyond the tourist industry, running a daily school train. Clearly, some of Kent's more ample visitors get a certain pleasure by corseting themselves into the seats.

The fog that had enveloped St Margaret's had not lifted. But the destination would be a weird one whatever the weather. As you approach the sea at Dungeness, two lighthouses appear, along with two nuclear power stations. Close to the headland, the railway takes a sweeping loop across the wide expanse of shingle and deposits you just outside the perimeter wall of Dungeness A. The following sign greets the innocent holidaymaker:

EXPOSURE TO RADIATION BY
- INHALATION
- INGESTION
- ABSORPTION THROUGH OPEN WOUNDS
COULD CAUSE HARMFUL HEALTH EFFECTS.

Well, welcome to Dungeness. Have a nice day.

As I arrived, two well-protected figures wearing dark glasses pulled mysterious pieces of luggage along the perimeter wall. Perhaps they were armed with Geiger counters to deal with a nuclear crisis that might endanger the planet. Perhaps they were just fishermen. There were a lot at the water's edge, having spent a day of their lives peering at the grey Channel in return for a few undersized whiting. Even so, it felt as though the apocalypse had already happened and that we were among the handful of survivors eking out a fragile existence in a perpetual nuclear winter.

There is no defined boundary between beach and anything else at

Dungeness. It is all just one vast expanse of shingle, decorated with the great blue spikes of viper's bugloss and dotted with, well, what exactly? Buildings of a kind, for sure, but what kind? Some of them looked like outcrops of the power station. But many of them seemed to be loved and lived in.

Most were just huts or shacks or converted railway carriages. It was a sort of village, of a peculiarly higgledy-piggledly kind. It had none of the indicators of an English village: no fences, most notably; hardly any sign at all of where the public ended and the private began. It might have been some marginal community in Arizona: what they call hardscrabble. Difficult to imagine that any member of the council planning department had ever set foot here.

Dungeness became known as a place to live because of the late film-maker Derek Jarman, who in this bleak setting endured his long, bleak final illness and reached the culmination of his bleak – indeed apocalyptic – artistic vision. But he also cultivated the garden of Prospect Cottage. The lighthouse being closed until July, and the power station permanently closed to visitors since the post 9/11 panic, the garden was the obvious place to visit, though it was a long, slow trudge across the yielding stones.

It was still maintained, nearly twenty years after Jarman's early death, by his partner, Keith Collins. It is not exactly Sissinghurst: the range of plants that will grow on this terrain is limited. But it constituted a defiant affirmation of life. Especially with the wisps of mist passing by, the sound of the foghorns to seaward and, most numinous of all, the shrill whistle of the second-last train of the day heading into the station.

As I waited to become the only passenger on the last train, I got talking to Peter, the station master, indeed sole employee. I remarked that some people might find this a strange place to be deposited. 'Hmmm, yes,' he said thoughtfully. 'Not everyone's cup of tea.'

It hadn't been his cuppa either, originally. But his wife had desperately wanted to get out of London and he had come to love Dungeness, especially after this improbably handy and agreeable job came up. It was a real community, he said, where everyone looked out for each other. Even the nuclear people were good neighbours; they had a lot of resources in case of emergency. And, this being south-east England, property was much in demand.

He pointed out a white-painted bungalow, the nearest house to the outer wall of the power station, and reminded me of a story that was in all the papers in 2009: it had been advertised for sale at £247,000 accompanied by a skilfully taken photo showing it alone in the open landscape against a bright blue sky. Following complaints from a flabbergasted potential buyer, the press showed the view from the other direction, complete with rather domineering neighbour.

'Remember that?' asked Peter.

I did, vaguely.

'Put the price up, all that publicity. Sold for £270,000 in the end.'

It might be a good long-term investment. Very long term. Dungeness A, unlike its neighbour Dungeness B, has already been decommissioned and, following the complex processes that attend the closure of a nuclear power station, will be demolished ... in 2097. I repeat, 2097. By which time the Queen's great-great grandchild may be on the throne of England, if the throne still exists, if England still exists. All rather Derek Jarman.

There was one last thing I wanted to do in Kent. On my very first day, I had driven past an old isolated, cottagey pub outside Plaxtol, between Sevenoaks and Maidstone: the Golding Hop, a name suffused with Kentish heritage. 'Beers from the wood,' said a peeling sign outside. It was early morning and there was no chance of a drink. But it had looked wonderful, a thought supported by an internet search: 'I've been visiting this pub for more than 30 years, and the place hasn't really changed at all, apart from the fact that the door now opens outwards,' reported one drinker.

And indeed it was as expected. The landlord was suitably indifferent to a stranger but not to his beer: a pint of Adnams, which was drawn, though not quite from the wood, from a barrel out the back. It was splendid. Except that, between the counter and the bar billiards table, was a television, blaring out an ITV soap opera. Not even one I had heard of.

The fog in the Channel; the diesel fumes that mingled with the perfume of roses; the beguilingly isolated bungalow right next to a nuclear power station; the near-perfect pub dominated by a fucking television set. Kent is a pearl of a county but there's a heck of a lot of grit in those Whitstable oysters.

June 2012

17. *Good morning, Your Grace*

DERBYSHIRE

In mid-August, four days before the big day, I rang Janet Quier just to double-check the schedule. Her husband answered, I got a one-word reply and then the line went dead. As one-word replies go, it was extremely helpful. The word was 'petalling'.

What it conveyed was that the Taddington Well Dressing and Flower Festival was going ahead as planned on the Saturday; that she was engaged in the most intricate and important part of the operation and was far too busy to talk to the likes of me; and perhaps (I never did discover whether this was true) that I had offended him by asking for Mrs Queer rather than Mrs Quire.

Taddington is a small, high, usually nippy village 1,000 feet above sea level in the Peak District, bypassed by the A6. Well-dressing is Derbyshire's defining tradition. From Chester Green in early May to Hartington in September, you could tick off several festivals every weekend and visit just about every parish in the county, marvelling at the inventiveness and skill of the inhabitants.

Each village decorates its well with a large work of art, usually with a religious or topical theme, made primarily from flowers. It is an odd custom, substantially confined to Derbyshire, perhaps because much of the county is on limestone, through which rainfall is inclined to slither away. This makes water particularly precious: something to be honoured, thanked and appeased and maybe indeed worshipped, even in a place as habitually wet as the Peak District. The notion is almost certainly pagan in origin, though the Church of England, in its adaptive way, eventually put itself centre stage. The current vigour of the tradition, however, is thoroughly post-religious. When I turned up at Taddington church, well before the 2.30 start, the attendant fete was already in full cry, complete with bouncy slide and pillow fights, and the centrepiece was getting comparatively little attention.

This village is not considered to be in the well-dressing premier league, which is headed by Tissington, north of Ashbourne, where the custom was first noted in the fourteenth century. But in Taddington it was still an awesome operation: months of preparation – soaking the wooden frame to make it thoroughly moist and holding; 'puddling' the clay base to create the surface; choosing a subject; creating a design; pricking out the template; finding the raw materials, especially begging or, *in extremis*, buying the flowers; and, then, in a final week of frantic activity by the ladies of the parish (these days – it used to be man's work), making it all happen. That's the petalling. Thousands of petals, plus bracken and bark and cones and moss and eggshells and, in the case of Taddington, hundreds of mussel shells, scrounged from a fish restaurant in Southend by a villager on holiday. Seventy-six different materials, the designer Diana Syder told me later, for a life-size but very temporary artwork. No wonder Janet Quier was unavailable.

In 2012 almost every village wanted a design incorporating the Diamond Jubilee and/or the Olympics. However, Diana, who is a poet and painter in real life as well as doing the well design *pro bono*, was rather keen on getting some creative satisfaction and was very anti the idea of doing the season's clichés. She opted for the moon landing, which did after all occur in the Queen's reign. 'The decision was democratic,' she said. 'We invite suggestions and then go away and make a decision. So not democratic.'

A respectable number of villagers and a few visitors dragged themselves away from the white elephant stall and the tea tent for a brief service. Then some of us processed up the hillside towards the High Well, where

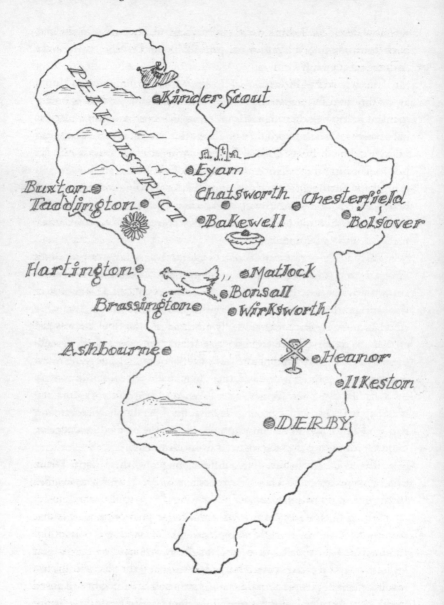

the children choose the design (they went for Union Jack and Olympic rings). There I met Janet Quier who – free of petalling for another year – was very friendly. Normally, the hill is alive with meadow cranesbill. It was now denuded. 'I think we've raided them all,' she said. On the way back down, we passed a garden still in full bloom. 'Ooh,' she said, 'those hydrangeas got away.'

This is a riveting little subculture, dependent on the flowers in bloom at the time and so completely different in Taddington, with its late summer slot in the well dressing calendar, to, say, Tissington at Whitsuntide. 'The flowers you'd think would work, like roses and geraniums, don't last,' Diana explained. 'So we do have to buy in some stuff like chrysanths. It's brinksmanship, whether you've got enough.'

The mussel shells were mainly for Neil Armstrong's spacesuit, along with (inter alia) cabbage, yarrow and sheep's fleece. His helmet was made from the cut-off bottoms of Camembert boxes. The moon's surface included grey gravel (squirrelled away when they resurfaced the road), dead lavender flowers, black banana skins, a whole variety of tiny shells and everything except green cheese. The petals go on last, because otherwise they might not survive the week. Diana's particular forte is the use of dead rhubarb leaves: her own discovery, she likes to think.

Much of this she told me later in an email. At the time she was just anxious to sit down: 'I'm tired beyond exhaustion,' she sighed, though there was another exhausting week ahead with a steam engine rally on the Sunday, quiz night on Monday, lanes race and barbecue Tuesday, variety night on Thursday (dress code: red, white and blue) and a summer serenade on Saturday, when the dressings come down, with luck, before they wither. That turned out to be the day Neil Armstrong died, making the design seem eerily perceptive rather than idiosyncratic.

'The lengths to which we go are not unique to this village,' Diana said. 'I'm interested to know why people well-dress, why people push themselves to do this. For me, it's an offering. I'm not Christian, but it's an offering.' I could suggest two other possible explanations. One is that winters are long, dank and dark up here, full of wind and wuthering: there is plenty of time to slump and watch television. The other is that well-dressing constitutes community art, which in most places in Britain involves council grants and paid team leaders and the whiff of organised worthiness. The whole process of well-dressing is based on oral tradition: there is no book to explain which petals work well and which don't. The knowledge is handed down, and everything happens from the bottom up, naturally, like water springing out of the ground. And that seems to me very Derbyshire.

It was the columnist Matthew Parris, once a Derbyshire MP, who put the thought into my head when he was commending the little market town of Wirksworth: 'It's one of those places that creates its own world.' Wirksworth is indeed unusually interesting. There are a fair number of what one resident calls 'lesbian potters and picture framers'. But here the relationship between different sections of the community is more balanced than in, say, Hebden Bridge: Top Ken's Discount Store stares at Traid Links and Le Mistral café du vin without looking threatened. And this mix of old and new gives the town an inner strength that would enable it to get along nicely if ever Brussels, Strasbourg, Westminster, Derbyshire County Council and Derbyshire Dales District all chose to mind their own business. Wirksworth might have been entirely taken over by camomile-tea drinkers but for its ugly name. Were it called Snowfield (as George Eliot rechristened it in *Adam Bede*), the whole place would be decamping to the new-agey Star Disc in Stoney Wood for Mind, Body, Spirit Events (as some do anyway), and I would fear for Top Ken and the chippy. But it isn't; it's called dreary old Wirksworth. And it wirks.

A lot of other places in the county have a similar air of self-sufficiency. Derbyshire is long and thin, and its only substantial place, Derby, is right down the bottom. Derby is a working-class city (Rolls-Royce, Toyota, Bombardier Trains). It does not have a university with a status to match Nottingham, Leicester or Sheffield. It does not have regional head offices or civil servants or even the county council (which is based in Matlock). So the middle class do not commute en masse into Derby.

The M1, the A61 and the Midland main-line railway serve the eastern edge of the county, between Derby and Chesterfield, which is the ugly bit. The only other route north is the A6, which, its low number notwithstanding, hardly has any dual carriageway (except, oddly, the Taddington bypass) and is not a fast route for commuting.

The railway across Monsal Dale once reduced Ruskin to lyrical fury ('The valley is gone and the Gods with it, and now, every fool in Buxton can be at Bakewell in half-an-hour, and every fool in Bakewell at Buxton'). It closed in 1967, mourned ever since by the sentimentalists who are Ruskin's heirs. But reopening it would be a disaster for Derbyshire. True, on summer weekends, the Peak is overrun by motorised trippers from Sheffield, who regard the area as an extension of their back gardens. But the absence of commuters and second-home owners (in any case a much weaker phenomenon in the North than the South) is the making of communities strong enough to dress wells.

A friend of a friend moved from the city into a big Derbyshire country house. Very quickly, he received a visit from one of the locals, who informed him that their garage was the petalling shed. The newcomer began to stutter and say that the garage was full of boxes and perhaps next year it might be a bit easier –

'So you'll be moving the boxes.'

He was further informed that it was customary for the ladies to be given tea and the gentleman helpers whisky. Wisely, he complied, and has been very happy in the village. You move to Derbyshire on Derbyshire's terms. I like that.

So where are we? Is this the North or what? Certainly, somewhere in Derbyshire, the North begins. Julian Glover, writer and historian, thinks there is a border just south of Brassington where the hedgerows give out and the drystone walls take over. Neil Hallam, journalist and naturalist, thinks it may come on the Via Gellia near Matlock, the most northerly redoubt of the clustered bellflower. John Beatty, photographer and geologist, says the North starts where the limestone of the low hills – what locals call the White Peak – gives way to the millstone grit of the real uplands, the Dark Peak. Indeed, as I drove around with John, we may have identified the very spot: Newhaven Cottage, in the village of Sparrowpit – its southern half built of limestone, its northern half of gritstone.

All these erudite friends agreed on one thing about Derbyshire: I had to visit Chatsworth, gracious home since 1549 of the Cavendish family, latterly Dukes of Devonshire. I kept trying to tell them, pompously but gently: this isn't a guidebook; I'm not interested in stately homes; I couldn't give a stuff about sodding dukes; I'm trying to grasp the *essence* of each county. Sometimes, as with the bloke who had bought the petalling shed, it takes a while to grasp what is going on. No one can understand a thing about Derbyshire without understanding Chatsworth.

Most stately homes sit behind high walls and iron fences past which the public may or may not be admitted at set times, to be ushered out with a sigh of relief. Here, the main road actually runs through the park. The house stands out against the ridge, beckoningly. There are no fences to speak of and no one demands any money until you approach the very door. Part of a Derbyshire childhood is turning up and swimming in the river on a hot afternoon, without handing the Devonshires a farthing.

Lightly disguised by their confusing title, the Devonshires *are* Derbyshire. It is a sort of grand duchy, like Luxembourg, and they are the hereditary, not rulers exactly, but distributors of largesse and centres of attention. Their memorials dominate Derby Cathedral. In some circles, their activities are the main topic of conversation: Is the 12th Duke, 'Stoker', a patch on his dad? What *has* the Duchess done to that restaurant? How is the dear old Dowager? (Debo, the last of the Mitfords). I expect there are some dinner tables where people still gossip knowingly about Georgiana, the Regency beauty and wife of the 5th Duke, or Bess of Hardwick (1521–1608), serial-marrier and matriarch of the dynasty. 'The people of Derbyshire are extremely proud of the Devonshires,' said Neil Hallam, who is a hardbitten kind of journalist, 'because they put themselves about. If you ask them to the opening of a WI tearoom, they go.' The late Duke certainly put himself about, when he was out of the county, in a different kind of way. He was and is still regarded with great affection, both within Derbyshire and, I believe, by several London ladies *d'un certain age*.

The beauty of Derbyshire owes a huge amount to the family's good taste. The estate village of Edensor (pronounced Ensor) is a marvel; built circa 1840 for the Chatsworth workers, it combines the unity of architectural theme of the best estate villages plus remarkable individuality. It is as if all the most charming Victorian country railway stations had been collected from their various branch lines and dropped in a single place. The different styles of chimney are peculiarly fascinating. It is only when you learn that Edensor was built because the previous village was spoiling the ducal view that one is reminded that the Devonshires did not get where they are entirely by philanthropy and their devotion to the physical process that produces dynasties. We shall return to this point.

If Chatsworth is a more convincing focal point of Derbyshire than either Derby or Matlock, this does not make it a one-dimensional county. It is more protean than most. The alluvial flatlands of the south are hard to distinguish from north Leicestershire or south Nottinghamshire. The pinched ex-mining towns of the east are a world away from the Peak. A journalist from *The Times* walked into a pub in Heanor in the 1970s and asked for a dry white wine. 'Are you taking the piss?' said the landlord. 'It's not fooking Christmas.' Dry white is easily obtainable, however, in frigid, genteel Buxton. And the mills along the Derwent Valley (or, more relevantly now, along the A6) have been declared a world heritage site by

UNESCO – in the words of one local, mingling delight and astonishment, 'on a par with the Taj Mahal'.

George Brown, deputy prime minister in the 1960s, an unforgettable yet seemingly forgotten politician who was MP for Belper, once expressed bemusement about the county: 'I can't make head nor tail of Derbyshire. Every time I think I've got it pinned, I find another bit where everybody's totally different.'

It is full of surprises, full of quirkiness, full of eccentricity. There is, for instance, Matlock Bath, the only inland seaside resort I have ever encountered. It has an esplanade complete with amusement arcades, aquarium (the old Victorian baths, now handed over to the carp), chip shops, a sort of beach pavilion, and pubs and cafés where you can sit outside and admire the view. Which is the traffic on the A6. There is the river behind that, but it is inaccessible and almost invisible. There is even a kind of Sunday afternoon *passeggiata*, which comprises the motorcyclists strolling up and down admiring each other's machines. In the autumn there are illuminations, just like Blackpool.

There is Chesterfield, an unprepossessing kind of town, given distinction by its crooked spire and Queen's Park, the loveliest of all county cricket grounds. (In the days of its best-known recent MP, someone said the word Chesterfield was famous for the four Cs: 'cigarettes, chairs, the crooked spire and Tony Benn.') And then there are the pubs. The Rutland Arms, Bakewell, is famous for Bakewell pudding, which was supposedly invented in 1820 when the cook got muddled as to the recipe for jam tarts. (Bakewell tart was invented much later, probably a long way from Bakewell.) To some, the pub is better known because it once had a chef who pissed in the soup.

Nearby is the Barley Mow in Bonsall, home of the world hen-racing championships, and once named as the world capital for UFO sightings, mostly around chucking-out time. And there are other pubs I found, in remote corners of the Dark Peak, including the one where I was immediately greeted by a baby ferret. I daren't name these places because (a) I may have imagined them and (b) if they do exist, the very act of mentioning them could cause them to implode and begin serving the pork scratchings on a bed of braised cabbage with a roast pepper coulis.

On a muggy, midgy Sunday morning John Beatty walked me up from the centre of Hayfield, past the Bowden Bridge car park, alongside the

Kinder Reservoir, until we rounded the bend. There ahead of us was William Clough – a place, not a person – and, above it, Kinder Scout, highest peak in the Peak and the scene, in 1932, of one of the most famous and most effective acts of civil disobedience England has ever seen.

If altering county boundaries ever made sense, there was a long-standing case for Derbyshire, which is not short of mountains, handing Kinder over to Lancashire as a gift to the populace of Manchester. On a clear day (even rarer in the smoke-ridden Manchester of 1932 than now) it can be seen from the higher points of the city. It stood taunting the substantial portion of the citizenry whose delight was to escape and tramp the mountains. An obsession with fresh air ran strong in Manchester, an antidote to the grimness of everyday life, summed up in what has become the ramblers' anthem, written by one of the participants, Ewan MacColl:

> *I'm a rambler, I'm a rambler, from Manchester way.*
> *I get all my pleasure the hard moorland way.*
> *I may be a wage slave on Monday.*
> *But I am a free man on Sunday.*

Several hundred walkers had arrived from Manchester to walk on Kinder, traditional common land which at that time was maintained as a private grouse moor with no public access. It was owned, natch, by the Duke of Devonshire. The intention of the trespassers was very clear: it had been signalled in the newspapers well in advance. The events of the day are matters of dispute and interpretation, along with the precise agenda of the organising body, the British Workers' Sports Federation. But after its leader, Benny Rothman, twenty years old and barely five foot tall, had fired up the group with a speech on a rock in the car park, everyone marched to the clough, where there was a confrontation with a platoon of ducal gamekeepers who had appeared over the ridge. Five ramblers, including Rothman, were jailed for up to six months on charges that included grievous bodily harm (an obvious exaggeration) after a ridiculous trial, in one of those mad acts of martyr creation to which embattled authority has been addicted from at least the time of Pontius Pilate.

The motives and methods of the trespassers were much criticised at the time, by older and more deferential ramblers. The case, however, was hardly disputed. As Christopher Hobhouse put it in the 1935 Shell Guide to Derbyshire: 'A very large proportion of the forty miles of open country between Manchester and Sheffield is denied to the teeming population of these towns for the benefit of ten or twelve sportsmen. There is, of course, nothing whatever to be said in defence of this state of affairs.'

The martyrdom sealed the outcome, since Kinder is no longer a private grouse moor and the right to roam is enshrined in legislation – and at appropriate intervals ever since the occasion has been marked with a ceremony on the spot. In 2002, for the seventieth anniversary, there was no Rothman, who had died a few months earlier. There was, however, someone else: the 11th Duke of Devonshire, then eighty-two. Since he was only twelve at the time of the trespass, he had an alibi. He did not use it.

He rose gingerly. 'I am aware that I represent the villain of the piece,' he said. 'I am only too happy to take this opportunity to apologise for the conduct of my grandfather seventy years ago. The great trespass was a very shaming event for my family. But from that great evil and those appalling sentences has come great good.' He said he loved to sit in his study and watch the ramblers crossing Chatsworth Park. 'I like to think that I have tried to redeem that evil.'

Amid the moors towards Sheffield is the village of Eyam (pronounced Eem). It would attract visitors in its own right had nothing ever happened here. But in 1665 it did. A box of cloth arrived from London, where the plague was raging. The recipient was dead within days. Within weeks, the disease had spread across the village. The rector, William Mompesson, persuaded his parishioners to isolate themselves so the plague could spread no further. It meant that most of the villagers would die: about 250, or three-quarters of the population, according to the usual estimate.

The most moving version of the story I have found is, surprisingly, in Arthur Mee's *The King's England*, the 'New Domesday Book' of the 1930s. His team of writers were obliged to use a style that was consistently florid, upbeat and cringe-making. But someone rose to this occasion: 'This village of grief and despair was a place of quiet heroism, the heroism of a little band who stayed to serve, of a panic-stricken people who in the very face of death resigned themselves to follow the path they were asked to tread.'

There are heartbreaking vignettes at every turn in Eyam. There is Cucklett Delf, where Mompesson brought his diminishing flock as the plague took hold, preaching from a rock to each family group, isolated from each other. Here one village girl, Emmott Sydall, would call plaintively to her lover, Rowland Torre from Stoney Middleton, until she herself fell victim and her calls were silenced. There was the woman from Riley Side who buried her husband and six children. And there was Catherine Mompesson, the rector's wife, who tended the sick until her own death, shortly before the disease faded away in November 1666. 'The passing bell ceased to toll, and the graveyard ceased to take the dead,' said Mee.

I had been to Eyam before and thought it was a 'thin place', in the mystical sense I learned at Little Gidding. It is the quintessence of Derbyshire self-sufficiency: the villagers understood what had to be done and did it (as usual, with a little help from the Devonshires, then mere earls, who arranged provision of supplies at the parish boundaries).

It is hard not to feel desolate on hearing this story. But Eyam is doing its best to wreck it. It had just acquired a new set of interpretative boards, which introduced the story thus: 'Eyam was not a good place to be between 1665–1666.' This is one of the few sentences on these boards that is not finished with an exclamation mark: 'The First Plague Victims Lived Near Here!' 'Eyam Stocks – still in use today!' 'Follow the Eyam Visitor Code!' 'We Like to Celebrate – it's a Tradition!' This is a place to come and be humbled by our forefathers' self-sacrifice, not be patronised by a subliterate dolt.

In Clay Cross, on the back of an electricity substation, there is a heroic-looking mural, of the sort often found in Ulster. It depicts a motley collection of protesters and the slogans 'Clay Cross UDC will Not Implement the Act' and 'People's March for Jobs 1983'.

This a little confusing, since Clay Cross Urban District Council did not exist in 1983. It had been abolished nine years earlier. The abolition was not personal – it was part of the general stuff-up of local government – but it might have been. The act that Clay Cross refused to implement was the 1972 Housing Finance Act, which insisted on rises in council house rents. In a way Clay Cross kept its promise, but only because it was about to disappear anyway.

The mass trespass is memorialised in the Bowden Bridge car park, on the wall of what used to be New Mills police station and in the hearts of everyone who climbs Kinder. Clay Cross has this absurd mural, scrunching together all the Left's lost battles. All the town's intransigence has ever achieved was sending to Parliament, as part of the Bolsover constituency, Dennis, the clownish brother of the leading Clay Cross rebel, David

Skinner. And there, for more than forty years, Dennis Skinner has sat, below the gangway on the Labour benches, making fatuous interjections.

The town and most of the people have the weary, run-down look common to old pit villages. But Clay Cross – with fewer than 10,000 people – now has a vast 24-hour Tesco Extra that overwhelms the place, ensuring the aged and lame, who seem to make up most of the population, have to walk a great deal further from the bus stops than they did to get to the old Co-op. There cannot be a smaller town in the country with a bigger Tesco. There's irony for you.

Near the mural I got talking to one ex-pitman, a bit too old now for a job on the checkout. 'That used to be a through road,' he said, with an air of resignation. 'But all roads lead to Tesco.'

We got on to the subject of the Devonshires, as one does in Derbyshire. 'Oh, Chatsworth is a lovely place,' he said. 'I met the old Duke once. Very nice gentleman. But it's a business, isn't it, Chatsworth?

'Got to make a living,' he added, almost breaking into song. 'Everybody's got to make a living.'

August 2012

~~~~~~~

In 2014 the Ordnance Survey calculated that the furthest point from the sea in the UK was Church Flatts farm at Coton in the Elms, seventy miles from the nearest mean low water line of The Wash. It was the home of Harry and Joyce Blackwell, who received the news with amused nonchalance. 'I don't think I've been to the sea since 1988,' Joyce told the BBC.

Deborah, Duchess of Devonshire, died in September 2014, aged ninety-four. There was much affectionate reminiscence.

18. *Damsons in distress*

WESTMORLAND

The Westmorland County Show, which dates back to 1799, takes place at Lane Farm, Crooklands, on the second Thursday of September and I was assured that the 2012 show, the 213th, would happen come hell or, what was far more likely, high water. War and pestilence have forced it to be cancelled, but never the mere weather.

'Bring your wellies,' warned the nice young man from the *Westmorland Gazette*. 'It always rains.' But I was travelling up by train, and one feels a prat changing at Crewe and lugging a pair of wellies across the bridge. Also, I wanted to fit in. My experience of agricultural shows is that they offer farmers a chance to dress up: get out their loudest clashing checks; a tie, yellow or green, whichever; and their best brown brogues, ready to schmooze with the nobs and the tractor salesmen. So I brought my own second-best brown brogues, the ones acquired at Bicester Shopping Village (see Chapter 14).

Which is when I discovered that here they wear wellies, and that one also feels a prat with trench foot. Even so, it was worth it. The Royal Show in Warwickshire, mother of all agricultural beanfeasts, is now defunct. Many of the old county shows have merged or declined, and village shows of ancient tradition have gone on life support after being rained on several years in succession. But this one is just amazing. The catalogue runs to 232 pages and the list of exhibitors went from the 'Able to Enable mobility centre' to 'Zoca Active'. The Freemasons had a stand; maybe MI5 did too.

In a way it is insane to hold an event on this scale on just one day – you can't hope to get round everything – and a weekday at that. But in another way that's what makes it so special: this did not feel like a show for farmers at which townies' money was welcome; it felt like a genuine gathering of the entire community of Westmorland. Only one dimension was missing – the county itself.

Westmorland encompassed the southern Lake District from the early thirteenth century until it became one of the three small counties to be wholly subsumed in 1974. Rutland fought back and ultimately returned; Huntingdonshire had insufficient sense of its identity to care; Westmorland accepted its fate as it phlegmatically accepts the weather. Everyone dutifully put Cumbria on their letterheads and took orders from distant Carlisle, and then the ex-county set about memorialising itself.

The little old county town, Appleby, became aggrandised into 'Appleby-in-Westmorland', almost as many letters as people. The Westmorland Way now stretches ninety-five miles from Appleby to Patterdale. The newish shopping centre in Kendal is 'The Westmorland'. Posthumously, the county has acquired a flag: red and white, with a golden apple tree superimposed. The name persists on the hospital and the *Westmorland Gazette*, one of those rural weeklies popular enough to survive Armageddon, never mind the internet. The Westmorland Motor Club had a stand at the show, as did the Westmorland Red Squirrel Society.

There is a Westmorland Arts Trust, Badminton Club, County Football Association, Cricket League, Geological Society, Horticultural Society, Music Society, Orchestra and Youth Orchestra. The Westmorland Damson Association represents the growers of the Lyth and Winster Valleys. And the Westmorland Step and Garland Dancers perform all summer and practise every Monday in winter. There is also a Westmorland Association, designed to celebrate all aspects of the historic county, but they failed to respond to enquiries, a sign of being either busy or useless. (The latter, I think.)

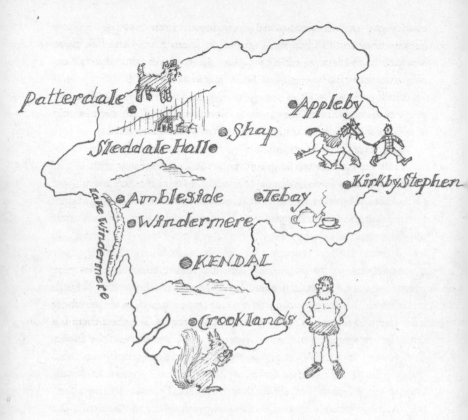

There was even a character at the show called Denis Westmorland, there with piles of his CDs, a dozen different ones, and his three British bulldogs. He plays accordion and writes and sings localish songs, though more in the village-hop than the folk tradition, and not quite my taste. Still, the name!

'Is it real?'

'Oh, yes,' he replied.

'Are you from Westmorland?'

'No, Cumberland. There's a whole colony of Westmorlands near the racecourse in Carlisle.'

'Any in Westmorland?'

'Not that I know of.'

This actually makes sense. Place names as surnames developed from medieval migrant workers, because their home village, town or, less often, county got used as a nickname (the cricketer John Hampshire was a Yorkshireman, and Martin Kent opened the batting for Australia). There wouldn't be much point calling someone 'Westmorland' in a pub in Kendal; it would be like saying 'Hey, Taffy!' in Aberystwyth.

Still, he is not much of a traditionalist, Denis. On his CD *Songs and Music of the Lakes and Cumbria*, the songs included 'My Cumbria Home', 'County of Cumbria', 'Thwaites of Cumbria', 'Fells of Cumbria' …

'Nothing about Westmorland?'

'I do mention it once in one of them. I'm a Cumbrian lad.'

Historically, Westmorland survived because communications were so terrible. The mountains on the northern border were, if not impenetrable, rather less than penetrable, and the journey north – by whatever means – involved getting across Shap Fell, the ridge north of Kendal and south of the village of Shap.

In Derbyshire the A6 is unavoidable. Heading north, it dribbles away into irrelevance. But in Westmorland it regains something of its old self-confidence. The presence of the M6 means it no longer matters anything like as much as it once did. But on the windy top of Shap Fell there is a reminder of how much it used to matter. A stone remembers 'the drivers and crews of vehicles that made possible the social and commercial links between north and south on this old and difficult ridge … and local people who gave freely of food and shelter to stranded travellers in bad weather'.

At least I think it says that. Unfortunately, someone tried to make it more legible by painting up the carved lettering but botched it by failing to wipe the wet paint from the surrounds, so the whole thing became hopelessly smudged. Below the inscription is a list of organisations that paid for the stone, and this is in Old English typeface and now almost wholly unreadable. But I could just make out the dread words Cumbria County Council, and I suspect their handiwork. The timing of local government reform in 1974 was fortuitous for its perpetrators, because Cumbria County Council might not have survived a single winter meeting before the M6 came through four years earlier.

There are still differences between Westmorland and Cumberland. Westmorland kids support Manchester United or City; by the time you cross the border to Penrith, Newcastle takes over. The Cumberland accent, from here, sounds rather Geordie. And historically, according to the cultural historian Mike Huggins, who lives in Windermere, most of Westmorland looked not north but south to Lancashire, partly because that was the most reliable way out. The A66, heading east to Scotch Corner, was (and still is) vulnerable to the weather – and Shap was notorious. 'The road was blocked regularly well into the 1960s, and it was a hell of a place to get stuck. The lorries would skid all over the place and it could take weeks to clear.'

Also, much of Westmorland's industry, such as it was, hinged on the making of wooden bobbins for Lancashire cotton mills: there were eight bobbin mills in Ambleside alone. Farming in Cumberland and Westmorland had much in common, but – as I discovered at the show – there was and is a Lancashire-and-Westmorland style of hedging which is entirely different from Cumberland hedging. The word Cumbrian is of ancient lineage but, says Huggins: 'It was hardly used until about the Second World War.'

Now Cumbria has won. And the public face of Westmorland survives for non-locals in only one, remarkably happy, respect: the M6 services at Tebay run, as the signs proclaim, by Westmorland Ltd, and built on their own farmland by the Dunning family. This is not only the least worst of Britain's seventy-odd motorway services; it is genuinely excellent. I had a pot of builders' (refill on offer) and Borrowdale tea bread overlooking a duck pond with a view of Blease Fell and the merest hint of passing lorry. In this landscape, even the M6 seems tame and inoffensive. I was tempted to stay for dinner.

And the reason Westmorland ought to have survived as a county is that it was excellent. It gets a bit noisy round the dual carriageway heading towards Barrow; the lime works at Shap are pretty ugly; and the Royal Oak in Appleby used to be run by a pair of miserable old sods who wouldn't allow you to have vinegar on the chips because it lowered the tone. Kendal is a town of grey stone and grey weather; but how can you dislike a place best known for making mint cake? And two miles out, heading to Grayrigg, you are already up on the moors with only the wind and the hills for company.

One also senses a remarkable solidarity, which the county show epitomises. 'During foot and mouth I remember going up and down the streets on the council estates in Kendal,' said Tim Farron, MP for Westmorland and Lonsdale. 'These were mostly people who had no connection with farming, and never walked on the fells. Yet they really felt the pain.'

Of course Westmorland was tiny. Roger Bingham, historian and councillor, remembers that when he first swam a length of the pool, he got a certificate signed by the county's chief education officer. Not printed:

he really signed it. And Westmorland always tended to get overlooked. *The Illustrated Counties of England*, the collection of *Illustrated London News* articles produced in 1985 and almost the last gasp of establishment sentimentality for the old counties, gave even Huntingdonshire a couple of thousand words. But Melvyn Bragg's essay was called 'Cumbria'; and he mentioned Westmorland just once, in the context of 'Cumberland and Westmorland wrestling', when he couldn't get out of it.

Westmorland was an anomaly. But a dazzling anomaly. Looking across Grasmere early one morning, from close to Wordsworth's cottage, I saw Silver How ringed with cloud like a pearl necklace. Doubtless Wordsworth would not care for the traffic, especially as red squirrels are being run over by cars on the A591. He wouldn't realise what a triumph it is that Westmorland actually has red squirrels to run over.

The talk at the showground was obviously all about the weather: it generally is. It was a particularly wretched year for the damsons. The food tent was packed with makers of damson wine, damson beer, damson gin, damson chutney, damson cheese and what-have-you, all now looking for simpler, more readily available alternatives to damsons like Kobe beef or goliath tigerfish.

'Diabolical,' said one grower. Damsons like the wet – they wouldn't be here otherwise – but the suspicion is that a cold snap sent the bees back to their hives just when they should have been pollinating. And the weather did for the grape harvest. Again. The High Cup winery near Appleby produces various fruit wines (the elderflower and apple is very drinkable) and might count as the most northerly commercial vineyard in the world. Except that they had not had a grape harvest since 2006, when they were still only amateurs.

It was bad on show day too. All morning there was a wind that reeked of November, and darkening skies. I was keen to catch the Cumberland and Westmorland wrestling. It started with a costume competition in which entrants posed in traditional gear, which comprises singlet and long johns with a pair of trunks on top, all of them handsomely embroidered with motifs. The sport is thought to have hints of Viking; the uniform seems to have Gypsy influences with an undertow of Turkish boudoir. It is not something one would lightly wear in places unfamiliar with the customs. To the intense irritation of some adherents, competitors are now allowed to wear conventional athletic gear to encourage newcomers sensitive to peer-group mockery. Yet the decoration, says Mike Huggins, was actually a concession to Victorian sensitivity: the bourgeoisie were shocked by the sight of men parading in what appeared to be their underwear.

The style of wrestling involves standing with the torso at right angles to the lower body and proceeding in a manner that may be similar to the mating rituals of the praying mantis. The costume competition had just morphed into the actual wrestling, starting with the under-eights, and I was just starting to relish it all, when the threat changed to reality and the rain started, leading to an unseemly rush to the car parks, which, shame-facedly, I joined. The farmers had all come in Range Rovers; my pathetic little hire car was not going to stand much chance of escape when the fields churned up.

This book, like life, is about what happened when I was busy making other plans. I decided to take one of England's strangest roads, which passes between the carriageways of the M6, flanked by unfenced strips of moorland, grazed by sheep, the odd goat, and cattle wearing luminous collars, who are accustomed to plonk themselves on the tarmac and dare you to budge them. They would not attempt such a manoeuvre on the motorway, certainly not more than once.

The lane leads to Scout Green, a rather Home Counties-sounding name for a hamlet in such a strange landscape. It is a good vantage point for anyone keen to photograph the trains on the main line to Glasgow, making either the climb to Shap, infamous in steam days, or the thrilling, surging, swerving southward descent. It was when I emerged back on to the A6 that I saw the sign 'Wet Sleddale'. It led to a car park by a reservoir.

There was one other car here, inhabited by an elderly gent who wound down the window for a chat. 'Is Sleddale Hall anywhere near here?' I asked, carefully pronouncing it Sleddle, trying to fit in. He pointed across the far side of the reservoir, towards the beck that fed it, and a tumbledown cottage halfway up the hillside behind: the least stately home on the tourist map, a place some way below the National Trust's radar screen.

Yet Sleddale Hall attracts a steady stream of visitors because it played the role of Crow Crag, Uncle Monty's rural slum in the cult film *Withnail and I*. The elderly gent turned out to be Bill Benson, who used to farm on the east side of the reservoir. He likes to come here, rather poignantly, as though hefted to the land like a Herdwick sheep. So he told me a bit of the story. Whatever hall-like pretensions Sleddale might have had were ruined, not just by normal agricultural decay, but because the reservoir ate up all the land on the valley floor in the 1960s. It is still said to be a wreck, though someone is supposed to have bought it to do it up, which might have seemed a good idea at the time, presumably a rare hot Westmorland day.

'Do a lot of people go there?'

'Aye,' he said. '*In summer.*'

Well, it was summer on some reckonings: the sun was shining at this point, the track looked puddled but passable, and it all seemed too serendipitous to miss. It has become a place of informal pilgrimage, like Jim Morrison's grave or Ringo's childhood home. Bruce Robinson, who directed the film, is a neighbour of mine: here was a chance for a little Sleddle-cred. So off I trotted, second-best brown brogues and all.

The track grew vaguer and boggier. I pushed on across moss and rush and grass that occasionally subsided into swamp. After half an hour I was more in need of another visit to Bicester than bloody Sleddale, but I refused to be daunted. Finally, I and whatever was left of my socks and brogues reached the edge of Sleddale Beck and the ford that led straight up to the hall.

What Bill had not mentioned was the effect of all the rain. The beck would have been easy enough to cross in trout fishermen's waders, iffy in wellies, unthinkable in my rig-out.

I gazed up at the hall, feeling like Moses denied access to the Promised Land, though as I recall Moses only had to go downhill, not trudge up a sodden fell with dusk approaching. And it seemed most improbable that Sleddale Hall had supplies of milk and honey.

September 2012

~~~~~~~~~

The High Cup winery failed to get a successful grape harvest even after the fine summer of 2013, 'too cloudy late in the season,' said the proprietor, Ron Barker. However, Barker managed to acquire grapes from locals who grow them in greenhouses, and was planning a grape wine to go with the likes of his damson, gooseberry and spiced beetroot. 'Grapes are a bit of a novelty to be honest,' he said. 'Temperatures are not predicted to rise enough to make them reliable for another thirty years.' A second Westmorland-owned service station opened in 2014 – on the M5 at Gloucester.

19. *Bowled by a floater*

HAMPSHIRE

The admiral and I sat on the deck of the cruising yacht *Seesaw*, heading out towards the middle of the Solent. 'Fifteen knots,' he said, sniffing the wind and observing the flags. 'Maybe eighteen. Bit stiff for small boats.'

Seesaw was part of a flotilla of fifty or so vessels, half from the mainland, half from the Isle of Wight, converging on the Bramble Bank, aka the Brambles, a small hazard to shipping a mile and a half out from Cowes. We might have been rushing towards a minor international incident, a skirmish for seemingly useless territory to plant the flag and claim the drilling rights. We were in fact going to a cricket match. Of course.

Almost all year the bank lurks just below the surface, the maritime equivalent of a golf bunker – a sand trap – ready to snare the unwary. Its greatest triumph was catching the *QE2* on her final arrival into Southampton. But on the lowest of low tides, a handful of times a year, about an acre of terra firma will appear for around an hour. And, since 1972, on a day

when one of the late summer spring tides reaches its ebb, the Royal Southern Yacht Club from Hamble and the Island Sailing Club from Cowes
have met halfway for a brief and barmy contest.

The game is not intended to be serious: no one keeps score and the
winner is preordained – they take it in turns. But the occasion has its own
rituals. Barbecues are often set up in the outfield; once there was an instant
bar, complete with optics; I had heard stories of bikini-clad lovelies wandering around, serving champagne.

This time, however, something felt wrong. We could see land ahead
of us all right, but experience suggested that was the seemingly permanent
island of Great Britain. Close at hand, what did we see? We saw the sea.
Low water was supposed to be at 6.30; it was almost 6 o'clock. 'Typical,'
moaned someone on board. 'We spend 364 days a year avoiding the Brambles. When we want it, it isn't there.'

Moments later, it was possible to glimpse some figures in the sea. Further investigation suggested they were not swimming but wading – chest-
deep: not ideal for cricket, but a start. Soon the little rigid inflatables – the
'ribs' – made a sort of landfall and the young men rushed into the waves,
as if it were D-Day. The water declined from knee-deep to ankle-deep, and
play of a kind began. A substantial group of people were clustered round
the bat, though it was difficult to tell who was fielding, umpiring or spec-
tating. They all appeared to be walking on water: the bank never appeared.

Sadly, I was not among the throng. The kindly people from the
Island Sailing Club had given me and my friend Hugh a cushy number
by billeting us on the *Seesaw* to escape the buffeting on the ribs. But the
wind was getting ever stiffer and time was too short; it was deemed too
risky to extract supernumeraries on to first the ribs and then the cramped
and crowded field. Even the Labrador, who was supposed to be the most
important outfielder, never made it.

So we sat, like staff officers, feeling dry, safe, cheated and guilty, next
to the admiral, watching from afar. The admiral was not a naval admiral,
in charge of whatever rust buckets and rowing boats the Royal Navy might
still have had at its disposal in 2012, but Robin Aisher, Olympic yachting
bronze medallist 1968, admiral of the Island club and a genial sort. He
adored the Brambles: when he was racing, it gave him an advantage – he
knew a safe short cut. He also said it really did have a bramble on it until
the Great Storm of 1703, which he talked about as if at first-hand, making
it sound like the hurricane of 1987 or last week's thunderstorm.

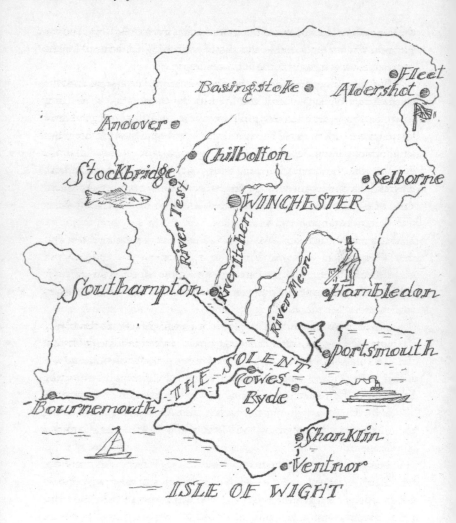

Aisher had played in the match every year until this one, having broken his wrist last time, aged seventy-seven, trying to chase a ball into the water instead of leaving it to the Labrador. But he was transfixed not by the game but by the fate of one of the ribs, which had got beached and then swamped. The Southampton harbour master and the Calshot lifeboat, which had been nonchalantly standing by, started to get serious. 'Probably about twenty knots now,' said the admiral. 'Gusting twenty-five.'

It was known from the start that the 2012 match might be a little iffy:

the tide tables indicated that the ebb would not be as low as usual. And the situation was compounded by the westerly wind. 'What we need for the cricket is a soft easterly,' was the admiral's judgement.

But the game continued. It was essentially aerial, like baseball, and the batsmen kept hitting and running, if a little mincingly. At 6.35, just after scheduled low water, the sound of cheering rose from the players, and there was a scramble for the ribs. The stricken boat was somehow refloated. But another, containing eight humans and the unemployed Labrador, broke down on the way home. Some of the younger players were said to have contracted hypothermia, though these reports came from their mothers, who, I think, meant their boys felt cold. The gusts were nudging thirty now. *Seesaw* began to live up to its name.

There was no champagne and no bikinis back in the club bar. But there were pints of Young's and plates of spaghetti vongole, and plenty of slightly rueful laughter. 'A bit hairy going off,' was the general verdict. 'It was very disorientating going for a run because the water was going across you,' reported one player.

Drinking with the admiral was a grizzled seadog bearing a resemblance to Captain Haddock. This was another Robin, Sir Robin Knox-Johnston, the first man to sail single-handed and non-stop round the world, and not a man to be perturbed by minor difficulties in the Solent. However, he complained that he had been bowled by a ball that had floated on to his wicket, which he thought quite unfair. By the time he had finished telling the story he had also been caught after the ball bounced off two boats and a fielder's head.

I couldn't see the injustice myself, either way. But wet bobs and dry bobs don't mix very often. Cricket and yachting both take large chunks out of summer weekends, even if the bobbing is just round the Solent, never mind the world. Not sure Sir Robin was used to what happens on dry land. Well, relatively dry land.

What this one annual event does is bring together what are perhaps Hampshire's two most distinctive sporting elements: boats and cricket. The Solent is a narrow strait, almost wholly sheltered (except when I'm out there): 'an inland sea', the admiral called it. It also has a unique tidal pattern, so that sailing is both gentle and piquant.

It is thought to have the greatest concentration of yacht clubs in the known world: sixty-six in Hampshire, including the island, and five major

ones in Cowes alone, among them the Royal Yacht Squadron, whose baronial headquarters (address: The Castle, Cowes) dominates the waterfront
with an air more forbidding than any mere fortification. Heaven help the
invading navy that ever tried to get in that way without a specific invitation from a member. 'Everyone in Cowes mixes together,' one yachtie told
me. 'Except the Squadron.'

The epicentre of it all is on the mainland, at the village officially
known as Hamble-le-Rice, where the River Hamble meets Southampton
Water, flowing past a forest of moored boats, their sails stowed, their masts
naked, with the delicate tracery of birch trees in winter: hundreds upon
hundreds of them, stretching as far as the eye can see, and emitting, on a
breezy afternoon, the strange music of marinas – the dink-dink-dink of
halyard on alloy mast.

It occurred to me that it would be extremely difficult for this lot to go
anywhere: the river's not wide enough; the Solent's not wide enough; even
the Atlantic would start having traffic jams. 'Absolutely,' said one expert.
'Even on the busiest day no more than 10 per cent would go out. And some
of them never go anywhere at all. They get damaged if you do that. Some
people just leave them there and invite friends round for drinks.' A bit like
having a country cottage, but not a secluded one.

About eighteen miles from Hamble, as the motorcar flies, is Hambledon, a very different kind of place. Just outside the village, on the
windswept expanse of Broadhalfpenny Down, cricket grew, in the late
eighteenth century, from a rustic pastime and gambling medium towards
a sport that conquered the world. Well, a part of it.

From the 1750s to the 1780s Hambledon was the leading cricket
club of all, regularly beating All England, mainly under the leadership of
Richard Nyren, who, by happy coincidence, was landlord of the Bat and
Ball, next to the ground. Hambledon fell as quickly as it rose, presumably because of the emergence of the upstart club at Marylebone and also
because, when it comes to exposure to the prevailing westerlies, they would
have been far more sheltered had they played in mid-Solent, or indeed
mid-Atlantic. The game continues, though the history of the ground is
chequered. Ditto the Bat and Ball, which fell on temporarily evil times a
decade ago when new owners made it clear they cared nothing for cricket
and tried to rename it 'Natterjack's'.

Both ground and pub have recovered, the field now being sympa-
thetically owned by Winchester College and run by a trust. And by happy

coincidence the last Sunday game of the season was taking place the day before the Brambles match: it was an old-fashioned clubbable contest between the Brigands, the notionally naval team who have made their home at Broadhalfpenny, and the Stragglers of Asia, whose origins lie with old Far East hands. Some people are disappointed when they go to Hambledon, but I wasn't, despite the customary keen wind. The ground is well kept and pretty and hospitable, the tea was lovely and, just before I left, the Pilgrim Morris Men from Guildford started performing a stick dance in front of the pub. Ah, Merrie England!

Hampshire is no longer the centre of world cricket, though they do now stage occasional Test matches in an inaccessible ground on the edge of Southampton. However, from the post-war resumption of the game in 1946 until his retirement in 1980, the very idea of England was embodied in the voice of a Hampshire man, John Arlott.

Arlott's cricket commentaries had both a poetic quality and a relevant discursiveness that on their own would have made him one of the outstanding radio broadcasters of all time. But the crowning glories were his voice and accent, always described as a Hampshire burr, which became throatier and more pronounced as the decades rolled by. It would be difficult, if not impossible, to find anyone who talks like that now. He came from Basingstoke, most Londonised of all the Hampshire towns, and, as he once remarked: 'My mum's the only person left in Basingstoke who was born there. And she doesn't go out at night.' However, there are those who believe there never was anyone in Hampshire who spoke like Arlott and that the accent was substantially his own invention.

He was and remains a hero of mine: a man of broad and humane sympathies. When I finally met him, shortly before I was to inherit his role as cricket correspondent of the *Guardian*, I was so overawed I couldn't speak. As a writer, Arlott was as distinctive (if not as brilliant) as he was a broadcaster. His policy was usually to enthuse about what he loved and ignore what he didn't like: as a book reviewer, if confronted by drivel, he would say that the margins were generous or the type pleasingly legible. His enthusiasms included cricketers, wine, cheese and Hampshire. Indeed, he helped preserve the county's own sense of itself, so much so that for *The Illustrated Counties of England* there can have been no second choice to do the Hampshire chapter. In his essay, he made one especially shrewd point: that in other counties, the main towns and cities recognisably take their character from the county, but in Hampshire this isn't true. They are on the edges, in a ring, looking outwards, with their own separate and essentially outward-looking preoccupations: the Royal Navy in Portsmouth, merchant ships in Southampton, tourism and retirement in Bournemouth, the army in Aldershot, London overspill in Basingstoke and Andover. He concluded: 'Thus the true heart of Hampshire does lie, in fact, at its physical heart.'

Which is surprisingly empty. Driving to Hambledon, the satnav told me to ignore my hosts' instructions, bypass rural Hampshire's best-known landmark, the crossroads pub known as the West Meon Hut, and take the back road. I drove for miles, along the edge of the South Downs towards the Meon Valley, past a vague hint of habitation at Beauworth and then miles largely devoid of life, two-legged or four, past sweeping hills turned into largely hedgeless fields of lately harvested grain. I had no idea one could feel so remote on the outer edge of commuterdom.

I was as awestruck as when I met Arlott. And I kept being amazed by the emptiness. It happened again near Chilbolton above the Test Valley. And then again on top of the zigzag the vicar-naturalist Gilbert White built behind his house at Selborne: nothing visible that might not have been there when he looked out 250 years ago except the white domes of the space tracking station at Oakhanger. And if you think of them as being particularly large puffball mushrooms, there is no need to be upset. Even Hampshire's most hackneyed gateway, the Fleet Services on the M3, is set among pine trees, lending it a pleasing heathland air; and the gorse-filled motorway verges, bright yellow in springtime, give an unusual lift to the spirits. Welcome to Happy Hampshire.

Contrast this with Portsmouth, notionally on an island, but one as pinched and cluttered as Manhattan, and with a great deal of associated sprawl. There are green lawns by the Southsea front and there must be a park or two somewhere. But it feels a long way from Hambledon. And though, as Arlott says, it looks out to sea not inwards to Hampshire, that's only to find out if anyone's coming. Portsmouth's job is to keep people out, which is I suppose why it feels so claustrophobic. Southampton is there to let people in and, though not a particularly attractive city, it is greener and more welcoming.

The Great Local Government Storm of 1974 took Bournemouth and part of the New Forest out of historic Hampshire and into Dorset (although the traffic jams of Lyndhurst were unmoved, as ever). The switch appears to have been popular and accepted: Hampshire being big and Dorset small, the change made Bournemouth the big I-am; and Dorset conjured up nice, cuddly feelings among housebuyers and thus bumped up property prices. The odd thing is that, since it moved, Bournemouth has become a lot less Dorsety and a lot more Hampshire. I had childhood holidays there and there was damn-all to do. Now it's full of students and St Andrew's Church in the town centre ('rock-faced outside with a tall apsidal baptistery') has been turned into a nightclub, with rock inside as well as out.

In 1974, the Isle of Wight was also finally detached from Hampshire. Is it a real county? It is a complicated case. It has had a county council since 1890. And postally, it was always treated as separate (pretty silly, putting Hampshire on an envelope destined for the island). But it was not one of the thirty-nine historic counties and until 1974 did not have its own Lord Lieutenant, for whatever that might be worth. There was, quite simply, nothing here, and hardly anyone (23,000 in the 1801 census).

There was a certain amount of royal patronage, both unwilling (Charles I was locked up in Carisbrooke Castle) and willing – Victoria adored the place and brought in her wake hordes of trippers, including one who reported: 'This island is a little paradise.'

I saw that quote in an advert on one of the ex-London Underground brand-new-in-1938 carriages used by the Isle of Wight's railway line from Ryde Pier Head to Shanklin. The line also retains old Southern Region station signs and generally cements the island's image as a 1950s theme park. The paradise quote is attributed to 'Karl Marx, political agitator', the assumption presumably being that visitors might get him muddled with Groucho. Karl took his holidays at Ventnor. Tennyson wrote 'Crossing the Bar' after crossing the Solent. Keats, Dickens and Swinburne all popped down.

But a county? Nah. Counties have their origins in the most distant swamps of time and are steeped in folklore even if the current inhabitants are unaware of it. This was a garrison with villages, an early-warning station for Portsmouth, a lookout point. Then it was an agreeable resort. Now what? It was granted a chapter in the *Illustrated London News* counties book, by Dudley Fishburn, but even he admitted: 'It is no longer an inspiration or an escape; it is rather a neat and well-ordered corner of calm.' It is certainly amiably sluggish, with that sense of community that comes from having a lot of the active-retired. But the indigenous architecture appears to comprise flat-roofed blocks of flats with their balconies guarded by bulbous balustrades: a less sunny southern Spain.

Winchester is Hampshire's obvious county town, since it is the only place of substance anywhere near the middle. It also has the main cathedral, barely visible even from the city centre; the longest in Europe but not much taller than a Shanklin bungalow, and equally unadorned – 'all is power at Winchester,' says Pevsner, 'nothing grace'. The most fascinating part of this cathedral is the jumble of memorials, mixing two Hampshire traditions, the military and ecclesiastical, with splendid illogicality: Sir John Campbell, Bt, who fell leading his brigade in the assault on the Great Redan at Sebastopol, and Lieutenant Colonel E. H. Merchant, 'shot by a fanatic at Peshawar, 1899', are commemorated amid all the prebendaries, clerks of the chapter, minor canons and precentors who stayed at home, leading for the most part longer lives, if less incident-packed ones.

Jane Austen gets the most attention. There is her tomb in the north aisle, where the inscription does not mention that she wrote anything, and the nearby wall memorial, which does. This is next door to Captain G. B. Gosling, who died in 1906 'at Nianguru, Congo State, while on an exploring expedition in Central Africa'. And next door to that, something much newer: 'In memory of the one thousand nine hundred and five British Officers Gurkha Officers and Men of the 10th Princess Mary's Own Gurkha Rifles who gave their lives for this country 1890–1994.'

Soon after Sir John Campbell Bt and many thousands of his contemporaries died in the Crimea, Aldershot became, as the signs still proclaim, 'the home of the British Army'. It was chosen because the area was hardly inhabited – the soil being thin and useless – yet handy for London. It remains largely a one-trick town.

Yet the centre of it did not feel remotely military. It felt to me more like an ex-mining town mysteriously transplanted to the stockbroker belt. I had imagined streets full of squaddies. Not at all. Admittedly, I was there on a weekday and the army does prefer to work office hours, like A&E departments and police stations. What I saw was a succession of sad-eyed elderly men, wrapped against the imagined cold on a fine early autumn morning. These were the Gurkhas.

One of the convulsions of the brief and troubled premiership of Gordon Brown was caused by the Gurkha Justice Campaign, aimed at allowing Nepalese soldiers who had fought for Britain to settle here. The campaign's public face was the sparky actress Joanna Lumley, who outmanoeuvred the government at every turn and forced it into a retreat of a humiliating nature not seen on the battlefield since the last time Britain chose to invade Afghanistan. Even while caving in, it looked niggardly and mean-minded towards people regarded by public opinion in heroic terms. It is arguable (and it seems to be seen that way in Kathmandu) that the Gurkhas are essentially mercenaries.

As the Gurkhas arrived, mainly in Aldershot, a safe Tory seat, the government then did damn-all to help settle them. Classic, really. The English being overtly polite, very little was said, though a post on the *Aldershot News & Mail* website may be taken to represent a substantial slice of public opinion:

> The Nepalese are ruining our community's! Taking our benefits and our houses and do nothing to contribute to our communities! Most don't work and also don't feel the need to learn the language. They have no comprehension of our basic manors and lifestyles, which causes friction in the Aldershot. If your in our army good on you but why should you get extra's. My brothers in the army and he gets nothing apart from a basic wage so why should they get special treatment! They should all go settle in there countries and fight to better there countries! The government should concentrate on looking after us English British people. Or they could take up residence with Joanna Lumley im sure she's got the money and the room for them!

Part of the argument was that the influx was damaging the education system.

Even without the Gurkhas, Aldershot appears to be getting the worst of every world. On the one hand, British governments have become addicted to ludicrous wars, with no clear purpose or exit mechanism. On the other, the army keeps being cut back. In times of war, garrison towns normally thrive. Aldershot has managed to suffer even as its residents are sent off to die, often at the hands of their alleged allies.

Just behind the town centre is Queens Avenue, a long, spacious – in some parts gracious – thoroughfare suitable for a triumphalist parade, if there were ever any triumphs to celebrate. But the horse chestnut trees, like the army itself, were giving off distress signals, long before the calendar would suggest the leaves and conkers should be executing their exit strategy.

Around them were the forceful and rather handsome Presbyterian and Catholic military churches, the army tailors Glover and Riding, acres of sports fields, boarded-up barrack blocks and a great many signs saying 'Aspire'. This turned out to be not a slogan but an outsourcing operation set up under the private finance initiative, which is a governmental accountancy scam.

The Anglican garrison church is some distance away, hidden behind trees, hard by one of the country's least-known yet most remarkable monuments, the equestrian statue of the Duke of Wellington. When you start to think about this (which I never had), it is odd that the great naval hero of the Napoleonic War is up there on his column in the heart of London, but the great military hero is commemorated mainly as a boot.

There is the Wellington Arch at Hyde Park Corner, though it is not much noticed amid the traffic. Nearby is a naked Achilles, which is also dedicated to Wellington, somewhat obliquely. Liverpool has Wellington's Column by Lime Street Station, complete with a list of his victories set out in the manner of stations on an exotic railway journey.

But his main memorial is here, showing him mounted on his trusty steed Copenhagen, more than thrice as large as life: thirty feet high, twenty-six feet long, set upon a mound known as Round Hill and surrounded by rhododendron bushes. The story is told, very well, on a pair of information boards. In 1846, with great ceremony, this statue was placed at Hyde Park Corner, on top of the arch. But there was a lot of chuntering: the aesthetes thought it was out of scale; Queen Victoria thought it ruined her view. But the Duke was still alive, and old, revered and crabby. So nothing could be done.

In the 1880s, however, the arch had to be moved because it was obstructing the traffic. With the Duke safely dead, the statue's enemies seized their opportunity. The Prince of Wales suggested moving it to Aldershot, where it might be appreciated. It was moved, though still not much appreciated, being neglected until a major clean-up and clearance effort shortly after the millennium.

It stands in parkland, by a football pitch. There was no one about except two elderly Gurkha couples. One of the men, Prem, spoke English more serviceable than my Nepali. Yes, he liked it here. Yes, the people were friendly. Yes, they wanted to stay. Any problems? He thought for a moment, then channelled Beruke, the Ethiopian I met in Birmingham.

'Too many Gurkha. Too many ex-army.'

There is another sport in Hampshire, more baffling and impenetrable than even cricket or sailing. Strangers are normally welcome to watch a cricket match or a yacht race even if they haven't the faintest idea what's happening. Try turning up at the Houghton Club in Stockbridge and asking where you can see the action. This is an institution that makes the Royal Yacht Squadron look as picky as the Tesco Club. There are just twenty-five members and it has exclusive fishing rights to thirteen miles of the River Test, the most famous trout stream in the world.

For a non-angler, simply setting foot in the shops of Stockbridge is like entering an alien world: Greenwells Glory; Tups Indispensable; Lunns Particular; Iron Blue Dun. Apples? Potatoes? Implements favoured by sadomasochists? Dry flies.

Nearly all the world's chalk streams are in England, most of them in the South-East, the best in Hampshire – the Test, which flows through Stockbridge, and the Itchen being the best of the best. They are gloriously clear, which enables trout – and salmon – to flourish, and creates an arena suitable for the contest between gentleman and fish. Coarse fishing, as the classless version of angling is disparagingly known, is like blind-man's-buff: cast your rod upon the waters and hope for the best. Fly-fishing is more like hide-and-seek, with a hint of hare coursing thrown in. One minute you see the fish; next minute he's slithered away to lurk in the luxuriant vegetation. With a dry fly, on top of the water, it is a game requiring infinite patience on both sides: a sport fit for a duke (at least one example belonging to the Houghton Club) or a mega-millionaire (several).

Such understanding as I have of this sport is entirely due to the patient explanations of Keith Elliott, editor of *Classic Angling*, which was enough to whet my appetite to learn more. Tricky. Owners of fishing rights on the Test are more adept than the trout at guarding their privacy, except at a very high price. There is a forty-nine-mile path called the Test Way; not much of it goes alongside the river itself. And the shrubs and reeds along the banks are encouraged to grow, the better to guard the arena for the aquatic *corrida*.

I did walk along the bank on the common south of Stockbridge: the Test looked as pristine as a mountain stream. But this is Hampshire, not heaven.

The chalk streams are under many competing pressures, abstraction above all. Every time there is a drought, the river levels get lower and the most vulnerable dry up completely, because more and more is siphoned off upstream, threatening entire ecosystems, not just ducal pleasures. Hampshire is extremely adept at pretending it exists in its own safe, unchanging world. The trout probably believe that until the final, fateful nibble. But it can never be wholly true.

September 2012

20. *Oh, Ena, where art thou?*

LANCASHIRE

It was a week in a thousand. To be more precise, ten days out of 7,305. Preston Guild happens once in twenty years. In Lancashire, it was a byword: 'He buys a drink about every Preston Guild' or 'My wife wants sex about every Preston Guild.'

It is a curious, fascinating survival. The origins date back to a royal charter in 1179; the first Guild ceremony may have been in 1328; there was definitely one in 1397; and the twenty-year cycle became immutable from 1542, with the pardonable exception of 1942, when there was a decade-long delay.

Something similar must have happened in half the boroughs of the kingdom. The local guilds operated as closed shops, protecting tradesmen from unwanted competition: there was a need to meet, just occasionally, to sort out the records and make sure the rights moved on to the next generation. It was a business meeting, but in Preston it turned into a fiesta, too well loved to let die when its original purpose vanished.

So it continues. Over the course of the ten days in 2012 there were four separate processions, some time-honoured civic pomp, balls, concerts and exhibitions, and a fringe thrown in. There are rituals understood between Guilds only by a handful of council officials: the wording of the Third Proclamation, who does what in the Trades Procession and so on.

This rendition seems to have been a success, after a sodden fiasco in 1992. Naturally muggins came up for the duffest day of the ten: the Thursday. 'Ooh, you should have been here Saturday,' said one Prestonian. 'It were mental.' Alas, the Guild attracted very little notice outside Preston, having to compete for oxygen with the Diamond Jubilee and the London Olympics and Paralympics, all of which are even rarer than Preston Guilds, mean men buying rounds and frigid wives getting randy. The *Lancashire Evening Post*'s contention that the place was being inundated by tourists seemed, um, fanciful. Those who did come were greeted by a series of used-car-forecourt-style flags along Fishergate and some rather baffling banners:

IT'S WELCOMING
IT'S INTERNATIONAL
IT'S BEING INVOLVED
IT'S GREEN
IT'S CREATIVE
IT'S BUSINESS

The Guild's very rarity is its biggest problem. Annual events build their own traditions from the bottom up. The Guild has to be reinvented every time by the council: there was a hint of organised fun, reminiscent of the ghastly Millennium Dome, the government's idea of how to celebrate a rarer event still.

The highlight of Thursday's programme was 'Business Day – the biggest networking event ever to be held in Lancashire'. I turned up, just a little late – as a serious networker should – and was admitted to a dark tent, which contained a small trade fair. There were a couple of dozen stalls promoting businesses that did not actually make anything, all of them with slogans starting with a gerund, and a slightly larger number of earnest young people in suits, most of them with large packs of business cards. The kind of people who call an H a haitch and call you 'yourself'. It was desperate. I came away with two Roses' chocolates inside a bag with various hortatory words: Grow, Influence, Inspire, Achieve.

Barrow-in-Furness

Lancaster

MORECAMBE
BAY

Blackpool

Preston

Blackburn

Nelson

Accrington

Southport

Bolton

Bury

Wigan

MANCHESTER

Crosby

Salford

CORONATION ST.

Liverpool

Warrington

River Mersey

As I left I passed a sign saying 'See you at Preston Guild 2032' and by the grace of God and the actuarial charts, I hope to do so, though not on the Thursday. This is the new Lancashire, I suppose, which looks much the same as everywhere else. What I was hoping to find was a remnant of the old Lancashire: a place where networking happened naturally, without anyone knowing the word; a place that was involved and welcoming without needing to mention it on banners. Is it still there, somewhere?

I arrived as a student in Manchester in the autumn of 1969. In pole position on Market Street, right next to Piccadilly, there was a UCP restaurant, then ubiquitous in Lancashire. It stood for United Cattle Products, which meant it sold tripe and the like. Mancunian kids' joke of that era: If UCP on it, don't eat the tripe. My advice, after a single visit: don't eat the tripe.

The centre of Manchester had only just lost its last coal mine, the Bradford pit. There were backstreets that could not have changed much since Victoria's reign, like Tib Street, which was full of little pet shops. Beer was cheap because there were at least a dozen competing local breweries, which nowhere else in Britain could match. George Best and Bobby Charlton were playing at Old Trafford. The *Guardian* was still in its ancient office in Cross Street and I went there on a university visit which, ten years later, after the building had been demolished, impressed the editor of the *Guardian* no end at my interview.

Manchester was no longer particularly smoky but it was grubby and, outside a few oases like the *Guardian* office and the Portico Library, rough. The only twenty-four-hour scene was at the Empire Grill in Albert Square. There was no Chinatown; gay activity was very covert. And it rained; it really did. It hardly ever poured. It was something more than drizzle. It rained with a soft relentlessness. Imagine a toddler drumming their fingers playfully on your head for three years.

Students did not venture north of Manchester very often but I once went to Oldham, to watch football. All I remember is the cold, the fog, the primitive terraces and Oldham Brewery bitter.

'Wren's Nest, Egypt, India, Victorious, Provident, Hawk, Cromer ...' said Mike Harding. Those were the names on the Oldham cotton mills, when Harding was growing up, most of them proudly emblazoned on the chimneys. Bernard Wrigley, 'The Bolton Bullfrog' – like Harding a humorist, actor and folk singer – grew up in Bolton and never left. He remembers walking on the moors above town and looking down on a forest of chimneys. Now there's just one left: the Falcon, which, oddly enough, was disused long before he was born.

The poetry of the names conceals the reality of life. Harding, growing up in Crumpsall in the 1950s, remembers gas lamps, cobblestones, clogs ('they were always said to be better for your posture'), rickets ('wishbone legs, still incredibly common then') and the arrival of the first car on the street. On the other hand, there was the sense of community that produces humour. Humour, always humour.

The list of Lancashire comedians goes on for ever. Harding scrawled down twenty-five names in a minute before pausing for breath, but he could have added dozens more. Some of them, you could say, just happen to come from Lancashire. For others, the whole of their humour was shot through with Lancy-ness, from George Formby, senior and junior, to the modern Boltonian, Peter Kay. Charles Nevin, in his beguiling book *Lancashire, Where Women Die of Love*, lists a dozen more. And both of them failed to mention Al Read and Ken Platt and Hylda Baker and Jimmy Clitheroe, all of them Lancastrian to their very bones, only four feet three inches of them in Clitheroe's case. There are Yorkshire comedians, of course, but their humour rarely depends on Yorkshireness: the particular shtick of Charlie Williams, who did lay on the Yorkieness very thick, was that he was black.

How do we explain this phenomenon? Why is Yorkshire so unfunny in comparison? Walter Greenwood, author of *Love on the Dole*, put it down to the weather: 'Yorkshire faces the full blast of the easterly wind' whereas Lancashire had a 'wild, warm, amorous wind, wenching with fat clouds and leaving them big with rain'. Ooh! Not much frigidity, then.

Harding puts it down to the Irish influence: the tradition of the music, the put-upon self-deprecation, the storytelling of the *seanchai*. Yorkshire was influenced by the Vikings, not a whimsical race. Bernard Wrigley thinks it was the claustrophobic way of life: the acres were less broad this side of the Pennines and humour was a response to shared privations in a confined space. He also thinks the accent uniquely lends itself to a deadpan delivery.

There was not much humour among the haitchers of Preston. This officially is the county town of the rump Lancashire created in 1974. No county was sodded around quite so royally as the County Palatine: bits added here, taken away there, creating a camel of a county including large swathes of rural Yorkshire (such as 'Barlick', see Chapter 7) but not, as it happens, a single rugby league team worth mentioning.

The true capital of Lancashire is quite obviously Manchester. It is a staggeringly different place now: the epicentre of new-found northern confidence, full of skyscrapers, whooshing trams (many of them heading to 'MediaCityUK', previously known as Salford Docks), and haitchers in suits with wallets full of business cards. Two hours from London by train, it is now London's northernmost exurb. I doubt if any tripe has been eaten in central Manchester this century unless it were served on a bed of rocket with a drizzle of raspberry vinegar.

Liverpool does not count in this context. Indeed, Liverpool could hardly ever count as part of Lancashire. It is too *sui generis*, too much a planet of its own. It has been far less susceptible to the kind of changes that have overwhelmed Manchester. I love it to bits, partly because it was physically spared the architectural ravages of the 1960s and 1970s. Lost in their own political fantasy, its councillors were too interested in changing the world than changing the face of the city. Hence the continuing splendour of the waterfront. Only recently has Liverpool got round to trying to bugger up all that.

Here, the Irishness is at its least diluted, to the point of Liverpool being Dublin's easternmost exurb. Scouse is, I suppose, the accent you get when you cross Lancy and Liffey.

And a very strange thing: it is years since I have been driven by, or even noticed, a taxi driver anywhere else in Lancashire who was not Asian. In Liverpool, I have never had one who was not white.

The epitome of New Lancashire, and its most dramatic sight, is not in either of its big cities. It comes as you turn off the A61 at Horwich, near Bolton, and head east and downhill. To the north is the great dividing line of Winter Hill with its TV mast, separating the last vestiges of heavy Mancunian vowels from the rolled Rs of the mid-Lancs mill towns.

Straight ahead is the Reebok Stadium, home of Bolton Wanderers Football Club – 'the Trotters' – who trotted from ghost-filled Burnden Park near the town centre to the outer edge, handy for car and train, and sold the naming rights to a company that makes plimsolls (or, as they called them here, pumps). In the words of the club website, 'the iconic Reebok Stadium is a versatile venue offering high end sport, entertainment, leisure and business facilities under one roof'.

Round it grew a whole new area, boringly named Middlebrook, and stuffed with shopping malls, car dealerships and the kind of chain restaurants that offer laminated menus the size of a tabloid newspaper, full of adjectives like 'tender', 'rich', 'creamy', 'succulent', 'soft', 'classic', 'great', 'almighty', 'crispy', 'delicious', 'tasty', 'fresh' and, very probably, 'iconic', a clear indicator that the food is none of these things. Except for the stadium being devoted to an un-American sport, everything here would be perfectly at home in the outer reaches of, say, Waco, Texas.

The stadium is certainly impressive, with the floodlights right on top of the superstructure, though the effect is to give them a strange droopy shape, as though in mourning for the club's latest defeat. The Lancashire mill towns were the seedbed of British professional football: the late Victorian industrialists who ran the teams paid big money to lure hungry (in every sense) Scots to play for them in an era when London was still treating the whole business as a jolly weekend runaround. Sixteen of the ninety-two clubs in football's top four divisions are in Lancashire – way more than in London – and more than half either are or have lately been in the Premier League.

It's not just the streets that were claustrophobic. Lancashire south of the Ribble is like the Middle East: first-time visitors to the Holy Land are staggered that Tel Aviv is an easy commute from the West Bank (or was until the Israelis stuck a dirty great wall in the way). And you don't realise from outside that if sentenced to a Tuesday night in the Premier Inn opposite the Reebok when there was a full football programme but Bolton were away, you could skip all the tender, rich, creamy, succulent food on offer, pick twenty or thirty alternative matches in Lancashire or just beyond, and still be back tucked up by midnight. What I was hunting was old Lancashire rather than brilliant football.

So I went to watch Accrington Stanley play York City.

'Wherever I go in the world,' David 'Bumble' Lloyd was telling his audience, 'they say "Where are you from?" "Accrington." And the first two words you hear are "Accrington Stanley".'

Since Lloyd makes his living as a cricket commentator and after-dinner speaker, and spends his life among sports obsessives, that's inevitable. In other company he might hear 'Accrington Pals', the battalion of the East Lancs Regiment devastated at the Somme, or the rich red bricks known as 'Accrington bloods'.

And he was preaching to the converted. He was addressing pre-match diners inside Accrington Stanley FC's unpretentious hospitality room, many of them members of the Lloyd family, since Bumble was personally sponsoring the match. The club's new chairman, Peter Marsden, had just announced the formation of a new board of directors, up from three to eighteen. This ran contrary to modern managerial thinking and, since it represented a board/average crowd ratio of less than 1:100, may be a world record. The Football League raised no formal objection but did think it might be better if they didn't all troop into the boardroom at every away game and start scoffing the prawn sandwiches.

There was method in this madness, for this is no ordinary football club. This was one of the places football began. Accrington were one of the twelve original members of the Football League. But, being about six miles from both Blackburn and Burnley, and smaller than either, they struggled. In 1962, confronted with an electricity bill of a few hundred quid, the board panicked and resigned from the League. Offers of help came in but Bob Lord, the Burnley chairman and a powerful figure, refused to countenance an un-resignation.

The club disappeared; the old ground, Peel Park, was demolished; Accrington were replaced in the League by Oxford, a place with infinitely more people, pennies and potential. It was a symbol of the decline of towns like Accrington and the rise of the rich South, even in a sport as northern and traditional as football. 'It's so easy to go to Manchester United or City and get on the bandwagon,' Lloyd was saying. 'This is an obligation to us.'

Accrington was an old weaving town. Lloyd's mum had to work eight looms starting at 5 a.m., coming home midday to make his dinner (the southerner's lunch) and then at 5 p.m. to make his tea (the southerner's dinner). His dad worked at Howard and Bullough – always known as Bulloughs – the vast engineering works that made, among other things, the spinning frames for the rest of the cotton trade. Most families led very similar lives. And it all faded and died, not dramatically like the football club, but gradually, a process so slow and inexorable it was hard to notice it happening. The mills closed; Bulloughs closed; the brickworks closed. And, like most of the Pals, they did not come back. But the football club did.

It was re-formed in 1968, and eventually found a new home, the Crown Ground, next to the remains of the most famous brickworks, the Nori Works (supposedly a misprint because the steeplejack put the letters on the chimney the wrong way round), just out of sight but not sound of the municipal tip.

And gradually the club roused itself from the deep obscurity of the Lancashire Combination until it found a go-getting chairman, Eric Whalley, who found a go-getting manager, John Coleman, who persuaded his Scouse mates to come and play. And in 2006, forty-four years after the electricity bill, Accrington Stanley returned to League Two, the rebranded old Fourth Division.

Nearly seven years later, they were still there, just about, having been rescued again in the meantime – by Ilyas Khan, the son of an Accrington bus driver, who became a Hong Kong banker. The aim now, said Peter Marsden, was to create a genuine community club, with £100 shares and no controlling sugar daddy. The board was not exactly community-based: Marsden was a London property developer and his colleagues included an Oxford professor and someone living in Brazil; even Lloyd, the purest of Accringtonians, has moved to Cheshire, as one does. So there is not much chance of them all turning up at once, for prawn sandwiches or even a meeting.

Loathing the excesses of modern football, I thought it was wonderful. The Crown Ground is tiny: though the crowd was computed at 1,506 it still looked well populated. It is so low-slung there was a 1,507th who was able to watch from his bedroom window above the stand. And they were so good-natured. The chanting between the rival fans was even borrowed from cricket. 'Lancy, Lancy, Lancy, Lancy – Lancashire,' chanted the Stanley ultras in the Sophia Khan Stand (named after Ilyas's mum). 'York-*shire*, York-*shire*,' chanted the York fans behind the other goal: deeper-throated, less tuneful, less humorous, less accommodating.

The York team were less accommodating too, but I found myself drawn to Stanley, playing in blood-red, like the bricks. I know about Fourth Division football, having spent years watching Northampton Town, behind a man who shouted 'Rubbish' at intervals for decades, win, lose or draw. Here I found myself close to an old bloke in a ski hat who greeted each attack with relentless positivity.

'Oh, look at that! At 'em, lads!'

'Come on, let's have a cheeky goal.'

'Oh, good try! Well played.'

Nothing came of any of the attacks, and the cheeky goal – almost inevitably – came from York, consigning Stanley to their fourth successive defeat. When it went in, the old boy just sat there, shaking his head with a hint of ruefulness. Everyone else did much the same. It was like being with 1,505 Nelson Mandelas. He spent twenty-seven years in jail; this lot had been deprived of forty-four years of their football-watching lives when Accrington were out of business, but they had no time for bitterness.

As we were filing out, I turned to my saintly neighbour. 'What did you do for forty-four years when you didn't have this lot to break your heart?'

'Well,' he said. 'It did help to have Manchester United to fall back on.'

Accrington's civic glory has faded. The borough is now called Hyndburn, whatever that might be, and the town hall has space for body toning and zumba. The market hall next door is rather handsome, with architecture fit for at least a provincial governor somewhere in South America. The tripe stall was just outside.

The market hall balcony was given over to tiny glass-fronted offices, one of which contained a lone reporter from the *Accrington Observer*, tapping away on her laptop. Her colleagues were all on the edge of Manchester, in a newsroom with seventeen other fading local papers. And the old Town Centre office was now a pop-up furniture shop. I worked out it was the old newspaper office because the sign said *ccringt Observ r*, though the middle R was now hanging loose so that in the next gale it would become the *ccringt Obse v r*.

But not all old music-hall joke Lancashire towns seemed to be struggling. Nearby Oswaldtwistle looked jaunty, with a pleasing informality so that Ozzy Computers sat next to Sheila's Wool Shop, Jack's Bakery and Jim's Barbers. And the centre of Wigan had an unexpected air of prosperity and charm, enhanced by a classical violinist busking outside WH Smith.

However, Wigan is famous for one thing above all. The brown 'tourist attraction' signs begin way out of town, all pointing to Wigan Pier. I followed them slavishly, through a half-hour town centre traffic jam caused by roadworks. The one-way system doubled back, the signs petered out and I found myself at the beginning of the half-hour jam again. So I dived off to the side, found a parking place and walked.

I had no idea what I might be looking for. The phrase Wigan Pier is world-famous. But most people outside Wigan, maybe inside Wigan too, have no idea what it means. George Orwell never found it. It turned out to mean a pub car park with a plaque commemorating that it had been opened by HM The Queen. I never knew she opened pub car parks.

What she actually opened, it turned out, was the Wigan Pier Experience, a 'heritage attraction' which closed in 2007, pending regeneration into the Wigan Pier Quarter. That regeneration was still pending five years later. Much of this was explained to me by Damien, the barman at the pub, a converted cotton warehouse which was inevitably called the Orwell.

The museum had gone. The Pier nightclub the other side of the canal had gone. Even the Tourist Information Centre had gone. 'It's all a bit of a dump really,' said Damien, a reasonable comment from his standpoint, a few yards from all the debris floating down the canal. The 'attractions' were now all boarded up.

The pier, however, still sort of existed, next to the defunct nightclub. A jetty, said Damien, but not much of one. It was not really even that, but a raised platform with a pair of what looked like broken railway buffers facing the canal. According to the information sign, it was a 'tippler', a place where coal wagons slid down tracks, hit the buffers and tipped their loads into waiting barges. In the Edwardian era, George Formby senior (father of the ukulele player) really did make Wigan Pier into a music-hall joke. But whether this bit of nothing was called the pier first or whether the name was a tribute to Formby's imagination is unclear. Either way, the original buffers were sold for scrap in 1929, before Orwell arrived to beat Damien with the story that Wigan was a dump, and called his book *The Road to Wigan Pier*.

I mentioned I was on my way to Blackpool, where there are three real piers. 'It's going downhill too, Blackpool,' he replied.

Oh, bloody hell, Damien, you're only young. Don't *you* start.

In the autumn of 1933 J. B. Priestley arrived in Blackpool on his *English Journey*, perhaps the most famous book of its kind. 'It is,' he wrote, 'a complete and essential product of industrial democracy. If you do not like industrial democracy, you will not like Blackpool.'

Credentials for what would now be called political correctness duly established, he continued: 'I know people who would have to go into a nursing home after three hours of it. (In the season, of course.) I am not one of those people.'

So now he has added his credentials as a tough and imperturbable traveller.

'I have never actually been in Blackpool at the crazy height of its season, during its various Lancashire "wakes" weeks –'

Aha!

'but I knew it before the war –'

The First War, that is.

'and I have seen something of it since. It is not, in my opinion, as good as it used to be.'

Damien, meet J. B. Priestley. J.B., Damien.

Exactly forty years later, the master-diarist Alan Clark attended the 1973 Conservative conference there. He did not become an MP until the following year, but he was not exactly one of those starry-eyed young candidates.

13 OCTOBER 1973 Isn't Blackpool appalling, loathsome? … dirt, squalor, shantytown, broken pavements with pools of water lying in them – on the Promenade, vulgar, common 'primitives', drifting about in groups or standing, loitering, prominently.

Well, I suppose Clark never pretended to like democracy much. And another forty autumns after that – well, thirty-nine, to be precise – I went back. And do you know, Blackpool's still going downhill. The town centre is so run-down the competition mainly comprises pound-shops being undercut by 99p shops. Its rather imposing red-brick semis go for prices that wouldn't buy you a beach hut in Bournemouth. It has ceased to be a venue for family summer holidays but, unlike the more southerly resorts, has found no real replacement. Its annual showcases for the benefit of respectable Britain, the party conferences, have migrated elsewhere, mainly inland. The Labour Party stopped going there in 2002, after the guacamole tendency had seen off the mushy peas tendency. The Tories, less fastidious, took a few years to follow suit.

The council spent many years trying to revamp the place as Britain's Las Vegas with its own supercasino. But a panel of great-and-gooders decided instead to send the project to Manchester, which was a bit like diverting regional aid to Park Lane. And when Gordon Brown, leader of Labour's no-fun-at-all tendency, became prime minister, he strangled the entire idea.

I am inclined to see Blackpool more as Lancashire's version of what New York is to the rest of the US: not the capital, and certainly not typical, but an exaggerated version of the whole. Lancashire is damp, dirty, funny, saucy. Blackpool is all that but a bit more so. It would be impossible to imagine it on the icy-fingered coast of Yorkshire. Mind you, if Blackpool were really New York, it would not have built its replica Eiffel Tower half-size; it would have been supersize. And were it really Las Vegas, it would have built not just the tower, but thrown in the Pyramids and the Taj Mahal for good measure.

Blackpool's trams have been upgraded: they no longer clank but take off with a Mancunian whoosh, which somewhat defeats the nostalgic object of having them. Other than that, the place maunders on. It is not appalling or loathsome, just a bit sad.

Nowhere is sadder than the Number 10 Bar at the Imperial Hotel, where the names of prime ministers are etched into the mirrors, and the walls are full of old political cuttings and cartoons. This used to be the late-night gathering place at conference time. Oh, I have seen Blackpool full of vulgar, common primitives all right, but most of them were in here, members of whichever party was in town, gossiping, shouting, laughing, drinking, boasting, lying, puking and trying to get laid. The barman said he had heard the conferences might come back once they had installed air conditioning in the Winter Gardens. I wasn't convinced.

Now the action belongs mainly to the stag and hen parties that have become Blackpool's most reliable source of both business and aggravation. Their gossip has more relation to reality than the politicians' version, but otherwise the pattern of late-night behaviour is much the same. On this occasion, however, the trouble was fiddling and small.

Blackpool was not empty: the guest houses were all displaying 'No Vacancies' signs. But the illuminations were lit and it was half-term, so there were more kids around than usual. Ken Dodd, just shy of his eighty-fifth birthday, was at the Grand Theatre, his fifty-fourth year of performing in Blackpool. It was also the weekend of the sixty-third Annual Sequence Dance Festival at the Winter Gardens. If I was quick, the programme suggested, I might make it in time for the final of the British Amateur Modern Sequence final: cash prizes for the first six, 'judging based on all-round efficiency in the Newchurch Waltz, Arcadia Foxtrot, Tango Callatina and New York Quickstep'; or the All Ladies Classical Sequence (the Regis Waltz, Saunter Shiraz and Waverley Two Step).

Despite the sudden popularity of dancing on TV, this was a subculture of which I knew nothing. Saunter Shiraz sounded like an Australian red; the others could be past winners of the Greyhound Derby. The box office being closed, I tried to blag and plead my way past the security men. It availed me nothing. Dressed for Blackpool in sweater and denim, I was passed by women dressed as though the Tory conference really had come home and it was the night of the prime minister's cocktail party.

Humiliated, I slunk away and wandered off to Funny Girls, the drag cabaret that has taken over the old art-deco Odeon. The dress code here was more relaxed; I would have passed muster in a cocktail frock myself. The DJ Zoe, aka Adrian, who has been here man, boy, woman and girl, was dressed in tarty pink and told some filthy jokes, one of which, involving a cheese toastie, sticks in my mind but is not going to make it into this book. The ensemble concluded with a splendid rendition of 'The Sun Has Got His Hat On'. All the stags, hens and some who might have been a bit of both had a splendidly raucous time and I concluded, only mildly pissed on the Saunter Shiraz or whatever, that the old town still had some life in it yet. Not sure what J.B., Alan Clark or Damien might have made of it all.

My adventures in New Lancashire were less uproarious. Next morning I drove to Crosby Beach, scene of *Another Place*, Antony Gormley's much-acclaimed installation of a hundred cast-iron moulds of his own naked body staring out to sea. It is said to represent the pain of emigration, though, for a successful artist, they might be staring towards Ireland or the Isle of Man and a more benign tax regime.

According to Sefton Council, their presence generates tourism (though only the hamburger and ice cream vans could possibly benefit) and 'extensive coverage of South Sefton in both the press and broadcast media'. A couple of feeble signs on the promenade warned people not to walk more than fifty metres from shore. This was separate from the eleven other thou-shalt-nots (not quite beating the record set the other side of the Mersey, see Chapter 15).

Yet the statues go out way, way further than that. So does the tide. And what's the point of any artwork if it can't be examined? The morning was dry, the sea calm, the tide out, the sand firm, the instruction ludicrous. So I strolled through the echelons of imitation naked Gormleys, stylised genitalia and all.

The most interesting bit was the way the barnacles and other marine life, invisible on the statues nearest shore, grew more and more encrusted as the lines headed out to sea and thus spent more time under water. I grew determined to reach the end of the line. By now I had gone a good quarter of a mile, the tide was on the turn and the sand was just starting to get squishy.

I was dauntless, having faced the far more dangerous tides of Morecambe Bay, under the guidance of the Queen's Guide to the Sands, Cedric Robinson MBE, the man the twenty-three Chinese cockle-pickers should have consulted before they were led to their doom in 2004. Nonetheless, the moment I sank up to my shins, just before reaching the furthest representation of barnacled Gormley, I concluded it was time to get the hell out.

A lifeguard buzzed round the beach in a 4×4 as the tide came in. Other people were out there, long after me. At least I think they were. It was a bit hard to tell from the promenade which ones were and were not Gormleys. One could imagine this ending in tears one day. That would get 'South Sefton' publicity all right.

The benchmark for old Lancashire is always the never-ending ITV soap opera *Coronation Street*, set in a fictional street in the fictional town of Weatherfield, always presumed to be Salford, very close to the Granada Studios, where the programme has been filmed since it began on 9 December 1960, before most of its current audience was born.

I suppose I was searching for some simulacrum of Coronation Street, somewhere in Lancashire – anywhere – bearing a resemblance to the way it was that December day when Ena Sharples, *sans* hairnet for once, marched into Florrie Lindley's corner shop and demanded, 'Are them fancies today's? I'll take half a dozen and no *e*-clairs.'

It certainly does not exist in *Coronation Street* itself. In its brilliantly written early days it was, in Charles Nevin's phrase, 'more sitcom than soap'; or, as Mike Harding put it, 'driven by character not plot'. It mutated, like the county itself. In 2002 a new production team decided, after years of rape, abductions, religious cults and transsexualism, to stop competing with rival soaps and reintroduce 'gentle storylines and humour'. For the upshot of that, I again have to quote that infallible source Wikipedia:

> In 2002, one of *Coronation Street*'s best-known storylines began, which culminated in 2003. Gail Platt married Richard Hillman (Brian Capron), a financial advisor, who would go on to leave Duggie Ferguson to die, murder his ex-wife Patricia, attempt

to murder his mother-in-law, Audrey Roberts, murder Maxine Peacock and attempt to murder Emily Bishop. After confessing to the murder of Maxine and his ex-wife, Hillman attempted to kill Gail, her children Sarah and David, and her granddaughter Bethany, by driving them into a canal. The storyline received wide press attention, and viewing figures peaked at 19.4 million, with Hillman dubbed a 'serial killer' by the media.

If the street really were in Salford, it would almost certainly have been demolished in the clearances of the 1960s and its inhabitants dispersed among the tower blocks. Is Ena's world still there anywhere? We can rule out the ring of mostly lower-division footballing mill towns north of Manchester, all the names redolent of hot Bovril, pools coupons, and the 5 p.m. radio reading of the results: Bolton, Oldham, Bury, Rochdale ... all of them transformed by de-industrialisation, commuterisation, embourgeoisement and immigration.

Even Accrington can be ruled out. Though the football clock was wound back to 1960, religious extremism now appears to be centred on the madrasas in a manner entirely alien to Jeanette Winterson's chapel-crazed (and in any case cruelly and lucratively fictionalised) mother. And Blackburn, even though it remains the global capital of the rolling R. 'Park the car *thurrr*!' I heard a man yelling into his mobile outside a betting shop. 'I'll pick you up *thurr*!' His face was black; his voice was purest Blackburn.

What about Rawtenstall? The very word typifies old Lancashire. It still has Fitzpatrick's, Britain's only surviving temperance bar, which appropriately (and not, one would guess, coincidentally) stands next to the imposing Methodist chapel. A fascinating place with a strange, not unpleasant, smell which could have come from any of the dozens of herbal remedies, Fitzpatrick's was once a chain to rival UCP. This one still stands, though it has become just a touch self-referential and postmodern ironic – it now bills itself as 'Mr Fitzpatrick's'. I can recommend the blood tonic, actually flavoured with rose hips and, I discovered after taking a bottle home, a good accompaniment to gin.

This may be a cruel trick on its teetotal inventor, Malachi Fitzpatrick, but it is hard to imagine that anyone left in Rawtenstall would care. Cheshire being too expensive, this has become prime commuter territory for Manchester media types. And the cafés have ciabatta on the menu and pot-pourri in the lavs. The Mancunian commuter belt is the best example, maybe the only example, anywhere in provincial England of somewhere that forms a counterweight to the madness of the South-East.

I kept asking knowledgeable Lancastrians where hadn't changed. Clitheroe, someone suggested. The name was promising enough. But take away the stone and the accents, and it could pass as Devon. Chipping, said someone. It turned out to be a village full of Mercedes. Downham was mentioned. In the Ribble Valley: a lovely spot, within sight of Pendle. It was here, just below Worsaw Hill, that I found (I think) the barn used in the 1961 film *Whistle Down the Wind*, that delicious black-and-white evocation of a 1950s northern childhood in which a group of children (led by Hayley Mills) mistake an escaped gunman (Alan Bates) for Jesus. The proposition now seems absurd. Of course, all the children would know about an escaped gunman. The question is whether they would have heard of Jesus.

Another source suggested the grim old mill town of Nelson. Unchanged? In some respects, yes. In the autumn of 2012, it still had terraced houses available for £17,000. Otherwise, Nelson has changed like no other small town in the country: Pakistanis constitute a majority of the town council. However, the jobs to which they originally migrated disappeared almost at once, leaving most bereft on the margins of society, their wives largely housebound, their children effectively segregated.

The town has one obvious success story. In a yellow-brick building next to the traditional indoor market – the Admiral's – now stands the Nelson Bazaar, 'the largest Asian market in Lancashire': opened in 2011 with about fifty stalls – far outstripping its neighbour – it sells hijabs and jilbabs; silks and cottons; bangles and earrings; saris in colours of a most un-Pennine exoticism.

We could have been anywhere in Pakistan, except for this. There I would have been a most welcome customer, a prize catch. Here I was a mere curiosity. The bazaar was crowded, on the build-up to the festival of Eid; indeed, it was planning to stay open next day until midnight. But there was no other white face in sight, except for an old woman who stared absolutely daggers through the window into what used to be Poundstretcher. The whites in Nelson all looked pained. That may have been caused by back spasms: the sleeping policemen here indulge in sleeping-police brutality, being built more like hills than humps. But I don't think that was the reason.

'Where do the saris come from?' I asked one of the traders.

'All imported. Mostly Pakistan. Karachi, Faisalabad, all over. Look,' he said, fingering an orange number. 'Only £30. This country too expensive.'

So Nelson has come full circle. Labour was imported to Lancashire from Pakistan to work in the cotton mills in a last-ditch attempt to compete with the subcontinent. Now the sons of those original migrants import their cottons from Pakistan anyway.

But I did know one candidate for Coronation Street. It was nearly a hundred miles from Salford. I had discovered it three years earlier when I briefly became public enemy no. 1 in Barrow-in-Furness.

North-West Evening Mail, 31 October 2009. 'NOWHERESVILLE,' roared the front-page splash. 'Anger as national paper reporter slams Barrow'.

It was all over pages two and three as well: 'FURY AT SLUR ON BARROW'. Next to a large picture of a handsome and dashing young journalist, nearby headlines read: 'Man awaits sex trial' and 'Search continues', which were not actually related but looked as though they might be. 'I found some of his comments quite bizarre,' said the Conservative council leader, Jack Richardson. 'It may have been a clever piece of writing,' commented the former Labour leader, Terry Waiting, 'but then so was *Noddy*.'

The leader columns and letters continued all through the following week, by which time some people had actually taken the trouble to read the original article, a profile of Barrow for the *Financial Times* magazine, and began to defend me. It's true I called it Nowheresville, quoted an anonymous source who described it as the 'arse-end of the Lake District' and poked fun at the rush hour – which is not even a rush minute, more like Sunday morning anywhere else.

I also wrote this:

Just five minutes' walk from the town centre is Hindpool, full of terraced houses – now with satellite dishes and double glazing and new front doors, but essentially little changed ... Hartington Street has little front gardens, and every one I saw was lovingly tended. The paper girl was walking down nearby Anson Street (the *North-West Evening Mail* still commands loyalty, a sure sign of a stable community), and everyone she passed said hello. The ice cream van trilled by, drawing attention from eight-year-old boys wandering around with plastic machine guns (a sign of innocence, not guilt). It felt like a fifty-year-old episode of *Coronation Street*. Maureen Whidborne, who runs the Neighbourhood Watch, admits she is not overworked: 'We hardly get any trouble, and we all know our neighbours. This is a lovely area.'

Barrow is the main town of what used to be known as Lancashire-across-the-sands, the detached portion that could only be reached from the rest of the county by a convoluted car journey via the corner of Westmorland; a slow train ride from Carnforth over the Kent Estuary and Cartmel Sands; or the perilous walk across Morecambe Bay, which should never be remotely attempted without the presence of the Queen's Guide, whether or not Her Majesty is accompanying you. Lancashire-across-the-sands was duly rationalised out of existence as an affront to straight lines and logic in 1974, to more than normal local annoyance, and the whole area dumped into Cumbria.

But I never saw anywhere that fitted that idealised portrait of old Lancashire more than Anson Street. When I went back to Barrow, I did not attempt to make my peace with the town hall. I did go and knock gently on Maureen Whidborne's front door.

She was never an Ena Sharples-type battleaxe but a woman of considerable energy who ensured that Anson Street got a kids' playground and anything else it needed: she was the fixed point on which the community turned. No more. Two months after my first visit, she had a stroke; then they diagnosed cancer. 'They gave her three weeks, and then three months. But she's still here,' said her husband, Bill. He was now nursing her full-time. There was no street party for the Diamond Jubilee in 2012 because Maureen was no longer able to organise it.

She was still sitting outside the front door on fine afternoons, with the kids coming by and saying hello. But she was no longer able to say much back. Bill thought of moving to a smaller house. 'But you don't know what your neighbours will be like,' he said.

Might they consider moving nearer their son? He's in Beaconsfield, Buckinghamshire. Bill shuddered a bit: 'Nobody cares who you are down there. They walk straight past you.'

September/October 2012

21. *The commuter homeward plods his weary way*

BUCKINGHAMSHIRE

The best-known suburb of Slough has only one industry, one in keeping with Britain's new emphasis on manufacturing for niche markets rather than the masses. It turns out precision-engineered human beings (male version only): a five-year process conducted in a factory that has been in continuous production since 1440.

The enduring success of Eton College rests on a handful of principles that, like so much in English, and particularly Etonian, life, are instinctively understood even if they have never been formally codified. The school is lavishly funded; it guards its reputation; and it aspires to excellence by being infinitely adaptable, changing slowly but then wholeheartedly, adopting new concepts (IT, male emotions) and discarding the old (flogging, fagging).

And it nurtures this adaptability under a thick mulch of tradition, which the boys find both intimidating and relishable, and outsiders both ridiculous and fascinating. Many of the country's most successful institutions share this knack, but even the monarchy finds it hard to out-detail Eton: a sign in the window of New and Lingwood, one of several competing school outfitters in the High Street, says there are 110 different designs for official Eton socks.

It was St Andrew's Day – actually it was thirteen days before anyone else's St Andrew's Day, but if Eton says it's St Andrew's Day, then so be it. And the crowds were gathering for perhaps the most impenetrable of all Etonian traditions: the Wall Game. The St Andrew's match takes place, and has done since the 1840s, between the King's Scholars, spiritual descendants of the original scholarship boys for whom the school was founded, and the Oppidans, which is everyone else. And no sporting event in the world offers a more compelling spectacle in the minutes before it starts.

The Collegers enter the field, arms interlinked, and march slowly forward like policemen scouring a ploughed field for a murder weapon. The Oppidans (literally, the townsmen, as any Etonian Latin scholar ought to know) climb over the wall from the street like intruders and leap down on to the field like SAS men. Both teams, their faces painted, form huddles to perform variants on the Maori haka, and everyone is duly enchanted. Even the referee, Angus Graham-Campbell, was delightfully dressed: in white tie, tails, green tartan trousers, a waistcoat in another green tartan, topped off with a red tartan handkerchief.

Unfortunately, the Wall Game then starts. *The Economist* once called this 'the world's dullest game'. This may be an understatement. For the next hour, most of the players sit on top of each other in an eternal scrum at the base of the wall, notionally trying to release the invisible ball into open space.

The players are not allowed to use their hands, or the customary violence that resolves a rugby scrum. And not much can happen even if they do because the pitch is only about six yards wide, so the oval ball soon goes out of play and the whole process resumes a little further along.

Not surprisingly, goals are rare. In fact, there has not been one in the St Andrew's match since 1909. They occasionally happen in the minor fixtures involving scratch teams and so on, but two world wars have been fought and dozens of Etonian Cabinet ministers have come and gone since anyone scored in this contest. A century and a bit is merely a blink of an eye in the history of Eton, but an hour of watching this stuff is a mighty long time, I can tell you.

The first 'How long does this go on?' that I overheard came after four minutes, though we already seemed to have been watching for ever. The game is sometimes decided by a lesser sort of goal, a shy, but by half-time there had not even been a chance of a chance of a chance and even Graham-Campbell admitted this was a particularly dreary fixture.

Despite the absence of any activity, it looked like a total mismatch.

The King's Scholars represent just one of Eton's twenty-five houses: they have seventy potential players against the Oppidans' 1,200-plus. They are also, ex officio, swots and, when they emerged from the huddles, one could see they were about half the size of the opposition.

The Oppidan supporters perched on the wall, where you might, if you happened to be precisely above the melee, actually see the ball. They were dismissive and footballish in their chanting: (to 'She'll Be Coming Round the Mountain') 'Have you ever seen a KS with a bird?' The KS had black-gowned choristers, who were at once more erudite and plaintive, adapting that most Etonian of hymns, 'I Vow to Thee My Country': 'We may not be the strongest, we may not be the best ...'

The game dragged on. The parents and siblings (the sisters were first to crack) and Old Etonians had drifted away, as did the Oppidan supporters on the wall. The Scholars' choir remained, and alongside the wall their players held firm. And with five minutes to go, SOMETHING ALMOST HAPPENED. The KS players broke upfield and launched an attack. The few remaining spectators grew animated, uncertain whether anything had actually occurred. It hadn't, and eventually the clock struck 12 and the contest was over: 0–0, as usual. Graham-Campbell thought the Scholars had won a moral victory, though.

I have long suspected that Eton doesn't really have lessons in the conventional sense; and that the college simply inculcates into the boys, over and over again, the mysterious Etonian art of exuding charm and generosity and still getting your own way.

I think now that even the seemingly pointless exercise of the Wall Game teaches something almost as important. The Scholars team, with its tiny pool of players, practises more and cares more about the result: it is important in counteracting their image as spotty and swotty. With the normal brutal methods of winning the ball banned, their persistence and determination were able to nullify what seemed like overwhelming opposition. What a wonderful lesson for life. Just because something looks stupid, it doesn't mean it is stupid.

I discovered that was even true of Angus Graham-Campbell's rig-out, when I plucked up the courage to ask. He pointed to his tartan trousers: 'Graham,' he said. Then the tartan waistcoat: 'Campbell.' And finally the handkerchief: 'Maclean. My mother was a Maclean.'

Buckinghamshire is the right place for Eton, because this is the county of educational extremism. Milton Keynes has the Open University, the one undeniable achievement of Harold Wilson's Labour government. Yet just up the road is its polar opposite: the University of Buckingham, the independent institution nurtured by Margaret Thatcher, and a bolthole for right-wing academics. I looked at the list of Buckingham's prominent alumni on Wikipedia. I hadn't heard of a single one.

More significant for most of the county's population is that Buckinghamshire has been the last redoubt of wholly selective education. In the early 1970s, Thatcher, as education secretary, supposedly closed down more grammar schools than anyone else. That process continued apace after the Tories lost power in 1974, but Buckinghamshire kept fighting in the courts to preserve its mix of grammar schools, for those who passed the 11-plus, and secondary moderns, for those who failed.

By the time Mrs T returned to government in her own right five years later, she had changed her tune. It was politically and practically impossible to revive the deceased grammars, but she called a truce: the 160-odd grammars that had survived in pockets round the country could remain, and the Buckinghamshire system was allowed to remain intact, a nostalgic relic. (It is still there, though not in Milton Keynes.)

In 2009 I visited two schools next to each other: Aylesbury Grammar for boys and the Grange Upper School. The first had blazers, crests, ties, manners, prefects, a cricket square, 400 years' continuous history, a fast track to Oxbridge and what the head called 'expectations', not rules; the other had bugger all. The Grange's head had never even been round the grammar school. The distinction was maintained by Buckinghamshire's own 11-plus, a test of verbal reasoning, evidently designed to find future Scrabble and crossword champions. The words 'pass' and 'fail' were banned by the county council in an uncharacteristic fit of political correctness, but effectively most were being passed or failed for life.

The first effect of this has been to make Buckinghamshire property even more of a magnet: the chance of a quasi-public school education at zero cost. What pushy parent could resist? The second effect has been to make those parents even more obsessed about their children's schooling than the rest of southern England's bourgeoisie. Whole dinner parties are given over to discussing what coaching schemes are available to get through the exam, and how to game the appeals system if it goes wrong (though I was also told that parents liked to keep good wheezes secret for fear of alerting the competition). Perhaps one day a sociologist can assess the third effect: the long-term consequences of near-total segregation from the eve of puberty onwards.

As if Buckinghamshire was not divided enough already. It was never a coherent county, being long and thin: sixty-six miles from Eton to the furthest northern border. Chesham and Amersham are on the Metropolitan Line; Stony Stratford is almost in Northamptonshire. Power and population have been shifting south since Tudor times: Buckingham lost the assizes to Aylesbury in Henry VIII's reign; 200 years later Aylesbury took over as the county town.

Ignored by the main roads and railways, Buckingham remains agreeably, indeed astonishingly, dozy, hard to relate to the county which takes its name. Although the university campus is within walking distance of the town centre, there is nowhere in England that feels quite so unstudenty. There are stories that the inmates get bused to Milton Keynes for a night out. Most are said to be foreign and obscenely rich. I'm not convinced they actually exist.

This was ever a county of class distinction and great country houses, many of them built by the Rothschilds, and a good few famous for their goings-on. There is West Wycombe Park, once home of Sir Francis Dashwood, leading light of the Hellfire Club; there is Mentmore Towers, home of the prime minister Lord Rosebery and later the Maharishi Mahesh Yogi, who briefly turned it into another outré Buckinghamshire educational establishment, the Maharishi University of Natural Law; there is Cliveden, where before the war the Astors entertained prominent Nazis, and after it Christine Keeler entertained John Profumo; and then of course Chequers, country home of British prime ministers since 1921 and where, during the reign of Mrs Thatcher (1979–90), the PM bused in strippergram hunks and women police constables from Princes Risborough to entertain voyeuristic visiting heads of government with acts of sexual depravity (*note to editor: please check this one*).

And yet here, amid all this splendour and fun, are the two most despised towns in the country ...

There is only one place to go in central Milton Keynes: the centre:mk, the giant shopping plaza, which in 2010 was Grade II listed as 'of national interest' architecturally, to the delight of the concrete-loving Twentieth Century Society and the fury of the owners, who saw themselves being sodded about by planners every time they wanted to change a window frame. They were lucky: it was nearly listed as Grade II*, which would have put it on a par with a lower-division cathedral.

The centre seems to be pretty much the only place to shop, other than outlying supermarkets, in a borough of 250,000 people. But it has its pluses: the first thing I saw – entering just before 6 on a wintry evening – was a branch of Patisserie Valerie with one of their *tartes aux framboises* giving me a come-on from the window. I resisted and walked around, eventually coming out into a frigid uncovered patch, to be greeted by Milton Keynes's most famous inhabitants, the original concrete cows, lurking grasslessly under what might have been a concrete oak tree.

By now I felt chilly and a bit disorientated: I was fixating on the *tarte aux framboises* but I couldn't find the way back, and the signs were confusing. The place was so huge, and I felt old, alien even. By the time I sorted myself out, though all the surrounding shops were in full pre-Christmas cry, the patisserie had pulled down the shutters.

There is something about Milton Keynes that makes it seem like the county town of Stepfordshire. The inhabitants radiate positivity: very defensive, a bit frightening. Uprooted from their families, they had to help each other from the start, and there is thus an exceptional network of local groups, which seem to be more to do with shared problems than shared interests. They know outsiders even hate their football team, moved here from Wimbledon in dubious circumstances. They get revenge by being extra nice and taking refuge in the thickets of their local codes: the H roads and the V roads and the redways and the colour-coded parking zones, all with complex regulations.

Twenty-two million trees were plonked down with the 125 roundabouts. (Or was it the other way round? One gets muddled.) And as the trees mature, there is a growing perception that Milton Keynes is maturing too: increasingly there are three-generational families, because grandparents are now moving here on retirement to be near their offspring.

But it looks to me like twenty-two million houses, and as I drove past them I began to hum Pete Seeger:

> *Little boxes on the hillside,*
> *Little boxes made of ticky tacky,*
> *Little boxes on the hillside,*
> *Little boxes all the same.*
> *There's a green one and a pink one*

And a blue one and a yellow one,
And they're all made out of ticky tacky
And they all look just the same.

Except that the colour scheme in Milton Keynes is nowhere near as daring and varied:

There's a beige one and a grey one
And a brown one and a russet one ...

The glory of England is that it is a palimpsest: every town, every village rests on layers of the past, all of them waiting to be rediscovered. Yet not this one: it is, by and large, a single daub – not a wholly ugly one, but painted in the style of the 1960s, when it was assumed that the motor car was the eternal future.

I had come here to look for the past, though. Without satnav it would have been unfindable, because it does not rate a proper mention on the signposts. Eventually it appears but only in brackets: Middleton (Milton Keynes Village). This was the original place, so obscure that in the 1960s it had the postal address 'Milton Keynes, Newport Pagnell, Bucks'.

'MILTON KEYNES,' wrote Arthur Mee. 'It lies among meadows through which wind the Ouzel and its tributary brooks, and has thatched cottages which must have looked for centuries much as they look today.' The second part of that is still true, though there was something themeparky about Milton Keynes Village: the thatched pub looked strangely pristine (it had been rebuilt after a fire, I discovered); Manor Farmhouse had obviously not seen a muddy hoofprint in decades.

The only person out on a frosty morning was the postwoman.

'Bit different from your other rounds?'

'I love this one,' she replied. 'It's so peaceful.'

Peaceful? The roar of traffic was constant. She directed me to the house where the church key was kept, and a grey-haired woman handed it over.

'Umm, you don't happen to know if there's anyone left round here from when there was just the village?'

'Well, yes,' said Catherine Held. 'Me.'

The church was pleasant, unusually light and airy. In Milton Keynes terms Catherine Held was also a reminder of a bygone age. Half a century earlier, she was a teenager, living in this same house with her parents when the plans were announced for a new city (technically, it isn't a city, but that has never bothered anyone) which ultimately was named after this little spot.

'It was a time when if you missed the last bus back on a Wednesday, the next one was on Saturday.'

'So the news was exciting?'

'Oh, yes. For me.'

The bus service quickly improved. The farmers were bought out, not especially generously. But for many years the original Milton Keynes remained largely unaffected by the huge surge of population into the area. Then it was announced that the fields round the village itself would be developed. The residents fought, but mainly to persuade the authorities not to use the name Milton Keynes Village for the new houses, so the villagers could maintain their own distinctiveness. So the estate was given the half-hearted name of Middleton.

'We weren't really part of the new city,' said Catherine. 'Now we're part of it. We heard the cuckoo for years and years. Then one year it never came back.'

'That field over there,' said her husband, Michael, pointing towards the back of his garden. 'It was going to be eighteen executive homes. Then it was going to be twenty-three superior homes. Then thirty substantial homes. How many did they build in the end? Fifty-four.'

But the Helds are not dog-in-the-manger about it all. 'If you get on your bicycle and go on to the redways [*Oh! So that's what a redway is!*] you get an idea of what the planners were after,' said Catherine. 'They could have made a much bigger mess of it,' said Michael.

And they have not done so bad themselves. Houses in the village fetch a premium. And the noise was nothing to do with the city. It was the M1, which came first.

An unknown resident once compared Buckinghamshire to 'a river delta in the rainy season, its swollen arteries (the motorways to London) bursting their banks and flooding everywhere so that – even literally from the air – genuinely rural Bucks appeared like islets of higher ground, with the flood water still rising ...'

I was pointed to that by John Gulliver, a retired farmer and gifted amateur artist living in the village of Preston Bissett, near Buckingham.

He remembered when someone moving in or out of the village was a major event. 'There used to be generations upon generations,' he said. 'For me, the village changed when they did away with the cobbled pavements and put kerbstones in. I think that's when it got a bit suburby.'

But the suburbanisation process gets hastened because Bucks has always beckoned to London as a useful, seemingly empty, not over-beautiful dumping ground for pretty much anything. Sometimes the locals fight it off: at one time the villages west of Leighton Buzzard – Cublington, Dunton, Stewkley and, appropriately enough, Wing – were favourites to be obliterated by the third London airport.

The Roskill Commission, which was set up to find a site for the airport, actually voted to plonk it here. But by the time the report appeared, it was the 1970s not the 1960s and the placid acceptance of progress that greeted the build-up of Milton Keynes had evaporated. 'Do you think these farmworkers would not fight?' cried the Rector of Dunton, Rev. Hubert Sillitoe. 'The English have always fought. I would give my blessing to people who fought because I believe it is licit for a Christian to bear arms in defence of his own home.' The government coughed politely and ultimately gifted the airport to Stansted.

Buckinghamshire was cunning as well as militant: note the rector's use of the emotive word 'farmworkers' rather than, say, 'management consultants'. Ever since, rural Buckinghamshire has been perpetually on its guard against fresh intrusions. Sometimes, I think the whole place just melds into one village that might be rechristened High Dudgeon or Great Umbrage. Cublington and Dunton are now at peace, or at least only low dudgeon and little umbrage. The places bearing arms, or at least up in them, lie south and west, on the proposed route of the HS2 super-duper railway line to the North-West.

Next to Preston Bissett is Twyford (not to be confused with any other Twyfords), a fair-sized village with a pub, a community shop, a school, a church with an ornate Norman doorway and a Chinese takeaway. Behind the church is St Mary's House, the old vicarage, containing the remnants of a medieval hall house which Gary Eastman, the director of a construction company, has been painstakingly restoring for the past twenty-five years. Seventy metres from his north wall, across a flood meadow, is the trackbed of the long-forgotten Great Central Railway. And behind that ...

Well, sometime in the 2020s (or, this being England, the 2030s or

2040s), there, according to the government, will be the route of HS2: on an embankment four metres above the meadow, with trains travelling up to 250 mph and emitting sound of around ninety-seven decibels. Comparisons in this area are complex, but this is just above the level of a pneumatic drill.

The Twyford Action Group, with Eastman in the van, has not surprisingly been prominent in the Stop HS2 campaign. The problem is that, unlike an airport, this cannot be palmed off on to Essex. It runs through Buckinghamshire or nowhere, and the politicians have been surprisingly steadfast. I am all for Nimbyism myself and would bear arms in defence of my home if I thought I could shoot straight. The problem is that if we Nimbies won every round, we would all still be living in medieval hall houses or mud huts. Eastman understands this. He is in construction: he even builds power stations; he believes the country needs infrastructure, and that the economy needs major projects to create employment. But not this version of it: 'The business case is just a joke.'

'So what should we be building instead?'

'The third runway at Heathrow.'

'Someone else's nightmare.'

'Of course it is. But it's absolutely necessary in my view.'

There was, I sensed, an air of impending doom in his voice. The case for the line rests not on the first leg to Birmingham, but its eventual extension to the North. Most of the antis I met just said, 'We wouldn't mind if there was anything in it for us' – i.e. we're agin it because there are no plans to include a stop nearby.

Eastman is hoping for mitigation, notably a berm between the village and the railway to deaden the sound. This, according to the HS2 company, depends on justifying it to the government and on the availability of spoil to build it. The villagers have already achieved one victory: the original plan was to build the new route hereabouts along the Great Central. It's now been agreed to site it 140 metres further away from the village. It was a victory for the villagers and one which Eastman helped achieve.

Unfortunately for him, that puts his house outside the zone whereby he could sell it to the government at market price. 'In theory my house is worth about £1.25 million right now. If I could sell it at all now, I would get half that. I've put twenty-five years into this and it's halved in value.'

There is another irony. If the Great Central had never been closed, there would be an extra route to the North, ideal for freight if not passengers, and there would be no case for HS2 at all.

I drove south to Stoke Poges and arrived, as one should, just before dusk, which, at the end of November, meant 3.30 p.m. I was looking for what is probably the most famous churchyard in the world, but it was impossible to find. Eventually, someone gave me directions to the church and I ended up at a modern block: St Andrew's Church. Luckily they were serving tea in there and, after a quick gulp, I was redirected to St Giles, nearly two miles away. There was no sign to it at all.

There is a car park but it closes an hour before sunset ('We've had quite a few cars torched'), which would have been mighty inconvenient had Thomas Gray been driving: he might have had to find another churchyard.

But somehow Gray parked himself here, probably in 1742, perhaps under one of the immemorial yews, and began the most famous, and perhaps the most beautiful, evocation of evening – that most magical English time of a day – in the canon.

Elegy Written in a Country Churchyard

The curfew tolls the knell of parting day,
The lowing herd wind slowly o'er the lea
The ploughman homeward plods his weary way,
And leaves the world to darkness and to me.

Now fades the glimm'ring landscape on the sight,
And all the air a solemn stillness holds.
Save where the beetle wheels his droning flight,
And drowsy tinklings lull the distant folds;

Oh yeah, right. Instead of a lowing herd, there was the lowing of successive take-offs from Heathrow and the traffic of the M40 and the drowsy tinklings of a chainsaw. But inside the church, the declining light through the stained glass bathed the place in a moody glow.

Gray is buried in a sarcophagus outside the east wall, along with his mother and beloved aunt. He is not mentioned on the tomb itself because there was no space: the curse of the writer through the ages. But there is a memorial stone on the wall and a monument hidden away in a wood – so discreetly that, in the gloaming, I originally failed to find it, although it is very large and rather coarse. Apparently, there used to be a regular traffic of American tourists here, on a coach from London that offered this as a package with Windsor Castle. And they would stand and recite the elegy in homage.

But that trade seems to have ceased. Perhaps American visitors have become less cultured; perhaps, like me, they were affronted by the racket; perhaps it was because the route took them through the one town in Britain more universally derided than Milton Keynes.

To my astonishment, it took more time to get from St Andrew's to St Giles' than it did from St Giles' into Slough. The very name Slough is the first problem; Betjeman compounded it ('Come, friendly bombs, and fall on Slough'); and its reputation has stuck ever since, as when the famously ferocious Mr Justice Melford Stevenson, uncharacteristically faced with an acquittal in his courtroom, told the defendant, 'I see you come from Slough. It's a horrible place. You can go back there.' The Slough Sewage Works is often held responsible for the stench on the M4.

In the First World War, a huge acreage round here was used as a dump. In the 1930s that turned into the Slough Trading Estate, which generated a light-industrial boom town that absorbed thousands of migrants from the depressed areas.

But the town never weathered. It evolved into a national joke, the obvious site for the Wernham Hogg Paper Company, whose regional manager was David Brent in *The Office*, the most resonant sitcom of the early twenty-first century. Its one tourist attraction (if we accept Eton as being elsewhere) might have been the observatory where Sir William Herschel discovered Uranus. But, with Slough's instinctive gift for marketing and PR, it got demolished in the 1960s.

Too tired to drive home, I resolved to spend Friday night in Slough. Some of the pubs were lively, including one known as the Herschel and a modern one called Wernham Hoggs. The High Street was almost deserted save for a few shadowy figures in hoodies, mostly lurking in doorways. I opted to eat in Pizza Express, which was deserted, perhaps the only Pizza Express in the country to have no trade on a Friday night. 'We've been busy all week and all day,' said the waitress. 'But people don't come to Slough to go out. They mainly go to Windsor.'

I took in the fact that we were only four miles from Windsor, two from Stoke Poges and less than three from Eton, the Wall Game and Angus Graham-Campbell's contrasting tartans. Is this a great country or what?

November 2012

~~~~~~~

By summer 2014 Gary Eastman had accepted that overall defeat was inevitable and that HS2 would be built. Twyford had achieved some tactical successes: the line past the village will now be protected by both a berm and an inner wall to deaden the sound. The government has also offered some compensation to homeowners outside the full buyout area: however, Eastman has been told the maximum available is £22,500. He has been advised his house is effectively unsaleable, and likely to remain so until after the line is built, whenever that might be. 'We're staying,' he says. 'We've got no choice.'

22. *Tally-ho, isn't it?*

LEICESTERSHIRE

After nightfall I parked, over-cautiously, on the edge of town and walked a long way past the 1950s semis. Many of them were decorated, as for Christmas, though it was too early for that. Some of them had fireworks issuing from the back garden, as for Bonfire Night. But it was too late for that.

The front gardens were paved for extra parking rather than tended, which was one indicator that this was not a traditional English suburb. The few houses with names were called Krishna Kunj or Sita Ram, which was a more obvious clue.

This was Melton Road in Leicester, which morphs into the terraced houses of Belgrave Road: 'the Golden Mile' and the centre of Indian life in Britain. Tonight was Diwali, the festival of light. It marks, among other things, the Hindu New Year (in this case the year 2069) and the victorious return of Lord Rama after his battles against the demon king of Sri Lanka. It is also an occasion to invoke the goddess Lakshmi, symbol of prosperity.

All the adverts and signs wished people 'a prosperous New Year'. None of your sentimental Anglo-Saxon 'happy' stuff.

The official action was centred on Cossington Street Recreation Ground, where the city council had erected a stage on which a succession of Indian dance troupes, all grace and arms like Lakshmi herself, performed attractively but repetitively, interrupted only by self-important speeches from officials. The real throng was on the street, mainly in family groups: the kids clutched their parents with one hand and let off handheld bangers with the other. It might have been a Matlock-style *passeggiata*, had it been easier to find a passage.

In contrast to Blackpool, Leicester's Golden Mile stretches less than half a mile but the golden bit is no exaggeration. The shops concentrate on three things: Indian sweeties, saris and jewellery. And the jewellers don't mess about: the focus is on gold. It suits the local taste: Leicester's Indians are mainly Gujaratis, well known in India for their business acumen and also their love of bling. But there may be another reason. Gold has always been the luxury of choice for communities whose roots are shallow ones. It is portable, hideable and famously gains value in difficult times. And this is a community still not wholly certain it might never have to uproot itself again.

'Is your job always as gentle as this?' I asked a relaxed-looking police sergeant, as he benignly savoured the atmosphere.

'I've had worse duties.'

'Because there's no drinking, I assume?'

He nodded. 'Bit different from the city centre on Christmas Eve.'

The crowd was, I suppose, about 90 per cent Asian. And it was huge: 10,000 in Cossington Street alone (according to the *Leicester Mercury*, though only on page 25, there being no trouble and thus no news), many thousands more on Belgrave Road. There were a fair number of white faces: the Golden Mile restaurants are where the communities intersect. But it was only as I was leaving, when I saw four youths in patkas, that I realised I had seen no other Sikhs at all, even though Diwali is a Sikh festival as well as a Hindu one.

I doubt if there were any Muslims either, not even from the substantial Somali bloc now centred nearby in St Matthew's. This was a night for Leicester's dominant community, who mostly came from Gujarat via East Africa in the early 1970s to what was then an overwhelmingly white city. It is an extraordinary, little-explored turn of history.

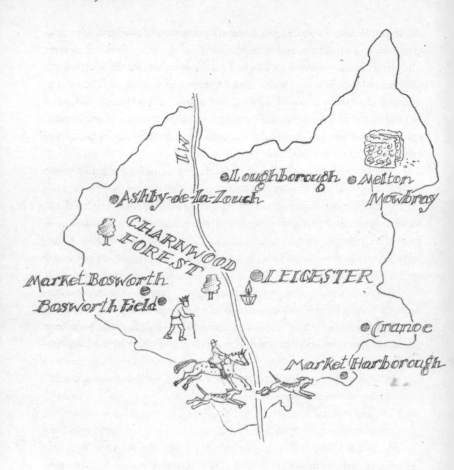

In the late 1960s the newly independent East African countries started low-level harassment of their Gujarati traders, who had sat uneasily in the middle of the social structure throughout the imperial era, hated by the blacks, despised by the British. At first Britain resisted letting them settle here, even if they held British passports. But in 1972 the Ugandan dictator Idi Amin shifted from harassment to expulsion, and the situation changed from a grumbling problem to a humanitarian emergency, and Britain had to respond.

A few of those smart enough to get out early had already settled in Leicester. So the city council took out adverts in the Ugandan papers warning that the city was full, which the Gujaratis took as an indication of milk and honey. There was a half-hearted attempt at dispersal, but once in, they were free to move, and soon enough the exiles gravitated to Leicester. But why? It wasn't just the adverts. According to one academic, Professor Gurharpal Singh, many of the East Africans had trading contacts there: some had actually been buying Leicester-produced knitwear and hosiery to sell in Africa. There was also cheap and available housing, partly because the Belgrave area had been blighted by an abortive motorway plan. And there were a fair few jobs.

Though right-wing MPs warned of fearful consequences, they never came. This was mainly because these were the ideal immigrants: they already spoke good English, and they were educated, resourceful, hard-working, instinctively self-reliant and entrepreneurial. These were, en masse, the nice Mr Patels (Patel being a Gujarati name) who were already starting to take over the nation's newsagents and keeping them open much longer than their predecessors, elderly English couples in cardigans.

Professor Singh also credits the city council, which was hereabouts taken over by funkier and leftier Labour councillors, for embracing the newcomers – many of whom turned into the kind of businessmen Labour lefties hate on principle if they're white. Leicester became the poster child for modern British race relations. According to the 2011 census, 'white British' were down to 45 per cent of the city's population. The news passed almost unnoticed.

However, there are embers here that no one wishes to poke just in case some resentment might still be smouldering. Asaf Hussain of Leicester University lectures in communal relations and specialises in organising tours – much appreciated by parliamentary candidates among others – of the city's places of worship: temples, mosques, Sikh gurdwaras, the cathedral and the synagogue. His much-respected wife, Freda, became high sheriff of Leicestershire and deputy Lord Lieutenant. 'We know *everybody*,' Asaf said.

But he isn't starry-eyed. 'This is still a multicultural city, not an intercultural city. Children of different races make friends with each other at school but afterwards they tend to drift apart. If the English eat Asian food, it's not because they have a close relationship with the culture, they just like the food.'

And the same applies in reverse. Successful migrants have begun moving out of the cramped terraces of Belgrave to more expansive suburbs, and a handful to the countryside. This does not imply integration into Leicestershire's traditional pursuits.

'Have you ever been invited to go fox-hunting?' I asked Asaf.

'Oh yes. I told them I wasn't interested. I've never heard of any Asian going fox-hunting.'

'The maharajas?'

'Only to impress the British. For Hindus it would not be very good. There's an elephant god and a cow god and they would be very angry.'

'There are supposed to be 300 million Hindu gods, aren't there? There's probably a fox-god somewhere.'

'Maybe. Who knows?'

There are close to a million people living in Leicestershire, a third of them in Leicester itself. The connection between city and county, still overwhelmingly white, was never very strong. And the link has become ever more tenuous, especially since Leicester regained its old independence from the county council (along with Rutland) in 1997.

The cathedral has become somewhat eclipsed by the more vibrant destinations on Asaf's itinerary, though it has been an important force in Leicester's strong interfaith relations. Though only an overgrown parish church, bumped up to cathedral status in 1927, it has a certain rustic charm, especially in the autumn when the leaves pile up among the gravestones.

It was also the first cathedral I visited where, far from demanding money at gunpoint, they made it hard to make a donation at all. 'Ah,' said Beryl, one of the volunteers. 'We used to have a glass thing by the door but it got rifled so many times we had to give up.' They now use a medieval chest that is harder both to find and to open.

This cathedral, rather than offering sanctuary to fugitives, is sited amid Leicester's most interesting section of higgledy-piggledy lanes and so offers a range of outward escape routes. Sometimes stuff that gets nicked – not the money obviously – makes its way back. Beryl gave me a tour of the returned treasures: 'That sounding board above the pulpit. That was stolen years ago. It turned up in Derby. And those carvings. They went walkies.'

The cathedral has been hoping for a little publicity boost. In 2012 what was thought to be the body of Richard III was discovered over the road, in what was formerly Greyfriars churchyard, now the council's staff car park. It was sent away to a secret destination for further forensic analysis, pending possible reburial inside the cathedral. I like to think of old

Crookback lying there for five centuries, orchestrating all the thefts like some regal Fagin: 'I hope you've been at work this morning, my dears.'

As things stood, there was a gaping hole in the car park, covered with a marquee as if for a garden party, and, in the cathedral, a tablet behind the altar, recording that he was buried nearby, but neither praising nor monstering him. It has been hard enough to find out where Richard was killed, never mind buried. Some years earlier, Leicestershire County Council invested in a heritage centre on Ambion Hill near Market Bosworth, where – it was thought at the time – the Battle of Bosworth was fought in 1485. Latest research, however, suggests it took place two miles away, on the flatlands near Stoke Golding.

The council responded phlegmatically. It could have been worse. One theory had been that the battle was in another county altogether. Ernie White, the councillor in charge of building the centre, was particularly relieved: 'My leader said, "If it turns out to be in Warwickshire, Whitey, you're sacked."'

Assuming he was in Leicestershire at the time, Richard III gave himself the best possible chance of a deal on his kingdom-for-a-horse special offer.

The roads of most counties are traffic-clogged. The roads of Leicestershire are horse-clogged. On an unpromising November morning, there they all were: on every B road, on every country lane, round the next bend; the ladies (mostly) of the county, riding with the hauteur that can only be achieved by an Englishwoman on horseback.

The county's emblem is the fox, which is odd because the fox's sole purpose in Leicestershire has traditionally been to get torn apart. But these days the fox has a city-sized bolthole. Reynard could swagger from Leicester Cathedral towards Humberstone Gate carrying a wadful of money and the snazziest kind of mobile, and no one would threaten him. He would be off limits even to the collection-box thieves. And this is not just because of the pacific Gujaratis.

I heard similar stories even in Melton Mowbray. Melton! Not just un-Gujarati but the fox-hunting capital of the universe, where the territories of the Quorn, the Belvoir and the Cottesmore, three of Leicestershire's four famous hunts, all converge. In theory, a fox ought to get eaten alive on sight. In practice, the fox has taken command of the suburban gardens, brazenly feasting, for instance, on the blood-fish-and-bone in my sister-in-law's pots of lamb's lettuce. And, in summer I dare say, he takes over the loungers on Melton's sun-kissed terraces, demanding plates of roast chicken, washed down by crisp Sancerre. And if everything is not to his satisfaction, barking at his hostess, 'Not this one, it's corked, you vixen.'

Asaf Hussain was not quite correct. I heard of an Asian doctor who was a regular with the county's fourth hunt, the Fernie. Very nice bloke, I was told. However, he wasn't from Leicester. He lived in Kettering. Northamptonshire.

Fernie country comprises the southern part of Leicestershire, from the Northamptonshire border and into the area east of the city known, misleadingly, as High Leicestershire. (Charnwood Forest, now largely deforested, is actually higher.) And as I drove through their territory to the little village of Cranoe, the road got ever more crowded.

Passing motorists, knowing their lowly place in the scheme of things, sat and waited while a stream of riders, in anonymous black jackets, turned into a farmyard. And there among the silage bales they gathered for the Wednesday morning meet of the Fernie. This is an event that would have received even less publicity in the *Leicester Mercury*. Furthermore, the weather had been sodden and the heavy Leicestershire clay certain to be cloying. Nonetheless, on a working day in November, about sixty to seventy riders turned up, plus a similar number of followers – following the hunt being a longstanding pastime of the rural peasantry.

The senior master of the Fernie, Joe Cowen, paid a special tribute to one of the regular followers, Trevor, who was having 'a big birthday'. The great thing about Trevor, he said, was 'he never gets in the way'. This is not necessarily a tribute one would want on a gravestone but it is a much-prized virtue among hunt followers.

There was also one outsider present and, though everyone smiled and nodded at me, they did so a touch warily. Everything the Fernie does now, as one of Cowen's joint masters announced before the start, takes place under the terms of the Hunting Act 2004. However, in 2011 two Fernie employees were convicted for digging out a fox from its burrow, only the third successful prosecution in the country since the act, after being secretly filmed by the League against Cruel Sports. Strangers with cameras are thus not welcome at the Fernie and even strangers with notebooks ring alarm bells. I absent-mindedly fished mine out of my pocket while talking to a woman about another member of staff, the red-tailed hawk employed to flush out foxes. Her voice suddenly got sharper: 'Are you from the village?' I made an excuse and went to grab a piece of fruitcake.

Joe Cowen is a remarkable man. He was a surveyor and a farmer, now sort of retired, but, as he admitted, to him the farming was always an adjunct to the hunting, not the other way round. He had his first outing with the Fernie in 1948, when he was seven, and has been master for forty years, which no one in Leicestershire has matched since the eighteenth century and even puts him ahead of the eponymous Mr Fernie. The joint masters now include his son. Suited and booted on horseback, Cowen senior looked fearsome. In repose in his office, he was affable and amusing, and a gold mine of information.

Leicestershire, he told me, became fox country because it was bullock country. From Victoria's accession until the Second World War, the bullocks of Britain would be brought down to these rich and springy grasslands to be fattened up for market. In the autumn, they would head indoors, the next step towards their plate-ward destiny, leaving the fields conveniently empty. Perfect.

So Leicestershire became the fox county, not as smart or as snotty as its only rival, Gloucestershire, but inviting enough for metropolitan enthusiasts to take homes for the winter in Melton or Market Harborough. There was, said Cowen, a particular style of Leicestershire hunting: 'It became known as the quick thing – a twenty-minute burst then stop for a drink. Jump ten fences than have a rest.'

'A sort of Twenty20 hunting.'

'Ye-es. Gloucestershire always looked down on this. But the countryside leads to a challenging ride at pace. Old grasses, big thorn hedges. And they do like the galloping and the jumping here.' In a way, he thought, the hounds in Leicestershire can become secondary to the ride across country.

But it does help to have a fox. And that has become problematic. Under the Hunting Act, the hunt now has to lay a trail somewhat in the manner of drag hunting (which apparently does not involve dressing in women's clothes) but not quite. So in addition to the huntsman, the whipper-in, the countryman, who looks after the fences, the terrier man, who spies out the land, the stable staff, the hounds and the hawk – all of them full-time with the Fernie – they now have a trail-layer. But his trail might cross the trail of a real fox. And since some of the hounds have not read all thirty-two clauses of the statute to discover what exactly is prohibited and what is exempt, there are, as the master delicately put it, 'accidents'.

The hunters have coped with embuggerances before now: towns, railways, motorways, fertilisers ('the hounds get very confused'); the Quorn lost part of its country to East Midlands Airport. They appear to be adapting to this one.

In the absence of busybodies with cameras, the countryside has sly ways of doing what it wants. And hunting does seem to be what rural Leicestershire wants. The farms are too large to appeal to touchy-feely new-agey smallholders; it's too far from London to attract many commuters; and the scenery is too dull for weekenders. Unless they like hunting, of course. 'There are about 600 farms in the Fernie country,' said Cowen, 'and I can count the number where we're not welcome on the fingers of two hands. We don't have much trouble because there's so much acceptance. And it's been like that for 200 years or whatever.'

The Hunting Act is palpably absurd. Lacking the political strength to ban fox-hunting completely, its proponents came up with a hodgepodge riddled with complexities and loopholes: it is not a crime to hunt a fox; it is not a crime to kill a fox; but it is illegal to hunt a fox with a dog unless covered by an exemption. The result has achieved none of the antis' objectives, except the not inconsiderable one of irritating the hell out of the rural upper classes. This statute, half-sentimental, half-vindictive, took up massive quantities of parliamentary time that Labour backbenchers might have better employed taking an interest in the war crimes being committed, with their connivance, in Iraq.

But although the act may have made only a marginal difference to the practice of fox-hunting, it has brought about one extraordinary social change. All over rural England, the old ruling class – the class that for centuries has provided the magistrates who dispense justice in the counties – now finds itself on the very edge of the law. Its members are at one with the speeding motorists, the dope smokers, the poachers and the red-diesel duty dodgers, the types they have customarily lectured and punished: at risk of conviction under a law they find oppressive. And the old hunt saboteurs, who used to revel in getting carted off by the police, now find themselves cast as coppers' narks. Whichever side of the argument you sit, you must admit this is rather funny.

Leicestershire is not that unattractive. The villages tend to be red-brick and straggly, their names blunt and businesslike: Barsby, Beeby, Tugby, Freeby. It also has the town of Coalville, no longer black, just grey. But the multi-barrelled names take on a strange enchantment: Kibworth Harcourt,

Peatling Parva, Newbold Verdon, Willoughby Waterleys, Breedon on the Hill and Frisby on the Wreake.

They can be somewhat disappointing in the flesh. But when the horn blew and the Fernie disappeared, they did so into rolling, very Midland countryside. I also crossed the county to the Vale of Belvoir, taking the route recommended to me by the cricket eminence and local cheerleader Jonathan Agnew, down the hill towards Harby. It afforded sweet views of the Vale, and also of the Ratcliffe-on-Soar power station.

Breedon on the Hill (like Pendle Hill in Lancashire) counts as a double tautology, meaning Hillhill on the Hill. Though it is not three hills, but half a hill, part-eaten by quarrying. It contains only the priory church, on a site devoted to worship since the seventh century; it has fine views and a whipping wind, as the Saxons would have noticed.

And nearby is the sweetest-sounding town in the kingdom, Ashby-de-la-Zouch – a place of ash trees (unless the wilt gets them) that belonged to the La Zouche family – and a sweet enough spot that once had pretensions as a spa. Its reputation as the epitome of English nomenclatorial eccentricity was enhanced in the days – ended in 1964 – when Leicestershire played an annual cricket match at the Bath Grounds. It was said that the great Denis Compton, struggling after a characteristically heavy night, went straight in to bat from his bedroom at the Royal Hotel. Which, I proved by staying at the Royal and recreating the incident, was theoretically possible. Were it not for the fact that there is no record of Compton ever playing at Ashby-de-la-Zouch.

Leicestershire now play all their home games in Leicester, at not very graceful Grace Road. No one much goes there these days, including and especially the supposedly cricket-mad Indians.

November 2012

~~~~~~~~

Two months later the body in the car park was confirmed as Richard III's. In May 2014, after a tug-of-war over the bones, a High Court judge ruled that they should be reburied in Leicester Cathedral and not York Minster, as a group claiming to be his descendants had tried to insist. This duly happened in March 2015, and the cathedral got its publicity all right: the country seemed far more interested in discussing Richard than the impending election.

23. *Loosen your corset, and stay*

HERTFORDSHIRE

The railway ticket office in Letchworth Garden City is an agreeable little red-brick affair, suggesting a station that does not see many trains, which is not the case. Across the bridge and in a dip, overshadowed by the new Morrisons, and half-hidden by trees even in winter, lies a factory.

It is an unusually attractive one, built in a style influenced by the Arts and Crafts movement, like so much of Letchworth. With some difficulty you can just make out the sign from the road: 'THE SPIRELLA COMPANY OF GREAT BRITAIN LTD. HIGH GRADE CORSETS'. When it opened in 1920 it was described as the Factory of Beauty. It was also known as Castle Corset.

Except for St Albans Cathedral, which is also very discreet, and the stately homes like Hatfield House and Knebworth, this may be the most famous building in Hertfordshire. Yet it is a puzzle. Corsets conjure up Victorian subjugation. Letchworth, the world's first garden city, was meant to represent a braver, freer new century.

The founding father, Sir Ebenezer Howard, imagined – in 1898 – a unique conjunction of *rus et urbe*: more than a suburb, since the surrounding farms were meant to feed the population. And his vision came to happy fruition because the architects, Parker and Unwin, made the place handsome and were generous with their gardens. And the people who came to live there were the third element. They tended to be progressive but prissy, keen on fitness and fresh air, unkeen on the old vices. It was the voters who stopped Letchworth having any new pubs until the 1950s. They would describe their houses as 'arty-crafty, ever-so-draughty', but they were often people who liked draughts.

And the corset factory was right too. These were no ordinary corsets: Spirella made the new version with flexible stays that replaced the old, occasionally stabbing, featherbones, which had themselves replaced whalebone. Spirella corsets were custom-made, with teams of corsetières going to clients' houses for private fittings. And the boss, William Wallace Kinkaid, was an only-the-best-is-good-enough-for-the-workers paternalist who fitted perfectly into the Letchworth ethos. He even built a ballroom at the top of the factory. I keep thinking of those corseted corsetières at the factory hop under the chandelier and the domed roof-light. But those were the man-short 1920s and as Joyce Grenfell sang:

So gay the band,
So giddy the sight,
Full evening dress is a must,
But the zest goes out of a beautiful waltz
When you dance it bust to bust.

Also in the 1920s came the second garden city, Welwyn. It is more Albert Speerish than Letchworth, with wide vistas down a boulevard fit for a marching army. The view is lengthy rather than compelling. But the principles are the same as those at Letchworth: you can live in the centre of town in an agreeable mock-Georgian with a walk to work and a view of John Lewis, which is a rather garden city-ish kind of shop. Welwyn's signature factory was Shredded Wheat, a starker, more imposing building than Spirella, though just as distinctive, with its thirty silos. And 'the Wheat' was loved in its own way, not least for the malty brewery-ish smell it emitted.

But garden cities were a dream that faltered, and the second war

finished them off. When the Attlee government wanted houses, it wanted them quick and cheap: cheerful was an optional extra. The first postwar new town was Stevenage, previously a dozy little burg with a pretty high street. The government imposed compulsory purchase orders on thousands of acres to construct a new town seven miles and several light years from both Letchworth and Welwyn. 'Stevenage will in a short time become world-famous,' boasted Lewis Silkin, the planning minister, in 1946. 'People from all over the world will come to Stevenage to see how we, here in this country, are building for the new way of life.'

The reality is better depicted by the fact that it became known as Silkingrad. But it proved to be a more durable template for the future of Hertfordshire than its predecessors. Similar projects came along in Hatfield and Hemel Hempstead. All of them were influenced by the principles established by Howard. However, they were funded by HM Treasury not philanthropy: corners were there to be cut. Still, the writer Gary Younge, who grew up in Stevenage in the 1970s and 1980s as a member of two tiny minorities – black and bookish – wrote a not unaffectionate memoir of the town for the magazine *Granta*. The schools were good, if undervalued, he said, the amenities 'great'.

The town, though, had a striking lack of self-respect: 'No one could ever really place it on a map, not even another person from Stevenage.' Younge felt the town deteriorated when Margaret Thatcher allowed everyone to buy their council houses. The people got richer, and more middle class, as rising prices across the South-East drove buyers into places like Stevenage, once considered beyond the pale. But Younge thought the actual community grew poorer – and rougher. When he told some kids in Luton he was from Stevenage, 'they sucked in hard as though I'd told them I'd grown up in the South Bronx'.

Lately Stevenage FC have climbed up the divisions, giving the town an identity at last. The council has been more proactive than most in supporting the arts, and the Gordon Craig Theatre looked lively, if not intellectually over-ambitious. However, there is one striking, overwhelming fact about the centre of Stevenage. It is hideous, repulsive, ugly beyond all belief. It is like the parade ring before the final of the competition to find the World's Vilest Building. The shopping centre, 'Britain's first purpose-built traffic-free shopping zone', opened in 1959, and the only decorative features are the anti-climb spikes. Not surprisingly, it appears to be falling to bits.

The garden cities have weathered more gently. The women of Britain discarded their corsets en masse in the 1960s and Spirella could not escape. Hertfordshire's other great interwar landmark, the art-deco Ovaltine factory at Kings Langley, by the main line to Euston, has also closed. But architecturally both stories have happy endings. Spirella has been lovingly restored to provide a centre for small firms; the ballroom is available for weddings and parties. Ovaltine has been turned into flats behind the preserved façade. The Wheat closed in 2008: the fashion for eating cereals less nutritious than their cardboard box has not abated, but the American owners moved production to Bath, leaving behind peeling paint, sad silos and a wistful Welwyn. An attempt to turn it into a Tesco has so far been rebuffed.

Letchworth also seems a bit forgotten by time, which is curious in a place with fast trains to King's Cross. It has retained something of its original atmosphere, produced by that strand of society that would now be stereotyped as sandalled-muesli-eating-beardie. The best-known shop is David's Books and Music, unimaginable in Stevenage. Nearby, the Arena Tavern, still one of only a handful of pubs, had a sign saying 'Welcome to all good-hearted people'.

The chief executive of the Letchworth Heritage Foundation, who, appropriately, was another John Lewis, gave me a tour, showing me the gloriously eccentric Cloisters, which began life as an open-air school and is next door to St Christopher, which still thrives as a first-names-for-everyone-even-the-head kind of school with a vegetarian menu. He also showed me Britain's first roundabout. I took a shine to Letchworth, starting to imagine myself joining the am-dram and the reading groups and the wine clubs; I could take up bridge again; a little light wife-swapping perhaps. With its safe, easy streets, it feels a terrific place to be over sixty or under thirteen, less so to be a teenager.

Public-enterprise Stevenage has been violently tugged between the Attlee and Thatcher conceptions of Britain, and the Treasury grabbed its money back. Letchworth was a product of high-minded property speculation. Buying vast acres of Hertfordshire farmland more than a century ago has produced a bonanza akin to striking oil. The Foundation is still the town's largest landowner but exists for the town's benefit. If Letchworth needs something it has a chance of getting it, which is a good place to be in the 2010s.

'Hertfordshire,' said the sign, 'county of opportunity'. What a pathetic, vapid slogan.

But then, what *do* you say about this county? Even Famous Potatoes wouldn't work. It's not famous for anything. There was a variant of skittles called Hertfordshire Roly-Poly but it seems to have vanished without trace. The county is said to have an unusually large number of village greens, often triangular. And there is something called Hertfordshire puddingstone, which looks like a lump of concrete but isn't: it's a mixture of rough stones held together with natural cement. 'hertfordshire: home of the puddingstone'. Well, it would take a brave council to opt for that.

If there was a Hertfordshire accent, it must have died with the actor Bernard Miles (born in Middlesex). That fine writer Richard Mabey, manfully trying to sum up for *The Illustrated Counties of England*, had to confess he had belatedly discovered that the woods which had meant so much in his childhood were actually in Buckinghamshire. He summed up the county rather sadly: 'It is hardly firm enough to grow roots in. Herts is more a kind of temporary mooring.'

Which was sort of Gary Younge's point. It is a place young couples choose to commute from when they don't have a better idea. Hertfordshire screamed out to have garden cities and new towns because it had the most open and available land close to London and was the last place anyone was likely to mind or notice. HERTFORDSHIRE: COUNTY OF OPPORTUNISM. For more than a century it has played the hinterland role previously fulfilled by Middlesex until that became no land and all hinter.

With the infinite perversity that attended the 1974 reforms, Hertfordshire, where hardly anyone cared, was left largely alone. It has so little identity largely because it has no focal point: the east–west communications are terrible. The Romans built the Icknield Way across the top and the moderns built the M25 along the bottom, but to drive cross-county in between involves all kinds of strange jiggling. By rail, it's impossible. Boxmoor knows bugger all of Bishops Stortford.

Though Hertfordshire has no personality, it is of good character. Indeed, if it were a person, one would recommend sending it off for asser tiveness training. The small brick-built towns are pleasant, good value, safe. When my nephew and his family moved from London to Berkhamsted, the police knocked on the door to say they were conducting a house-to-house search: 'We are investigating an egg being thrown at a car,' an officer intoned solemnly.

The countryside is inclined to disguise itself in its neighbours' clothes: chalky soils and big skies in the east; woods and clay and Chilterny bits in the west, with various subtle gradations in between. Has anyone even told Hertfordshire it's a county? '*TOWIE* extra smashes skull in mystery Thai accident,' said the headline in the *Hertfordshire Mercury*. Not 'Stanstead Abbots man smashes skull', as you would expect. *TOWIE* is tabloid-speak for the TV programme *The Only Way Is Essex*, about another county entirely. Is that all Hertfordshire is? An extra in the dramatic life of the big, blowsy, boisterous county next door?

In the spring of 1937 a writer – a pretty dire one, but that's not the point – called Owen Hamilton left London for the summer to inflict a book on his publishers. 'I am joyed to find, despite the trivial troubles that were mine, that all is yet right with the world,' he announced in his 'prelude'. 'I wander along the lanes, welcomed everywhere; accepted by the trees; greeted by the little mill-stream; hailed by the birds and flowers; kissed by the lips of a wind that never kissed me in London's streets.'

So where is he? Grasmere? The Scillies? Tuscany? '... Installed at the small picturesque place of Ware, so Bruges-like with its barge-life, bridges, poplars and swans, but lodged at the Saracen's Head Hotel ...' On he babbled, did Hamilton: 'One thinks of some medieval German town of the Meistersingers' period. What a sketch Vermeer would have made of the old bridge!'

Where? Ware! Less than twenty-five miles from Charing Cross. Ware was famous in its day as the Watford Junction of the coaching age: first major stop on the road north. There were sixteen coaching inns on the High Street, but the Saracen's Head is the last one left, and that's not the original but a 1960s rebuild from the Stevenage school of architecture, which now wrecks the view from the bridge. Vermeer would have vomited.

But get past that and Ware turns out to have a down-at-heel charm that is partly typical of the older Hertfordshire towns, especially those that have gone a bit out of style, and partly all its own. Several of the former inns, now turned to all kinds of more mundane uses, still have riverside gazebos built for the customers. And the river itself, the Lea ('the wanton Lea that oft doth lose his way' – Spenser) or Lee, retains a place in the hearts of the few Londoners old enough to have snogged before the war, when the riverbank was the venue of choice.

Peter Wilbourn, growing up in Ware in the third quarter of the last century, had trouble finding such hiding places. 'If I met a girl in Baldock Street, then by the time I got to my grandparents' house up the hill, they would know who she was, where we'd walked and how much time I spent with her.' He also found it hard to get a drink: his father ran a pub, so all the other landlords knew exactly how old he was.

'Do you think it might be like that for a kid in Ware these days?'

'Nah,' he said instantly. And then he thought. 'Actually, probably yes.'

Ware has only sluggish trains to London, making property about 10 per cent cheaper than in nearby hurry-rush Hertford, and the community less transient. Not only is it not a dormitory town, it does not have its most famous artefact: the Great Bed of Ware. At least, not normally. But by happy chance, it was paying a year-long visit home – to the museum in the High Street – for the first time since it was removed to the Victoria and Albert Museum in London eighty years earlier.

I had heard of the Great Bed of Ware but, to be honest, had no idea what it was. For all I knew, it might be a geographical feature lightly disguised as an item of household furniture, like the Great Artesian Basin or the Bog of Allen. It turned out to a bed: a four-poster, lovingly carved, dating back to the late sixteenth century, which was used by a succession of Ware coaching inns as a selling point, being somewhat warmer than the banks of the Lea for a twosome and not out of the question for an orgy. Both Shakespeare and Ben Jonson gave it a mention, in what one takes to be examples of the mucky topical jokes now confined to panto.

Allegedly it's ten feet long and eleven feet wide, and has variously played host to six butchers and their wives, and whole platoons of soldiers. I am not convinced: it does not look that much bigger than the beds provided in up-market American motel rooms. The V&A, boringly, no longer permit the bed to be used for any of its proper purposes. And if the museum ever does decide to unleash this potentially lucrative revenue stream, the bed might be hard put to bear the weight of two modern middle-aged Americans.

Wilbourn worked for the National Association of Master Bakers, whose appropriately small-scale offices happened to be in Ware, in the south-east corner of the county, through the years when the trade withered almost to vanishing point under the onslaught of Big Bread.

The main weapon of Big Bread was the Chorleywood Bread Process, developed in and named after the town in the south-west corner of the county, thirty-five miles from Ware. The CBP was created in 1961 and, according to the food writer and campaigner Felicity Lawrence, 'dispensed with all the time and expensive energy required by traditional methods'.

Air and water were mixed into the dough, plus a double quantity of yeast to make it rise, chemical oxidants to get the gas in and hardened fat to stop it collapsing. And a lot of salt. The result tasted worse than neat Shredded Wheat but was long-lasting, cheap to buy and profitable to make, especially when backed up with winsome retro adverts of the sort that made Hovis and Mother's Pride sound wholesome and homely.

The number of artisan bakers is now slowly growing, but they have a tiny slice (as it were) of the market, compared to the big factories and the supermarkets' in-store bakeries – derided by purists as 'tanning salons' – where the bread generally arrives literally half-baked.

Fifty years on from Chorleywood's main claim to fame or infamy, it was named in 2011 as the least-deprived and most desirable area in Britain. In keeping with Hertfordshire's chameleon habits, it is more like the plutocratic towns of South Bucks than the rest of the county. You can even buy real bread, though it is baked in Chalfont St Giles, not Chorleywood, a point made to me very firmly by the store manager, who understood the significance of the question.

Chorleywood does not even care much for its other claim to fame. 'So is this really Britain's most desirable place to live?' I asked someone in the café where I stopped for a bite.

'It *was*,' he said. 'Then as soon as all that stuff appeared in the paper saying so, the burglars descended en masse.'

January 2013

~~~~~~~~

Berkhamsted also has burglaries, as well as eggings; my nephew found out the hard way. In 2013 the National Association of Master Bakers rebranded itself as the Craft Bakers' Association. The president, Christopher Freeman, called the old name 'sadly outdated'. He might have added that it led to schoolboy sniggering.

24. *The silence of the trams*

NOTTINGHAMSHIRE

Some counties don't have to work too hard to find a symbol. Across Nottinghamshire, he's everywhere. There is Robin Hood Street, Robin Hood Close, Robin Hood Way, Robin Hood Chase. There are two Robin Hood Avenues, three Terraces and three Roads.

There are Robin Hood farms; pubs, hotels and guest houses; a theatre, an industrial estate, a primary school, a railway line, a travel company, a garage, a boxing club, a fish bar, a tyre company, a firm of party organisers and another of private detectives, which is a nice touch. Nottinghamshire's Harley-Davidson dealers are called Robin Hood. And then there are the Friar Tuck restaurants and Maid Marian Way. Little John is a pub, a riding school and a fishing lake and above all the deep-throated bell on top of the city Council House on Old Market Square (universally known as Slab Square).

Robin Hood and King Arthur are England's only quasi-historical figures to have broken out of the vault that holds Jack o' Lantern and Gog and Magog, and made it to Hollywood. However, there is a problem for Robin's home county. It is easy enough for a coach firm or chippie to seek a little reflected glory: no threatening letters need be expected from solicitors representing the Hood family.

But there is a problem of provenance. Some tinpot little airport had the idea of calling itself Robin Hood. It serves Doncaster and Sheffield, in Yorkshire. And, although the association of Robin with Sherwood Forest and Nottinghamshire is a strong one, the county has found the connection difficult to monetise.

There may be a Robin Hood Theatre (just outside Newark – small but enterprising) but it can't match Stratford by endlessly performing the master's plays, or indeed performing them at all. No active pensioner can show you round Robin Hood's birthplace: we have no idea when, where or if he was born. Indeed, everything anyone thinks they know is almost certainly wrong. If he was extant in the reign of Richard the Lionheart, as most stories suggest, then – according to Emrys Bryson's *Portrait of Nottingham* – he can't have used a longbow (not invented); can't have consorted with a friar (none around); and can't have thwarted the Sheriff of Nottingham (there wasn't one).

There is a Robin Hood statue, symbolically sited outside the walls of Nottingham Castle, rather than inside: he is being remembered as an outlaw not a nobleman. The statue did not come until the 1950s, more than 700 years after his presumed death, and it is a decidedly odd one: Robin has thighs like Sherwood oaks but is wearing a very silly hat indeed.

Some entrepreneur tried to make money up the road from the statue with a sort of tourist trap called Tales of Robin Hood. It didn't trap many. Twenty miles away in Edwinstowe a remnant of Sherwood Forest has been turned into a country park, and the county council has been planning 'a world-class visitor attraction', the kind of phrase that strikes terror into one's heart. But there is a further problem: though the woodlands are lovely, dark and in some places deep, the Nottinghamshire countryside is uneventful. It is far less varied than Yorkshire; much flatter than Derbyshire; has no coastline, unlike Lincolnshire.

The world-class attraction in Sherwood Forest, aside from the elusive local hero, is the Major Oak, which, having lived through three millennia, is now thirty-three feet thick with a ninety-foot spread. Gnarled and pollarded, it is not especially tall and leans wearily on metal crutches like a very old, very fat man whose only remaining desire is to fall down gently

and go to sleep. But no one will let him. He is surrounded by a ring of much taller and very feminine birch trees, who appear to be nursing him, and fussing.

Over its long life, the tree has been known as the Cockpen Tree because fighting cocks were kept inside the hollow trunk awaiting their punch-ups, and then the Queen's Tree, before Major Oak stuck, because it was immortalised in print by the eighteenth-century soldier-turned-anti-quarian Major Hayman Rooke. Queen's Tree just feels wrong as a name; it looks so indisputably masculine. And there is something about the whole of Nottinghamshire that makes these distinctions more than normally sharp.

When Emrys Bryson first arrived in Nottingham from the Black Coun-try just after the war, he was struck by the city's self-confidence: 'People walked and talked as though they owned the place, instead of just scut-tling around. It was as though they were on holiday. Everyone seemed full of themselves.' He loved it and spent forty-five years on the *Evening Post*, mainly as the drama critic.

Neil Barnes, later a BBC producer, arrived at the university in 1956, not from the industrial North but from Portsmouth. He was immediately dazzled. 'When you went into Slab Square, there were all these gleaming white buildings. The university was the same. Gleaming, and set in park-land. It was an amazing place.'

John Holmes also arrived as a student, started broadcasting on BBC Radio Nottingham in 1970 and was still at it more than forty years later. But he did disappear for ten years to work in Bristol: 'They've got no balls in Bristol. In Nottingham they're always up for rebellion. There's no proper castle because the buggers kept burning it down. You could say it started with Robin Hood.'

'They don't pretend to be particularly blunt in the way of Yorkshire-men,' says Bryson. 'But if they don't like something, they *make it known.*'

One might even say the refusal by most of the Nottinghamshire miners to join the national coal strike in 1984 was a manifestation of this. There was a hint of self-interest: a belief – false, it turned out – that the newer Notts pits had a chance of surviving Margaret Thatcher's mass clo-sure. But the refusal of the miners' leader Arthur Scargill to call a strike ballot offended their sense of fair play.

This extends into many aspects of life. In the 1970s and 1980s the local cricketing hero Derek Randall kept being dropped from the England team in favour of Mike Gatting from posh, metropolitan Middlesex even though Randall was making more runs. 'If the Yorkshire Ripper had come from Middlesex,' said an unusually daring cartoon in the *Evening Post*, 'they'd have given him another chance.'

Cricketing wounds tend to heal, though. There are said to be families in the old pit villages still riven because they took opposing sides in 1984. And when Notts County play teams like Chesterfield and Rotherham, they are apparently even now greeted by terrace chants of 'scab, scab, scab, scab' from opposing supporters who were not even born at the time.

In national folk myth, particularly male folk myth, the city of Nottingham was most famous for its women. This certainly helped bump up applications to the university, even more than the gleaming buildings. The belief existed on three different levels. Firstly, that women were in the majority: four to one in the most optimistic versions. Secondly, that they were more outgoing and more up for, um, it, than those anywhere else. And thirdly, that they were better-looking.

Oddly, there appears to be a smidgen of truth in every one of these. Census evidence suggests there were indeed more women than men (128,000 v 112,000 in 1901, for instance). These women would have had a degree of independence, and cash, because there was work for women: first in the lace industry and then for at least two of the big local companies – Boots the chemists and the tobacco firm John Player. And thirdly, all this was at the daintier end of the old working spectrum, so that the bloom of womanhood would have taken longer to fade in Nottingham than elsewhere. Furthermore, Boots workers got discounts on cosmetics, all the better for first titivating and then titillating. 'The Queen City,' it sometimes gets called, but perhaps only by the tourist office.

There was always a rougher, manly side to Nottingham too. It wasn't just the penchant for rioting. In the early nineteenth century it had the worst slums in the country. As some of those were cleared, the railway was built across the Meadows, which might otherwise have remained as open space but instead turned into another notorious rookery. The third big factory, Raleigh, was very male-dominated, presumably by characters not wholly unlike Arthur Seaton, Alan Sillitoe's creation in the most famous of Nottingham novels, *Saturday Night and Sunday Morning*. Graham Greene, who got a subediting job on one of the Nottingham papers in the 1920s, was appalled by the general squalor, turned to Catholicism as solace and exacted revenge in one of his least accomplished novels, *A Gun for Sale*, in which Nottingham, thinly disguised as Nottwich, is portrayed as a right dump.

Modern visitors mostly see a benign face: the Trent gleams too, on a good day; the cricket ground is efficient but still charming; you can live in a nice house in the Park and walk to town. But Nottingham is ringed by vast, depressing estates. And by the dawn of the twenty-first century the city had acquired a reputation as 'Shottingham' for the level of gun crime.

This was mainly due to the activities of one Colin Gunn, leader of the 'Bestwood Cartel', who was jailed in 2006 for life with a minimum of thirty-five years and was later deemed so dangerous that he was reported to be imprisoned in conditions similar to those used on Hannibal Lecter in *Silence of the Lambs*. Those who have seen the film will be aware how effective those turned out to be: so one should not be too condemnatory – that nice Mr Gunn's return to Bestwood may be imminent.

Gunnless and largely gunless, the city now has instead Nottingham Contemporary, a cutting-edge art gallery produced by the great public-money boom of the early 2000s. 'You can sit outside there with the new trams going by and really think the whole city has gone cool and continental,' said one regular visitor. 'Then you go a few yards and it's the same old crap.' The trams are wonderful, partly because you don't (as in Manchester) have to wrestle with ticket machines on the cold platform: they have chummy conductors. They are also very quiet; maybe too damn quiet – 'park and glide' is the official exhortation. Gliders are lovely too, but they don't sneak up on you as you're coming out of Debenhams. The trams might cause more casualties than Colin Gunn before someone decides to install an artificial clanker. And behind all that cool is an almost unimaginable despair. When a new branch of Costa Coffee opened in the suburb of Mapperley in early 2013, there were 1,700 applications – a fair number from people with PhDs – for eight jobs, several of them part-time.

Presiding over this strangely confused city is not Robin Hood, or Colin Gunn, or Arthur Seaton, or Jesse Boot the chemist. Pride of place, above Slab Square, at the junction of King and Queen Street, goes to a statue of Brian Clough, an original, innovative and highly successful manager who took Nottingham Forest, a once-bumbling football club, to two successive European Cups in the late 1970s.

There is, however, a great deal of anecdotal evidence to the effect that Clough took kickbacks on transfer deals on an industrial scale. Though he was fond of posturing as an anti-establishment leftie, he robbed the average football supporter to enrich himself. That Robin Hood: he didn't understand how the world worked.

Nottinghamshire is a self-conscious county but self-contained. Its accent is little known and hard to imitate: Emrys Bryson says that neither Albert Finney nor Ian McKellen, who both played Arthur Seaton, got anywhere close. But it is persistent and distinctive, if not easy for an outsider to sort out from Derbyshire. Nottingham remains the capital of the East Midlands m'duck zone ('Duck' or 'm'duck' being the asexual term of vague endearment analogous to the general northern 'luv'). There is also the Nottingham O-ending: Stapleford is Stabbo; the Cockington Road, Cocko; late, lamented Shipstone's Brewery turned out pints of Shippo's. And so on.

Local accent joke (1): Man takes cat to be seen to. 'Is it a tom?' says the vet. 'Nee-ow, av gorritt wimmee in this box.'

Local accent joke (2): Golfer hits solid drive down the fairway. 'That's a nice tee shot,' says his non-Nottingham partner. 'Ta verry mooch. Burritint a tee shot, it's a pullova.'

A friend told me of overhearing amid the crowd (or smattering) in the stands at Notts County: 'It's a bit Derby Road tonight.' Rhyming slang for cold.

Pronunciation can be very complex in this county. It is said that people brought up in the old mining villages, populated between the wars by miners migrating from the already worked-out pits of the North-East, emerged with Geordie accents without straying from Nottinghamshire. Also, take the case of Southwell, or Suth'll, an amiable if rather bunged-up little town where the Norman minster beat St Mary's Church, Nottingham, to cathedral status in an act of late Victorian giant-killing. (Nottingham and Leeds are the most significant English cities to be thus deprived.) The church always calls the place Suth'll. So does everyone in horse racing – the possession of a manky all-weather track being the town's other claim to fame. But I had long understood that the locals called it as spelt: South-well.

Nothing so simple. Boots on King Street seemed a suitably Nottinghamshire place to start asking the name of the town we were in.

'Southwell,' said the girl on the checkout with total assurance.

'Suth'll,' said a man just walking out of the door.

'South-well,' said a woman behind me, joining in. 'But I suppose it depends how posh you are.'

'I went to the Minster School,' said the checkout girl, pointing up the road. '*Everyone* says South-well.'

To the bank. 'I grew up here,' said the teller. 'Suth'll.'

At that moment the postman walked in. He must know. 'South-well,' he said. 'But I'm a Newark-er. People here usually say Suth'll.'

'Suth'll,' said the cathedral guide.

'I say Suth'll,' said a man in the street. 'But I wasn't born here. My children were. They all say South-well.'

'Suth'll, mostly,' agreed another passer-by.

There seemed to be something generational involved, so I stopped two teenage girls. 'South-well,' they shouted in unison. One tried a bit of explanation. 'People who live in Suth'll all call it South –

'Oops,' she said.

I gave up.

The annual Nottinghamshire rite of autumn is Goose Fair, held on Slab Square until 1928, when it was exiled to the Forest, a very unforested suburban open space. Approaching it at night down the Mansfield Road, it looks like Las Vegas, shamelessly illuminating the desert sky.

Not a goose in sight these days, though plenty of sitting ducks. No shepherd fleeces his flock as gently as a showman at a travelling fair. Everyone expects to be diddled on the sideshows, just as everyone expects to be terrified by the high-tariff rides. The newcomer in 2012 was Atmosfear ('Includes violent motion of loops of 360 degrees'). The list of exclusions ruled out anyone under fourteen, below 140 cm and over 200 cm. 'Persons of certain body shapes may not be able to ride,' the sign added tactfully, and it further excluded those with epilepsy, heart problems, asthma, loss of control of limbs, neck problems, back problems, recent surgery, fractured bones and pregnancy. It did not rule out the disease which, as a parent, I have rechristened teenile dementia. And its sufferers made up, at £4 a pop, all the users and queuers for Atmosfear.

In other respects Goose Fair is extremely inclusive. Like the cinema, the fair is not merely recession-proof but actually benefits from bad times: it constitutes a cheap treat in years when families have to axe their summer holidays. There are no cultural taboos, so there were a lot of Asian families, indeed groups of Asian girls. Goose Fair repels only the fastidious bourgeoisie, and outsiders. It is a very local occasion, surpassed for its size and place in local folklore only by Hull Fair, the fiesta of an even more secret and unfrequented city.

The Nottinghamshire of the global imagination, in so far as it exists, is very different from the reality. Robin Hood constituting indifferent business, he just seems like a cliché. The old mining town Eastwood used to dismiss its most famous son, D. H. Lawrence, as 'that mucky man'. And even now the low-key trade brought in for tours of Lawrence's home in Victoria Street and the museum up the road is dwarfed by the hordes attracted by the jumbo-sized branch of IKEA.

Coachloads of schoolchildren are brought long distances to the outskirts of the rather remote village of Laxton, east of Ollerton, for the Holocaust Museum. This is something to which it is hard to object, though its positioning is decidedly random – the house belonged to a Methodist minister's family who became transfixed after a visit to the Yad Vashem museum in Jerusalem. And it does slightly detract from Laxton's extraordinary significance as the only village in England that has retained the medieval system of open-field farming. This is living history, which, in this particular spot, a Holocaust Museum is not.

The fields' survival is a complete fluke. In the eighteenth century, when the fields all around were being enclosed, Laxton was relatively prosperous and the lord of the manor, Earl Manvers, was drawing high rents, so the economics of creating big fields with a single owner was not as clear-cut as it was elsewhere. A century later, when the subject came up again, the then earl was distracted by rebuilding his stately pile, Thoresby Hall. There was a certain amount of bickering between local landowners. By the time everyone got their act together, they decided to leave the village alone. And by the twentieth century it was clear that here was now something very, very special.

The Manvers family sold up in 1950 and the Ministry of Agriculture took charge of Laxton until the Thatcherite sell-off thirty years later. The threat was such that the agricultural historian Joan Thirsk compared it to 'dismantling Stonehenge for the sake of the building materials'. The Min of Ag kept the peace by selling it to another arm of the state, the Crown Estates.

The system has not survived intact. Some land has been hived off. The strips of land are no longer the elongated cricket pitches which the peasants ploughed in Robin Hood's day; most are now about half as wide as a football pitch. Some land has been enclosed and there are 168 strips instead of a couple of thousand.

But the principle has been maintained. There are three huge fields, each one divided into a patchwork, split between Laxton's fourteen farms in a manner ensuring that each farmer has his share of big bits and small bits; good land and bad. The fields have to be planted on a strict rotation – wheat one year, then another cereal or beans the next, then fallow. And each strip is separated from its neighbour only by a double furrow, leading to all kinds of border skirmishes. My guide, Stuart Rose of Bottom Farm, was told by his dad that the way to avoid problems was to make sure you got on to the land first. In practice, Laxton self-polices, with the Court Leet meeting in the Dovecote Inn every December, levying small fines on each other for infringements, and letting the ale soften any grievances.

In theory, this is unworkable. Farmers *hate* anyone else sticking their noses into their business. They *hate* wasting time and diesel trudging from one field to the next. But there are some interesting consequences. For one thing, farming in Laxton is a lot more sociable than it is elsewhere. When everyone's out in the fields, says Stuart, 'there's a lot of stopping and nattering'. Secondly, Laxton may be the most vibrant village in the county. The fourteen farms – plus a few smallholdings – are all grouped down Main Street and High Street, with small strips of their own land out the back. Contrast this to the other villages in the area, without an agricultural worker in sight and dead in the daytime.

The farmers moan, of course. But still. 'You'd think it'd be a struggle to get tenants,' said Stuart. 'But whenever a farm does come up, which isn't often, there are forty or fifty applicants.'

At the end of the Victorian era, William Straw opened a grocer's shop in Worksop. The business prospered and in 1923 the family moved to 7 Blyth Grove, on the edge of town: not a trophy house, exactly, but a solid semi, which Mrs Straw decorated richly in a manner that may already have been a bit old-fashioned.

The Straws had three sons. The youngest died as a toddler; the middle one, Walter, went in to the business; the eldest, another William, went off to London to teach English and Latin at the City of London College. But after his father died, the younger William – rather improbably – returned to Worksop and there he stayed. When his mother died too, in 1939, he took over as housekeeper for Walter until his brother died, whereupon William lived alone until infirmity forced him into hospital in 1985.

When William himself died five years later he left the furniture to the National Trust. When officials arrived to inspect their gift, they were at first thoroughly sniffy, the individual items being worthless. 'It was only as the afternoon wore on,' as one of them explained later, 'that the spell of no. 7 took hold of us.' The place was a time capsule. Nothing had been touched. A 1932 calendar hung on the walls; the father's hat and coat were still on their peg; the mother's domain at the back had been preserved. Much of the stuff had been carefully labelled. There was no TV, no radio, no gramophone, no telephone. In an upstairs cupboard, there was a random collection of food in tins and jars: perhaps in case of Worksop coming under nuclear attack; perhaps in preparation for what did happen – the National Trust not just taking on the furniture but buying the house and opening it as one of its most appreciated properties, and certainly its most improbable. 'It's just like seeing all your granny's bits and bobs,' as one early visitor put it.

Half-aware of the story, I had imagined something along the lines of the Collyer Brothers, the reclusive hoarders from Brooklyn who died horribly amid tons of their own debris. (The room in which I am writing this is held by some to be *un hommage* to the Collyers.) But absolutely not. No. 7 is a shrine to order: a house unused to visitors that has been readied for important ones. Perhaps William Straw had been preparing for us all along.

The Straws were not recluses either. Walter was said to go dancing. William was involved in church and civic groups. They went to the theatre and the Scarborough Cricket Festival. Much, though, remains mysterious. Evidently, William was a non-combatant in the battle of the sexes that so preoccupies most of humanity.

But there is something in his life – quiet, self-contained, in touch with the past, purposeful to the point of bloody-mindedness – that seems to contain the very essence of Nottinghamshire.

October 2012/February 2013

~~~~~~~

Alas, Nottingham did away with its tram conductors in 2014.

25. *That nice couple at no. 45*

MIDDLESEX

One of the great joys of writing this book is setting off on a new adventure, armed with an old guidebook to see the delights that remain. Today's text is *Highwayman's Heath* by Gordon S. Maxwell (1935):

> Turn down from the Bath Road by the Three Magpies, and you
> will come upon a road as rural as anywhere in England. It is not,
> perhaps, scenically wonderful, but for detachment from London,
> or any urban interests, it would be hard to find its equal; there is
> a calmness and serenity about it that is soothing in a mad rushing
> world.

He promises further rustic pleasures ahead: a hamlet with a pub, the Harrow; two 'fine old farms', one of them reminiscent of 'one of those delightful old farmsteads met with in the Weald of Kent'; and some cottages 'which might be in the heart of Devonshire for their antiquity, their picturesqueness and lonely situation'. Maxwell proves this with a picture showing the half-timbering and lovely, curving thatch.

The Three Magpies is still there, and the road, Nene Road. You pass a little upturned-cannon memorial to William Roy, the pioneer of tri-angulation and forefather of the Ordnance Survey. And then the open space stretches in front of you. However, the walk is now necessarily a brief one: there have been one or two small changes. A high fence bars the way, topped by razor wire and adorned with signs uttering blood-curdling threats under the Aviation and Maritime Security Act 1990.

The original hamlet was demolished in 1944, when public inquiries on planning matters were out of fashion. The place has since become rather famous. It was originally known as Heath Row, but it has lost the space. Which is a metaphor for the whole of Middlesex.

Heath Row was a row of houses amid the crops of Hounslow Heath. Its fate was extreme but not untypical. I could have been following *Our Lanes and Meadowpaths: Rambles in Rural Middlesex* by H. J. Foley (1887): 'How luxuriant is the wood on every hand! ... And yet could pasture be richer, or could any meadows be more full of beauty than these?' He was writing about Mill Hill.

'Notice,' he went on, 'how the surface of the meadows reflects the varying moods of the sky.' By now he was in Edgware. 'Lovers of rural nooks and corners can hardly do better than pay a visit to Kingsbury,' Foley advised.

And then: 'We come to the gates of Wembley Park, with an ivy-grown and thatch-covered lodge guarding the entrance ... 250 acres, beautifully wooded.' Towards the centre of London and 'what can be more peaceful and secluded than ... Neasden? ... Little altered or disturbed, consisting chiefly of a few scattered cottages with a fair sprinkling of good old houses planted in large grounds'.

As late as 1951 Norman Brett-James, in *Middlesex*, commended the 'completely rural surroundings' of Scratch Wood, some time before it became a motorway service station.

So it goes round here. The land of the Middle Saxons was first mentioned in AD 703 and officially abolished in 1965. It is not uncommon in south-east England to have one's life bedevilled by aggressive, noisy neighbours with no respect for your boundaries. Such problems only rarely end in murder. Middlesex happened to be next door to the most raucous, most

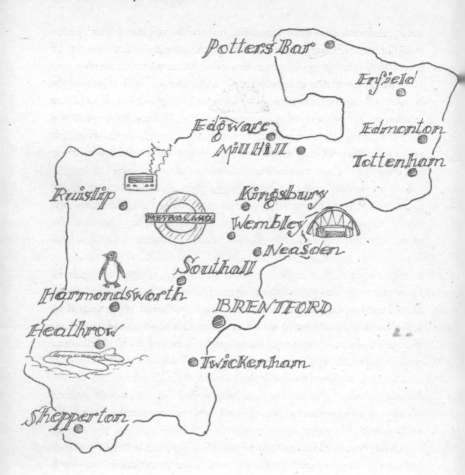

expansionist place in Britain and was subject to an endless campaign of suffocation that lasted nearly a millennium, followed by a comparatively rapid process of dismemberment lasting less than a century.

The thirteenth-century antiquarian Matthew Paris said the woods of Middlesex were almost impenetrable and 'infested by outlaws and beasts'. But by 1709 the county was being described as 'but the suburbs at large of London, replenished with the retiring houses of the gentry and citizens thereof' (although Hounslow Heath remained very wild, because it was an infamous hunting ground of highwaymen, regarded as both outlaws and beasts). William Cobbett famously wrote in 1822 that 'All Middlesex is ugly'. A decade later Lord Macaulay, just as famously, wrote that 'an acre in Middlesex is better than a principality in Utopia', which in terms of what happened to property prices was a much shrewder comment.

Middlesex at that time was a far grander place than it subsequently became. The city of London was just that: the City of London. Everything in what we now consider London north of the Thames and west of the City was part of Middlesex: Charing Cross, Parliament, Buckingham Palace, the lot. Russell Grant, entertainer, astrologist and Middlesex partisan, still contends – from his thirteenth-floor flat in Soho – that he lives in Middlesex, with fine views of Surrey and Essex. The Boat Race crews still toss for the choice between 'the Middlesex station' and 'the Surrey station' before racing from Putney to Mortlake, and in the early days that was the undeniable truth. But even then Middlesex was the second-smallest county, more compact than Huntingdonshire, ahead only of Rutland.

In 1889 London itself acquired its own county council. Its neighbour lost a chunk of its already paltry territory and much of its population; Middlesex County Cricket Club, based at Lord's, no longer played in administrative Middlesex. And when a new Guildhall was built in 1913, the site chosen was not in the county town, Brentford, but in Parliament Square, opposite the Commons. Pevsner called the building 'art nouveau Gothic'. It looks to me more like the parliament of Ruritania.

The Guildhall was some way away from its own dominion, which was now a croissant-shaped thing stretching from Shepperton and Staines in the south-west to the distant north-eastern habitations of Tottenham, Edmonton and Enfield. Post-1889 Middlesex commanded the river from just west of Hammersmith, so the Boat Race stations remained half-right. Much of the redrawn county was still at least semi-rural, complete with the undulating pastureland of Mill Hill.

By the 1960s it was not. Administrative logic was in fashion, and the patchwork of councils that governed the areas within the supposed green belt was deemed unfit for purpose: six county councils, seventy-three boroughs and county boroughs, twenty-eight urban districts, three rural districts, six parishes and the City of London were all considered ripe for abolition. To the Conservative government, the fact that Labour had controlled the London County Council undisturbed for twenty-six years was even more germane. The City escaped change; nothing else did.

And so in 1965 Middlesex, aged at least 1,262, quietly expired. Its body parts were redistributed, mostly to the new Greater London Council, but with a small bone (Potters Bar) thrown to Hertfordshire and some larger ones to Surrey, which was allowed to extend north of the Thames as small compensation for the chunks it was itself obliged to disgorge to the new monster.

In contrast to the changes that would occur outside London nine years later, postal Middlesex – which did not cover all the old county – was allowed to survive. The cricket club also lived on, but the county's second most famous institution, the Middlesex Regiment, was amalgamated out of existence less than two years later. It had grown out of the old 57th Regiment of Foot, which, during the notably bloody Battle of Albuera in the Peninsular War, had been instructed by its severely wounded commander Colonel Inglis, 'Die hard, 57th! Die hard!' He obeyed his own command, living on for another twenty-four years, until 1835, and the regiment became known as the Diehards. Middlesex, however, passed away with barely a murmur. The name is probably best known now as an American novel about a hermaphrodite.

The Middlesex Guildhall had an afterlife as a Crown Court before, in 2009, becoming the site of Britain's newly created Supreme Court. At the back of Court 3 there hangs one of the county's old treasures, the ornately framed Sir Joshua Reynolds portrait dating from 1762 of the Earl (later 1st Duke) of Northumberland, Hugh Percy, who later became – in the geographically flexible manner of these characters – Lord Lieutenant of Middlesex.

Scattered about this room, and elsewhere in the building, are various remnants of the deceased county, including the foundation stone, complete with county crest of a crown and three swords ('three Seaxes fesse-wise', to be more precise). Court 3's main purpose is to be the centre of the Supreme Court's export trade, in which the judges sit as a committee of the Privy Council and dispense justice to distant corners of the Commonwealth. In that capacity, it sometimes has to hear appeals from prisoners who have been sentenced to death. The collection of Middlesex memorabilia is not the room's only source of grim nostalgia.

In 1973 John Betjeman recorded the best-loved of all BBC documentaries: his prose-poem 'Metro-land', a journey on the Metropolitan Line's route out of Baker Street through Middlesex towards Hertfordshire and Buckinghamshire. The brilliant wheeze of the then-independent Metropolitan Railway was that, like the American railroads, its owners understood that the way to make money was to build the lines and the communities together. Betjeman's genius was to be completely non-judgemental. There is, to be sure, an elegiac undertone. But the programme was made without even the hint of an intellectual sneer about suburban pretensions.

And thus, throughout the first half of the twentieth century, London trampled over Middlesex. Not mindlessly or brutishly: much of Metroland was built in the same agreeable style that lay behind Letchworth. And it was probably true that, as the ditty went,

> *Hearts are light, eyes are brighter*
> *In Metroland, Metroland.*

I don't suppose my Uncle Mendel promised Auntie Regina a rose garden in 1946 when they paid a few hundred quid to buy 48 Trevelyan Crescent, Kenton (alight at Preston Road – as I did, many times). He wasn't that sort. But she got one, both at the front and, more substantially, at the back. By then Kenton was no longer what one old-time writer had called 'a dream little hamlet'. But it was always their dream little home: leaded lights; herringbone-patterned brickwork; an arched porch.

These were never, in John Major's striking phrase, 'invincible green suburbs', except in terms of their Conservative majorities. It was the houses that were invincible. Metroland exacerbated the inclination of the English to be self-contained, a bit fearful, home-birdy and dull. The suburbs were never without neighbourliness: Auntie Regina became dependent on their kindness towards the end of her fifty-three years as wife, mother and widow at no. 48. But in Middlesex neighbours could never be taken for granted. No one in Metroland ever really knows what goes on behind the other houses' leaded lights and net curtains. And not far from Trevelyan Crescent was the most startlingly secret home of them all, the epitome of suburban improbability. The address was 45 Cranley Drive, Ruislip.

This was the home of a Canadian couple, Peter Kroger, an antiquarian bookseller, and his wife, Helen. In early 1961 police knocked on the door and were invited in; Detective Superintendent George Smith of Special Branch asked politely if the Krogers could tell them 'the name and address of the gentleman who comes and stays with you each weekend'. 'Well,' said Mr K. after a pause to stare at his wife, 'we have lots of friends.'

Having failed to elicit any mention of the friend that interested him, the Superintendent decided to arrest the Krogers. Mrs K. asked if, before they went, she might stoke the boiler. Yes, said the Superintendent, if I can see what's in your handbag. It turned out to contain a six-page handwritten letter in Russian and a piece of glass with three embedded microdots, advanced spying technology of the era. Very easy to hide in antiquarian books. Around the house were various items not normally found in Ruislip, even at that time of growing prosperity and modernity when the houses of Metroland were becoming full of gadgets.

The cigarette lighter on the table had an unscrewable base containing secret codes; the radiogram had a special band for receiving high-frequency broadcasts; the talcum powder container in the bathroom had a secret compartment with a miniature telescope; and under a trapdoor in the kitchen, guarded by rubble and a concrete slab, was a shopping bag holding a metal box with a wireless transmitter.

'That wireless transmitter,' the Attorney-General, Sir Reginald Manningham-Buller, later revealed in court, 'has no maker's name on it, is not of commercial design, and is fitted with a non-British plug to fit into the house mains and fitted with an earpiece and no loudspeaker ... it had an aerial and earth and was suitable for transmission ... [*and here I like to imagine a theatrical pause*] TO MOSCOW.'

It is hard to explain at this distance just how thrilling and chilling this was in 1961. About half the British population had lived through not one world war but two. A nuclear Third World War with the Soviet Union was considered a possibility, bordering on a probability. Less than two years later, during the Cuban Missile Crisis, it almost happened. And here was a link to the very heart of darkness. *In Ruislip.*

Whenever mystery is unmasked in a suburban English home, it is customary for the neighbours to say, 'Well, they kept themselves to themselves.' But this was not true of the Krogers. Though he undoubtedly smuggled out messages in his antiquarian books, Peter Kroger was also a well-regarded and knowledgeable dealer. They gave famous parties, at which the lighter and the radiogram were doubtless well used for their obvious purpose. Helen, childless herself, was a kind of universal aunt, dishing out presents to the neighbourhood children. She was particularly nice to Winifred Spooner's baby two doors away at no. 41. Mrs Spooner is now the last of the old neighbours left. 'I always used to joke with my eldest that he was the only baby who had had his tummy tickled by a spy.' The Krogers were hiding all right, but hiding in plain sight.

It was their ordinariness and niceness that made such an impact, not least on a nine-year-old with an overheated imagination like me. Could I trust *anyone*? What did my dad really do when he went off 'fishing'? Why was my mum always so vague on details? (It must have made an even bigger impression on Manningham-Buller's daughter, Eliza: she became head of MI5.)

And Ruislip! The Krogers could have chosen – probably did choose – the suburb for its English blandness. They certainly chose the house carefully. It was not a typical semi, like 48 Trevelyan Crescent. It was not a house at all, but what the press called 'a chalet-bungalow' at the end of a cul-de-sac. The current owner, John Paulo, an engineer from Liverpool, kindly let me in for a snoop. He's quite used to it: there was another writer lurking in the street on my first visit; the Paulos have had actors popping round before productions of plays on the subject, like Hugh Whitemore's *Pack of Lies*; they once had half a dozen Chinese tourists outside taking photos – 'They were very polite. They knocked on the door and asked if it was OK.'

The Paulos have done the place up, very nicely actually, turning the loft into a genuine top floor. They have kept the trapdoor that led to the transmitter, but moved it. It's a sort of conversation piece. And, as I was shown round, slowly I began to realise the thought processes behind the Krogers' choice. There is no house directly opposite; the bungalow is set back so the garden is not overlooked; and there was a field – now a football pitch – behind. A Metroland gem for anyone wanting privacy. What's more, the streets were built with a network of alleys, now blocked off to avoid annoyance by kids. But in the Krogers' time, had they sensed danger, they could have nipped over the fence at the back unobserved and had dozens of possible escape routes.

But they didn't sense danger despite being very skilful operators. The only flaw in their plan was that their contact in the Underwater Weapons Establishment at Portland – then a major concern for the Soviet Union – started spraying his cash around. The trail led by a devious route to Cranley Drive. The police wanted to watch the Krogers, but the only way to do that was from the house that was sort of over the road, though actually on Courtfield Gardens. There they lurked behind the little side window, after pleading with the Search family, who lived there, to put their patriotic duty ahead of loyalty to their charming neighbours.

The Krogers were really Morris and Lona Cohen, two American

old-style pre-war communists, idealists who had never recanted, and escaped the country after being implicated in the Los Alamos spy case. They had the second-last laugh. Sentenced to twenty-five and twenty years' jail, they were swapped for a British agent after serving eight. They returned to the East in glory and were awarded the Order of the Red Banner and the Order of Friendship of Nations, and posthumously were depicted on post-communist Russian stamps. However, before they died in the 1990s, they had to live most of their days in Poland and Russia, in the turgid empire ruled by Leonid Brezhnev, and when interviewed for a TV documentary in 1991, they sounded somewhat wistful.

Against that, had they returned to Ruislip in 2012, they would have seen the place festooned with front-garden placards with the less-than-catchy slogan: 'SAY NO TO ANOTHER FLOODLIT AND FENCED ASTRO-TURF PITCH ON KINGS COLLEGE PLAYING FIELDS'. Which doesn't make the suburbs of the capitalist West sound very lovable either.

Outside no. 45 the tree-rose that Helen Kroger planted still blooms every summer.

'Red?'

'No,' said John Paulo, 'pinky-white.' Ah, she did do her utmost not to give even the smallest clue.

Urban Middlesex has existed for less than 100 years. But already it has proved as dynamically protean as London itself. The Metroland suburbs have been through one existence as the epitome of dreary English respectability. But now many of those in the inner ring and what you might call mid-Middlesex have mutated again, into largely Asian communities. Neasden, besides being a running joke in *Private Eye* (whose printers were there in the early days), also has a giant, arrogantly painted branch of IKEA (which the company likes to pretend is in Wembley) and the first Hindu temple in Europe.

'Beyond Neasden,' Betjeman told his TV audience, 'there was an unimportant hamlet where for years the Metropolitan didn't bother to stop … slushy fields and grass farms.' Then he told the stories of the failed attempt to build a tower that would dwarf Eiffel's; of the football stadium; and of the British Empire Exhibition of 1924. The Indian Pavilion at the exhibition, with its twenty-seven courts – one for every province – was the nearest thing Britain had seen to the Taj Mahal until the Neasden Temple was built. Now Wembley itself is a major Gujarati centre.

Of an evening the new Metropolitan trains, comprising one long single compartment like a giant sausage, are full of exhausted Asian commuters going home to Wembley, Kenton and Harrow. Their Jewish predecessors have pushed north into Hertfordshire. The very week I stole a look at my aunt's old house came news that the large Kenton Synagogue, where I had my barmitzvah, had just put its rabbi on short time.

But no change can match the one that has overtaken Southall, away to the south-west on Brunel's line out of Paddington. It was once a nondescript suburb best known for its bus factory and a substantial contingent of Welsh migrants. In 1979 the police bashed and killed a left-wing activist, Blair Peach, during an anti-Nazi demonstration; in 1981 it was the centre of riots between Asians and skinheads which ended with a pub burning down. But these battles became a rout. Southall found peace by becoming overwhelmingly Punjabi – the front gardens of the Metroland-ish semis bricked over to provide parking for two, three, four cars – and most especially Sikh.

It is nondescript no more. Its shopping streets are perhaps the least cloned in Britain, even down to the exotic Asian banks, and bookmakers that advertise Indian cricket matches in their window rather than football or racing. Just about all the other shops are Asian, creating an impression of bottom-up enterprise that might be regarded as an object lesson to the cautious and non-entrepreneurial English.

The springtime Vaisakhi parade is Southall's celebration of its Sikhness. Vaisakhi was the day in 1699 when the Sikhs, having already narrowed down millions of Hindu gods to one, shrugged off the Hindu caste system: their last living guru, Gobind Singh, told them that henceforth 'the lowest will rank with the highest'. In the villages of the Punjab the occasion is said to be marked by wild dancing. In the suburbs of Middlesex it has taken on local characteristics by becoming a gigantic traffic jam: a stately, rather lugubrious procession. In the vanguard were swordsmen, performing a ritual battle startlingly reminiscent of the Morris Men's rapper dance.

At its centre was a giant float containing the holy book, the Guru Granth Sahib, resting on a cushion, covered with a cloth like a shroud, while priests recited verses and wielded the brushes known as *chauris*, in the manner of punkah wallahs, protecting their scriptures from insects and heat.

Neither was a problem in Southall this April. Nor were Nazis and skinheads. There was a great deal of food: even the Punjab National Bank had a tent frantically trying to keep up with the demand for naan. It was all free too, a fact I was slow to twig until a passing Englishman urged me to tuck in, before adding, 'It's cold. But it's hot.' The heirs to the police who killed Blair Peach were relaxed, confident in the improbability of trouble. It was, frankly, a bit dull.

But it was at least the re-enactment of an ancient and meaningful tradition. And in Middlesex that is strikingly rare.

The Middlesex Village Book, published in 1989, was one of a series produced round the country by Women's Institutes at the time. It contains essays of varying quality and some very nice line drawings. It is very difficult for anyone this close to London or any other major city to use the word 'village' without sounding pretentious. But this book is unusual for listing communities that would make even a cabbie scratch his head.

Many of the places mentioned are palpably not villages: Feltham, Greenford, Harrow on the Hill, Shepperton, Twickenham ... But what about Botany Bay (not the one in Australia)? Charlton (not the one with the football team)? Cowley (not the one in Oxford)? Cranford (not Mrs Gaskell's)? And on to Field End, Halliford, Laleham, Lampton, Littleton, Longford (not the one in Ireland) and beyond to the likes of Roxeth and Sipson. Near-at-hand places with strange-sounding names.

Among the WI villages in the north-east are Ponders End (known to old-timers as Ponders Plonk, for obscure reasons, and now very Asian) and Winchmore Hill, which did indeed have an unusually self-contained, forgotten air that one might almost call villagey. Then I headed down the North Circular past Neasden, singing Willie Rushton's wonderful hymn to the place ('It'll work out so much cheaper if you buy a seasden'), towards the more plausible-sounding villages in Middlesex's south-west corner, the remnant unwanted in London and handed to Surrey. However, they just merged into one another; struggling to find something memorable about Laleham, I found myself in Littleton.

I went west to Staines, a town so bedevilled by its unfortunate name and the unwanted residency of the comic character Ali G that it has uneasily rebranded itself as Staines-upon-Thames. Not such a bad place, I was thinking, as I sat on the Thames-side terrace in the Swan Hotel eating a tuna sandwich and watching the scullers and the narrow boats. Then I realised that, having crossed the river, I had broken the first rule of this book: I was actually in Egham Hythe, which was always in Surrey.

The lesson of Middlesex is that it has long been a place that offers the promise of a better life: for the eighteenth-century gentry; for their contemporaries, the highwaymen; for the homesteaders of Metroland; and in this corner too. The Middlesex WI still lists thirty-eight branches, and I bet they do their utmost to make a community in places that look deeply unpromising to sneery outsiders.

The 1989 book tells the story of a London family that moved out after the war from a cramped upstairs flat to a new house on the edge of Feltham, backing on to Hounslow Heath: 'Our garden when we moved in was a field of knee-high lush grass left over from the cows on Sparrow Farm. The children could hide if not willing to come in for meals or bed. They spent that entire summer building camps in the woods and, we learned later, trying to dam the Baber Brook.'

Within the year, the council had bought Sparrow Farm and it was turned into a housing estate. The family's access to the heath was severed. 'Soon there were too many cars for the small roads,' the anonymous resident continued, 'but perhaps some of the families had also come from upstairs flats and needed to share the space and freedom with us.'

Across the A4 from the Three Magpies and the road 'as rural as anywhere in England' is the turning to Harmondsworth, a village famous for its huge medieval timbered tithe barn; for being the former HQ of Penguin Books (built on a cabbage field in 1937); and for the presence of two 'immigration removal centres'. Less than a mile from modern Heathrow's perimeter fence is Harmondsworth Church, St Mary's: a much-admired Norman doorway, a brick-and-flint tower and some of the shapeliest yews in any churchyard in England. Some lovely cottages, two shops, two pretty pubs, a school. A real village and a beguiling one too. There is a dull background hum all right, but the village is not under the flightpath; the only really offensive noise came when two motorbikes roared through, which doesn't happen often because the road leads nowhere.

Among the graves I met Michael and Valerie Coombes, who had moved up from Devon fifty years before when Michael came out of the RAF. 'It's a lovely community,' said Valerie. But if you camp by an active volcano long enough, sooner or later you get buried by hot lava. For years Harmondsworth has lived under the threat of a third runway. Ostensibly this was lifted in 2010 when the coalition came to power. Then the government had second thoughts, but lacked the guts to say so, and chose to prevaricate until after the 2015 election. The latest thinking is that the expansion will obliterate the more transient village of Sipson next door. Harmondsworth, meanwhile, will be ruined without being demolished, meaning the compensation will be pathetic.

But Plans X, Y and Z will be along soon enough. 'It's the uncertainty that's so awful,' said Valerie. 'If it's going to happen you accept things and get on with it. But we don't know.'

Even closer to the airport, the Three Magpies has a sign by the door asking patrons to be respectful of their neighbours and leave as quietly as possible. I thought perhaps the pilots might have complained about the racket. I now see it as an indicator of people wanting to make the best of life in difficult circumstances. Which is very English, and very, very Middlesex.

April 2013

26. *Where the winds hit heavy on the borderline*

NORTHUMBERLAND

The Border Counties Railway between Hexham and Riccarton Junction closed in 1958, five years before Dr Beeching could have had the pleasure of strangling it personally. It ran for forty-two miles – single track, sometimes a single passenger – through the loneliest countryside in England, and some of the loneliest in Scotland.

North of what was once Kielder Station, where the road jinks away to cross the little North Tyne, the old line now carries on as a path and cart track, towards even more remote territory at Deadwater. But just after Kielder, a walker can turn off left, head up a boggy field, and there it is: a barbed-wire fence dividing the English county of Northumberland from the not-quite-yet nation-state of Scotland to the south.

I repeat, *to the south*.

It is the merest sliver of Scotland: a field 200 yards wide. No skirl of the pipes, nor hint of tartan, nor whiff of deep-fried Mars Bar, nor swig of Irn-Bru. Then comes Bell's Burn and the edge of Kielder Forest and

England starts again. It is a sort of peninsula, a mysterious product of the strange and bloody medieval process that created the Anglo-Scottish border.

People sitting much further south sometimes imagine that Scotland begins at Hadrian's Wall, which is wrong by up to sixty miles; that the border is a straightish east–west line; or that it largely follows the River Tweed. In reality it is almost unimaginably complex: sixty miles long to a passing crow, about 110 to an earthbound human, and it runs mainly north-east to south-west. Scotland's southernmost point, the Mull of Galloway, is about the same latitude as the northern tip of Yorkshire, near Redcar. And the western land border at Gretna is on a par with Newcastle, which is a helluva way from haggis.

Historians have terrible trouble sorting out the logic of the border. Some emphasise the significance of the Treaty of York (1237); others ignore it. It does seem clear that the line was pretty much fixed in the thirteenth century with the exception of medieval Britain's most marginal constituency, Berwick-upon-Tweed, which was captured once and for all for England by the future Richard III in 1482.

Nigel Tranter, author of *Portrait of the Border Country*, found the abrupt and capricious deviations of the border unfathomable but 'no doubt explainable once by the ambitions and positions of the properties of influential magnates, the apprehensions of wardens, the intrigues of courtiers – or by uneasy compromise or sheer accident'. It took me two hours and two separate conversations with the patient owner of Bells Burnfoot Cottage to be reasonably confident I had it right in 2013. Doubtless it will become better marked if Scotland ever becomes independent. Possibly the markers will include Hadrian's Wall-style forts, lookout posts and armed guards.

The Anglo-Scottish border, however, is what it is and what it has been for centuries – unlike the borders of most English counties. Which is one reason why Scotland has become a country of growing self-awareness, self-assurance and ambition. And why the English often have no idea where they live.

Tranter was equally baffled by the 'strangely arbitrary line' that marks the most northerly point of England and the most northerly of the border crossings. It is merely a kissing gate by the solitary meadow – known as Seabreeze – that lies between the London–Edinburgh railway and the edge of the cliffs at Marshall Meadows Bay, across the Tweed from Berwick. Marshall Meadows comprises just an agreeable-looking country

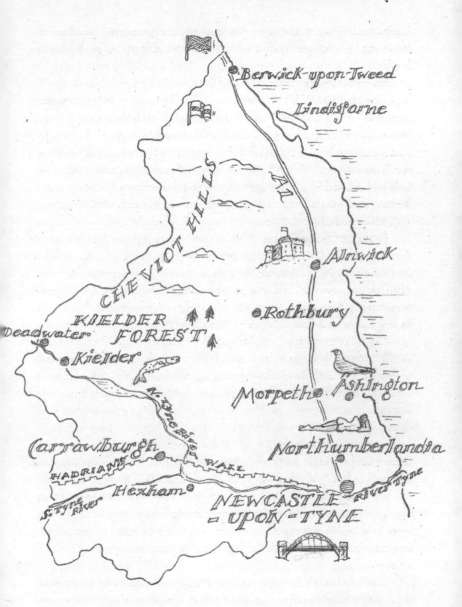

house hotel and the Fairbairn family's sheep farm, three-quarters in England, a quarter in Scotland. On a bright but windy morning (most mornings must be windy up here), I wandered along the cliff path past the

Fairbairns' holiday caravan site, picked up England's most northerly wind-blown bit of black plastic, passed its most northerly plants (a dead heat between a thistle and a stinging nettle), crossed into Scotland, watched a southbound express go by and headed back into Northumberland.

The Fairbairns have minor extra complications with government paperwork. John Fairbairn was born in England; his brother and parents in Scotland. He has no problem about who to support at football or rugby since he isn't interested. He was a bit worried about the possibility of Scottish independence: 'That might come difficult for us.' Already, there are wild legal anomalies around here: for instance, the River Till, a tributary of the Tweed, is wholly in England, but governed by Scottish fishing laws.

Thus the border has nothing to do with Hadrian's Wall, which is a sad, patchy old thing. No one is quite sure of its purpose. Was it aggressive? Defensive? Or just a means of control? It looks now as if it could hardly have deterred a wandering ewe. I considered the possibility that Hadrian had promised his wife he would finish the job, but never quite got round to it, as one doesn't. But in a single respect Hadrian did get it right. England's natural, defensible, logical line runs the way his wall does, between Solway and Tyne, not Solway and Tweed.

Travelling through Northumberland, which is essentially the land between Tyne and Tweed, I was at different times reminded of almost everywhere I had ever been in my life. The one place it never felt like was England.

It struck me first at the Temple of Mithras, the archaeological relic by the Wall at Carrawburgh. Mithraism was a cult, its adherents the Moonies or Scientologists of the day; they were into sun worship and bull sacrifice. It was popular with Roman soldiery across the Empire and one can see how appealing both elements of Mithraism might have been to the troops posted to this bleak outpost, the wind scything across the moor, a long, long way from Mediterranean sunshine and mamma's meatballs.

Northumberland is a breathtaking county, full of big, ever-changing skies, and landscapes that normally belong to more spacious nations. At times, it felt to me like the Wild West: Montana or Wyoming, maybe, with more rounded peaks. At others, it might have been Russia: where there are trees, there are trees (150 million in Kielder Forest); where there ain't, there ain't. There were even moments when the sun was on the beige land and I fancied, in a fantastical way, that it was Saudi Arabia. I finally decided it was Britain's Minnesota: a place with one big urban sprawl (Tyneside playing the role of Minneapolis) and not much else; a tough history of mining; and a reputation for being remote, cold and northerly, notwithstanding that in both cases there is another country even further to the north.

What Northumberland is not is English-pretty or cosy. 'Toto,' I thought, hunching away from the gale at Carrawburgh, 'I don't think we're in the Home Counties any more.' It is not just a matter of landscape. There is something forbidding about the place: it defies the middle-class homesteaders who have spread across the rest of the English countryside. I have known sensible, sensitive people – and heard of more on this trip – who have tried to settle in rural Northumberland and failed. It was simply too foreign.

There are a lot of factors: the old rural Northumbrian burr has almost gone now but, by golly, it was a daunting barrier to conversation – as guttural as German or, perhaps more to the point, Danish. Even so, the infinite local variations that increasingly get lumped together as Geordie still remain, to the unattuned, both inimitable and largely incomprehensible.

On the upper reaches of the Tyne, especially the North Tyne, any conversations become less likely. Someone dared me to go into the Black Bull at Wark and endure the stares. In the event, no one stared: it took some time before even the barmaid acknowledged my existence. I did not attempt Part 2 of the dare, which was to order a Campari. Places like Wark have never known a yeoman class or a bourgeoisie.

No other county is so dominated by an eponymous duke: the 12th Duke of Northumberland, unable to match his forebears by governing Middlesex, still sits in Alnwick Castle, which the Percy family acquired a mere 800 years ago, with 100,000 scattered acres at his command. The rest of Northumberland is full of minor aristocrats and gentry – and what one might rudely call peasants. Bill Lancaster, former director of the Centre of Northern Studies, explained that there were open and closed (or 'close') villages. Open ones had multiple landowners, and thus tended to be comparatively free-and-easy; the others were controlled by a single man. 'In Northumberland you don't even get closed villages. What you get are farming hamlets, with a terrace for the workers. In Victorian times the Duke didn't want villages: they could be centres of dissent.'

Oh, it would be easy enough to shift from Surrey to the more genteel suburbs of Newcastle, or to the camomile-tea towns of Alnwick and Hexham. Lots of like-minded souls. There is a Shakespeare group in distant

Allendale. And the Coquet Valley has its adherents. But beyond that, well, it's remote. There are issues of transport as well as culture. The East Coast Main Line bombs up the coast, and a glorious stretch of rail it is. But the trains often forget to stop on the 125 miles between Newcastle and Edinburgh. The only other line worth mentioning is the one following Hadrian from Newcastle to Carlisle. But, in the sad absence of the Border Counties line, there is a vast empty trainless quarter between the two.

And the roads! North of Morpeth the A1 – *the A1!* – suddenly goes down to single carriageway for the first time since Hampstead Garden Suburb, and stays like that most of the way to Berwick. This event is marked by signs reading 'DON'T SPEED'. Fat chance of that when you're in a line of lorries behind a tractor and a muck spreader.

The babbling North Tyne gets 700,000 young salmon every year from the hatchery at Kielder. But it's no use for navigation, never mind commuting. This was Reiver Country and the history lurks close to the surface. The Robsons, Charltons and Milburns were famous for plunder long before they became famous for football. And many of their heirs remain. 'The North Tyne had such a reputation for violence and theft that even in Victorian times the Newcastle shipyards wouldn't take apprentices from there,' according to the Hexham-based writer Harry Pearson. 'Into the 1980s the men from Wark used to head to Haltwhistle for a massive traditional fight on Bank Holiday Mondays. This was something that dated right back to the reivers.'

I stopped in Bellingham, which looked just the sort of little English town where people often say good morning in the street. I tried. But as the old ladies scowled by, the words died in my throat. Bellingham is pronounced 'Bellin-jam'. They probably sensed I was the sort of the person to get it wrong. This is just one of a whole pile of Northumberland shibboleths designed to entrap an outsider. Wark is prounced 'Waark'. Alnwick is 'Anick'; the village actually spelt Anick is 'Eh-Nick'; Alnmouth is 'Alanmouth' ... And of course Newcastle is 'New*cass*el'.

Over the years, Newcastle has probably been the least-worst run of any British big city. It has had its moments, especially in the era when the corrupt T. Dan Smith led the council in the early 1960s. But Smith did not quite achieve his ambition of turning the city into a chilly Brasilia. Its heart still derives from the architecture of the early nineteenth century, mainly by the architect John Dobson and the spec builder Richard Grainger, thrillingly topped off by Robert Stephenson's High Level Bridge. 'The only major city in England with a planned centre,' enthused Pevsner, 'classical, competent and resourceful'.

I was lucky to have a living, breathing guidebook with me as well: the playwright Michael Chaplin, who was able to point out not just, for example, the Corinthian portico of the Theatre Royal but the site of its former neighbour, the public lavatories on Shakespeare Street, known to the locals as Anne Hathaway's Cottage. Mike gave me a tour of Newcastle's own Athenaeum, the Lit and Phil, and then led me to Grey Street, 'one of the best streets in England', according to Pevsner, a judgement that seems to me unduly cautious. Sinuous and sloping from the Grey Monument down towards the Quayside, it was also, when Pevsner wrote in 1957, soot-blackened and ripe to be stuffed up by mindless modernisation. But the actual centre was remarkably unruined in the 1960s and 1970s, perhaps because, like Liverpool, the city was too mired in industrial decay: the great empire built by the Victorian arms tycoon and shipbuilder William Armstrong was fading away.

But somewhere along the line, Newcastle was revitalised. It is hard to pin down when and how it happened. Part of it was benign neglect: the redundant docks were not turned into some grandiose Canary Wharf but allowed to redevelop organically. Part of it was forethought: in the 1980s, when Thatcherism was raging through the North-East, a load of redundant old railways were patched together into a Metro system, second in Britain only to the London Underground. (It is fair to say that this happened by seeing the two sides of the Tyne – Northumberland and County Durham – holistically not historically.)

And then Newcastle became trendy. In the 1980s it was the setting for the very un-Thatcherite Channel 4 rock programme *The Tube*, which started to make the place seem cool. Like Manchester and Leeds, the city reaped the benefit of being a magnet for regional offices. It was a big winner from the universities boom, not just in numbers but because it was seen as a lively, party kind of city, so it attracted sub-Oxbridge students from the southern middle class who headed to New*cass*el to learn Geordie as a foreign language. It benefited from the great football revival: Newcastle United hardly ever won anything, but they were always major players in the sport's grand soap opera. And Michael Caine's 1971 gangster film *Get Carter* was set on Tyneside. A flop on its release, it slowly acquired cult status, which was either one cause of the city's growing status or an effect.

The invasion of students certainly added a new dimension to a city where working-class males had always been heavily alcohol-fuelled. And so two boozy cultures collided. Here began the meteorologically insane habit of young people going out pubbing and clubbing wearing bugger all, dressed not so much to kill as to catch their death. I took a Friday night wander down Grey Street to observe this old-hat but ongoing phenomenon. There was so much bass-thumping coming out of the basements that at any moment it felt as though Dobson and Grainger's well-constructed buildings might all tumble down the hill into the Tyne.

And yet the cultural collision was not violent. The Friday night atmosphere seemed very amiable. Even so, I took refuge from the noise and goose-pimpled flesh in the Crown Posada, by the Quayside, a joyous wood-panelled pub where the music came from 1950s LPs on a 1950s Dynatron record player. Fairly quickly, a drunken granny from Blyth started snogging me, until her husband led her gently away. At some point during the second pint, discussing Muddy Waters (I think it was) with some bloke at the bar, I realised there was no city in England where one was more likely to strike up a bar-room conversation with a stranger and none where one was less likely to understand what the hell they were on about.

Northumberland is a big county (no. 5 in area, smaller than only Yorkshire, Lincolnshire, Devon and Norfolk). Newcastle is emphatically not the geographic centre of it and has been separately administered throughout modern times. But the whole county looks to Newcastle and almost unanimously supports/endures the football team: it has nowhere else to go.

The city in return regards the county as a kind of country estate, much as Sheffield regards the Peak. Any Tyneside childhood is suffused by memories of days in the small, mostly down-at-heel resorts up the coast which can be a match for the Mediterranean or Caribbean on at least, ooh, four or five days in an average summer. And the rest of Northumberland – that vast Saudi-style Empty Quarter – is seen as theirs too, but something more distant, more haunting. Out There.

In July 2010 Raoul Moat, thirty-seven, a small-time hoodlum with anger management problems, came out of prison and shot three people with a sawn-off shotgun. He wounded his ex-girlfriend, killed her new lover and blinded a policeman, before apparently conducting an armed robbery in a chip shop at Seaton Delaval. His car was found near the small town (or village, as the locals call it) of Rothbury, in the Coquet Valley, and a manhunt began which for a week transfixed the nation.

The *Financial Times* sent me up to Rothbury to report this. I arrived to find a huge cast of police (including one-tenth of Britain's firearms officers) and media doing their best to rub along with a small population that was at once bemused, irritated, fearful and, without ever quite admitting it, relishing the extra business and excitement. Initially, the locals would point towards the Simonside Hills – Out There – and say he could be anywhere.

For this was a very Northumberland manhunt: Out There was miles and miles of nothing. And there was an inclination to treat Moat in what may have been his own grandiose self-image: as a man against the world but resourceful enough to live alone indefinitely amid the crags and summer-high bracken. In a country as settled and CCTV-ed as this one, there was something exhilaratingly American about the very idea.

As the days passed, evidence started to point in a different direction. A reporter saw a beefy and suspicious late-night man in a baseball cap on the street. Local resident Rob Herdman saw a figure moving near his greenhouse and reported the mysterious disappearance of his salad crops. An abandoned camp was discovered nearby.

Early on Friday evening, six days after the initial shootings, Moat was cornered on the edge of town. He had been living almost within earshot of the speculation, in a storm drain by the river, from which – had he lasted long enough – he would have been literally flushed out. A tense night followed, in which the marksmen pointed their guns at Moat and he pointed his gun at himself. It was a weird night too: among the arrivals was the troubled ex-footballer Paul Gascoigne, armed with a chicken and some cans of lager for his mate 'Moaty'; in the Queen's Head, the media, trying to make sense of what was happening behind the police cordon, were joined by a group of wedding guests, barred from reaching the reception at a hotel the other side of the river. So they had their own breakaway, bride-and-groomless, party instead.

Just after 1 a.m. the police decided to use an experimental Taser on Moat to stop him killing himself. It had the reverse effect: it never became wholly clear whether his death was reflexive, brought on by the jolt, or a considered decision. The inquest jury decided on suicide. In early 2012 the blinded policeman, David Rathband, also killed himself, perhaps the saddest aspect of a sad, sad story.

And on a Saturday morning a year later I drove into Rothbury and wandered down the High Street. All the police and journalists had gone; everything else seemed as it was and should be, although the *Big Issue* seller outside the Co-op was an improbable touch. The sign on Bill Kirkup's toyshop said 'Closed' but no one was taking any notice, including Bill, who was in his normal place behind the counter, dealing with a stream of kids brought in for a little Saturday morning treat. (There is nothing more fascinating to a child than a small-town toyshop.) I had met Bill first time round and he remembered me instantly, and not unkindly; his accountant had brought him the *FT* cutting and he had approved.

Rothbury had a new preoccupation: the road was closed by Cragside, William Armstrong's old country home, just as it was on the night of Moat's last stand – this time because of a landslide. There was talk of it being closed until Christmas, with unfortunate effects on the summer tourist trade.

'After the Moat business, the village was quiet,' said Bill. 'But we had a lot of eerie visitors who used to ask for the site where he was shot. One family wanted to take a picture of their child posing in the drain. How bizarre is that? And bikers would arrive with a few cans and sit there, you know. The family came up to spread his ashes on the river and they used to put flowers down there. The locals would kick them in the water. We didn't want to make a shrine of it. We just wanted to make it go away.'

But he had kept the cuttings. And, as he admitted, it was part of Rothbury's history. The biggest thing that had happened there since 1878, when Cragside became (probably) the first house in the world to be lit by electric light.

Back on the border, in Berwick, I met Simon Duke, a reporter on the *Berwickshire News*, who also had to contribute to its sister paper, the *Berwick Advertiser*. The *News* circulates mainly in the Scottish county of Berwickshire, which starts across the line at Marshall Meadows; the *Advertiser* in and around the English town of Berwick-upon-Tweed. Both papers report on the generally subdued doings of Berwick Rangers, the English football team who play in the Scottish League. All clear?

'People in Berwick definitely see themselves as English,' Simon said. 'But I wouldn't say they were particularly proud. They're not that bothered. There isn't much fuss if there's a football match or something. Whereas the other side of the border is *very* Scottish.'

Reporters here have to wrap their heads round two very different legal systems since they may have to cover both Scottish and English courts, never mind such complications as the River Till. For Simon Duke, the main difference between the papers was not English/Scottish but urban/rural. The townie *Advertiser* gets a response if it tries to involve readers via social media; the rustic *News* doesn't. The *Advertiser* is obsessed with parking (Berwick wants more) and the seagull menace (Berwick wants fewer). The *News* focuses mainly on agriculture.

Not the week I was there, though. 'HUMAN REMAINS UNDER INVESTIGATION', yelled the front page of the *Berwickshire News*. The man who wrote the splash was delighted: 'It was a dream story for us,' said Simon.

Mike Chaplin was a trainee reporter on the *Newcastle Journal* forty years ago. Early on, his news editor beckoned him over and said portentously, 'I've got a job for you.' He handed Mike the tide tables for Holy Island and told him to write the paragraph showing that day's times. He would have caught the aggrieved look at once. 'It's the most important job on the paper,' the news editor hissed. 'Get it wrong, someone will die.'

The tides at Northumberland's oldest tourist site have been a matter of life and death since at least the seventh century AD, when St Aidan arrived to found the monastery at Lindisfarne. The essence of the problem has not changed. You can drive to the island by the causeway just over half the time; the recommended times on foot across the sand are more conservative. But, essentially, two or three hours either side of high tide the waters close in. The *News*, the *Advertiser* and the *Journal* all still list the safe crossing times. On the day I crossed, the deadline was 13.35.

> *The tide did now its flood-mark gain,*
> *And girdled in the saint's domain;*
> *For, with the flow and ebb, its style*
> *Varies from continent to isle;*
> *Dry-shod, o'er sands, twice every day,*
> *The pilgrims to the shrine find way;*
> *Twice every day, the waves efface*
> *Of staves and sandalled feet the trace.*
>
> 'The Holy Island', Sir Walter Scott

This struck at one of my deepest obsessions. I mentioned my childhood fascination-cum-psychosis about floods, storms, tsunamis and inundations back in Dunwich (Chapter 13). I felt drawn to Holy Island, but also terrified. That was before I had lingered too long in Berwick and then got lost in the outskirts. It was 11.30 when I finally crossed and even then the water was lapping the tarmac in places.

In theory, nothing ought to go wrong, even if you don't buy the papers. There are electronic signs at the start of the causeway, flashing the magic figures, 13.35; notices all over the island; and blood-curdling pictures of drowning cars. The first person I met was the postman, who comes from Berwick to deliver to the few dozen homes and businesses. 'Some days I have to get on and off, whoosh.' Today he was relaxed. I wasn't.

Normal people come to Lindisfarne to seek spiritual renewal in the spirit of St Aidan, St Cuthbert, St Eadberht and St Eadfrith, or to twitch rare birds or drink the monkish mead or explore the castle, refurbished by Lutyens with a garden designed by Gertrude Jekyll, or buy tat in the souvenir shops. Not me. The castle? Oh no, no time.

It was a classic Northumbrian morning: bright but cold-breezy, with clouds forming and re-forming. Everyone seemed to me to have a sense of urgency: the tourists, a gang of builders dismantling some scaffolding; even the birds sounded as though they were singing with one eye on the clock. I opted for an early lunch in the Ship but confined myself to a sandwich, being further discombobulated by a poem on the wall in praise of lifeboat men, with the rubric 'LET NOT THE DEEP SWALLOW ME UP'.

By 12.45 the High Street was eerily deserted; by 1.15 the car park had virtually emptied. The ice cream man was reassuring. 'I'll leave at 1.45,' he mused. 'Let the tourists get off first.' The issue was a classic one for a reporter. What does 'a deadline' mean exactly? There are little white lies involved. 'We must have your copy by 6 at all costs' means 'We will be mildly inconvenienced if it's later than 6.30.' Do the Holy Island safe crossing times work the same way? Logic and the ice cream man suggested yes. But was I sure?

I pressed the panic button at 1.20. The lapping water hadn't moved in nearly two hours. I stopped on the bank on the other side and waited. I reckon I would have had time to walk to the castle, inspect Gertrude Jekyll's garden, have sticky toffee pudding, coffee and brandy in the Ship and a nap in the car, and still get off safely. More sensibly, I might have spent a night, a week or a lifetime, allowed myself to be girdled in the saintly domain to contemplate the infinite mysteries, like tides. However, I was off to see something traditionally unavailable on Holy Island: a naked woman.

Northumberlandia is the county's newest tourist attraction, billed as the 'world's largest landform sculpture'. It was commissioned by Viscount Ridley, owner of Blagdon Hall, an eighteenth-century pile which, as its downbeat name somehow suggests, has managed to maintain its amenities through the proximate, but not too proximate, presence of large quantities of coal.

The title lightly disguises one Matt Ridley, a journalist known for his heterodox views about climate change (he thinks it exists but may be a good thing, which is certainly true for tourist projects in Northumberland). He was also formerly chairman of Northern Rock, a building society-turned-bank which went spectacularly belly-up on his watch in 2007, thus helping precipitate the financial crisis, an event which might mitigate anyone's enthusiasm for the ideas of Viscount Ridley.

The plan was conceived to enable the Blagdon Estate to overcome objections to a new open-cast coal mine, and involved shifting a million and a half tons of waste, which were then lightly grassed over to create a simulacrum of an extremely large woman, designed by the American 'architectural theorist' Charles Jencks. She is known to some as 'Fat Slag'.

From a helicopter she might indeed look fairly convincing. But the Blagdon Estate does not provide helicopters or, at the time of my visit, toilets or a cup of tea; and the explanatory leaflet was only proffered from someone's pocket as I was leaving. Happily, there was no admission charge.

One has acquired over the years a certain superficial familiarity with the female body. But it would not have been one's first guess at Northumberlandia. It felt to me like a particularly hilly and difficult golf course. I know she had a face because there was a sign saying 'PLEASE KEEP OFF THE FACE'. I think I found a hip because someone said it was a hip. And I feel pretty sure I stood on one of her windblown bosoms, but she did appear to have four of them, two of them very strangely positioned.

Atop the bosom there was a fine view of the open-cast mine and of a classic Northumberland cloudscape, full of wonderful and definable shapes. One definitely looked like a dragon. Another like a flying pig.

From early April until mid-September the Hirst Northern Homing Society normally gathers at Friday teatime in a back room at the Northern Social Club in Ashington: a handful of humans and several hundred of their best friends, crated and ready to be freighted.

The humans were nearly all male and mostly grey; the birds were sleek, well fed. These are the rich cousins of the urban pigeon, anxious not to get begging letters from their ne'er-do-well relatives. If they were human, they would probably get out of Ashington and head south for good. Instead, every weekend they are driven south – further and further as the season progresses, concluding in Bourges, in central France – and every weekend they fly home at the first opportunity. There is an attrition rate which John Snowdon, the society chairman, thinks might average out at 10 to 15 per cent a year, usually caused by bad weather or the pigeons' multiplying enemy, sparrowhawks. But week after week, most get home, at an A1 dual-carriageway-ish average speed of 60 mph if the winds are favourable, and a single-lane-ish 40 mph if not.

None of the old pit communities is as imbued with north-eastern culture as Ashington. It is a town 'rich in associational life', in the words of Bill Lancaster. This was the town that produced perhaps Northumberland's three greatest footballers: the Newcastle 1950s hero Jackie Milburn and the Charlton brothers, Jack and Sir Bobby. It was a centre of leek growing and whippet racing as well as pigeons. It was also the home of the Pitmen Painters. And its accent remains distinctive, even in this region of elongated vowels. (Northumberland joke: Ashington woman goes into the hairdresser, says, 'Can I have a perm?' and gets the reply, 'I wandered lonely as a cloud.')

There is an explanation for all this, says Lancaster. The Ashington Coal Company was a Quaker-run consortium which took a broader view of its responsibilities than most pit owners. The firm thought long term, concentrating on high-quality coal which had a high reputation – it was even exported to Germany in the 1930s – and it was inclined to a kindly, paternalistic view of its employees. Hence decent wages, and the strong sport and social side – which all led to a stable workforce and thus to a particularly introverted accent.

But I still didn't understand what made the pigeons keep coming back. 'What is it,' I asked the folk at the social club, 'apart from your cooking and care, of course?'

'That's just it,' said George Drury, who was helping with the checking process.

'And sex,' said John Snowdon. 'Remember when you were young and you'd go any distance for sex?'

George nodded: 'It'll do anything for sex, a pigeon.'

I was just musing on how I might compare in that matter to a youthful pigeon when in came Bob Bell, seventy-eight, a Renaissance man worthy of study at the Newcastle Lit and Phil and a legend in his own home town: former face-worker, former professional footballer, former world champion leek grower and pigeon man par excellence.

I can well understand the appeal of pigeon racing – its intricacies, its strategies and the notion of airborne freedom to men confined underground. But why leeks? Nasty vegetable: Shakespeare had it right – Fluellen would have brought the Globe down with knowing laughter when he forced Pistol to eat a whole one in *Henry V*.

'Why didn't you compete with cucumbers or carrots?'

'We did,' said Bob (or, this being Ashington, 'Burb'). 'But the money was in the leek shows. And the radiograms. And the televisions. And the washing machines. And the fridge-freezers.'

But it's gone now. Bob said there used to be fifty-two leek shows in Ashington, offering prizes that in the 1950s and 1960s could transform a pit family's life. There was one for every social club – and there are still dozens of those. 'They don't want to know these days. They just sit at home with their computer games.'

'Whippets?'

'Why-aye. Never see a whippet race now.'

'What about the pigeons?'

'Dying the death.'

It didn't look that way at the back of the Northern Social, as nearly 300 birds were brought in and filled the small room with their soft cooing. But John said they loaded up to 800 here in the old days. And, whatever drives the pigeons home, this hobby can be a bit of a passion-killer for the humans.

It is not a sport that lends itself to holidays, or to weekend togetherness. The lorry arrived only a fraction after the scheduled hour of 6 to get the birds to the starting point in Peterborough. And once they are released, it is reasonably easy to calculate when they might return. But that release can be delayed and delayed if the weather isn't right. In the North-East, most pigeon men have their lofts on their allotments. And there can be a lot of £1-a-time calls to the 'Liberation Line' and long, long waits with the Thermos. But what joy when a champion bird comes home preening, and looking for his tea and his oats.

Whippet racing may have gone towards extinction even more surely than the Northumbrian burr, though there is some suggestion of a revival

in leek growing: younger gardeners are said to be enthused by the traditions of skulduggery and the notion of fertilising the trenches with dead
cats and dogs. And the Ashington accent is still famous in the North-East.
The very funny magazine *Newcastle Stuff* included, as well as a column
called Tyne & Weird, an Ashington Dictionary:

> Stern: A small piece of rock
> Sure: Light downpour of rain
> Talkies: Large hen-like creatures eaten at Christmas.

The last pit closed in 1988 and the town seemed rather sad. I stood
outside the Nisa Extra store and every shopping bag clanked. Reopening
the railway station would really help, even if it did dilute the accent.

Before returning south, I took the advice Bill Kirkup gave me in Rothbury: drive to Corby Craggs on the B road to Alnwick, sit on the bench
and admire the view. That view is north-westwards stretching towards the
distant, snow-capped Cheviots across a vast country where Raoul Moat
might be lurking yet had he put his mind to it. Every bird in creation
seemed to be singing, with the possible exception of the racing pigeon.
The sun was shining but still the Northumberland sky was filled with its
signature large, fluffy clouds. Methinks I saw one shaped like a naked
woman.

April 2013

27. *Land of the rising sap*

DORSET

It was just before 7 and coming up to Moira reading the Radio 2 News. Melvin the cheesemaker and his assistant Phil were already there: in white uniforms and wellies and black gloves. They were deep into their work, fooling their boss, who thought he would show me the start of the process.

This is the cheesemaking plant at Woodbridge Farm in King's Stag – the domain of Michael Davies, the man who brought back Britain's most mysterious cheese from the edge of oblivion. This is the home of Dorset Blue Vinny.

The cheese (and cricket, and wine) connoisseur John Arlott wrote about Blue Vinny in 1958 and, even then, he said, 'Of all the cheeses still made, it is the hardest to find.' But he declared, 'It is worth the search. It is amazing that a skimmed milk cheese should be so noble and round and rich, without a trace of the pungency we find in so much of the Continental blues.' That was shortly after de Gaulle had declared that only fear could unite the French because you couldn't bring together '*un pays qui compte 265 spécialités de fromage*'.

He said that at a time when most British consumers thought cheese meant Cheddar or Dairylea. Now there are more than 700 named varieties made in Britain, though it hasn't made us less biddable. I do wish we possessed a fraction of France's localised bloody-mindedness.

Michael Davies was bloody-minded all right. In the 1950s, said Arlott, the cheese came only from a Mr Vincent of Sherborne. By 1982 it had disappeared completely. Someone was selling something called Blue Vinny to the grockles: it turned out to be second-grade Stilton. That was when Michael first began experimenting in the garage, ripening the cheese in his wife Christine's pantry. (Declaration of slight interest: Christine is my wife's first cousin.) 'The first time I opened up a cheese it was solid blue,' he recalled. 'I think it had a shelf life of twenty minutes.'

Everything else turned blue, including the corn flakes, and he was ejected from the pantry. It took him seven years to get it right. The blue was always the problem. There were certain traditional Dorset ways of getting the mould that would produce the blue veining into the cheese – muddy horse-harnesses, old boots, damp hay – but these would nowadays raise eyebrows at the Food Standards Agency. The modern answer turned out to be one known to the Romans: the fungus *Penicillium roqueforti*. The tricky bit was getting the quantity right – less than a teaspoonful for a vat full of unpasteurised Friesian milk.

On Day 1 had come the starter mixture – a sort of sour milk – plus the mysterious blue and the rennet. At Woodbridge this is veggie-friendly plant rennet and not the traditional rennet that comes from the fourth stomach of an unweaned calf (or maybe the blood of a Dorset virgin, I hardly know what to believe). Then it turns custardy and becomes curds and whey, last heard of being eaten by Miss Muffet.

By the time I got there next morning and Moira read the news, the whey had drained away and the curds were in the cooler, exhibiting the consistency of scrambled egg and a taste something like cheese, though of a bland and mass-produced kind, which is not the nature of the finished product. By lunchtime on Day 2 it will have hardened enough to be put into moulds to stand in the first of my sort-of cousin Michael's three storage rooms, each cooler than the last, to be given the most mystical ingredient of all: time.

At first it looks, frankly, like an industrial-sized roll of toilet paper. But then the tinges of blue appear. Within twelve weeks Michael will have

Sherborne

Shaftesbury

King's Stag

BLACKMORE VALE

Beaminster

Cerne Abbas

Blandford Forum

Charborough House

Tolpuddle

DORCHESTER

Poole

Lyme Regis

Poundbury

Abbotsbury

CHESIL BEACH

Weymouth

Corfe Castle

St Aldhelm's Head

Portland Bill

tested the cheese and pronounced it good, or not. Arlott called the taste 'subtle yet round', and that's right. It's not an in-your-face blue cheese like Stilton or Roquefort itself. It has taste, but above all aftertaste. Blessed are the cheesemakers.

Blue Vinny has to be a rarity. Almost nothing in this process is mechanised; it cannot be mass-produced. Dorset was never Somerset, which unleashed its cheese on the world; a few dozen American Cheddar-eaters could eat up Woodbridge Farm's entire output. The Blackmore Vale traditionally made its living from dairying, selling its cream to London and, when the railways arrived, the milk as well. The cheese was always an afterthought. Much of Dorset did not even make cheese, since it is on chalk, where dairying is unpromising. Hence, so the locals insist, 'chalk and cheese'. Reference books deny it.

Dorset's most conspicuous resident is pure chalk and not cheesy at all. Beefcake, more like. Everybody knows the giant of Cerne Abbas, trilled

Arthur Mee in his 1939 guide to Dorset: 'He equals thirty tall men standing one on the other, each of his fingers measures seven feet, and the club
in his hand is forty feet long.'

All of which may be true, but it is not his fingers or his club that
anyone notices. In Sussex, not an especially demure county, the hillside
chalk figure of the Long Man of Wilmington is almost well enough clad
to pass at a garden party arranged by the Hove Conservative Association.
His Dorset rival would be wholly unacceptable even on Brighton's nud-
ist beach. The Cerne Abbas giant is in possession of Britain's biggest,
most famous and longest-lasting erection. Estimates of its size range from
twenty feet, which looks like an underestimate, to forty. But perhaps it is
so realistic it varies according to the quality of the company.

Estimates of his age vary too. Scholars argue whether he might be
Celtic or Saxon; yet no evidence of his existence has emerged before 1694,
which adds credence to the notion that he might be a landowner's parody
of Cromwell. It is hard enough to believe he could have survived the Victorians, let alone generations of pre-Reformation Cerne Abbas abbots; the
Bishop of Salisbury was trying to organise a cover-up as late as the 1930s.

The National Trust has now fenced the giant in, allegedly to preserve
the downland rather than to prevent him escaping and terrorising the
neighbourhood. In a sense, it doesn't matter. The best views come either
from the air or from a lay-by on the main road, where on a May morning
he could be seen in his full glory, just above a field of, um, rape.

But it is an easy walk up the hill, and though he is largely invisible
behind the fence, his thighs lie close to early purple orchids, themselves
a symbol of fertility, like the giant himself. The fence is not impregnable
and it would be nice to think that worried village maidens might, as of old,
steal up there, lie close to his mighty organ and dream of babies; and that,
perhaps on Midsummer's Eve, couples might also sneak through the fence,
maybe thinking of babies, maybe having taken precautions.

All around everything seemed to be growing, almost visibly, the sap
rising and rising as if the whole landscape were an extension of the giant's
dick. Everyone seemed to be at it: the swannery at Abbotsbury was full
of new-hatched cygnets and the flutter of tiny, fluffy wings. Over most of
England, the default weather is usually an uncontroversial, unmemorable
mid-autumn grey. But this place is different. Springtime feels the natural
time of year. It's an illusion of course. And this illusion is entirely the creation of Dorset's best-known former resident.

'Dorset,' the signs say, 'Home of the Jurassic Coast'. This slogan is regarded with contempt by all the local intellectuals I met, partly because it's such an obvious attempt to cash in on the film *Jurassic Park*, which had nothing to do with Dorset. It would be just as accurate to call it the Triassic or Cretaceous Coast, which doesn't quite do the business marketing-wise.

It is also misleading. As surely as the image of Devon and Cornwall was created by the Great Western Railway, which was only a minor presence in Dorset, this county was fixed in the public mind by the novels of Thomas Hardy. It used to be marketed as Hardy's County, and it is hard to think of it any other way. In the novels, of course, he avoided the word Dorset, renamed the towns and reinvented a Wessex that sprawled across six counties. It is a wonder he was never appointed to a committee to reform local government.

This fictionalisation bought him freedom to exercise literary imagination beyond the reach of both geographical pedants and paranoid neighbours. But South Wessex, aka Dorset, is at the heart of his work. And he is at the heart of Dorset. Many other writers have been drawn to the county, including Jane Austen, John Fowles, Ian McEwan, P. D. James and J. Meade Falkner, author of *Moonfleet*. The difference is that in Hardy's work, Dorset is more than a setting. It is, in effect, one of the lead characters, a player.

You can still stand on High West Street in the thoroughly satisfying town of Dorchester and, if you ignore the traffic and the vulgar canopy over the entrance to Ladbrokes, imagine yourself back in the 1880s. But Hardy's countryside has largely vanished.

The most powerful of his landscapes, 'Egdon Heath', was based on the vast tract of open land that once stretched nearly all the way from his birthplace at Upper Bockhampton into Hampshire. No more does twilight fall on Egdon, as it does in *The Return of the Native*, 'to evolve a thing majestic without severity, impressive without showiness, emphatic in its admonitions, grand in its simplicity'. It's now slightly scabby woodland and scrub, which various bodies are trying to restore to something like its old self by reversing the whole drift of millennia of agricultural history and taking nutrients out of the soil.

But it still feels like the real Dorset, which the coast does not. For Dorset is not a coastal county, not in the way that Devon and Cornwall are. It is an instinctively inland place that happens to have a coastline.

Yes, the fossils are amazing and the story of Mary Anning, the Lyme Regis carpenter's daughter and pioneer of palaeontology, is inspirational.

And Poole Harbour is enormous: sixty miles of coastline, if you allow for all the little inlets and headlands, with five large islands. Sailors can be as lonely as Noah, notwithstanding a couple of hundred thousand people living on the east side of the bay. But, frankly, the coastline is either hard to get at or too damn easy. There are not that many sandy beaches, except in woebegone Weymouth. And, as soon as a yachtsman gets out of Poole Harbour, the prospect, if the weather is even slightly iffy, is not a pretty one.

'When you get past Swanage,' explains one local sailor, David Burnett, 'this is a ferocious coast. At St Aldhelm's Head there's a tidal race, which is nasty at the best of times. There's nowhere to take shelter until you get to Weymouth and there you have to get right inside the marina. There's another race off Portland. You have to get right round Portland Bill and then you're in Lyme Bay, where there's nothing at all. Lyme Regis has only got the Cobb. There's no proper protection until you get to Exmouth. It's a brute of a coast.'

Even walkers on the coastal path have to plan carefully because of the risk of being shot at by the army. And serious fossil hunters, whose perfect moments come after winter storms, are thus inherently at risk from rock-falls. Mary Anning had one very narrow escape; her dog did not survive.

Burnett is the living embodiment of Dorset's real appeal. He arrived at Stanbridge, near Wimborne, in 1972. The locals thought he was some daft hippie. His company, the Dovecote Press, has since become one of the most successful of all small-scale publishers, turning out 120 books about Dorset alone.

His timing was ideal. It was the moment when the frantic progressivism of the 1960s was starting to fade and the English were starting to rediscover their countryside; cottages that were unsaleable in the decades after the war started to acquire the allure that has never faltered. Globally, those years were producing the first great surge of environmental awareness. And nationally, Hardy, then far more fashionable than soppy old Jane Austen, made Dorset a kind of collective fantasy. Somehow he made the place seem irresistible, despite filling his novels with a never-ending trail of injustice and misery.

For Burnett's business, offset printing had just arrived, making small-scale book production much more economic, and all the towns had an infrastructure of little bookshops that lapped up stuff like his Discover Dorset series. It's become harder, but even now he shifts about 1,200 copies a year of his bestsellers: the volumes on geology and the Romans.

There is, however, another side to Dorset. 'Introspective' was the word chosen by Sue Clifford, founder of the support-local-distinctiveness charity Common Ground, which was based until her recent retirement on Gold Hill in Shaftesbury. One incomer told me he was astonished by how many of his Dorset friends – intelligent, educated people – did not own passports and had hardly ever been to London. And it was an old friend from Weymouth who told me of the local boy whose view of the world was based on induction rather than deduction. 'Oy don't loike them Frenchies,' he said. 'They do roll their bogeys up and down their lilo.'

There is another word that kept cropping up unprompted: 'feudalism'.

Tolpuddle is just east of Dorchester, a pretty village but stringy and noisy: the A35 to Poole now bypasses the village, but not by much. In 2013 it was also being threatened by a rural power station, otherwise known as a wind farm. At one end of the string is a row of early twentieth-century farm workers' cottages, now given over to a celebration of the village's most famous sons: the six men who in 1834 began something slightly resembling a trade union and were transported to Australia.

Knowing only the headline, I had assumed that Dorset was an improbable hotbed of agrarian radicalism. In fact, the reverse was the case. The Tolpuddle Six, Methodists rather than advance-guard Marxists, were doing what was by then legal, if not yet perfectly legal. Elsewhere in England their Friendly Society of Agricultural Labourers would have passed without comment.

But this was Dorset. There was little industry to compete with landowners for labour. And even after the 1832 Reform Act had extended the franchise, the local grandees were still able to convince themselves that the very thought of raising farm wages was the first step on the road that led to Robespierre and the tumbrils. So the local landowner James Frampton schmoozed the Home Secretary to invoke the Unlawful Oaths Act 1797, designed to prevent naval mutinies, and put the men on trial. This was enough to convince a Dorchester jury and get the men transported. (Or, as the *Daily Mail* might now put it, 'SOFT-TOUCH JUDGE GIVES UNION THUGS FREE SUNSHINE HOLIDAY'.)

It was not enough to prevent a large and ultimately successful furore which got the men pardoned. Thus Tolpuddle became a byword in the history of trade unionism. And the occasion is celebrated every year in the village with a festival run by the TUC, which used to consist mainly of droning Labour Party speeches – like the irrelevant part of the Durham Miners' Gala – but has now been Billy Braggified into a jolly old music-and-fun-led shindig.

But the history has not gone away. For many locals, the defining monument in Dorset is not Corfe Castle, nor the Portland Bill Lighthouse, nor the monument to Admiral Kiss-Me Hardy on Black Down – it's the Drax Wall, separating Charborough House, home of the Plunkett-Ernle-Erle-Draxes, from several miles of the A31. It's a dark wall, shaded in places by huge copper beeches that almost demand the use of headlights. It's not a security measure: any kid could scale it. It's not an aesthetic addition: the brickwork reeks of the early railway era. It's a statement. The latest scion of the family emulated at least six of his forefathers in 2010 by being elected MP for South Dorset, though, for political purposes, he understandably calls himself Richard Drax.

The P-E-E-D family (good God, didn't anyone spot the acronym at Harrow?) are by no means alone. In Dorset people talk about the land-owners the way Londoners distinguish between suburbs ('No really, dear, that's not Islington, it's Dalston'). Here is Pitt-Rivers land; there are the Ashley-Coopers; there the Cecils; much of the coast (and the Abbotsbury swannery) belongs to Charlotte Townsend, daughter of Viscount Galway; then there are the Digbys at Sherborne, the Martens at Crichel Down. (Most unusually, the Martens were reputedly in the process of selling up.)

Several of the old county bridges still have a sign on them, which appears to date from the late 1820s:

DORSET

ANY PERSON WILFULLY INJURING ANY PART OF THIS COUNTY
BRIDGE WILL BE GUILTY OF FELONY AND UPON CONVICTION
LIABLE TO BE TRANSPORTED FOR LIFE BY THE COURT.

T. FOOKS

This law applied everywhere: indeed, defacing Westminster Bridge was for a long time a hanging offence. But I have never seen such a sign anywhere else. Sure, it's all a joke now: you can buy that sign on a key fob. But I also have not seen another county where the social order of the pre-Victorian era seems quite so intact.

This is not necessarily a bad thing. At Wimborne St Giles, the estate of the Earls of Shaftesbury, the 12th Earl has been restoring the family estates and fortunes after the unfortunate murder (by his trophy wife) of his father, and the even more untimely death of his elder brother. The Earl still has 6,000 acres, with 1,000 head of cattle grazing in Constablesque water meadows, flanked by bridleways along which Tess of the d'Urbervilles might have trudged. I didn't use the word 'feudal'; the villagers did, in the bar of the Bull, after an idyllic evening's cricket on the little ground inside the gates to the park. But they weren't complaining, and nor was I. The place was suffused by a pleasing air of noblesse oblige, without obligations on the peasantry.

Yet the one place in Dorset that best represents England's unchanging hierarchy is an entirely new one. Poundbury is Dorchester's new suburb (though that word is frowned on), built by the Duchy of Cornwall, which 'seeks to implement the principles' expounded in the Prince of Wales's 1989 book, *A Vision of Britain*. The architect, Leon Krier, was challenged to create 'a self-contained new extension to the town in harmony with traditional Dorset architecture'.

Poundbury is a puzzle. By design, it is less spacious than Letchworth or Welwyn. Yet it is not thrown together, like most of the later new towns: the buildings are full of curly bits. It is clearly meant to be urban and not suburban, yet – on a weekday lunchtime – there was no buzz. It is so bourgeois the shop in the square was a mini-Waitrose and there was a bead shop, rather than a bread shop. Yet the ration of social housing to owner-occupied is 35:65 in the latest phase. The royal prerogative is less intrusive than it was early on, when the Duchy reputedly specified which roses were allowed, yet there are still stern princely rules about building materials. On the other hand, when I was there the verges were a disgrace, with the dandelions reproducing themselves as exuberantly as the Abbotsbury swans.

The district councillor, Andy Canning, admits Poundbury is a Marmite place which people either love or hate. But he thinks it has three great pluses: the cheek-by-jowl societal mix; the blend of housing with offices and workshops; and the architecture, which he personally likes. There is a pub, and a school is imminent. But I couldn't sense a real community there. Many of the homeowners are retired, either downsizing and happy to have a house with almost no garden, or dividing their time between England and abroad. This is not a mix likely to reproduce, say, the beleaguered camaraderie of Milton Keynes. It is not a malign place; this is benevolent paternalism, twenty-first-century-style. It just seemed a bit bloodless, unreal; a bit like its progenitor, his future Majesty.

There is certainly no rush to create future Poundburys. But, up the road in Sturminster Newton, where does the redeveloped town centre most resemble? This place. Many local architects and builders have had work from the Duchy here and seem to have gone a bit native. Poundbury does not remotely look like the rest of Dorset. And yet it may be that Dorset will come to look like Poundbury.

There is a similar disconnect in Sandbanks, reached by a lovely clanking old chain ferry across Poole Harbour. Though on the Hampshire side of the water, Sandbanks was always in Dorset, despite feeling more like an outpost of southern California (waterfront home: lots of acute angles, very ugly – £7.25 million).

It really is full of surprises, Dorset. A couple of miles from Corfe Castle, you can turn off near the steam railway, drive down a forested country lane, pass a 'Beware of the Deer' sign, ignore a couple of 'Private Road' notices, before finally being stopped by a security man who, in my case, appeared not so much threatening as baffled as to how I knew anything was there. For in this enchanted woodland glade, too hidden to be remotely controversial, is Wytch Farm, the largest onshore oil well in Western Europe. And wytch farmer wouldn't fantasise about retiring to Sandbanks or California after a discovery like that?

And then, on the coast road from Bridport to Weymouth, you crest a rise and suddenly there appears what looks like a causeway akin to the one leading to Holy Island. (Oh, Gawd! Not more tide tables!) This is in fact Chesil Beach. And beyond it, like an elongated Rock of Gibraltar, stands one of England's most mysterious places: Portland. There is something mind-blowing about Chesil, a unique stretch of shingle eighteen miles long, 300 trillion stones allegedly, on which a blindfolded expert can locate himself by the particular scrunch underneath, the stones subtly getting bigger, from mushy peas in the west to baked potatoes in the east.

It is this fragile link that, in theory, stops Portland being an island. Now it has a bridge rather than a ferry, it seems less like an island geographically. In every other respect, this is a world of its own. You approach it now past the Chesil Beach centre, a pleasant baguetty/vin-rouge kind of café-cum-information point surrounded by sharp un-Chesil-like gravel, brought in presumably by lorry. Truly: they imported stones to a place with 300 trillion of them.

But once on Portland itself, the baguettes fall away: there is no less vin-rougey place anywhere in southern England. It is also very, very distinctive: the Barrow of the south. Careful readers of this book will recognise that as a compliment.

Portland is busy trying to remake itself after the withdrawal of the navy and the closure of the Underwater Weapons Establishment that was the centre of attention for the Ruislip spies. But it still has its greatest asset: the stone that provides the gleaming whiteness for many of Britain's most prominent buildings, including Buckingham Palace and St Paul's. It is set about not just with quarries but with fields of grey rocks, like mini-Stonehenges. The houses themselves are not gleaming but very, very grey. The explanation seems to be that the stone is porous and needs attention to keep it clean, which is more likely at St Paul's than in the terraces of Portland.

Famously, no one in Portland can say the word 'rabbit', the wretch that can spell death to quarrymen. This is a far more rational superstition than the one that stops actors naming the Scottish play. But everything about Portland is particular. It is incredibly ugly, right down to the beach huts on Portland Bill. Yet it is utterly true to itself: the epitome of Dorset introspection. It does not seek the approbation of the likes of me. And for that reason I am delighted to offer it.

It has very little competition on the coast: Bridport is very nice and welcoming but Weymouth's buildings were savaged by the Germans and Poole's by the council. However, inland Dorset is full of towns competing with each other to smile. There is Blandford Forum, the Georgian town that manages simultaneously to embrace influxes of urban escapees and army recruits: an unusual mix of tisanes and tattoos. And then there is the wonderful hilltop town of Shaftesbury, best known for Gold Hill.

As I approached the summit a woman was standing at the top, yelling into her mobile: 'You know that advert? *Duh*-duh-duh. *Duh*-duh-duh. *Duh*-duh-duh-duh-duh ...'

Dvořák, dear. And Hovis. The film was shot here originally in 1973, by Ridley Scott, and was widely believed to have been set in Yorkshire. This is a trick of the memory, because the accent on the voiceover on YouTube is definitely Mummerset. The advert was brilliant; the street, mostly barred to passing traffic, is beautiful but overrun; the bread's disgusting.

The connoisseur's Dorset place is, however, Beaminster ('Beh-*minster*'). Charmingly set among the hills and the spring breezes, the square has not been touched since Hardy's day. It has wisteria, unwrapped sherbet lemons and ladies called Marjorie. But it also exudes an air of Hardyesque struggle, which was exacerbated in 2013 by the enforced closure of the Beaminster road tunnel. But that was not the whole story. The square is a gem architecturally, but clearly in a long-term battle economically. The bank had gone; so had the Wild Garlic restaurant; and two other shops were for sale.

Beaminster exists in the uneasy twilight that divides a large village from a small town. It is not big enough to be self-sustaining, but too big not to worry about it. It is not quite chi-chi enough or set dramatically enough to draw the crowds: a great place to grow old, but not to grow up. It is the epitome of the Dorset dilemma.

May/June 2013

~~~~~~~

The winter storms that ravaged the country in 2013–14 uncovered a virtually complete 200-million-year-old skeleton of a five-foot ichthyosaur ('a fish-lizard') at Black Ven, near Charmouth. It took eight hours to dig out. Fossil hunter Paul Crossley told the BBC that had it not been discovered, the next storm would have wrecked it.

Chesil Beach also had a battering, making the slope to the sea much steeper. 'The beach will sort itself out,' said Angela Thomas from the Chesil Centre. 'It might not always. There may be a time – we've no idea when – that the sea does overtop Chesil.'

28. *The ascent of Mount Toebang*

CUMBERLAND

One morning in early June I awoke in Rosthwaite on the edge of Derwent Water. It is just a couple of miles from Seathwaite, the wettest habitation in England. The sound outside was that of incessant rain, mitigated only by interruptions from the cuckoo, a bird now increasingly confined to damp corners. Obviously our plans would have to be aborted. That was agreed: if the weather was ridiculous the mission was off.

Slowly I opened the curtains. The sun blazed in. The supposed rain was the water in the beck tinkling over the rocks. There was no possible excuse now. After kippers, we drove – my old school friend Anselm and I – to the car park at Seathwaite, which was another national landmark ticked off. I had already been to the southernmost and westernmost place in England (Chapter 11), the easternmost (Chapter 13), the northernmost (26) and the lowest (10). To come: the driest. Ahead of us, though still far out of sight, was the highest: Scafell Pike.

'C'mon,' said Anselm gently, in the fatherly tone he would use when

I was nine and he was ten. He had always done mountains, including this one, several times; I didn't. He was a lawyer; but I was a great respecter of the Law of Gravity. My back and right knee had been hurting for days, but I had been desperate not to cancel even though I was quite petrified.

Scafell Pike is an odd record-holder: everyone in Britain knows about Ben Nevis and Snowdon. But the highest mountain in England is strangely anonymous. Many people – and even the memorial at the summit – call it just 'Scafell', which is another mountain entirely. This certainly confuses the walkers and may cause occasional chaos at Mountain Rescue HQ. Even most of those who know the name pronounce it 'Scaffle Pike', while the aficionados go for 'Scawfell Pike'. It is a very English kind of confusion.

It is also not a greatly loved mountain, even among mountain-lovers. When I mentioned the project to one climber he told me it was his least favourite anywhere: 'uncomfortably steep with stretches of sharp rubble, real ankle-risking stuff. And sharp enough that you don't want to put your hands out either'. He suggested misreading the map and doing Snowdon instead.

In his *Pictorial Guide to the Southern Fells*, the sainted Alfred Wainwright is ambivalent. He also doesn't make it sound attractive – 'tarns are noticeably absent on the arid, stony surface ... the landscape is harsh, even savage, and has attracted to itself nothing of romance or historical legend. There is no sentiment about Scafell Pike.' But he adds, 'The ascent of Scafell Pike is the toughest proposition the "collector" of summits is called upon to attempt, and it is the one above all others that, as a patriot, he cannot omit.'

Seathwaite did not look as though it gets 140 inches of rain a year, not far off half an inch a day. There was even a sign by the campsite banning ground fires, as though this were the Australian bush in a drought. And indeed it hadn't rained in a week. You could spend a hundred summers in the Lake District and hardly find such an ideal day for climbing: we had layer after layer in our rucksacks but we never needed more than a T-shirt.

There are at least half a dozen routes to the summit, but Wainwright called the route up Borrowdale 'pre-eminent'. So we marched along the narrow valley, me prattling the while to avoid thinking about what might lie ahead. Even now I was nervy. But it was not just a commitment, it was evidently my patriotic duty. Onwards.

What struck me most was the complete absence of prohibitions,

imperatives and instructions. Just after Seathwaite the farmer had a 'Close the Gate' and 'Dogs on Lead' sign. Beyond that, nothing: no warnings, no commands, no signposts even. Back along the valley there was a hire car that would order me to put on my seat belt and would not shut up until it was obeyed. All around us was the most spied-on country in the world, a place that abhors self-reliance. Up here we had only our wits and our Wainwright.

On such a day, we could hardly be alone, but the company was never overwhelming. And what also struck me, as other walkers overtook us (which most of them did), was their capability, their good nature, their responsibility. It was an honour to be among them. There were a couple of plastic bottles at the summit, and one of my satsumas rolled fifty feet down a precipice into Ruddy Ghyll, where it bobbled beguilingly for a long time. That aside, there was almost no litter anywhere.

Except that God had indeed dumped all his builders' rubble here instead of hiring a skip. At first, along the valley, the view was dominated by the green mass of Great End ahead of us. It was Great, but very far from the End. All this time, Scafell Pike, instead of dominating the landscape, was maintaining its distaste for publicity, remaining totally invisible. But then we reached the mountainside Piccadilly Circus of Esk Hause. Anselm pointed to an outcrop beyond a stony plateau. 'There it is,' he said.

Herein lay my one bleak but indisputable triumph. I knew nothing of the terrain, but consider myself expert in identifying the too-good-to-be-true. I seized the Wainwright: 'Ill Crag is prominently in view from the section between Esk Hause and Calf Cove. It is the highest thing in sight, and wishful thinkers will assume it to be the summit – until the Pike itself is finally revealed, indisputably higher and still far distant across a waste of stones.' Moral superiority was some compensation for the hour that preceded the final ascent, which comprised mostly what Wainwright called 'delectable clambering', the adjective not being the one that sprang to my mind.

Someone had told me you could always find the summit of Scafell Pike, even in thick mist, by the sound of cheering and popping champagne corks. But it wasn't like that. There were thirty or forty people up there, and a few dogs (on leads, as per the only instruction). The mood was contented, excited even, but not triumphalist. There was a pervading sense of respect for the place: hardly any graffiti on the stones even – one said 'DEAN & STE', as though the writer had been caught in the act and urged to desist.

There was also, very touchingly, a framed wedding photo, late 1940s at a guess, placed on the flat-topped cairn which is much favoured for souvenir pictures and takes the 3,209 feet of the summit to about 3,213. Otherwise there were just a few windbreaks, roughly constructed from the stones, and the trig point. No information, other than the misleading sign built into the cairn, which serves as both a First World War memorial and a record of the land being given to the nation by Lord Leconfield. No café, no railway station – the English leave such fripperies to Snowdon – not even a guide to the view: Wainwright's monopoly of the wisdom is unchallenged.

So everyone just ate their sandwiches and pointed to the panorama. There was a touch of heat haze rendering Mont Blanc, Everest and Australia invisible, but still: Skiddaw and Derwentwater to the north; Windermere and the Pennines to the east; Morecambe Bay and the real Scafell to the south; Sellafield and the Isle of Man to the west. Then people began pointing upwards, puzzlingly, towards the few fluffy clouds. And there, way, way above us, was a lone paraglider. Bloody typical. No matter how high you get, there will always be some swine who outdoes you.

The descent was very untriumphant. I queried Anselm's navigation, this time wrongly, thus forfeiting the moral high ground while still hugging the actual high ground by lagging behind. I had long stopped worrying about my back and knee but everything else was hurting, most particularly my left big toe, which is a very Scafell Pike-ish kind of injury. As you tire, you start bashing the stones more and more often.

There seems to be some kind of mountain truism here: the descent is always harder. Mentally, you've done it and imagine yourself home. The world starts to intrude on your thoughts. And, gravitationally, a slight stumble is now more likely to be disastrous, as suggested by the fate of the satsuma. We took longer going down than up.

But, as Sir Edmund Hillary put it in more trying circumstances, 'we knocked the bastard off'. Anselm was congratulatory. No one back home seemed impressed by what I had done; I was, though. Next morning I sat, achey but self-satisfied, in the garden by Crummock Water belonging to the Lakesman and writer Hunter Davies, who once published three bestsellers in a year. I mentioned the difficulties of descending.

'It's a metaphor for fame and life,' he said sagely. 'The fun and satisfaction is getting there. But coming down is hard.'

A couple of months earlier, in a bitter-cold March when the snow was still on the bottoms as well as the tops, I had come to Keswick, where a big man in claret breeches praised the 'purity of the lakes and the pointed mountains' and raised his arm roughly in the direction of the four peaks that overlook the town, and rolled them round his tongue: 'Catbells, Glaramara, Skiddaw, Blencathra'. His view was somewhat obscured, not just by the mist, snow, murk and dark, but because he was on stage and pointing at Row L in the back of the stalls.

The role was that of Francis Herries: 'Rogue Herries', protagonist of Cumberland's most famous saga, which was being dramatised in one of Britain's most remarkable playhouses, the Theatre by the Lake. The building, though new, is attractive. But in other British theatres the architecture and stage design do not have to compete with such a brilliant backdrop outside. Other theatres tend not be to be seventeen miles from a railway station. Nor set in towns like Keswick, with a population below 5,000. Nor quite so far from a serviceable pair of spare underpants, never mind claret breeches. Keswick has dozens of shops selling anoraks, parkas, cagoules, wind jackets, fleeces and what-have-you. The nearest M&S is another seventeen miles away, in Workington.

Since *Rogue Herries* required, as well as the eight professional actors, more than thirty locals on stage as extras and chorus, this meant the ratio of performers to a full house was about 1:10 and to the town's entire population not far off 1:100. Artistically, *Rogue Herries* may not have been the theatre's finest achievement – there were times when it seemed to be going on longer than the entire eighteenth century in which it was set. It was, though, a triumph of ambition, even audacity, enterprise and local pride. A triumph of planning too, though everything at this theatre constitutes that.

The spring show, designed mainly for local consumption, is nothing to the summer season, which runs from May to November (a somewhat optimistic length for a Cumberland summer) and involves, in a manner unmatched in England, an extraordinary self-imposed challenge. Six plays run in *repertoire*, as opposed to *repertory* – two a night, one in the main house, one in the little studio – with fourteen actors engaged for the duration to appear every night in one or the other. Just casting the plays is an extraordinary balancing act between the artistics and the logistics. If Keswick did have a railway, it would be a doddle to run in comparison.

Somehow it all works. Since the current building opened in 1999, the theatre has always turned a profit; its grants make up only a small proportion of its revenue, giving it a solidity many bigger theatres would envy. The trick, says Patric Gilchrist, the executive director, is the balance. 'In the main house we give them what you might call "take the money and run". In the studio we find that anything with a warning about language and content goes down particularly well.'

I think Gilchrist was being unduly self-deprecating: Oliver Goldsmith in the main house is not unambitious. But it seems to me that Keswick's theatre may have found a virtuous circle to go with the dress circle. If the summer is fine the town is packed with tourists; if it's not, then those who are there will need to find somewhere dry, and where better?

On midsummer evenings it is still light when the interval comes, and it is possible to wander outside with a G&T and stare at Derwentwater and Catbells etc. It struck me that Gilchrist had missed a trick. He could have saved on the set for *Rogue Herries* and staged the play even more spectacularly outside, on the little lakeside beach with the waters lapping the shore. True, cast and audience would have got hypothermia. And I suppose drama here will always require a balance between artistics and logistics.

When Herries talked about the county in his play, he knew where he was: 'Half the girls in Cumberland have wanted to marry my son,' he said. These days the word Cumberland has almost totally disappeared. Outside the county it conjures up only a sausage. Inside, the name has gone far more completely even than Westmorland. In 2013 there was still the *Cumberland News*, the minor county cricket club and the Cumberland Building Society. Not much else.

Of the new county names instituted in 1974, nearly all are already consigned to the dustbin of history: Cleveland is back in Ohio; Avon is just a river again. None gained such widespread acceptance as – I will try to say this without obvious distaste – 'Cumbria'. Here, in a manner I otherwise experienced only in Huntingdonshire, I felt like a throwback, a refugee from the past. When I said in advance to the locals, 'I'm coming up to Cumberland', they would reply, 'Oh, you're coming to Cumbria, are you?'

This is partly because the name is perceived to have historic resonance, dating back to the Dark Ages; partly because, even before 1974, it was already being used as a generic term for the Lake District; partly because Cumbrian was previously used as the adjective for someone from Cumberland; and partly because Cumbria has, more than any other modern entity, found itself on the news for countywide catastrophes: foot and mouth in 2001; the floods of 2009; a mass shooting in 2010.

But also Cumbria represents Cumberland's imperialist triumph: incorporating the whole of Westmorland, a slice of Lancashire and a soupçon of eviscerated Yorkshire, which was rendered into the Poland of English local government. If you're Cumbrian, especially a Cumbrian councillor, what's not to like?

Personally, I love the rolling syllables of the old name: one can almost hear Herries's horse galloping over the moor or John Peel's view-halloo: *Cum-ber-land*. A land, not an 'ia', a real place. The Wikipedia page for Cumbria has to warn people not to confuse it with Cumbia (a Latin American dance), Umbria (Italy) or Cambria (the classical name for Wales).

And, as I understand it, the alleged Dark Ages history is largely mythical. It hinges on the legend of Dunmail, now referred to as the last king of Cumbria, supposedly killed in AD 945 on Dunmail Raise, the hillock on the A591 separating Cumberland's Thirlmere from Westmorland's Grasmere. But his very existence is dubious, and Professor Angus Winchester of Lancaster University said on Radio 4 that the geography is misleading: 'Even in the tenth century there was no suggestion really that Dunmail's territory extended into the southern half of what is now Cumbria. So calling Kendal and Barrow and Millom part of Cumbria is probably a complete misnomer historically.'

Wordsworth refers to Dunmail as

He who once held supreme command,
Last king of rocky Cumberland.

And people with a sense of place still see the Raise as a significant boundary. '"There's nowt good comes over t'Raise," we always say,' the Keswick-based writer Keith Richardson told me. 'And I'm sure they say the same thing in Westmorland.'

There is nothing left there now to advertise the Raise's significance to the casual motorist, just a discreet water treatment plant and an antique AA phone box. Not even a Dunmail Theme Park and Souvenir Shop. And certainly not a county boundary sign. You could whizz through and think

Dunmail Raise was an offer of improved pensions to retired postmen. Cumberland existed as a recorded entity from 945 to 1974. Its abolition was classically English: thoughtless and pointless.

Even in its historic form, the county was always an uneasy coalition. There is Carlisle, shorn of its medieval strategic importance. It lies there, making McVitie's ginger nuts and custard creams, with a pleasant but pint-sized cathedral and a well-preserved castle, awaiting the day – should Scotland choose independence – when it can become England's El Paso or Panmunjom. There is the fat arable land of the Eden Valley. Avoid the M6 and take the ubiquitous A6 from Carlisle to Penrith, and you pass the smuggest-looking farms in the kingdom, so neat an errant buttercup would be shot on sight.

There is the tourist country of the Lakes, and even that may be divided into two: the lowlands of the coach parties, and the lonely tracks. You can switch from one to the other quite rapidly: straight after leaving the hordes in Buttermere, you can turn on to the Newlands Pass and fancy yourself the last motorist on earth.

And there is West Cumberland: a coast that is at once industri-alised and undiscovered; repellent and ravishing. The towns race each other to the reputational bottom; each knowledgeable local has their own unfavourite. Cumbrians competed to feed me names of places that they assured me were the pits of the earth, all in places where the earth no longer supports pits: Frizington, Rowrah, Cleator, Cleator Moor ... But I couldn't quite see it. Every ex-mining village in England exudes despair: voting for only one party, their people can thus safely be forgotten by all of them. Yet these, set between the sea and the mountains, all had a strange, savage beauty about them.

The big coastal towns turned out to be sharply differentiated, one from the other. I had a strong childhood holiday memory of Dad driving us from Westmorland to Whitehaven for Sunday lunch: a hotel with a view out to sea over vast railway sidings full of coal wagons; and my mum asking the receptionist the way to the promenade, to be greeted with a you-must-be-out-of-your-mind kind of look. (No one I found could remember such a hotel, suggesting it was me who was out of my mind.)

Whitehaven lives up to its name in several ways. It is less than 1 per cent non-white. It also has the most sensational setting. Given a differ-ent industrial history, culture and above all climate, this might have had not just any promenade but one for the *beau-monde*: the Monte Carlo of the North, a Cumbrian Cannes. There but for fortune. It has improbable admirers: Candida Lycett Green (John Betjeman's daughter) of *The Oldie* fell in love: 'A tremendous place ... one of the best and most undiscovered Georgian towns in the country'. But being undiscovered, no one cherishes it, and the buildings are shabby.

Its neighbour Workington is bedevilled by its unlovely name, though working would be a fine thing for people in its more deprived wards. And it looks away from the sea, gazing mainly at its own not very pretty navel. Yet in Portland Square it has a cobbled, tree-lined piazza of exceptional charm, not so much Cumbria as Umbria (or Umberland).

Further up the coast is Maryport, where in 1979 the *Guardian* sent their reporter Melanie Phillips. 'The inhabitants appear to be paralysed by apathy,' she announced. The only virtue she could find in a town of dismal poverty was that there was little juvenile delinquency: 'Social workers say that the children do not have enough spirit or initiative to get into trouble.' Maryport roused itself enough to complain furiously. Now it has a new aquarium and the beginnings of touristy self-confidence. And it really does have a promenade, though everyone else on it seemed to know each other. The toilets had been vandalised and locked up. 'Kids!' said a kindly local, advising me to piss in the bushes. In context, this suggests the new generation may be more energetic.

In fact, this whole coast is less poverty-stricken than one might expect. There is one reason for this. I discovered it by taking the slow coastal train down from the little resort of St Bees (best known as the start of the coast-to-coast walk) alongside a beach so stony it might have been Scafell-Pike-on-Sea. Then we stopped at the least welcoming station in all England: Sellafield.

Once the HQ of Britain's nuclear industry, Sellafield was known as Windscale and had a visitors' centre. It no longer bothers. I was told to expect armed guards. I saw none, though I expect they saw me. The perimeter fence was high, and topped with razor wire, and the guardhouses made Checkpoint Charlie look like Liberty Hall. But, oddly, a short distance away there was an open gate in the fence, unattended, seemingly unnoticed.

I did consider exploring the possibilities: marching into the control room like Homer Simpson and pressing buttons at random. But it would be cruel to try to mess up Cumberland's *grand projet*: Sellafield still employs 10,500 people directly, plus about 1,500 contractors, which, since the meltdown of Ford Dagenham, makes it the largest single-site source of employment in the country. But perhaps trespass might not have been that easy. And the last train back to St Bees was at 18.27 and the conversation with the armed guards might have involved missing it. Such a discussion could go very badly for anyone wearing a 'No Nukes' T-shirt.

Most of West Cumberland loves Sellafield, even though it does not produce power any more; it merely reprocesses spent nuclear waste. It is a symbol of modern working life: most of us spend our days doing very little of what we were designed to do, we merely try to clear our inbox. Final site clearance at Sellafield is scheduled for 2120, even more distant than at Dungeness.

There were two Windscale piles, where the plutonium for Britain's nuclear weaponry was developed. No. 2 has been dismantled but no. 1 remains, because that was the site of the infamous fire of 1957, which did more than anything to discredit nuclear power in Britain – Windscale became so notorious it had to be rebranded – and there are still about thirty tons of melted, contaminated fuel at the bottom.

As the train drew away, two other beacons in the landscape came into view briefly, before disappearing into cloud: Scafell Pike and Scafell. Both, with luck, will still be there after 2120, probably along with my unemptied inbox.

The most impressive and distinctive inhabitants of Cumberland have four legs not two, and that is not a mutation caused by nuclear fallout. These are the 50,000 Herdwick sheep which graze the very summits of all the fells, avoiding Scafell Pike only because it grows rocks instead of grass.

They are extraordinary-looking beasts, with a fleece so thick it is useless to anyone else but damn useful to them on a winter's night. Their meat, however, is gamy and much valued, even though the animals are tough as old boots. The ewes have white faces and mostly off-white wool to go with their aquiline noses, erect ears and fetching little topknot. Yet their lambs are generally all-black, making the fellsides the most multiracial-looking place in the county, until they grow lighter with age.

They look smarter than the average sheep, so much so that one senses they could open information booths and point lost climbers in the right direction. At their mother's knee the lambs get to know their 'heaf', their own area of the fell. Only rarely do they stray to the far side of the mountain. It is an astonishing, mystical branch of agriculture, its continuation largely made possible by Beatrix Potter, who put her Peter Rabbit earnings into buying up farms threatened by development or the Forestry Commission.

Their existence was briefly put at risk again by foot and mouth in 2001 and now again by the scientists and bureaucrats of Natural England and Defra, the rebranded Min of Ag who – as every farmer in the country will insist – invariably put their feet in their mouths and talk through their arses. Gavin Bland, who has 2,000 sheep in the narrow valley between Thirlmere and Dunmail Raise, is no exception.

This is the final element of the Cumberland coalition. Bland's world bears little relation to that of the arable men by the A6. And he believes it is threatened by the insistence of Whitehall that the ewes be taken off the tops in winter to let the flora regenerate, thus endangering the transmission of knowledge from ewe to lamb that is fundamental to the survival of the Herdwicks and their masters: 'The Herdwick sheep is happiest where it lives. It's just the boffins dictating theory. They have no idea about farming sheep.' He pointed across to Helvellyn. 'That hill produces lamb in summer. There's no input. No fertiliser. It's sustainable.'

Five times a year the sheep have to be gathered: for shearing, dipping, drenching, tupping and lambing. It's the July gather – for the drenching against fluke and worms – that's the hardest, because by then the Herdwicks have moved high up the mountain to find fresher grass and cooler air. Which means Bland has to climb the mountain himself to round them up and count them. He counts them in twos and in English, not the old Cumberland way (where 1-2-3 becomes yan-tan-tethera). Does anyone still count like that? 'Only if someone's listening.'

It all makes these farmers Cumberland's second most impressive inhabitants. Gavin Bland was British fell-running champion in 1999: 'Half my training was just work. You can't do this job if you're slow.' His uncle Billy was even better, said by some (including his nephew) to have been more dedicated and determined than the most famous fell-runner of all, Joss Naylor. Billy Bland holds the record for the Bob Graham Round, which involves ascending at least forty-two peaks over 2,000 feet inside twenty-four hours. He did it in thirteen hours fifty-three minutes. 'I walked round with Uncle Billy once,' said Gavin casually. 'We still did it in twenty-four hours.' We were talking the day after I had made a big fuss about simply going up and down Mount Toebang.

It is said of the old Cumbrian farmers that they could be more easily understood in Oslo or Stockholm than in the West End of London, because their dialect was still heavily influenced by their Norse ancestors. It is also said that in the primary schools of rural Cumberland, almost every child is blond, but they get darker as they grow older. Another Norse characteristic. Which is strange, because it makes them the precise opposite of the Herdwick sheep.

March/June 2013

By 2014 Gavin Bland had no sheep on Helvellyn: it had been fenced off. He still ran his Herdwicks on High Raise and Ullscarf. The contest between the farmers and officialdom – plus writers like George Monbiot of the Guardian *who says the fells have been 'sheepwrecked' – goes on.*

29. *A midsummer night's mare*

WILTSHIRE

As the title may not immediately suggest, the play *Jerusalem*, widely regarded as the best British drama of the early twentieth-first century, is set in Wiltshire.

The central figure, Johnny 'Rooster' Byron, is a small-time drug dealer and big-time character, a Romany anarch presiding over a perpetual Saturnalia from his filthy caravan in the woods. He spends his life infuriating the council, the constabulary and the residents of the spanking-new housing estate just offstage. Rooster was played, in the West End and on Broadway, by Mark Rylance in a performance at once so glorious and domineering that it is hard to imagine another actor ever risking reputational death in the attempt.

The writer, Jez Butterworth, lives in Somerset, and in some ways Wiltshire is an odd setting for the play. 'I leave Wiltshire, my ears pop,' says one character, which doesn't seem quite right: Wiltshire is a county with little sense of unity. The main roads and railways run east–west; it takes an age to get between the two main centres, Swindon and Salisbury. People habitually shop in Bath or Bristol. In Cornwall, Devon or Dorset one might meet a trans-county ear-popper. But in Wiltshire? Hardly.

Maybe Butterworth was just following Hardy's rule for rural writers: he wrote about who and what he knew but made sure they were well enough disguised not to sue. But in another way Wiltshire is the perfect setting. In London's inexorable campaign for a total takeover, Berkshire has fallen; Somerset is under sporadic bombardment but still behind the lines. Wiltshire is now the main theatre of war: Swindon is commutable; Salisbury and Chippenham just about; the new estates are comparatively affordable and attractive, as long as any lingering Rooster Byrons can be cleared out; and the thatched cottages are simply divine for the weekend.

There is something else about Wiltshire. As *Jerusalem*'s hero-villain-victim approaches his Calvary, he calls to his aid his ancestors, actual and then spiritual: 'Rise up! Rise up, Cormoran. Woden. Jack-of-Green. Jack-in-Irons. Thunderdell. Búri, Blunderbore, Gog and Magog, Galligantus, Vili and Vé, Yggdrasil, Brutus of Albion ...'

In this county, that lot are frankly parvenus.

It was 3 a.m., and misty, as we trudged across the darkling plain, hordes of us. At that hour, it was a long way from the car park. 'This walk's bullshit,' said someone. It felt as though we were clocking on for the early shift at a distant coal mine, probably in midwinter, possibly on the steppes. The way was lit only by occasional banks of arc lights, which did their job well enough to fool the occasional skylark into thinking dawn had already come. Dawn had not come, or we would be heading the other way.

Finally we went through one last checkpoint and the scene seemed suddenly more like a funfair, with a row of food stalls: gourmet burgers, an Oriental noodle bar, vegan and vegetarian. Then another field. I still couldn't see our destination but the noise preceded its appearance. When it did emerge, Stonehenge looked fiddling and small. Unreal. I don't mean unreal, wow! I mean unreal, it looks like a film-set replica.

This might have been to do with the goings-on inside the circle. Hundreds were crowded in, dozens of whom had climbed on to the fallen lintel that lies on top of the Altar Stone and were jiggling endlessly about to the sound of bongos, waving their arms and their mobiles. We might have been filming a new teen blockbuster: *Meet the Halfwits*.

This is the world's most famous celebration of the summer solstice:

the shortest night followed by the longest day. In these circumstances I was hoping for an appearance by Arthur Pendragon, formerly John Timothy Rothwell from Wakefield, one-time head of the Gravediggers' biker gang, campaigner for access to Stonehenge and crowned 'Raised Druid King of Britain'. And, even more, for an appearance by the sun.

What is alleged to happen is that the sun pokes his head up just to the left of the Heel Stone, which in 2013 was next to the perimeter fence dividing the site from the A344. 'I've been coming here for twelve years and I've never seen it,' said a copper. 'I think there've been two clear mornings and both times I was called to do something at the wrong moment.'

No one even seemed to know when sunrise was meant to be: 3.52, someone said; 4.27, 4.35 and 4.43 were other suggestions. I was armed with the correct time: 3.52 GMT would have been right but, on British Summer Time, sunrise was due at 4.43 in London and, according to English Heritage, which runs the place, 4.52 at Stonehenge. Wrongly, I assumed that someone would call for silence and the artist formerly known as John Timothy Rothwell would appear and provide a sense of occasion, maybe even dignity.

Naturally, there was no appearance from the sun, which was not on English Heritage's email list. More surprisingly, King Arthur did not show his face either. The sky did lighten somewhat. But 4.52 came and went and no one noticed; the jiggling continued regardless on the Altar Stone.

At this point anyone with a beard, a robe and a knowing air could say anything and be believed, and they did. One such figure told me the druids would appear by the Heel Stone shortly. So I got past the Hare Krishnas ('They're from Scunthorpe,' a bystander was explaining), picked my way through the sleeping bodies and the empty cans of Skol and Strongbow, and headed to the fence, where indeed some white figures were prancing around, one of whom was administering knighthoods to anyone who asked.

This might have been the real King Arthur, returned from the island-valley of Avilion, where falls not hail, or rain, or any snow, nor ever wind blows loudly. This might have been the fake-real or real-fake King Arthur, aka John Timothy Rothwell. Or it might have been any old fake King Arthur. By now, I was beyond caring and joined the throng heading out. ('We're going! McDonald's!' said a voice.) It took two hours to get out of the car park.

I had been here before for the solstice, in 1976, when I was a young reporter and the stones were probably still under guarantee. I have distant memories of a small and enjoyable occasion, graced by the presence among the druids of Bill Roache, who even then was Ken Barlow of *Coronation Street*. But each year interest was building and soon the fields nearby were turned into a summer-long campsite.

In 1985 came the Battle of the Beanfield, when the police smashed up a convoy of New Age travellers heading to the site. For years thereafter access to the circle was heavily restricted. English Heritage relented in 1999, partly at the instigation of Arthur Pendragon, and allowed 'managed access'. These two protagonists battled each other through the court for years, though they seem to have been roughly on the same side. Hence, before the 2014 solstice, Arthur was due to achieve his objective, with the demolition of the old Visitors' Centre, the completion of a new one a mile from the site and – that rarest of modern phenomena – the permanent closure and grassing-over of a major road, the A344.

What happened in 2013 was something that offered the worst of every world: a takeover by pig-ignorant students and backpack-tourists, without regard for this place or its meaning. There is a growing urge by the young, who spend almost their whole waking lives vicariously, looking at screens, to see something for themselves. This is wonderful, provided they don't wreck the occasion with their own self-regard. For 363 days a year English Heritage runs Stonehenge with an iron fist, admitting only carefully vetted small groups into the circle. A discerning and hardy minority is allowed in for the winter solstice. On the 365th, the most important, authority stands back and allows a free-for-all without purpose or dignity.

I had been warned it would be ghastly. The cool Wiltshire place to go for the solstice is Avebury, twenty-two miles away. The stone circle at Avebury is older, bigger, more complex, more ravaged by time and desecration, more mysterious, more beautiful in its setting and less hackneyed: in the phrase I learned at Little Gidding, a thinner place. It also has a beckoning, half-timbered pub. The little village itself is absolutely darling, with particularly fine stone. It would be, because the old peasants built their homes by ravaging the sarsens that lay around the fields, little realising that they were recklessly endangering their descendants' fortune. The remains were not obvious, and it was the 1930s before the archaeologist Alexander Keiller arrived, bought Avebury Manor with the proceeds from his family's marmalade fortune, excavated the site and then tried – with partial success – to evict the inhabitants and make Avebury as famous as Stonehenge.

I was there the evening before, in bright sunshine, as a far smaller, older set began to gather, and came back the next. Avebury is big enough to allow everyone to find their own stone and stage their own solstice. The default Avebury-goer – and this may be true all year – is an ageing hippie with a grey ponytail, beads and/or a floaty dress. Folk songs wafted over from outside the pub. Everyone smiled at everyone else, and began conversations in which they explained at length their theories about crop circles and ley lines. A woman from New Mexico in a floppy hat wished all-comers 'Happy Solstice'. One might have had a very happy solstice, leaning against a rock and waiting for Rooster Byron to appear, offering a very large spliff. Unfortunately, I felt this strange obligation to bear witness to the Stonehenge horror instead.

Even without the aid of a Chippenham carrot, Avebury offered a sense that the Wiltshire landscape has a quality almost totally absent from England south of the Pennines. It's not just pretty, it's breathtaking. Chalk downland hardly exists outside England. And this is the heart of it, in a landscape less broken by development than further east. I came off the North Down near Milk Hill, descending into the Vale of Pewsey in the evening light. A near-full moon had risen over the midsummer landscape and would be glinting on the chalk when the late June night finally fell. It was exhilarating.

The downs themselves have a sinuous shape, and the huge, near-hedgeless landscape, broken only occasionally by trees or copses, has an unearthly air. Everywhere there are strange shapes. Is that a round barrow up there? Or is it just a bump? This is country fit for Thunderdell and Woden, big and bold enough to attract dreamers and theorists and outlaws like Rooster. Funny thing is, Wiltshire's other big business is the one most calculated to repel such types. This is the army's county.

The village of Copehill Down stands out starkly in the midst of the plain, and might be a little incongruous in any case. But then there are the steep-pitched roofs and the un-Englishly neat line of young beeches planted on the high street. It seems, well, just a bit Germanic.

Indeed, you can almost smell the *apfelkuchen*. Copehill Down was built by the army in the 1950s to prepare troops for the war that was never fought: the one where its soldiers probably got wiped out as the Soviet Union swept across Central Europe. The population of the village is zero: the houses, authentic in outline, are short of trivial details like windows; and the climbing frames in the front gardens look a bit severe for even a Prussian pre-schooler.

Time has also damaged the purity of the conception. Copehill Down has had to adapt to the wars Britain actually did fight. 'Bosnia didn't look out of place at all,' said our guide, the anagrammatically named Lieutenant-Colonel (retired) Nigel Linge. But the Afghan compound thrown up in the square would completely baffle a future Pevsner. The village was also now protected by fierce lines of razor wire. This was nothing to do with military training: it was to stop the metal being nicked.

Less than four miles away is another village – even more remote, same population (zero), very different history. Imber is thought to date back to Saxon times; it lasted until 1943, when the army – having acquired all the surrounding land – decided to evacuate the inhabitants in the run-up to D-Day. It was always a lonely place: 'There stands Imber on the down, Seven miles from any town,' said an old verse. And the pre-army track is still lit only by 'Wiltshire street lights', piles of chalk by the roadside. Nonetheless, Imber has inspired in death a sentimental following it never had in life.

Colonel Anagram had never been enthusiastic about taking me there. He thought too much fuss had been made about Imber already – 'much bigger places than this were evacuated' – and was worried I would write about nothing else. He agreed to go under mild protest. And we glimpsed the spire of St Giles' Church through the trees, passed the new housing on the edge of the village (Potemkin houses, with no actual existence, though these were built to resemble Ulster blocks of flats) and eagerly awaited the rest of it. Then, whoosh, before we knew, we were out the other side. True, except for the church, the Baptist cemetery and a single farmhouse, there is not much left of Imber, but it would have been nice to have a gentle look round; it would have been a good spot to have our sandwiches, at least. But the colonel did have a valid excuse: the area was being pretty much enfiladed by live artillery fire at the time. The red flags were flying above the village, though not to indicate a Communist takeover.

He was a good sort, Nigel, with an endearing weakness for liquorice. After forty years' service, he had taken the civilian job of Lands Liaison Officer at Salisbury Plain. The army controls 94,000 acres here, a stretch twenty-six miles long from Bulford and Tidworth in the east to Warminster in the west; and up to ten miles wide, almost half of the plain on most reckonings; and 11 per cent of Wiltshire (with a sliver of Hampshire thrown in). And it has acquired an unlikely reputation as a good steward. Here the chalk downland not only lives on, but does so with a minimum of heavy agriculture; the ox-eye daisies and lady's bedstraw, being impervious to bombardment unless they suffer a direct hit, can flourish. The survival of this vast tract can largely be credited to the army's presence, in terms of both keeping out the developmental threats that assail the rest of southern England and showing a surprising amount of institutional and individual sensitivity. The nesting boxes for owls and kestrels that dot the trees near Imber are down to the enthusiasm of a single officer, Nigel Lewis. 'We're trying to get a symbiotic relationship so soldiers can train and animals can graze, but not overgraze,' said Linge.

Salisbury Plain feels like a kind of thoroughly un-Disneyfied theme park of millennia of British history: the remains of Neolithic causeway camps; Bronze Age burial barrows; Iron Age hill forts; Romano-British villages; medieval lynchets ... The army's own additions merely add to the effect. As well as Copehill Down and the Imber flats, there is a patch of land designed to represent the damper parts of Afghanistan. There are Iraqi touches too, so that it adds up also to a history of modern British foreign policy.

In some places it felt almost Jurassic: standing on Sidbury Hill with a helicopter hovering over the valley, I fancied it was a pterodactyl in flight. And yet it was all very English: the background music in my head was 'The Lark Ascending', punctuated by occasional bursts of gunfire. And the extinct birds are not entirely imaginary: behind a high and rather militaristic fence, we caught a glimpse of a pair of the great bustards – the world's heaviest flying birds and extinct in Britain since the 1840s – being reared for release. With luck, they will one day outnumber the helicopters.

In the meantime the landowner has to balance military needs – which in themselves often conflict with each other – with ecological needs, archaeological needs, leisure needs and local needs. 'It keeps me in a job,' says Linge. He has to worry about badgers, rabbits and off-road racers. It all seems to work remarkably well: there is access to almost all the plain some of the time – even Imber Church, though officially redundant, is opened up for carols and a St Giles' Day service. Keeping the locals happy is not that big a problem because, more than any other county, Wiltshire just loves the army.

Wootton Bassett is a market town near Swindon which used to be famous for the St Ivel yoghurt factory and as a major junction on the Great Western Railway. Mostly, the inhabitants just call it Bassett, though these days they like to practise its new, sonorous full title: Royal Wootton Bassett. For four years the town became famous – a regular on the evening news – because of its impromptu repatriation ceremonies when dead soldiers were brought home from the wars in Iraq and, particularly, Afghanistan.

I was in the High Street near the war memorial when I became aware of an old man tending the flowers and talking to a couple of obvious tourists. They were asking him how the Wootton Bassett phenomenon started.

'I started it,' he said simply. His name turned out to be Ken Scott. He was ninety-eight and spent three years with the Eighth Army in North Africa, before taking part in D-Day. The bald statement might have been a slight oversimplification. But he is certainly the embodiment of an extraordinary story and an exceptional town.

In the spring of 2007, said Scott, he was standing on the High Street with a couple of his pals from the British Legion Club when they saw a hearse come by carrying a coffin draped with the Union Jack. They thought it might have been one of their members whose funerals, in the nature of things, happened pretty frequently. They made enquiries and discovered that the High Street was on the route between RAF Lyneham, where the bodies from Iraq and Afghanistan were being brought in, and the mortuary in Oxford. They got the mayor – one of their members – to have a word with Lyneham, so that next time the Legion would know in advance and could pay their respects. So a group turned up – in their blazers, grey trousers and regimental hats (no medals) – and waited to bow their heads.

As the mad Iraq war faded into the background, thousands of squaddies would be dispatched to what became the even madder war in Afghanistan, excited by the chance of real soldiering instead of yomping round the moors, even as their mothers became tearful and fearful as they flew out. Dozens – a small percentage, but too many for anyone's comfort – would fall victim: sometimes to something resembling conventional action; more often to roadside bombs, rogue local allies or the other cockups of a more than normally cocked-up war.

And so Wootton Bassett entered the vocabulary of the time, along with Helmand and Camp Bastion and the like. Passers-by started joining in; then the shopkeepers began to close their doors and come outside; then nearby villagers would come in specially; then they came from further afield; and, with them, the TV crews. Once the tenor bell of the church was tolling, by chance, because the ringers were practising. And that seemed a nice touch, so it became part of the ritual. Word came that the families were appreciative and the town grew in confidence.

News coverage of this war was scanter than of any since before the Crimea, and tightly controlled. But Bassett was not subject to military censorship and PR. And even as the politicians lavished praise on the town, one sensed their discomfort. They wanted a narrative of inexorable progress towards victory. But this was a war that had gone on longer than the two world wars put together and hardly anyone could remember what the hell the British Army was doing there. And all the public were seeing were the hearses down Wootton Bassett High Street.

Lyneham was due for closure anyway, as its fleet of Hercules transporters grew ever older, so the full conspiracy theory cannot be valid. But as Linda Frost, who became mayor in 2013, put it, 'I don't think the government liked the publicity we attracted. It really brought the war home. On the occasions when there were two, three, four soldiers, it was totally heart-wrenching. It didn't matter what age you were, the minute the hearse came through, it was so powerful.'

The last Hercules were moved to Brize Norton in Oxfordshire in 2011. The geography there was different and it was possible to keep the hearses out of any town centres that might have wished to take on Bassett's role. In compensation David Cameron organised the Royal prefix. It is impossible to avoid the thought that he did so with the same kind of relief with which he might hand over a peerage to an irritating colleague he wanted out of his hair.

But the story didn't end for Ken Scott. He kept finding flowers on the war memorial, so he would get a vase to make them last longer. There would be cards too, getting drenched and windblown. So he began to collect them and they are now in a memorial book in the council offices. One reads, 'My darling son: I'm sure that somewhere you are leading men again.' Another says, 'All the funny times we had together. Sleep tight, Bob.'

I asked Ken Scott if he regretted the end of the repatriations. At ninety-eight, his wits were clearer than those of the three prime ministers who had created the tragedies. 'What I regret is that they happened. One army can't go into another country and try to change their culture. The Nazis tried that. I think Tony Blair's a war criminal. Those young boys. Handsome young boys. It's very sad.'

And yet for Wootton Bassett there was a war dividend. Lyneham did not offer much employment, so it was not a major loss. In a country full of high streets dominated by charity shops and pawnbrokers, this one exudes an air of unusual perkiness and prosperity. And Linda Frost says that it has given the town a lingering unity: even routine local events are better supported than they were before. There is nothing like a sense of purpose to keep an old town vigorous.

An old bloke too. Look at Ken Scott, as the flowers and cards kept appearing for him to nurture and cherish.

Wootton Bassett is the only Wiltshire town I saw that could match the county's poster boy, Marlborough, where the economy is buoyed up by the presence of a major public school. Marlborough also has what is said to be the second-widest high street in Britain, beaten only by Stockton-on-Tees. An information board says the town had had 'a quiet history since the Civil War'. This ignores the fact that the High Street carried the traffic from London to Bath well into the twentieth century. And the story of the punch-up between two old ladies trying to get into a single parking place.

The council meet in Trowbridge; the police are in Devizes; Salisbury has nothing to say to Swindon, a town whose exponential growth has not erased its old baleful reputation. Victorian travellers knew it as Swindleham, because it had a monopoly on the Great Western Railway's catering in the days before buffet cars, and took full advantage. It is now best known as the home of the Magic Roundabout, a vile set-up near the football ground involving five mini-roundabouts round 'a contra-rotational hub'. The locals have got used to it, are even perversely proud – the jokey nickname has become official – but, like everything else in the town, it repels visitors.

Even its rival Salisbury seems to be feeling the twenty-first-century pinch a little. It's a wonderful town – like Oxford without all those cleverclogs kids – but the traffic is ghastly and, even here, I saw a street with four charity shops in a row of five. The cathedral is fabulous of course, especially the needle-like spire: tall and grey and old and lovely. But it is best seen nowadays from the hill fort of Old Sarum, which like sunken Dunwich used to return two MPs before 1832 despite having no voters, an arrangement that at least had the virtue of being relaxing for the politicians.

I think that Wiltshire's glories are in the villages: not the obvious chocolate-boxers, like Castle Combe – which even in midweek had the bee-buzz of noise from its motor-racing circuit – or the tourist honeypot Lacock, but the workaday places, all of which seem to have a ration of gorgeous thatch looking more natural and homely than in any other county. I took a particular shine to Bishops Cannings, an architectural mishmash but tucked away all snug and secret beneath the stirring downs north of Devizes. This is one of the villages associated with Wiltshire's favourite legend, the moonrakers: the locals who, one moonlit night, were retrieving a barrel of smuggled French brandy (or similar) which they had hidden in the pond, when the excise man rode by. They told him they were collecting cheese – the moon's reflection. The exciseman thought they were idiots and rode off.

Not daft, these people. But it is a county where one can start to believe the impossible ...

I met my old friend Bryan McAllister, the reformed *Guardian* cartoonist, in the Barge Inn at Honeystreet. Or as the sign in the bar has it, 'Honeystreet twinned with Roswell, New Mexico', global centre of ufology, and maybe home town of the floppy-hat woman at Avebury. The Barge is the global centre of crop circles.

Another sign offers a prize of 100,000 pints of the pub's own brew, Croppie Ale, to 'any genuine alien in possession of a valid passport from another world' who could reproduce the most famous of all crop circles, the Galaxy Formation, which appeared at Milk Hill in 2001. The Barge has achieved something almost as hard as finding a winner of its competition: a USP to sustain the profits of a country pub.

The crop circle phenomenon appeared to be fading, having lost its last vestiges of mystique. Too many jokers created too much elaboration, snapping the last skeins of doubt that there were any kind of natural forces at work. And yet. The first report of something resembling a crop circle dates from 1678, in a Hertfordshire oat field. The researcher Terence Meaden found an account in an 1880 edition of *Nature* magazine, submitted by a well-known amateur scientist in Surrey. The first Wiltshire account, from Tilshead, goes back to about 1904. 'All the complex circles are man-made', said Meaden. 'But some of the single circles would have been made by some kind of whirlwind or vortex.'

There was a more compelling puzzle centred on the Barge: what happened, under a previous regime, to more than £400,000 in Lottery funds supposed to be used for refurbishment of the pub and other community projects. But in Wiltshire there is always that sense of mystery. At Avebury I met a bloke who swore convincingly that his grandfather had seen crop circles. And at the Barge the kitchen staff had apparently been captured by aliens and were unable, even after half an hour, to offer a menu.

Having spent the previous night sleepless and wretched at Stonehenge, I made my excuses to Bryan and left early. But I made a final detour down Stonehenge's dying highway, the A344, and stopped by the perimeter fence. About a dozen other people had done the same. Now there were no clouds, the moon was full and the circle was deserted except for a couple of security men. The thousands of lager cans had been cleared away. Stonehenge looked real again: broody, impressive, genuinely mysterious. The real meaning of solstice to an Englishman struck me forcefully: it means that henceforth the days start getting shorter. Bloody winter can't be far away.

June 2013

~~~~~~~~~

Ken Scott returned to Normandy for the D-Day commemoration in 2014. He told journalists of the horror of wading past the dying: 'They had met the machine guns and you couldn't help them. They were crying out, "Give us a hand, buddy." Some of them were calling for their mothers. We just had to keep going – we pushed them to one side, we just couldn't help them.'

The 2014 sunrise at Stonehenge was magnificent, apparently.

30. *Let's party like it's AD 43*

SOMERSET

'Good evening,' I said to Allen Powell, landlord of the Crown at Pilton.

'That would be an exaggeration,' he replied.

It was Thursday. All week cars had been going through, past and round Pilton. Some of them had stopped at the pub. The occupants asked the landlord whether a rival pub, the Apple Tree, was open; whether they could recharge their phone; use the toilets; have a glass of water; buy a ticket for the event down the road; and, on rare occasions, whether they might buy a drink or some food. He was remarkably affable, really.

The village already looked like a place under occupation: stewards in hi-vis jackets, the storm troopers of the leisure age, patrolled and controlled the streets. In the valley, there was already a vast tented encampment. In the English countryside any unfamiliar sight towards the horizon usually turns out to be a new type of polytunnel. But this was the size of a Middle Eastern refugee camp. Friday, Saturday and Sunday the pub would be closing. These marked the three business days at the camp, officially known as the 2013 Glastonbury Festival.

An immeasurable part of the success of this almost-annual ritual is its name. Michael Eavis, the founder, did not, after the first year, call his little shindig at Worthy Farm the Pilton Festival. He did not name it after the nearest town, Shepton Mallet. Instead he gave it the name of the most mystical town in Britain, which was not obvious geographically. Now there is a most astonishing invasion: 180,000 people, two Cup Final crowds, descend, except in the occasional fallow years, on what they might think is Glastonbury but isn't, among villages that have no infrastructure whatever.

It was a masterful piece of branding, as clever as naming a piece of technology after something yummy: Apple, Orange, BlackBerry. The second part of the trick was being in the most mellifluous of all the counties. Somerset is named after Somerton, the original (until 1366) county town. *Somer* may or may not mean summer, but it sounds as though it does. Somerset was a summer county perforce, because in winter vast areas of it were under water (often in summer too, as any festival regular would attest). But to our ears there is another implication. Where better to be at the end of June, when the countryside is at its most ravishing, than the county whose name trips so sweetly off the tongue? *Somer-set.*

Another aspect of Eavis's skill has been his ability to keep his most important neighbours happy. Everyone in Pilton gets a free ticket. The surrounding farmers get in the loop by renting their fields out. There is work for local contractors and for the kids, not least as stewards. Villagers get the milk franchise. For the three-day weekend itself this is a frontier village, and so there is also scope for smuggling rackets: in this case people-smuggling of the kind that used to go on at the Berlin Wall. Only this racket is designed to get people in rather than out.

Until 2000 gatecrashing the festival was a rite of passage: if you didn't get in you were a wimp or a non-trier. Now there is a security fence and the trade is far more clandestine. The ticket-holders, meanwhile, just drive through Somerset as if through a cordon sanitaire. Once in the site, they stay in, and so – perhaps uniquely for an event of this magnitude – there is very little spin-off for local traders not directly involved.

The Crown shuts mainly because there is no point opening. Surrounding B&Bs have 'Vacancies' signs, which they would not expect on any other midsummer weekend. Glastonbury, nearly seven miles away,

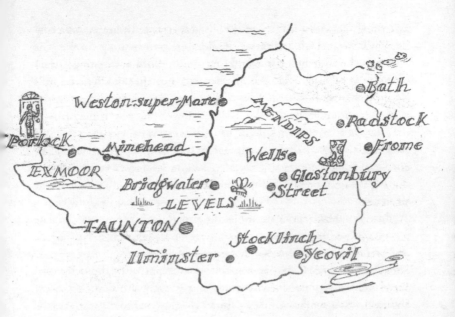

gets a little pre-festival business from passers-through panic-buying sleeping bags and wellies. Thereafter it is deserted and the owners of the funky shops have time to moan to passing writers.

'It's terrible for business,' said Caroline Harris of Natural Earth. 'Nobody comes here.'

'It's like a ghost town,' said the Hundred Monkeys café.

'Even the locals are at the festival,' reported Conscious Clothing.

'The old ones?'

'Definitely.'

In the early days the very words 'Glastonbury Festival' used to terrify one's mother. Now you take both Mum and Gran. That's the history of modern popular music.

Allen Powell said he was going to go out for the three days, go to things the way publicans never do.

'There's something on in the village, isn't there? A garden fete or something?'

He put on his weary face. 'Yes, something like that.'

Somerset is The Hedonistic County, the County of Self-Indulgence. They can put that on their leaflets and road signs, and credit me. It was a conclusion I reached while wearing my floral-pattern bathing cozzie, lying back nonchalantly in a bathtub-warm rooftop pool and staring dreamily towards Bathwick Hill over the best cityscape in the kingdom. All I needed for total nirvana was one of the bikini-clad fellow bathers to lean over and peel me a grape.

Bath is surely the only inland city in Britain constructed essentially for pleasure (Bradford? Wolverhampton? Maybe not). The Romans settled there not because it was a defensible position, offered mineral wealth or had fast trains to London. They chose the site because it offered one of the delights of home, thanks to the only really hot springs on a chilly island. And as Tacitus said, taking the waters is 'one of those luxuries that stimulate vice'. It sounds like advertising copy, though he was actually being censorious; on this subject it comes to the same thing.

Bath has played the same role intermittently throughout the two intervening millennia, most famously in the eighteenth century, when the real-life counterparts of Jane Austen's characters used the waters as the backdrop to their mating rituals. The springs continued to be central to the city until the late 1970s: kids used to have toga parties in the Roman bath. Then years of neglect and the death of a child from meningitis led to closure for nearly three decades. Restoration came in the years of *fin-de-siècle* plenty thanks to a millennium grant plus the discovery that the health issues could be resolved by tapping much, much deeper into the spring, down to water that is said to have fallen as rain before the Romans ever got here.

The project was much delayed and became a byword for official hopelessness. But in 2006 the locals got their bathright back. And the council and the operators are very keen that it should be seen as a public bath, not a private one. They like to tempt workers away from the rush hour with their twilight package. It seems to me rather a triumphant comeback, making the waters once again the centrepiece of a city that, for all its traffic and pretensions, retains its infinite charm.

I went into the pool with a pain in my right shoulder blade, my right kneecap, my left collarbone and my left *quadratus lumborum*. Afterwards, some of the pains had definitely shifted around, if nothing else. But my brain felt startlingly refreshed. Anyway, how can you not love a place where even the post office looks like a temple of Athene?

In Xanadu did Kubla Khan
A stately pleasure-dome decree.

That was written in Somerset – until Coleridge was interrupted by a man from Porlock, the late-eighteenth-century equivalent of a courtesy call from BT. Bath is on the eastern edge of a county that stretches a long way west and has a strong literary tradition. James Crowden's *Literary Somerset* lists 300 writers of various kinds from Adelard of Bath to Thomas Young. What it lacks is a single, overwhelming Hardyesque author who embodies the county. Even the Brontës can be said to represent a certain grim overarching Yorkieness. But Somerset is too heterogeneous. It's hard to imagine what Austen's characters might say to those of R. D. Blackmore, the thick end of three hours' drive away even now. But let's try:

CATHERINE MORLAND: I hope I shall have the pleasure of seeing
    you again soon. Shall you be at the cotillion ball tomorrow?
CARVER DOONE: I will fling thee senseless into the river if I ever
    catch thy girl-face there again.

The pleasure principle is surprisingly widespread. Exmoor, aside from blood feuds, was a place for stag-hunting. Then take Bridgwater, a town once known for the Bridgwater Smell (it came from a cellophane factory), but now that's gone it can enjoy its carnival. This is the centrepiece of a series of autumnal bacchanals that are widespread in Somerset, in a manner analogous to the Lewes-centred Guy Fawkes Nights of East Sussex. Bridgwater notionally raises money for the event and also makes charity donations, averaging around £20,000 a year. *Twenty thousand? From a whopping great carnival?* They could probably raise more from a few well-run coffee mornings or beetle drives.

No one much cares for the Somerset coast from Weston-super-Mud to Butlins, Minehead, though it perks up when it meets Exmoor a few miles from the Devon border. Otherwise it is not very beautiful and the Bristol Channel's massive tidal range ensures that the sea is often invisible. But I can commend the retro-funfair, complete with 1950s penny slot machines and Victorian sideshows, that camps at Weston for high season. Somerset's most famous school is Millfield, best known for its sport. Even the holy little city of Wells has a street, hard by the cathedral, that used to be known (a sign dutifully records) as Grope Lane. Above all, what is

Somerset's best-known – almost its only – industry? Cider, the drink of choice for the revellers at Worthy Farm (they are always called revellers in the media), because I suppose they think it's what they ought to drink, and also because it's cheaper and stronger than the beer.

The local heroes are all bringers of joy, like Eavis himself. ('You see him in Wells,' said one sceptic. 'He has an aura about him. And he jolly knows it.') And Julian Temperley, maker of cider brandy. And the smokery people from Hambridge. Somerset's cricketers have always made the game, above all, *fun*.

Cider aside, Somerset never did make much. There was a small coalfield centred on Radstock; Clarks made shoes at Street, until they didn't; Morlands sheepskins still come from Glastonbury, just about; there were gloves and, even now, helicopters round Yeovil. It is too easy to categorise the locals as mañana-ish; they do that better themselves: 'Sometimes oy just sits and thinks. But when that gets too stressful oy just sits.' But there is a strange undertow of masterly small-scale engineering and construction. 'If I was stranded in the desert,' said the sculptor Gordon Young, who came down from Carlisle thirty-four years ago, 'I'd want a Somerset bloke to bodge me out.' He introduced me to his very-Somerset neighbour, Brian Hill, who was – among many other projects – restoring a Paxman agricultural steam engine, the last of its kind. He was creating a lot of new thingummies to replace the old wotsits and it was absolutely marvellous, even though I understood almost nothing of what he was doing.

'Brian, do you think this is a particularly Somerset thing to do?'

'Yes, I do. There's loads of clubs for restoring old engines.'

Gordon Young, from cold old Cumberland, thinks they're all a bit soft. 'You'd be hard-pushed to starve in Somerset. Everything bloody grows. It's so fertile. The season's so long, they think they're in clover. They *are* in clover. It's the land of lush. Somerset's never produced an England footballer, you know. I know they aren't all softies: the Somerset Light Infantry had a great record. But they're spoiled rotten.'

There is a much rougher working-class culture too. I sometimes caught glimpses of it decades ago when Ian Botham was in his rampaging pomp in the backstreet pubs of Taunton. Botham's home town, Yeovil, is considered the HQ of this. Yobville, as it is sometimes known. Or Yeovile. Or, as it was sometimes spelt in Old English, Evil.

But everything is relative. Somerset is not that rough. What it does have is a delicious weirdness, just below the surface. 'MAN BEATS LEWD

MASCOT' said a poster for the *Central Somerset Gazette*. In Long Sutton I saw a sign saying 'BEWARE. POLICE OPERATE IN THIS AREA'. Usually, such signs say 'THIEVES'. Maybe it was placed there by the National Union of Marijuana Farmers. And Glastonbury has an estate agent called the Real Ralph Bending, who has modelled his adverts on those of Roy Brooks, who half a century ago was the last man to try to bring humour to this grim trade.

> WESTBURY-SUB-MENDIP: One-bed ground-floor apartment out
>   in the sticks. Suit someone whose brother is also their uncle.
> GLASTONBURY: Two-bedroom retirement home. Suit someone
>   on their last legs.

I have had to clean up Mr Bending's spelling, which suggests he should be careful making fun of rural ignorance. But I applaud his efforts.

The notion of Somerset as ground zero for two-headed bumpkins is deeply ingrained in the wider culture. When a friend's wife began teaching in a Devon comprehensive, a kid asked where she came from. 'Somerset,' she replied. 'Ooh, aaarrr. Ooh, aaarr,' the class went in mocking unison. Counties without big cities have that effect on their neighbours.

But it is a substantial agricultural area and unusually varied: a bit of everything. However, the hierarchy of farming is not quite the usual counter-intuitive arrangement with the low ground at the top. In complete contrast to Dorset, there are few big landowners and some of the farms are exceptionally small. The big cheeses make the big cheeses. But everyone looks down, literally and metaphorically, on the Somerset Levels. Or, as they are usually called, the moors. These are not, though, anything like the upland moors of Exmoor, Dartmoor or the North.

Anyone driving down the M5 will get a sense of the Levels as they drive across Sedgemoor, a journey otherwise notable only for the vast Morrisons depot at Bridgwater and some particularly repulsive service areas. It is like a miniature East Anglia: flat fields fringed by willow and reeds rather than hedgerows, and broken up by the artificial drainage ditches known as rhynes or rhines (usually pronounced *reens*).

As I wandered the fields near Muchelney, just outside Langport, on a July morning, the rhynes were unpleasantly stagnant and covered in duckweed. A year earlier, it would have been a very different story.

The Levels were drained, but not as quickly or determinedly as the Fens: when James I's chief fen-reclaimer, Sir Cornelius Vermuyden, arrived to have a go at Somerset, the rustics, with their eternal suspicion of busybodies sent from London, saw him off. And the Levels never did get the big arable fields that made East Anglia rich.

So the area has remained relatively poor – 'bogtrotters', I heard one incomer call his neighbours. Certainly the -ey suffix indicates that Muchelney was an island, and to this day Muchelney Abbey and its adjoining church have always remained above the waterline. 'The monks knew what they were doing,' said one villager ruefully. Locally, the village has long had a certain celebrity as the home of the Lowland Games, a jokey celebration of what might be called bogtrotter culture.

Most winters there is some flooding on the moors, which is not a problem as long as the stock is removed in time and the roads stay dry. Even then, canny villagers normally park elsewhere and hitch rides out by tractor. In November 2012 this was impossible: the only exit was by boat. Several of the outlying homesteads, not necessarily new, were inundated. At least in hindsight and/or in public, villagers like to play up the joy of these occasions. 'It is lovely, the peace,' said one woman. 'We have flood parties in the church and we bring what we've got a lot of. "Have you got potatoes? I've got carrots."'

But in 2012 that wasn't the half of it. The moors flooded in summer as well, for weeks on end, creating a vast and foul insect-ridden swamp. 'I never had bites in thirty years in Somerset,' said Gordon Young, way above the waterline in High Ham. 'Now I've got bites that still haven't healed.'

'Is Somerset malarial, do you think?' I asked lightly.

'I did wonder. I asked the doctor.'

In Muchelney itself, one could sense the unease, even in a summer that was tending towards drought. Anecdotal evidence suggests several incomers have been trying to find a permanent way out. Graham Walker of School Farm has a popular farm shop, selling stuff from his polytunnels. Which is lucky. The grass on about half his moorland fields had not recovered a year later. He had no doubt who was to blame: 'Too many people sitting on their backsides refusing to do any work.'

This was a not very veiled reference to the Environment Agency, which for years had refused to dredge the rivers, mainly to save money but rationalised by all kinds of theories that appear to have collapsed under the weight of water. 'The swampists are in headlong retreat,' concluded Anthony Gibson, the former regional director of the NFU.

And so rural England's battle to keep its head above water takes on an extra urgency in the Levels. One local branch of agriculture, peat-cutting, is withering away because it is palpably unsustainable. But the place does need to stay reasonably dry if it is to retain its local culture and cuisine: jugged hare, smoked eels, the occasional badger steak and, behind locked doors, so I heard in whispers, a very occasional, illegal, roast swan.

People in Somerset do seem curiously self-deprecating about their county. Several I met referred to it as 'a drive-through county' and it is true that it is not, for the most part, a destination in the way of Devon, Cornwall and Dorset. Partly that's due to the dreariness of the coastline and the gentleness of the hills. There is also an absence of great houses, with the single major exception of Montacute, ancestral home of the Phelips family; even the Duke of Somerset's place, Bradley House, is in Wiltshire.

And yet the place is quite stunning architecturally. Pevsner, who normally worked on the historic boundaries, found he had to split this volume, and merge North Somerset with Bristol. Far bigger and more obvious counties were not so honoured.

In part, this seems to be because Somerset had a late surge of church building in the fourteenth and fifteenth centuries, when the county had a quarter of the English wool trade and a good deal of money. Parishes competed with each other to build the biggest towers (Somerset never went in for spires much). It was also a beauty contest: these towers were not just fat and solid, as in Norfolk; they were dolled up. In the words of Julian Orbach, who has been writing the new edition of Pevsner: 'the stone was so good you could play games with it'.

There was an extraordinary variety of such stone too. Somerset straddles several of England's great geological belts. So it goes from Bath stone, through the blue lias limestone-and-shale that makes the ancient county town of Somerton look so calm and self-possessed, to hamstone ('the loveliest building material in England' – Simon Jenkins), which gives so many Somerset villages the colour of different types of marmalade, sometimes orange, sometimes lemon.

In places, this becomes decidedly over the top, as at Barrington ('startlingly beautiful' – Candida Lycett Green) or Hinton St George, described by Alan Bennett as 'absurdly picturesque', the emphasis for me being on the absurd. One survey suggested this was the place with the longest life expectancy in the country: long enough for the populace to get crabby and install bins for doggie-doos, as if this were Hampstead, and signs like 'Private Drive. Church Property'.

For me, the glory of Somerset does not come from the stone or the gastropubs. It comes in the places that live quietly and unshowily with their own integrity. Throughout this book, I have been searching for the perfect small town. I had hopes of Wells, before discovering that just about every shop on the High Street was a chain, from Country Casuals to Waterstones. Some Somerset towns, notably Frome and Bruton, have already started to feel the influence of displaced Londoners. Yet it is still possible to find somewhere like Ilminster, as self-contained and unself -conscious as a small town in Gascony. It seems to have survived even Tesco.

Anyone might be thankful to be in a Somerset village. And it was Arthur Mee, children's encyclopedist and begetter of the sentimental 1930s county guides, *The King's England*, who is credited with the phrase 'thankful villages' to cover the tiny number of places that sent their young men off to war in 1914 and got them all back again.

There are thought to be fifty-one of them (excluding various doubts and complications, all explained on the website hellfirecorner.co.uk). And, of these, nine are in Somerset, a remarkable number; Yorkshire is second with five. There was a later, inevitably much smaller, list: the villages that repeated the trick in the Second World War as well. There are said to be fourteen 'doubly thankful' villages, two of them in Somerset: Stocklinch and Woolley.

I came upon Stocklinch, not far from Ilminster, early on a summer's evening. Inside the little church was a brass plaque 'in gratitude for peace and victory' listing the nineteen men who took part in the Great War. Below it is a framed parchment listing seven who served and came back from 1939 to 1945. By the village hall there is a commemorative stone bench. There is of course no war memorial.

The bugles called from sad shires with such regularity that one middle-sized county's over-representation in this list seemed as though it must have an explanation. Norfolk did not have a single thankful village, nor Devon, nor Surrey. Small villages obviously stood a better chance, but that does not appear to be a particular Somerset phenomenon. Did the agricultural exemptions in the conscription system work more kindly here? Did Somerset lads' mechanical skills get them safer jobs behind the lines?

Father Geoff Wade, the vicar of Stocklinch, rejected these explanations, and Rod Morris, one of the researchers behind the Hellfire Corner project, was just as definite: 'The Somerset Light Infantry took heavy losses on the western front. You'll get a fairly starchy response if it's suggested Somerset did not play its full part.'

Morris lives in another thankful village, Rodney Stoke, which sent twenty-one men out in the First World War and got them all back. Its neighbour Draycott, so close that the boundary is indistinct, lost eleven. His collaborator Norman Thorpe concluded, 'We have tried many times to find any reason for the completely erratic distribution of thankful villages, and each time we have concluded that it seems to be pure chance.' The vicar, being both C of E and an ex-naval officer, did not attempt to tell me that thankfulness was a sign of God's special benison. It was blind chance, he thought. Which is lucky, because God's benison can be mighty capricious. Flixborough in Lincolnshire was one of the original thankful villages; in 1974 it was the site of one of Britain's worst modern industrial disasters when a chemical works blew up, killing twenty-eight.

There is one last very Somersetty explanation. Rod Morris mentioned a theory that all the Somerset thankful villages lie on the St Michael ley line, devised/invented by the late John Michell. This is the great western line – more direct than Brunel's – which links Glastonbury Tor with St Michael's Mount to the west and with Avebury and Bury St Edmunds to the east. If there are any answers, they have to come at Glastonbury.

A month later Glastonbury was back to what passes for normal there. The characteristic shops of a small English market town were all thriving again: the witchcraft supply store, the non-toxic hairdresser's, the Sufi charity shop, the Ethical Elegance beauty salon and so on. Ralph Bending, the subversive estate agent, was still in fine form:

> WEST PENNARD: Two-bedroom cottage. No heating and plenty of
> fresh air await a tenant with the constitution of an ox.

Glastonbury now had an event of its own, indeed one that can hardly be imagined anywhere else: the 18th Goddess Conference, 'a unique transformative, spiritual, emotional, psychological and physical experience', which in 2013 was devoted to celebrating 'Eartha, our Great Earth

Mother'. We were enjoined to honour her by wearing autumnal colours, which I did: a khaki shirt spattered with a shade of plum, an overripe one which had squirted over my collar.

This looked a feeble effort beside the flowing orange and russets that otherwise filled the hall. About 100 women, mainly of the Earth Mother type themselves, and a handful of men, had gathered in the town hall under banners depicting goddess icons from round the world – Grandmother Spider Woman, the Cumaean Crone, the Luristan Birthing Goddess – some of which looked like stylised depictions of page 3 of the *Sun*.

The heterodox archaeologist Terence Meaden explained to the gathering his theory about Stonehenge: that there is a four-minute gap between the sun rising by the Heel Stone and the shadow penetrating the stone circle itself. For Meaden there was an obvious interpretation about rising, penetration and consummation (although, as we have learned, the Wiltshire sun does not always get it up in the first place).

This notion was greeted with not only applause, but cheering and whooping. Indeed, cheering and whooping greeted just about everything, even a very arcane lecture on German Earth Mother theory. Through this, it was possible to sit at the back and applaud politely, if not whoop, with everyone else. But looming up were Earth Circle Gatherings 'for Connection, Discussion and Support' and 'a Feast of fabulous two-and-a-half-hour workshops'. One of these was specifically about Avalon, and thus seemed to link the very heart of Glastonbury's ruling mythology and Somerset's deepest secrets. However, the programme promised that 'We will Inhale, Embrace, Ground, and Embody this Energy with Earth Goddess and Avalon Essence Dance'. Terrified, not least by the capital letters, I fled into the High Street and made for what looked like an old stable block, site of the Goddess Temple.

This is a lilac-painted room, strewn with cushions and suffused with incense. A woman sat cross-legged in front of the altar and kept lighting candles, at a rate of about two per minute, below a picture of an unnervingly busty goddess figure with flowing tresses. Even so, it was profoundly relaxing, just like the bath in Bath, if a bit like how one imagines George Harrison's living room circa 1969.

I had grasped one fundamental, I think: the belief that Neolithic humanity worshipped goddess figures, often representing the fecundity of the earth fertilised by the masculine heavens. This would make sense, wouldn't it? But it was quickly suppressed by patriarchal Judaeo-Christian-Islamism and has not gained much traction anywhere outside Glastonbury.

But is this a religion, a cult, a belief system, or what? I wanted to ask the conference organiser, Kathy Jones, Priestess of Avalon, who had been in the hall wearing a fetching headdress which might have passed as a fascinator at Ascot. I was directed instead to her husband, Mike, which seemed somewhat patriarchal.

Not a religion or any of the above, he insisted. 'Goddess is an experiential spirituality.' It was, he said, primarily but not exclusively, a path to spirituality for women, adding that 'for us, the goddesses will arrive through the priestesses'.

Have you experienced this?

'Oh yes', he said. 'Eartha appeared last night. At the opening ceremony in the town hall.'

He was not immune to sensing I might be sceptical: 'This is not historical, it is not theological. The scholarship is not important to us. It is what we feel. If anyone turns round to us and says, "That's not right", we say, "It is right for us."'

I found this answer rather attractive. It made a change from religions claiming a monopoly on wisdom. He was also arguing for a small gesture to sexual equality. 'In this county there are about 2,000 houses devoted to God and only one to Goddess.' It also seemed very Glasto, I said. He didn't disagree with that. 'Everyone who comes here to do spiritual work finds it a very intense experience.'

Back at the Crown, Pilton, Allen Powell was in more relaxed mood. He was a little warmer about the festival now. 'Always pleased to see it come financially. Always glad to see it go personally.' The financial gain, it transpired, comes not from the festival-goers, still less from any festival non-goers, but from feeding and victualling the contractors before and afterwards. 'I'm not anti-festival in any way,' he insisted. 'It's been good for the village, brought people in.'

Thus Michael Eavis borrowed the existing aura of Glastonbury to bump up his own project; nowadays the town, excepting that one hopeless weekend, basks in the warmth generated by the festival. Glastonbury really does have some very unusual people; the festival mostly belongs to chartered accountants from Beckenham, but deep down they must believe they are unusual too. This is the kind of symbiosis of which the Earth Mother must surely approve.

June/July 2013

~~~~~~~~

Gordon Young, I learned later, was not quite right in his assertion that Somerset had never produced an England footballer. John Atyeo, who played six internationals in the 1950s, was born in Standerwick, just inside Somerset, though he was essentially a Wiltshire boy.

The horrendously wet winter of 2013–14 produced yet more flooding on the Levels. This time it also affected places like Surrey and Berkshire, thus creating more interest among the media and politicians. The government suddenly discovered the money, and the Environment Agency the rationale, for an urgent programme of dredging the rhynes. Ralph Bending was keeping his spirits up. TO LET:

>   STREET: *Eco-friendly two-bedroom first-floor apartment. Suit someone who farts in a bottle.*
>   GLASTONBURY: *Handy one-bedroom flat. Suit someone in touch with themselves.*

31. *Very good in Parts*

LINCOLNSHIRE

Within two hours of arriving in Lincolnshire, I was recognised. In the café of a fenland garden centre.

'You do double glazing, don't you?' said the woman behind the counter.

'Not exactly,' I said.

She seemed mildly affronted, as though there had been some deliberate attempt at deception. 'You're *not* the double-glazing man from Bourne?'

'I could always try to do double glazing, but I'm not from Bourne. I'm from Herefordshire.'

She switched tack quickly. 'Oh, nice county.'

'Lincolnshire's a nice county too,' I said.

If she had ever been paid a compliment in her life, she had never accepted one on behalf of her county. 'Flat,' she said, flatly. 'We like it, though,' she added in that tone people use to justify a taste for something completely uncool. It was my first experience of what I came to know as the Lincolnshire backward defensive: an apologetic remark, very lightly seasoned with a pinch of truculence.

Did I mean it? Is Lincolnshire a nice county? Yes. At any rate, it is intriguing, distinctive, full of the unexpected. But it has what you might call issues. And the most serious of these is low self-esteem.

It was not always so. When the county rebelled against the Reformation in 1536, Henry VIII's response was withering, even before he embarked on wholesale vengeance: 'How presumptuous then are ye, the rude commons of one shire, and that one of the most brute and beestelie of the hole realme, and of leest experience, to fynde faulte with your Prynce.' (He would have made a brilliantly provocative newspaper columnist.) It was the brute and beestelieness that gave Lincolnshire its strength as a county. It was near-enough impenetrable, guarded by the sea, the Humber, the Trent and, worst of all, the Fens.

To that extent not much has changed. Very big, Lincolnshire: famously second only to Yorkshire. But the internal communications are primeval. The roads have encouragingly low A numbers and look invitingly straight on the map, but are curiously inimical to overtaking. The A16 used to unite the county from Grimsby in the north-east to Stamford in the south-west, each town approximately sixteen miles apart from the other. (Supposedly that allowed everyone to get to market and back in a day.) There has been some tinkering with the road numbering in the bottom corner, but it is still more than eighty very slow miles. The once-extensive railway network is now vestigial. And the external communications are no better. There is only one main-line station, Grantham, which sends a few phlegmatic commuters 105 miles to London every day. Nearby, the A1 skirts the outer edge of Lincolnshire, but not helpfully.

So hardly anyone comes by. Lincoln Cathedral is amazing, but only the most intrepid visitors get there. On the coast, Skegness still attracts its trippers, especially from the East Midlands. But in the words of the Lincolnshire polymath, David Robinson of Louth: 'They drive like hell into the sun in the morning to get there and they drive like hell into the sun in the evening to get back, and they don't see anything in the middle.' Who does?

There is a perception that the county is indeed flat and boring, though its Wolds are the highest bit of far-eastern England. But no one

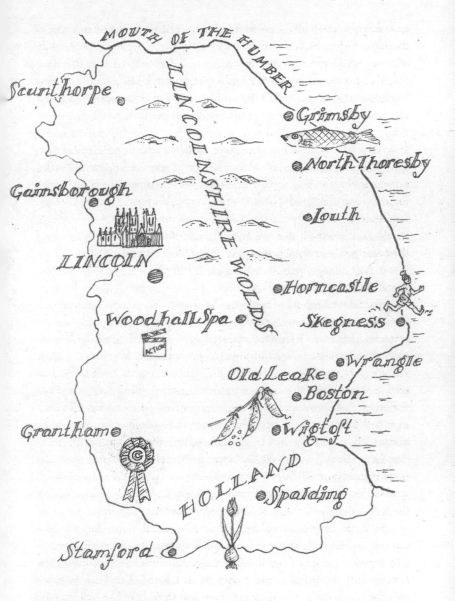

knows quite what to say about Lincolnshire, whether they live there or not. Few outsiders even know the nickname for Lincolnshire people, 'Yellowbellies', which Robinson, the acknowledged expert on such subjects, insists comes from the yellow facings on the regimental uniform – not because the soldiers all ran away, and not because the Fenmen were all yellow from bog fevers.

The word one kept hearing was insular, emphasised by the BBC Radio Lincolnshire headlines I caught while stuck behind a gravel lorry for about an hour on the A16: 'Lincoln City Council is holding consultations on this year's Christmas market and seventy-seven people have been killed in a train crash in Spain.' It was mid-July. 'There is a certain feeling about the place, without anyone quite knowing what it is,' explained the local author and broadcaster Alan Stennett. 'There is a pride in being different, there's a pride in being insular. We don't want anything to do with that lot, be it London or Poland.'

Lincolnshire joke: Carload of Cockneys passing through a village; they see an old yokel and aim to have some fun. "Ere, mate, you seen a lorry load of monkeys pass this way?' 'No. Why? Have you fell off?'

It is a county with 600 churches, most of them striking, some amazing. Robinson of Louth told me, as he approached his eighty-sixth birthday, that after a lifetime of studying the county, there were still places he didn't know and wanted to explore. But the pride is limited, partly because it has never been fostered. The county has never had a county council as such. It used to be divided into three Parts (a word that has no singular), analogous to the Yorkshire ridings – Lindsey, Kesteven and Holland. In 1974 it was top-sliced instead, with most of the county getting its own council and the north placed in something called Humberside. Of all the new counties this was the most total failure, not just unpopular but wholly misconceived. The Humber is not some piddling stream like the Tyne or Tees: it is a barrier, even with the then newly built bridge. The two sides had no interest in each other, and the council was dominated by Hull.

When this ill-starred invention was abandoned in 1997, two new unitary councils were created called North Lincolnshire and North-East Lincolnshire, which have no connection with official Lincolnshire. So even now, eight slow miles south of Grimsby, as you approach North Thoresby and Utterby, you pass a sign welcoming you to Lincolnshire. Which is Utterby stupid. Here is a county with an identity crisis making the problem much worse.

Lincolnshire has always had problems finding warm supporters. In its chapter in *The English Counties* (1948), James Wentworth Day, a right-wing polemicist as trenchant as Henry VIII, strayed from the celebratory tone of the book and called Lincolnshire people 'uncompromising, dour in parts, ugly in patches'. He went on: 'They believe in work and making money. The humour is unsparing but seldom subtle. There is a take-it-or-leave-it spirit of local pride, a box-your-ears defiance of people from other parts and a knock-down rivalry between town and town, village and village.'

This gets somewhere near the nub. As an actual county, Lincolnshire is a waste of a great deal of space. But as a slice of England it has virtues matched almost nowhere else. There is an unusually widespread sense of continuity and stability. Rich Londoners steer clear, partly because the transport links are so dire, partly because the villages, if not the people, are indeed ugly, and not just in patches.

So much of Lincolnshire has changed remarkably little. This is best appreciated in one of the typical small towns – Louth or Horncastle for preference – over a pint of Bateman's 'Good Honest Ale'. Or perhaps in bosky, golfy, eccentric, totally untypical Woodhall Spa, with its enchanting half-timbered Kinema in the Woods and its general air of the Kenyan White Highlands, shortly before Mau Mau. And there is *space*: on a summer's morning on the wide expanse of sharp sand at Anderby Creek there was only one other mammal in sight – a distant seal, who took one look at me, decided even this beach wasn't big enough for both of us and opted for the frigid sea instead.

Lincolnshire does have incomers, and not just east Europeans: there are loads of refugees from south-eastern England, working-class pensioners who did well out of council house sales and cashed up to bolster their pension in a place where property prices are more like Poland than Pimlico. Static caravans are advertised for £5,950; semis in Boston below £100,000; Skegness bungalows not that far from the sea below £150,000. Lincolnshire hospitals are said to do an unusual number of hip replacements.

But it remains above all insular. Would-be achievers have always left to explore and/or change the world: Sir John Franklin from Spilsby; George Bass from Sleaford; Captain John Smith from Willoughby; Matthew Flinders from Donington; Joseph Banks from Revesby; Isaac Newton from Colsterworth; and Margaret Roberts, aka Margaret Thatcher, from Grantham. They tended not to come back: Franklin and Bass failed to return from their travels; Flinders also died young; Smith might have died in Virginia had he not been rescued by Pocahontas; Thatcher escaped the IRA in the Grand Hotel, Brighton, and died in the Ritz Hotel, London.

In the same tradition, the airfields of Lincolnshire sent out the RAF to bomb Germany and save the world; many of those men never came back either. And, should Her Majesty be in need of support, she can always turn to Lieutenant-Colonel John Lindley Marmion Dymoke of Scrivelsby Court, the thirty-fourth hereditary King's/Queen's Champion, though if the danger is immediate and physical he might need some help, since he was born, like her, in 1926 and acquired the job six years before she ascended the throne.

The great men of Lincolnshire who found fame might all have thought their childhood companions a little wanting in vigour; Mrs Thatcher certainly did. Those stiff North Sea breezes seem to induce an unexpected lethargy. Were I to settle here I might find selling double glazing far too stressful to contemplate. I might just about summon enough spirit to ascend the highest point in the Parts of Holland, Pinchbeck Marsh, twenty-six feet above sea level, before taking a nap. But there is much to be proud of. In particular, these lowlands of Holland do more than anywhere else to feed their compatriots.

The pea harvesters at Wigtoft lined up like an army of invasion: four gigantic juggernauts proceeding at the pace of little old Lincolnshire ladies. They left the lay-by and proceeded into Matthew Tunnard's seventeen-acre field to chomp up the plants.

The machines separated the pods, stalks and leaves and then shat them out from their rear end. From deep in the innards the peas themselves were then tipped into a trailer while still on the move, like a mid-air refuel or a drive-by sex act. From the trailer they went on to lorries whose drivers were commanded to get to the factories at Long Sutton or King's Lynn within two hours. Longer than that, the product starts deteriorating. The Lincolnshire air was suffused with the sweet smell of fresh peas. 'Wonderful!' I said. 'You get sick of it after seven weeks,' said Steve Francis.

Francis is managing director of Fen Peas, one of the two large conglomerates that dominate the UK pea-picking business. This is an almost wholly Lincolnshire branch of agriculture. All harvests are stressful but the pea harvest is recognised as the most fiendish of all, because peas – far from being easy-peasy – are temperamental little sods. They don't like it cold; they don't like it dry; they don't like it wet (which is what wrecked the 2012 crop); and they don't even like it hot, which, after three weeks of heatwave, was piling pressure on Francis in 2013. 'There is now no such thing as a normal summer,' he said. 'Or winter, autumn or spring.' Then there are the crows, pigeons, slugs and snails (which get into the packaging). The harvest lasts about seven weeks from late June to August: 'You go to sleep thinking about it,' says Francis. 'You dream about it. You wake up thinking about it. And you dread the phone ringing because it will be bad news.' This is farming; if there is good news no one would mention it anyway.

But it's true about peas being difficult. Even the most zealous grow-your-own gardener is usually content to leave them to the pros. A good garden harvest might deliver a few hundred peas. I did a rough calculation with Francis, who is responsible for 5,000 acres round the county, and we reckoned he produced about 100 billion.

Fen Peas is the kind of collaborative effort now out of fashion in agriculture: the farmers do the planting; Francis organises the harvest. For the seven-week season he employs the grand total of fourteen contract labourers round-the-clock, working twelve-hour shifts. There would be no sleep in Wigtoft tonight for the workers nor, I imagine, the neighbours.

But the balance of power round here is different from that of a Home Counties village where rich incomers move in and moan about crowing cocks and church bells. One paradox of Lincolnshire is that residential property is cheap but agricultural land very dear. This alluvial soil is fantastically fertile. A bit further north from Wigtoft, round Wrangle and Old Leake, are the Boston silts, 'the best farmland of all', according to Alan Stennett. The soil is dark and soft and crumbly, suggesting mystical properties; even the cabbage fields looked strangely yummy. Putting a seed into the soil here is like igniting a firework which will go whoosh any moment – light the blue touchpaper and retire. Possibly to Barbados.

The problem is that the land is so expensive it is unaffordable for a normal farmer. 'These kinds of farms are fetching up to £30,000 an acre. You couldn't get a return on capital because your income wouldn't service the loan,' explains Stennett. Prices are dictated by outside investors seeking to make use of farmland's exemption from inheritance tax. And there are *fields* over 100 acres, the size of a small farm in the west of England.

Francis's team will not even have the satisfaction of producing the finest petits pois; that's a different part of the business. The best of the 100 billion may end up as supermarket own-brand garden peas; the lowest grade may end up in tinned stew. If these peas are too tender, I was told, they can explode. But they make good mushy peas. To be eaten with chips made from Lincolnshire potatoes. And of course fish.

At 7 next morning the bell rang and business began at the Grimsby Fish Market, as it has done every Monday to Friday, bank holidays excepted, since shortly after our own ancestors crawled out of the freezing waters. There is a sense of departed glory.

The market is a long, low, cold building and it was far from full, either of people or fish. About 100 merchants stood around and followed the three auctioneers in a game of follow-my-leader round three separate stashes: cod, haddock and mixed, which meant everything else.

In the way of business between professionals, the details were barely comprehensible. The auctioneer pointed to a box, mentioned a seemingly random number, went up or down – usually down – and, without any response being audible or visible to me, announced the name of the successful bidder. Then a handful of tickets were strewn on to the box to indicate the deceased fish's new owners. Only the cod appeared to register any emotion whatever: a wild-eyed surmise about the sudden turn of fate that brought them to captivity and this indignity.

It was all over inside three-quarters of an hour, which was middling kind of business, normal for midweek. Monday is a busy day, when the weekend catch comes in, and there can still be 4,000 boxes for sale, each containing maybe four or five large cod or up to fifty tiddlers. But a couple of decades ago there might have been 30,000 boxes.

Grimsby flourished from the mid-nineteenth century, when the combination of trains and primitive refrigeration allowed its fish to reach London. All Lincolnshire's great summits are man-made, most of them being ecclesiastical, but the 200-foot brick-built, wafer-thin Grimsby Dock Tower is perhaps the most startling of the lot. Completed in 1852 to provide hydraulic power for the dock gates, it was based, with Victorian swagger, on the Torre del Mangia (the Tower of the Eater, which is appropriate) in Siena. The tower still lords it over an area that is otherwise rotting away and classically ripe for redevelopment: it is easy to imagine the chi-chi bars and restaurants and apartment blocks that might follow.

Except that this is Grimsby, which is very un- all that. And the docks have considerable resilience. The fish market has suffered not just from the decline, almost to nothingness, of the Grimsby trawler fleet but also because many big buyers now bypass the middle men. Against that there are an increasing number of restaurants (not necessarily in Grimsby) that care about quality, and the market's owners felt confident enough to do a big modernisation job on the hall in 2012. The docks themselves still have a certain vibrancy, supporting the new offshore wind farms. And Carl Hunnysett, the market's operations manager, was keen to explain to me – as my mother used to say whenever there was girlfriend trouble – that there were plenty of fish in the sea.

By the market reception desk there were black-and-white pictures of the old market from 1965: more crowded; somewhat less bio-secure, with the smoking not confined to fish; but recognisably the same place and the same all-male bantering world, with a tubby auctioneer making notes in the same sort of account book. 'Probably the same book,' said Hunnysett. A few years back, the market tried to stage its own Big Bang with auctions being conducted electronically from a different room. But the buyers wanted to smell the fish.

That morning, across the county, a more familiar kind of market was also gearing up. This was Boston, a famous old town, once a port second only to London, home of the Boston Stump, the country's biggest parish church, grander than half of England's cathedrals. It dwindled into an obscure and elderly town: I was greeted by signs urging me towards a big exhibition – for hearing aids. Now it has had an influx of energetic, young, go-getting people anxious to better themselves. Boston is not happy.

It is a town where market day still matters, partly because it is at the centre of such a fertile area: the stalls sell produce that looks as if it has come from the soil and not a conveyor belt at a Chinese lettuce factory. More than that, market day is a social occasion, a chance to chat to friends, and also to whisper sotto voce about the change that has come upon this part of Lincolnshire – suddenly, unexpectedly, unwontedly.

By the war memorial I met Sue Ransome, matriarch of the most formidable political dynasty to emerge from anywhere called Boston since the Kennedys. There the analogy ends. Sue and Don used to run rival taxi firms until they formed their own coalition and got married. They flirted with all the mainstream political parties until they heard Nigel Farage, the UKIP leader, and thought he talked sense. The offspring agreed. In the 2013 county council election the Ransome family stood en masse in different Boston wards as UKIP candidates for Lincolnshire County Council. Sue and her daughters Felicity and Elizabeth stormed in; Don and eldest daughter Jodie narrowly missed out. Their son, Sam, was going to stand too but, at nineteen, he shied away for fear of being thought weird by his mates.

Sue Ransome was edgy when I called. 'What do you want to talk about?'

'The issues that got you elected.'

'Oh, you mean potholes.'

Potholes, Poles; similar word, same hopeless anger. Stable, sleepy, hearing-aidy Boston grew by almost 16 per cent from 2001 to 2011, almost entirely due to the arrival of migrants to work in agriculture and its associated processing plants, which form Lincolnshire's main business. Though peas require almost no human input at all, Lincolnshire's other vegetables – like cabbages, caulis and sprouts, are highly labour-intensive. It is not soft work.

Sue Ransome's complaints about the migrants were not venomous, but not always convincing either. 'If you see Boston at 2 in the morning, it's just vile. They're urinating in the street. Don't get me wrong. It's English and foreigners. But the foreigners don't seem to have any regard for our way of life.' Some allegations had the ring of truth ('I've heard of Russians going to Latvia and Lithuania to buy EU passports for £100.') and she was not without sympathy for the migrants themselves: 'It's exploitation and it's being done by our own people. We've heard from the workers how much they pay for transport, rent and everything, and the conditions in which they live.'

Don Ransome looked back to the old days: 'Fifteen years ago a good cauli-cutting gang would earn £500 a week each. True, they might spend it in the pub and it would all be in cash. But I don't think anyone gets the chance to get that money now. The locals don't get the chance to get those jobs.' Quite. First, the Portuguese undercut the English. Then the East Europeans undercut the Portuguese. The next step was assumed to be a great influx of Romanians and Bulgarians, who were due to receive full working rights across the EU and the chance to undercut everyone else.

And so Boston finds itself at the sharp end of modern agribusiness. The public buy on price, not quality; the supermarkets screw their suppliers to get their edge; the suppliers screw their workers; the migrants, for whom bad British wages beat good money back home, climb in. It's modern capitalism. We will come back shortly to the woman who made Britain embrace that.

Skegness is a classically down-at-heel east coast resort, made famous by its prancing railway-poster symbol, the Jolly Fisherman (created in 1908 by a jobbing artist, John Hassall, who had never been near the place) and the accompanying slogan: 'Skegness is SO bracing' – i.e. freezing cold.

A few miles up the road, nearer to Ingoldmells, is Skeggy's other claim to fame: the first and almost the last Butlins holiday camp, opened in 1936. Once these camps dotted the coast. Just three are left: Stalag Luft Bognor (see Chapter 8); Minehead, where its presence appals the bien-pensant Somerset incomers; and Skeggy, where somehow – out of town and on this bleak coast – it still seems to work. Like Charles Ryder returning to wartime Brideshead, I mouthed the phrase, 'I have been here before.'

I was either four or five, and now have only a handful of memories, all vivid: the chalets; the toilet blocks at the end of each row marked 'Lads' and 'Lassies'; the communal meals in a vast hall ('Good morning, Glouces-ter House,' a voice would say over the loudspeaker); the Glamorous Gran and Knobbly Knees contests; and being forced to remove my vest on the beach and having a screaming fit – the weather must have been SO bra-cing. My father had urgent business to prevent him from joining us: that's not a memory, it's a certainty.

The chalets, which had a basin with a cold tap, have been replaced by low-rise blocks with mod cons. The boarding-school-style house names have been replaced by terraces with signs saying 'Pebblestone Place' or 'Cuttlefish Walk'. The best look like well-designed housing estates; the worst like the Bates Motel. The camp is guarded by an eight-foot spiked fence on a berm rendering the sea invisible except from a few of the upper-most rooms. This is (a) the sea defence that is essential on this frangible coast, (b) to keep out intruders, and (c), I suspect, because Butlins can-not quite shake off its regimental mentality. There is an exit to the beach, though it is hard to find. I assume there is more profit in keeping people in.

On the whole I was impressed with the way Butlins – sold on twice since Sir Billy Butlin's heyday – has adapted to the modern world. There is a fancy new swimming pool, almost as warm as the Bath spa, and a tented entertainment complex built like the Millennium Dome. I was just too late for Billy Bear's *Buzz Boom Bang Show*, but could have queued for the *Barney Photoshoot*.

As I wandered, I came across one very nice touch: an original chalet, preserved and listed. The original furnishings – the sailing-boat pattern curtains and B-monogrammed pillow cases – have all gone, so the interior looks grimmer than it actually was. But the outside still looks attractive in a mock-Tudor Woodhall Spa-ish kind of way.

A lot of campers passed by and peered, usually approvingly. 'Nice, isn't it?' said one.

A boy of about ten rushed up to the window and stared inside for a moment. 'Weird!' he cried, and rushed off.

The Living Health Chiropractic Clinic and Holistic Retreat takes up two terraced houses on a busy corner on the edge of Grantham town centre. It offers Lava Shell Massage, Body Wraps, St Tropez Tanning, Waxing and Pedicures. Level with the first-floor windows there is a marker stone with gold-leaf lettering. It is both grander than the blue plaque norm, and further out of reach, to deter vandals. 'BIRTHPLACE OF THE RT. HON. MARGARET THATCHER, M.P.,' it reads. 'FIRST WOMAN PRIME MINISTER OF GREAT BRITAIN AND NORTHERN IRELAND.'

This was Alderman Roberts's famous corner shop, where his daughter Margaret began her long life's journey to a funeral at St Paul's. One had imagined a poky backstreet shop – but this must have been a premium site even in those days. The clinic's remedies sound evanescent and subject to fashion, but it has been there for twenty years, succeeding a restaurant. It seems very un-Mrs T and there is nothing left of her days except a rather lovely fireplace, of dark wood with leaf-pattern tiles, and that has been moved. Carol Thatcher turned up once for a treatment but her mother never did. 'I don't think she liked Grantham,' said Sandra, the practice manager, who has grown bored with such questions.

One tries to imagine what might have happened had Margaret Roberts remained in Lincolnshire. She would never have stayed in the shop. But she might have married an estate agent, settled in one of the unprepossessing villages and turned herself into Lynda Snell, pouring all that furious energy and intellect into ensuring the success of the summer fete and the Christmas pantomime, reducing her neighbours to terror-stricken admiration.

She might have joined the council herself and devoted herself to Lincolnshire, perhaps stiffening its backbone and trying to give it some self-respect and identity as a county and not just a random collection of communities. She might even have had a statue by now. As it is, that issue is problematic. Too much hatred, even in a county without much energy for it.

I wish she had got to work on Lincolnshire, great Yorkshire's little brother which has drifted into obscurity. Oh, big, amiable lummox of the shires, pull yourself together, take some pride in yourself, move those signs to the proper borders. You're not flat, you're not boring, you're not ugly. OK? Hail to thee, good, honest county. Now buck up.

32. *The horse has bolted*

BERKSHIRE

Two old boys called John and Jim were reminiscing about life in the Huntley & Palmers biscuit factory that used to dominate Reading. They had started there as apprentices and remained until it closed in 1976.

'Do you remember they used to play *Housewives' Choice* and all the women and girls used to sing along? ... Certain places you thought "this is a dirty filthy hole", like the fruit room, you stuck to the floor with currants ... The worst place, that was the cheese room ... You had some good smells, though, didn't you? No. 6 especially, the one that did the ginger nuts, that was the one people remember the most, wafting across Reading ... When Huntley & Palmers closed down you couldn't believe it ... We were brought up that the factory was there ... All the manufacturing was going from the town ... I watched the last Cornish wafers come out of no. 2 oven, some of the bakers had been there since the 20s and 30s, they were in tears ...'

I didn't meet John and Jim, with their ripe, almost extinct accents that would once have been described as Berkshire. They were interviewed as part of the remarkable BBC exercise in recording ordinary life known as *The Listening Project*. I happened to catch it when it was broadcast on Radio 4 in 2012 and was captivated. It was the story of a living and a way of life that had vanished not because the world had changed – the world has not lost its taste for shortbread and ginger nuts – but because the attitudes of industry had changed and, above all, Berkshire had changed.

Reading was known for the three B's: beer, bulbs and biscuits. Suttons the seedsmen went west (Devon) in the 1970s. The remnant of the old Simonds' brewery (later Courage) closed in 2010. Reading is hardly struggling without them: it has become a high-tech hub and grown so much its phone numbers have had a digit lopped off the code and added on to the number, the British indicator of a serious metropolis. In 2012 it was reported that Reading's residential property was worth over £50 billion, second pro rata only to London; ahead in total of far larger places like Edinburgh and Liverpool. There is an American swagger to the place.

The last remnant of Huntley & Palmers' once-vast Reading estate is a single red-brick building on the corner of Gas Works Road, a name no longer allowed even a road sign. The building itself is equally discreet. The biscuit company name is on the gable but there is just an anonymous side door with bells, and the ground-floor windows are tinted, in a mind-your-own-business way. Maybe flats, maybe not.

As in most American cities, the heart of Reading is now out of town. I drove to Green Park, which has large plate-glass office buildings with generous space for cars set amidst the vegetation categorised in *The Flora of Berkshire* as 'botanically stereotyped post-industrial shrubbery'. It is not an ugly place. Indeed, on a gorgeous early September day at the end of a warm summer, there was a delicious hint of Silicon Valley. Even the numbering is American-style – i.e. inflated and illogical: Brook Drive goes 100, 200, 250, 300, 350, 400. Green Park has everything a high-tech young executive might need: a nursery, a gym, inter-company fun runs. There is even a branch of Costco, the American members-only discount warehouse which functions as a cult for people obsessed with bulk-buying vast quantities of washing powder. Costco has a strange system of class-related faux-exclusivity: retired insurance salesmen are welcome to join; retired biscuit factory workers are not. (And nor are writers.)

Next door is the football stadium, named – like much of Berkshire – after the businessman, philanthropist and American-style self-promoter

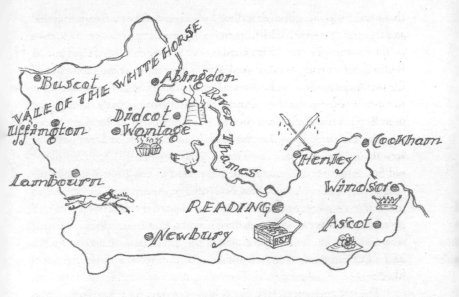

John Madejski. The ground is the home of Reading FC, who used to be known as the Biscuitmen but changed their nickname to the Royals. Had I known at school that it was possible to change a nickname I would have got my marketing department to come up with something more appropriate than 'Worm' and 'Bogsy'. It is a different world and one must embrace it. For Green Park is perhaps Britain's most perfect example of its type: a nowhere place for nowhere people.

The traditional shape of Berkshire is that of a boot: not a sexy, slithery, high-heeled boot like Italy, but an old working man's boot – hard-worn, toe curled upwards, the leather misshapen. A seedsman's boot, perhaps. This was because the entire northern boundary – bar a little jiggle round Oxford – was formed by the Thames, meandering north, south, east and occasionally even west along much of the river's 215 miles.

In mileage and in the English imagination, Berkshire is the quintessential Thames-side county. The eastern stretch is that of blazers and Bolly, of *Three Men in a Boat* ('I call the whole thing bally foolishness,' said Montmorency the dog as they set off). Upstream the river becomes more contemplative; this is the countryside of *Wind in the Willows*, a work that has never dated even as the water voles, Ratty's descendants, flirt with extinction. And everywhere, in the mind's eye, glide the swans, with their air of serene contempt for all human endeavour.

Two months earlier, with the heatwave of 2013 in full cry, I had joined the gathering at the Compleat Angler Hotel on the Berkshire bank of the river opposite Marlow. The dress code, as at nearby Ascot, was ludicrous. As the temperatures soared into the eighties, the principals had to wear thick braided blazers; the rest of the cast were dressed for bit parts in *The Pirates of Penzance*. A small flotilla was about to set out on Day 3 of Royal Swan Upping week.

Swan-upping! The very phrase is redolent of English summer, of languid days on the river, even though hardly anyone can explain its purpose succinctly. This includes the participants. What's it about? Well, um, it's about languid days on the river. Very languid. I sat in the press launch all morning. Not much was missing from the idyllic picture except, for us, the chilled Sauvignon Blanc being served on the attendant pleasure boats. And also the attendant swans.

Three groups of rowers in their G&S outfits took to the water – those representing the Worshipful Company of Dyers in blue, the Vintners' Company in white, royalty in scarlet, as though it were a more complicated version of the Boat Race. Swans have only four possible owners under British law: the Abbotsbury swannery in Dorset, which is not relevant here, and the two livery companies under rights going back to the fifteenth century; the rest, by default, can be claimed by the Crown, represented here by the Queen's Swan Marker, David Barber. This is not the same as being owned by the Crown, as you might discover if a swan smashed through your window and you tried to sue Her Majesty.

Notionally, the aim is to decide which of this year's cygnets belong to which owners. This is fairly pointless: anyone who has seen a swan will know they belong only to themselves. The Uppers give the cry 'All Up!' whenever they spot a family, whereupon they converge on the brood, surround it, truss up the parents and claim the cygnets as their own, according to a complicated formula of heredity. The swans decreed not to belong to the Crown used to get a nick on the beaks – one for the Dyers, two for the Vintners, hence the old pub name the Swan with Two Necks, a corruption of nicks. These days they are ringed instead. The Queen (the 'Seigneur of the Swans') always gets the benefit of any doubt.

Then the Queen's Swan Warden, Professor Chris Perrins of Oxford University, puts each cygnet in a little hammock resting on coat hangers

('It's not high-tech but it works and it's cheap'), weighs it and measures its head to determine its age. Sometimes a cygnet might have a fish hook attached and this can be removed. If it's very sick, it can go to a swan rescue centre. Then the party moves on upstream, leaving the swans potentially healthier but perhaps mildly traumatised. There is no means of communicating in Swannish 'We come in peace'.

My colleagues on the press launch were photographers, mostly working for local papers, getting a nice shot for the *Henley Standard* or the *Windsor Observer*, or, with luck, getting a cracking shot for the nationals of, say, the Vintners' Swan Marker falling in. This had happened earlier in the week but the snappers were too far away.

The small-town papers could make more of swan-upping:

LOCAL FAMILY IN KIDNAP HORROR

—

Swans trussed up: 'We thought we'd all die'

—

GANG ESCAPES UPRIVER

These temporary kidnaps should have been a regular occurrence on this fine morning but they weren't. There were only three uppings all morning and only once, at Earley, did our boat get a really good view. The ride not having been interrupted much by swans, we arrived in Henley, the lunch stop, an hour early. This pattern continued for the rest of the week, Professor Perrins told me later. The stately progress begins at Sunbury and ends at Abingdon, lasting five days and seventy-nine miles. 'The first two days were very good, Wednesday was poor, Thursday was poor, Friday was very poor,' he reported. This was an extreme manifestation of a trend over the past few years, which even the Swan Warden cannot wholly explain. He thought the cold March may have been one factor, delaying and inhibiting breeding.

Nonetheless it seems to tie in with the curious and under-explored history of the swan on the Thames. Their numbers rose after 1900 when gravel pits began to be developed and provided lovely breeding grounds. War was unhelpful: swans were more likely to get eaten. Between the wars they expanded to culling point. Then they shot up again in the 1950s, before falling again because, it was eventually realised, they were ingesting the lead weights used by fishermen. When the lead was banned they surged once more. But now it's tricky. They are probably being hampered by the creeping urbanisation of the riverbank: the decline of the gentle sloping edges and little beaches that make ideal nests, and the growth of concrete moorings.

But in another sense the swans are natural townies. They don't care for London much, but the cygnets, once they leave the nest, increasingly congregate by the bridges of the smaller towns. There is an extraordinary parallel with the behaviour of the human student population. In town they can find company, lark about and eventually, after two or three years, get a mate. And they should acquire a veneer of education, in their case enough local knowledge to find a good site for a nest. In the meantime, there is an infinite supply of nice old ladies who will chuck them bits of bread on the way back from the shops, the avian equivalent of the pizza delivery man.

Thus it seems possible, as the humans migrate upriver from Middlesex into Berkshire, the swans are moving back the other way and becoming, like the fox, suburban rather than rural. At the end of the week the Swan Marker compiles a report on the swan population of the Thames. But swan-upping seems to lead to theories rather than hard evidence. Is it any use? 'The only historical records we have of swans anywhere in the country are from the swan-uppers,' says Professor Perrins. 'It's not high science but it's useful and no one else does it. It does no harm, it does some good.' And it is jolly good fun and the continuation of ancient tradition. And that, in Berkshire, is being rapidly eroded.

In 1998, long after the great carve-up of 1974, Berkshire County Council was abolished, as happened later in Bedfordshire and Cheshire, although the county – for ceremonial purposes – was deemed to be still in existence. The Lord Lieutenant of Berkshire at the time asked a Downing Street official where Berkshire now was exactly. '*You* are Berkshire,' he was told.

Perhaps the average Costco-haunting Green Park screen slave is unaware that Reading is even meant to be in Berkshire. But at least Berkshire is in Reading, to be found in a small but agreeable office shared with the county archivist. Berkshire's name turned out to be Mary Bayliss, which is a plain, un-Lord Lieutenanty kind of name, though it did disguise the fact that her father was Viscount Bridgeman and himself a onetime Lord Lieutenant of Shropshire.

Mrs Bayliss is a pleasant, conscientious, discreet woman, looking nothing like as close to the retiring age of seventy-five as she claimed, who had emerged through the arcane process that governs appointment to her arcane post after several decades as a magistrate and a lifetime of good works, rendering her well suited to her quasi-royal duties.

She was only mildly discommoded by having to deal with six 'unitary authorities' rather than one county council, though its absence meant that there was no one whose job was to cherish the county, promote it and maintain the signs on the borders which have now started to vanish. Her prime responsibility is for the 'arrangements of royalty on official visits to Berkshire'. This is slightly more onerous and interesting than in most counties because the royals are on hand and it is not unknown for the Queen to pop out after breakfast in Windsor, open a surgery or a school, and be back home for elevenses. The Lord Lieutenant is not expected to be present if she pops out to Sainsbury's, or for events in Windsor Great Park or Ascot Racecourse, which count as her back garden.

Still, this is not just any old county but, uniquely, *Royal* Berkshire, its status giving it the right of audience; its incarnation, Mrs Bayliss, was able to deliver a loyal address in which she told Her Majesty how proud Berkshire was to have provided a royal bride, Kate Middleton of Buckle-bury, aka the Duchess of Cambridge. Occasionally, the Lord Lieutenant is called upon to deputise for royalty by presenting minor gongs and, she says, 'I do see it as part of my job to try to keep the county together,' which is harder than it ought to be.

The White Horse stands above the village of Uffington – home of Thomas Hughes and John Betjeman – on the edge of White Horse Hill, overlooking the Vale of the White Horse. Unlike other chalk figures, the horse's 3,000-year-old antiquity is not in doubt. But it is oddly stylised and anatomically bizarre, as though designed as a logo by some Bronze Age whizz kids. That may be somewhere near the truth: one explanation is that it was cut by the Atrebates, the tribe whose territory evolved into Berkshire, as a standard to rally their forces against their enemies. It is thought that the Atrebates were the allies of the Romans against the recalcitrants north of the river. Later the Thames would be the frontier between Wessex and Mercia. It was probably always a boundary. It still is, in London ('Sarf of the river, guv!? At this time of night!?').

And the horse served as a symbol, *the* symbol, of Berkshire until the 1970s. Its limbs being oddly shaped and disconnected, the horse never looked as though it was going anywhere – not even along the brow of the hill towards the long barrow known as Wayland's Smithy, where, so the legend goes, the god of smiths will reshoe any horse for a groat. Then it was decided that the Thames no longer constituted a proper boundary, and the horse was captured by Oxfordshire. Indeed, the whole ankle section of the Berkshire boot was detached, including even the old county town of Abingdon, leaving Berkshire as merely a feeble slipper, never a good move orthopedically, and in this case the first step towards rendering the entire county meaningless. In its favour, the change slightly eased the arrangements for rubbish collection in villages west of Oxford.

The Flora of Berkshire has the discreet subtitle 'Including Those Parts of Modern Oxfordshire That Lie to the South of the River Thames'. Its author, Mick Crawley, Professor of Plant Ecology at Imperial College, likes to describe himself as the leader of POFLOB, the Popular Front for the Liberation of Occupied Berkshire. He calls the boundary change 'Mercia's belated triumph', adding, 'It robbed Berkshire of its county symbol, along with much of its botanical diversity.' I did hear the phrase 'Occupied Berkshire' a few times while I was there.

POFLOB is of course just a professorial joke. But there was correspondence in *The Times* in 1974 that had very chilling echoes. The paper had reported on the last-ditch, unavailing efforts to prevent the transfer of the White Horse and then published a letter from the archaeologist Jacquetta Hawkes, wife of J. B. Priestley: 'A small, harmless thing in a world of great and terrible things?' she asked. 'Not at all. This disregard of people's feelings, of the power of symbols to give us meaning and identity, is slowly destroying us.'

There followed a strange and convoluted response from the Conservative MP for Abingdon, Airey Neave, suggesting that since Uffington was moving counties, the White Horse had to go too otherwise his constituents in Uffington would 'violently resent' its removal from the parish. (He ignored the obvious solution of not meddling.) Five years later Neave was brutally murdered, blown up in his car by an Irish Republican splinter group, weeks before his ally Margaret Thatcher would become prime minister and almost certainly have made him her Northern Ireland Secretary. He was victim of a dispute where people really did 'violently resent' the imposition of ill-judged boundaries from outside.

In Berkshire the changes merely encouraged the county's drift into anonymity, driven by incomers, forcing up property prices and pushing out old biscuitmen and other relics. Berkshire has been undergoing Londonisation for centuries, but the process has taken an unusual path, very different from that of other commuter counties. In one sense, it began early: courtiers and other riff-raff have been hanging round Ascot and Windsor for centuries. But, against that, royal influence kept the railway away from Berkshire's south-eastern corner until the late 1850s: the trains to Waterloo are still much slower and feebler than the Paddington services direct from Reading, which, with its proximity to Heathrow, the M4 and M25, is the best-connected town in a generally ill-connected country.

Of course, east Berkshire is full of commuters. But west of Reading there are very few stations. You could commute from Reading itself, but what would be the point? It has not, as Betjeman feared, become a suburb of London but an alternative honeypot within the general sticky gloop of the South-East. So to some extent has Newbury, HQ of that twenty-first-century behemoth, Vodafone.

Pevsner called Berkshire 'half home county, half West Country'. Betjeman, writing in *The English Counties* in the late 1940s, saw Berkshire, 'this battleground of the centuries', becoming once again 'a prominent seat of war ... in the latest battle, that between the old agricultural way of life and the new industrial one'. That isn't quite what has happened. The old way of life has been smothered all right, but not by industrialisation or even commuterisation, but by a more subtle process. That has spread from the Home County side towards the west, where Berkshire shades pictur-esquely into the chalkiness of Wiltshire and Hampshire.

If anyone still reads *Tom Brown's Schooldays*, written by Thomas Hughes of Uffington, they probably skim the opening chapters describing Tom's pre-boarding school life beneath the White Horse. It includes this fogeyish grumble:

> O young England! young England! you who are born into these racing railroad times ... You're all in the ends of the earth, it seems to me, as soon as you get your necks out of the educational collar, for midsummer holidays, long vacations, or what not ... All I say is, you don't know your own lanes and woods and fields. Though you may be choke-full of science, not one in twenty of you knows where to find the wood-sorrel, or bee-orchis ... We had to cut out our own amusements within a walk or a ride of home. And so we got to know all the country folk and their ways and songs and stories by heart, and went over the fields and woods and hills, again and again, till we made friends of them all. We were Berkshire, or

Gloucestershire, or Yorkshire boys; and you're young cosmopolites, belonging to all countries and no countries.

He was obviously addressing the kinds of boys who went on to Rugby. Now the country folk and their ways are going too. The yokels used to scour the chalk outlines of the White Horse like affectionate stable lads and make a party of the process. They are all but gone now. Instead Berkshireness may be defined by one family. As the *Evening Standard* once memorably put it, 'Prince William is known to love the middle-class ordinariness of the Middletons' lives and frequently enjoys kitchen suppers at Carole and Mike's £4.8 million home in Bucklebury.' Not every girl in Berkshire actually marries a prince, but a lot of them would be plausible contenders.

'The fact is that the area is almost entirely populated by wealthy people,' says Professor Crawley. 'The scenery is going to stay good or maybe get better, if they knock down the Didcot power station. You won't have wind farms here because they'll fight them. The countryside's affected by more insidious things.' No one sees the nitrogen pollution that's in the very rain, rendering the flora ever less diverse, more post-industrial, more Green Parkish. Berkshire's most distinctive fauna – the ground-nesting nightjars, woodlarks and Dartford warblers of the heathland near the Surrey border – can only be protected in official reserves because their most virulent enemies are not the wicked humans but their doggies.

The last fragile bloom of pure Berkshire eccentricity was the artist Sir Stanley Spencer (1891–1959), who was obsessed with women, Jesus, his home village of Cookham and himself. He appeared to be working towards bringing all these themes together in his unfinished masterpiece *Christ Preaching at Cookham Regatta*. Spencer liked to tell people he felt ill crossing the Thames to Bourne End. Since he was actually quite well travelled, I am inclined to think this was all part of his shtick. Alas, Berkshire has no one left even to play the game now.

The towns and villages of west Berkshire used to be dotted with racehorse stables, taking advantage of the springy downland in a county with three racecourses: Ascot, Newbury and Windsor. Most of the stables have gone: Wantage is not even a one-horse town. The great horsey villages of East and West Ilsley are down to one yard each. And so on. In a county of ordinary middle-class £4.8 million houses the land is just too, too tempting.

Even in the mini-Newmarket of Lambourn, only one trainer is left on the High Street: Harry Dunlop at Windsor House. 'I don't think it's sad,' says Dunlop. 'It's probably a natural progression. The village is obviously expanding. The important thing is that new yards are being built up the road closer to the gallops.' About thirty trainers remain, not so much in the village itself, but mainly in Upper Lambourn, where they are less prone to irritate the school-run mums by clogging up the morning traffic.

I fell in love with Lambourn, partly because the Lambourn Valley looked amazing and partly because it is a true working village where the horsey business mixes seamlessly with real life – Goff's Bloodstock office next to Cream Hairdressers; Racing Welfare opposite the George; retired stable lads shuffling into the pub via the Co-op to whisper rumours about the favourite in the 3.30 and yarn about the day their colt won the St Leger. The pubs have suffered a bit because the cast has changed. The Irish stable staff were replaced first by East Europeans (who mainly drink at home) and now by South Asians (who hardly drink at all). The normal reasons apply – they want less money and come to work more readily – plus an extra one: they weigh less.

Christina, Harry's sparky wife, kindly drove me up to Mandown, where the gallops are concentrated. They are under the control of the Jockey Club now, bringing both investment and protection. She showed me the all-weather canters and the straight mile, which arrows its way in the direction, appropriately enough, of the White Horse. At least the racehorses have not yet been rustled by Oxfordshire.

At the top of the hill we looked down on the gallops belonging to the champion jumping trainer Nicky Henderson, one-time master of Windsor House but now with his own private domain at Seven Barrows. His last lot of horses were doing their morning work, while in the fields all around the farmers were frantically working to get their harvest home.

It was blazing hot for September and the scene looked timelessly idyllic. But English idylls are never timeless. These fields used to be full of sheep – East Ilsley once had the largest sheep fair in England – but in wartime the farms switched to arable and mostly stayed that way. West Berkshire was famous for elm trees, but they all died just after the local government reform, as if they had themselves been uprooted. And the forecasters were warning that summer would be gone by the following morning, hence the farmers' rush. Trainers always feel vulnerable: a star racehorse is always just one bad stumble away from the vet's rifle. But at that moment this seemed like England *in excelsis*.

I went down to Seven Barrows, to the barrows themselves – Neolithic long ones, dating back to 3500 BC. I wandered for a couple of hours along the Ridgeway, with Didcot power station my constant companion. I slipped into horseless Wantage, with its statue of King Alfred.

Finally I took myself to the river again, to Buscot Weir, in the north-westernmost corner of historic Berkshire. The day was starting to decline and so was the summer. Some teenage boys were drying themselves off after a dip and picnickers were just packing up for the drive home. I was a little puzzled by the geography, since the path to the river was hidden, and got into conversation with the lock-keeper. He told me this was the border of three counties: Wiltshire, Gloucestershire and Oxfordshire.

'As far as I'm concerned, Berkshire's in there somewhere,' I said.

'I suppose you don't believe in metric either.'

Well, actually, now you come to mention it ...

I had to cross over to the north bank to follow the Thames Path, so heaven knows what county I was in, ancient or modern: Gloucestershire, maybe. All was peaceful in the sunlit afternoon: Ratty and Mole were probably dozing nearby. I got as far as a wartime pillbox, one of the hundreds erected along the Thames to protect against a possible German invasion to match the Roman one 2,000 years earlier. It was a long-lost cousin to the one miles downstream at my school near Wallingford, where we used to sit and smoke, pretending to watch out for Jerry, in reality watching out for Josh, the tyrannical housemaster.

I had a sudden sense that some day, sometime, in a future I cannot possibly imagine, the Thames might become an important border again.

July/September 2013

~~~~~~~

Three of Didcot's six cooling towers were demolished in July 2014.

33. *First we take Hunstanton ...*

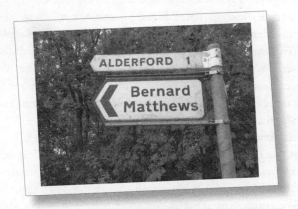

NORFOLK

O wing to personal circumstances, I arrived in England's fourth-largest county a week later than originally planned. By that time, it had moved closer to being the fifth-largest and further away from being no. 3, several chunks of its territory having opted to secede from Norfolk and merge instead with the North Sea.

It happened in Happisburgh, which is pronounced 'Hazebruh', happy not being exactly the word. The first big storm of autumn had taken several lumps away from the cliffs along Beach Road. This is an ongoing process. In particular, it had removed yet more of Bryony Nierop-Reading's back garden, leaving her bedroom about fifteen feet from the cliff edge, the last part of that being overhang.

Mrs Nierop-Reading had not intended to be on the front line of the nation's feeble costal defences. When she bought her bungalow six years ago it was two houses back from the sea. 'I've got a beautiful view,' she said, looking out of her patched-up living room to what was left of the garden. 'Getting better by the day. Unfortunately.'

Mrs N-R is a grandmother, a retired maths teacher and a plants-woman, the sort one might find running the pony club, the sort usu-ally called 'redoubtable'. And that is precisely what her house now is: a redoubt, increasingly surrounded by an implacably advancing enemy. The two houses in front of her have fallen; the two behind her have been demolished. She had refused all blandishments to leave.

She admitted that this last assault had frightened her and that she was starting to waver. The roof on the extension went and the wind had hurled some huge timbers clean over the shed. The problem is that this coast does not only collapse when you might expect it. Most of the dam-age was done on the third day of the storm, when the wind had largely abated. And even after that, two days before I got there, her neighbour Arthur Richmond, who runs the Seaside Tea Rooms, was blithely walking his dogs along the other spur of Beach Road: 'I saw a crack in the tarmac that hadn't been there before. Then I turned away, heard a thud and it had gone: about a six- or seven-foot stretch of road.'

Bryony showed me what was left of her domain, though mercifully she did not attempt to show me the back garden. Instead we went out the front, where the road now came to a halt at an earth bank left by the tempest.

'That's what's really scary. People walking up the bank to see what's on the other side. On the other side there's nothing.'

'You're terrified for *them*? They're terrified for *you*!'

Happisburgh is in the vanguard of a battlefront stretching up eastern England. There have been half-hearted attempts to defend it but essen-tially government policy is to let this lonely, often forlorn coastline take its chance. The houses behind Bryony's were known as Railway Cottages; and the Hill House pub in the village has a half-timbered signal box at the back, now used as a sea-view holiday let. But the trains never did reach Happisburgh, which is one reason it was always a resort for the caravan-ners and a few bloody-minded devotees who relish the cliffs and beach, even though these are not always where they were last time they visited.

There is something far stranger about this place. In the past few years, archaeologists have found dozens of sharpened flintstones on the beach. They are thought to represent hand-axes used by our forefathers, *Homo antecessor*, between 700,000 and 950,000 years ago – shall we say about 35,000 generations? I saw one at an exhibition in Norwich: it was about the size of a large brooch, brightly polished and rather nasty-looking, and

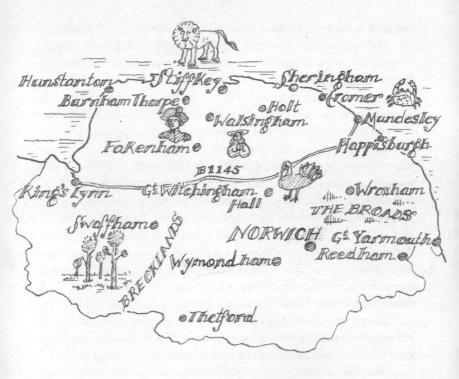

not very handy. Maybe they used it to cut up the roast mammoth for Sunday lunch.

The blurb described it as 'evidence of the oldest settlement in North-West Europe' – here, where human existence is now so evanescent and marginal, where Bryony's bungalow might not survive the next northerly and where the lighthouse, the pub and even the church may not last until the 35,003rd generation. It does not seem the obvious place to set up camp.

Bryony disagrees even now. 'I was very, very lucky to get this house and even if I have to leave it, I have had these years of absolute bliss living here.'

'What bliss?' I asked, looking out at the grey sea and the debris.

'The sheer pleasure of waking up at dawn and watching the sun rising over the sea, moving over the lighthouse and setting behind those trees.'

It is not just Happisburgh that one can imagine being decoupled from

England. 'If the rest of Britain sank beneath the waves, and Norfolk was left alone, islanded in the turmoil of the seas, it would, I think, survive without too much trouble,' wrote James Wentworth Day. 'Norfolk has always stood alone and aloof.'

Topographically, it is more likely to be the other way round, with Norfolk doing the sinking. But one can certainly imagine it floating off like a giant raft and hardly even noticing. One can argue it is pretty much an island already: the Little Ouse and Waveney both rise at South Lopham, the one heading west and north towards the Wash, the other turning east to meet the sea. These still form most of the landward boundary of the county, which has proved more stable than the seaward one. Or, as someone put it – possibly Malcolm Bradbury: 'Norfolk is cut off on three sides by the sea and on the fourth by British Rail.'

It is, quite obviously, the end of the line, to an extent matched only by Cornwall. No one passes through by chance. But Cornwall has more incomers and tourists and is more dependent on Plymouth, over the Devon border. Norfolk is thoroughly self-contained. Norwich is more than just a county town, more like a capital. It even feels like a capital, of an agreeable and small continental country: all those huddled, companionable streets complete with Dutch gables – plus repulsive modern additions that hint at a phase of joyless Communism. A bit like somewhere round the Baltic, maybe.

The fastest way to cross the world from here is to fly from Norwich Airport (sometimes described as an experience almost like owning a private jet) via Amsterdam, and stuff Heathrow. It is quicker to get to Schiphol than to Liverpool Street. This is the modern manifestation of Norfolk's old tradition of looking out to the once herring-rich sea and the Continent beyond, not inward to England.

Professor Peter Trudgill, the acknowledged expert on this subject, has argued that Norfolk dialect was heavily influenced by Dutch migrants fleeing religious persecution during the Inquisition, not just in its vocabulary but also in the S-less verb forms he calls East Anglian zero ('She look just wholly bee'tiful, she do.'). The old dialect has faded to vanishing point, as it has almost everywhere. The writer D. J. Taylor, who returned to live in his native Norwich after years in London, says he hasn't heard the old Norfolk male-endearment 'Bor' in years. But the accent hasn't gone, nor the zero verbs, nor the complete inability of the acting profession to get it right. It is, quite literally, inimitable. 'What you do hear all the time are the inflections, the way the sentences are put together,' says Taylor. 'I heard a woman in a shop quite recently say to her child, "Wha' d' yew want, one o' them ones then?"'

It was Taylor who alerted me to the traditional exchange that can be used to identify a proper Norfolk man anywhere in the world, the way spies have to complete a prearranged conversational exchange before being handed the secret papers:

'Dew yew fa'er keep a dickey, bor?'

'Yis, en e wan a fule ter roide 'im, wi ye come?'

The first line translates as 'Has your father got a donkey, old chap?' The reply should be self-explanatory.

Keith Simpson, the erudite MP for Broadland, was told by his grandfather that the characteristic local sentence was 'People in Norfolk, they speak so slow, that by the time thcy've got to the end of the sentence, why, blas' me, they've forgotten what the beginning was.'

Underlying all this are a deadpan manner and sense of irony that, Taylor insists, far eclipses the generic British irony that so foxes foreigners. 'I remember asking my brother to do something he didn't want to do. "Reckon I will," he replied. And it didn't just mean "Reckon I won't." It was much more complex than that.' There are countless stories of outsiders having baffling encounters in rural Norfolk that leave them completely confused as to who was the idiot in the conversation, but suspecting it might be them.

There is a tradition of agrarian radicalism that dates back at least to Kett's Rebellion (1549) and continued, if furtively, in the first three decades after the war when two rural constituencies regularly returned Labour MPs. But they did so with the perversity implied by the old Norfolk saying 'Do different'. In an era when voters across Britain used to swing between the parties at elections with an almost eerie national uniformity – in that respect the nation has become far more diverse – Norfolk seats used to delight in heading in the opposite direction.

The rules for place-name pronunciation are of course impenetrable. Every BBC newsreader knows Wymondham is 'Wyndham'. Everyone in Norfolk knows Hautbois is something like 'Hobbies'. But then many very-locals call Hunstanton 'Hunston' and Stiffkey 'Stookey', for example, although I was advised that it would be pretentious for me, or even someone from Norwich, to try to copy them. My researches suggest even that summary is an oversimplification. Some in Stiffkey say Stookey should only be used to refer to the local cockles, Stookey Blues.

This sort of richly textured local culture is one indicator of a county with a strong sense of self-identity. Another is possession of a first-class cricket team, which Norfolk does not have. But it has something more powerful. Norwich City, the Canaries, are a *county* football team in a way matched only by Ipswich next door in Suffolk. Football being both more popular and worse-tempered than cricket, it gives the rivalry with 'Silly Suffolk' an edge that these days may surpass Yorkshire v Lancashire. It is all of a piece: this flinty, wilful, almost mischievous, occasionally intense semi-detachment from the rest of us. It is no coincidence that the Norfolk morning paper, the *Eastern Daily Press*, retains a rare vigour (despite being run by the usual avaricious dolts) and is said to outsell the *Sun* in its area.

Outsiders think of Norfolk as part of the South-East. But it isn't. King's Lynn has a similar latitude to Stafford; Burnham Market – 'Chelsea-on-Sea' and Norfolk's answer to the Range Rover-infested coast of north Cornwall – is level with the Derbyshire pit villages. The roads and railways being slow, the county has few daily commuters. And the north coast is a challenging distance from London for a weekend cottage.

The county still has its own heroes. A fairly random trio are depicted in a rusting metal tableau at the back of Norwich Station: Horatio Nelson of Burnham Thorpe; Edith Cavell of Swardeston; and Stephen Fry of Booton. The real local heroes are less universally beloved: for some (mostly *Daily Mail* readers rather than *Eastern Daily Press* types) there is Tony Martin, the west Norfolk farmer who in 1999 shot two intruders, killing one of them, a sixteen-year-old boy. It was a complicated case, reduced to simplisms by much of the press. Martin was jailed for murder, toned down to manslaughter on appeal. There is also the late Bernard Matthews, pioneer of mass-consumption turkeys, who became famous for his mass-consumption version of Norfolk dialect ('Bootiful!') on his company's adverts.

For those with a long memory there is the Singing Postman, Allan Smethurst, who in the mid-1960s briefly made the Beatles quake with the popularity of his self-penned signature number 'Hev Yew Gotta Loight, Boy?' I still remember the chorus

> *Molly Windley, she smook like a chimley,*
> *But she's my little nicoteen gal.*

although the lyrics of 'Dew Yew Fa'er Keep a Dickey, Boy?' now escape me

(I think his managers must have changed 'Bor' to 'Boy' to reach a Bernard Matthews-size market).

It all ended sadly, as sensational success in pop music tends to do. Being very Norfolk and some distance from the archetypal 1960s heart-throb in appearance, Smethurst needed a great deal of Dutch courage to get out on stage. The novelty faded fast, and he spent his last twenty years in a Salvation Army hostel in Grimsby. His songs, which he continued writing even in the hostel, were homely and humorous, evoking both lost Norfolk and lost love. His work helped perpetuate the first, but he never did find the second.

One might add to the county hall of fame Alan Partridge, the disc jockey created by Steve Coogan, first on radio, then on TV and, in 2012, the film *Alpha Papa*. The Partridge character began as a crass chat show host reminiscent of that other 1960s meteor Simon Dee. As with Dee and the Singing Postman, Partridge's star fell rapidly, and he ended up doing the graveyard shift on a radio station in Norwich. I happened to meet Steve Coogan at the kind of glitzy showbiz party to which an author of my stature gets invited, ooh, pretty much every night really. So I asked him why he picked Norwich, not a city regarded as inherently funny. That was the reason, he said: 'I didn't want somewhere northern and obvious. It hadn't been degraded.' Coogan had never even been there. When he finally did go, he found he liked Norfolk for all the reasons one should like it ('There's a kind of otherness about it.'). More surprisingly, once the connection became established, Norfolk decided it liked him too: 'When I went back I was treated as a returning hero.'

Now this might be taken as a sign of provincial stupidity. But the thing about Alan Partridge is that he has no self-awareness, and the joke is always on him. So, as a stupid incomer, he fits Norfolk's idea of itself.

There are two lines about Norfolk that have turned into clichés. One is N4N, the notation supposedly used by doctors at the Norwich Hospital to indicate Normal for Norfolk. Usually applied to patients from Dere-ham, according to one version. The implication of local stupidity is, I think, more than countered in the other direction.

The other cliché is 'Very flat, Norfolk', an exquisite line in the context of Noël Coward's *Private Lives* ...

AMANDA: Have you known her long?

ELYOT: About four months. We met in a house party in Norfolk.
AMANDA: Very flat, Norfolk.

but exceedingly boring when repeated by twerps every time you happen to mention the county. Well, I dare say the tourist trade might be improved if the next earthly upheaval deposited a Kilimanjaro or two somewhere near Thetford. But Norfolk rarely gives the impression of flatness, the way, say, much of Lincolnshire does. And it isn't dull.

That's because of the sheer variety of the county, which includes two mysterious and unique landscapes. In the west there is Breckland – 'the English Steppes', according to Simon Barnes – the arid, flinty, piney land once dominated by rabbits and sheep, who picked it so clean the diarist John Evelyn compared it to the Libyan desert. The army and the Forestry Commission have had most of it, but the fragments that remain are large enough to be haunting and a touch forbidding.

Then there are the Broads, which have always sounded to me redolent of rainy 1950s family holidays where we never did what *I* wanted. Not that I had ever been there. But the moment I glimpsed the Wroxham boatyards I felt a slight shudder. Oh, my dear, the noise and the people! One could just imagine.

But it wasn't like that at all. We did have privileged access. John Blackburn, warden of the Hickling Broad nature reserve, took Simon and me out in his electric boat, as silent as a Nottingham tram. There was barely a sound except the wind in the reeds as we glided into Hickling Broad itself, which lives up to its name – the largest expanse of water in the system.

The Broads are far more enigmatic than the old post-Christmas *Radio Times* ads made them sound. It was 1960 before it was shown they were not natural but man-made: medieval peat diggings which were flooded by rising sea levels to create an accidental canal network. That afternoon Hickling Broad was empty but for a lone fisherman, a fair quantity of rather exotic birdlife, and us. Above was a Norfolk sky of the sort that, in keeping with the normal pattern round here, the Norwich watercolourist John Sell Cotman got more right than the occasional visitors Turner and Constable: always a streak of purple somewhere, always a streak of purple.

'I bet it's bedlam in summer,' I said.

'Not necessarily,' said John. 'It depends on the water level under the bridge at Potter Heigham. If it's too high for the bigger boats to get through. And if you come in the evening when the other boat people are in the pub. And if you pick the nights when the sailing club isn't meeting, you can have the place to yourself then too.'

Which puts the Broads one up on Venice. Also, Norfolk has grander churches.

There is another, far more secret transport route: what the humorist and singer Sid Kipper ('Like a Rhinestone Ploughboy') calls the Trans-Norfolk Highway, which the Department for Transport hides under a bland *nom de route* as the B1145. But it really does cross the county: from Mundesley on the coast to King's Lynn in the west, disappearing momentarily a couple of times, then magically reappearing. All the way the signs, like Sirens, beckon the motorist to deviate from the straight-ish and narrow to see Norfolk's most tantalisingly named villages: Whissonsett, Weasenham St Peter, Weasenham All Saints, Tittleshall, Wending, Booton (actually very bootiful, I thought), Themelthorpe, Drabblegate, Fiddler's Green, Stratton Strawless, Trunch.

But the road itself is bewitching enough. Except for a northward turn near the coast it runs roughly level with the bottom of the Wash, about three-quarters of the way up the county. The highway aside, communications are almost non-existent. This really is deepest Norfolk, where the Black Shuck might appear on a winter's night, floating in canine form on a bed of mist. But it was a lovely drive, beneath magical cloudscapes. Not flat.

D. J. Taylor had lent me the CD of a terrific radio documentary he did about the Singing Postman a few years back, so I listened to that. Rather less appropriately, I then put on Leonard Cohen. I got to his great revolutionary anthem:

> *First we take Manhattan*
> *Then we take Berlin.*

But it seemed a bit odd in this setting. It seemed time to rewrite it:

> *First we take Hunstanton*
> *Then we take King's Lynn.*

I commend my version to the Norfolk independence movement. It doesn't scan if you call it Hunston.

Norwich Cathedral is more than normally lovable: it has an unusual architectural integrity; it is very welcoming; and the set-up feels as though it is part of the life of the modern city rather than a demanding old nuisance. On a mild autumn morning, the walk down to the river through the Close, intermittently alive with the dawdling pupils of the 900-year-old school, is an unusually cheering and timeless urban experience. The cathedral itself has a spire second in height to Salisbury, but it is low down and does not show off.

But then Norfolk is so full of show-pony churches that the cathedral is not that special. It is unusual in having a spire: the characteristic sight of the Norfolk countryside is of a medieval tower poking above the treeline. But, the spire aside, no other expense was spared on these churches. The county was rich from wool in the Middle Ages, and religion was how it flaunted its wealth. I went into some churches that had fonts almost as large as a Welsh chapel.

There is generally a steady traffic of Pevsner-wielding travellers pootling from parish to parish swapping favourites. 'I think one is either a Salle or a Cawston man,' Betjeman said somewhere, as though the relative merits of Sts Peter and Paul, Salle, and St Agnes, Cawston, were one of the major issues dividing the nation: United or City; Tory or Labour; Salle or Cawston.

I'm a Salle man myself. Cawston church is stark and uncompromising, and the massive tower looks military rather than ecclesiastical. Salle ('Saul' in Norfolk-speak) is more homely, as well it might be, since it hardly has a parish to go with it. This enables it to have a more enchanting setting, just opposite a cricket ground. A Cawston man urged me to forget Salle ('one man's vanity project') and concentrate on the great wool churches: Aylsham, Reepham ('Reefum') and Worstead.

To be honest, the best thing about Norfolk churches is not the architecture but the vicars. I stopped off at Weston Longville, living of the eighteenth-century diarist and gourmand Parson Woodforde ('... soals boiled and fryed, couple of boiled chicken and tongue, beans and bacon, stewed beef and an haunch of vension ...' And that was just for starters.). They probably did not, in his day, have 'Messy Church' at 4 p.m. in the hall, every second Sunday.

There are, however, few things messier in the history of the Church of England than the life – and especially death – of the famous Rector of Stiffkey ('Stookey' or maybe not), Rev. Harold Davidson, 'the prostitutes' padre'. He died in 1937, but his story is one of those ancient newspaper sensations that still exerts a fascinating power. With good reason.

Davidson was not your average country clergyman. He had been on the stage before being ordained and never quite lost his taste for theatricality of all kinds. When he came back from the war to discover his wife had become mysteriously pregnant, he began spending his weekdays in London ministering to fallen women, a category that did seem to include not just prostitutes but the waitresses in Lyons Corner Houses and other teashops.

The inference might have seemed obvious, but the evidence of his wrongdoing was curiously elusive, as shown when an ecclesiastical court finally convened and heard evidence against him that was both circumstantial and thin. Nonetheless, the court had him 'removed, deposed and degraded' from the priesthood, of which he had become the best-known member, far surpassing the archbishop of Canterbury.

Broke and indignant, he campaigned for reinstatement while preaching from a barrel at Blackpool before escaping what he called 'the blatant vulgarities' of the place to go upmarket and play Daniel, delivering sermons from a lion's den in Skegness. And it was there, one summer's evening, that a lion called Freddie, who had perhaps omitted to take his medication, grew weary of the sermonising, picked up the rector in his mouth and mauled him to death. The version of the story on the church noticeboard says that much of the audience thought this was part of the act and laughed uproariously.

Though he had his enemies all right, most of the villagers wanted the rector buried among them. Thousands attended the funeral, not all of them journalists. And there he lies, in a corner of Stiffkey churchyard, not hidden away but in a grave that might be described as uncharacteristically discreet. Perhaps the mourners repaired, as I did, to the pub named, of all things, the Red Lion. They probably discussed the question, which remains unresolved, of where the rector stood on the spectrum between holy innocent and dirty old man. Or argued about whether to call the place Stiffkey or Stookey.

There was an even more famous religious figure in Norfolk: Richeldis de Faverches, a Saxon noblewoman who in 1061 had a vision of the Virgin Mary in Walsingham. The site became an Augustinian priory and one of the world's great centres of pilgrimage. A succession of kings came to the shrine, including the young Henry VIII, who walked the last couple of miles from East Barsham barefoot. The older Henry VIII had the place destroyed with more than normal thoroughness, complete with several exemplary executions.

And then for more than three and a half centuries Walsingham mouldered, a forgotten symbol of the Catholicism England had rejected. But the medieval Slipper Chapel, outside the village, had survived the carnage. This was where less energetic pilgrims than Henry would remove their shoes for the final push. It had eked out the succeeding centuries in such lowly incarnations as a poorhouse and a cow barn. But in 1895 it was bought by a Catholic family; in 1938 it was reconsecrated.

By that time the Church of England had begun to take an interest, or at least a segment of it had, and the Vicar of Walsingham created his own shrine in the village with its own Marian statue. Eventually, the Orthodox Church built their version in the old railway station, and pretty much everyone was in on the act except the atheists and the Jedi Knights. Walsingham began marketing itself as 'England's Nazareth'. It was a rebirth, not least of the village's ancient marketing skills, for as one resident put it, 'There's no one who can turn a penny into a pound like those Augustinian canons.'

It may indeed be England's Nazareth in the sense of it being a possible flashpoint for holy war. What one senses in Walsingham is not so much an aura of sanctity but of the kind of quietly simmering resentments that led to the Reformation in the first place. The Slipper Chapel is a sombre and appropriately brooding place, but the Anglican shrine is bizarre: ponging of what might have been either incense or industrial floor polish and with enough gold on the altar for Walsingham to stage the next Olympics. 'My dear,' said one local Catholic. 'They're much Higher Church than we are.' Hard to believe all this was being built while Harold Davidson was enduring life with the lions. Extremists from the puritan wing of the Church of England have been known to picket the annual Walsingham procession.

Walsingham is a pretty village of darling little cottages, whose interiors often reveal medieval wall paintings when the builders move in. It has only a handful of shops, but two of them specialise in religious knickknacks. It is a sort of Lourdes for the carriage classes. But there is a fourth place of pilgrimage: the ruins of the original priory, at the back of the old courthouse, in the garden belonging to the Gurney family.

The main relic comprises the leftovers of the ruined priory, most obviously the remnant of the east wall, which stands in the middle of the lawn looking like either a folly or a giant croquet hoop. Other remains are scattered about and integrated into the garden; the west tower looks like a little garden well, set about with rose bushes. On a kindly afternoon, the breeze rustled the beech trees and the first leaves were starting to drop on to the lawn. It really did seem as though God might be hereabouts, and possibly the Virgin Mary too.

In haste, I rushed past Roys of Wroxham, 'the world's largest village store'; languorously, I crossed the River Yare on the chain ferry at Reedham. I took a peek at Great Witchingham Hall, a mix of Tudor and Victorian with a few echoes of onion-dome Muscovy. It looks like a country house hotel. It is actually the HQ of Bernard Matthews. It was here in the 1950s, when great mansions cost buttons, that he shelled out £3,000, kept two rooms to live in and filled the other thirty-three with turkeys: they were, the *Independent* reported, 'hatched in the dining-room, reared in the Jacobean bedrooms and slaughtered in the kitchens'. The turkeys now live and die up the road and round the back, protected by security.

I enjoyed cosy Reepham and genteel Holt, marvelled at spacious Swaffham, surely the only town in England that has both a market cross with Tuscan columns and a Russian restaurant. I went through Fakenham, which has a Museum of Gas and Local History, and also a tattoo shop adjacent to the Tudor Tea Rooms, a conjunction that sets the mind racing: 'Excuse me, Muriel. You just finish your teacake while I nip next door and get a tramp stamp on my buttocks.'

I began to understand the logic of the classic Norfolk town: by the river a small industrial estate where the station used to be; the market square on what counts in Norfolk as a hill; and somewhere round the back the supermarket, usually the same one – Fakenham, Stalham, Aylsham, Downham Market ... Tesco towns all.

And now there is another: Sheringham, the little seaside resort that had spent the past seventeen years – *seventeen!* – trying to keep Tesco out. It was perhaps the most epic battle in the history of British retailing – Sheringham as Stalingrad – and on more than one occasion it appeared that the antis had won. But they were up against an implacable opponent who hurled unimaginable resources against the district council in pursuit of victory.

I first went to Sheringham to report the story in 2009. When I mentioned the town in a phone call to a Tesco press officer there was an audible gulp. The company was not that keen on the world being aware of its existence.

Throughout, Tesco's opponents have been fond of wartime metaphors, but this was not a case of a united band of brothers defying the wicked invasion force. The town was split down the middle. 'You've heard of Ambridge, an everyday story of country folk?' said the owner of my hotel when I arrived. 'Well, welcome to Umbrage, an everyday story of seaside folk.'

A lot of the residents were fixated by the allure of having a real supermarket just like a grown-up town, instead of having to drive for a full *ten minutes* to get to Morrisons in Cromer. And there was a reasonable case for wanting shops that would stay open as advertised instead of shoving off of an afternoon because it was raining and quiet. However, these did tend to be the people whose roots in the town were shallowest, especially the young, who were mostly going to shove off anyway. The pro-Tesco Facebook page was run by a student from Holt.

Sheringham does not have the best beach in the kingdom – it only gets sandy at low tide; it is north-facing; it is buffeted by winds. The town's USP was that it was a theme park of nostalgic shopping: three greengrocers; three fishmongers; two butchers, one of them called Icarus Hinds; a bookseller called Bertram A. Watts; a wool shop with such a variety of different coloured threads that it was almost as lip-smacking as the retro sweetie shop; and one of the nation's great ironmongers, Blyth & Wright. Everything that Tesco has a history of killing off.

Tesco had long since taken Hunstanton and King's Lynn and it was utterly determined to get Sheringham. Its costs must have been staggering. North Norfolk District Council was, narrowly but consistently, keen to oppose the project but was constrained by a strange secret agreement signed by two former council officers years earlier. In 2010 it caved in.

Three years later I came back to discover that the new store was just a week away from opening. That very morning the *Eastern Daily Press* had splashed on the news that Sheringham's traders were summoning a '1940s spirit', which was a very Sheringham thing to do. The town had just had a wartime-nostalgia weekend and the windows of the Lobster, one of the pubs by the seafront, were covered by pictures of Captain Mainwaring and Sergeant Wilson. And indeed a 1940s spirit was what I found. Some were phlegmatic: 'If my son was coming into the business I'd be scared to bits,' said Peter Scotter the fishmonger. Some were defiant. 'I've had eighteen good years here,' said Steve Fulcher the greengrocer, 'and I plan to be here for a few years yet.'

And the Tesco that was preparing to open was not as hubristic as the one that had won the battle. The company had just announced a 25 per cent fall in profits and had been forced into humiliating retreat in both the US and China. Perhaps in Sheringham it will try to make nicey-nicey with the new neighbours, at least in the short term.

The week before, Sheringham had suffered some damage in the storm that almost took Bryony's bungalow in Happisburgh: water seeped under the sea wall. But, like most of Norfolk, it is not in imminent danger of being swallowed by the sea. The threat is to landward: the danger that the county's distinctive charm will be wrecked by an onslaught of homogeneity.

October 2013

~~~~~~~~

Less than two months later, in early December, a tidal surge hit Happisburgh and Bryony Nierop-Reading's bathroom caved in. The house was then demolished. She was unhurt, having removed herself and her belongings in time. The council declined to offer her any compensation, claiming that she should have moved earlier. She said she was better off than those next door in Walcott, who were taken by surprise. 'I've seen floods,' said resident Jane Knapp. 'But this was so quiet. The water crept up; it was like bath water overflowing.'

In 2014 the British Museum announced that a year earlier scientists had found the oldest human footprints ever seen outside Africa – 800,000 years old – in the mud on Happisburgh beach. And six months after Tesco arrived in Sheringham Steve Fulcher said business was way down, but was unsure whether that was due to Tesco or the wet winter: 'People say if you can survive the first twelve to eighteen months, trade does come back, so fingers crossed.'

34. *Not not proud*

STAFFORDSHIRE

We walked up the stone steps leading to the main entrance of the ancestral home of the earls of Shrewsbury – passing by the Talbot hounds, the family symbols flanking the door, and under the family crest. We went through the armoury, past the statuary and into the Octagon, the centrepiece of this extraordinary house.

'Fantastical,' Pevsner called it. Indeed, the whole experience was dream-like. The long corridors were dark and grew ever more mysterious as we approached the Octagon. There we were shown a film depicting the 15th earl being cursed by an old crone who had been spattered with mud by his rushing carriage. The earl was described as 'cruel' and 'arrogant', which was the best indication yet that the current earl, no. 22, was not actually at home.

Then we were led into another chamber, where we were invited to take a seat. We began swaying up and down. Then the walls began moving until we seemed to be doing a full 360-degree turn. And then … no, I didn't wake up. We were all ushered outside into the light, where it became clear that we had been not in one of the rooms of the stately home but in a green prefab within the shell of the original house, which is known as Alton Towers.

Ah, the A-phrase, never to be spoken by fastidious parents in front of children for fear they will have to go. As alarming in its way as the D-word, Disney, the only company which outstrips Alton Towers' owners, Merlin Entertainments, in 'location-based, branded family entertainment'. The Earl of Shrewsbury and his family, the Talbots, are indeed not at home, and have not been since 1924. The witch's curse has had some effect.

The ride inside the Towers, 'Hex', is a gentle middle-aged kind of jaunt. On the far side of the house, however, is Merlin's new pride and joy, the Smiler, opened early in 2013: the world's first fourteen-loop roller coaster. The queues for the Smiler have lasted all summer long, peaking at three hours. Three hours' wait for a thrill you can't help anticipating but which lasts just two minutes forty-five seconds? Sounds like dating.

And indeed the Smiler is aimed squarely at the post-pubescent market. Even now, in late October, with the season nearly over, the wait was over an hour. God bless the smartphone! Indeed, the imminent autumn half-term has now become the park's busiest time of year, branded as Scarefest, and featuring Franklyn's Freaky Fun Zone, Skelvin's Spooky Storytime and Phil's Petrifying Penalty Shot.

I was there as a guest of the management, and my guide, Liz Greenwood, was much nicer than her bleak title of 'corporate communications manager' suggested. Nonetheless, at this point we had a disagreement. One of us thought it would do no harm for a single time-pressed VIP to be given preferential treatment and allowed to queue-jump to experience the park's star attraction. The other refused to contemplate such an injustice to the patient paying customers. You will of course have gathered that it was me doing the refusing. Actually, I was even more frightened by the thought of having to endure the adjoining ride, Oblivion, which concluded with a sheer drop, as down a lift shaft.

What Liz wanted me to experience most of all, though, was the look of the place. When the Talbots left, a local entrepreneur opened up the gardens and the banqueting hall, and it remained a small-scale attraction until the 1970s. The Corkscrew arrived in 1980, the first double-looper in Europe, so popular it caused chaos. Since then, there has been rollercoaster hyperinflation. It all got too big for small business. Enter Merlin,

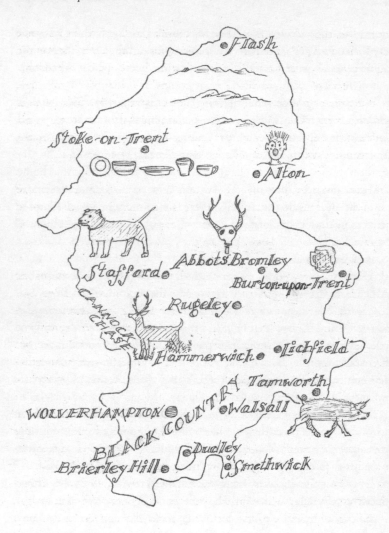

now also operators of Legoland, Sea Life, Madame Tussauds and Black-pool Tower.

The house had been carefully rendered uninhabitable just before the listed buildings regime came in. But the gardens – zestfully put together by the 15th earl – were intact, and Liz wished to make clear how well Merlin was nurturing and indeed restoring them. As you enter the grounds, the impression is of a stately home and park. Even the Smiler remains beneath the roofline and the treeline. Alton Towers is the reverse of a Disney operation, centred on a fake Mickey Mouse's Castle. Here is a fairy-tale castle that looks fake but isn't. You could ignore all the rides, send off the adolescents to queue for the Smiler and picnic quietly amidst the cedars.

'We try to appeal to different age groups,' said Liz. 'We want people to bring their children, who will bring their children, who will bring their children, who will ...' The same dynastic principle as the aristocracy. And indeed I am happy to offer them my own slogan to appeal to the reluctant bourgeoisie: 'Alton Towers – not nearly as dreadful as you think.'

Merlin, owned mainly by private equity, is an instinctively secretive company. It does not like to reveal its visitor numbers. Liz Greenwood tried to tell me Alton Towers was simply 'one of the biggest attractions in Staffordshire'.

'*One of?*'

OK, she eventually admitted, nearly half the visitors to Staffordshire go there. It takes a moment to think where the bigger half might go. Not the beach. This is not a magnet of a county. This is the not-as-dreadful-as-you-think county. Before the Industrial Revolution it was considered infamously primitive: they were already making pottery round Stoke, but had to transport it by packhorse across tracks so appalling that the breakage rate was phenomenal. Then everything changed, and Staffordshire splintered into several different pieces that had almost nothing to say to each other but were busy as industrialists by appointment to the nation and the world. The Potteries now pottered triumphantly, sending their wares safely by canal and then rail. Burton-on-Trent quenched the country's thirst. The Black Country sent just about everything, everywhere.

In between there was rich farmland, the lovely wooded valley round the River Churnet – which included the then little-known village of Alton – and bleak moorland in the north. But it never did cohere as a county. Until 1959 there was not even a county regiment: there were the South Staffords (two VCs at Arnhem) and the North Staffords (four VCs in the First World War and a reputation for industrial-scale swearing, I read somewhere). And the single regiment was merged again soon enough.

Tim Cockin from Barlaston, south of Stoke, is the author of *The Staffordshire Encyclopaedia* – a county could not have a more assiduous enthusiast – but even he has to admit that Staffordshire is fragmented, and not just between the Potteries and the Black Country. 'We don't have much to do with Burton, but we are very aware they are in Staffordshire and they are very aware they are in Staffordshire.' It is, as he likes to say, very diverse.

But all this understates the reality of Staffordshire's divisions. It is not just that one part of the county doesn't speak to another, this is a place of strong but tiny communities, intensely local to an extent unimaginable elsewhere in the country. Jo Moody, the senior curator of the Black Country Living Museum, told me that, after the reorganisation and the merger of councils, Tipton's records were moved to Smethwick: 'So nobody consulted them any more.' Smethwick was about ten minutes away. Keith Hodgkins of the Black Country Society was at Tipton Grammar School, where a minibus of children would arrive from Brierley Hill, five miles away: 'They sounded almost alien.' All across urban Staffordshire are boundaries invisible to the naked eye that the locals regard as impenetrable walls. The Wolverhampton *Express & Star*, once the country's most successful evening paper (and now the least unsuccessful), built its reputation by producing multiple editions to ensure one town should not be befuddled with news about the next one. Upper and Lower Gornal, twin pit villages, were said to have had accents so impenetrable that neither place could understand the other. And even now, Hodgkins thinks, there is a difference between south of the Dudley Ridge and north, where the accent is harsher.

Stoke-on-Trent, which is of course six towns rather than one, is even more complex for an outsider to unravel. The situation is not helped by its most famous chronicler, Arnold Bennett, with that fierce commitment to truth that marks out the great writers, rechristening Stoke the Five Towns, because he thought that sounded better.

For most outsiders Staffordshire remains a county to rush through as fast as possible. Not an easy proposition on the M6, though the expensive alternative, the M6 Toll, is a nostalgic reminder of how joyously empty motorways were in their early days: a theme-park ride for the over-sixties. And one day, there might be an even faster way through ...

Whittington Heath Golf Club, just outside Lichfield, is an inviting course, good enough to attract occasional national boys' and ladies' championships, if not quite the Ryder Cup. It is not cheap (£1,400 joining fee even before the subs kick in), but nor is it snotty: on an autumnal weekday afternoon the eighteen holes, and the nineteenth, were alive with men with diamond-pattern sweaters and Midland accents. Its great asset is being built on fast-draining heathland: it had poured earlier in the week, yet the fairways still had a September springiness.

I can claim – without false modesty – to be one of the worst golfers in the game's history, and have a particular terror of long par fives. But there was something very appealing about the 505-yard ninth hole: oak trees to the left, oak trees to the right, but a nice straight bouncy fairway ahead. I am not the only one who has taken a shine to it. The first phase of HS2, the projected north–south rail line, is due to run, straight as a perfect clattering drive, past the clubhouse and down the ninth fairway. Tee to green in five seconds. There will be collateral damage to about half a dozen other holes. The railway will cut the course, very neatly indeed, in two.

Despite the obsessive nature of golf, this is not quite like losing one's house. And though members are joining in the ritualised protests, the main battle is to mitigate the damage. The club has extra land on which to rebuild: it hopes the line will be tucked away in a cutting; that it will not be too noisy (though it can hardly create more noise than the A51); that there will be a bridge or tunnel to get golfers and carts from one side to the other; and that the club can keep going during the building phase. The first rule of golf (this much I know) is never to allow outside thoughts to impinge on your concentration. And HS2 has been a long-lasting cloud on the horizon, which may or may not unleash its terrors. 'To be honest I think the members worry more about their swing,' said Mike Raj, the club professional.

The problem, here and elsewhere along the route, is that there is bugger all in it for those most affected: it is a line to transport people between big cities, and the aggregate national good is in conflict with individual damage. I think the case for HS2 is a strong one, yet the government has been cruel and churlish in the way it has dealt with individual grievances, irritations and indeed tragedies. There are no plans for a stop in Staffordshire. It will be a county, more than ever, to rush through, a role it has played since the pottery stopped falling off the packhorses.

No wonder Staffordshire people look inward, to the resources of their own communities. This book has not been much concerned with the twee end of local tradition – cheese-rolling, pancake races and furry dances, charming survivals all, but not saying much about the county in which they take place. The Abbots Bromley Horn Dance, I was told, was different: untwee and untouristy. And also very Staffordshire.

The dance dates back at least to 1532, maybe to 1226, maybe to Saxon times. It takes place, as the T-shirts say, on the first Monday after the first Sunday after 4 September. All its rituals are as precise and obscure as the date. There are twelve dancers, all male, based round two families: six carry reindeer antlers, the largest weighing nearly two stone. There is a very butch Maid Marian ('I married into the job,' he said), a Hobby Horse, a Fool, a boy archer, a boy playing the triangle to beat time and an accordionist. The standard uniform is an elfin pink-and-green panto-mime outfit.

And it does involve something of the very English kind of effort – serious but not serious – that other villages would put into a panto. But obviously its roots are way deeper than that. The first person I met was Steve from Bradford, who had bagged the dry slot under the Butter Cross to sell his books and CDs, mostly about morris dancing.

'What's this event got to do with morris dancing?'

'Nothing whatsoever,' said Steve.

'What is it to do with?'

'It is to do with the Abbots Bromley Horn Dance. It's its own tradition.'

The day proceeds on its own strict-ish timetable between 8 a.m. and 8 p.m., involving a lunchtime trip out to Lady Bagot's place at Blithfield Hall and then processing through the village at teatime, though tea was not foremost on the menu. The dancers stopped at the four pubs, the Bagot Arms, the Goat's Head, the Crown and what was the Royal Oak and is now Ruchi's Balti, where they got Cobra lager rather than ale, and at several private houses too.

It really is old-fashioned man's work, what with the lugging of the antlers and the downing of the beer. The music was eclectic, involving tunes as local as 'Lili Marlene' and 'The Wearing of the Green', and the dancing looked amateurish. But it must be more carefully choreographed than it looked, otherwise the participants would keep getting a face full of antlers. Maid Marian did rattle the collection tin and the couple of hundred spectators were made welcome. The atmosphere was affable and humorous. But always one felt that this was a day for Abbots Bromley, not for outsiders. And that, one senses, is why it has survived.

But what does Staffordshire have to offer the rest of the world, beyond Alton Towers? Pottery, of course. There is an agreeably tangy cheese, only recently revived. There are Staffordshire oatcakes, but they are largely con-fined to the Potteries. There is the Staffordshire Hoard, a collection of what someone described as 'bloke's bling' – gold pommel caps for swords and so on – found in a field near Hammerwich in 2009. But Staffordshire managed to keep that quiet for about 1,300 years.

There is the Staffordshire Bull Terrier, visually unnerving but claimed by its supporters to be so gentle it is known as 'the nanny dog'. If true, that might make it a more appropriate county motif than the Staffordshire knot, originally the crest of the earls of Stafford. The Smiler at Alton Towers is said to look, from certain angles, a bit like the knot. But surely the county must have some way of presenting itself, to itself and its inhabitants, other than at Alton Towers? Perhaps not. In Burton I asked a girl if she was proud of being from Staffordshire. She thought for a moment. 'I'm not not proud,' she said.

Even the smaller places struggle to get good publicity. The Mid-Staffs Hospital Trust (slogan: 'Because we care'), based in Stafford and Cannock, became embroiled in a scandal about uncaring nurses and neglectful management. Tamworth was recently named as the obesity capital of Britain, although the people have some eating to do before they catch the customers of Morrisons, Jarrow. It might, however, have a reasonable chance in an ugliest-town-centre contest (possible slogan: 'Burned by the Danes circa 874! Wrecked by the planners circa 1974!')

There was a time when the otherwise inoffensive town of Rugeley was the most notorious in England, owing to the infamy of William Palmer, 'the Rugeley Poisoner', hanged in 1856 for the murder of a racegoing companion. The case was a sensation at the time, and it still bewitches researchers, some of whom believe in his innocence. On the other hand, Palmer may also have poisoned his wife, four of his infant children and countless other victims. He was, of course, a doctor.

Staffordshire towns exist to please themselves, not sniffy visitors, and that's fine. And there are unexpected pleasures. Triple-spired Lichfield Cathedral, for instance. Having had an overenthusiastic makeover from the Victorians, it is not to everyone's taste as a building – somewhere round the bottom of the second division of the ecclesiastical league table – but its setting is champion, by a lake in a particularly congenial close. Inside, it was unusually sunny and airy near the altar, which gave the building an invigorating feel. This arose, one eventually realised, from the absence of stained glass. The cathedral authorities are very proud of their stained glass: the sixteenth-century Herkendrode Windows. But they had gone away for restoration.

'Is it just me?' I asked a guide. 'But might the cathedral actually be nicer without them?'

She looked around furtively. 'It certainly isn't just you,' she whispered. 'But we're not allowed to say so.'

Outside, the scene was completely placid: most of the pupils at the cathedral school must have been in lessons. The peace was broken only by a bearded schoolmaster, staring with an agitated air in the direction of a small knot of teenage girls and focusing, as the profession has always done, on the kind of great issue that really matters in education: 'Izzy, tuck your shirt in, please!'

But you can never accuse Staffordshire of being samey. Barely an hour's drive away I stood outside a more modest school building: the Flash Church of England Primary School (motto: 'Reaching Ever Higher'). The motto was not a random cliché. Flash is the highest village not just in England, but in Britain. In 2007 experts from the Ordnance Survey ruled, for the benefit of a BBC programme, that it was more than 100 feet higher than its rival, Wanlockhead in Dumfriesshire.

This is not what anyone expects in Staffordshire. But the signs say Flash is 1,518 feet above sea level, and the true figure was said to be 1,558 feet. I would have been willing to accept a nought on the end. The Staffordshire sliver of the Peak District is widely recognised as particularly uncompromising and this is no postcardy, tea-shoppy, bed-and-breakfasty English hill resort; even on a sunny autumn afternoon it felt wide open to the east wind. The few natives I met were very friendly, but the hours before the New Inn was due to open stretched too far ahead to encourage lingering. And the school, alas, will reach no more. It closed in 2012 after enrolment fell to zero. Staffordshire as a whole would hardly know that Flash was there.

So here is the problem: a county of localised distinction but general incoherence. It is bipolar, but neither of the poles – the Potteries and the Black Country – is regarded as attractive. Some of it is clearly northern; much of it palpably Midland. Its eastern outpost is certainly distinctive and, one might say, attractive: Burton-on-Trent was and, to an extent, still is the brewing capital of Britain.

Burton had nineteen breweries in 1921 and it still has eight: the sprawling old Bass plant is now owned by the North American giant Molson-Coors and almost entirely devoted to lager; Bass itself, the beer that quenched the empire's thirst, is now brewed under licence at the Marstons plant; and there are half a dozen bijou breweries as well.

There being no obvious alternative, I followed the signs to the National Brewing Museum. However, perhaps in obeisance to the British tradition of eccentric licensing laws, it shuts up shop shortly after lunchtime. I did have a chat with one of the guides, Des McGonigle, who went to school in the town and remembers how the air was suffused with the mingled smells: the wort from the mash tuns, with underwafts of Marmite and Robirch pork pies. If you stand on the bridge by the station now, the rebuilt Coors plant still dominates the townscape, but only a few puffs of smoke escape, and the town is usually smell-less, just as Coors products are largely tasteless.

In the north, there is Stoke-on-Trent, whose traditional industry collapsed, partly because British womenfolk lost interest in Sunday-best tableware, but mainly because Asia could easily undercut even low north Staffs wages. There has been a small-scale revival, led by ceramicists operating at a level somewhere between the craft fair and the old manufacturers. The *Sunday Times* reported in September 2013 that there were 231 ceramics-related firms in the city and gushed, 'Now Stoke is cool.'

Well, that's good news. But the city's biggest private employer is the online bookmaker Bet365. And Stoke-on-Trent remains the least inviting city to visit in Britain and perhaps (vying with Naples and Charleroi) in Western Europe. The problem with the Six Towns is just that: separate places and no obvious centre – the station is in Stoke and the shopping centre is in Hanley. 'I call it Britain's Los Angeles,' said one regular visitor. He did not mean it was cool. 'You have to drive to get anywhere. And you get traffic jams all day every day.'

In a rainy dusk I wandered round Tunstall, northernmost of the Six, and found Bond Street, where in 2012 the council offered terraced houses for £1 to people willing to do them up. I wanted to stay in one of the Six Towns, but buying a Bond Street house would have required time to organise, and I never did discover the exotic alternative of a hotel. The only available shelter I saw anywhere was the bus station.

In the south there is the Black Country, removed from the county in 1974 and plonked, to local disgust, in the West Midlands. If Staffordshire inspires a certain indifference elsewhere in England, West Midlands is even less popular, and neither can match the negativity evoked by what might be the least-loved geographical expression on earth: *Black Country*.

No one quite knows how the name originated, probably the obvious one: the coal was so thick and so close to the surface, and the air was almost the same colour. Here was the very engine room of the Industrial Revolution:

the whole producing the raw materials of coal and steel and iron; the individual towns having their own specialities – Willenhall for locks; Walsall for brass and saddles; Cradley Heath for chains; Wednesfield for traps; Netherton, in the old Worcestershire enclave of Dudley, for anchors. And so on.

It is hard to know what came first in the Black Country, the fierce hyper-local pride or the contempt of the wider world. Whatever has replaced all that activity, call centres are not high on the list: for other Britons, a friendly Bangalorean voice will always beat a thick Black Country accent. Years ago, when industrial dereliction was at its worst, I used to pass through regularly on the train and see a huge sign near Smethwick: 'WHERE WILL YOU SPEND ETERNITY?' Oh, Gawd, I used to think, please, not in Smethwick.

I repent. There could be far worse fates than an eternity comprising fish and chips in beef dripping washed down with pints of mild amidst warm people with such a powerful sense of community. And it is reasserting itself. Firms now like to use Black Country in their title (Black Country Jaguars; Black Country 4×4; Black Country Balti; Black Country Decorations ...). Say it loud! I'm Black Country and proud!

Brummies are particularly prone to patronise their Black Country neighbours as 'yam yams' ('yow am' being one of the usages), but there is a resurgence. Keith Hodgkins gives much of the credit to the Black Country Living Museum, which is a particularly fine and painstaking (if smoke-free) recreation of the old townscapes. 'To me the museum is the most powerful piece of propaganda to the outside world,' he said. 'It's a constant struggle for identity, and losing the old county was a terrible tragedy because it lumped us in with Birmingham.'

Staffordshire's contribution to Britain's economic history is not in doubt. Its contribution to political history rests on one speech, made in Birmingham by the MP for Wolverhampton South-West in April 1968. Enoch Powell, the Shadow Defence Secretary, warned an audience of fellow Conservatives in Birmingham of the dangers of the mass influx of non-whites. This was the speech known as 'Rivers of Blood'.

In his very precise yet very Brummie accent, Powell demanded that immigration should cease and that existing migrants should be encouraged to leave. He also warned about the pending Race Relations Bill, designed to prevent discrimination but which, he implied, would lead to violence. The title came from his closing quote: 'Like the Roman,

I seem to see "the River Tiber foaming with much blood". It was that sentence that did it. Powell, the classicist turned politician, later regretted not keeping it in Latin: the newspapers might not have bothered to translate it.

Within hours his party leader, Edward Heath, had dismissed him from the Shadow Cabinet, and Powell never held high office again. He drifted away from the Conservatives and finished his career as an Ulster Unionist. 'The Wolverhampton Wanderer', some called him.

Good grief, it was nearly fifty years ago. The impact at the time was extraordinary. Opinion polls showed that about three-quarters of voters agreed with him. But the political elite was both horrified and terrified and, although Powell was ostracised from mainstream politics, the speech had massive effects on what was to follow. His intervention became both a self-fulfilling prophecy and what you might call a self-rejecting one.

On the one hand, it made discussion of immigration so taboo in polite society that violent extremism – or even Powellite extremism – could not get a foothold in the debate. British cities, with rare aberrations, have been largely placid. On the other hand, there *was* no debate. Scared to raise the subject, politicians did not attempt to formulate a policy either – even during the long reign of Margaret Thatcher, who was not unsympathetic to the Powell thesis. And thus his projections of numbers were proved pretty much correct: in the 2011 census 14 per cent of the population of England and Wales was described as other than 'white British'.

That's the macro-picture. The speech, however, had an unexpected effect on the city he represented too. 'Race relations in Wolverhampton have been some of the best, if not *the* best in the UK,' said one prominent resident. 'When there were mini-riots in the North-West about ten years ago, it turned out the local religious leaders hardly knew each other. That's been unthinkable in Wolverhampton for almost forty years. And the direct reason for that was Enoch Powell.'

This opinion, improbably enough, comes from Rob Marris, who held Powell's old seat for Labour from 2001 to 2010. 'Not Powell's doing. It was a reaction against him. After the speech, the great and good got together to make sure that they knew and trusted each other. It's a continuing process of hard work.' Marris lost the seat to a Conservative, but hardly a Powellite: his name is Paul Uppal and he's a Sikh. 'Regrettable though it is to me personally and to Labour that he won,' said Marris, 'it is a measure of how far Wolverhampton has travelled.'

The other controversial passage was where Powell read out a letter telling the story of one of his constituents, a widow 'in a respectable street' whose house was now surrounded by immigrants. She was followed to the shops by 'charming, wide-grinning piccaninnies' chanting 'racialist' at her and had excreta put through her letter box.

Powell had got this story in a letter that was anonymous but detailed and evidently rational. For nearly forty years, however, there was no corroboration; his many enemies took it as urban myth. However, in 2007, the BBC and *Daily Mail* identified the woman as Druscilla Cotterill of 4 Brighton Place, a wartime widow, childless – and now long dead – who saw her area change around her and, perhaps not unreasonably, took to drink. I spent nearly an hour looking for Brighton Place. The satnav and *A–Z* showed it as being off the Merridale Road, but there was no sign of it. I asked one passerby: 'No idea,' he said. 'Wouldn't live here if you paid me. All snobs.'

That was not the picture Powell had painted. We were close to the city centre. The houses were mostly Victorian/Edwardian, with front gardens, big but a bit faded. The few people around did not seem overwhelmingly non-white. None of them had heard of Brighton Place. I was baffled. Then an elderly bloke (white) came by, with a knowing air. He tapped two bits of concrete that had once held a street name, leading up an almost rural green lane. 'That's what you're looking for.' I was not the first.

Fearful of this story's continuing potency, he was not going to give his name. But he sounded convincing. He had lived here for ever. He remembered Brighton Place, a cul-de-sac demolished years ago. He remembered Druscilla Cotterill: 'She was a little bandy-legged lady but if you said anything you didn't like, she'd clock you one.'

'She drank?'

'Not 'alf. But she was happy as a pig in shit. All those black people who lived round her, they looked after her.'

'So did it happen? The excreta through the letter box?'

'Yes and no.' He became a bit vague now. It happened, he seemed to be saying, somewhere round here, but not to her.

He was unhappy about what was happening along Merridale Road now. The houses were being bought up by non-white landlords. The colour was not the issue: they were turning them into flats and bedsits, and then no one looked after them. 'Look at the front gardens,' he said with disgust.

He also directed me to a large white-painted, bay-fronted Edwardian semi about 100 yards down the road. It still looked pristine, except for the 'For Sale' sign, which appeared to have been there a long while. Its owners, a West Indian family ('very nice people'), were selling up. There was no plaque to mark its most famous former owner: Enoch Powell had bought it in 1954 for £1,500 and made it his constituency home for the next twenty years. For two decades Powell had regularly walked down this street, always ready to stop for a chat, according to my informant. Whatever anyone said about him, no one ever denied he was an assiduous, well-attuned constituency MP.

So why the hell did he need an anonymous letter telling him what was going on 100 yards up the road from his own house?

According to the 1978 Shell Guide, in Upper and Lower Gornal, the allegedly non-communicating twin villages, 'pure Chaucerian English is still spoken'. I went into the post office and asked a pink-haired girl if we were in Upper or Lower?

'*Wyd was his parisshe, and houses fer asonder,*' she replied. '*But he ne lafte nat for reyn ne thunder.*'

Actually, she just said 'Lower', rhyming it with 'Power', which may indeed be Chaucerian.

'Is it true that Upper and Lower Gornal can't understand what each other says?'

'Hey!' she said, with great indignation. 'My nan lives in Upper Gornal!'

I made an excuse and left.

September/October 2013

~~~~~~~

In November 2013 a primary school headmaster in the Black Country announced a zero-tolerance policy against local dialect phrases like 'I cor do that' (instead of can't) and 'It wor me' (instead of wasn't). He did not specifically ban anyone from calling him a 'blithy-ed', which is Black Country for prat.

35. *A va-whatle?*

ESSEX

I arrived in Frinton on a crisp, sunny morning, after the first frost of the season. I parked next to a discarded package for 'Mixxed Up Classic Stimulating Drink', also a Bounty wrapper and a used Greggs bag.

It was my first visit to this legend among seaside resorts: the late Victorian town that strove to keep the horrors of the twentieth century at bay – litter, public houses, fish-and-chip shops and omnibuses. Frinton shut itself 'inside the gates', the railway crossing that guarded the only obvious way into town. They were more than a piece of routine street furniture and a nuisance to motorists; they were a symbol, of enclosure and defiance.

The frost was just burning off the grass as the first conscientious bag-carrying dog walkers of the day accompanied their charges along the sweeping Greensward, the swathe of grass between the Esplanade and the shore. On a morning like this even the North Sea looked inviting, as the tide turned to reveal the spectacularly sandy beach. But the legend of Frinton is such that disappointment is inevitable. For a start, the thatched toilet block was boarded up for the winter. So much for one Essex joke, the one at the expense at Frinton's demographics: 'Harwich for the Continent! Frinton for the incontinent!' Not in November. Now it's 'What's the matter with you? Can't you wait till Easter?'

Furthermore, having ignored one century Frinton has succumbed to this one: the chippie was the harbinger, in 1992; the first pub, the Lock and Barrel, carefully designed to look unlike a pub, arrived with the millennium. There was furious opposition to both. Offshore, the wind turbines of Gunfleet Sands go about their obtrusive business. Even the level-crossing gates have gone, to be replaced by a barrier. Which caused another hullabaloo: in other countries, whole towns have disappeared with less ululation. There was even a report of a couple retreating back to London because they hated the noise of motorbikes. And heaven help us, the golf club is trying to get down with the kids: 'A club for all ages', insists the sign.

I do admire Frinton's determination to go its own way in a country that expects conformity from its communities. Close to the pub there is still the British India restaurant, serving Mountbatten Mushroom and Viceroy Bhavan. The town has so far seen off the normally irresistible force of Tesco. And there is still nothing that smacks of artificial seaside enjoyment. It is the perfect resort for perfect children: the sort who will build sandcastles all day and read a book all evening without saying a word until they are ready for adult conversation.

It was with relief that I headed down the coast to Clacton. For one thing it was easier to find a toilet. And Clacton was a pleasant surprise. Expecting another disastrous seaside town to match Lowestoft or Margate, I thought the seafront, the beach (well, some of it) and the pier all rather jolly. Essex is a place that defies preconceptions. One does wonder what Frinton is doing in Essex. But, in the words of the writer Julia Jones: 'Whatever you say about Essex, the opposite will also be true.'

Just past Clacton, and a mere nine miles by road from the British India restaurant, is Jaywick, the eastern side of which in 2010 was decreed by the Index of Multiple Deprivation to be the most deprived area in the country. Posh-paper journalists find it an easy place to commit a bit of misery journalism, about the flimsy housing, youth unemployment, flooded streets, whatever. These reports sometimes lack a bit of context.

Jaywick is the best surviving example of the Essex plotlands, built up between the wars on sites that were considered useless, either on marginal

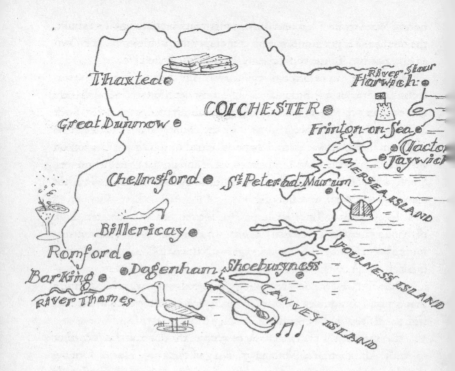

portions of the coast or on the heavy Essex clay known to dispirited farmers as 'three-horse land'. A generation of men whose escape from the slums had been the trenches found it liberating to buy their own little patch of England, however humble.

And they were resourceful enough to build their own holiday cottages or, as outsiders usually called them, shacks. Many were hardly bigger and perhaps less salubrious than a Frinton beach hut, but slowly – and against considerable opposition from the council – their owners made them just about habitable, into homes where many of them would choose to retire. There were complex disputes with the council and other authorities, one of which reached the Court of Appeal in 1936. Lord Justice Greer refused to believe that people were living in Jaywick by choice: 'Nobody of ample means would go and live in this marsh!'

The anarchist scholar Colin Ward and a colleague met many of Jaywick's original settlers: 'What struck us was their enormous attachment to their homes, their defensive independence and their strong community bonds,' Ward wrote. He found that for fifty years, before a sewer was built, the residents had got groups together to empty the primitive toilets known as Elsan closets. Those who did it were called 'the Bisto kids'.

This spirit has, perforce, not gone away. The 'avenues' behind the sea-front stretch known as Brooklands – the most deprived section of all – are named after pre-war car marques: Alvis, Sunbeam, Talbot, Bentley, Swift ... They have still not been adopted by the council and are thus not its problem. Officials have instead dumped a load of spoil from Clacton on wasteland and invited the residents to use it and do the roads themselves. Some of the avenues looked almost Frintonesquely neat; others, in a not especially wet week, were flooded.

The place staggered me. In parts it looked like an American slum, perhaps post-apocalypse New Orleans, which is not an absurd comparison: thirty-five people died here in the 1953 east coast floods. Indeed, amid these gimcrack renderings of Essex timber buildings, it all felt more American than English, and not just in looks. It needs rugged individualism, a pioneer spirit, to thrive here. And some do. 'I wouldn't live anywhere else,' said one pensioner on Brooklands.

But there really are two classes of people: the descendants (actual or spiritual) of the original plotlanders, living in their own houses, forming about 40 per cent; and a more transient majority who came here solely because there are a lot of near-slums to rent very cheaply. Hence the crime, the unemployment, the deprivation. The local Conservative MP, Douglas Carswell, says the problem derives from well-meaning officialdom, trying so hard to prevent a repetition of 1953 that it banned all new building in Jaywick. No one has been able to convert their shack to anything more substantial. 'If you've got a plot of land with brambles growing on it, it's rendered worthless because you can't build on it,' according to Carswell. 'And if you've got a wooden house, you can't build a brick one.'

This is changing. Developers can now amalgamate the tiny plots and build more substantial houses – but on stilts, as protection from the next tidal surge. 'People may only have a home worth £20,000–30,000 but they've scrimped and saved so that they are not living on a council estate,' says Carswell. Just down the road there was discovered, in 1911, the Clacton Spear, now in the Natural History Museum and believed to be 450,000 years old. Jaywick may be the spiritual home of an entity even more interesting to future palaeontologists. This could be the real birth-place of Essex Man.

Essex is an exception to a great many rules, and it is a spectacular exception to the general decline of county loyalty and identification that has taken place elsewhere. This is the county that turned into a concept. Or rather a series of linked concepts.

Basildon is often seen as the epitome of Essexness. It was built on old plotlands after being designated a new town in 1949, in Colin Ward's words, 'to make some kind of urban entity out of Pitsea and Laindon, where by the end of the war there was a settled population of about 25,000 served by seventy-five miles of grass-track roads, mostly with no sewers and with standpipes for water supply'. None of this had any place in the Attlee government's brave new England and the owners were duly enticed with the offer of a snug and sanitary new home with garden in the new town. And if the inducement failed, they were forced out.

To those who had not yet migrated from the war-ravaged East End, Basildon was a popular destination. It wasn't Letchworth, but nor was it Limehouse. There was for one thing plenty of work, mostly in factories that were not too heavy-duty: Ilford cameras; Carreras tobacco; Ford radiators; Yardley cosmetics; Standard telephones. In the early days, the town was much admired by bien-pensant outsiders; they especially liked the pedestrianised town centre.

But mistakes were made. The architects (consultant: the revered Sir Basil Spence) failed to notice that the shopping precinct would be a wind tunnel. And they failed to provide enough parking spaces anywhere, a problem exacerbated when, one by one, the factories began to close and Basildonians were forced, by hook, crook, car or train, to hunt far afield for work, often in London. A certain discontent crept in.

In 1979 Margaret Thatcher became prime minister on a swing that was especially high in all the south-eastern new towns. In Basildon an improbably camp right-winger called Harvey Proctor overturned a five-figure Labour majority. Four years later the seat was split up because of population growth. Proctor took the more Tory portion, Billericay. His successor in Basildon was a more appropriate Essex boy called David Amess, but he had what seemed an intractable Labour constituency. 'I had no HQ, I had no money, I had an inexperienced cousin running my campaign,' he recalled. 'There was a sea of red posters. I got all my supporters together when the polls closed, said we had come a good second and they were not to show their disappointment.'

He won, for one overwhelming reason: by 1983 Mrs Thatcher had

introduced her policy of liberating/bribing (delete to taste) council tenants by letting them buy their houses at ridiculously low prices. 'What I
had sensed on the doorstep was that people were thrilled to own their own
houses. She tapped into the idea of giving people a leg up.' Amess would
hold the seat for fourteen years, most famously in 1992, when his result –
among the first to be declared – was the first indicator that Thatcher's heir,
John Major, had retained power. His grinning mush across the nation's
TV screen was a stab to the heart of the Labour Party.

Amess identifies the Fryerns estate (pronounced 'Free-uns'), one of
the first to be built, as a crucial element in his victories. It is now largely
owner-occupied with three-bedroom 1950s-built terraced houses selling
for around £165,000. Bill Archibald, who left the pits in Sunderland in
1961 to take a job in the oil industry, is one of the councillors from the
Fryerns Ward. A Labour councillor. I asked him what the major issue in
the Fryerns was now.

'Council housing,' he replied. 'People come to me and say, "What
about my son and daughter? They can't get on the housing list." So I say,
"You bought your council house, didn't you? That's why. We've hardly got
any." And I think "That's another vote lost."'

But Basildon did well in the 1980s, not just from the Thatcher subsidy. There was plenty of work, in London if not locally. The character
created by Harry Enfield, Loadsamoney, epitomised the flashy wide boy
with a wallet full of tenners, gleaned perhaps from the City or the motor
trade or the fringes of crime. He sounded very Essex, though the phenomenon of Essex Man was not taxonomised until a *Sunday Telegraph* profile
in 1990 (anonymous but written by the Essex man Simon Heffer):

> Ownership, independence, a regard for strength and a contempt
> for weakness underpin his inarticulate faith in markets. Above all,
> he believes in getting things done ... For spiritual purposes Essex
> Man is to be found all over the newly affluent parts of the outer
> London suburbs. But he is discovered in his aboriginal state and
> in the greatest abundance in the triangle between Brentwood,
> Southend and Dagenham Marshes.

Later the *Guardian* columnist David McKie proposed that Essex
should be split into two counties: the northern, largely rural portion,
which represented a different kind of Essex; and the southern portion,

identified by Heffer, which McKie proposed calling Gormandy, after Teresa Gorman, an even louder right-wing Tory who had succeeded Proctor as MP for Billericay (after his sad habit of spanking under-age rent boys had found its way into one of the more disagreeable Sunday papers). Cartoon Essex Man was not necessarily averse to giving someone a spanking, but it was more likely to take place non-consensually in dark alleys after closing time. The typical Essex Man was an Adam in need of his Eve and, happily, she was on hand and – famously – available.

Like Essex Man, Essex Girl was a phenomenon of the 1980s who was not widely identified until the 1990s, by which time she was probably safe-ish behind a pushchair. By then everyone knew what she looked like: 'big blonde hair with tasteful black roots, their layers of make-up, tottering along in micro-mini and white stilettos for a Malibu at the wine bar, en route to the night club', as the *Mail on Sunday* put it. However, the social historian Pam Cox of the University of Essex (where else?) places her in a wider context, allied to the Valley Girls of California and also in a long line of historical equivalents: 'the Lancashire mill girls of the 1840s, the so-called "girl of the period" in the 1860s, munitions girls in the First World War, the "Docklands degenerates" of the 1930s and the "good-time girls" of the 1950s. All were attacked for their immorality, for their vulgarity, for their sexual laxity, and for their frivolous spending.'

There was a third element in the rise of Essex, and it pre-dated the formal identification of both Man and Girl.

> *Good evening I'm from Essex*
> *In case you couldn't tell*
> *My given name is Dickie, I come from Billericay*
> *And I'm doing very well.*

The great music revolution that had started in Liverpool in the early 1960s found its way to Essex a decade later. Dr Feelgood from Canvey Island, a pub band playing what is sometimes called Essex Delta music, had a cult following but limited commercial success. They are now seen as precursors of punk – in particular because they sang in what was recognisably their own voices. And punk, in the words of Billy Bragg, who was at the serious end of the same movement, represented 'a rejection of the rock aristocracy that lived its life on Lear jets and tour buses in the USA. Punk was the tearing down of that edifice and replacing it with the urban everyday experience.'

And along came Ian Dury, inventor of both Billericay Dickie and what might be the most beautifully constructed stanza in the whole of English poesy:

> Home improvement expert Harold Hill of Harold Hill
> Of do-it-yourself dexterity and double-glazing skill
> Came home to find another gentleman's kippers in the grill
> So he sanded off his winkle with his Black and Decker drill.

Dury, stricken with polio and an uncompromising self-awareness, was not actually an Essex boy: he was born in Barnet and his first band was called Kilburn and the High Roads. But, perhaps more than anyone, he gave Essex its voice. Pop music had always thrived on place names – Tulsa, Wichita, LA, Frisco Bay, Memphis – but not Billericay. Meanwhile, the writer Giles Smith was growing up round Colchester, the genteel end of Essex, wanting to be a rock star but believing that a scion of the Colchester bourgeoisie was ineligible for such a career – at least until the emergence of Damon Albarn of Blur ('whose parents were neighbours of a friend of mine') and Nik Kershaw, so posh he came from Suffolk. In the meantime Smith looked longingly westwards to the Duryish end of the county: 'I think we perceived Romford as slightly naff but also exciting.'

Since then the epicentre of Essex naffness has definitely moved somewhat nearer Colchester ...

Brentwood is a medium-sized town with middle-class people who aspire to send their children to the local middling public school. As McKie said, it was a frontier town between Gormandy to the south and west, and technically-we're-in-Essex-but-we're-practically-in-Suffolk-really to the north. One of the few half-attractive buildings on the High Street is or was an old coaching inn called the White Hart, though it has lately been rebranded as the Sugar Hut. 'What's this place?' I asked the barman. 'This is basically where we do the TV show,' he replied. 'Twice a week.'

The show is *The Only Way Is Essex*, a twenty-first-century manifestation of so-called reality TV, featuring the county's next generation, now sort of grown up, perhaps the great-grandchildren of the plotlanders and children of the Essex Girls. It has had ten series on ITV2 since 2010.

Though its audience has hardly ever exceeded two million, its influence has been immense: as a beacon to impressionable teenagers nationwide and as a hammer blow to the residents of practically-Suffolk-really, who keep hoping they might wake up and find themselves living somewhere normal.

Reality TV in Britain is usually dated back to 1974 when a producer called Paul Watson persuaded the mildly dysfunctional Wilkins family from Reading to let him film almost every aspect of their daily lives. Such programmes soon became ubiquitous and the term reality TV was later used to describe souped-up talent contests, a form of cheap telly first shown in the black-and-white era. Reality documentaries soon evolved into a tacit conspiracy between the programme makers and the audience. Honey-voiced researchers would talk their way into the homes and workplaces of humdrum people whose ambition in life was to get on telly; the resulting footage would then, more often than not, be cut to make the participants look as entertainingly idiotic as possible.

TOWIE, as the Essex programme became known to aficionados, was a variation on this theme. It is described as 'structured reality', in which the plotlines are agreed in advance, although the conversation is not actually scripted. That is not how reality works. What we have here is a different kind of conspiracy: the film-makers and the sort of actors ganging up on the poor old audience to milk the programme's inevitably limited lifespan for all it's worth. Nine of Brentwood's businesses, including the Sugar Hut, are now said to be owned by *TOWIE* regulars. This, says Pam Cox, is very different from the Essex Girl phenomenon: 'The first time the joke was on Essex. The second time Essex is in on the joke, and acting up to it.'

I did not attempt to see the Sugar Hut in full cry, because I had no wish to spend Friday or Saturday night in Brentwood, and because I would never have complied with the dress code: 'funky, fashionable and glamorous' (this does not apply to the dancers, the Sugar Hut Honeys, for whom the dress code is 'almost nothing'). I did go in before lunchtime for tea and a currant bun. Even then, the *TOWIE* effect was obvious. Outside, girls were having their photos taken in front of the sign. Two of them came in giggling and asked if they could use the Ladies. 'Of course,' said the barman affably. The room was decorated in what might be called tart's boudoir-style, but the boudoir of an upmarket tart, with representations of Hindu gods looking over the leather and plush. The tea and bun were surprisingly good.

But the *TOWIE* look has spread far beyond Brentwood. It involves designer brands, hair extensions, spray tans, sculpted brows, big hair, false eyelashes and – for intimate moments – vajazzling ('adorning the pubic area (of a woman) with crystals, glitter, or other decoration' – *OED*). This definition may already be out of date, since male vajazzles (or pejazzles) have apparently arrived. And the month before my tea and bun the *Guardian* reported that an Irishwoman charged with drug trafficking in Peru was 'wearing a hair doughnut from Lauren Goodger's product range'. Lauren Goodger was in the first six series of *TOWIE*. I don't know what a hair doughnut might be, but maybe you can lick the sugar off.

If this version of Essexness has spread to darkest Peru, it has certainly spread all over the county. Brentwood is not a frontier any more. I was having a cream cheese and cucumber sandwich in a teashop in Thaxted, a candidate for capital of practically-Suffolk, surrounded by people whose accents were not those associated with cream cheese and cucumber sandwiches. 'She's awright, innit?' said a woman at the next table.

Perhaps these distinctions are long out of date. In 1990 David Thurlow noted a peculiarly high incidence of murder in the area between Colchester, Great Dunmow and Tolleshunt d'Arcy and wrote a book called *The Essex Triangle*. Perchance the practically-Suffolks are being wiped out.

I wandered down to Romford, once the HQ of all the edginess that so fascinated young Giles Smith. There are still two large nightclubs facing each other just by the station: Fiction and Voodoo. Romford is only just down the road from Brentwood but was part of the territory lost to London in the 1965 upheaval and is officially part of the London Borough of Havering. There were two ladies behind the desk of the information centre. I asked them whether they thought they were in Essex or London.

'Oh, Essex, definitely,' said the senior of the two. 'We all think that.'

'The older people do,' said her colleague. 'As far as I'm concerned I live in Havering. I don't want to be associated with those idiots. I think it's insulting.'

But there is a different Essex. This is the county reputed to have more islands than any other: about thirty of them – some substantial (Canvey, Foulness, Mersea), some not – but enough for imagination to expire to the extent that at least two are named after the lapwing: there is both Pewit and Pewet Island. Most are in groups, tucked away in the estuaries or guarding them, like the Walton Backwaters or, around Foulness, the Essex Archipelago (maybe also the Essex Delta; not to be confused with the Murder Triangle).

Most of these islands do not yield their secrets easily. Northey Island is pretty much in the suburbs of Maldon, down a side road on the edge of town. The turning is unmarked, and it has one of those nerve-wracking tidal causeways. Just over a thousand years ago Northey was the most strategic point in England.

It seems that the Vikings – after raiding other east coast ports – camped on the island with a view to attacking Maldon and demanding protection money to go elsewhere. The Saxon leader Brithnoth assembled his forces at the end of the causeway, blocking the exit. The next bit can only be described as Pythonesque: more *Spamalot* than *Camelot*. Despite being outnumbered, Brithnoth allowed the enemy off the island so the chaps could have a proper battle: the Battle of Maldon (991). Brithnoth was beheaded; his army was routed; and King Ethelred had to pay the Vikings to go away ('the Danegeld'), which they did before returning for further instalments. Visitors are supposed to obtain a permit in advance from the National Trust, but getting no reply, I wandered on anyway, gambling correctly that the warden and the geese would be less heavily armed than the Vikings. Northey is a calm and evocative place, while being, as the Vikings spotted, very handy for town. The warden could be at Marks & Spencer inside ten minutes (provided shopping hours and the tide table coincide).

It is this sense of edgeland that gives Essex wildness a special appeal, like the Rainham Marshes, firing range turned bird sanctuary. Dick Durham, Essex man and news editor of *Yachting Monthly*, loves to sail up Yokefleet Creek at the back of the Foulness shooting gallery: 'You've got lugworms popping up as the tide goes out and then a curlew strolls by. There'll be a boom as a gun goes off on one side, and you get a glimpse of Southend on the other.'

The coast at the arse end of Southend, from Shoeburyness northwards, is very much devoted to expending as much ammunition as the Ministry of Defence can still afford. This was, in the 1970s, supposed to become the site of London's third airport. The original choice of Stansted being unpopular with the residents, the government considered at least

100 alternatives, including practically every patch of land in the south-eastern quadrant of England (and even beyond) where there was a chance no one important would complain. Foulness was chosen until the birding lobby got agitated about the Brent geese that winter there, and the Treasury grew nervous about the cost. So in the end, a quiet decision was taken to expand the existing small airport at Stansted after all, without ever quite spelling out the implications.

So Foulness was left to the soldiers and the shelduck and a couple of hundred residents leading a strange life over a bridge and behind a military barrier. Security has been outsourced to a firm called Qinetiq, who must have the big advantage of being cheap to counter the minor drawback of being useless. I rang up and was assured the barrier would be open and access allowed to the public on Saturday morning. Complete rubbish, said the staff on the gate: 'It's not the first Sunday of the month, is it?'

Except for the first-Sunday open house, there are two back doors on to Foulness, both via Wakering Stairs, the steps on to Maplin Sands that are open unless there is actual live firing. One involves taking the footpath along the sea wall to the bridge, though opinion among the dog walkers was that I would get picked off by the guards in no time that way. The other is by the ancient six-mile track across Maplin Sands known as the Broomway. This also had disadvantages. It is notoriously dangerous, even for the well prepared and well shod. Contrary to the general health-and-safety trend, it has evidently become more dangerous: the causeway has been allowed to crumble and many of the broom-like poles used as markers have disappeared. Sudden mist can be a killer in this Morecambe Bay of the South. The dog walkers reckon the degradation is deliberate Ministry of Defence policy to discourage visitors. And even to start the journey, the tide has to be ebbing, which it was not when I arrived. Plus, in the unlikely event of unauthorised landfall on Foulness, security may hurl you back into the sea. Otherwise no problem.

Anyway, they said, there's bugger all on Foulness. There was a pub, the George and Dragon, until 2007. But outsiders had to ring in advance to arrange a permit, which was one deterrent to trade. After a pint or six, customers often came to grief on the narrow access roads. And it was a notoriously unwelcoming pub anyway. 'More Dragon than George,' said one source. It takes a lot to deter an intrepid adventurer like me. That was a lot.

It is not necessary to leave the mainland to discover strangely beautiful places in Essex. Some find them in the most incongruous settings. Billy Bragg, growing up in Barking in the 1960s, used to sneak off with his mates down to the Beckton Marshes, by then more wasteland than marsh. He recalled, 'It was a place of burnt-out cars, nudie books, tramps, fly-tipping, feral kids and the acrid air of the gasworks. It was a scrape-kneed I'd-kill-for-a-bottle-of-Tizer kind of place. And you felt if you went far enough towards the river, you'd come across the nineteenth century. It was like going through the back of the wardrobe.' A magical world, just by the Northern Outfall Sewer.

More obviously magical is St Peter-ad-Murum, the chapel built on the wall of a former Roman fort fourteen centuries ago by St Cedd, who sailed down from Lindisfarne to try to convert the Saxons. What's left is the original nave, with stone walls – purloined from the Roman ruins or imported from Kent – thirty inches thick. 'The interior has a great but homely solemnity,' says the official guide.

It is next to the other wall: the one that tries to keep Essex separate from the sea. The chapel is at the end of the Dengie Peninsula, between the Rivers Blackwater and Crouch. It is a very Essex mishmash: to the west, the Bradwell nuclear power station; to the south, windswept fields of winter wheat; to the north, a distant view of Mersea Island and the coast stretching round to Clacton and beyond; to the east the North Sea.

In Essex the sea is always murky. All the estuarial muck heads this way out of the big city, metaphorical as well as literal. In 1949 a local wildfowler was hunting for supper on the marshes when he saw an odd-looking shape. It turned out to be the torso of one Stanley Setty, a small-time racketeer and spiv who had been stabbed to death with an SS knife, cut in pieces and dropped from a great height: a small plane, it turned out. The murderer, Donald Hume, had got muddled between the marshes and the open sea. An easy mistake.

On the wall, I met June and Phil, from the North-East Essex Badger Group.

'Lot of badgers round here?'

'Oh yes,' said June. 'We're very pro-badgers, but when they undermine the sea wall they've got to be moved on. The whole peninsula could be at risk.'

For the sea also gets muddled between its space and ours. On 31

January 1953, just over three years after Setty was killed, the Memorial Hall on Canvey Island, commemorating the war dead, was officially opened. The MP performing the ceremony told the gathering that people were at their greatest in adversity. Within hours they were to face adversity of a kind they had never known. That night there was a high spring tide and a severe storm. Nearly 2,000 people died in the Netherlands, more than 200 at sea and more than 300 on the east coast of England and Scotland. Fifty-eight were lost on Canvey, four more than died in the war, to go with the thirty-five at Jaywick and eight at Harwich. On Canvey, nearly all the dead were under six or over sixty. In a country where nature is meant to behave gently, it was the worst natural disaster of modern times. People in coastal Essex use the floods as a chronological reference point, whether they are old enough to remember them or not, the way the rest of England talks about before and after the war.

Hidden away, shielded by trees, beside St Peter-ad-Murum is the Othona Community, a Christian retreat founded by Norman Motley, an RAF chaplain. He was hoping to build reconciliation and understanding after the Second World War, an event whose trauma, disruption, horror and heartbreak have been sanitised by the British through decades of being wrapped in heroic myth. It offers tea and empathy to all-comers and seems a haven not so much of religion as of common sense.

But somehow the spirit of St Cedd has found a wider application. Essex became a centre of heterodox thought of all kinds. In the 1830s a reformed drunk from Rochford called James Banyard founded the Peculiar People, a literalist sect with a belief in divine healing, which did not help its spread, owing to the mortality rate of its adherents. The sect still exists, its views somewhat toned down, under the less striking name of the Union of Evangelical Churches, still fifteen of them, almost all in east Essex. Southend has surprisingly few pubs, supposedly because of the non-conformist influence.

In the twentieth century other groups made their way east to practise beliefs ranging from the primitive to the avant-garde. In Essex, land was cheap and plentiful, yet still close to London. There was room to pray or sing or strip off without offending the neighbours the way you would in Kent or Surrey. The capital was certainly spreading this way, but here the bourgeoisie were not in the vanguard. This was the lee side of the smoky city, and thus inherently undesirable.

The working-class first started to move north-east towards places like Walthamstow in the late nineteenth century; the Great Eastern Railway, out of Liverpool Street, offered particularly cheap workman's fares, making it possible for the very people whose homes in London had been demolished by the railway companies to commute back in again.

After the First World War the London County Council was given permission to build the Becontree housing estate in the little parish of Dagenham. This was a novelty, since it was outside the LCC's own area. In 1935, fourteen years after the first tenants moved in, the population on the estate reached 100,000. By that time Ford had opened a factory with its own Thames port and there was soon work for everyone who was not too fussy. The choice was football (Alf Ramsey, Martin Peters, Jimmy Greaves and Terry Venables) or Ford. And that remained substantially true until late in the century, when the Ford factory began to be run down and then partly demolished.

The first inhabitants of Becontree, with its inside loos, little gardens and privet hedges, were pioneers of a kind. That was even more true in the new towns and, above all, the plotlands. It was the Wild East.

The river! The river! Billy Bragg urged me never to underestimate the importance of the Thames. 'The river is the key to understanding Essex,' he insisted. 'It's made it very outward-looking and given it the ability to absorb people. Other counties don't have the same speed of change.'

And I kept finding, even well away from England's Mississippi, curious echoes of America. In the next-door county there have been cases of people being ordered to paint their houses Suffolk Pink. In rural Essex the palette seems more vibrant, the rules more relaxed. The Recorder's House in Thaxted ('a remarkable sight' – Pevsner) is now painted Pugin Red from the Dulux Heritage catalogue: the planners retreated from opposition, apparently because the village backed the owners. Elsewhere, there are lilacs, rich greens and a general sense of anything goes. Surprisingly close to a city like Chelmsford, one can find secretive houses down remote lanes that might belong to Romany-blood hustlers or shabby-chic intellectuals but clearly not routine commuters.

And everywhere there is this sense of restless pioneering. From the Peculiar People to the habitués of the Sugar Hut, this is a county full of folk breaking free of old constraints and following new rules, whether from the Gospels or the gossip mags. Looking east from the M25 at the

Dartford Crossing, you get the ugliest view in England: industrial river-side Essex looks much like northern New Jersey. But from other perspectives this county, like nowhere else in Britain, has the characteristics of godly Utah and hedonistic Nevada. Maybe the Murder Triangle equals the Badlands.

And quite often Essex villages give off little architectural hints of New England. The wooden clapperboard houses are of course very American – but maybe it's the other way round and America resembles Essex. After all, as they like to say in Essex, the *Mayflower* was launched in Harwich (well, maybe, say scholars). In Great Easton I passed a striking white building with a cupola. It might have been a Massachusetts Baptist Church; it turned out to be the 1980s-built showroom of P&A Wood (world-famous in rather refined circles), repairers and restorers of vintage Rolls-Royces. A Silver Ghost 1920 4-Door Open Torpedo Tourer at £550,000, anyone? In Great Bentley there is a massive village green that belongs in a far more spacious land. Even Great Wakering (it's a Great place, Essex), now an ugly sprawling village, seemed to me American in its very mindlessness.

Furthermore, just outside Clacton is St Osyth, where Lee Wick Farm was for many years recognised as the driest place in Britain: an average of just under twenty inches' rain a year. According to my weatherman friend Philip Eden, Essex is in two separate rain shadows: of the Welsh mountains for westerly winds and of the Pennines when they are more north-westerly. The winds descend the lee side of a mountain range, making the air less humid, hence less rain. So if the answer is not St Osyth it will be somewhere nearby.

It's a title Lee Wick Farm is unlikely to get back, simply because Robert Faulds, the previous farmer, has now retired and given up the daily routine of measurement. (You have to be in it to win it.) But the figures don't lie, says the current farmer, Robert Clarke. 'In my experience, it's either boggy-wet or dry like concrete,' he says. 'Some years I think we're officially classed as desert. We've got no irrigation so we have to plant drought-resistant potatoes, and barley never grows as well as it does elsewhere.' These are not problems that often face farmers like Gavin Bland in Cumberland. But twenty inches a year is exactly what they get on many ranches in South Dakota.

It was no coincidence that Billy Bragg chose the A13 to Shoeburyness for his parody of Route 66. And come to think of it the A12 is the most frightening road I have driven since I last tackled the Washington Beltway (excluding a back alley near Naples that turned out to be a footpath). The A12 is not well enough engineered to cope with the number, speed and murderous intent of the motorists.

All of Essex's infrastructure seems to be creaking. The trains are jammed solid; Chelmsford's big new estates are built on flood plain and there will be tears one day, insist knowing locals. Yet even this Little America contains multitudes. Maybe it's the element of American-style risk that gives Essex its vibrancy, its edge. Who knows what trick that inscrutable brown river – he must know somethin', he don't say nothin' – and unpredictable sea might pull next?

And, to push the analogy even further, there is something, just like America, about all the Ess-excess that makes more respectable counties nudge each other and roll their eyes. The centrepiece of Basildon's wind farm-cum-shopping centre is a fountain incorporating a bronze statue of a mother and child. The mother, arched beyond horizontal, is cradling her infant; both are naked. Close to, it is very beautiful. Basildon was so proud that it turned the statue into the town crest. Unfortunately, when reduced to a miniature, the image is less clear; it looks like the activity that produced the child. Poor old Essex: it just *asks* for trouble.

Until I was eleven, my grandparents lived in Westcliff-on-Sea. Every few weeks we would make the four-hour pre-motorway drive from our home near Northampton to see them. My father was usually less than delighted; I was thrilled. Grandpa would habitually accompany me to Southend Pier, where we would take the little train on the one-and-a-third-mile journey to the pier head and play the old mechanical penny-slot machines, which usually involved flicking a ball-bearing and trying to get it to roll into the hole that won you both the penny back and another go.

Those outings, I suddenly realised as I walked past the old Peter Pan playground, took place more than half a century ago. But the pier has been even more ravaged by the years than I have. Born in 1829, it reached its full world-record length on its hundredth birthday and continued serenely until it got to 130. Then, as old bodies do, it became accident-prone.

1959: major fire at shore end, destroying Pier Pavilion
1971: child injured, forcing rebuild of the walkway

1976: fire destroying most of pier head, including the amusement arcades
1980: threat of closure
1986: (just after railway rebuilt) tanker slices through structure, leaving seventy-foot gap
1995: bowling alley burns down
2005: pier head goes to blazes, again
2011: barge crashes
2012: fishing boat crashes

But, by golly, it was resilient. And in July 2013 the Duke of Kent, looking across the estuary to his own domain, opened the new prefabricated (and, so the council keeps repeating, iconic) Royal Pavilion at the pier head.

And so, on a brisk but pleasant November afternoon, I took the train once again. It is diesel now, not electric, and the carriages have got smaller – not my imagination – though this was not a problem, since on both journeys I was the only passenger. A few well-wrapped tourists, mainly Asian, were doing the walk, which misses the point, I've always thought. And, about three-quarters of a mile out, there was a lone figure in the water, carrying something long and thin.

At first I thought he was taking a dog for a rather wet walk. Then I decided my old eyes were playing up again: it must be a buoy. Then I wondered if it was another bloody Antony Gormley statue. All wrong: it was a bait-digger, apparently. The Southend tide goes out so far that fishermen are often sighted in waders near the end of the pier, hunting for bass and herring.

The iconic Royal iconic Pavilion contains a very un-iconic café, serving tea nowhere near the standard of the iconic Sugar Hut, and a large empty room with chairs stacked at the sides.

'What's it used for?' I asked someone official.

'Weddings, conferences, concerts, anything really.'

'What's there for kids to do?'

'Not a lot. They can have ice cream sometimes. Not today.'

Well, they can visit the lifeboat station. Or read a book. I was told amusement arcades are a fire risk. But not the old penny slots, surely? Can't they bring in the company that runs the retro funfair at Weston-super-Mare?

Oh, Essex! You're awright, innit? Please be yourself, you bundle of contradictions. Give us a bit of the old razzle-dazzle, even vajazzle. Don't try and turn the whole county into frigging Frinton. I know the rest of us take the piss. But, honestly, we love you just the way you're meant to be.

November 2013

~~~~~~~~

The eleventh series of TOWIE was shown in 2014, but it was announced that future series would be aired on something called ITVBe. Next stop: the knacker's yard.

The thoughtful Conservative MP Douglas Carswell (page 435) improbably defected to UKIP in 2014.

36. *Percy and the parrot*

SHROPSHIRE

In the weeks before the five-ringed circus came to London in the summer of 2012 the Olympic Games' country cousin was also celebrating. It was the twenty-seventh time the Olympics had been staged since their reinvention in 1896. Shropshire could do better than that. This was the 126th Annual Wenlock Olympian Games.

The event at Much Wenlock was established by the local doctor, William Brookes, to 'promote the moral, physical and intellectual improvement of the inhabitants'. In 1890 a young Frenchman, Baron Pierre de Coubertin, came to the town to watch the sports and talk to Brookes about his ideas on physical education. Six years later he started his own version in Athens, which became rather famous.

De Coubertin's Olympics recognises the connection: one of the mascots chosen for the 2012 Games was called Wenlock, though this was an honour the town could have done without; it was a hideous one-eyed thing that could give even a robust child nightmares, the product, as one columnist put it, of a 'drunken one-night stand between a leło tubby and a Dalek'. Or merely the usual ghastly issue of a marketing meeting.

Much Wenlock gets no rights in return. It has to stick to the word 'Olympian' not 'Olympic'; it cannot touch the five rings – the self-selecting International Olympic Committee being very keen on what it considers its intellectual property rights. But no one can stop the town running, jumping, swimming and performing such not quite Olympic activities as bowls, cricket and gliding.

The athletics took place at the William Brookes School just twelve days before the opening ceremony of the so-called real Olympics. The town was full of people, not all of them young, in tracksuits and tight black running shorts, exuding an air of good health and Brookesian enthusiasm. The sport, however, was somewhat inhibited by the running track, which was a figure of 6 rather than the traditional oval, and more suitable for racing whippets than humans.

In this of all years, so close to the great London fiesta, I thought there might be more outside interest. Much Wenlock's equivalent of the opening ceremony was a parade through the town led by a little boy in princely robes on a white pony. He looked as pleased as a prince too. It was not a very grand parade, and was watched by a few dozen townspeople and a Japanese camera crew who appeared to constitute, discounting myself, the full complement of the global media.

At first I was puzzled. Then I thought how very Shropshire that made it. In theory Much Wenlock is not especially distant from London. But this is the only English county without a direct train to the capital; the roads are pretty convoluted too. Campaigners are trying to get a train from Shrewsbury restored, but as one local put it, 'It's not that they actually want to go to London. It's just they think they have a right to go.' A few Scottish-border villages perhaps excepted, nowhere in England *feels* more remote from London. And the same applies in reverse; if the Wenlock Games took place in Surrey, there would have been camera crews everywhere. Shropshire gets ignored by the world. The world's loss.

Even Shropshire's bard went there only occasionally. Next to Hardy of Dorset's entire canon, no writer's work is seen as the embodiment of a single county so much as A. E. Housman's *A Shropshire Lad*. Yet he saw it mainly from a distance, from a viewpoint near his home in Worcestershire,

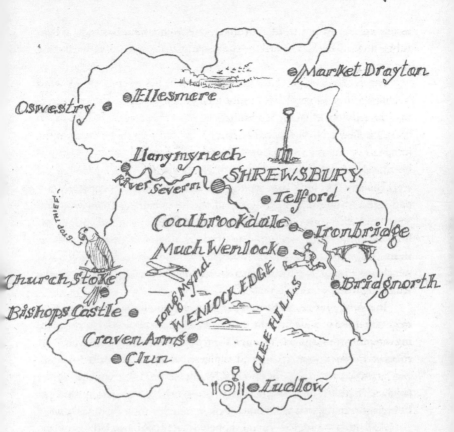

whence he stared at the Blue Remembered Hills of the county next door.

Housman himself shed little light on his connection with Shropshire. The scholarly consensus is that he was traumatised, first by the death of his mother on his twelfth birthday and then by his homoerotic longings. Read in this light, the undertones of the sixty-three poems that make up *A Shropshire Lad* become overwhelming. Shropshire was Housman's own imaginary land of lost content.

Originally he planned to call the work 'The Poems of Terence Hearsay' but was talked out of it. And, in the words of Jim Page of the Housman Society: 'A Bromsgrove Lad just wouldn't have worked, would it?' Housman was some way into the sequence before he was persuaded to make Shropshire the motif, hence the curiosity that one of the most famous of the poems, 'Bredon Hill', is set miles away. But what is most

overwhelming is the way that, in the reader's mind, he seems to have captured the landscape:

> *On Wenlock Edge the wood's in trouble*
> *His forest fleece the Wrekin heaves;*
> *The gale, it plies the saplings double,*
> *And thick on Severn snow the leaves.*

I walked along the Edge on a still day in late November. Many of the
trees remained in leaf. They were gently decaying after a happy summer
and a douce autumn, preparing to fall off their perch in their own good
time. And what more can you hope for from life, be you leaf or human?
This seems a very Shropshire way to get through our mission: passive,
uncomplaining, contented. The wood was *not* in trouble. The Wrekin was
not heaving. It was *not* the land of lost content. If anything, it might be the
land of found content.

It is not necessary to be an acknowledged poetic genius to manipu-
late the evocative power of Shropshire place names. 'As soon as the train
left the platform my mother would begin her recitation: "Condover, Dor-
rington, Leebotwood, All Stretton, Church Stretton and Little Stretton,
Marshbrook and (pause for effect) Wistanstow Halt." It was a litany of
delights.' That was Julian Critchley, recalling a visit to his grandmother in
Wistanstow in his well-liked but ill-remembered autobiography, *A Bag of
Boiled Sweets*. Critchley was a journalist turned liberal-minded Conservative MP who, once preferment had finally passed him by in the Thatcher
years, allowed full rein to his humorous subversive tendencies.

Wistanstow Halt existed for just twenty-two years: opened 1934,
closed 1956. Driving north from Craven Arms on the A49, I saw a turn to
Wistanstow and, on a whim, took it, passed over the railway bridge close
to where the station must have been and found a perfectly formed village,
essentially a single street. Not the county's most obviously beautiful. But
there, huddled together, was everything required to take one from cradle
to just short of the grave: nursery and school, community shop, church,
village hall, a pub with its own brewery, defibrillator – even a 3G signal to
call the final ambulance and maybe email the next of kin.

The shop, in the old forge, had been part-funded by the actor Pete
Postlethwaite, who lived nearby. It was very welcoming and, though not
overstocked, happy to accommodate its regulars' special requests. There

didn't seem any urgent need ever to leave such a place. I met one woman, an incomer, who rarely did. Critchley himself ended up here and indeed there are worse places to spend eternity than Holy Trinity churchyard, though myself I would prefer to be buried by the oaks rather than the leylandii. Wistanstow felt, as Critchley's mother had intimated, like the epitome of Shropshire. Housman's ashes have a grander resting place, in the churchyard of Ludlow's quasi-cathedral, St Laurence's. There is a stone in the north wall with the lines:

> Goodnight; ensured release,
> Imperishable peace,
> Have these for yours.

Not Housman's most memorable. I might have gone for:

> Leave your home behind you,
> Your friends by field and town.
> Oh, town and field will mind you
> Till Ludlow tower is down.

Shropshire was not always a model of rural calm. In 1709 a Quaker industrialist called Abraham Darby took over a run-down blast furnace at Coalbrookdale and began to experiment with the use of coke rather than charcoal in the manufacture of iron. Perfecting the process took three generations and most of the century, but its moment of glory came in 1779 when the grandson, Abraham Darby III, produced the dynasty's showpiece, the iron bridge over the Severn.

England was running short of wood, but the seams of coal were staring at the Darbys from the steep banks of the river. It was a revolutionary discovery. What would become known as the Ironbridge Gorge was for a time the innovative centre of the world, the Silicon Valley of its day. It was a honeypot for factory owners and for workers.

But the first three Darbys all died young, and the family fortunes fluctuated. The whole Ironbridge phenomenon was short-lived too. The east Shropshire coalfield was small and by the mid-nineteenth century the area began to be outcompeted by areas like the Black Country, which had more space and more coal. Just when most of England was becoming industrial, Shropshire became post-industrial. Ironbridge and

Coalbrookdale became relics. Neil (later Sir Neil) Cossons was brought in to make something of its heritage in 1971. 'The gorge was a scene of complete decay and dereliction,' he recalled. 'If you said you lived in Ironbridge, you were looked at with pity. The whole place was populated by old people.'

But the remnants were there, and Ironbridge 'Birthplace of Industry' became what must be the most popular destination on Britain's longest river. In landscape terms, the gorge has regenerated itself and become wooded again. And the architecture has a touch of class because the Georgians were stylish even when building factories. The bridge itself is exquisite, though long ago declared too fragile for traffic. You could not replicate Ironbridge's current success in the average ex-pit village. Nonetheless, there is a huddled, claustrophobic feel, as in the Rhondda; there were too many cars for comfort even in late November.

This is a problem of success. There are now ten – *ten!* – museums in this little valley, plus the modern versions of ancillary industry: teddy bear shops and curio centres. The only sign of continuing industrialisation came from Ironbridge power station, on the opposite bank, emitting smoke but in a wispy, lazy Shropshire kind of way. It was due to close by the end of 2015. In the meantime, this remnant of the world's first industrial powerhouse was burning coal from places like South Africa, Poland and Colombia and biomass from Louisiana. The English run the museums. I don't suppose they have ten of those in the whole of Colombia.

As a failed superpower, Shropshire settled back into a very happy torpor. Not much happened. The twentieth century made only one major incursion into the landscape: the building of Telford New Town for displaced Brummies which subsumed several undistinguished coalfield towns from the 1960s onwards. Telford was particularly helpful to the Ironbridge Project because it meant there was money sloshing about.

In 1974, the great local government mash-up left Shropshire unscathed. Instead of revelling in its escape, a rare survivor of the April Fool's Day massacre, it opted for self-harm instead. The word 'Salop' had long been used as the county's abbreviated form, as an adjective – 'Salopian' – and also as the official name of the old county council. No one took much notice. But in a fit of national compliance, the new county names were now being adopted for all purposes, postal addresses included. The new council decreed that Salop was in and Shropshire was out, and the populace found that the place they thought they lived in had in effect ceased to exist.

In Old English, the area was known as Scrobbesbyrigscir, derived from Shrewsbury. When the Normans arrived, they had understandable problems pronouncing this, hence Salop. Later, Latinists argued that the title Shropshire County Council was tautologous. Actually, 'shire' and 'county' are not the same, but it was the sort of argument that could win the day in the 1880s, when county councils were being set up, and Shropshire was full of parsons with Oxon and Cantab after their names and too little to do. It was somewhat more surprising that it had any credence in the 1970s.

The new Salop lasted just six years. A campaign led by Colonel John Kenyon of Oswestry forced the council to vote 48–6 in favour of reverting to Shropshire. One of the issues raised was the meaning of *salop* in French, something that must have post-dated the Normans, and its possible deleterious effect on the tourist trade. This point was drawn to my attention by Shirley Tart, the doyenne of Shropshire journalism, who has spent her life trying to deal with the very same problem in good humour. According to my *Collins Robert French–English Dictionary*, '*un salop*: bastard, sod, swine; *une salope*: bitch, cow, tart'.

The locals – especially older ones – do use the word Salop sometimes, but not as a synonym for the county. It is their way round the problem of pronouncing the county town: *Shrows*-bury, which is considered posh; *Shrews*-bury, a bit common; or even *Shoes*-bury, dead common. Country folk often say, 'I'm going up to Salop today.' Shrewsbury football fans are even said to chant '*Sa*-lop' occasionally.

Differences of opinion in Shropshire tend not to be too vituperative and I have not come across a county quite so comfortable in its own skin. The post-2010 coalition government liked to distinguish between 'strivers' (good) and 'skivers' (bad). The mainly Tory voters of Shropshire fit into neither category: this is a county for the conscientious but unambitious. It has had people who go off into the world and make names for themselves, but this does not always turn out well. The trouble started with Old Parr, Thomas Parr of Alberbury: born 1483, so it was said, died 1635. For nearly all that time, he appeared to be doing rather well on a diet of 'green cheese, onions, coarse bread, buttermilk or mild ale (and cider on special occasions)', with none of that new-fangled tobacco but a good deal of old-fashioned sex: he married at eighty, committed adultery at 105 and remarried at 122. There is no evidence that any of these numbers were remotely correct, but he was obviously knocking on a bit yet absolutely fine, until, having allegedly passed the 150 mark, Parr was discovered by the Earl of Arundel. His lordship insisted on taking him to London to be exhibited at court, where he took ill and died. The royal physician William Harvey proclaimed that he had been seen off by London's rich food and pollution.

You see what happens when Shropshire men get above themselves? There was Robert Clive of Market Drayton, who conquered India, then slit his own throat. Captain Matthew Webb of Dawley, the first man to swim the Channel, who drowned in Niagara Falls. Andrew Irvine of Shrewsbury School, who really got above himself and disappeared on Everest. And what about Andy Lloyd of Oswestry, who in 1984 became the first Shropshire-born cricketer to play for England since Victoria was on the throne? He remains the only England opening batsman never to have been dismissed. That's because he got bonked on the head by a West Indian fast bowler after half an hour and was never picked again. *You see?* Best to stay home. Shropshire probably still murmurs disparagingly about Charles Darwin of Shrewsbury and his crazed ideas about monkeys.

I exaggerate a bit. But Shropshire can seem a bit small-minded and backward. This is one of several counties where incomers snigger about the natives who, when they say tomorrow, mean mañana but without the same sense of urgency. There is an obverse to this: a powerful sense of community. Shirley Tart's newspaper, the *Shropshire Star*, did not even exist before 1964. In the heyday of the evening papers, no one thought it worthwhile to give Shropshire its own.

Fifty years on, provincial press circulations are falling fast and the *Star* is not immune. But even in 2013 its sales were still above 40,000, in the top six nationally, above the local papers in such trivial places as Birmingham, Leeds and Glasgow. It is partly a sign of good, solidly rooted management. It is also a comment on the place, a sign of an ageing, stable community where people know and care about their neighbours. That's Shropshire.

Readers of fiction persistently refuse to accept its essential premise: that the characters and locations do not exist. A great deal of time is wasted by analysts of P. G. Wodehouse's work trying to pinpoint the exact location of Blandings Castle, home of Lord Emsworth and, far more important, his prize pig, the Empress of Blandings. Evelyn Waugh once told a radio audience, 'The gardens of Blandings Castle are that original garden from which we are all exiled', and the books do refer to Shropshire, which indeed has Edenic characteristics.

But Shropshire is also completely inconsistent. The biggest of the inland counties, it veers between the soft and the muscular. North of Shrewsbury it is relatively flat and meadowy, morphing gently into the Cheshire plain. But the south is startling, which makes it the reverse of the two counties to the east, Staffordshire and Derbyshire, where all the drama is in the north.

South Shropshire can feel Alpine: passing through Church Stretton one day with the Long Mynd under snow, I could swear I heard the tinkling of cowbells. On the other side of the Mynd is the most challenging drive in the country: the 1 in 4 ascent, with a sheer drop to one side, from Asterton up to the gliding club on the summit. I thought the bell was tolling, not tinkling, and the wind on the moorland plateau was savage. This bleak and beautiful landscape bears puzzlingly little resemblance to the English Midlands. The answer to the puzzle must be that, deep in its soul, this is not the Midlands but Wales.

Upland Shropshire gives the county a very un-Midland elemental power; the last fair before Christmas at Church Stretton used to be known as Deadman's Fair, because so many farmworkers failed to cope with the journey home through the snow and the alcoholic haze. But above all, this is not a county of mountainsides, nor even of farms, nor small villages. It is a county – *the* county, along with Lincolnshire – of small towns, now almost all forgotten by the railways, and often by major roads, and to some extent by time itself.

David McKie of the *Guardian* once described Bridgnorth as the ideal-sized town: 'large enough to be varied and interesting but small enough for the locals to know which of the traffic wardens is the most vindictive'. Personally, I prefer towns small enough for the locals to know that the traffic warden only appears on alternate Tuesdays. And Shropshire has a lot of candidates, hardly known to the outside world. Much Wenlock is delicious, and has its name in its favour. Newport is trafficky but stylish – the Shell Guide described it in 1951 as 'the centre of the district where two-bottle squires are still said to live'; the southern approach to Market Drayton, heading towards the hillside church, is pregnant with promise that is not entirely fulfilled by the town centre.

Bishop's Castle was once the terminus of what may have been the second most eccentric branch line in England, surpassed only by the hero-ically mad Potts Line west out of Shrewsbury. It misses its railway badly, since the streets are steep and narrow and barely adequate for a horse and cart, never mind a juggernaut. It also misses Ron Davies's ironmon-gery and the greengrocer and even the market, dating back to 1249 but now removed – perhaps for ever – to nearby Lydham, where access is less complicated. Bishop's Castle does have a deli and a sprinkling of book-shops, being the westward edge of what one resident calls 'the brown rice belt'. This is centred on gastro-Ludlow, where traffic wardens are perforce very active indeed. South of Bishop's Castle is Clun, a town so remote and secluded it never did get a railway. In this least angry of towns is the improbable last resting place of the eternally angry John Osborne. Bish-op's Castle looks down on Clun as being a bit, well, clun-nish.

I think my favourite of all Shropshire towns is probably Ellesmere, in the deep north, a place – I confess – I had never even heard of until arriving with my family, on a enchanted summer's evening, by narrowboat along the Llangollen Canal, and discovering not just a town with an air of quietly assured permanence but the eponymous and lovely mere: 113 acres of it.

Bishop's Castle, Ellesmere and Clun are all tight against the Welsh border, as is Oswestry, a railway town that no longer has a railway. It did have the golfer Ian Woosnam, who liked to call himself Welsh. ('Where is Wales?' demanded an American journalist after Woosnam won the 1991 Masters. 'Is it in Scotland?') The border, created after Henry VIII decided to blunt the power of the Marcher Lords in 1536, is more like a coastline than a political frontier, full of peninsulas and inlets. It is far less obvious than Offa's Dyke, built to keep the Welsh out of Mercia, or the Offa's Dyke Path. Only rarely do even two of these three lines run close to one another.

The oddest manifestation of the border comes in the large village of Llanymynech, where it runs along the main street, though not down the middle, the roadway being in Wales. The line then lurches eastwards, to bisect what used to be the Lion Hotel. Thus, in the days when Welsh pubs closed on Sundays, drinkers were obliged to head for the back bar. The Lion had closed by the time smoking bans came in. These took effect in Wales three months before England, thus leading to a temporary exodus from the Dolphin on the Welsh side to the Bradford Arms over the road. As the Welsh Assembly gets more powers, there will be more such weirdness.

As it is, one of Shropshire's most famous characters lives just in Wales, in Church Stoke, which occupies a phallus-shaped protuberance of Montgomeryshire (in England for ecclesiastical purposes) north of Bishop's Castle. His name is Sam and he watches over the front entrance of Harry Tuffins. Harry Tuffin's mini-chain of supermarkets began here in 1955 and spread, mainly across Shropshire. Harry died young, in 1976, and most of the expansion occurred under his son-in-law Roy Delves. There were shockwaves across the county when the family sold out, in a complicated deal, in 2012. They were matched by the shock a year later when Sam disappeared.

Sam is a twenty-five-year-old African macaw, the stores' mascot and Roy's pet. 'Roy was devastated, he was,' said the woman on the checkout, with genuine affection for both boss and parrot. There was a quick and happy ending. A man from Staffordshire was seen loading him into a van, quickly traced and sentenced to 100 hours' community service. This was not Sam's first adventure; on a previous occasion he was found in a pet shop in Shrewsbury. But, so soon after the sale, it seemed like another blow to the comfortable certainties Tuffins inspired in their customers. The shops are low-ceilinged, unflashy, in the style of both Poundland and a market stall. There is a hint of good-natured hustling behind it. Sam's presence is not just a nice touch, it's retailing genius. His presence turns a child's trip to the supermarket into a delight. Mine too. I asked him if he regarded himself as English or Welsh. 'Ullo,' he replied. 'Ullo.'

The real epitome of Shropshire man was another incomer, not as ravishingly coloured as Sam but more reliably articulate. To anyone in Britain throughout the third quarter of the twentieth century, Percy Thrower was more than that: he was the personification of the affable, knowledgeable man of the soil. He came from Buckinghamshire but just after the war, aged thirty-two, was appointed parks superintendent of Shrewsbury, a town whose parks were much admired and whose flower festival (its prizes much coveted by Lord Emsworth, among others) was ranked second only to Chelsea.

Thrower made Shrewsbury even more famous by becoming famous himself. Long before Alan Titchmarsh and the woman with no bra, he was the face of BBC gardening, first on *Gardening Club*, then, when colour TV demanded more reality than a fake greenhouse in a studio, *Gardeners' World*, often set in the large garden of Percy's own bungalow, the Magnolias, at Merrington.

He exuded the air of a countryman of his generation: tweed suit, tie, pipe, Labrador. He had the attitudes of his generation too, witness his response when asked about chemicals in gardening: 'DDT ... that's not too dangerous.' And he knew his worth as well: his BBC career ended in 1975, when he opted to do commercials for a gardening subsidiary of ICI. He died in 1988, as boss of the Percy Thrower Garden Centre, which is still there, on the edge of Shrewsbury, though now without much family involvement. Thrower was not wholly a cliché: on nights alone in London he would visit casinos. But maybe rustic non-censoriousness is also part of this county's mixture. The old *Sunday Times* journalist Maurice Wiggin once wrote a piece about Shropshire, theorising: 'Perhaps it is because the landscape is fey that it builds resilient and down-to-earth people.'

Shirley Tart was once at an open day at the Magnolias, talking to Percy as he leaned on a gate with his pipe and an air of Salopian contentment. She spotted a man with a plastic bag and secateurs, looking furtive.

'He's nicking cuttings from that plant!' she told him in a do-something tone of voice.

'I shouldn't bother about that too much,' replied Percy. 'How do you think I got it in the first place?'

July 2012/November 2013

~~~~~~~~~~

Direct trains between Shrewsbury and London were restored in December 2014.

37. *Say, is there Beauty yet to find?*

CAMBRIDGESHIRE

A chill January evening: the kind of night when Evensong at even the most famous cathedrals becomes more contractual obligation than tourist attraction, let alone a joyous affirmation of faith. This, however, was not a cathedral, merely a college chapel. Yet outside there were maybe 150 people, huddling against the cold by the 'Keep off the Grass' signs, awaiting admission.

'Gratifying attendance?' I remarked to the usher as we filed in.

His reply had an airy smugness rarely seen in an English house of worship since Anthony Trollope's time. 'Quite normal for a weekday,' he said. 'Weekends we have about 800.'

'Cathedrals get about ten!'

'Our choir does seem to attract them.'

I spent the entire service in King's College, Cambridge, trying to puzzle this out. After all, Ely Cathedral up the road is one of the wonders of the nation, and my inexpert ear actually preferred the harmonies on offer there. And it didn't look as though my fellow congregants – mostly young and foreign – were obvious connoisseurs.

Perhaps they were drawn by the unique appeal of the candlelit chapel, with its architectural consistency and its Rubens and its fan vaulting and its rather cosy kind of grandeur. More likely it was that we were in Cambridge, with a lot of tourists slopping about and nothing to do between the shops shutting and dinner time: King's College Chapel gets a lot of stars in the guidebook.

Maybe there was something else too. Cambridge is a city of locked gates and 'Members Only' signs and forbidding head porters guarding mysterious archways and quadrangles, leading on to more archways. And here we were, admitted free of charge, not just to any college but to the ultimate Cambridge college – the home of Keynes and Forster and Turing – enabling us to bask momentarily among the elite of elites, the rarest of rarefied minds.

And afterwards it was possible to cross the road and peer into the college's window on to the workaday world: the Shop at King's. What could such an august institution display to give us an insight into the thinking of the truly first-class brain? The answer was a choice of mugs, mouse pads and tote bags, all with a KEEP CALM AND CARRY ON motif. What genius! What originality! How can your average, humdrum tat-seller compete?

King's was somewhat besieged that month, and not just by tourists. There was a Wages not Wine demonstration following revelations that, of all the Cambridge colleges, it had both the highest wine budget (£338,559) and the highest number of workers paid below the living wage of £7.65 an hour (123). The college argued that it was important to take into account fringe benefits, such as car parking. You have to be quite clever to think of that one.

If Oxford is an uneasy coalition between town and gown, in Cambridge the order of priorities is much clearer: almost everything feeds directly or indirectly off the university, and its dominance is accepted with much less demur. The city centre is smaller, less fascinating than Oxford's, less riddled with intriguing alleyways before it dwindles into suburban terraces, largely in the grim local yellow-grey brick. I sometimes think of Cambridge as an ugly city with beautiful buildings. It is certainly the more open city of the two, in the sense that several of the colleges are more exposed to public gaze: 'Welcome to the zoo,' a King's don remarked to a friend of mine.

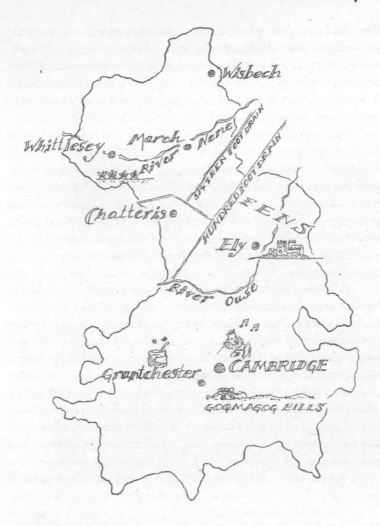

However, the buildings are guarded not just by the locked gates but by the porters, the magnificent breed of salt-of-the-earth, more-than-my-jobsworths epitomised by Skullion in Tom Sharpe's *Porterhouse Blue*. The only implausible aspect of the novel is that Skullion, with all the power that attends a head porter, would ever accept demotion to become mere master of his college.

The city *is* the university. Here even the river has been co-opted and rendered semi-private. The only ways to see the Bridge of Sighs, perhaps the second most famous structure in Cambridge, are either by kind permission of St John's College, which requires either an invitation or payment, or by punt. Yet I could not detect the level of tension that still lurks below the surface in Oxford. The 800-year town v gown conflict is over and gown has won, largely by hiding away gowns, scarves and all other badges of overt superiority.

Allan Brigham – BA (Sheffield), Cambridge roadsweeper for thirty-five years, tour guide, historian and now honorary MA (Cantab) – remembers a graffito soon after he arrived saying 'Bash a Grad in '78'. That would be unthinkable now, he says. 'You wouldn't know who they were. The students look like everyone else. They speak like everyone else. They probably go to the same clubs.' As at Oxford, the growth of a second-division institution ('Home of Anglia Ruskin University' say the signs on Cambridge station), plus dozens of sometimes dodgy third-division colleges and language schools, has narrowed the divide, evened up the gender balance and made it easy to tell the folks back in Shanghai that you studied at Cambridge.

The real University of Cambridge has always been the Avis of British universities: the no. 2, so it has to try harder. It is never Cambridge and Oxford, which would make alphabetical sense, always the other way round, and Oxbridge not Camford. It is an upstart, dating back only to 1209, a spin-off. To be fair, the two have marched in lockstep pretty much ever since: the Old Firm. Their prestige and reputation and lead over all other British universities are as great as ever, maybe greater – it being much harder to gain admission on the old pals' act and doss around getting a pass degree in land economy and first-class honours in puking and practical jokes.

It is a crazy way to run a university system, with two teams and hundreds of also-rans, but there we are. Like other ancient but enduring British institutions – Eton, the monarchy, the City of London – Oxbridge has thrived by responding rapidly to societal change, backed up by being exceedingly rich. And yet there is always this slight air of Oxonian superiority over its rival: Cambridge (to oversimplify wildly) was always Roundhead rather than Cavalier; Low Church not High; turned out lab-coated scientists not high-minded aesthetes. Oxford has provided nine of Britain's thirteen post-war prime ministers, Cambridge none. Cambridge politicians have tended to get within sniffing distance of 10 Downing Street before bumping their heads on the political ceiling: Rab Butler, Willie Whitelaw, Ken Clarke, Nick Clegg too (one assumes). 'Oxford has produced prime ministers and bishops; Cambridge, poets and mathematicians,' sums up Dr Elisabeth Leedham-Green, author of *A Concise History of the University of Cambridge*.

The historian Hugh Trevor-Roper, Oxonian to the core, was exiled to Cambridge as Master of Peterhouse and called it 'a torpid introverted village ... surrounded by dreary Fens'. One recent incomer I know has found it most unwelcoming: 'No one speaks to you in Cambridge. They're too snooty, either because they're upper-class, or because they're not and have moved heaven and earth to get there. Or they're from the Fens and too shy to say anything.' This is not Allan Brigham's experience. 'I've always found Cambridge very friendly. Sometimes on my barrow I felt like a Catholic priest. People would recognise me but didn't know me. And they would tell me all sorts of things.' And it is hard to ignore the advantages of living in a walkable city with the cultural advantages of somewhere far bigger.

There is another way of looking at Oxford v Cambridge. It was expressed by the nineteenth-century economist H. S. Foxwell in a letter to John Neville Keynes, father of the more famous John Maynard, after Keynes senior had been offered a chair at Oxford:

> Pray don't go. Think of the effect your move might have on your son. He may grow up epigrammatical and end by becoming flippantly the proprietor of a Gutter Gazette, or the hero of a popular party; instead of emulating his father's noble example, becoming an accurate, clear-headed Cambridge man spending his life in the valuable and unpretentious service of his friends, venerated by the wise and unknown to the masses, as true merit and worth mostly are.

And, indeed, Cambridge has specialised in fields of which the masses have minimal comprehension. Introverted, though, is not the word.

The old Cavendish Laboratory was housed in mock-Gothic splendour in Free School Lane, just round the corner from the Eagle, where Francis Crick interrupted the drinking one lunchtime in 1953 to announce that he and James Watson had discovered the secret of life. (There are always know-alls in pubs, whether or not they have just cracked DNA.) Its replacement is a soulless but functional 1970s building surrounded by a science park two traffic jams out of town. There is a single external grace note – the quotation above the door: 'The works of the Lord are great, sought out of all them that have pleasure therein' (Psalm 111). Trust the scientists to find something incomprehensible.

I had as personal guide Professor Malcolm Longair, astrophysicist and Jacksonian Professor Emeritus. The Jacksonian chair, dating back to 1782, is considered a touch inferior to the physics department's other great title: the Cavendish Professorship. Five of the eight eligible Cavendish profs have won a Nobel Prize, compared to just three of the Jacksonians. (Between them they are level with Spain.) Still, I was most honoured by his attention, and Longair is a wonderfully zestful advocate for physics in general and Cav physics in particular, which for him is essentially experimental rather than theoretical.

There was the small drawback that I took in only a fraction of what he told me. I just about understood that the Cav had discovered neutrons, electrons and pulsars. It was a little harder to grasp the full implications of the SQUID (Superconducting Quantum Interference Device) and the SLUG (Superconducting Low-inductance Undulatory Galvanometer). 'The bread and butter of condensed matter physics,' the prof said helpfully.

He also said there had been three great boom-times for Cambridge science. The first derived from Isaac Newton; the second came in the late Victorian era, when engineering and physics started to march hand in hand; and the third is right now. Although I had no idea what all the huge expensive clobber in the Cav actually did – in computing the machines get ever smaller, in physics it goes the other way – I could see the boom clearly enough. It was all around us, in the labs and office buildings that have shot up round the Cav and across the flat countryside now known as Silicon Fen; and in a surge in house prices (perhaps 40 per cent in three years) that has made London look like a sluggard: million-pound flats; half a million for bog-standard bungalows.

This has everything to do with Cambridge being Cambridge. In 2013 the pharmaceuticals giant AstraZeneca, an Anglo-Swedish mutation of what was once dear old ICI, announced that it was closing its research and development operation in Cheshire and moving it into the biomedical gold-rush area next to the new Addenbrooke's Hospital, transferring a thousand jobs from where they are needed in the North to where they are absolutely not. 'Our people will be able to rub shoulders with some of the world's best scientists,' said the chief executive.

And like microscopic particles in a laboratory experiment, money oscillates between the tech start-ups, the multinationals and the university, sometimes landing large piles on the lap of whoever happens to discover something commercial. All of which is more pleasing to government than funding bachelor claret-glugging dons to sit round old quadrangles translating Sanskrit.

What worries Elisabeth Leedham-Green is that as Cambridge's scientists get further and further from the core of the university – a huge new cluster is planned north-west of the city – they will commune less and less in the university itself. 'People won't be coming in to lunch as often as they used to. It seems to me a real hazard.' More than half a century ago the novelist C. P. Snow, a Cambridge physicist himself, very publicly worried about the gap between the two cultures, arts and sciences. It is getting more extreme than ever.

I drove out to Great Kneighton, a 'brand new community' with 2,500 homes, being flung up close to Addenbrooke's. The architecture is no more attractive than that of the Cav, but one salesman I met was in raptures: 'People are coming from everywhere. Local, outsiders, China. Cash buyers. Buy to let. I had one woman in who said she didn't really want to live here, she wanted to live out in the country. But she said she'll do that in ten years' time because she didn't expect the same capital growth out there.' This is not a recipe for community.

And the biggest local player wants its share of any action that's going. Already the richest university in Europe, Cambridge has been using American-style methods to bump up its war chest nearer to those of Harvard and Yale. It manages its £5 billion endowment with great seriousness, and has just created another fifty jobs in the fund-raising department for people to harass the graduates by cold-calling and begging.

But how would a postgraduate working in the Cav, living in a rented house in Great Kneighton with a pushchair in the hall and minimal connection with a college, gain any part of the traditional Cambridge experience? Intellectually, this place is a powerhouse. In other respects, it did feel a bit like Slough.

Cambridgeshire was always a feeble county, small but disunited. Its northern half, the Isle of Ely, was under the control of the Bishop of Ely until 1837 and had its own county council until 1965. Nine years after that Cambridgeshire was changed again, bloated by the inclusion of

Huntingdonshire, the old Soke of Peterborough and a sliver of Essex, because that fitted Whitehall's idea of what a county ought to look like. The new version had even less identity.

As a county, Cambridgeshire's major claim to distinction is, as you might expect, educational. Henry Morris became the chief education officer in 1922, when rural education right across England meant confining children – barring a handful who won scholarships to the grammar schools – in frigid village schoolrooms until they were fourteen and could be released on to the farms. Morris stayed in his job for more than thirty years and set up a string of 'village colleges' that were both pioneering comprehensives and community centres: he talked about raising the school leaving age to ninety. Sawston Village College, the first of the breed, still boasts of its public facilities for adult education, sport and culture; it even has a cinema run by the kids.

In the nineteenth century Cambridgeshire was also the main centre for the quarrying of coprolite, or fossilised shit, which had commercial value as a fertiliser. Perhaps one day university scientists will find a similar use for KEEP CALM AND CARRY ON mugs.

The dominant feature of the county's landscape is not specific to Cambridgeshire. The Fens stretch across south Lincolnshire, Huntingdonshire, Norfolk and a bit of Suffolk. But the heart of them lies here. Take out the city and a doughnut of rich but decreasing countryside that surrounds it, and Cambridgeshire is Fen. It is hard for a modern traveller to understand what that once meant: a vast bog, uninhabitable except on the bumps.

Theoretically, this is dry country because rainfall is low, and Fen farmers are as obsessed with water as if they were grazing the Australian outback. But not in the same way: here the perpetual danger is not too little water, but too much. It does not normally arrive from the sky, at least not directly. Were it not for the sea wall, it would arrive from the North Sea every high spring tide. And it does arrive from the big Midland rivers that snake their way into the Wash. If it pours in Northamptonshire, the water heads into the Nene and Great Ouse, and potentially all over Cambridgeshire.

Historically the Fens were remote, sickly and, to outsiders, primeval. The inhabitants, clustered on whatever slightly higher ground was going, made a patchy living catching wildfowl and summer-grazing cattle on the flood plain; they never starved because they could always live on eels.

Everything changed in the seventeenth century when Charles I asked the Dutch engineer Cornelius Vermuyden to work out how to drain the Fens. The locals hated him. Capital took a different view: what emerged was a vast new area of fertile, if still vulnerable, agricultural land, with the inestimable advantage for the new owners that you could make money without having to live in the bloody place. They were, in effect, inland colonists. 'The Fen people,' as Allan Brigham put it, 'were the Red Indians.'

In the new Fens there was work, and Vermuyden's network of drains and washes – canals and flood meadows basically – enabled the 'Fen Tigers' to maintain vestiges of the old way of life into the twentieth century. They remained a breed apart: silent and mysterious in outsiders' estimation; down to earth, tough and resilient in their own. I was lucky enough to find Rex Sly, who carried on his family's 400-year tradition of farming the Fens until settling into semi-retirement as an author, producing a fine history of the place, *From Punt to Plough*. He agreed to escort me. Alas, in the midst of a very mild, very wet January, we picked the one day of ferocious freezing fog.

I drove from Chatteris to meet Rex on the dead straight yet rather alarming back road that runs only inches from Vermuyden's Forty-Foot Drain. One false move and the car's a goner: it's a regular occurrence after closing time. Rex took me on past Whittlesey Washes, which was now – after the downpours – a vast inland sea. Or so he said. Visibility was down to a few yards and for all I knew, there were vast herds of wildebeest sweeping majestically across the horizon. It all added to the mystique of the place. But even when the fog lifts, there is almost nothing to give any definition to the landscape; a miserable wind turbine or a pile of sugar beet comes as a relief. Sly can get lyrical about the big skies, as a Kansan or a Nebraskan might. But it is an acquired taste.

Most never bother to acquire it. The whole county is remarkably short of great houses. And up here the pattern of modern agriculture has created an empty quarter which is astonishing given its proximity to crammed Cambridge. From the 1970s onwards the whimsical nature of European agricultural policy created ideal growing conditions for large-scale arable farming. But increasingly this is undertaken not by the owners but by what are in effect landless plutocrats. They rent huge acreages every year – not necessarily or even normally the same land – to grow industrial quantities of veg, often without needing the help of East Europeans, never mind locals.

The surviving cottages are not attractive to weekenders or incomers. Rex Sly admits many of the villages feel hollowed out. The Fen traditions are fading: wildfowling is rarer; hare coursing is illegal; even the innocent delights of Fen skating (still going strong when I attended the Duddleston Cup during the snows of 1981) have become moribund due to mild winters and uncooperative landowners. All over Cambridgeshire the countryside seemed unusually fearful, full of locked gates and 'Keep Out' signs. There is a reason for this: this kind of agriculture uses massive bits of kit; they say a £100,000 tractor can be stolen at midnight, disguised, and parked safely on an eastbound freighter in one of the smaller ports before cockcrow.

But it goes wider than that. Wisbech, the classic Fen town, has one of the most handsome Georgian terraces anywhere in England, North Brink. But behind this façade lurks a town ill at ease with its new arrivals – not just from East Europe. The roaring demand for property in Cambridge appears to have led to an export trade in problem families.

Evensong in Ely Cathedral was wonderful, even though the choir far outnumbered the congregants – the pleasure increased, as at King's, by avoiding the admission charge, £8 in this case; the cash register closes before the service. I did regret not arriving in both daylight and better weather to see whether Newmarket Heath could be seen from the cathedral; the reverse is certainly true. The racing industry should look more to the diocesan seat; it has much to learn about extracting money from the public.

Next day, feeling the need of a little mountain air, I went back south of Cambridge to reach the summit of the Gog Magog Hills. Now the sun was out, along with the first snowdrops and aconites. Without recourse to crampons, ice axe or oxygen, I reached the trig point in the middle of Wandlebury Hill Fort after an ascent from the car park which took about ten minutes. There was some question, however, as to whether this was indeed the summit; the suggestion was that the neighbouring field might have a hummock 243 feet high rather than a mere 240.

I descended to sit near the river in Cambridgeshire's best-known village, as generations of undergraduates have done, having cycled, punted upriver or walked across the meadows ('the Grantchester Grind').

> *Say, do the elm-clumps greatly stand*
> *Still guardians of that holy land?*
> *The chestnuts shade, in reverend dream,*

The yet unacademic stream?
Is dawn a secret shy and cold
Anadyomene, silver-gold?
And sunset still a golden sea
From Haslingfield to Madingley?
And after, ere the night is born,
Do hares come out about the corn?
Oh, is the water sweet and cool,
Gentle and brown, above the pool?
And laughs the immortal river still
Under the mill, under the mill?
Say, is there Beauty yet to find?
And Certainty? and Quiet kind?
Deep meadows yet, for to forget
The lies, and truths, and pain? ... oh! yet
Stands the Church clock at ten to three?
And is there honey still for tea?

Rupert Brooke wrote 'The Old Vicarage, Grantchester', his most famous non-war poem, not on some benighted battlefield, but in a Berlin café in the spring of 1912, three years before he died of blood poisoning en route for the Dardanelles. So what might he have seen more than a century on? Elm trees? Alas not. Chestnuts? Yes. Dawn and sunset? Not yet abolished. Hares? Unlikely. Water? Absolutely. Beauty? Some. Certainty? No. That vanished in the trenches. Quiet kind? No, there's the M11.

Always ten to three? On the contrary, the clock was unpoetically accurate. Honey for tea? Oh, yes: 60p for a small pot in the Orchard, the long-established café next to Brooke's old lodgings in the Old Vicarage. Brooke is commemorated on the war memorial in the churchyard in the alphabetical egalitarianism of death, between Walter Bolton and Arthur Cutter. 'Men of Splendid Hearts,' reads the rubric, rather patronisingly, I thought.

The Old Vicarage, late seventeenth century, is now in the hands of another writer, one Jeffrey Archer. Incumbents of St Andrew and St Mary tended to shun the place, but I thought it was a really attractive house, in far darker, richer brick than the Cambridgeshire norm: the sort of place one would like to believe could inspire great writing from its occupant. Whether it has worked for the present owner is a matter of opinion. What one can say is that Lord Archer has never written anything quite as elegant as the crossword clue that appeared in the *Guardian*, courtesy of Araucaria, the late Rev. John Graham: 'Poetical scene with surprisingly chaste Lord Archer vegetating (3,3,8,12)'. A scholar of King's was Araucaria. One of its most fertile minds.

A few weeks later I returned to Whittlesey Washes on a non-foggy morning to see if they really existed. By now the flooding had spread across the road, which was closed off not just with signs but with concrete blocks strong enough to thwart a terrorist attack: the detour to Thorney is so long and frustrating that too many drivers had skirted round the original barriers and chanced the water, with unfortunate consequences.

There was indeed an inland sea, about four feet deep across the fields. The morning was cold, breezy and sunny, and the water was rippling and glinting around the bare roadside willows, and as far as the eye could see, which this time was a long, long way. Suddenly the Fens looked as beautiful as any place on earth.

January/February 2014

~~~~~~~~

In late February 2014, King's College caved in and agreed to pay all staff the living wage, the pressure from public opinion and undergraduates having become unendurable. As its great alumnus J. M. Keynes once put it: 'When my information changes, I alter my conclusions. What do you do, sir?' In May, AstraZeneca successfully staved off a bid from the even larger American pharmaceuticals company Pfizer, which was suspected of wanting to move jobs out of Britain altogether.

The answer to Araucaria's conundrum is an anagram of the clue's last four words: The Old Vicarage, Grantchester.

38. *And no one to call me m'duck*

IN THIS COTTAGE JOHN CLARE
THE POET WAS BORN
JULY 13:1793,
THIS TABLET IS ERECTED BY THE
PETERBOROUGH MUSEUM SOCIETY
1921

NORTHAMPTONSHIRE

I awoke in Northamptonshire, as I had done many thousands of times before. But this time it was different. There was no birdsong from the garden. The view from the window offered not Dad's dahlias but a flooded flat roof covered with what looked like the innards of a nuclear power station. Actually they were the necessaries for the Sol Leisure Centre: 'The Regions [*sic*] Premier Leisure Complex'.

Since I left the Barratt Maternity Home a few hundred yards down the road, an experience I do not recall, those thousands of nights – from the dummy to impending decrepitude – were nearly all spent in my parents' various homes.

But Mum died first, and Dad on his own was not quite so insistent on seeing children and grandchildren. Still, I was a fairly regular visitor. And even after he died, my brother and sister-in-law were just outside town, and very hospitable if I happened to be passing; any traveller round England is bound to pass Northampton quite regularly.

Then in 2012 they moved away. Thus it was that, obliged to stay in Northampton for the first time since, I booked myself into the Ibis Hotel, handy for the station, in the midst of the regions premier leisure complex and just opposite a tattoo parlour ('Tattoos by Dick'). I chose the Ibis because it sounded particularly horrid; it offered a kind of mortification of the flesh. It was a misjudgement as it was a perfectly decent hotel. Sources told me if I wanted somewhere crap, I should have stayed in the Travelodge, which has taken over the shell of what was once Northampton's grandest hotel, the Grand.

Anurag, Sergio and Krisztina behind the Ibis desk could not have been kinder. But far from home themselves, they could not know that I was not just an anonymous salesman or contract worker staying in an anonymous hotel in this anonymous town; that, after thirty-seven outsider's chapters, this one was to be personal and heartfelt; that I had come home, even though there was no one to greet me. They did not welcome me with the traditional Northamptonshire endearment 'm'duck'. And nor, all week, did anyone else.

Not only did I have nowhere obvious to stay, there was no one even to drink with. I would have loved a game of cheese skittles – Northamptonshire's great invention – with my mate Dave Hickey, if there was a pub left in town that had a table. But Dave had died absurdly young. And the crowd of newspapermen that used to gather in Shipman's drinking hole had long scattered. The lovely old bar (established 1790) was still there. But it was, in the mysterious way that afflicts a struggling pub, never quite open. Outside hung a 'For Sale' sign, including the ominous phrase 'suitable for renovation'.

In 1939 George Orwell published *Coming Up for Air*, in which his hero, a fat, middle-aged insurance man called George Bowling, goes back to his home town, Lower Binfield. The visit was not, on the whole, a success: 'Where was Lower Binfield?' Bowling wailed. 'Where was the town I used to know? It might have been anywhere. All I knew was that it was buried somewhere in the middle of that sea of bricks.' Bowling stayed miserably in his old local, which had gone upmarket, but found he had nothing in common with anyone there; I had a perfectly nice steak in what I was advised was now Northampton's best pub, the Wig & Pen, formerly the Black Lion.

There was even a kind of cabaret. The woman at the next table was yelling at her husband: 'That's it for me now. I'm not fucking coming home.

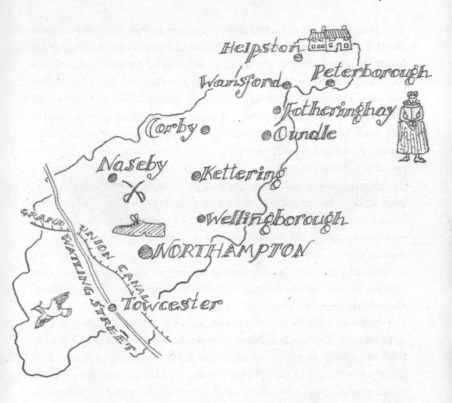

I want a divorce. I'm desperate.' His replies were discreet and inaudible, which is how marriage break-ups used to be conducted in Northampton. Behind them, two drunken young men intermittently harassed the happy couple before being thrown out. This was the best pub in my home town, just before 9 p.m.

At the start of the 1970s the brilliant and wayward architectural writer and broadcaster Ian Nairn came to Northampton and made a brief TV film about the Emporium Arcade, which was about to be demolished. Nairn was enchanted by the market square – reputedly Britain's largest – and appalled by the impending fate of the Emporium, the Edwardian building that dominated its north side. He almost fought back tears as he wandered along its echoing balcony.

As an enterprise, the arcade can never have been a roaring success. As Nairn pointed out, it never led anywhere and drew no passing trade.

And, as the borough council said at the time, it was 'a hotchpotch of small shops, many of them on the seedy side – an illogical use of a modern town centre'. 'That's exactly what a town centre is about,' wailed Nairn. Despite a 10,000-signature petition, the logicians won. Down it came: Nat Bloom the tailor, Harrison's Records, Roy Douglas Stamps and all. And the café where the reporters from the evening paper, the *Chronicle & Echo* – which had the building next door – would go for the mid-morning moan before the lunchtime moan in Shipman's.

Demolition came in 1972, just before the arrival of the *Chron*'s junior-most but mouthiest journalist. The mid-morning moan was moved to the coffee shop in Adnitt's department store (aka Debenhams) and I now like to believe that I occasionally ceased whingeing about the chief reporter and subeditors to state my unflinching view that the council had made a massive strategic error.

For the sentimentalists were not just right, but spectacularly right. Given a rear entrance and a refurb, the Emporium Arcade would have been Northampton's central attraction: a place of boutiques and galleries and vibrant enterprise. It would have been a *destination*. The bog-standard chain-store shopping centre that replaced it was neither big enough nor good enough. Now, all the way from the market square to Marefair, there is almost nothing but pound shops, tattoo parlours, cheap booze stores, Polish grocers and nightclubs: and not nightclubs with tinkling pianos and Ingrid Bergman in an evening gown. Not the Golden Mile, the Dross Half-mile. A destination all right – for kids who want to get bladdered, puke and fight. In 2013 the *New York Times* chose it as Ground Zero for a censorious story about Britain's binge culture.

The end of Emporium coincided with the start of Northampton's expansion from a county town of 100,000 to one above 200,000, a similar size to its neighbour Milton Keynes. But having lost its old county-town cosiness, it has not acquired big-city sophistication, nor even Milton Keynes's own no-one-likes-us-we-don't-care kind of spirit. Nor its vast and popular shopping centre. Northampton is doughnutted by vapid estates full of transient incomers who don't know their neighbours and go to Milton Keynes to shop.

Brian Binley, the Conservative MP for Northampton South, did his utmost to talk the place up, and listed all the things that are happening, including the demolition of the old bus station ('the mouth of hell', according to a more recent TV presenter, Kevin McCloud), known to us fogeys as the new bus station. It went up just after the Emporium Arcade went down, obscenely violating what could have been the arcade's stunning new entrance. 'It's the biggest town in England,' Binley said with a show of pride. 'I don't want it to be a mediocre city.' But the truth is that this town would love to be mediocre again. Last time city status was on offer (when Chelmsford was upgraded in 2012) Northampton wasn't even mentioned in the betting.

Northampton is not a complete catastrophe. The Royal and Derngate, the theatre complex built on the site of the old-old bus station, is a triumph, though it would be more of one if the town itself were more attractive. The new and improbable university is a success, and says it is no. 1 in the country for graduates finding jobs: it does construction and leather technology, not philosophy or medieval poetry. The town has always had great parks. Some days the market square is still vibrant. And Tony Clarke, who was the Labour MP before losing to Binley, loves to tell the story of the old lady in town who got a Somali family as her new neighbours. 'Oh, they're lovely,' she said. 'They're so kind and friendly, it's like the old days.'

But the real story of Northampton is epitomised by the fate of its newspaper. The old scruffy, smoke-filled, graffiti-ridden offices of the *Chronicle & Echo* where I worked are long gone. It moved into spanking-new premises: with expansion on the way, the bosses talked of upping the circulation from 50,000 to 80,000. Instead it collapsed to 15,000. The old-new offices lie empty and the remnant of the paper – now a weekly, not a daily – is housed in a terraced building that would suit a small firm of chartered accountants.

This is of course largely to do with the collapse of local journalism; though Northampton now appears to be vying with Milton Keynes as the biggest metropolis in the English-speaking world without its own daily paper, neither may hold that title for long. It is partly to do with the ineptitude of the owners, Johnston Press. And yet there is something particularly chilling about the speed and extent of the *Chronicle & Echo*'s downfall. Local newspapers depend on people who care about their community. Northampton is what happens when they don't.

And yet good things persist. R. E. Tricker Ltd, English Shoemakers since 1829, still operates behind its russet-brick frontage just beyond the town centre, as it has done as long as anyone can remember. It is now under the control of a fifth-generation family member. The family is actually

Barltrop not Tricker; the firm's name changed in 1862 when a Barltrop married a Tricker and was shrewd enough – long before firms paid brand consultants to state the obvious – to decide which name sounded sexier.

The current Barltrop, Nick, is known to be a shy man and managed to escape the building before I arrived. Thus I never got the chance to ask if he might be related to Mabel Barltrop of the Panacea Society next door in Bedfordshire. But his co-director Barry Jones was welcoming, and kind enough – even as he displayed the £1,200 hand-crafted shoes that are his firm's pride and joy – not to comment on my £39.99 made-probably-in-China-untouched-by-human-hand slip-ons.

Northamptonshire depended on footwear at least from the time Cromwell camped in the county and divined that, contrary to cliché, an army actually marches on its feet. The industry began because the county had cows for leather, wood for tanning and rivers for transport. Now thousands of jobs have gone east, in the normal way. But a residue remains, both around Northampton and in the cluster of small towns further north on the A6. The county no longer sells shoes to the ignorant masses, but to a discerning clientele who appreciate what they are getting: a welted shoe, stitched rather than stuck together. 'A welted shoe is designed to be resoled and heeled time after time,' said Barry. 'Send a pair back after thirty years and it will be made to the same specification.'

I was briefly the *Chronicle & Echo*'s boot and shoe correspondent, though I learned little and remember less. So he gave me the tour: the clicking room, where the leather is cut, through closing, lasting, making, finishing and the shoe room, for the final polish. There was a lovely smell of leather, with a slight underlayer of glue. Tricker's turn out just 1,400 pairs a week, 200 of them by hand. 'Our biggest markets are Italy and Japan, where people have a different concept,' said Barry. 'They'll spend more on their footwear because they care more. The Japanese will spend a day here trying things on and taking photographs. The same as I'd like to do at the Ferrari factory.'

A handful of old Northamptonshire names have got big and stayed, like Barker, Church's, John Lobb, all owned by conglomerates now. Tricker's and Crockett & Jones fly the flag for family firms. The old single-handed really specialist shoemakers, like Albert Whiting, who made buckskin boots for professional cricketers, have nearly all died off. The mass-market stuff has gone abroad, even Doc Martens, though its current owners are reportedly moving some production back again.

And one firm turned into a star of stage and screen. I knew Barry would wince when I mentioned it. In 2005 *Kinky Boots* became the most successful film ever made about Northampton (possibly the only one), then a Broadway musical (definitely the only one). It told the story of a young man who inherited his father's shoe business and discovered it was going bust. He then met a drag artist who solved the problem by persuading him to make feminine footwear strong enough to fit masculine feet. And, after many travails, everyone lived happily ever after. Which was all sort-of true except the last bit: Steve Pateman, the young boss of W. J. Brookes of Earls Barton, did diversify into 'Divine Footwear' and all was well for a while. Then the cheap knock-offs arrived from abroad. The factory is now a housing estate.

Filming was done, inside and out, at Tricker's. What the film could not convey was the smell and feel of the leather. The shoemaker's art is concentrated in the clicking room, where the clicker has to choose the best leather for the front of the shoes and the second-rank stuff for the back. I was invited to stroke the best. It was beautiful: smooth, sensual and, given enough time, quite probably arousing. Very kinky indeed. All the while Barry was explaining precisely where the leather came from. Eventually understanding dawned.

'You mean to say I'm stroking a cow's arse?'

'We prefer to call it the butt.'

Even on modern maps Northamptonshire looks a long thin county. Historic Northamptonshire is even longer, a county and a half since the Soke of Peterborough had a separate county council and ancient liberties that, for instance, allowed the magistrates to try murder cases. This right continued until 1971, on the promise that they would never invoke it.

The county was defined by the transport links between Northampton and Peterborough: the River Nene (pronounced Nen in Northampton and Neen up there), and the Trans-Northants Express (my little joke), which ambled between the two until the day it didn't. I took the line from Castle Station in Northampton just before it closed, alone, as twelve-year-olds were allowed to do in the 1960s, went into a café in Peterborough, played Del Shannon on the jukebox and then took the train back again. Just after that, Peterborough was removed from Northamptonshire and placed in Huntingdonshire, an arrangement that lasted less than a decade before all that was subsumed into Cambridgeshire.

Thus Peterborough appears to be moving eastward, a process which, if it continues, should soon lead to its meeting the onrushing North Sea as that batters its way westward. Then it'll be soked all right. Football fans in Northampton used to hate Peterborough and their fancy nickname 'Posh'. 'Death to Posh,' said the graffiti. This has been replaced by Northampton's psychopathic obsession with Milton Keynes, which has almost nothing to do with football. And Peterborough can wander off to Norfolk or wherever, though it would be helpful if it dismantled its cathedral first and moved it to Northampton, which needs a little something.

For the whole county, including the Soke, location has been crucial to its modern existence and fate. This is now the logistics centre of Britain: basically, it's one big warehouse. It borders nine of the other thirty-eight counties, more than anywhere else. There are several points on country lanes west of Northampton where it's possible to cross in quick succession the Romans' Watling Street (now the A5), the Grand Union Canal, the West Coast Main Line and the M1: the entire history of English transport in a few hundred yards. It is extremely difficult to get from London to the North without passing through Northamptonshire.

This is also just beyond what used to be considered the edge of commutability. In other words, it was right in the target area. In the 1960s almost all the major towns – Northampton, Peterborough, Corby and Wellingborough – were earmarked for massive expansion, a process that looks likely to go on until the last meadow is converted to grow a crop of motorway cones. Nowhere have the Nimbys been more comprehensively routed.

Among the casualties is believed to be the battlefield at Naseby, the decisive encounter of the Civil War: Britain's Gettysburg. In 1989 it was decided to drive the new A14 through this neglected site, against the anguished screams of historians crying 'desecration'. The problem, a planning official told me later, was that while all the historians consulted were certain where the battle was fought, each one's certainty was different from the others. So Whitehall shrugged its shoulders and pushed on with the route it wanted.

Anyway, my school history book claimed Naseby was in Leicestershire. Outsiders always belittled Northamptonshire. No one even knew where to place it. Was it North, as the word implied? Or South? It's sort of in the East Midlands but not quite. Sometimes people called it South Midlands or South-East, or the Home Counties, which is definitely wrong. The TV programmes come from Norwich, which is insane. I once overheard someone utter the phrase '*Very* Northamptonshire!' But Northamptonshire is the county that was never seen as very anything. Except maybe very nondescript. A folk music researcher once triumphantly discovered two songs that came from the county – then found out they really came from Lincolnshire. The Northamptonshire Regiment sometimes marched into battle to the tune of 'The Lincolnshire Poacher'. This was a county that timidly wanted to fit in.

It was on a characteristically bland new housing estate on the edge of Corby that I met Chris Eilbeck and John Tye, two incomers actually, both from London. But they helped change my increasingly despairing perspective of my own home county. They are both members of the Northampton Ramblers, which has a long-established route called the Northamptonshire Round, though it actually takes the form of a ring round the county town and is thus is in danger of being tarmacked itself.

So the two devised their own route round the edge of the (Sokeless) county. Clockwise from King's Sutton in the south to Easton-on-the-Hill in the north and then back down the east side. Fourteen days; 204 miles. You could take a fortnight's holiday and do the whole thing, as with the Coast-to-coast walk across the Pennines, though funnily enough no one ever has; there might be an issue camping in some of the publess villages. Only eight people have done it at all, even in stages.

The route leaves the county just twice: once because the path goes the wrong side of a hedge; and once to take in a pub in Leicestershire. 'All the locals belittle the county and say there's nothing here,' said Chris. 'They're not getting out and about. They just see the towns and the charity shops and think that's it.'

'There's noise in places, obviously,' said John. 'But a lot of the time you could be the only people in the county.'

'My favourite place is the stone bridge at Cosgrove,' said Chris. It is rather lovely: shaped like the top of an ace of spades. Then they started batting the highlights about.

'The view of King's Cliffe.'

'The windmill at Hellidon.'

'And there's Blatherwycke.'

'And nobody knows.'

'You don't have to fight the crowds when you get there.'

'That's the whole point, isn't it?'

I left inspired. I had forgotten how fond I was of the old place, how strong my memories were: the Blisworth Arm of the canal; the Royal Scot thundering through; fields full of lapwings; the walk on a summer's night from Newnham to Badby; haunted Fotheringhay, where Mary Queen of Scots was imprisoned, tried and beheaded; watching Northampton Town beating Leeds and Villa in their one and only season in the top division; nineteen-stone Colin Milburn smashing sixes. And how much I always planned, living in London, to come back home again for good.

Suddenly I was seeing it with freshened eyes. The sun had come out, in this rainiest of winters, which helped. I had forgotten the beauty of the building stone: grey at the top end, then turning to a wonderfully varied brown. Honey-coloured, it's often called, but it varies from mousy to marmalade. And at its absolute best – Rothwell Church, maybe – like a brown-haired girl just emerging from a salon with blonde highlights.

I had lunch in Oundle, the smartest of Northamptonshire towns ('so snooty you can get arrested for watching ITV') and went to see the white-washed cottage at Helpston where the peasant poet John Clare was born in 1793. It is now owned by a trust and open to the public. It's a very nice set-up but, in tough times, in this most untouristed area, a bit of a struggle. Clare himself called Helpston 'a gloomy village in Northamptonshire, on the brink of the Lincolnshire Fens'.

At first sight he might seem a rather soppy nature-lover, celebrating a timeless prelapsarian countryside. In fact he was beset by change and what he perceived as decay, most particularly by the enclosure of the surrounding fields, which transformed the ancient rhythms of the village and curtailed his productive wanderings.

> *Autumn met plains that stretched them far away*
> *In unchecked shadows of green, brown, and grey.*
> *Unbounded freedom ruled the wandering scene;*
> *No fence of ownership crept in between*
> *To hide the prospect from the gazing eye;*
> *Its only bondage was the circling sky.*

But then:

> *Now this sweet vision of my boyish hours,*
> *Free as spring clouds and wild as forest flowers,*

Is faded all – a hope that blossomed free,
And hath been once as it no more shall be.

Change disorientated Clare, especially after he achieved brief celebrity but, of course, bugger all money. He became depressed and had what we would now call a breakdown. This worsened after he moved to nearby Northborough to live with his large but sickly family. Eventually, he was confined to the asylum in Northampton and the poetry dried up. Twenty-seven years later, he finally returned to Helpston on the new railway, in his coffin.

I chose to study Clare at A level because, if I'm honest, he was a famous writer from Northamptonshire, which is what I aspired to become. But Helpston is only a few miles from Peterborough and so has now been plonked in a different county entirely. As Byron Rogers wrote in the *Guardian*: 'For 150 years he was "the Northamptonshire Peasant Poet"; this is chiselled into his grave and memorial ... Now he is Cambridgeshire's Peasant Poet. The skewer has been removed and the man, for whom a move of three miles brought on the anxiety which became madness, is spiralling through eternity in no man's land.'

The Northamptonshire accent is a very distinct one – I still reckon I can spot it anywhere – but it is hard to imitate and impossible to define. Even David Wilson finds it a struggle and he is probably the foremost expert on the subject: a Higham Ferrers boy who studied dialectology in the great specialist unit at Leeds, taught English and produced *That'll Lern Yer, a Dictionary of Northamptonshire Dialect*.

The accent might be a cross between Cockney and Brummie, which is geographically as it should be, but it bears no obvious resemblance to either. Nor is it northern: it's long *grarss* not short *grass*. But in Corby, where thousands of Scots poured in to work in the now demolished steelworks, it has spawned a weird mutation, a sort of twangy Glaswegian.

The great exponent of the language was an artist called Reg Norman, who reputedly got his inspiration from hearing the women queuing at Saxby's pie shop in Rushden and turned them into a pocket cartoon that appeared in the *Northamptonshire Evening Telegraph*, 'Air Ada' (Our Ada), who was always talking to her friend 'Mawd'. This was not very funny, nor intended to be; it was, however, very precise and popular.

Wilson had his favourite overhear on a bus back to Higham Ferrers:

'Is them seats took?', which goes along with another bus-chestnut, 'Ent much room, wuz they?' Lynda Needle, who has translated Bible stories into dialect to read on Radio Northampton, is fond of the ultimate expression of apathetic obstinacy: 'Ah enna gunna do it.'

The accent is always said to be strongest in the inward-looking little shoe towns like Rushden. I am not best placed to judge whether women still address each other, as Ada and Mawd did, as 'gal'. But even in Raunds, supposedly the strongest-accented town of the lot, no one used the gender-neutral m'duck on me. It is not a usage unique to Northamptonshire; in this matter, the county was at one with the rest of the East Midlands.

'When were you last called m'duck?' I asked Brian Binley MP. 'All the time. In my surgery.'

Probably it gets used by wheezy pensioners in doctors' surgeries too, but not among the puking youth of the Northampton nightclubs. And maybe there are still mullocking (awkward) people who scrat about (rush around) pointlessly. But I fear the worst. Binley, from Finedon in the A6 belt, does pass the acid test of Northamptonianism. He refers to the town as N'*thamp*ton. No need to stress the first syllable. No one round here is ever likely to get it mixed up with far-off *South*ampton.

When the call of home was loudest, I always imagined I would settle for ever in south-west Northamptonshire. Here the countryside not just rolls but even pitches a little. Some of the villages are Cotswold-scrumptious but the stone is more handsome, the houses and horses less expensive, and the incomers less snotty.

I became particularly fixated on the village of Eydon (pronounced Eden): lots of nice stone, a splendid old pub, the Royal Oak, and a farm called East of Eydon, which suggested that at least some of the inhabitants had a pleasing sense of humour. Driving by in the 1990s, I stopped at the post office to be greeted by a sign on the door, 'No Directions Given', which suggested that some of the inhabitants might also be miserable sods. I gave up on moving to Eydon. This time, I paid another trip to see if the sign was still there. Naturally the post office had closed down years ago.

The post office had also gone in the village I grew up in, Milton, as it used to be known, now poshified back into its medieval name of Milton Malsor while at the same time being almost engulfed by surging Northampton. Though the main A43 now bypasses the village, the place seems noisier. The shop that went with the post office hangs on, though perhaps not for long; Tesco, the killer of commerce, is dangerously close. The smaller, more villagey of the two pubs, the Compass – once famous for its skittles team – seems equally on the brink. Yet the village is much cherished: the Historical Society has a wonderful website.

I went to see our old friends Monty and Pat Kutas, still newcomers when my parents chose to move back into town after sixteen years, traumatising their youngest son, who could remember nowhere else. Now they have been there almost half a century, a tribute to Milton's healthy air: Monty, well past ninety, was debating whether or not he was up to another summer's golf. But the place has changed, a magnet for people whose main aim is a home handy for the motorway. 'We don't get together the way we used to,' sighed Pat.

The church was locked, a sure sign of encroaching urbanism. In the graveyard I saw the old village names of a generation I can just remember – Tack, Mackintosh, Judge, Mallard, Pell, Yates. If memory serves, they all called me m'duck.

February 2014

~~~~~~~~

The 'mouth of hell' bus station was demolished with a very satisfying six-second controlled explosion in March 2015. Nothing was said about blowing up any of the equally ugly buildings nearby. First reports suggested the new building was even worse: it got clogged up with buses, causing gridlock all over town.

39. *The Great Wen-will-it-implode?*

LONDON

The morning I was going up Britain's tallest building dawned improbably clear: cloudless and un-Londonish. Naturally, by the appointed time, the sky was starting to grey up, though it was still possible to see the distant outlines of the Chilterns, far away to the north-west. As if they mattered. The Chilterns are not the point. The stars of the show are in the foreground.

It takes two separate lifts to get to the viewing platform 800 feet up on the seventy-second floor; and there, around and beneath you, is the rest of London's galaxy of new skyscrapers. Huddled together just north of the river is the dominant constellation, a cluster of lustre: huge twenty-first-century buildings with homely names – the Gherkin, the Cheese-Grater, the Walkie-Talkie, the Helter-Skelter. These overpower the faded veterans of the last century, the NatWest Tower (aka Tower 42) and Lloyd's of London, which caused shock in the innocent 1980s when it displayed all its undies as outer garments.

To the east, Canary Wharf; to the south, the Strata, whose USP was three wind turbines (which are rarely switched on); to the north-west, almost forgotten now, the Post Office or BT Tower, and much-loathed Centre Point; to the north-east, looking rather like a gasometer, the Olympic Stadium. And way down, down, down, barely visible, are the buildings that once defined London: St Paul's Cathedral, the Houses of Parliament, Buckingham Palace. Even the Tower of London, just along the opposite bank, looks merely like an elaborate doll's house. All that's missing is the biggest building of all, the Shard, because we're in it.

Not on top of it. There are another fifteen levels, and steps leading up to a small glass room accessible only to Important Persons with more Vs in front than I can muster. I had managed to blag my way round the £24.95 admission fee (£29.95 on the day) but it's tough getting to the top. In any case, altitude does not define the quality of a view: you often get an impressive view of London flying into Heathrow along the Thames, but the townscape looks too Dinky Toy-ish to offer any sense of reality. In the Shard, you can get a very decent view for the price of a cup from the thirty-second floor coffee shop. At a similar height, the London Eye has been a huge success. The connoisseur of the capital Simon Jenkins swears by the view from the Monument, a mere 200 feet up.

The Shard is not just London's tallest building but the tallest in Western Europe: 1,017 feet. Or 1,016. Or 1,012. Or 1,004. It depends how you do your calculations. However, this is merely like being European baseball champions: it's not our thing. On the global list, the Shard is only sixty-third. Or thirty-ninth. Or sixty-first. Or seventy-fifth. This is a surprisingly inexact science. By the time you read this, London's finest may have fallen near the relegation zone. If even some of the planned stratosphere-scrapers, mostly in Chinese cities, actually get built, this will be regarded as non-league architecture.

Even London will soon be throwing up new rivals. My own favourite view comes entirely free of charge. It is the scale model of the capital in the foyer of the Building Centre in Store Street, just off Tottenham Court Road. This was an ill-starred project: its opening party was scheduled for 7 July 2005, the day of the London bombings. But it has survived, and been regularly updated: the older buildings in grey; the newest, like the Shard, and the forthcoming in gleaming white. On the model big white ones are everywhere. This is the brave new city, where additions are invariably described as 'iconic' or 'world-class', even if, like the height of the Shard,

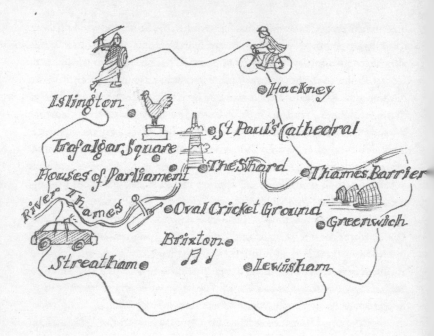

they palpably are not. Their architects promote themselves like TV chefs and are treated solemnly by the media on their own terms.

In London beautiful old buildings are not normally knocked flat: they have too many staunch allies. They just get bullied until they are left cowering, like St Andrew Undershaft (a largely redundant church, not a character in a Restoration comedy), which has survived the Fire and the Blitz and everything else to eke out a continuing but purposeless existence in the shadow of the Gherkin.

Barely visible from the Shard or on the scale model is St Mary-le-Bow, perhaps Wren's second most famous creation, close to his most famous, and in the very heart of one of the world's great financial centres. This church is the home of Bow Bells, within the sound of which all Cockneys are meant to be born. This would be difficult these days, since St Bart's Hospital no longer has a maternity unit, and it would probably need to be Christmas morning with a favourable wind for the bells to be heard at the Royal London or St Thomas's. By this definition any new Cockney would have to be born in a pew, or maybe at a trading desk, to a mother who was *much* too busy to take an hour off. That assumes the bells are working properly. I arrived at 6 p.m., just as I swear I heard the clock strike four. 'Am I going mad?' I asked a man in a dog collar. 'Ah, I think one of the hammers is broken,' he replied.

The occasion was a lecture given by the biblical scholar Dr Jules Gomes entitled 'Prophets of Justice Challenge Profits of Injustice'. Dr Gomes had come down from the Isle of Man, where he lives, presumably obeying the call of God rather than the advice of his accountant. 'The God of the Bible is the polar opposite of this goddess of the markets,' he proclaimed. And he called in aid Isaiah, Amos and Ecclesiastes: 'I have seen all the works that are done under the sun; and, behold, all is vanity and vexation of spirit. That which is crooked cannot be made straight.'

His interpretation was very clear: 'I don't think I want to throw out capitalism entirely. It is unbridled capitalism that is the problem.' And this he told to an audience of two dozen, while outside the hundreds of thousands who form the rest of the City's workforce made their way home on a winter's night after another day of unbridled capitalism.

I love London. I always have loved London. It is so ingrained that I have probably never, until now, thought about how much I loved London. In the school holidays, I would come down from Northampton to stay with my grandmother in her flat in Temple Fortune where the trolley buses ran past the window. And from the age of eleven or twelve I wandered off alone from Golders Green station and met friends from boarding school or just explored. It wasn't that Nana didn't worry – she was worrying about Vietnam before Lyndon Johnson could find it on a map. But she didn't worry about *me*. Adults were adults and children were children, and they didn't get in each other's way: 'Bye, darling.' It was marvellous.

And so I was an Underground boy. At twelve, I could tell you exactly how to get from Bayswater to Queensway (Circle or District to Notting Hill Gate, then take the Central). It was many years later, when I actually lived in London, that I realised the smarter answer was to walk a few yards down the street. I don't know exactly when it was that I was in Soho gazing into a strip club with my friend John, and he wanted to go in and nervy little me said I would rather stick to the plan and go to the Oval; it might have been last week.

Nana died, and I lost my freedom pass. But years later I came back and settled in Islington. Peter Ackroyd, author of *London: A Biography*, is very good on the sense of London as a palimpsest. Other cities cannot compare: New York is too new, Paris too planned, Berlin too jerky in its history. In London the gentle dust of time accretes and settles; every brick, every inch has an amazing story, usually untold. And nowhere exemplifies this more than Islington: a site where Boadicea fought the Romans, which became a resort, beyond the City boundary. Generations of citizens would come to ride, drink, play ball and you know what. This was where Raleigh first sampled tobacco. 'A haven of carelessness', in Ackroyd's phrase. Then the pace of history quickened. It was built up to become a home for Pooterish clerks, then degenerated into a slum. Next, the old houses were either demolished to become council flats or gentrified to provide houses fit for the likes of the young Tony Blair.

When I arrived, its current incarnation was still in a relatively early phase. Islington was trendy all right, but still more shabby than chic. Ten years after the abolition of shillings and pence, two establishments on Upper Street refused to deal in decimal currency: one was the King's Head theatre-pub, which thought it was a cool gimmick and, with beer still well under a pound a pint, a viable one; the other was an old draper's shop whose owner simply couldn't be bothered to change her ways. There were almost no chain stores or restaurants. Now there is little else. But, as Ackroyd says: 'The area has regained its reputation for hospitality and conviviality which it possessed long before it ever became part of London. The old presence lingers beneath every change of appearance.'

And there I was: young, single, not poor, living in the most exciting district of the most exciting city on earth. Did I take full advantage? Did I explore this great megalopolis? Who does? It was only now, with a book to write and a deadline to keep, that I reverted to being a twelve-year-old and wandered again. In a city that seems so expensive, it is amazing how much you can do free of charge if you put your mind to it. I have an inflexible rule that, with half an hour to spare in the West End, I always go into the National Gallery, pick a room at random and immerse myself. I had a spare half-hour as recently as 2006, I'm sure of it.

You can tiptoe into the Supreme Court; you can go to Evensong at St Paul's; indeed, on a Sunday in South Kensington you can attend seven different masses at Brompton Oratory (choosing between English, Solemn Latin and Tridentine Latin) and pop next door for any or all of four more with the vibrant Anglicans of Holy Trinity, Brompton; you can stand on a platform at Waterloo and watch the sinuous progress of the colour-coded South West trains; you can see what's on the Fourth Plinth (a striking blue cockerel last time I looked); you can see the Hogarths at Sir John Soane's Museum or the skeletons at the Grant.

With notice, you can observe the London Metal Exchange, the last 'open outcry' exchange in Europe and certainly the best free theatre in London: a group of young men in jackets and ties with furious energy and no self-consciousness setting prices in a glorious flurry of signals that brings together the atmosphere of Speakers' Corner, a confrontation between football fans, Prime Minister's Questions, a West End musical and a Victorian Derby Day.

Though it's a pig to find by land, there is the Thames Barrier, which is all that stands between the city and inundation from the North Sea. It is not exactly Sydney Opera House, which is said to resemble nuns playing leapfrog, but the Barrier does look like a line of mummy nuns and baby nuns (clearly from a very liberal nunnery) playing on see-saws.

Within the square mile of the City half a dozen churches were built devoted to Marian devotion alone: besides the aforementioned St Mary-le-Bow, there is St Mary Abchurch, St Mary-at-Hill, St Mary Aldermary and St Mary Aldermanbury (of which only the footprint remains), all by Wren, and St Mary Woolnoth, by Hawksmoor. With a little forethought and luck you can get yourself into the sumptuous Guildhall for the Silent Ceremony, which marks the inauguration of each new Lord Mayor (686 so far), not to be confused with the upstart Mayor of the whole of London (just two). This brings out of the woodwork the Remembrancer, the Common Serjeant, the Common Cryer, the Ward Beadles, the Aldermen below the Chair, the Aldermen above the Chair, and a bloke in a ludicrous furry hat who turns out to be the Swordbearer.

And there is the sheer serendipity of the streets, where you come across such oddities as the grave of Giro the Nazi dog, tucked away by Carlton House Terrace; he belonged to the German ambassador and fatally chewed through a live wire left by builders in 1934 to be buried with full Nazi honours. The Nazis were far more sentimental about animals than people, just like the English.

There are pockets of quite improbable rusticity. I love the pretty Keeper's Cottage in St James's Park, whose occupant could have popped into his nearest neighbours, the Prime Minister and Chancellor of the Exchequer, to borrow a cup of sugar in the days before Downing Street was turned into a fortress. There is East Acton station, on the Central Line but with the look of a halt on a long-closed branch: alight here for

Wormwood Scrubs, known to non-locals for its prison but, beyond the high wall, one of the largest and most unexpected (if litter-strewn) open spaces in London.

It is a city of endless mysteries and anomalies. As even novice tourists know, London traffic goes on the left (except in Savoy Yard as they may not know). And, as they soon discover, you stand on the right on a tube escalator or risk curses and humiliation. But no one knows what to do on the stairs leading to and from the escalators: the rules, where they exist, vary from station to station.

Some things you really cannot spot by chance, like 23–24 Leinster Gardens, Bayswater, where, between two hotels, in the midst of a stuccoed terrace, is a house that does not exist. It was knocked down when the Metropolitan Line was pushed through in a cutting in the nineteenth century and then rebuilt as a dummy. Andrew Martin, in his book *Underground, Overground*, tells how he confronted the staff of both hotels, who had no idea, and soon had them standing outside saying to each other, 'But we thought it was part of *your* hotel.'

Still, the more you walk the more you allow for delightful happenstance. Outside one nonconformist chapel I saw a group of men dressed for a funeral unloading a car full of things that did not look corpse-shaped: they were crates of champagne. Walking down Victoria Street, with storm clouds building to the south-west, I caught a shaft of sunlight illuminating the towers of Westminster Abbey with a violet sky behind. What a fabulous, golden, mysterious treasure house of surprises and pleasures this place is. I had forgotten that London had such a thing as weather; I think most Londoners have also forgotten. That is because they lead the life of Londoners.

Back in the days when I travelled the Underground for a half-fare of tuppence, the tubes were dominated by adverts for temp agencies, and something called the Location of Offices Bureau, which encouraged employers and workers to migrate to cheaper, less crowded places where commuting might not be so stressful. It is said that 24,000 jobs a year moved out of London in the 1960s.

The population of London was declining, which was assumed to be a good thing, leading to a more sensible and equitable distribution of the nation's population and its diminishing share of global wealth. The bureau continued to assist the process through the 1970s until Margaret

Thatcher came to power and axed it. In the thirty-five years of right-wing government since Mrs Thatcher's accession (including the thirteen when Labour was in power) the wealth has gone both up and down, but no one in authority has given a damn about whether it was spread fairly.

In that time, London's status has risen again, both globally and nationally. Unquestionably, this is a world city, maybe *the* world city, whatever that might mean exactly. Within England, it has been the unrivalled dominant force for a millennium, and over the past couple of decades it has extended its lead further and further over its toiling rivals. I now realise that in a sense this entire book has been about London. Every county can be defined by its distance from the capital, not just geographically – though someone could probably construct a workable algorithm using mileage and transport links – but economically, culturally, spiritually, even linguistically.

In those years, British industry (concentrated in the North and Midlands) has declined massively, while finance and tourism (concentrated in London) have grown to compensate. Though political power has been devolved to Scotland and Wales, and given away upwards to Brussels, England has become ever more London-centric. No major country is as centralised as this one. Many countries – the US, Canada, Australia, Brazil ... – do not have their largest city as the capital. German finance is centred on Frankfurt, not Berlin. Even once-monolithic France has been devolving; and in any case the south is a long way from Paris. In little England, the pinnacle of excellence in almost every single field of endeavour is in London. The only obvious exceptions are academe and football. And, frankly, Oxford and Cambridge are now pretty much outer suburbs. And in most recent seasons London's top football teams have been pretty much equal to Manchester's and superior to Liverpool's.

In many fields the path of ambition leads *only* through London. And so do the transport links. In late 2013 and early 2014, as the banker-induced slump gave way to recovery just in time for the next election, the statistics of those years constantly exemplified the extent of London's overlordship. Some 80 per cent of UK private sector jobs between 2010 and 2012 were created in London; the overall growth rate in London in the planned pre-election boom year of 2014 was expected to be twice as high as in the rest of the country; and – a splendid stat, this – 80 per cent of all the cranes operating in the UK in 2013 were in London and the South-East. England is not so much a country as a solar system, in which a searing sun is surrounded by frigid little asteroids and then reverses the law of physics by drawing the heat out of them.

The mayor of London, Boris Johnson, has a riff when he speaks to the Conservative conference whereby he lists all the provincial nowhere-towns that have made small contributions to his city's *grands projets* – the Olympics, Crossrail, Thameslink, the new sewer – by providing some of the rivets or widgets. This draws cheers from the local delegates. It is like listening to a billionaire detailing the coins he has put into charity boxes.

The relationship between London and the provinces (that telling word) has always been domineering; it has now become abusive, and one senses it in all kinds of strange ways. Journalists always had a rough idea of what a life was worth in news terms: one Briton dead = ten Americans = twenty Europeans = 500 Africans = 1,000 Bangladeshis, something like that. Now it needs amending: maybe one Londoner = five provincials. It is astonishing how much more solemnly a storm is treated if, by a rare mischance, it should brush the South-East instead of merely attacking the periphery.

As a visitor to the city, I always bought *Time Out*, with its comprehensive listings of all the plays, concerts and exhibitions: a range of culture and entertainment matched nowhere else on earth, so vast no individual can do more than skim the surface. Now *Time Out* is given away free and imposes its own choices, merely picking out the newest and what it considers the best: the metropolitan elite imposing its own criteria about what to see and do. Non-Londoners get this sense even at home when they are bombarded with news of London events.

In the wonderful London Library (note the name), books about London are not housed with those on the rest of England but as a separate country, between Lithuania and Luxembourg. The three main countries of Western Europe might be considered as Germany, France and London, and the best illustration of this comes from the Olympic Games.

In the late 1980s Britain felt self-confident enough to start bidding to host the Olympics again. But the Games are awarded to cities, not to nations. Birmingham put in a bid once and Manchester twice; every time they got a derisory number of votes among the members of the International Olympic Committee, the self-appointed body that decides these matters. The late John Rodda, the *Guardian* journalist who understood the Olympics better than anyone, just laughed; he said repeatedly that Britain could only hold them in London 'because it goes where the wives of IOC members want to go shopping'. The rest is history.

London was a pretty frantic city in the 1980s, but it had its down times: before dawn; around 9 a.m. on Saturday, which was a wonderful time to whizz round in a car and do jobs; Sunday afternoon, when the shops were shut. Now it never ceases. It is a marvellous place to be young and rich: I was told that German bankers have to be not merely bribed to be posted back to Frankfurt but offered free tickets to London at the weekends.

Most Londoners experience life differently, even those who work in the City. The crushiest moment of the London rush twenty-four hours is said to come at 8.25 a.m. on the narrow northbound platform of the Northern Line at Bank. The passengers there do not look like masters of the universe in either dress – between the smartly suited, the smart casuals and the scruffs, the scruffs have a slight edge – or demeanour. They look cowed, put upon, heading through the throng for a few moments in the half-light before entering whatever building offers them the next phase of their half-life.

Recent London novels, even from really good writers, seem to reflect this by being deeply depressing: Ian McEwan's *Solar*; Zadie Smith's *NW*, John Lanchester's *Capital*. At the launch of the Labour manifesto in 2010 I sat by one of London's most famous and successful journalists. The back-drop on the stage was a clever-clogs computer graphic of a field of waving barley. 'Look at that grass,' said my neighbour. Perhaps he had never seen any real grass, let alone barley.

A well-judged career in London offers three stages: a joyous single life; then perhaps thirty years on the hamster wheel, coping with the job, the children, the commute and everything else, above all the thumping mortgage; but then, for those who bought their houses a boom or two or three or four earlier, there comes the payout. *The payout!*

In 1971 an organisation called the Houseowners' Association pro-duced a small volume: *Where to Live in London*. It gave star ratings to the various districts and suburbs for the benefit of potential buyers; the tone would now be considered politically incorrect, but some of the judge-ments were pretty astute:

BRIXTON*: The place most people love to hate.
HACKNEY**: Distinctly working-class but not entirely without
   hope.
LEWISHAM**: Very grotty.
GREENWICH***: Clearly coming up in the world. Parts still rough.

HAMMERSMITH***: As Irish as they come. But some parts are
  beginning to look interesting.

right up to:

ST JOHN'S WOOD*****: An area where money is the only
  password. Even small luxury town houses fetch £20,000 ...
  and £70,000 is not unknown.

Oh, it's very funny indeed (talkin' about my generation). By 2014
ordinary three-bedroom terraced houses in distinctly ** or *** parts of London, which would still have cost four figures in 1971, were nudging ever
closer to the million-pound mark. To have maintained their value against
inflation they should perhaps be worth £100,000. Even four decades ago,
when mortgage tax relief was on offer, house purchase was perceived as
a shrewd investment. No one knew how shrewd, any more than the tech
multi-billionaires, pursuing their theories in their basements and garages,
knew quite how clever they were being. And the techies can be said to
have brought about some improvement to the world; they even pay taxes
on their riches, sometimes. House price inflation has offered life-changing
tax-free windfalls, for nothing.

This is not just a London phenomenon. Property owners across Britain have benefited, but to nothing like the same extent. As *Where to Live
in London* noted: 'The average price paid in London for a home is nearly
£5,900 – well over £1,000 higher than the national average and nearly
£2,000 more than in the poorest parts of the country.' That gap has got
wider and wider and wider.

Most of the great buyers' market phases in London since then have
followed a familiar course: prices would surge in the capital, then ripple
outwards in a year or so as young couples were priced out and found
themselves forced to settle for the suburbs, exurbs or even provinces. The
post-2010 boom has been much slower to spread, partly because of London's stranglehold on desirable jobs, but mainly because the pressure at
the top end has been caused not by residents' need for somewhere to live,
but because every oligarch, princeling and money launderer on the planet
saw a London property as an essential status symbol, bolthole, occasional
holiday home and a seemingly infallible and very lightly taxed investment.

The constant search for new and undiscovered districts has now taken on a frenzy not seen since the European powers competed to grab tracts of Africa. As a young woman wailed to Simon Jenkins, 'I'm too late for Shoreditch. I'm desperate for Hackney. I may get something in Catford.' She was not interested in west London, now seen as very uncool.

This phenomenon is typified by the story of Hoxton, which the 1971 book did not even think worth mentioning. I suspect many Londoners had still never heard of it, except perhaps from the opening scenes of *Pygmalion*/*My Fair Lady* when Henry Higgins is showing off his ability to pick up the slightest variation of accent: 'Where do I come from then?' asks one man.

'Hoxton.'

'Blimey, you know ev'ryfink, you do.'

In so far as it had a reputation it was a fearful one. This was enhanced by a 1969 book, *A Hoxton Childhood* by A. S. Jasper (a pseudonym), which recalled growing up in a rough family – drunken, dishonest father; loving, put-upon mother; thieving brother and brother-in-law – around the time of the First World War. This was backed up by Ted Williams, son of a road sweeper, who was interviewed for a brilliant 1980s ITV series (the sort that hardly gets made these days), *The Making of Modern London*:

> One reason that the posher people who used to live in Hackney moved out, the managers of department stores, foremen, people like that, was because they didn't like living so close to us lot in Hoxton.
>
> It was a common saying 'If you put a net around Hoxton you'd have half the criminals of the world.' They'd do a bit of house-breaking in places where people could afford to lose it, like De Beauvoir. If we saw a college boy, we'd snatch his hat off and fill it up with horse shit, then give it to him back. We were rotten when we went into the posher areas, we wouldn't do it in our own street.
>
> When the police tried to arrest anybody they'd have to come in pairs, and there was a riot then because people used to get on to the roofs and chuck stuff down at them.

By the late twentieth century Hoxton had started to morph into an artists' quarter; by 2014 the artists had been priced out, partly due to what is perhaps the most important contribution to London of its first mayor, Ken Livingstone: stitching together bits of forgotten railway into the new

Overground network. I went to dinner in Hoxton Square (three-bedroom apartment: £2 million) at Zigfrid von Underbelly, a restaurant with a lot of TV screens, the sort of place that asks how you want your burger cooked, though I'm not sure the answer makes much difference.

Hackney Council, being barred from imposing a sensible amount of tax on £2 million 'apartments', ekes out its feeble public services by charging £5 an hour for parking in Hoxton Square right up to midnight. No one was seen vandalising the cars, chucking stuff from the penthouse rooftops or putting horse shit in hats. Down the road, into once equally no-go-for-respectable-people Shoreditch, was a nightclub called Cargo. That week's programme read: 'Monday – Resident DJ; Wednesday – Bloomberg Corporate; Friday – Deep Disorder'. I'm not at all surprised by the Bloomberg Corporate, just amazed there isn't more Deep Disorder.

The old places still attract older people's money. In both 2012 and 2013 Egerton Crescent in South Kensington was named as the most expensive street in the UK, with houses changing hands at an average of £7.4 million. It is a terraced row with most of the front doors opening straight on the pavement, not unlike pound-a-house Bond Street in Stoke-on-Trent, where (extrapolating) you could buy 7.4 million houses for the price of one in Egerton Crescent, with homes that are more pleasingly proportioned and handy for the museums, but honestly ...

In reality, although too few properties change hands for it to show up in surveys, the most expensive street is probably Kensington Palace Gardens, a bit further north, where the Sultan of Brunei and Britain's presumed richest man, Lakshmi Mittal, live next door to each other (Oh, the chats they must have over the fence: 'Yer onions doin' awright this year, Lakshmi?') in houses that may be worth over £50 million, within hailing distance of the Duke and Duchess of Cambridge ('Mornin', Kate, pet, 'ow yer diddlin'? Oo, in't the baby lookin' bonny?'). Most of the street is taken up with embassy residences and many of these buildings seem somehow to reflect their nation's image – Finland: unpretentious and bourgeois; France: elegant and fussy; Russia: cold and forbidding. The continuing value of many of these houses depends partly on them not collapsing into their vast new basements.

Despite all this, London property is becoming less and less about location, location, location. The streets are far safer than they were in the 1990s, in keeping with a trend across the Western world, helped a little by

Britain's North Korean-style mass surveillance system. Singles in particular, fuelled by desperation, are becoming more adventurous about where they live. Brixton, which used to be described as diverse, meaning black, is now diverse meaning diverse. Deptford, only six minutes from London Bridge, has always been resistant to change, mainly because so many of the old do-up-able terraces were bombed out in the war and rebuilt as council flats. Even so, on Deptford High Street you can already smell the macchiato. At the Elephant and Castle – such a pretty name, such an ugly place – the huge Heygate Estate is being demolished to be replaced by something more appealing and market-friendly. The population has been dispersed by the council.

The once gentle rise and fall of neighbourhoods has been succeeded by a dizzying momentum, almost all of it upwards. London was never a truly segregated city, like Johannesburg or Washington, DC. Charles Booth's great survey of the 1890s, *Life and Labour of the People in London*, includes maps, coloured to indicate the wealth of the inhabitants in each street: the very rich in gold, the very poorest in black and described as 'lowest class, vicious, semi-criminal', gold and black nuzzling surprisingly close to each other.

One of the black areas was the south side of Chadwick Street between Victoria and Westminster, barely five minutes' walk from Parliament itself. The residents were described by Booth as 'labourers, hawkers, flower-sellers, bottle-gatherers and organ-grinders, also thieves, beggars and prostitutes'. I went to Chadwick Street and found myself standing outside the headquarters of Channel 4.

All this is what is normally described as 'regeneration', a friendly, wholesome word. Regeneration usually means government-assisted gentrification, or embourgeoisement. What we are seeing is a variant of the Paris-ification that we saw in Oxford in Chapter 14: the poor being shoved towards and beyond the periphery. But there is a mitigating influence: new developments are expected to have a small proportion of 'affordable' houses (as opposed to the unaffordable ones). This means that the inner London of the future will probably not conform to our old notion of an inner city. It will be confined to the rich and a few of the poor: in other words, the tycoons, bankers and oligarchs plus their nannies and cleaners. There will be a few middle-class people with grandfather-rights, living in the homes their grandparents shrewdly bought after reading *Where to Live in London* four decades ago. But most of the teachers, journalists, nurses, policemen, even doctors of tomorrow will be elsewhere. In terms of the future city's balance that is not so much regeneration as degeneration.

For reasons lost in the smog of memory, I have on my shelves the S–Z volume of the *London Post Office Telephone Directory*, April 1959. It is a feast of nostalgia, complete with advice about how to make calls from a telephone without a dial or on a party line (i.e. a shared one and less fun than it sounds). Then there are the old exchanges with their strange-sounding names, of which you dialled (if you had a dial) the first three letters. Some were boringly geographical (FULham, KILburn, SWIss Cottage); but others were regal (MONarch, ROYal, TUDor); heroic (CUNningham, RODney, FRObisher); artistic (ELGar, KIPling, VANdyke); or pastoral (ACOrn, CHErrywood, SPEedwell).

And, darling, simply everyone was there. The British were not yet addicted to going ex-directory for fear that someone might phone them. Harold Wilson MP, of 12 Southway, NW11 (MEAdway 2626) was in, just five years before he became prime minister and entered a gateless Downing Street with a lone copper outside the door of No. 10. There were two pages given over to representatives of our old friends from Hertfordshire (Chapter 23), Spirella Corsetières; and less than half a column of Singhs. C. M. (Molly) Matthews used the 1961–2 phone directory as the basis for her classic work *English Surnames*, reasoning that it was a fairly representative sample of the country. It was a very different London.

In 2014, on an Overground train between Brondesbury Park and Stratford, I could eavesdrop on – no, was unable to block out – half a dozen simultaneous mobile calls, conducted in half a dozen languages, the one in English being heavily accented. This is not a stretch of line obviously frequented by tourists.

There were always foreign voices and non-white faces in London; it was that kind of city. However, there was no organised large-scale immigration until the arrival of the *Empire Windrush* and 500 migrants from Jamaica in 1948 to alleviate labour shortages in those heady years of full employment.

In the years that followed, more West Indians arrived, then Asians, and the trickle became a steady stream. This soon produced growing concern within the Cabinet, which struggled to find a way to stem the flow without, on the one hand, alienating people from the white Commonwealth who still perceived themselves as distant sons and daughters of the Mother Country and, on the other, being seen as overtly racist.

The first act designed to restrict post-war immigration was passed in 1962, but still the numbers grew, (a) because the British economy was growing too; (b) because it was held to be inhumane to restrict the admittance of families; (c) because crises came – particularly the persecution of Asians in East Africa – which required an urgent humanitarian response; and (d) because successive governments hadn't got the foggiest idea what they were trying to achieve (let alone how to achieve it) and veered between laxity and harshness. And of course the first generation now had children born here who were clearly British, but sometimes had trouble grasping that themselves.

The pre-existing British fell into two camps: a largely elite group who felt that immigration was so obviously a Good Thing that it must never be discussed, for Fear of the Consequences; and a largely non-elite group who felt, usually without much venom, that things had got out of hand. The first attitude prevailed, and perhaps deserved credit for the fact that, except for the original Notting Hill riot of 1958, the racial violence that did take place only rarely involved the local white population as such, and more often directly centred on the police as provocateurs or victims, depending on one's perspective.

This was particularly true in London. People grew to like their Gujarati newsagents and Polish plumbers, who worked longer and harder than their home-grown predecessors. This did not mean the capital embraced the newcomers but, in the tradition that governs behaviour on crowded tubes, paid them 'civil inattention'.

Any kind of control gradually became more difficult because European Union laws insisted on free movement of labour, although the British government declined to join the Schengen Agreement allowing passport-free travel across the Continent, a decision which was more a nuisance to its own citizens than a deterrent to anyone else. In 2004, much of Eastern Europe joined the EU, and Britain, unlike the other rich countries, imposed no interim controls. Hence the arrival of, most obviously, the Poles.

But the immigration of the twenty-first century is altogether harder to explain. It extended far beyond the Commonwealth and the EU: migrants came from Somalia, whose residents sought refuge as their country disintegrated; from southern Europe, as the euro crisis took hold; from Francophone Africa, South America, everywhere. 'Who?' was now anyone on an increasingly mobile planet: the footloose, the love-struck, the ambitious, the knowledge-hungry. 'How?' remained a bit mysterious, given the toughness of ministerial rhetoric and the difficulty of getting through Heathrow even for the natives. It was also hard to be sure how these newcomers lived, given the property market, though there was evidence of a vast penumbra of life in relentlessly subdivided houses in the more unfashionable boroughs.

'Why?' was easy enough. From Dick Whittington onwards, it has been believed that the streets of London are paved with gold. And London, if not exactly welcoming, ignored you benignly, was full of one's own fellow countrymen, had a language that was far more accessible and pliable than any other, and made few demands – certainly no expectation of adaptation to the new surroundings – as long as you remembered to stand on the right of the escalators.

The effect has been stunning. According to the 2011 census only 44.9 per cent of the population of Greater London was 'white British'. Tony Travers of the London School of Economics has surmised that the figure has now dipped below 40 per cent, in part because of higher birth rates among the incomers. This is not the product of any coherent political will of the sort that governs migration into a country founded on immigration like Australia; it stems from a situation of which the government lost control the moment the *Empire Windrush* docked.

The deeper mystery is what has become of the aboriginals. Even ten years ago the default voice you heard on arrival in the capital was that of the fark-me-guv-cor-blimey-my-ol'-man-said-follow-the-van kind of Cockney who has dominated London since Bow Bells first sounded. Such people still drive taxis but off-duty the drivers are often parked in Hertfordshire or Essex. Cockney can be heard all over south-east England and beyond, but less and less in the capital itself.

The migrants have made London an even more heterogeneous, varied and fascinating place than it was before, exemplified by what is now its most popular free event: the bottom-up Notting Hill Carnival (originated 1966) having surely now overtaken the top-down Lord Mayor's Show (originated circa 1215) after shrugging off a once-fearful drug-ridden reputation to become the kind of multi-culti celebration which, in the white liberal middle-class imagination, sums up day-to-day London.

There, as the London School of Samba sashayed through the street, I met Cecilia Beckett who came to Hackney from Barbados, involved with the carnival since 1988, when there were twenty bands rather than the current seventy or eighty. For her, carnival is not about the day itself so much as the preparation: all the costume-making and practising. 'It's about giving young people something to do over the summer holiday in a place where they don't have much to do,' she said. 'Teaching them about their heritage, about calypso, about steel bands and about carnival. But it's changed. It used to be about doing your own thing. Now it's about putting the right thing on the form so you can get funding.'

Meanwhile, those white liberal middle classes are being driven out by the conversion of London homes into 'a global reserve currency' – a phrase given resonance in a much-read article by London-based American writer Michael Goldfarb: 'The property market is no longer about people making a long-term investment in owning their shelter,' said Goldfarb, 'but a place for the world's richest people to park their money at an annualised rate of return of around ten per cent' – all abetted by council tax rates, at the top end, of staggering generosity. It may be significant that the piece was published by the *New York Times*, rather than any London paper – whose senior executives are almost all among the beneficiaries of the ever-reverberating boom.

In March 2014, which may or may not prove to be the peak of the lunacy, a property investment company called London Central Portfolio offered a new fund. It was quite conservative in a way, suggesting that if top-end flats continued growing at only 9 per cent, a small opportunity (formerly known as 'a home') worth £1.5 million now at that rate would become £36 million by the middle of the century. 'Firmly sustainable,' said Hugh Best, LCP's investment director. 'They have been growing at that level for forty years and we see no reason for that to change.' The possibility of bloody revolution may not have been factored into the calculation.

Overall, the presence of the migrants has not necessarily been unpleasant. There is evidence that in this unmelting pot, many were importing the sterner attitudes of their backgrounds rather than fitting in with their new come-day-go-day domicile.

'The effect has been to shift London to a more conservative version of itself,' says Travers. 'There are more children born in wedlock in Greater London than anywhere else in the UK. Smoking figures are lower in London. Alcohol consumption is lower in London. The homicide rate continues to go down. What we're seeing, paradoxically, is Britain shifting back to the 1950s.' Perhaps we could mark this development by restoring ACOrn, CHErrywood and SPEedwell to the telephone system.

Everywhere is churning. Brick Lane, E1, the most chameleon street in the ever-changing city, is starting to shrug off its Bangladeshi phase, undergoing a Hoxtonisation process as the retro clothes shops march southwards and the area takes its character from the ultra-cool kids at the London campus of the Italian fashion college Istituto Marangoni. The curry house owners appear to be cashing in and moving out, many following the same path from here to the north-west suburbs established by the Jews a century earlier. One curry house almost opposite the Brick Lane mosque had magically transformed into an Argentinian cantina the week before I was there. The mosque itself, formerly a synagogue, before that a chapel, may have to find yet another incarnation. A nightclub probably.

A few streets away on Whitechapel Road is the Blind Beggar, a pub with an extraordinarily rich history. It was named after the thirteenth-century legend of Henry de Montfort, blinded at the Battle of Evesham, who became so downwardly mobile that he ended up craving alms in Bethnal Green. And it was outside the pub that William Booth, founder of the Salvation Army, preached his first sermon.

But nobody cares about that stuff. What they want to know is this:

> On 9 March 1966 Ron Kray walked into the saloon bar of The Blind Beggar and shot George Cornell in the head using a 9mm Mauser. Legend would have it that this happened because Cornell had called Ronnie a 'big fat poof', in public, to which Ron obviously took offence and sought revenge. This story seems highly unlikely, according to reliable sources, and it is more likely the shooting occurred due to a 'business disagreement' involving the Richardson brothers.

That story comes from the pub's own website. And at the bar you can buy not just T-shirts and 'authentic Kray memorabilia' but a splendid little booklet guiding you on a Kray Twins Walk as a memory of the days when Whitechapel did not have Bengali markets but was terrorised by nice white boys like Ronnie and his twin brother, Reggie. Among the stories in the booklet is an exchange between Ronnie and his Auntie Rose about why his eyebrows met above his nose. 'It means you were born to hang, Ronnie love,' she told him.

A few years earlier he would have done. But by the time the Krays were convicted of murder in 1969 (Ronnie for Cornell; both for the stabbing of

Jack McVitie; neither for the other murders they might or might not have committed or ordered), capital punishment had been abandoned and so they mouldered in prison, trading on their celebrity, before emerging for some of the East End's last great funerals, their own. Among the hundreds of wreaths at Reggie's funeral, according to the booklet, were those saying 'Legend', 'Free at Last' and 'Hero'.

Much of the Whitechapel in the booklet has gone now, including the Krays' own home in Vallance Road. Many of London's tourist destinations – the Tower of London, the Chamber of Horrors, the London Dungeon and so on – are based on a barbarous history. This one, well within living memory, does seem a little raw.

The other traditional redoubt of the gangsters was always Soho. More than anywhere, Soho is ever-changing; it is never what it was, as the locals are quick to mention, last year, last month, last week or last night. The characters have always all just died; some much-loved enterprise has always just closed. On another level it remains gloriously itself: a lake isle of louche living surrounded by conformity. Ronnie Scott's is still there, opposite Bar Italia. Two Italian delis survive, as does the Algerian Coffee Stores. The Gay Hussar, home of cold cherry soup and goulash, is clinging on.

In autumn 2013 the police raided eighteen brothels, complaining that the workers were victims of human trafficking, which is not what the girls seemed to think. Prostitution has resisted control by the authorities throughout human history, a situation not expected to die out before humanity itself does. In Soho, as in the wider world, there has always been a homosexual subculture, which remained well hidden in the years of persecution. That has certainly changed. An area largely dedicated to the old Adam now caters somewhat less for Adam seeking Eve and more for Adam seeking Adam.

I was intrigued to know whether the crackdown had put paid to Soho's most obvious brothel, located in a building whose ground floor, since last year, is now given over to a large emporium specialising in male underpants not available at M&S. As the sign in the window puts it: 'Latex, Leather, Neoprene, Vinyl, Steel'. (*Steel?*) The door to upstairs was open and an 'OPEN' sign hung in the window, suggesting business as usual. But, as cautious now as when with John from school, I was reluctant to climb the stairs for fear of having to make an excuse and leave.

So I went into the shop. Behind the counter were a girl decked out as a punk, complete with holes in her head, and a young man. I asked if upstairs was still in the business it used to be in.

Responding with the righteous *froideur* of a 1950s landlady who had just discovered goings-on and insisted that hers was a respectable house, the indignant punk said loftily, 'We have no idea about upstairs.'

I said that seemed surprising.

'Seriously,' said her companion. 'We have no idea what you're talking about.'

Oh well, they do say Londoners are less and less likely to know their neighbours.

It was William Cobbett who first called London the Great Wen (wen being a sebaceous cyst). That was when London was a fraction of its present size, both in administrative theory and in practice. But in every era London had quiet unknown areas where the essential but unsexy services could be maintained.

I first took the Docklands Light Railway to Pudding Mill Lane Station on 14 July 2005, eight days after London had been awarded the right to stage the 2012 Olympics, seven after the tube and bus suicide bombings that convulsed the capital and killed fifty-two innocent people, along with four guilty ones. The exit led on to Marshgate Lane, a street of reclamation yards, car-parts depots, concrete crushers, hotdip galvanisers and steel-fencing and wire-mesh distributors – plus a factory that prepared smoked salmon for the restaurant trade. The road also led to a small gut feeding the Lee Navigation Canal. Nothing had navigated there in many years except a great deal of weed and what looked like half a motorcycle. There was a heatwave: the streets were fly-blown as well as litter-strewn, and felt more like Delhi than London. Nothing to do with the people: there was no one about. Somewhere along the way I must have crossed what would become, seven years later, the finishing line in the Olympic Stadium.

I returned at intervals over those seven years, as the businesses were pushed out, like many of their workers, into the middle distance. This did not involve the brutal mass evictions that have taken place in other Olympic cities: an estimated 720,000 in Seoul before the 1988 Games; at least 1.25 million before Beijing 2008; an as yet unknown number prior to Rio 2016. It was a very English process: grinding, petty, niggardly. Lance Forman, the head of the smoked salmon firm,

H. Forman & Son, managed to get a site nearby without being exiled to Essex – an offer made hours before he was due to take the authorities to court – but only after years of devoting himself to the struggle rather than his business. When I returned in 2010, the area had already been sealed off. During the Games Pudding Mill Lane station was also closed; many signs advised spectators to walk to West Ham, a distance that might have taxed some of the athletes.

The Olympics themselves were a great triumph: opponents melted away (or at least kept quiet); the weather behaved; the volunteers smiled and had fun themselves; Britain won heaps of gold medals; and even non-sports lovers enjoyed the party which, mainly at the beach volleyball on Horse Guards Parade, sometimes took on the character of a drunken debauch rather than a sporting event.

Normally after a city has hosted the Games the hangover is extreme. But London has been in a strange mood, at odds with the quiet desperation of the rest of the country. The Olympics have been admitted to the small pantheon of British institutions that are too holy to criticise except in the most guarded terms, along with Stephen Fry and Christmas. In March 2014 the area remained largely sealed off, with a security man forcing pedestrians off the Queen's highway without any plausible basis in law, while facilities the country did not need were readied for their post-Olympic afterlife.

The alleged cost of the Games has remained fixed at £9 billion since it was upped from £3 billion in the early days of preparation, and this is almost never queried. Figures this glib are inherently untrustworthy. How many of us have any inherent understanding of what £9 billion gets you? Quite a few houses in Kensington Palace Gardens, for sure.

It would seem, at the very least, to people living across England in places where the councils can't even repair the potholes, a great deal of money to spend on a new football ground for West Ham United, an oversized swimming-pool complex, a few bits and pieces, and a boost to the regeneration/gentrification of the East End, which would have happened anyway.

Wandering in Woolwich, I got a bit lost and found myself on a road that led nowhere in a Thames-side industrial estate. Moored there was a hulk, rotting away in a rather Dickensian manner and falling gently on the ebbing tide. This was the *Royal Iris*, an old Mersey ferry, built in 1950 and retired in 1991, as her bones started to get a bit too creaky for full-time working.

On Merseyside she was regarded as one of the great local characters: 'the fish and chip boat', because you could buy your supper on board. And the original plan was for the ship to stay in Liverpool as a nightclub. Then she was sold to a consortium who wanted her to be a nightclub in Cardiff instead. During the operation to remove her she broke free of her towline, like a cornered animal, and got injured in the process. She was removed to Cardiff anyway, where she rotted some more. There was an attempt to bring her back to the Mersey. It failed.

And so she was brought to Woolwich, where no one knew or cared about her. There was a nightclub plan here too. That was in 2002 and nothing has happened since. A pleasant young man called Darren is employed to look after her and is clearly a little bit in love. 'You go down there,' he said, pointing to the mud round the bow, 'then look up and she's really beautiful.' Restoration, he insisted, was going to start soon. 'There'll be events on board. Not a nightclub. Corporates.'

Not here, I presumed. Darren shook his head and pointed upriver towards the glittering towers of Canary Wharf and beyond. This part of the capital is not an immediate candidate for regeneration. But it is London, and London has to have it all.

August 2013/February/March 2014

〜〜〜〜〜

When the hotel inside the Shard, the Shangri-La, opened in May 2014, it emerged that the surrounding glass acted at night as a mirror, enabling guests in some hotel bedrooms to have a perfect view of goings-on in others. Details! Details!

40. *From the Black Hill*

HEREFORDSHIRE

The parishioners made their way towards Holy Communion shortly before 6 a.m. At the head of the procession was the Reverend Nicholas Lowton, vicar of Clodock and Longtown with Craswall, Llanveynoe, St Margaret's, Michaelchurch Escley and Newton, who is not one of the younger breed of clergymen. Even so, Sunday best was not expected. The vicar himself was in dog collar and jeans. The dress code for most of the congregants comprised woolly hats and plenty of layers.

It was Easter morning and, despite having half a dozen relatively cosy churches to choose from, the vicar opted to celebrate the occasion on top of the spur off the easternmost ridge of the Black Mountains which hereabouts divides England from Wales – officially known as the Black Hill, usually referred to by the locals as the Cat's Back. At dawn.

In practical terms the exercise was a great success. About fifty congregants made the short but stiff climb to the summit, compared to the zero who might have attended indoors at this hour. In spiritual terms the setting enabled Nicholas to make his point: 'Moses met God at the top of the mountain. Elijah heard the still small voice on a mountain. Peter, James and John saw Christ transfigured on a mountain.' Aesthetically, there was a problem. The idea was to see the sun rising in front of us to caress the soft Herefordshire countryside in the spring of the year. Not a chance. Thick fog engulfed the top: it was possible to see Nicholas, gamely bare-headed, grey hair flapping in the wintry breeze. Behind him, not exactly a pea-souper, but a thin grey gruel.

He urged us to go down to the land which we would be looking at if we could see it, and to spread the word of Christ's love. But he is a shrewd as well as an eloquent preacher and knows when to stop, which was at the moment 500 toes were starting to go numb, so he just added, 'Have a Happy Chr – Easter! Easter! It's early!' and bade us farewell. My immediate concern was not to spread any word at all but head back to bed. Still, Christ rose on Easter Day under far more difficult circumstances, and we all felt a little holier for having risen ourselves.

Had the weather permitted, we might have seen the Malverns, the ancient boundary between Herefordshire and Worcestershire, and perhaps even on a very clear day the Wrekin in distant Shropshire. And beneath us we would certainly have seen those parts of the vicar's far-flung parishes not too tucked away in the clefts of the foothills: fifty square miles, bigger than Bristol, a third the size of Rutland; 1,150 people, three pubs, one shop, one vicar.

The area is known as the Golden Valley. Technically, that refers to the valley of the River Dore, which belongs to another priest, Ashley Evans, who until recently looked after fourteen churches, now rationalised to ten (plus a chapel). But the name is generally used to delineate all the little crinkles that occupy the whole south-western corner of Herefordshire.

Geographical details around here are a bit confused. The sixteen-mile-long ridge behind us that runs north to Hay-on-Wye and makes Wales invisible even on a clear day is one of the most striking features of the entire British landscape but has no name as such. Visitors tend to call it Offa's Dyke, because the Offa's Dyke footpath runs along it. But down here Offa didn't need to build his pathetic dyke to keep out the Welsh; God had done his utmost by erecting a far sterner barrier.

The area became more widely known because of Bruce Chatwin's exquisite 1982 novel, later a film, *On the Black Hill*, about two bachelor identical-twin farmers whose lives spanned most of the twentieth century.

Such a pair of twins did live locally but, though the border was said in the book to run through their farmhouse, the Black Hill is entirely in England. The book/play/film *Shadowlands*, about crusty old C. S. Lewis falling in love, uses the Golden Valley as a motif: a half-remembered paradise. However, the only identifiable landscape in that film is Symonds Yat, on the banks of the Wye, miles away and a completely different part of Herefordshire.

Then again this border is in itself foggy: neighbouring Monmouthshire was technically part of England until 1974, though no one ever thought of it as English. This border is more elusive, more protean than the Scottish equivalent. Ashley Evans has a church inside Wales, which does not happen up north; in rugby there are unpredictable loyalties; it is often hard to know who lives on which side of the line; and a pure Herefordshire accent has Welsh cadences. Welsh place names can be found halfway across the county, though the locals take a robustly English approach to pronunciation: the hill called Mynydd Ferddin is usually referred to as Money Farthing or Muddy Ferdin; the hamlet of Bagwyllydiart is just Baggy.

The situation is typified by the status of the eccentric book town of Hay. The Royal Mail thinks it's in Herefordshire and the Welsh government thinks it's in Wales; years ago Hay famously declared itself an independent kingdom, which was a stunt but one with a kernel of truth. And no one (yet) seriously envisages this as an international frontier. These are the Welsh Marches, decidedly plural.

We settled in the Golden Valley a quarter of a century ago. No time at all. There are church-school-shop-pub villages around here that look recognisably English, but the pattern of settlement is distinctly Celtic: scattered farmsteads, most with a damp sheep meadow or two but nothing like enough even to scratch a living. We live in one parish, have a patch of land over the brook in another; the muddled old Royal Mail insists we live in a third.

One recent visitor – from Worcestershire – told us we were in the most beautiful place he had ever seen: 'What a wonderful life you must have!' I rarely have the time to see it that way myself; nor, I suppose, had the generation upon generation who lived, fucked, strove and died on these unforgiving hillsides. But it is true that I pine whenever I am away from them, November to February partially excepted. My ideal retirement plan would be to continue living here with four clearly-defined seasons: spring, summer, autumn and Australia. But I hope to leave for good only horizontally and even then merely to St Margaret's churchyard up the road. The place has that effect.

The Golden Valley is changing, but it does so only slowly. In Craswall, 'the highest and wildest parish in Herefordshire', according to the 1955 Shell Guide, 'the farmers ride about on horses as they always did'. Electricity came here only in the 1960s, around the time everyone else's novelty was BBC2. Even now there is a clear delineation between the old farming families – Powells and Prices and Prossers, Watkinses and Williamses – and those whose forebears are not in the churchyard.

Twenty-five years is several centuries too short to understand all the interlocking kinships and ancient feuds that govern life here. Incomers have to learn Golden Valley ways as a foreign language, and a native speaker can always tell the difference. We try to tread lightly, but sometimes fail. The farmers have a holy terror of outsiders telling them what they can't do, which is the best explanation as to why, though it is an area of outstanding natural beauty, it is not an Area of Outstanding Natural Beauty (unlike large chunks of Kent, Surrey and even Lincolnshire). We may regret that next time some damn fool wants to build a wind farm.

But if there is hostility, it is either hereditary or personal. There is a mutual dependency, a recognition that without fresh blood the place would have withered long ago, and an underlying strength. When they tried to build a wind farm on the Cat's Back, and when the council tried to close the schools, the community rose as one. When the roads flood or the valley's white and blocked by snow or you drive the tractor into a ditch or the sheep break out, there is someone to help. There is an aristocracy here, but not in the normal sense; it comprises the kindly, the sociable, the capable, the quietly knowledgeable and the adaptable.

In all of that, the Golden Valley is merely a distillation of the rest of Herefordshire. 'I think borderlands have a very special quality,' Michael Tavinor, the Dean of Hereford, told me. 'That's why they're more liberal. The population have to deal with Welsh people and the Welsh language and get on with it. They are used to accepting differences.'

That applies within the Church too. 'There's no real sense of extremes of churchmanship,' the Dean went on. 'Partly because clergymen look after a large number of churches. Any differences would tend to be ironed out.' Hereford was keen to appoint a woman as its 105th bishop but the resignation of no. 104 came a touch too soon for the Church as a whole. This liberality extends to what might be described as the Church's polar opposite: Herefordshire's most famous yet most secretive group of humans, the SAS. No regiment in the army depends less on blind obedience and more on individual decision-making. That above all is an aristocracy of the adaptable.

But, long before women bishops, the city of Hereford never managed to be among the nation's pacesetters. This was one of the last cities to get a railway (1854), a multiplex cinema (2014) and a bypass (sometime never). The London trains take for ever, or longer on a bad day: much of the route is single-track ('You are held in a queue. Please hold the line.'). There are only one and a bit road bridges over the Wye, which the shoppers and commuters have to share with all the traffic crawling its way through the unbypassed city centre on the A49 – a sluggish enough road anyway. The longest hour of my life was spent following a Somerfield lorry from south of Leominster to Shrewsbury. Hereford itself has more traffic to less purpose than anywhere else I know.

The irritated motorist may catch a glimpse of the cathedral. However, the defining sight of the city was for many years a rear view of a row of grim shops that fringed the old cattle market by the Edgar Street round-about. The market was demolished last year to be replaced by a new and controversial shopping-and-entertainment complex. The visitor is now greeted by the brick wall of a branch of Debenhams and a multi-storey car park. There are two schools of thought about this among Herefordians: either it is slightly less ugly than the previous monstrosity or actually uglier. 'Couldn't they afford an architect?' asked one incredulous visitor.

Poor Hereford: too small (55,000) to be urbane, too big to be intimate, too badly connected to be businesslike, nor quite beautiful enough to make a living from its looks. But the genius of this county does not lie in the city, nor even in the pleasant small towns like Ross, Ledbury and Leominster. Nor even does it lie in the villages, handsome though many of these (Pembridge, Weobley, Eardisley, Bodenham ...) may be, especially the half-timbered black-and-white villages towards Leominster. It lies down the obscure lanes in places you can find only by satnav or accident: parishes and hamlets and valleys and wooded hills the world has passed by.

Most of Herefordshire is more conventionally, more quintessentially English than the Golden Valley: the fields are larger, the farms more arable, the springtimes earlier, the Welsh influence less obvious. But these Shangri-Las of the Marches are dotted everywhere (Aylton, Brinsop, Kings Pyon, Knill, Snodhill, Preston-on-Wye ...).

Everywhere too are hidden valleys, lush hillsides, sudden breathtaking views and remote homesteads any Briton genetically imprinted with the urge to buy houses wants instantly, even those who are lucky enough to have one of their own already. The pornography of this quasi-sexual urge can be found in the property supplement of the *Hereford Times*. These urges are related to those found in Surrey and Cheshire too, but they represent a different kind of kink. Herefordshire houses do not habitually include swimming pools and are not guarded by electronic gates. They tend to be scruffy, often draughty and damp, but divinely positioned. These days they are often inhabited by liberal, unstuffy, well-travelled baby-boomers who have made enough money elsewhere, thank you, but not all that much. But there is a price to be paid. And it is paid, as ever, by the young.

One of Hereford's most successful institutions is the Sixth Form College, founded in 1973 when the county's schools went comprehensive. It was one of the first in the country and is recognised as one of the best. The college now has nearly 2,000 students, about 80 per cent of the county's A-level cohort, giving them much of the personal freedom of a university but perhaps more insistence on academic rigour. There are only two drawbacks. One is the extent to which the college adds to the city's rush-hour gridlock. The other is more profound, and Dr Jonathan Godfrey, the college principal, is well aware of it.

'Almost a performance indicator of our success is the percentage of our students who go away to university,' he says. 'And not many come back.' There are a few professions in which it is possible to build a respectable career in a place as provincial as this one. 'We're doing our bit,' Godfrey adds. 'We've got about twenty ex-students on our staff.' But simple reality, never mind ambition, means that most of Herefordshire's brightest and best feel they have to leave. That includes many of the farmers' children who helped their parents lambing and milking at the hours when London kids were just getting back from parties. Their departure is not always reluctant.

In an era when almost everywhere has a university of its own, the Marcher counties have been a sad exception. This has been an important factor in Hereford's stagnation. There has been talk of a university for some time. Godfrey insists it has gone beyond a pipedream and become a serviceable plan for an institution concentrating on (that word again) 'liberal sciences' which has been garnering at least notional support within government. All that is still missing, as normal in Herefordshire, is the money.

'What we can't offer are the fleshpots of Manchester, Liverpool or Leeds, or the cultural life,' he admits. 'But that cart would follow the horse of a university.' Worcester now has a university. Worcester has a bypass. In some versions of the story, Worcester made damn sure of that.

The county of Hereford and Worcester (born squalidly: 1974; died unmourned: 1997) is the *locus classicus* of the wretchedness of the local government botch. Originally, this malformed entity was to be called Malvernshire; protesters won that argument, but none of the others. Hereford's name went first but it was to be second in everything else. It was not a minuscule minority, as Rutland was in Leicestershire, but, with less than a quarter of the combined population, it was a perpetual minority nonetheless and Herefordshire did feel itself oppressed.

This is a county that has always had a powerful self-awareness. Opposition to the original plan was universal and theatrical: a black flag on the Shire Hall in Hereford, a bull led up to Downing Street, a coffin paraded before a Hereford United game. Discontent continued during the twenty-three-year occupation. It was felt most acutely by Herefordshire's contingent of councillors, whatever their politics, who sensed total indifference to their concerns, exemplified by the decision to build a new council HQ – on the *other* side of Worcester.

I don't recall dawn raids by Worcestershire storm troopers on the homes of suspected dissidents or crowds of independence supporters being tear-gassed by armed traffic wardens and health and safety officers. Worcestershire didn't much care what we thought. I do remember my heart leaping every time I saw that the HEREFORD AND WORCESTER sign on the Monnow Bridge south of Ewyas Harold had had the 'AND WORCESTER' bit whitewashed out once again. It would always take ages before anyone bothered to restore it. The persistent rumour is that Worcestershire stole all Herefordshire's treasures and never gave them back. David Taylor, who has represented the village of Clehonger on various councils since 1970, is dubious: 'Well, they may have had *something*. But we hadn't got much treasure to start with.' And though it is true that Worcester got a bypass and Hereford did not, this was largely because Hereford kept bickering about the route.

When the government said it would consider a demerger, a poll showed Herefordshire more than 90 per cent in favour. And the night before it happened, in 1997, regional TV brought the leaders of the newly elected separate authorities to the restored county border on the crest of the Malverns. Terry James, the first leader of the new Herefordshire Council, said it was like the end of empire. 'It was very funny. I talked about all the parties and how every church in the county would be ringing its bells. Then they asked, "What's happening in Worcestershire?" And their leader said, "Nothing."'

But, as happened in post-colonial Africa, the first flush of liberation-enthusiasm did not last long. James avoided being toppled by an army general who then made himself president-for-life, but each winter now the lovely lanes become more pothole than tarmac, and the public lavatories were closed as expensive fripperies, and a new rat-friendly dustbin regime is imminent. Most of this is due to cuts outsourced by government to the council to palm off the blame. But David Taylor is a little wistful about the loss of the neighbours' stronger tax base: 'It was always Them and Us with Worcestershire. But we were getting quite a good return, financially, in those days. We're in the S-H-ONE-T now.'

As in Africa, no one would seriously seek a return to colonialism. But there are reports, from one of the county's borders, of a new act of creative vandalism. The current clever-dick signs read:

Herefordshire
You can

Supposedly one of these has been amended to:

Herefordshire
You can't go to the toilet

The livestock market, banished from the city centre, is now several miles out of town. The new site is far less cramped and far more practical. But its departure marks a major severance of the link between town and country: the Farmers' Club, as run-down as the old market, has closed and been sold off, and the special character of market day has gone for ever.

As a business, the market seems to be reviving. But it's not the same. 'People used to do ten minutes of sheep selling and four hours of chatting,' says Steve Hancorn. 'Now it's a place of business. Soulless but functional.' Hancorn is the scion of a Golden Valley farm family who did come back and still keeps his sheep. 'Most of the farmers do a bit of hedging, a bit of ditching, a bit of shearing or a bit of contracting. I was lucky enough to go to university so I can do a bit of teaching in the warm.'

Meanwhile, Debenhams, Waitrose and the new multiplex (a measly six screens) stand on the market where the cattle used to low. Since the market moved, the only bull now seen anywhere nearby is the life-size bronze statue in the city centre. It is supposed to be a Hereford bull, but lacks the white face which is its defining feature. It does have what must constitute the most impressive display of male genitalia on permanent display in any shopping street in the land. It is just outside the local branch of Ann Summers, its head slyly half-turned towards the window as though he were wondering whether the flimsy pink bra-and-knicker set on display would suit one of his paramours.

On a quiet side street nearby is the HQ of the Hereford Cattle Society, which dates back to 1878, since when it has recorded the productive matings of Hereford cattle across the county, the country and the world: these are beyond question Herefordshire's most successful exports and have become synonymous with the roast beef of Olde England.

The breed dates back more than a century before that, to when a group of local landowners began to experiment with breeding from their oxen and discovered that the animals with white faces and markings on a reddish-brown body tended to thrive best. The pioneers did their work secretively, a characteristic which is bred into the Herefordshire farmer.

The animal that resulted was short and stocky, like a rugby fly-half, and it had the great Herefordshire adaptability gene. But it was big enough until, in the twentieth century, it began getting smaller. David Prothero, the breed secretary for the past thirty years, says the Americans wanted smaller animals for their indoor feed-lots. Then they changed their minds and decided bigger was better, and British breeders were slow to catch up. So Herefords went into decline, especially in Britain, even in Herefordshire.

When Prothero joined the society, as a teenage driver, in 1971, it was an organisation with thirty-nine staff. Now it has five plus one part-timer. That is partly because the laborious record-keeping has been computerised. It is also a reflection of bad times. The sturdy old Hereford went out of fashion. Farmers wanted bigger, fancier, continental animals; consumers wanted beef less often and they wanted it leaner.

But the British Hereford was saved. Extinction was never likely, but it might have become a cutesy novelty. The breeders bought in new genes from overseas, to put some bulk into the breed. It was, says Prothero, a thirty-year process, and not universally popular. A minority refused to turn their cows into GI brides and insisted on sticking to the time-honoured British bloodlines. They remain inside the fold but are treated rather like the anti-feminist fundamentalists in the Church, with semi-affectionate exasperation. The Traditional Herefords are marked in the herd book with square brackets and an asterisk, [*].

David Powell is an eighty-year-old bachelor farmer from the cidery village of Much Marcle, whose great-grandfather first bought some Herefords in 1834. He took over his father's farm in 1972, bought a bull and went on from there, building up a herd that is very much [*]. 'Mine are shorter and slower-maturing, but the meat cooks better, the fat going through the grain of the beef. People are coming back to them. I've got a butcher in south London who will take as much as I can produce. And we're now getting enquiries from South America and Australia for embryos because they've gone too far changing the breed: they're too tall and too narrow.'

With his personal bloodline dying out, Powell has done a deal with a charity and runs his farm partly as an education centre. This has been an education for him too. 'We get students from London, and they all shout because they say you can't hear yourself in London. We also had a girl who thought to get milk from a cow you had to kill it. And a boy who thought potatoes came off a tree. They weren't from London, though, they were from Ledbury.'

Some of his cattle were grazing amidst the trees in his cider orchard, which were just coming into blossom. God was in his heaven. His star turn was at the far end of a meadow, looking across to May Hill and Gloucestershire beyond.

'Come here, Laura,' he called. 'Come on, Laura. I want you.'

And over she ambled, for a small bit of grub and a pat on the head.

'She is a bit of card, this one,' he admitted. 'But there you are. Most docile breed in the world. Would your wife come to you if you did that?'

In his office in town, David Prothero has his triumphs to report too. Within the past couple of years Waitrose, the Co-op and now Sainsbury's have all started marketing Hereford beef. Square brackets and genetic purity are not part of the deal. There is an asterisk on Sainsbury's promotional leaflet: 'Hereford means sired by a Hereford bull, registered with the Hereford society.'

Still, there is a certain reflected glory for every male in the county. There are counties symbolised by roses, swords, bears, foxes, what-have-you. But where else is represented to the world by a bollock-naked professional stud?

David Garrick was born in Hereford. So was Gilbert Harding. And Beryl Reid. Nell Gwynne, maybe. Mott the Hoople and most of the Pretenders were Hereford boys. Blanche Parry, Elizabeth I's confidante, has a memorial in the church at her home village of Bacton. Much Marcle prefers not to mention its own local boy, Fred West.

Sir Edward Elgar from Worcester worked on *The Dream of Gerontius*, and much else, in a small cottage at Birchwood. The poet laureate John Masefield was born in Ledbury. Painters? There are some very fine locals. But Herefordshire's most famous resident artist was undoubtedly an incomer, and far better known as Australia's most famous artist.

Sir Sidney Nolan made his name after the war for his Ned Kelly series. He then lived in London for many years until, in disarray after the suicide of his second wife in 1977, he sought refuge in a remote house in the Golden Valley with Mary Perceval, who became his third. In 1983 the Nolans bought the Rodd, a farm north of Kington, where he lived and worked for the nine years until his sudden death, aged seventy-five.

The Rodd is surrounded by low hills in the Hindwell Valley, and already had an antipodean connection: it was from here that Australia reputedly received its first Hereford bull, Sir Archibald. And Nolan was evidently enchanted by the place, even establishing his own herd of cattle (not Herefords). He kept painting in one of the barns, often using spray paints: the studio has been preserved and looks as though it belonged to a particularly finicky vintage car restorer. He worked under fierce lamps designed to recreate the light of the outback, here, in this soft, damp borderland. All his artistic life Nolan relished harsh light and harsh landscapes: Australia, China, Greece, Antarctica. Never once, apparently, did he paint Herefordshire.

He wrote once about the special challenge of painting in Australia: 'The light will not let you amalgamate the forms, whereas in Europe you have the unity emanating from floating skies.' This most painterly of counties was, it seems, all too easy.

Outside, the sky was floating across the Hindwell Valley and the campion was flourishing in the hedgerows. All over Herefordshire it was the sweet o' the year. Near Putley, the apple blossom was out – less showy than the plum in Worcestershire but more trustworthy, and wild hops were clambering about abandoned hop yards. There was a serenade from linnets and blackcaps, with occasional interventions from the cuckoo, a bird that has got rarer in my own corner of the county these past three years. I suspect social services may have intervened, in disgust at its domestic habits.

I waited for the weather and went up the Black Hill one more time.

On this occasion the only other congregant was a gentle Labrador and we climbed in companionable silence, before 7, on a perfect May morning. The grass had a gentle anointment of dew and everything glistened. Below us was no patchwork – it was too green for that – but everything was already in its summertime splendour except the lazy ash. To the east there was a little grey fair-weather cloud of the sort that can make it hard to distinguish a mountaintop from the sky, but it was possible to look across to the Malverns whence I looked across to Herefordshire three years and thirty-nine chapters ago in a springtime every bit as gorgeous as this one.

Then I braved the Hereford traffic and went into the cathedral – on a site that has been a place of worship since the eighth century at least: a span of 1,300 years. And by the tomb of St Thomas Cantilupe, the learned bishop of Hereford from 1275 to 1282, I lit two final candles for my children, the living and the dead.

I thought about those 1,300 years and tried to think into the even more unimaginable future, 1,300 years from now. And I offered a sort of prayer: that there might then still be a Herefordshire to cherish. And an England.

April/May 2014

ACKNOWLEDGEMENTS

In my head, I am Barbara Cartland, who wrote 723 books and sold a billion copies of them. I have hundreds of ideas for books, but by morning I can't always remember what they were.

This one, however, has been in my head for thirty years or more. It emerged after a lunch with Andrew Franklin of Profile Books. He wanted me to do one book, which I was not then keen to write; I wanted to do another, which he was not so keen to publish. I think there was a silence over the coffee before I said, 'Well, there is another possibility . . .'

My first thank you is to Andrew for leaping on the thought and inspiring me to get *Engel's England* out of my head, where it was serving no purpose, and on to the screen, page and shelves – and for much sagacious advice along the way, some of which I listened to. It has been a great pleasure to work with Andrew and the whole Profile team, especially Penny Daniel, Lesley Levene – a heaven-sent copy editor – Ruth Killick, Pete Dyer, Diana LeCore, Cecily Gayford and Stephen Brough. Susannah English's maps adorn the book. And none of this would have happened without the help and support of Marilyn Warnick and Christopher Lane.

During three years of travel, I have always depended on the kindness of strangers, which has been remarkably forthcoming. I met large numbers of lovely people who were extremely generous with their time and their knowledge. Luckily, I also had a large network of strategically placed relatives and friends who were generous not just with their knowledge, but also their spare rooms. A special medal should be struck for Simon and Cindy Barnes, who had the decency to move house while I was in the midst of this book, so I could conveniently sponge off them while researching both Suffolk and Norfolk. A suggestion that they might like to move again to one of the counties I still hadn't done was understandably rejected.

Others who were kind enough to dispense shelter and sustenance were: Steve Barnett and Alexandra Marks, Steve and Alice Bates, John and Jan Beatty, Calum and Emma Byrom, Alexander Chancellor, Mike and Sue Chaplin, Hugh and Tess Chevallier, Simon and Karen Clegg, Kate and Daren Collis, Michael and Christine Davies, Andy and Judith Denwood, Jane Doust, William and Naomi Duffield, James and Lisa Engel, Richard and Liz Engel, Tony and Sally Engel, Julian Glover and Matthew Parris, James and Jenny Halse, Martin and Sue Hesp, Jon and Margaret Holmes, Susan and John Lloyd, Nick and Jane Mason, Andrew Nickolds and Catherine Hurley, Nick Pitt and Alison Lang, James and Rose Rouse, Rob Steen, Martin and Penny Wainwright, and Francis Wheen and Julia Jones.

Hugh Chevallier and Christopher Lane were also both kind enough to read the proofs and make many helpful suggestions, as did my wife, Hilary. Hugh accompanied me on a couple of my adventures in Hampshire and Wiltshire; Anselm Shore tolerated me while I tentatively put one foot in front of the other up Scafell Pike; in Derbyshire I was lucky enough to have both Neil Hallam and John Beatty as erudite and companionable guides; and in Dorset I was delighted to have lunch with Sue Clifford, founder of the charity Common Ground, whose book *England in Particular* (co-authored by Angela King) was an inspiration as well as a source.

I would like to thank everyone else who helped along the way, especially: Jonathan Agnew, Robin Aisher, Joy Allison, David Amess MP, Mike Amos, Jori Ansell, Lesley Archer, Bill Archibald, Chris Arnot, Mike Austen, Alex Balfour, Ian Ball, Matthew Banner, Ron Barker, John Barnes, Neil Barnes, Rupert Barnes, Julie Bartram, Mary Bayliss. Richard Beaumond and the audience at Bookworms (Shropshire), Roger Begy, Sir Alan Beith MP, Edward Bevan, Charlie Bibby, Roger Bingham, Brian Binley MP, David Bishop, John Blackburn, Gavin Bland, David Boothroyd, Dr Karin Bottom, Jane Brace, Billy Bragg, Steve Brenkley, Isobel Bretherton, Allan Brigham, John Bright, Terry Broomfield, John Brown, Sir Peter Brown, Emrys Bryson, Charlie Burgess, David Burnett, Andy Canning,

Amanda Carson, Douglas Carswell MP, Andrew Charman, the late
George Chesterton, Kitty Chevallier, Professor Carl Chinn, Sue Clarke,
Tony Clarke, Christine Cleaton, Tim Cockin, Dick Cole, Pat Collins,
Anthony Collis, Mike Coombes, Ted Corbett and Jo King, Sir Neil Cos-
sons, Nigel Costley, Paul and Polly Coupar-Hennessy, Joe Cowen, Dr
Pam Cox, James Coyne, Bernie Cranfield, Professor Mick Crawley, Caro-
line Cunningham, Stephen Dalzell, Paul Davey, Max Davidson, Hunter
Davies, Patricia Davies, Ron Davies, Garth Dawson, Glen Dawson, Tim
de Lisle, Graham Dines, Paul Dixey, Carolyn Dougherty, Simon Duke,
Harry and Christina Dunlop, Dick Durham, Gary Eastman, Philip Eden,
John Edgeley, Simon Edwards, Chris Eilback, Keith Elliott, Simon Fan-
shawe, Tim Farron MP, John Florance, Martin Forwood, Steve Fran-
cis, Linda Frost, Jane Full, Chris Game, Andrew George MP, Anthony
Gibson, Sarah Gibson, Patric Gilchrist, Dr Jonathan Godfrey, Angus
Graham-Campbell, Russell Grant, Rob Guest, John and Evelyn Gulliver,
Steve Hancorn, Charlotte Hanna, Mike Harding, Robert Hardman, Kay
Hardy, Norman Harris, Clive Hay-Smith, Tim and Penny Heald, Simon
Heffer, Catherine and Michael Held, Bill Hensley, Ian Herbert, Francis
Hicks, Professor Michael Hicks, Sue Hicks, Brian Hill, Keith Hodg-
kins, Derek and Doreen Hodgson, Nicola Holland, John Holmes, David
Hopps, James Hosking, Professor Mike Huggins, Carl Hunnysett, Mark
Hurrell, Asaf Hussain, Matt Jackson, Paul Jackson, Tom and Sally Jaine,
Brian James, Terry James, Conor Jameson, Peter Jinman, Richard John-
ston, Barry Jones, Robert Jones, Jonathan Kindleysides, Bill Kirkup, Steve
Knightley, Christine Knipe, Monty and Pat Kutas, Dr Bill Lancaster, Mark
Lawson, Helen Leadbeater, Philippa Lee, Dr Elisabeth Leedham-Green,
Harry Legg, Steve LeMottee, John Lewis, Lieutenant-Colonel Nigel
Linge, Danny Lockwood, Professor Malcolm Longair, Steve Lowe, Rev.
Nicholas Lowton, Hugh Lupton, Steven Lynch, Bryan McAllister, Tony
McWalter, Sean Magee, David Makinson, Vic Marks, Rob Marris, Chris
Marshall, Rodney Masters, Bob and Joan Mawson, Dr Terence Meaden,
Rev. Alan Middleton, Tim Minogue, Brian Montgomery, Jo Moody,
Rhodri Morgan, Charlie Morris, Rod Morris, the late Gerald Mortimer,
Paul and Lynda Needle, Bryony Neirop-Reading, Charles Nevin, Pete
Nichols, Geoff Nickolds, Mike Nixon, Richard Norris, David North-
wood, Gerry Northwood, Janet Oldroyd-Hulme, Julian Orbach and Kate
Pawsey, Maggie Osborn, Marc Oxley, Jim Page, Maggie Papas, John Paulo,
Professor Philip Payton, Harry Pearson, Andy Peebles, Professor Chris

Perrins, Barbara Piranty, David Powell, Rev. Jemima Prasadam, Gordon Prentice, Trevor Pressley, David Prothero, Rick Pushinsky, Janet Quier, Andrew Radd, Mike Raj, Don and Sue Ransome, Fiona Rawlings, Dr Barrie Rhodes, Peter Rhodes, Keith Richardson, Canon Mervyn and Sue Roberts, Chris Robinson, David Robinson, Paul Robinson, Stuart Rose, Alan Roxborough, Very Rev. Michael Sadgrove, Professor John Salt, Ken Scott, Carmela Semeraro, Chris Simmonds, Keith Simpson MP, Professor Gurharpal Singh, Keith Skipper, Wendy Skirrow, Dan Sleat, Rex Sly, Alison Smedley, Sir Tim Smit, Giles Smith, James Smith, John Snowdon, Richard Spiller, Jon Spira, Laura Spira, Ian Standing, Jeff Stanyer, David Stead, Alan and Sue Stennett, Jack Straw MP, David Summers, Diana Syder, Bruce Talbot, Shirley Tart, Robin Tatlow, Very Rev. Michael Tavinor, David C. Taylor, David J. Taylor, Chris Thomas, Norman Thorpe, Rev. Tom Thubron, John Thurston, Angela Tidmarsh, Professor Tony Travers, Adam Trimingham, Dr Nigel Tringham, Professor Peter Trudgill, Peter Tuke, John Tye, Professor Clive Upton, Wendy Varcoe, Rev. Mike Vockins, Father Geoff Wade, Lyn Walsh, Ben Ward, David Ward, Pam Ward, Michael Watkins, Ruth Watkins, Margaret Watson, Paul Weaver, Dr Ian West, Andrew Whittle, Peter Wilbourn, Very Rev. Bob Wilkes, David Willis, David Wilson, Julian Winder, Robert Winder, Chris Witts, John Woodcock, Bernard Wrigley, Derek Wyatt, Gordon Young and Gary Younge. With apologies to anyone I have inadvertently omitted or, almost as bad, misspelt.

The staff of the British Library and London Library were always helpful, and the Association of British Counties' website was a far more accurate guide to the real boundaries of the counties than the confused information available elsewhere. The Inn Signs Society have kindly helped with pictures. I have also been grateful for the company of the Radio 4 newsreader Kathy Clugston, the Ulster-flavoured voice on my satnav. Without Kathy, I would never have known which way to turn on each 'roan-de-boat'. Sometimes I shouted; and I had to cope with one county (Nottinghamshire) without her when she got left behind. But no matter how much she was provoked and abused, she did not grumble, sulk or answer back.

Finally, and above all, my thanks go to my wife and daughter, Hilary and Vika, who avoided almost all the journeys. They phlegmatically tolerated my absence and, even more trying for them, my presence. Without them, I wouldn't be anywhere at all.

A NOTE ON PICTURES

Most of the pictures that serve as a motif for each chapter were taken by the author, which may explain a lot. But I have been very grateful for help filling in the gaps.

The picture of the Stewartby chimney (Bedfordshire) is from adarkertrantor.co.uk. The Inn Sign Society kindly provided the pictures for Devon, Cheshire and Somerset.

In many cases the setting of the picture will be obvious from the photo or mentioned in the chapter. But readers may be interested in the whereabouts of some of the others.

Chapter 3 (Surrey): The cricket scoreboard is in the village of Normandy.

Chapter 5 (Devon): The Tom Cobley pub is in Paignton.

Chapter 14 (Oxfordshire): Bicester Shopping Village.

Chapter 15 (Cheshire): The Cheshire Cat is at Christleton.

Chapter 17 (Derbyshire): The Quiet Woman is at Earl Sterndale.

Chapter 21 (Buckinghamshire): A shop window in Eton High Street.

Chapter 22 (Leicestershire): Melton Mowbray.

Chapter 26 (Northumberland): Marshall Meadows.

Chapter 28 (Cumberland): This delightfully demotic notice was near Buttermere.

Chapter 30 (Somerset): The Ancient Mariner is opposite Coleridge's cottage in Nether Stowey.

Chapter 31 (Lincolnshire): Near Boston.

Chapter 36 (Shropshire): Ellesmere.

Chapter 39 (London): Kensington. Of all places!

Chapter 40 (Herefordshire): This bull is above the front door of the Hereford Cattle Society offices and is not to be confused with the one peeping into Ann Summers' window.

That leaves the opening chapter, which is a bit problematic. Both my memory and the date on the picture insist that I must have taken the picture in Worcestershire, presumably in a churchyard. But I failed to remember or note the village and, though I have pestered just about every vicar and church official in the diocese, no one has yet come up with the answer. If you know, matthew@matthewengel.co.uk would be delighted to hear from you. The solution, if it materialises, will be on the matthewengel.co.uk website, along with corrections, updates and quirky matters arising.

A note on the paperback

The response to publication of the hardback edition of Engel's England in 2014 was very gratifying. And I have had many kind notes from readers saying how much they enjoyed the book.

Some correspondents did mention the occasional error; I am glad to say that (a) they all did so 'gently and politely', as requested in the introduction and (b) none of the mistakes were horrific. Corrections have been made where possible and appropriate for this edition, along with some updates.

So in addition to my earlier list of acknowledgements I would like to add Peter Clear, Colin Flint, David Gouldstone, Anni Holden, Edward Keene, Colin Lane, Nick Lowe, David McKie, Terry Marriott, Gabriel Milland, Mary Milne-Day and Ed Pearce. I would also like to repair the omission of Sam Llewellyn, editor of *Marine Quarterly*, from the original thank yous, especially because I asked him the same ignorant maritime question *three times*, forgetting the answer twice.

Alas, no one has yet identified the mysterious Worcestershire churchyard. I live in hope, and will report on *matthewengel.co.uk* if and when.

Matthew Engel
Herefordshire, April 2015

INDEX OF PLACES